1

A Complete Guide to the Arts Section of the National Board Exam for Funeral Services

David R. Penepent, PhD

Program Director of Funeral Services Administration
State University of New York at Canton
Canton, New York

President of Anubis Publications Inc.
3 Harrison Street
Norwood, New York

ESTD 2020

A N U B I S
PUBLICATIONS, INC.

Copyright © 2024 Anubis Publication Inc.

No part of this publication may be reproduced, duplicated or transmitted in any form, means, including photographing, recording, or other electronic or mechanical methods, including but not limited to emailing, without the prior written permission of the publisher, except in reviews and certain other non-commercial use permitted by copyright laws.

ISBN: 979-8-9891595-6-7 **(Paperback)**
ISBN: 979-8-9891595-5-0 **(Hardcover)**
ISBN: 979-8-9891595-7-4 **(Digital)**
ISBN: 979-8-9891595-8-1 **(Audiobook)**

The glossary of terms and content outlines used in this publication are the intellectual property of the American Board of Funeral Service Education and are being used with expressed permission. No part of the outlines or glossary of terms may be reproduced, duplicated or transmitted in any form, means, including photographing, recording, or other electronic or mechanical methods, including but not limited to emailing, without the prior written permission from the American Board of Funeral Service Education, 992 Mantua Pike, Suite 108, Woodbury Heights, NJ 08097.

Published and Distributed by:

Anubis Publication Inc.
3 Harrison Street
Norwood, New York 13668
585-356-4929
dpenepent@deatheducationassessmentdrills.com

Printed by: Lightning Press
Totowa, New Jersey 07512
www.Lightning-Press.com

Contributing Authors

David R. Penepent, PhD is the President and Owner of Anubis Publications Inc. Dr. Penepent has been a funeral director and embalming practitioner for over 30 years. A graduate of the Simmons Institute of Funeral Services in Syracuse, New York, he earned a Bachelor's of Arts degree in Psychology from the University of Wisconsin Oshkosh; A Master's of Arts degree in Organizational Management from the University of Phoenix; and a Doctorate of Philosophy degree in Leadership and Organizational Change from Walden University. Currently, he is the Funeral Services Administration Program Director at the State University of New York at Canton. Dr. Penepent wrote the Business section, FTC, OSHA, Cemetery & Crematory, Communications, and Funeral Law sections of this book. He lives in Norwood, New York with his wife and has three children and three grandchildren.

Darien B. Cain, M.S., B.S, B.Tech., is a New York State Licensed Funeral Director/Embalmer for Cleveland Funeral Home Inc., in Watertown, NY. After growing up in Clayton, NY, Darien obtained a Bachelor's of Science in Biology from the State University of New York (SUNY) at Potsdam. She then completed a Bachelor's of Technology in Funeral Services Administration at SUNY Canton. In 2020 Darien became a full-time Lecturer for SUNY Canton's Funeral Services Administration program. She recently completed a Master's of Science in Management from SUNY Potsdam and earned the Chancellor's Award for Student Excellence. Currently, Darien is currently pursuing her doctoral degree at Liberty University. Darien contributed to multiple sections of this book, including Accounting, Funeral Directing, Funeral Home Management, and Merchandising. She lives in Watertown, NY, with her husband, Captain Ian Cain, U.S. Army, and her new born, Wesley. We all honor Captain Cain's service to this country and dedicate this book to the brave people who serve and have served.

Christina Lesyk, LMSW is an Associate Professor of Applied Psychology at the State University of New York at Canton. She earned her Master of Social Work degree from Hunter College School of Social Work in New York City and her Bachelor of Arts degree in Women's Studies from Columbia University/Barnard College, also in New York City. She has been a New York State licensed social worker since 1992. Prior to teaching at SUNY Canton, she taught in the certified Bachelor of Social Work degree program at the State University of New York at Plattsburgh. At SUNY Canton, she teaches in human services, psychology, and social sciences. She has also taught Business Communications, Death, Dying and Bereavement, and Crisis Intervention courses. She has been recognized with awards such as the SUNY Chancellor's Award for Faculty Service, the Phalanx Service Award, and the Stellar Advisor Award. She also currently serves as the elected Board Secretary for the New York State Chapter of the National Association of Social Workers. She volunteers annually to provide review sessions for the Arts portion of the National Board Examination for Funeral Service Directors. Professor Lesyk wrote the Sociology, Psychology, Grief Counseling, Ethics sections of this book. She lives in Norwood, New York with her husband, Alex.

Dedication

This book is dedicated to the men and women of the military. Their bravery and devotion to defend this country's freedoms is greatly appreciated by many funeral directors in the United States. Thank you for your great service to this great country and the Constitution you defend.

From the Bivouac of the Dead
By Theodore O'Hara

The muffled drum's sad roll has beat
The Soldier's last tattoo;
No more on life's parade shall meet
That brave fallen few.

On Fame's eternal camping-ground
Their silent tents are spread,
And Glory guards, with solemn round,
The bivouac of the dead.

God Bless the United States of America

Table of Contents

Domain IV

Cemeteries & Crematories

Domain V

Funeral Home Merchandise

Domain VI

Bereavement Counseling

Acknowledgements

A review manual of this magnitude takes a considerable amount of time and effort to complete. Dr. Thomas Taggart was my professor when I attended the Simmons Institute of Funeral Services in Syracuse, New York 35 years ago. He developed the concept of taking the ABFSE outline and using it as part of the review process. There is a plethora of information to be covered that could potentially be on the National Board Exam. Dr. Taggart's notes became crucial to creating a summary of the information in concise form. Over the years, he updated the information as the outlines changed and information was added, deleted and revised. When he retired in 2016, the review manual went unedited, and over the past eight years, the ABFSE outlines for the Arts section has been revised twice with no edits to Dr. Taggart's NBE Review Manual. His review manual was a starting point for this book which incorporated all the changes in the curriculum outlines made by ABFSE. We have added graphics and diagrams to better serve the students in preparing for the NBEs. Finally, we created an audio version for students who learn best by listening to the material. This book was greatly influenced by Dr. Taggart's initial notes.

Words cannot express my sincere gratitude to my colleague Darien Cain for the hours of work she put into writing the various sections in this book, in addition to editing the many drafts. While funeral directing was not her original career path, her choice to become a funeral director has blossomed into a vocation in which she has applied her knowledge in the profession to become an outstanding professor of funeral services at the State University of New York at Canton. Her teaching style and ability to connect with the students has earned her the Stellar Advisor Award in 2023. In addition, while pursuing her Master's degree at SUNY Potsdam, Darien earned the Chancellor's Award for Distinguished Student, an honor very few students achieve. Recently, she earned the Distinguished Faculty Award at SUNY Canton. These three honors distinguish her as a valuable asset to the profession. The contributions she has made to funeral service education and the profession has undoubtedly been advanced because of her career choices five years ago.

Christina Lesyk is a highly decorated faculty member at SUNY Canton. Her outstanding leadership, teaching and advisory skills have earned her a great deal of recognition and honors including the Chancellor's Award for Faculty Service, the Phalanx Service Award, and the Stellar Advisor Award. Her knowledge as a social worker has served the Funeral Services Administration program at SUNY Canton well with her instructions in Psychology and Death, Dying and Bereavement. Her dedication to the program even extends to participating in annual NBE review sessions. Her knowledge, skills as a social worker practitioner and devotion to this project have enriched this publication immensely.

I owe a great deal of gratitude to Zachery Micheal Smith for designing the cover of this book.

And finally, a special thank you to Captain Ian Cain for his service to this great nation in the US Army, 10th Mountain Division. I appreciate the countless hours that Darien spent working on this book, which meant family sacrifices. With a humble heart, words cannot express my appreciation for your understanding.

David R. Penepent, PhD

TIPS on How to
Pass the National Board Exam

The National Board Exam (NBE) should never be taken for granted. Even if you received good grades in mortuary school, a considerable amount of preparation is necessary to successfully pass the Arts section of the NBEs. The following are some tips on how to prepare for the exam.

Tip 1: Know the Exam

According to the Conference National Board Exam Arts Study Guide (2022), the exam is divided into four specific areas, with a specific number of questions per section:

- ➢ Funeral Arranging and Directing comprises - 34% of the questions – 51 items
- ➢ Funeral Service Marketing and Merchandising comprises –
  14% of the questions – 21 items
- ➢ Funeral Service Counseling comprises - 13% of the questions – 19 items
- ➢ Legal and Regulatory Compliance comprises - 23% of the questions – 35 items
- ➢ Cemetery/ Crematory/Other Disposition comprises - 16% of the questions – 24 items
- ➢ The Conference Beta Test questions for future exams comprises - 15 questions, but these questions don't count towards your final score.

Total 165 Questions

Tip 2: Preparing to Study

Identify what you do not know as a starting point. Using the Death Education Assessment Drill (DEAD) simulator, take a 150-question Arts test. The first test will become an indicator and provide a roadmap of what needs to be studied. Identify what types (subject matter) of questions you got wrong. Use this textbook to look up the right answer. The key here is to develop an understanding of why you got the questions wrong and why your answer is not the right one.

Use the DEAD simulator to focus in on specific areas. For example, if you got 10 merchandising questions wrong, use the simulator to create mini quizzes to further narrow the scope of material that needs to be studied. DO NOT memorize the questions and answers; that is not studying. Memorizing questions and answers is low level learning, and retention of the material will be minimal.

Tip 3: Test Smart, Not Hard

Questions on the NBE have four answers. Try to make it a 50/50 question by reducing the answers down to 2 possible answers. For example:
> Bill died with a will and when his will was Probated, Thom was declared to handle the final affairs of Bill's estate. What was Thom's title?
> > A. Administrator
> > B. Administratrix
> > C. Executor
> > D. Executrix

Two of the answers can automatically be eliminated simply by knowing their definitions (Administra**trix** and Execu**trix**). The suffix *trix* denotes a woman, thus B and D can be eliminated. The remaining possible answers, A. Administrator and C. Executor, requires you to know the difference between the two terms. Administrator means that the deceased died without a will and the courts appointed an Administrator to handle the final affairs of the estate. Since Bill died with a will, he declared in this legal document who would be handling the affairs of his estate, thus the answer would be C.

Tip 4: Scenario Questions

Scenario questions are comprehension of the material questions. If you understand the material, you will understand the scenario question:
For example:

Bill dies intestate. Thom was appointed by the courts to handle the final affairs of Bill's estate. Who is Thom?
A. The Judge
B. The Attorney
C. The Executor
D. The Administrator

Dying *intestate* means that the person died without a will. Answer A and B would be eliminated because both are officers of the court. There is only one possible answer – D because when a person dies without a will, the court appoints a person to handle the final affairs of the estate (Administrator). An Executor is a man who is identified in the will to handle the final affairs of an estate.

Bill died intestate. What document gives Thom the legal authority to handle the final affairs of Bill's estate?
A. The Will
B. Letters of Administration
C. Letters of Testamentary
D. A Writ of Habeas Corpus

A Writ of Habeas Corpus has nothing to do with wills or Probate. Bill died without a will, thus A is incorrect. Answers B and C require a comprehension of the legal process that takes place when a person dies without a will. The will is the Last Will in Testament, thus when a person has a will, the judge would issue Letters of Testamentary. However, if the person dies without a will, the judge appoints an Administrator or Administratrix and the legal document declaring Thom's authority to settle the final affairs of the estate would be **B. Letters of Administration.**

Tip 5: DO NOT Change Your Answer

Once you select an answer, move on! Don't second guess your answer. The majority of time students change their answers, they usually select and change the answer to the wrong one. Your first answer is usually the correct answer.

Tip 6: Use DEAD to your Advantage

Use the DEAD simulator nightly and do between 150 and 300 questions as part of your study ritual. The key is to consistently score 85% and above on each quiz and full-length test. Research has shown that students who have scored consistently above 85% on five or more practice exams usually pass the NBEs. Several factors influence the outcome of the exam, but like any exam, the more you study and prepare for the exam, the more likely the chance of receiving a favorable outcome.

Tip 7: Know Vocabulary Terms

Arts is straightforward and most of the questions revolve around a comprehensive understanding of the vocabulary terms. There are flash cards that can be purchased; however, creating your own flashcards is more effective. Each chapter has the current American Board of Funeral Service Education glossary. One of the problems with definitions on Quizlet or purchased flashcards is that some of the definitions have changed and are outdated.

Creating flashcards involves a thorough process that aids in remembering the terms. Only create cards on terms you need to review.

Tip 8: Do Not Get Nervous

Test anxiety does play an important role in the outcome of the exam. Being a little nervous prior to the NBE is normal and is part of a heightened awareness of the importance of the exam. Worrying and self-doubt are negative feelings that could shift positive energy to negative energy, causing the mind to lose its focus on the goal of passing the exam. Having a positive attitude and doing the necessary studying prior to the exam will reduce some of this anxiety. Effective study habits that limit distractions (cell phones, social media and procrastination) will help to create a feeling of accomplishment, which could reduce stress.

Tip 9: Take a Review Session & Private Tutoring

Most mortuary science programs have a capstone course that reviews all the material learned throughout the curriculum. Anubis Publications offer five 2-day review courses, throughout the year, for the Arts section. See **www.deatheducationessdrills.com** website (under *Resources*) for more information.

Some students need to have concepts re-explained. Some tutoring experiences are very expensive and require students to make long term commitments. Anubis Publications offers semi-private tutoring sections at $30/per hour. The sessions are led by experienced mortuary science professors who tailor the session to your needs. See **www.deatheducationessdrills.com** website (under *Resources*) for more information. Students who benefit the most from this session come prepared with questions about specific topics.

Tip 10: What if I Fail?

Failure is good as long as you learn from your mistakes, correct your behavior, and move forward towards success. Failure is bad when you keep making the same mistakes repeatedly and expect a different outcome.

If you fail the NBE, keep your results and bring them to a tutoring session. In January 2023, the Conference began providing information on the concepts missed on the exam. Even though the actual questions are not known, these concepts can be remediated in a private review session with our professors. During the tutoring session, these concepts can be the focus for remediation.

Domain I
Human Response to Death

Funeral Directing

Preparations for Final Disposition

Funeral Rites and Ceremonies

Funeral Directing and Preparation for Disposition

Preparation of Human Remains for Final Disposition

Preparation for disposition is the entire purpose of funeral services. Helping families to take leave of their loved ones with respect and dignity should be in the mission statements of all funeral firms. The funeral director is responsible for caring for the dead while helping the bereaved begin their grieving process. However, there is much more to operating a funeral home, such as personnel management, facilities maintenance, community outreach, financial management, and advertising which are not directly involved with the preparation of remains. This section focuses on the variety of methods that must be applied to suit society's needs for the different types of dispositions which exist today.

Each of the potential dispositions begins either with a body that has been embalmed in a typical or common way or with remains that have not been embalmed, thus presenting different challenges for disposition.

1. Long-Term Storage Prior to Viewing

Death happens at the most inconvenient time. In the practice of funeral directing, more and more families are unable to travel to the location of the visitation for a week or two, requiring a delay in viewing and services. If the situation is known at the time of embalming, extra arterial injection with a specialty fluid, supplemented by a humectant co-injection (ex. Sorbitol or Lanolin), could retard decomposition and maintain the appearance of the fullness of the tissues. Water will evaporate from the body tissues over time, resulting in shrinkage and darkening of the tissues; humectants should prevent dehydration. Additionally, the use of massage cream on all exposed surfaces delays dehydration. If the potential need for extra arterial injection is not known at the time of first embalming, a six-point injection may be utilized to re-embalm the areas that the embalmer feels are not entirely preserved. Hypodermic injection could be used to address difficult areas of distribution. Sacrificing the natural feel of the tissues and losing the flexibility of extremities for easier dressing are tradeoffs for a higher level of preservation. This is an unusual situation; atypical treatment with paraformaldehyde gel may be necessary to firm flaccid tissue.

The signs to look for that indicate the problems associated with dehydration include separation of eyes and lips, shrinking of tissues, discoloration of different areas, pockets of gas under the skin, flies or maggots, shrinking of fingertips, and foul odor.

The remains should not be dressed, cosmetized, or casketed until shortly before the actual viewing will occur. Moisture evaporating from the body could absorb into the clothing and casket interior, supporting mold and bacterial growth, with the potential for reversal of embalming by excess moisture or humid conditions. This will re-hydrate the muscles and protein tissues. Cooling to normal room temperature is preferred; embalmed remains kept in a cooler close to the freezing point (32° Fahrenheit) leak excess embalming fluid through the skin, resulting in moisture or condensation of bodily fluids. The refrigerated human remains require a daily inspection to determine the condition of the remains and, if necessary, corrective measures should be taken to deal with small problems (such as mold development or dehydration) as they arise. The human remains placed in a cooler should be properly labeled with a toe tag or wrist band and placed in the cooler, head-first. A cooler manifest should be posted on the outside of the cooler identifying the proper location of the human remains in the cooler. The remains should be covered for dignity and privacy.

Dignity and respect should be given to the human remains at all times. The remains should be dressed in a hospital gown and wrapped in a sheet when placed in a cooler for extended periods of time. The sheet will draw moister away from the remains and towards the material. The sheet will also serve as an indicator of points that need to be treated post-embalming, such as IV holes or bodily fluid discharge. Plastic garments should be placed on the human remains shortly before dressing for visitation or services.

The FTC allows a storage fee to be charged for each day that the remains are on the funeral home premises and no other funerary treatments (such as embalming) were performed. Custodial care fees can be charged to the consumer only on days of waiting to engage for services.

For example:

> Day 1: Mr. Thompson dies on Monday, and the funeral director makes the removal and embalms the remains;
> Day 2: On Tuesday, the family makes arrangements, and the funeral director arranges for the service a week away.
> Day 3: On Wednesday, the funeral director files the death certificate, publishes the obituary, and finalizes all the plans for the visitation Monday afternoon.
> Day 4-7: The remains are in the prep room, covered on the embalming table.
> Day 8: The hairdresser and the funeral staff dress, casket, and cosmetize the remains for visitation. Family viewing is from 1:15 PM to 2:00 PM.
> Day 9: Church service followed by committal service at a local cemetery.

In the above scenario, only on Days 4-7 can the funeral director charge a custodial fee because the funeral home was storing the remains and not engaged in the practice of funeral directing during those days.

Human remains that have not been embalmed can only be held in a mortuary cooler as a means of delaying decomposition. The FTC requires the funeral director to offer the "use of the cooler" as an alternative to embalming, if a cooler is on the premises. Some state regulations require the funeral firm to have a cooler on the funeral home premises as a condition for charging for the use of a cooler. Charging for the use of the cooler and charging a custodial fee is considered "double-dipping" and is frowned upon by most state regulatory agencies.

Assuming embalming or other chemical treatment is not allowed by family preference, the best that can be done is to treat the surfaces of the face, neck, and hands with a very thick layer of massage cream (which contains a humectant such as lanolin), adding more when necessary. Posing the features is important, but if permission has not been given, it is mutilation to use an invasive technique like injector needles or mandibular sutures. The mouth may be kept closed by placing a strip of cloth around the chin and tying it on top of the head towards the back. A chin rest positioning device may also be used.

The use of a mortuary cooler requires careful documentation. Each time human remains are placed in or removed from the cooler, the time, date, and employee performing the task is documented on the Refrigeration Log. Remains should be placed in the cooler, head-first, so the ankle ID can be quickly and easily observed. No matter how many calls a firm makes annually, all human remains in a cooler should have an identification tag on the remains and on the body bag. The longer and more often the door is open, spilling out cooled air, the more expensive the cooler is to operate. It is legal to charge for refrigeration as long as no other service was performed on the remains during that day.

A family member (or a family agent) must make a visual identification of the human remains, no matter what type of final disposition is selected. To prepare for visual identification, The funeral director should ask for permission to do minimally invasive procedures, such as shaving, closing the jaw and mouth with injector needles (wires), closing the eyes with adhesive, and injecting cavity fluid. Be certain that the permission for limited treatment is specific to avoid legal jeopardy.

Can a funeral director charge for this limited invasive procedure? Identification is considered part of the cremation or direct burial process and is incorporated in the package fee. If, for example, the family does not choose to embalm but would like to view their loved one's remains prior to direct burial, with permission, the funeral director could charge for topical disinfection and a preparation fee.

2. Mausoleum and Entombment

The general idea for proper mausoleum entombment is to allow the slow evaporation of moisture from the remains as well as control any leakage. Modern mausoleum crypts are built to allow liquids to drain into a type of gutter system, as well as bodily gases to escape through a roof vent. Well-prepared human remains will allow evaporation to occur easily and control the amount of leakage. Cemeteries with mausoleums have entombment rules which need to be followed.

Remains that will be entombed in a mausoleum should be embalmed with a more concentrated arterial solution than normal to reduce the amount of water introduced into the body tissues. Regional injection to address areas of deficiency may be required.

Prior to casketing human remains, a leakproof pouch should be placed in the casket to collect any leakage that may occur over time. The pouch can be concealed underneath the human remains during visitation and services, and prior to final disposition, the remains are zippered into the pouch. It is not recommended to use a liquid adhesive around the zipper in this situation because this will prohibit off-gassing. Bodily fluids that accumulate in the pouch will evaporate over time in wooden caskets. Some wooden caskets have a plastic tray in the base of the casket to accumulate bodily fluids. Metal caskets with a gasket are designed to off-gas when the internal gas pressure reaches maximum capacity. Non-gasketed caskets will off-gas similar to wooden caskets. A mold-inhibitor chemical that will prevent mold growth, often paradichlorobenzene, should be placed in the casket. Local requirements, usually promulgated by the Department of Health, may vary. Some cemeteries require that the casket be wrapped in a membrane that will maintain a hermetic seal over the long term. Some cemeteries place casketed remains on a plastic tray before entombment. Allowing moisture to evaporate is generally a better method for long-term storage. After all, some Egyptian mummies have lasted for thousands of years just from pure desiccation (removal of moisture).

3. Transportation by Common Carrier

Common carriers are companies that are hired to transport goods. Examples: buses, trains, trucks, and airlines. Generally, human remains are transported long distances by airlines because they travel faster than land-based carriers. Human remains that will be transported by airplane must have certain preparations made in order to have a safe journey to their final destination. Most airlines require that the body be embalmed. In some cases, religious practice prohibits embalming, and some airlines will transport those cases. Unembalmed remains must be placed in a leakproof container with gel packs applied for cooling. Two packs go on the front of the body, two packs on the back, one pack under the head, and one pack goes under each leg. Hands should be bound over the abdomen. Dry ice is prohibited for shipping human remains because the off gassing (release of CO_2 gas) was causing live animals stored next to the human remains to perish. Human remains that start to exhibit beginning or advanced stages of decomposition, should be transported using private carriers, such as a removal van or contracted removal service. Creating a biohazard in an airport could result in hazmat cleaning fees for the shipping funeral director. This could cause unnecessary delays and layovers in shipping.

Different types of containers can be used to transport the remains by common carrier. If the remains are not in a casket, they can be transported in a **combination unit.** *This unit has particle board sides and top, a plywood base, and a cardboard cover over the entire unit.* The remains are stabilized by straps built into the unit and usually have padding to protect the remains. This is the most cost-effective container for common carrier transportation due to weighing the least. If the remains are already in a casket, then an **air tray** is utilized. *This system uses a plywood base to which the casket is attached with straps, and the unit is covered with a plastic casket sheet and a cardboard cover.* Be sure to check with the airlines regarding weight limits. Due to the extra weight of a casket, this is the more expensive method of shipping. Air trays are used properly when there are services at the forwarding funeral home prior to shipping the human remains for final disposition. If the forwarding funeral home does not have public or private services prior to shipping, ethically, the casket should be sold by the receiving funeral home. This keeps shipping costs down (ethical treatment of the family) and allows the receiving funeral home to care for the family's needs as if the person died near home to provide the full service (ethical treatment of other funeral directors).

When shipping by a common carrier, it is necessary to affix the Burial Transit Permit and shipping information to the outside of the combination unit or air tray. The receiving funeral home's name, address, and telephone number must be displayed on the combination or air tray unit. Air freight may be paid by either the shipping or the receiving funeral home. Air trays and combination units are single-use items and must be destroyed after one use.

When shipping internationally, it is necessary to have additional documentation. The process begins by contacting the consulate for the country where the human remains will be sent. This will ensure that the requirements, policies, and procedures are adhered to prior to shipping.

Most countries have similar rules about what documentation is required for shipping human remains to another country. These are some of the most common documents required for international shipping of human remains:

1. Burial Transit Permit.
2. Copy of the Death Certificate.
3. A statement from a Department of Health official stating that the human remains are not infectious, contagious, or communicable.
4. Citizenship information, such as the passport.
5. The destination funeral home receiving the remains needs to be declared.
6. Embalming report
7. Caskets might have to be inspected by Customs and sealed before they can be placed on the airplane. Transportation Safety Administration (TSA) regulations need to be followed at all times.

Some countries have a consulate fee that needs to be paid prior to shipping. Trade services should be utilized to process shipping human remains out of the United States. There are too many varying factors to consider, and professional trade services seem to know each of these requirements and they have a system for processing these types of air transports.

Since 9/11/2001, the Transportation Security Administration (TSA) has imposed rules and regulations on shipping human remains via common carrier. For a funeral home to send human remains on a common carrier, they must become a Known Shipper prior to shipping human remains. Each airline has an application that needs to be processed with TSA for a Known Shipper ID to be assigned to a funeral home. Each airline will issue a separate Known Shipper ID.

When sending casketed remains on an airplane, it is necessary to account for severe changes in cabin pressure. Wooden caskets do not seal, so they may be latched in their usual fashion. Metal caskets that seal present a unique problem. The gasket and locking mechanisms on sealer caskets are designed to relieve pressure from the inside - out. This gasket mechanism is designed to allow gases produced by decomposing remains to escape when the internal pressure increases, potentially causing the casket to rupture. For burial purposes, this is necessary. If the cargo hold of an airplane loses its pressure, the air inside the casket will flow out. However, when pressure is restored in the cargo hold or when landing the aircraft, the air pressure cannot go back into the casket, because the gaskets prevent airflow inward. The result is that the casket top itself will be crushed by atmospheric pressure. Metal caskets can be locked; however, the plug over the key locking chamber needs to be placed in the document envelope affixed to the top of the shipping unit. This opening will allow easy airflow in and out of the casket regardless of pressure change, preventing damage. If this procedure is not done, the forwarding funeral home could be liable for replacing the damaged casket.

When possible, air transportation needs to take into consideration various routes to avoid extremes of weather conditions. During summer months, use a northerly route to avoid high temperatures at airports. Conversely, during winter months, use a more southerly route, if possible, to avoid freezing temperatures and weather delays. Sometimes using airports that are in areas of extreme weather conditions cannot be avoided.

Another concept with shipping during high-temperature seasons or shipping to tropical countries is to prepare the remains by using cotton soaked in lamp oil inserted into each nasal cavity. This would prevent the development of maggots if there were flies present previously or upon arrival of the remains. Prior to public viewing or prior to shipping human remains, the best funeral practice is to always keep the face covered to prevent a fly from using the nasal cavity as a receptacle for laying their eggs.

Another factor to consider in common carrier transportation is unembalmed remains or a decomposing case in which embalming has failed to retard the natural decomposition of the remains. Human remains in advanced stages of decomposition can be shipped using a container known as a Ziegler case. This is an eight-sided (octagonal-shaped) metal casket that is welded and used for extreme conditions or cases. A Zieglar case is a one-piece lid with a rubber gasket. The lid is placed on top of the container and is screwed down, then soldered or welded shut. Once properly closed, it is completely sealed. The strength of the seal prevents the outflow of air if there is a pressure drop (discussed above), so when pressure is restored, the container will not collapse. The Ziegler case can be placed in a regular burial casket with the interior removed. The corners are tapered diagonally to allow the removal of straps or other devices used to lower it into the casket.

4. Green Burial

Green burial refers to human remains which are interred in the ground, without any chemical treatment, and usually in a biodegradable burial unit or wrapped in a burial shroud. This concept of human remains disposal is based on the notion that it allows the remains to naturally decompose fully back to the earth. The general tenets of green burial are that there will be no synthetic chemicals introduced into the ground, that the burial container can fully decompose, and that there is minimal marking of the gravesite. Most green cemeteries use latitude and longitude coordinates to locate the grave. There are hybrid cemeteries which are traditional cemeteries that have a green section in addition to their regular areas for burials. Generally, there is no embalming, no vaults, no metal caskets, and no wood caskets with finish. The strength of green cemeteries is that they are an ecologically sensible alternative to cremation, where a large amount of fossil fuels are used during the cremation process.

Green cemeteries in the northern portion of the country have a problem with winter burial. When the frost is too deep in the ground to open a grave, the body must be stored until spring. This requires embalming because an unembalmed body would have to be kept in a cooler for a long time. That would be expensive, as well as defeating the conceptual idea of reducing the *carbon footprint*. There are fluids manufactured by at least two chemical companies which are approved for green burial. These fluids contain naturally occurring chemicals that break down completely into harmless molecules, thus meeting the requirement for full decomposition in a green cemetery.

Some of the green embalming chemicals are supplied in their fully diluted form and can be used in the embalming machine with no further dilution. Preservation of the cellular tissue is minimal; firming and long-term preservation is noticeably different from conventional embalming with formaldehyde or glutaraldehyde-based chemicals.

5. Preparation for Cremation

The Burial Transit Permit is obtained from the Registrar in the locality where the death occurred after the death certificate has been filed. Cremation is a means of final disposition which uses intense heat to incinerate the human remains and reduce them to their calcium and carbon components. A Burial Transit Permit is issued and needed prior to cremation. Once the cremation has been completed, the crematory operator will file the completed Burial Transit Permit with the Registrar where the cremation occurred. The cremated remains from that point forward are not considered a legal entity. They may be treated in any way that is legal, which mostly means not littering and scattering cremated remains in public or private areas, where doing so is prohibited. Crematories will provide a Certificate of Cremation (that authenticates the cremated remains as being those of the person brought to the crematory), which can be taken to a cemetery to prove that the cremated remains in that urn are a particular person. The Certificate of Cremation replaces the body transit permit required by cemeteries for the burial of cremated remains. This certificate is needed for shipping cremated remains, as well as traveling with an urn on a common carrier. Burying cremated remains is not considered the final disposition; the cremation process is the final disposition of the human remains.

The most important aspect of cremation is being absolutely certain that the proper person is being cremated. *Identification of all human remains begins at the point of removal when an ID bracelet is affixed to the wrist and ankle.* In some states, like Ohio, this is a state regulation. Each time that the remains are moved for various treatments (such as embalming or cosmetology), the ID bracelets should be checked and verified. Human remains need to be identified by the family (or their appointed representative) prior to cremation in the container selected by the family during arrangements. A family member needs to sign a statement declaring that they identified the remains of their loved one. No human remains should be cremated prior to proper identification by the next-of-kin or person making the funeral arrangements.

The direct cremation package price for cremation includes the treatment of the remains for sanitary purposes, and there is no additional charge allowed for this preparation. Prior to having the family identify the human remains, the following procedures should be implemented to prepare the remains for positive identification by the person making the arrangements:

1. The deceased hair should be combed.
2. The face should be disinfected and sanitized.
3. Orifices should be swabbed with a disinfectant spray, and any visible signs of bodily fluids should be removed.
4. The oral cavity should be secured to the closed position
5. Eye caps with stay cream on top should be inserted under the eyelids.
6. The deceased should be prepared and placed in the cremation unit selected by the family during the arrangements.

7. The remains should be in a state of repose that presents a positive memory picture.
8. Human remains placed in an alternative container should be covered from the chest down with clothing, a hospital gown, a blanket, or a quilt.

Preparing the human remains for an identification session is included in the direct cremation package price. If the family wishes for a private viewing session with immediate family and the funeral home has a policy in place for viewing unembalmed remains in such a setting, the funeral home can charge for such viewing, provided that such a session appears on their General Price List.

Crematories have a capacity that cannot be exceeded. Capacity is the measure of how large a person may fit in the retort. The common capacity of a retort is 450 pounds, meaning that a larger person needs to be taken to a crematory that can accommodate excessive weight limits. A similar term to capacity is burn rate which is a measure of how fast the body is consumed by heat and flame. When more than one human remains are being cremated during the day, larger remains are cremated first because the retort needs to be set at a low temperature to burn off the adipose tissue (body fat) gradually. Cremating large human remains, too fast, could cause the retort to catch fire, creating damage to the retort and possibly the crematory. The person with the least amount of weight is cremated last and poses minimal threat to crematory operations.

Sample question:
A crematory had human remains that weighed 375lbs. When were the remains, cremated?
A. 8:00 a.m.
B. 11:00 a.m.
C. 3:00 p.m.
D. 4:00 p.m.
Answer: 8:00 a.m.

Tooth extraction is Prohibited.

Tooth extraction at the request of the family can only be performed by a dentist. A funeral director is not trained to remove teeth, and doing so could cause a liable situation and be considered a form of mutilation. Dental gold is not the same as jeweler's gold. Dental gold has little resale value…it is made mostly of various alloys in order to be durable and withstand oral acids.

Preparation of the human remains for cremation includes:

1. Removal of any pacemaker, defibrillator, or device that has a cell battery as a component. The small pill size pacemaker embedded in the heart poses little risk and may be left in place. Only remove subcutaneous battery units. Battery cells that are not removed will explode in the retort and could cause damage to the retort. In addition, shrapnel from a battery-operated device could be life-threatening to the crematory operator.

2. To remove a battery-operated device that is subcutaneous, an incision is made over the device to expose the device. Connective fascia tissue might have to be removed to expose the unit. Using an aneurism hook, the device should be extracted from the body and pulled tight. The leads that are attached to the heart can be snipped with wire cutters. The device should be disposed of properly and not in the biohazard waste container because usually, this material is incinerated and will pose the same hazard as previously stated.
3. The funeral home may charge an extra fee to remove pacemakers because it is not done for each and every case. This fee should be nominal and must be on the GPL.
4. All belongings should be documented on an inventory sheet and signed by the family. Remove all personal items that should be returned to the family, such as hearing aids or jewelry.
5. The human remains should be placed in a leakproof pouch specially designed for the cremation process. Note: Disaster pouches will emit toxic chemicals such as benzopyrene (BAP) and polyaromatic hydrocarbons (PAH); both are a violation of the Environmental Protection Act (EPA).
6. Radioactive implants, active or inactive, need to be removed by a trained surgeon prior to cremation. An embalmer is not licensed to remove such an implant. Knowingly cremating human remains with radioactive implants is also a violation of the EPA. If a surgeon is unwilling to remove the implants, the family should be counseled on other options of final disposition.
7. The human remains should be dressed in a minimal garment, such as a hospital gown or clothes brought in by the family. If the deceased is wearing the clothes from the removal, the pockets should be checked prior to cremation and any contents should be documented and returned to the family.
8. The cremation container should have the head end clearly marked with the decedent's last name and the name of the funeral home written on the exterior.
9. A numbered metal medallion that can withstand the temperatures during the cremation process is placed on the cremation container prior to being placed in the retort and remains through the cremation process.
10. After the cremation process is completed, the medallion should be attached to a plastic bag containing the pulverized cremated remains. If possible, that medallion should be included in the urn when presented to the family.

Recap: All human remains should be identified by the person making the arrangements (or designated representative). The remains need to be checked for a pacemaker or other device with a battery pack; the remains should be checked head-to-toe for jewelry; and finally, the remains should be in a leakproof pouch acceptable for cremation.

Documents required for cremation include:
1. Burial Transit Permit.
2. Authorization for Cremation form or Cremation Authorization forms specific to state regulations, which authorizes the crematory to perform the cremation.
3. In some cases, a cremation permit is issued by a coroner, medical examiner, or Department of Health. This requirement varies from state-to-state.

4. Further documentation includes a statement about what will happen to those cremains if they are not retrieved within a certain period of time. This, too, varies among the states, ranging from 60 days to four years (Customer Designation of Intention form).
5. If, for religious reasons, the family requires an intact bone fragment, a written notarized statement from the family must accompany the authorization form. The bone fragment should not exceed 3" in length.
6. The family should be informed that cremation is an irreversible process by which intense heat is used to reduce the human remains to their calcium deposits. This disclosure should be a part of the informed consent section on the cremation authorization form and should be reviewed with the family at the end of the arrangement process.

A funeral home should not retain cremated remains for an extended period of time. Cremated remains may be buried in the ground (interment), placed in a niche or columbarium (inurnment), placed in a common receptacle for many different cremated remains (ossuary), or returned to the family for their retention. There is no law specifying that they need to be disposed of in any specific way or time frame. Some states have provisions within the law that allows the funeral director to properly dispose of unclaimed cremated remains in a prescribed manner. In New York State, for example, a Customer Designation of Intention form is used during the arrangements to identify the consumer's wishes for the cremated remains after the cremation process has been completed. This form also indicates that after 120 days, if the cremated remains are unclaimed, the funeral home has the right to dispose of the cremated remains in a prescribed manner.

A funeral director may transfer the cremated remains from a temporary container to a final container, such as an urn selected during arrangements, as a service to the family. A funeral director may not comingle the ashes of two or more people in the same container. There are companion urns that have two sections but do not mix the cremains. Inurnment may be in one urn or several small ones; it is allowed to divide into smaller units for burial in different places. When the urn has been filled, it is important to be certain the outside is clean, showing no dust or other indication of what is inside. If transporting cremains on an airplane, it is requested that the content material must be transparent to X-Ray so it can be checked by TSA.

Human remains with radioactive implants cannot be cremated unless the radioactive implant has been removed. Knowingly cremating human remains with radioactive implants is a violation of EPA standards and could result in a federal violation for the crematory operator and the funeral director. Removal of radioactive implants can only be done by a trained medical professional who can properly dispose of the radioactive material. If no medical professional is willing to remove the radioactive implants, the funeral director needs to counsel the family on alternative means of final disposition. Radioactive implants whose shelf-life has expired are also covered under this rule.

Sending Cremated Remains via Mail

Cremated remains can only be sent via United States Postal Services Priority Mail Express. The postal service has a specific box marked "Cremated Remains," in which the cremated remains must be packaged for shipping and can be obtained without charge from the Post Office. The package needs to be sent by registered mail, and a signature receipt is required. A tracking number will be issued.

Funeral Directing and Preparation for Disposition

First Call:

Funeral directors are not able to proceed with a case until they receive an official notification of death, generally known as the "first call." With the rise of cell phones, almost all notifications of death are made via telephone (at least 98%). The notification of death is most commonly made by the family, an agency, such as a nursing home or hospice center, a hospital, a medical examiner's office, a police agency, or even a friend. Gathering important preliminary information regarding the caller and their relationship to the decedent is the essential part of the first call.

The person answering phones on behalf of the funeral home must use an appropriate tone of voice and proper language. Neutral language should always be used to ensure that respect is given to every person equally. When answering phones, the person's tone and diction should be clear, crisp, moderate volume, and slightly slower than normal speech, and use appropriate enunciation and pronunciation. The person should sound understanding and empathetic, not too cheerful or somber. The person should also not sound bored, annoyed, or angry. This is the first interaction the funeral home and director may have with the family and will set the tone for any future interactions.

When gathering first call information, the person receiving the call needs to **determine the nature of the call**: That is, is the caller calling regarding an "at-need" case in which someone has died or "pre-need" case in which someone wants to pre-arrange their funeral services, but death has not occurred yet, or death is imminent (very close).

Acquiring Vital Information: The removal process begins by **obtaining vital information**. The preliminary information obtained on the *first call* must be accurate and informative. This information, if wrong, will affect other information obtained during the conference arrangements. Misinformation could cause delays, cost the firm money to correct errors, and is unprofessional.

The person taking the call needs to obtain the following information:
1. The name of the decedent.
2. The location of the deceased. If an institution, has the deceased been transferred to the morgue, and the remains been released?
3. If the caller is a representative of an institution, the question should be asked if the deceased is ready for the funeral home to make the removal.
4. If the person dies at home and the death is attended by an agency (such as Hospice or Home Healthcare), usually the representative from the agency calls the funeral home. During this conversation with the healthcare worker, the funeral director obtains the majority of the information:

a. Address where the removal will take place
b. Who will be signing the death certificate
c. Time of Death (TOD)
d. Name of the next-of-kin or contact person who will be making the arrangements.
e. Contact person's phone number and possibly an alternative phone number
f. Obtain pertinent information about the location of the removal.
   1) If there are stairs, sharp corners, multiple floors,
   2) The decedent's weight, state (decomposition, rigor mortis), and cultural/religious beliefs needs to be obtained to ensure that appropriate removal measures are taken.

5. If the caller is a family member and the death was an unattended death, the funeral director will inform the caller to call 911 and notify the authorities that a death occurred. This could be alarming for some family members. The funeral director should inform the caller that calling the authorities is a normal procedure when a person dies without medical personnel attending the death. The funeral director should explain the process of involving the authorities:
   a. After the caller calls 911, a uniformed officer, such as a police officer or sheriff, will show up at the house and take some preliminary information.
   b. The coroner/medical examiner official will come to the home and authorize the removal.
   c. The coroner/medical examiner or police officer will then call the funeral home and authorize the removal. If the death was suspicious or no doctor would sign the death certificate, the coroner/medical examiner personnel could require the human remains to be taken to the ME's office or local morgue.
   d. At that time, the removal personnel will come to the home and bring the deceased back to the funeral home or do as directed by the authorities.
   e. Reassuring the family that the funeral home is always there for them, the funeral director's cell phone number (optional) should be offered, or the funeral director should provide the best number for the funeral home. Reassure the family that the authority will be expeditious, and if no one replies within 30 minutes, the next-of-kin should call the funeral home.

Medical Facility Notification: If the caller is the next-of-kin, and the decedent is at a medical facility or other agency, additional information may need to be obtained, such as:
   1. Medical Record Number (obtained from the institution)
   2. Date of Admission
   3. Location of facility or room where the patient is residing or
   4. Has the deceased been transported to the morgue?
   5. The physician who will be signing the death certificate
   6. The next-of-kin contact information

Most medical institutions will provide a face sheet that has this information. Some institutions are reluctant to provide this information because of HIPPA (Health Insurance Portability and Accountability Act) regulations. Unfortunately, such institutions are misguided regarding the information that funeral directors can obtain information about the deceased. The following is the **HIPPA regulation** *with respect to disclosing information to the funeral director:*

Standard: Uses and disclosures about decedents.

(1) **Coroners and medical examiners.** A covered entity may disclose protected health information to a coroner or medical examiner for the purpose of identifying a deceased person, determining a cause of death, or other duties as authorized by law. A covered entity that also performs the duties of a coroner or medical examiner may use protected health information for the purposes described in this paragraph.

(2) **Funeral directors.** A covered entity may disclose protected health information to funeral directors, consistent with applicable law, as necessary to carry out their duties with respect to the decedent. If necessary for funeral directors to carry out their duties, the covered entity may disclose the protected health information prior to, and in reasonable anticipation of, the individual's death.

Source:

http://www.hipaasurvivalguide.com/hipaa-regulations/164-512.php

Occasionally, funeral homes will receive calls from "price shoppers," a person who will call many funeral homes to compare and contrast pricing for funeral services. Under Federal Trade Commission (FTC) Funeral Rule, firms are required to disclose current pricing information to the consumer, both in-person and over-the-phone inquiries. While accurate pricing over the phone is a triggering event for pricing disclosure, under the Funeral Rule, the funeral director is not required to mail or email a General Price List (GPL). The key to these types of inquiries is to provide accurate information while engaging in a conversation as to what types of services are available and how the firm can best serve their needs.

The Removal: After the first call information has been obtained and authorization has been granted, the decedent can be removed from the residence/institution. Funeral home personnel should not be dispatched until proper authorization has been obtained. However, the funeral director should begin the removal process by notifying additional staff of the pending removal. Coordinating and preparing the removal vehicle with the proper equipment and organizing personnel in the midst of other scheduled events, like funerals and visitations, may require freeing up personnel in order to comply with state regulations governing removals.

Once the first call has been received and permission to remove the human remains has been granted, the removal can be made from the place of death. **The removal** is *the transfer of human remains from the location of death to the funeral home.*

Various vehicles may be used for removals. Some firms solely use a hearse for all removals and funeral services. Some firms utilize a removal vehicle which is usually a minivan or SUV that has the space for a removal cot. The choice of vehicle may depend on factors such as availability, location of the removal, number of decedents, and the family's wishes (some families are adamantly against a hearse coming to the house). Most states require that a removal vehicle has tinted windows to impede the view from the public.

Vehicles should be properly maintained, including necessary inspections, registrations, and oil changes. The removal vehicle should have an adequate supply of gas, especially in the event of midnight removals when gas stations may not be available. The vehicle should also be cleaned, both interior and exterior, to maintain a professional appearance and a clean environment. The vehicle should also be equipped with the proper removal equipment, which includes, but is not limited to:

1. A mortuary cot to carry the decedent, a pillow or head block, sheets,
2. Alternative moving devices like Reeves Carrier or a MedSled First Call,
3. Mortuary/body bags (a/k/a, disaster pouch). This is a regulation in some states,
4. Hand sanitizer/wipes,
5. Relevant paperwork (General Price List, Embalming Authorizations, Business Cards, Information sheets),
6. Appropriate PPE (disposable gloves, masks, shoe covers, disposable gown).

Mortuary bags vary in size and thickness and should be chosen based on the conditions and location of the decedent. Severely obese or decomposing decedents should be placed in a Disaster Pouch, which is thicker with reinforced straps.

Depending on the age of the decedent, a different removal device may be used. A baby or infant will be too small for a standard cot; therefore, the funeral home may use a bassinet or infant carrying container.

The removal staff should be trained in proper ergonomics and lifting techniques to ensure proper lifting occurs without injury. Lifting in the funeral industry is an occupational hazard, and under OSHA regulations, removal personnel need to be briefed on each various removal situation to ensure the deceased is being handled with care and respect while maintaining employee safety. At least one removal personnel should be appropriately licensed (unless state regulations don't require a licensed funeral director). Some states require a licensed funeral director to be present to sign discharge paperwork. Additional non-licensed removal personnel may be utilized for additional help, especially on removals when the deceased is obese. The general rule of thumb is there should be at least two people for each removal if the deceased is under 250 lbs. In some cases, police agencies and fire departments may be called to do lift assists with difficult removals. All removals should be completed, caring for the human remains with the utmost dignity and respect.

All removal personnel should be neat and professionally presentable because they are the first representation of the funeral home to have contact with the family. Their attire should conform to the standards of the funeral home. The social norms established by the community will influence funeral home policy regarding proper attire. For example, a rural farming community may not want removal staff to wear suits. In this situation, dress pants and a dress shirt with the funeral home logo affixed may be appropriate.

Home Removals:

Once at the removal site, the funeral director should first speak with the family to introduce the staff and discuss the removal process. If there is only one person making the removal, the deceased should be removed last after the family has been briefed by the funeral director. Before the removal occurs, the deceased needs to be properly identified and checked for personal belongings. The funeral director should confirm with the family their wishes with these personal effects. A wedding ring or other jewelry should be removed at the next-of-kin's request. Other items, such as clothing, glasses, dentures, and personal mementos, should be taken only at the next of kin's request. All items should be appropriately documented in the file, with instructions on what is to happen with each.

If there are two funeral home personnel on the removal (which should be in the majority of cases), the removal should be done first after the initial contact with the family. Universal precautions should be used on all removals. The remains should be shrouded in a bed sheet (with the face covered) for a smooth transition from the bed to the removal cot. **Someone should always remain with the decedent to ensure safety and confidentiality**.

If the furniture is moved during the removal, the furniture should be moved back after the human remains have been secured in the removal vehicle. If the decedent is in a bed, the best practice is to either fold up the bedding or re-make the bed for the family. If a bed sheet was used for the removal, the sheet should be washed and given back to the family at the time of arrangements. If the sheet is badly stained and is deemed a biohazard, the family needs to be informed that the sheet was properly disposed of because it was a biohazard.

Once the removal has been completed and the deceased is secured in the removal vehicle accompanied by another removal person (**never leave the human remains unattended**), the funeral director returns to the resident and discusses with the next-of-kin the following information:

1. What type of services are desired?
2. If services include public viewing or a public funeral with the human remains present, verbal permission is needed for embalming. A simple nod of the head is not considered permission.
3. If the family chooses cremation as a means of final disposition, the funeral director should ask, "Is that before or after public or private visitation?" Presenting options to the family is a way to allow the family an opportunity to choose the type of services that best fits their understanding of how to honor the life accomplishments of the deceased. A family that chooses cremation doesn't always mean direct cremation without services. Most family's welcome options to make an educated decision.
4. The next-of-kin may inquire about pricing information. A GPL is required to be available during the removal process. This is a triggering event (under the Funeral Rule) and requires the funeral director to physically hand the next-of-kin, for their retention, a copy of the GPL that explains the cost for such services:

For example: "Mrs. Thompson, you asked me how much embalming costs. To be in compliance with state and federal regulations, I must present to you a copy of the General Price List which lists all the funeral goods and services we provide at the Jones Funeral Home. (Open the GPL and point to the charge in question). You asked me how much embalming costs. Our cost for embalming is $750.00."

5. Establish a meeting time for the arrangement conference.
6. Some funeral homes present the family with a cloth or canvas garment bag that has a laminated card attached, with instructions on what to bring to the arrangements. Each side is gender specific, with information that may be required during the arrangement conference and the appropriate clothing necessary for public visitation and services.

Institutional Removals:

The decedent needs to be appropriately identified, tagged, and labeled. If the decedent is in a mortuary pouch, the best practice is to open the bag and check the toe tag or hospital bracelet that may be affixed to the decedent. The name on the ID tag should match the name on the mortuary pouch. Be sure to complete all required paperwork at the institution to ensure that there are records of the removal.

A Registered Resident/Apprentice or Licensed Funeral Director may have to provide their Resident/Apprentice/Funeral Director License as well as Driver's License to the institution. Licensed personnel should also be the ones signing any agency documents during the removal process.

➢ *Who may sign for removal may vary from state-to-state.*
➢ *Some Veteran Administration Hospitals have their own registrar and death certificates are completed at the time of removal. In these cases, only a fully licensed funeral director could sign for the removal, as residents/apprentices cannot sign death certificates.*

Arrangement Conference:

The purpose of the arrangement conference is to obtain vital statistical information for the death certificate, coordinate and plan the preferred method of disposition and services desired by the family, fill out the necessary paperwork and authorizations, and review the financials.

Traditionally, arrangements are held in the funeral home shortly after the death. However, as more and more people live away from their families, arrangements may be made in a variety of formats, including both in person and virtually through phone, email, and fax. Arrangements may also be held in other locations besides the funeral home, such as the family's house or in an institution, such as Hospice or nursing home.

Arrangements should be a form of client-centered counseling in which the client helps guide the arrangement conference with encouragement from the funeral director. The funeral director should allow the client family to tell them stories about their loved ones to learn more about their life and details that could be pertinent to the funeral services. The funeral director should use open-ended questions to guide the conversation.

Arrangements should be made by the legally appointed person. The hierarchy of who is entitled to make arrangements varies from state-to-state. Traditionally, the first in line is a legally appointed agent, followed by a legal spouse.

> ➤ *Health-Care-Proxy and Power of Attorney cease after the death occurs.*
> ➤ If the decedent has pre-arrangements that are pre-funded, the wishes of the deceased should be honored.

The death certificate is a legal document containing vital statistics, dispositions, and final medical information pertaining to the deceased. The death certificate contains vital statistical information about the decedent, as well as the manner and cause of death provided by a medical professional and is certified by the registrar where the person passed away. Most death certificates in the United States are filed on the Database Application for Vital Events (DAVE) system. Most states use the DAVE system; however, there are some municipalities that still utilize paper filing of death certificates.

The funeral director provides the following information for the death certificate. Required information may vary from state-to-state:

1. Name of decedent
2. Date of birth of the decedent
3. Date of death
4. Time of death
5. Last known address of the decedent
6. Address or institution of death
7. Decedent's race
8. If the decedent is of Latino/Hispanic background
9. Decedent's highest education
10. Decedent's occupation and last known workplace
11. Decedent's parent one birthname
12. Decedent's parents' two birthname
13. Decedent's veteran status
14. If a decedent is a veteran, years that they served in the military
15. Name of informant (person giving the information)
16. Address of informant
17. Method of disposition
18. Name and location of the place of disposition (crematory, cemetery, medical facility)
19. Funeral Home name, address, and registration number
20. Funeral Director's name and registration number

Vital statistics are entered and electronically signed by the funeral director. The cause and manner of death are signed by the licensed medical professional. Once the local registrar receives the signed death certificate electronically, the document is processed, and a burial transit permit is issued.

An important concept to know: What is the difference between a Death Certificate and a Burial Transit Permit? A ***Death Certificate is filed*** by the funeral director, and a ***Burial Transit permit is issued*** by the registrar.

Some states may need additional information for their death certificates. Some municipalities also require a medical clearance to be obtained before cremation can occur. If information is not known, "unknown" may be written on the line requesting the information (check state requirements). Don't leave blank spaces on a death certificate. Cause of death is how the person actually died. Example: myocardial infarction. Manner of death is the broad classification of the mode of death: natural, homicide, suicide, accidental, and unknown.

With the DAVE system, the voluntary filing of the **SSA-721** Statement of Death by the funeral director is no longer required. Once the death certificate is filed with the Registrar's Office, Social Security is immediately notified that the decedent's social security number is no longer active. If the death certificate is paper filed, the funeral director will need to complete form SSA-721 and file it with the local Social Security office. A surviving spouse or child, under the age of 18, may be eligible for the lump-sum death benefit of $255, which utilizes form **SSA-8**, Application for Lump-Sum Death Payment. SSA-8 is a form completed by a case worker at Social Security.

Once the funeral director has the vital statistical information, the **Death Certificate** *is filed with the local registrar* to obtain certified copies for the decedent's family, as well as obtain the **Burial Transit Permit**, *which is issued by the registrar allowing the disposition to take place*. Most death certificates are filed with the local registrar using the Database Application for Vital Events (DAVE) system. Certified copies of the Death Transcript can be ordered on DAVE, and the Burial Transit Permit can be downloaded and printed by the funeral director at the funeral home. Certified copies of the death certificate are needed for any property or assets that are in the name of the decedent. Including but not limited to titles, deeds, insurance policies, retirement, bank, and utility accounts.

Methods of Final Disposition

The first service detail that needs to be selected is the method of disposition. This selection will dictate what type of paperwork is necessary, as well as the type of treatments and preparations needed for the human remains. The methods of disposition are:
1. Burial- when the body is placed in a casket and buried in a cemetery or entombed in a mausoleum.
    a. Traditional burial - will have a funeral service before burial.
    b. Direct burial – will not have any services before burial.
2. Cremation- when the body is incinerated in a retort.
    a. Services with cremation after - the body is present for the services, and the cremation takes place afterwards.

      b. Services after cremation - a memorial service will be held after the body has been cremated, with or without the cremated remains present.

      c. Direct cremation - the body will be cremated, and there will not be any services.

      Legalities of scattering cremated remains vary from locality-to-locality.

3. Body Donation - in which the decedent is donated to a medical institution for research. (Note: many medical facilities cremate the decedent when they are finished with their body).

4. Burial at Sea – this may be a full body in a casket or cremated remains.

5. Alternative disposition - sustainable "green" forms of disposition.

      a. Green burial – no casket or vault and no carcinogenic embalming fluids.

      b. Alkaline hydrolysis (not available in most states) – water cremation is a process in which the human remains are placed in a pressure chamber that is filled with a mixture of water and potassium hydroxide and heated to a temperature around $160°$ C or $320°F$. The soft tissue is dissolved, and the bone fragments remain. The remaining bones are processed similarly to the manner used in the cremation process.

      c. Natural Organic Reduction (NOR), a/k/a Human Composting, is a process of the final disposition of human remains in which microbes convert the human remains into compost material (not available in most states). This process requires the body to be wrapped in a biodegradable shroud. The remains are placed in a reusable container and organic material is placed on top of the remains. Microbes, overtime (30 to 60 days), will dissolve the human remains, depending on several factors. After this time, much of the human remains will decompose and become compostable material, leaving behind the bones.

      d. Cryonics – the freezing and long-term storage of human remains for possible restoration of life in the future. A process that is extremely rare.

There are a wide range of services that could be selected. These include but are not limited to:

1. Calling hours or visitation - to allow friends and family to come and give condolences

2. Home funerals - Services at the decedent's or family's house

3. Memorial Service - These are services without the body present may or may not have cremated remains present.

4. Funeral Service – These are funeral services with the body present.

5. Humanistic service - in which there is no religious connotation.

6. Adaptive service - non-traditional services but may have spiritual or religious connections.

7. Graveside service – The services only take place at the gravesite.

When selecting services, various items should be discussed, including but not limited to

1. Date and time

2. Location of services

3. Cemetery name and lot/plot location, if applicable

4. Desired clergy, celebrant, or speaker

5. Pallbearers (casket bearers) - will the family provide pallbearers, or will the funeral home provide this service?
6. Desired merchandise: casket, vault, urn, alternative container, memorial packages, prayer cards
7. Use of hearse if applicable or desired
8. Military honors, if eligible and requested
9. Order of the procession vehicles
10. Desired restoration, cosmetics, hairstyle of decedent - may obtain a photo for reference.
11. Clothing wishes for the decedent
12. Ways to personalize the services

The family may also desire a death notice or an obituary. A death notice is a short publication stating someone has passed away and may include service information. An obituary is a longer publication containing a biographical sketch of the person's life, including information about the person and the service details. Families may wish to write the obituary on their own but may also want input from the funeral director or may wish to have it written completely by the funeral director. Grammar and proper sentence structure is the responsibility of the funeral director since the name of the funeral home will be publicized. Obituaries will vary from family-to-family, but many include surviving relatives, deceased relatives, school/work/activities/organization involvement information, and donation requests.

Once the disposition of the decedent and the service information has been discussed and decided, completing all required paperwork is an important part of the funeral directing process. The following are some of the standard forms prepared and processed on each case:

Death Certificate	A legal document containing vital statistics, disposition, and final medical information pertaining to the deceased.
Cremation Authorizations	Forms authorizing the cremation of the decedent.
Embalming Authorizations	Form authorizing embalming of the decedent.
Right to Control Disposition	Identifies the person who has the legal authority to handle funeral arrangements. Usually, it is the next-of- kin.
Designation of Intentions	Designates what is to happen with cremated remains after the cremation (return to next-of-kin, burial, etc.)
Identification Authorization	Obtains signature identifying the decedent.
Itemized Statement of Goods and Services	Itemized costs of services and merchandise selected. Includes payment contract.

Financials:

After the paperwork has been completed, the financial information may be reviewed. The pricing should be taken from the General Price List following Federal Trade Commission (FTC) guidelines (*See FTC section*), and *the selected goods and services should have their itemized prices recorded* on the **Statement of Goods and Services**. The Statement of Goods and Services should be prepared during the arrangement session and reviewed with the client's family. As the charges are being reviewed, the funeral director should use the statement, "You selected ___, and this is the charge for that service or merchandise." Explaining all the services and merchandise selected with the corresponding charges will give the consumer one last opportunity to determine if these are the services they choose for their love-one.

During this explanation, the family should understand which charges are declinable and which are non-declinable, also known as the Basic Arrangement Fee. On the Statement of Goods and Services, there are two sections with funeral home charges, that is, Services and Merchandise and Additional Services and Merchandise. Cash Advances are third party payments for services rendered, such as a cemetery or crematory. The practice of charging for cash advances is a convenience for the family so that the consumer only pays one bill for all the services. The disadvantage is that the final amount appears to be higher, and the consumer could perceive that the cash advances are funeral home charges when they are fees that are passed on to third-party vendors. Only the amount charged by a third-party vendor is the amount that can be charged to the consumer. Charging a fee for cash advances is a violation of FTC and some state regulations.

The Statement of Goods and Services form should be signed by the client's family, acknowledging that they are being charged for the goods and services they selected, and they assume financial responsibility for services rendered. Payment for services rendered should be discussed at the end of the arrangements. The funeral home payment policy will dictate the terms and conditions of the contract. Sometimes arrangements need to be made for a third party, such as Social Services, the Veterans Administration, a charity, or a life insurance company, to pay for the funeral expenses.

If the person is on Medicaid, Social Services, or disability services, they may be eligible for public assistance (sometimes referred to as indigent burial funds through the county in which they reside). The eligibility requirements and the documentation requirements vary from municipality-to-municipality. The amount that is covered by social services also varies.

Military and Veteran Benefits

If the decedent is a veteran or active-duty Service Member, they may be entitled to Military Honors and benefits. Veteran benefits generally must go through the Department of Veterans Affairs to ensure and verify status and qualifications. These would include burial allowances and interment costs.

To be eligible, veterans must meet the VA's criteria:

1. Veterans with an honorable or other than-honorable (general) discharge are entitled to a burial flag.
2. To obtain the burial flag, a copy of the **DD214** (a/k/a Separation Papers from the military) or another discharge form must be present. The discharge form must state the type of discharge.
3. A burial flag may be obtained using **VA form 27-2008** (*Application for United States Flag for Burial Purposes*) from the United States Postal Service.
4. Veterans are also entitled to a Military Marker. There are a few different markers and medallion options, which may be selected by the family using form, **VA 40-1330** *Application for Headstone or Marker* (marker) or **VA 40-1330M** (medallion), usually affixed to a headstone or mausoleum crypt. On the marker application forms, there is a box to indicate if the family would like a Presidential Memorial Certificate.
5. If a person was dishonorably discharged from the military, they are usually not eligible for military honors or benefits. Verification of questionable eligibility for Veteran benefits can be made with the local Veterans Affairs Office.
6. **VA form 21-530** *is used for Veteran Burial Allowances,*
7. **VA form DD 1375** *is the request for payment for funeral expenses and interment expenses.*

Request for Military Honors

The family may also wish to have Military Honors rendered at the end of the funeral or committal services. Military Honors vary depending on the status of the Veteran (veteran, retiree, rank, etc.). Honors may include the playing of taps, three-volley salutes, folding and presenting of the flag, and casket bearing. Coordinating with the Casualty Affairs Unit or Military Honor Team on what items the decedent is eligible for is the best way to determine the type of honors.

Arranging for Military Honors varies depending on branch and location, as honors are rendered by the branch in which the decedent served. The branches of the military and armed forces include the Army, Navy, Air Force, Marines, and Coast Guard. For example, in New York State, Army Honors are rendered through Fort Drum's Casualty Affairs Department, and Navy Honors are rendered out of a Reserve Unit located in Syracuse, NY. Each branch and location have different paperwork that needs to be filled out, and the DD214 (discharge form) must accompany the request for honors.

If the decedent dies while on Active Duty, the military may handle the preparation and arrangements. Active-Duty deaths may be prepared at Dover Air Force Base in their Mortuary Affairs Unit in Dover, Delaware. When a death occurs out of the country on deployment or rotation, 95Ms (Mortuary Affair Specialists) are tasked with retrieval and examination of the body, along with preparation to return their remains to the United States. The military also has specific embalming requirements and standards that must be followed in the event of an Active-Duty death.

Burial may take place in a military, veteran, or National Cemetery. The decedent or their dependent must meet eligibility requirements for burial in a National Cemetery. To establish eligibility and arrange for the burial, the funeral director will need to contact the National Cemetery Scheduling Office and submit the proper documentation. There are additional eligibility and scheduling requirements for Arlington National Cemetery and Airman's Home National Cemetery.

In some instances, a veteran organization, such as a VFW or an American Legion, may ask to be part of the funeral services. They generally have their own short service that is given after the celebrant or clergy has concluded. If the decedent was only eligible for the folding of the flag and the playing of taps, or the military lacks the personnel for a full honor team, the VFW or the American Legion may assist with the three-volley salute and other honors. Generally, the funeral director will coordinate these details with the organization commander or leader on behalf of the family.

When a full twenty-one honor team is provided, the general order of personnel is:

1. Chaplain – Military, religious speaker *Chaplains may be of different faiths
2. Bugler – to play taps *Generally, they hold the bugle and play a recording
3. Color Bearers
4. Color Guard - Carry the flags
5. Casket bearers – (Carry the casket, also known as pallbearers)
6. Firing detail
7. Commander of the firing detail
8. Detail Commander

Burial at Sea:

Some personnel may be eligible for a burial at sea. These include members and former members of the Armed Forces, US Civilian Marine Personnel of the Military Sealift Command, dependents, and United States citizens deemed eligible by their notable service to the United States. There are specific burial requirements for casketed remains and cremated remains.

To set up a burial at sea, the director, along with the next-of-kin, must complete and file a request form with Naval Affairs. The DD214 and a VA copy of the death certificate must accompany this request. Note: A VA copy of the Death Certificate is provided free of charge for all veterans by the local Registrar. If cremated remains are being scattered at sea, the Certificate of Cremation must be presented to the Naval Base of Choice (Norfolk, VA; Jacksonville, FL; San Diego, CA; Bremerton, WA; and Honolulu, HI). Once the paperwork has been received, the Commanding Officer will contact the funeral home to ensure the human remains are properly encased, according to military regulations.

Casketed remains require the following:
- ➤ Casketed remains must have 150 lbs. of extra weight added to the casket with the following:
- ➤ 6 - 1" nylon bands placed around the casket. Two on the head end, two on the foot end, one lengthwise, and one around the sides.
- ➤ Twenty holes (4 in the head cap, 4 in the foot cap, 8 in the bottom, 2 in the foot end, and 2 in the head end) must be drilled into the casket as well to ensure the remains sink.
- ➤ Casketed remains can be placed in water at least three nautical miles from shore, as long as the water is 600 feet (100 fathoms) deep.

Cremated remains require the following:
- ➤ Cremated remains need to be sealed in a bio-degradable container.
- ➤ Cremated remains can be placed in water at least three nautical miles from shore.

Upon approval for burial at sea or scattering at sea, the funeral home will be contacted, and a time will be scheduled for the casketed remains (or cremated remains) to the base. Along with the human or cremated remains, copies of the paperwork and the burial flag should be given to the Commanding Officer.

The Burial at Sea Ceremony Procedure:

- ➤ Once the remains are with the Navy, they will bring the decedent onto the ship or aircraft for the burial at the sea ceremony.
- ➤ Generally, these burials take place during a deployment or rotation; therefore, families are not able to be present.
- ➤ On the request form, the next-of-kin designates a particular religion for the service, if desired.
- ➤ The Navy will then record and take photos of the service and take GPS coordinates of the final disposition.
- ➤ The Office of the Naval Commander will send the next-of-kin the folded flag and shell casings.
- ➤ This process can take 6-12 months, depending on the deployment or rotation length.

Pre-Arrangements

Pre-arrangements will have similar conversations as at-need arrangements; however, they are more geared toward the future. The same attention to detail needs to be given to pre-arrangements as if they were for an at-need case. Pre-arrangements may be made anywhere; at the funeral home, the family's house, an agency, or other locations. Many people opt to set up pre-arrangements for a variety of reasons, including:

> - imminent death,
> - diagnosis of a terminal illness,
> - aging,
> - traveling,
> - living in two different places,
> - lack of family,
> - applying for Medicaid (which requires people to spend down their assets),
> - social service allotments, rehabilitation center allotments, and
> - moving into a nursing home or hospice facility.

Pre-arrangements generally allow people to make their own wishes known and recorded to ease the financial and planning burden on the family. This allows the funeral director to make an initial connection with the client and their family. Pre-arrangements may just be **pre-planned,** in *which the service and disposition details are discussed and recorded in a file,* or maybe **pre-funded,** in which *the beneficiary or other relevant person (caretaker, next-of-kin, power of attorney) begins funding a pre-need account.*

Pre-funding a funeral account should determine if the client qualifies for a revocable contract or an irrevocable contract.

A **revocable contract** *is a legally binding contract that can be terminated by the purchaser at any time prior to the death of the beneficiary with a refund of the money paid on the contract as prescribed by state law.* Depending on the type of pre-need revocable contract, if there are funds in excess of the cost of the at-need services rendered, these funds are returned to the estate of the deceased. Depending on how the funds are deposited in a fiduciary (a third-party entity, like a bank or credit union) and depending on state or federal regulations, upon the request of the purchaser, the funds can be withdrawn at any time prior to death. All principle and interest should be returned to the purchaser upon request, barring any contractual penalties for early withdrawal.

An **irrevocable contract** *is an agreement for future funeral services that cannot be terminated or canceled prior to the death of the beneficiary.* The funds, however, are portable and can be moved from one funeral home to another; however, they can never be refunded to the purchaser. Excess funds after the services have been rendered must be surrendered to the governmental agency from whom the purchaser was receiving public assistance. Only individuals spending down or who are on Medicaid/SSI benefits can establish an irrevocable trust account. This type of account is created to prevent Medicaid fraud.

If a person wishes to create a pre-need contract that cannot be changed or canceled by a family member prior to death, a written instrument, such as a Designation of Agent form, should be created to outline the pre-need arrangements and also to designate an agent to handle the at-need affairs of the purchaser when death occurs.

Pre-funded funeral contracts may be guaranteed or non-guaranteed. **Guaranteed funeral contracts** *are agreements where the funeral firm promises that the services and the merchandise will be provided at the time of need for a sum not exceeding the original amount of the contract plus any accruals, regardless of the current prices associated with providing the services and merchandise at the time of the funeral/services rendered.*

Non-guaranteed funeral contracts *are agreements in which the funeral firm promises to apply the amount of pre-paid funds plus any accruals to the balance due at the time services are rendered. However, the cost of the funeral will be based on the current price for the services and merchandise at the time the death occurs.*

Many funeral firms will guarantee the prices for the funeral services and merchandise; however, non-guarantee cash advance items. This practice is common because funeral homes cannot guarantee third-party vendors' costs for providing their services in the future.

Some states have Pre-Need Insurance policies that can be purchased as a means of funding funeral arrangements. Such policies must be sold by a licensed insurance agent and are regulated by the insurance laws within the state. Some states, such as New York, prohibit the sale of such policies because they are not consumer friendly. If, for example, a policyholder misses a payment (a/k/a premium), the policy lapses, thus voiding the policy and forfeiture of all the premiums paid to date. In a pre-need contract established with a funeral home where the funds are set aside in an interest-bearing account, if a payment is missed, the funds that are set aside are still the asset of the beneficiary until death occurs.

Preparing for Services

Upon completion of the arrangements, the funeral director coordinates and implements all the necessary paperwork and personnel for the services selected by the client's family. This includes contacting the clergy or celebrant, church or another venue, cemetery or crematory, merchandise manufacturer if not in-house, vault company, military or fraternal organization, musicians, cosmetic/hair personnel if not done by the director, and funeral home staff (including funeral attendants, drivers, and cleaners).

The decedent should also be appropriately prepared with desired clothing and restoration if necessary. Merchandise will also need to be ordered or created for the services. If the firm prints its own memorial items (such as prayer cards or register books), it is important to be sure they are printed correctly and timely. Most funeral homes use computer software that generates these items; however, accuracy when the data is entered, is essential; an error in the initial data entry will cause errors throughout all the documents and sundry items.

The funeral home should also be cleaned and set up for the services. This would include being mindful of which religious and cultural items are in the service room. If the firm is decorating for a themed or personalized service, all items are placed in the desired location for display. Flowers should also be appropriately arranged, keeping in mind who sent the piece and the relationship to the deceased.

The exits should be in compliance with the state fire code with illuminated emergency exit signs. Accessibility services, such as ramps, elevators, and restrooms, should be cleaned and in ADA (Americans with Disabilities Act) compliance. The funeral establishment should be in compliance with the local building code. The establishment should have appropriate safety measures such as proper fire extinguishers, fire alarms, carbon monoxide detectors, and labeled exits.

During the Services

The family should be escorted into the facility or service room for their first viewing of the decedent to ensure their satisfaction with the preparations and setup. The funeral director should answer any questions the family may have and make any changes that are desired. If adjustments need to be made to the deceased, the funeral director should ask the family to step out of the room and make the necessary corrections in private. Witnessing the adjustment of the deceased could be traumatizing to some family members.

During the services, funeral home personnel should be visible and available to assist patrons with opening doors, answering questions, navigating the funeral home, as well as beginning and dismissing services. Personnel should be clean and dressed appropriately as they are a representation of the image of the firm. The staff should be knowledgeable and familiar with the service details and the facilities.

The Procession

The funeral director ideally should have cars parked and lined up for the procession before the start of the services. The pallbearers should be identified and briefed as to what is expected prior to the services. They should possibly be seated together for an easy exit after the conclusion of the service. Once the service has concluded, the pallbearers should be gathered and organized accordingly to move and carry the casket to the hearse.

A traditional funeral procession:

1. Escort- Law enforcement vehicle and personnel, if desired and available
2. Lead Car
3. Clergy's Car – clergy may ride in the lead car
4. Pall Bearers if they are not riding with their family
4. Hearse/coach
5. Family
6. Friends

In a funeral procession, the family and funeral coach (hearse) should never be separated. Funeral flags or funeral placards need to be visible. Four-way flashers and headlights should be on during the procession and turned off once at the cemetery. The hearse and lead car should have a purple hazard strobe light on top of the vehicle to indicate the funeral procession. Without an escort or proper traffic controls, all traffic laws must be obeyed.

The Committal

After the funeral service is the committal service at the gravesite, funeral personnel should be at the head and foot of the casket during the casket carry to the grave. The funeral director should ask the pallbearers if anyone has any lifting or health concerns that would restrict them from carrying the casket to the grave. The funeral director should maintain proper decorum while the casket is being carried to the grave and inform the pallbearers of any obstructions, hazards, or obstacles that need to be avoided. The clergy should lead the casket to the grave. The funeral director directs the proper movement of the pallbearers to ensure their safety and the smooth transition of the human remains to their place of rest.

Once at the gravesite, the casket should be placed on the lowering device, and the pallbearers should be thanked for their service. The clergy or celebrant should be positioned at the head of the casket for the short committal service. Once the committal service concludes, the funeral director thanks the attendees and provides them with directions, such as a request from the family for the participants to join them for a reception (repass) and its location. Usually, the vault lid is placed on the base after the family has left the burial site. The funeral director must stay at the cemetery until the lid is placed on the vault.

After the Services

Once services have concluded, the funeral director should meet with the family to give them copies of the paperwork, certified copies of the death certificate, relevant merchandise that may not have been taken from the funeral (prayer cards, register books, cards), and flowers requested by the family.

Aftercare

After services have concluded and all documents have been given to the family, checking in on the client's family is an essential part of providing quality services. After the funeral services, some families may have questions about settling their loved one's final affairs. The funeral director could serve as a resource to direct the family to various services and community resources. This may be in the form of a phone call to see how the family is doing or a drop-in visit to the client if they are in the area. Follow-up could also be through email, letters, or cards. Many firms send cards on holidays or after the first year of death. This allows the family to feel that the funeral home truly cares about them and that their loved one was not just another case. Aftercare is a great way to maintain a positive reputation and possibly gain more client families through positive word of mouth.

Funeral homes can also organize community activities such as events, gatherings, and seminars to invite and connect with the general public. Some firms host holiday remembrance events, information sessions, and support groups. Some firms may also have an aftercare pamphlet or booklet to give clients at the end of services that contain information about grief and other resources, such as counselors in the area or literary suggestions on grief.

Religious Funeral Customs

Religion is a culturally entrenched pattern of behavior made up of sacred beliefs, emotional feelings accompanying those beliefs, and overt conduct implementing the beliefs and feelings. Following the religious customs and guidelines, as it pertains to funerals of your decedent is important because these customs help facilitate the grieving process. The funeral directors should not do anything that goes against the religious beliefs of the decedent to maintain their respect, dignity, and wishes.

Each religion,* denomination, sect, etc., have various customs, beliefs, and funeral practices. Understanding each of their funeral practices is an important part of the funeral directing process to be able to carry out these wishes. When following religious customs, attention to detail is key, as the funeral home should not have any objects or perform any rituals outside of the faith that would or could be perceived as offensive. For example, a funeral home that mainly serve Catholic clientele would need to remove any Christian symbols when serving a Jewish family and covering the mirrors in the funeral home would be an important part of the Jewish mourning rituals.

Each religion will have a specified clergy member or religious leader. Honorariums for these personnel will vary from institution-to-institution.

Funeral directors should also be mindful of religion and cultural ties** and be able to conform to those norms for services, regardless of the personal beliefs of the funeral director. The religious leader may be a part of the funeral arrangements depending upon their religious custom.

*Although each religion has specified funeral customs, there may be variations between institutions, groups, and localities of the same religious belief.
**For those who are adherent in their faith, and devoted to their religious community, the religious leader may be contacted regarding the death and services before the funeral directors.

Liturgical Denominations

Types of Christian Religions

Christianity - *Generally divided into two branches: Catholicism (Roman Catholic and Eastern Orthodox) and Protestant*

In this broad section terms will be reviewed that may be utilized in the various Christian denominations and services.

A liturgical church and a non-liturgical church differ primarily in their approaches to worship and religious rituals. Liturgical churches follow a set order of worship, often characterized by formal rituals, prescribed prayers, and a structured liturgy that is repeated regularly. The liturgy provides a sense of continuity and tradition, with specific rites observed throughout the church calendar. Examples of liturgical churches include the Roman Catholic, Eastern Orthodox, and Anglican traditions. On the other hand, non-liturgical churches, often associated with Protestant denominations, emphasize flexibility in worship, allowing for more spontaneous and informal expressions. These churches often prioritize preaching, congregational participation, and individual interpretation of scripture, with less emphasis on a standardized liturgical format. The distinction between liturgical and non-liturgical churches reflects diverse theological and worship preferences within the broader Christian tradition.

Roman Catholic

In the Roman Catholic Church, the Sacred Scripture is the Bible, and utilizes Canon Law (church law), and the hierarchy of personnel is as follows:

- The **Pope** (or Bishop of Rome) located in the Vatican, is the head of the church, followed by the
- **Cardinals** (a dignity conferred upon Bishops or priests making them princes of the church), followed by
- **Archbishops**, serves over a large geographical group of dioceses.
- **Bishops**, serves over an individual diocese.
- **Monsignor**, an honorary title conferred by the Pope, that means "Papal Household." This title is rarely used since Pope Francis. The priest should be addressed as, Monsignor.

➢ **Priests** (may be known as the Celebrant or officiant). He is addressed as Father. A Priest presides over one or more parish(es) within a Diocese.
➢ **Deacons** (subordinate officers). There are two types of Deacons; Permanent and Temporary Deaconate. Permanent Deacons are usually married men in the church who have been ordained by a bishop to carry out special duties in the church. Temporary Deacons are men waiting ordination to the priesthood. This is usually a 6 month to one year title.
➢ Finally, **the laity** (congregation members). Non-ordained but trained to perform special duties, such as, Eucharistic minister or lecturer.
➢ **Nuns** are women who are members of the religious order, or convent, and are bound by vows of poverty, chastity, and obedience, and are led by the **Mother Superior**.

Clergy members wear religious garments known as vestments, including a **scapular**, which is a piece of cloth or a medal worn around the neck. These vestments vary in color depending on the religious time of the year. In the liturgical traditions of Christianity, the colors of the vestments worn by priests play a symbolic role, reflecting the different seasons of the liturgical calendar and conveying theological meanings. The liturgical year typically revolves around cycles, and the colors of the vestments change accordingly. White or gold vestments are often worn during festive seasons such as Christmas and Easter, symbolizing joy, purity, and the resurrection. Red is associated with Pentecost and commemorates the Holy Spirit's descent, symbolizing zeal and the fire of faith. Green is used in Ordinary Time, representing growth, hope, and the Christian journey. Purple or violet is employed during seasons of penance, like Advent and Lent, conveying themes of repentance, preparation, and reflection. Additionally, white vestments may be used during funerals, symbolizing the hope and joy of the resurrection. The use of liturgical colors adds a visual dimension to worship, helping to convey the theological significance of each season within the Christian calendar.

Usually, the vestments worn during funerals of laity are usually white. Vestments worn during funerals of religious, are usually red or white. Red vestments signify martyrdom, meaning, the person's death was a direct result of persecution because of their faith.

(Pope Francis with the Metropolitans - equivalent to a Cardinal in the Christian Orthodox Church)

Modern Catholic churches often exhibit diverse architectural styles and designs, reflecting a balance between tradition and contemporary aesthetics. Many contemporary Catholic churches emphasize simplicity, functionality, and a sense of community engagement. Architects often employ open spaces, natural light, and minimalist designs to create a welcoming atmosphere for worshipers. The traditional cruciform layout, with a central nave and transepts forming a cross, is still prevalent, but some modern churches may deviate from this structure to explore innovative designs that encourage community interaction and participation. Architectural elements like large windows, geometric shapes, and sustainable building materials are commonly integrated to enhance the overall aesthetic and environmental considerations. Additionally, modern Catholic churches often incorporate advanced audio-visual technology to facilitate worship and outreach. Overall, the design of modern Catholic churches aims to harmonize traditional values with contemporary sensibilities, creating spaces that foster spiritual reflection, communal worship, and a connection to the divine.

Traditional Roman Catholic Churches are in the shape of the cross with distinct areas:

The **narthex** (vestibule) of the church is the entryway which leads to the **nave** (the large area of the church where the parishioners sit during Mass) in which the pews are located. Under the pews are the **prie dieu*** (kneelers). In front of the pews (depicted as the horizontal bar of the cross) are the north and south transepts (between the pews and the altar). In front of the church is the **altar** and a lectern where the sacred scriptures are read. Both the Hebrew and Christian Scripture (old and new Testaments) are read from the same lectern. This has been a significant change in the Catholic Church since Vatican II Council. Before This Church conclave, the lectern on the left was reserved for the Gospel readings, and the lectern on the right was reserved for the Epistle readings. These two lecterns are not used in modern Catholic Church worship. Behind the altar is the **chancel**, the area for the clergy where the consecration of the Eucharist takes place.

There are many religious items of importance in the Roman Catholic faith including but not limited to the **crucifix** (a cross with the Corpus Christi - body of Christ is depiction), **Rosary beads** (beads and crucifix used to recitation of prayers), **sacred heart** (religious picture of Jesus that depicts a glowing heart), and **holy water,** which the faithful use to bless themselves (except during the Lenten season, as they enter and exit the church. Prior to sitting in their pew, the Catholic parishioner will genuflect on their right knee, and make the sign of the cross with their right hand, towards the **tabernacle,** a box shaped object in the front (or to one side) of the church where the consecrated Eucharist are stored, awaiting distribution.

In the Roman Catholic Church, the inscriptions **INRI** the Latin abbreviation for Jesus of Nazareth, King of the Jews (or Jesus of the Nazarene King of the Jews); and **IHS** (The first three letters in the Greek word for Jesus- Ιησούς) are commonly found.

When someone in the Roman Catholic faith is dying, a Priest may perform a Sacrament known as the **Anointing of the Sick,** to prepare the soul for eternity. When death is eminent, and the family contacts the funeral director regarding pre-arrangements, it is appropriate for the funeral director to ask the family, "Has your loved-one received the Anointing of the Sick?"

*Prie dieus are also found in funeral homes and placed in front of caskets for family to stop and pray during visitations.

Once death has occurred the traditional method of disposition is embalming, followed by a wake and Mass of Christian Burial. The human remains, after the Mass, are to be entombed or interred in consecrated grounds.

Cremation has become accepted by the Church but is still not the preferred method of final disposition in the United States. There are some regulations within the Church that need to be followed if cremation is chosen as a means of final disposition:

1. The Church prefers that the human remains be present in the church, prior to the cremation process.
2. If cremation occurs prior to the funeral Mass, the cremated remains can be displayed, in front of the altar, by the Easter candle, on a table. The urn should be covered with an appropriate size cloth (known as a pall) during the Mass.
3. After the Mass, the cremated remains need to be either entombed or interred in a consecrated burial plot or niche.
4. The cremated remains should never be placed on display (such as behind a glass columbarium or retained by the family for display) or scattered. The total cremated remains need to be entombed or buried and the practice of retaining a small portion of cremated remains is frowned upon by the Church.

Typically, there will be a **wake**/visitation the night before the funeral service, with vigil lights at each end of the casket. A crucifix is usually displayed in either the head panel of the casket or at the foot of the casket, on a tripod. A **prie dieu,** is placed in front of the open part of the casket and if the casket is closed to mourners, the prie dieu is placed in the center of the casket. Family may wish to offer **prayer cards** (cards with the decedents name, birth/death dates, and a prayer/poem) at the visitation and/or funeral services. Funeral attendees may also wish to purchase mass cards or **spiritual bouquets**, which are documents indicating the offering of a Mass for a specific intention, in these cases offering a Mass in memory of the decedent. The funeral home should have a tray or locked box for these cards.

Either at the end of the visitation or at the funeral home before the procession to the church, **morning prayers** may be held. The funeral director will then process to the church and will bring the casket into the narthex feet first (unless the decedent is a Priest or Deacon, then they are headfirst). Once in the narthex, the Priest will bless the casket with Holy Water, and the **pall** (a symbolic white cloth representing the decedent's baptismal garments when they "Put on Christ, now they are clothed in Christ's glory") is placed on the casket, by the funeral directors. Only religious items, such as a crucifix or the Bible, can be placed on the pall. If the person was a veteran and the casket is draped when entering into the church, the flag needs to be removed and set aside during the Mass. Once the Pall has been removed in the back of church at the end of Mass, the flag can be placed on the casket, prior to exiting the church.

After the placing of the pall and the blessing of the casket has taken place, the ecclesiastical (of the church) processional continues in the following order to the front of the church:

> ➢ Crucifier (person who carries crucifix),
> ➢ Alter attendants/acolytes,
> ➢ Clergy,
> ➢ Funeral director and a funeral attendant on either end of the casket with the pallbearers flanked on either side,
> ➢ Followed by family.

(Incensing the casket during the Song of Farewell)

At the front of the church the casket is placed perpendicular to the altar in front of the **Paschal candle** (the Easter Candle) that signifies everlasting light (replacing the previous use of requiem candles, a series of three candles on each side of the casket. In the Tridentine Church, this custom is still practiced).

The funeral director should then **genuflect**, bending of the right knee, or bow in front of the altar as a show of respect to the Blessed Sacrament, before proceeding to their seat for the service. Genuflecting or bowing should also be performed by speakers and readers before and after their reading. Funeral directors should also genuflect before recessing the casket out of the church.

Catholic funeral Mass known as the **Funeral Liturgy or Mass of Christian Burial** is liturgical and centered around the Eucharist (distributed to those who are properly disposed within the faith), and will include readings, a homily (preaching of the Word of God), songs, possibly eulogies, and ends with the **final commendation prayer** and the blessing by the Priest. Services are similar to the Church's traditional Mass offered on Sundays except the funeral rite is inserted into the liturgy. After the service the casket should be turned around for a feet first exit utilizing the same order as the procession. If the deceased is clergy, the casket should not be turned, since the casket is in the proper position for a feet first exit.

At the burial site the priest will perform the Committal prayers and the grave is blessed with Holy Water. Burial should be in a consecrated burial site with feet facing the east. If the decedent is being buried in a Roman Catholic Cemetery a **Christian Burial Permit** may be required in addition to a Burial Transit Permit. While this document is rarely used in most dioceses, this could be testable on the NBE. Such a permit is a document by a priest that confirms the eligibility of burial in a Catholic cemetery.

Generally, services are prohibited on All Saints Day, Easter, Christmas, and Holy Week. Sunday Funeral Masses are usually not available, due to normal Mass schedules.

In conclusion, the rituals associated with a Mass of Christian Burial in the Catholic Church encapsulate profound moments of faith, remembrance, and hope. The liturgy unfolds with prayers, scripture readings, and hymns that offer solace to the bereaved and express the Christian belief in the resurrection. The Eucharistic celebration, a central element of the Mass, underscores the promise of eternal life through the Body and Blood of Christ. The commendation of the deceased affirms the community's collective prayers for the soul's peaceful journey. The use of incense, holy water, and the pall further symbolize purification, baptism, and the unity of the faithful. The Catholic funeral rites, steeped in centuries-old traditions, provide a meaningful and comforting framework for the grieving, blending reverence for the deceased with the enduring hope found in the Christian faith.

Tridentine Requiem Mass

The Tridentine Funeral Rite, also known as the **Requiem Mass** according to the Roman Missal of 1962, was the liturgical form used in the Roman Catholic Church before the Second Vatican Council. In this traditional funeral rite, the emphasis was on supplication for the soul of the deceased, seeking God's mercy and intercession for the departed. The liturgy included prayers and chants in Latin, such as the Dies Irae, focusing on themes of judgment and redemption. The priest, clad in black vestments, expressed the Church's traditional teachings on death, judgment, heaven, and hell, emphasizing the need for prayers to aid the soul's passage through purgatory. The Tridentine Funeral Rite featured ceremonial actions like the use of holy water, the offering of incense, and the ritual covering of the casket with a black pall, six candles flanking both sides of the casket, each carrying symbolic significance tied to the Catholic understanding of death and resurrection, prior to Second Vatican Council.

In contrast, the modern-day Roman Catholic funeral rite, influenced by the liturgical reforms of the Second Vatican Council in the 1960s, emphasizes a more pastoral and communal approach. The liturgy is often celebrated in the vernacular language, allowing for greater understanding and participation by the mourners. The focus has shifted from emphasizing judgment to celebrating the deceased person's life and the hope of resurrection. The modern rite incorporates scripture readings that speak to the Christian understanding of death and life, and the prayers are often more inclusive and consoling, addressing the grief of the bereaved. Additionally, while elements like the use of incense, holy water, and the pall are still present, their symbolism may be explained in a more accessible manner. Overall, the modern Roman Catholic funeral rite seeks to bring comfort to the grieving while affirming the Christian belief in the resurrection and God's mercy.

Orthodox Christian Church
a/k/a Eastern Orthodox Church or Orthodox Catholic Church

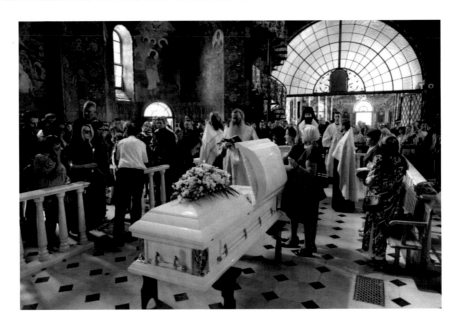

The Eastern Orthodox Church and Roman Catholic Church split during the reign of the Byzantine Empire. In 1054, a doctrine dispute between the church leaders led to the Great Schism that divided the Eastern and Western Christian Churches. The Eastern Church believed that their beliefs were the true teaching of the church. The word *orthodox* ("right believing") has traditionally been used in the Greek and Slavic speaking Christian world to designate communities or individuals who preserved the true faith (as defined by those councils), as opposed to those who were declared heretical, that is, the followers of the Western Church. Although similar to Catholicism, there are a few key differences between the Eastern Orthodox Church and the Roman Catholic Church in matters of doctrine and the Primacy of the Pope. After the Vatican I Council in the 1960s, the relations and some of the theological differences have been resolved, (*see picture on page 47*) with Pope Francis and Orthodox Bishops) although the Orthodox still hold to their traditions and rituals for religious services and burial customs.

Cremation is strictly prohibited in the Orthodox faith. Orthodox believe that the human body is a Temple of the Holy Spirit and cremation is seen as the deliberate destruction of God's creation. Traditional burial and embalming are generally selected as a means of final disposition in this religious group. There does not seem to be any strict regulations regarding the preparation of the human remains for final disposition. The **Priest** is the religious leader in the Eastern Orthodox Church, and a **Deacon** is a subordinate officer who assists the priest. The Eastern Orthodox Church has a few key components that are unique to the faith.

The **Solea** is the open area in front of the altar, where the casket is placed during the funeral service. The altar and body of the church are separated from the sanctuary by the **Iconostasis**, a solid screen partition that is covered with **Icons** (religious pictures). In the middle of the Iconostasis are the **Royal Doors** that only clergy may use to access the altar.

Eastern Orthodox services are Liturgical, centered around the **Divine Liturgy**, the celebration of the Eucharist (communion). A few symbols that are unique to the Orthodox church is the crucifix that portrays Jesus' feet nailed side-by-side as opposed to the Roman crucifix where Christ's feet are nailed on top of each other. Usually, on the top of the Orthodox church steeple is a cross with a slanted bar at the foot end of the cross. This sloped bar has religious significance which represents the ascension of Christ in addition to the theological concept that 'the Cross is the true scales of justice.

Typically, Eastern Orthodox funerals begin with the **Parastas** or Parastasis (vigil) of which candles are placed at each end of the casket, an Icon is placed at the foot end of the casket, and a cross is placed behind the casket.

Trisagion, three short services or blessings that are performed at various stages:
1. The evening before the funeral (at the funeral home),
2. The morning of the funeral (at the funeral home before going to the church),
3. and finally, at the committal.

Once the funeral procession arrives at the church, the human remains are brought into the entry, and the casket is opened, placing feet first in front and perpendicular to the altar in the Solea. The liturgical services are performed by the priest and may have songs performed by a cantor (religious singer). Organ music or other instruments are not part of this religious custom. The singing is chanted and performed acapella. After the completion of the service by the priest, the casket is turned parallel with the altar and the Iconostasis, and the decedent is anointed with oil and covered with sand or ash. Before recessing out of the church, a **last kiss** ritual is performed in which funeral attendees pass by the casket and kiss the deceased and the **Icon** (a holy picture, typically painted wood or mosaic) placed by the head of the casket.

The committal rituals vary based on cultural traditions and locality. In some Orthodox Churches, they pour the oil and sprinkle the ash on top of the closed caskets, during the graveside service. In some orthodox churches, the family members fill in the grave and the women will then adorn the top of the grave with flowers or tree bows. Usually there is a repass back at the church after the committal prayers.
Funerals may be prohibited on Sundays and certain holy days.

Protestant Denominations

Protestant denominations are those who broke away from the Catholic Church starting with the Protestant Reformation in 1517 by Martin Luther. Beliefs and services vary from denomination-to-denomination and from church-to-church within a denomination. Denominations may be liturgically based in which worship is formalized and centered around the Eucharist, such as the Anglican Church. Or they may be non-liturgical in which worship is less formal and centered around the bible or scripture, such as the Baptist Church.

Due to the differences within churches and denominations it is crucial to discuss the funeral service with the minister, pastor, or reverend who oversees the church. Liturgical churches are generally in the traditional shape of the cross with similar sections as the Roman Catholic churches, while non-liturgical churches may be in a different shape. Funeral services in liturgical denominations may be held at the church, while those in non-liturgical denominations are generally held anywhere (funeral home, church, other venue). The order and rituals of the wakes, services, committals, and burials will vary depending on the denomination and church. The preference in burial and cremation will also vary.

Anglican or Episcopalian Church

The Anglican Communion, of which the Episcopal Church is a member, began in the sixth century in England, and evolved as a part of the Roman Church. It separated from the Roman Catholic Church during the reign of Henry VIII, but it was during the reign of Elizabeth I that it began to have a formal structure. Unlike the Catholic Church, which is organized under the administration and authority of the Pope, Anglicanism is bound together by the shared belief and tradition, and in particular by the common tradition of prayer as it is embodied in the *Book of Common Prayer,* which was first commissioned by Elizabeth I in 1549.

The Anglican or Episcopal Church is a derivative of the Roman Catholic Church. The split in the church originated with King Henry VIII when the pope refused to grant King Henry's second divorce from his wife. The Anglican Church rejects the authority of the pope, however many of their customs, rituals and theological understandings are rooted in Catholicism.

Like the Catholic Church, their ecclesiastical structure is unique to their traditions and customs to the Church of England. This is the official religion of England, and the King (currently, Charles III) is the Supreme Governor of the Church. The Archbishop of Canterbury, (currently, the Most Rev. Justin Welby) is the most Senior Cleric. Like the Catholic Church, the Anglican Church have established dioceses that govern a geographical region. The diocese is presided over by a bishop who oversees the various parishes under their jurisdiction. One of the major differences in the Anglican Church is they allow females to be ordained clergy. Anglican Parishes are led by a:

> **Rector** - (origin: from the Latin word '*regere,*' which means ruler or teacher).
> The priest is addressed as Father and the female priest is addressed as Mother.
> The Rector is the pastor of the local church.

Visitation is usually held in the funeral home prior to the funeral mass. No crucifix, prie dieu, or vigil lights on either ends of the casket, are displayed unless requested by the family, or local customs. During the arrangement conference, the funeral director should ask the family as to which of these items should be displayed.

Funeral services are preferred to be held in the church. A pall is generally used to cover the casket. The rubric for the funeral services is taken from the *Book of Common Prayer.* There are two rites for burial: one rite, with more traditional language and the other rite has more contemporary wording. The priest meets the casket in the back of church and after a blessing, proceeds down the center isle to the front of the church, led by an acolyte bearing a cross. Often a Pascal Candle will proceed the cross. If not, the Pascal Candle is generally placed in front of the altar, near where the casket or urn is placed. Instead of a processional hymn, the priest generally recites an anthem during the procession. The funeral directors follow with the casket, flanked by the pallbearers. The family follows the casket and will sit on the Gospel side of the church. If the pallbearers are not family, they will sit together on the opposite side of the isle. Communion is offered to all Christian believers. Following the funeral service there is a procession to the grave.

Once at the cemetery, the priest will lead the casket to the grave, reciting prayers from the *Book of Common Prayer.* At the grave the final committal prayers will be offered. During these prayers the priest will take a hand full of dirt (some use white sand) from the grave and make the sign of the cross, on the casket, with the dirt reciting: "We commit this body into the ground, earth to earth, ashes to ashes, dust to dust. In the Name of the Father, and of the Son and of the Holy Ghost, Amen." There is a final blessing that is given to the bereaved.

The Anglican Church don't have any restrictions against cremation as a means of final disposition. Some local churches, however, prefer that the cremated remains be placed in a columbarium within the church. These niches are restricted in size and before a family selects an urn, the funeral director should be aware of the internal dimensions of the niche.

The church keeps accurate records of the members who die. When providing the church with a clergy record, they may ask for the cause of death. Due to confidentiality issues, the funeral director should obtain permission from the family before disclosing this information to the church.

Lutherans

The origins of the Lutheran Church date back to a Roman Catholic priest and theologian, named Martin Luther, who protested the selling of plenary indulgences, and other non-scriptural practices the Catholic Church was doing at the time. The origin of the word Protestant (means, to protest) came about when Luther nailed his Ninety-Five Thesis (ongoing concerns with the theology demonstrated by the Catholic Church) to the doors of a Wittenberg Church in Germany. Having harshly criticized the Roman Church, Luther was confronted and eventually excommunicated. Many in northern Europe, having read his writings, became followers, despite persecution from church authorities, and followed his spiritual guidance and direction. As the church developed, over the years, various sects developed, which interpreted and adopted church teachings differently. These sects are known as Synods.

Today in the United States, there are four main church bodies:

1. Evangelical Lutheran Church of American
2. Lutheran Church – Missouri Synod
3. Wisconsin Evangelical Lutheran Synod
4. Lutheran Church of America

Each of these churches have some unique cultural and theological differences and the funeral rituals may vary depending upon the Synod affiliation. The more liberal Synods accept women as ministers, while others, more conservative groups, prohibit women from being ordained or holding a leadership role in the church. The minister is usually addressed as "*Pastor*."

Depending on the Synod, visitation is usually held at the funeral home the night before the funeral service. Some Synods permit the casketed remains to be placed in the narthex, and opened, prior to the church service. The Lutheran Church is classified as a liturgical church because of its rites and rituals which have similarities to the Catholic Church order of worship.

Usually, the Pastor will say a prayer with the family before the casket is closed and brought into the sanctuary for the service. A pall is placed on the casket and once in the front of the church, the casket is positioned parallel to the altar. Prayers, liturgical readings, music and a eulogy comprise the funeral service. Normally, communion is not offered as part of the services. If communion is offered, different Synods have different rules on who can receive the Eucharist.

Lutherans sometimes have funeral services at the funeral home. The use of the pall is usually not required however, the casket is closed prior to the beginning of the service. In such services, the family is asked to say their final good-byes and then the funeral director and attendant will lower the bed and close the casket. Locking the casket (not in front of the family) is usually done prior to leaving the funeral home for the cemetery.

The committal prayers are recited at the grave and the Pastor will use either sand, earth or flower petals to create a cross on the headcap of the casket. This symbolic gesture signifies that the remains are returned to the basic elements to which they were created.

Non-Liturgical Churches

United Methodist Church

The origin of the Methodist Church began at Oxford University, in 1729, by two brothers, John and Charles Wesley, who founded, the "Holy Club." The brothers found the Anglican Church to be both political and not Biblically sound for faith formation. This group developed methodical habits centered around prayer and ministry to the poor, imprisoned and sick. As a mocking ridicule by their classmates, members of this club were called, "Methodist." Methodists from their beginnings focused on the Word (Biblical teaching) and not on rituals. At one time, the Methodist Church in the United States was quite large, however with an aging population and the recent schism in the church over theological and cultural issues, the church is dwindling in membership. Many parishes have lay ministers serving the pulpit needs of this community. The churches that do have a significant number of parishioners have a pastor to minister to the congregation's spiritual needs. The minister is usually addressed as *Pastor.*

These are usually non-liturgical churches and void of any ritual, and subsequently, the funeral service could take place either in the church or the funeral home. There is no formal procession in-or-out of church and usually the funeral directors process in with the casket and place it parallel to the altar. Flowers are permitted to be on the casket and the casket is never opened in the sanctuary. One duty of the funeral director may be to light the altar candles before the church service begins.

The funeral services, either at the funeral home or in the church, consist of some scriptural readings, music, prayers and a eulogy. A great deal depends on if a minister or laity is leading the services. Following the funeral services in the church, the minister leads the casket out and pallbearers assemble at the back of church to assist the funeral directors with placing the casket in the hearse.

Once at the cemetery, the pallbearers assist again with carrying the casket to the grave. The procession to the grave may or may not be led by the minister. The committal prayers are recited at the grave and the Pastor will use either sand, earth or flower petals to create a cross on the headcap of the casket. This symbolic gesture signifies that the remains are returned to the basic elements to which they were created.

Presbyterian Church

The word Presbyterian, derives from the Greek word, Presbyteros, meaning, "elder." The elders within a given church include the ordained pastors as well as men and women elected by the congregation. The minister serves as the moderator, and the elders form a session, which is the decision-making and governing body within the church. Sessions located within a certain geographical location compose the next governing level. The presbytery functions similar to the session, except over a larger geographical region. The presbytery is the governing body of the church that has jurisdiction over the sessions of all Presbyterian Church (USA) congregation within its bounds and its ministers' members. It is composed of "all the churches and ministers of the Word and Sacrament within a certain district." (G-11.0101). Three or more presbyteries form a Synod. The final governing body in the church is known as the General Assembly.

There are no restrictions in the church as to the type of services for the deceased, nor prescription for the form of final disposition. Cremation or burial is accepted as a means of final disposition. The Book of Order of the Presbyterian Church states that the funeral services or memorial services should be "held in the usual place of worship in order to join this service to the community's continuing life and witness to the resurrection." This is a non-liturgical church, and the place of service is usually the decision of the pastor and the family.

The order of worship is usually determined by the pastor, in consultation with the family. Casketed remains are not open in the sanctuary and some churches have a pall that is placed over the casket during the service. Normally, funerals held in the church would begin with a procession and end with a recession out of the sanctuary. A plain cross leads, followed by the pastor. Funeral directors are at both ends of the casket and the pallbearers are flanked on both sides. The family follows and once in the front, in most churches, the pallbearers will join their family. The family will sit in the first two rows in front of the pulpit. Upon the conclusion of the services, the casket will recess out in the same order as it came into the church.

Since the Presbyterian Church accepts cremation and donation of human remains to medical science as a means of final disposition, most funeral and memorial services will conclude with committal prayers as part of the services. Like other protestant committal services, these services are very brief and commit the body to the earth as its final resting place.

Baptist Church

There are many different groups of Baptist and all these churches, while doctrinally follow the same theological premise, are independent entities within themselves. Their traditional standards are modified and vary from church-to-church, to fit their congregational needs. Therefore, to advise as to the funeral customs and rituals for the Baptist Church is dependent upon the customs and traditions established within the community of believers. Thus, consult with the local pastor prior to any funeral service as to the order of worship. This is a non-liturgical church, and the minister is usually addressed as *"Pastor* or Reverend."

One tradition that is customary in the Baptist Church is having the human remains lie in state in the sanctuary prior to the services. Family and friends will gather and pay their last respects before the funeral services commence. About 15 minutes before the scheduled services, the funeral director will escort the family up to the casket to pay their final respect. This is a time for the family to say their "good-byes" before hearing the pastor's message of comfort and healing. Some Southern Baptist Churches do this ritual at the end after the pastor delivers their message. While customary, such a tradition tends to reignite grieving wounds which may be contrary to the spiritual message from the church leader.

Like other protestant committal services, these services are very brief and commit the body to the earth as its final resting place. Usually, the pastor will lead the procession to the grave quoting scripture verses at various points. Some ministers use two flowers, which they place on the top of the head panel of the casket in the shape of the cross, while others use flower pedals. A repass (or gathering), sponsored by the women of the church, is usually held back at the church for the attendees.

Pentecostal

Pentecostal churches are highly emotional and a non-liturgical church. An example of this type of church is Assemblies of God who emphasize that the work of the Holy Spirit can only be experienced directly through the presence of God by true believers. Such powerful experiences of faith are not found through rituals or thinking, but rather in an emotionally charged religious experience that is revealed in the Gift of Tongues. Glossolalia (Greek for Speaking in Tongues) is the phenomenon of (apparently) speaking in an unknown language, especially during religious worship. What may sound like gibberish to some, is an expression of faith, by believers, that God is speaking through them in a foreign tongue that can only be interpreted by another believer with the Gift of Interpretation. This notion is scripturally based and is a sacred belief among Pentecostalist.

There are a variety of Pentecostal churches, therefore the funeral services are dependent upon the traditions established by the local church. In some Pentecostal churches, cremation is shunned and considered disrespectful to God's temple, the human remains. Some services are one hour in length and others could last for two to three days with the human remains lying-in-state in the funeral home, church or in the family's home, for a public visitation. The church service could be a two-to-three-hour event and attendees will engage in singing, telling of stories, reading of letters of condolences, reading the obituary, and a spiritual message from the church leader (Pastor). Speaking in tongues is not an uncommon experience in some of these funeral services. Some churches call this type of service a, *"Home Coming,"* because the bereaved believe that the deceased is being welcomed into their final home in heaven. Prior to the services, the funeral director should obtain an order of worship from the pastor and ask, "at what point will the services be concluding?" This is an important consideration for such services with respect to scheduling, military honors, vault and cemetery personnel.

Like other protestant committal services, these services are very brief and commit the body to the earth as its final resting place. Usually, the pastor will lead the procession to the grave, quoting scripture verses at various points. There may be a song sung at the grave followed by the committal prayer. A repass (or gathering) is held back at the church for the attendees. A living fund is set up by the Pentecostal Assembly for donation in lieu of flowers to support mission projects in the decedent's memory.

Quakers

Quakers are also known as the Society of Friends. George Fox, an English religious man in the seventeenth century," trembled at the Word of God." People who were inspired by this reflective introspection, met frequently and embraced the notion that God spoke through them during periods of silent meditation and spiritual reflection. The people who rejected this form of worship and prayer, mockingly nicknamed the followers, "Quakers." This group of believers gather in a Meeting House and have no minister or religious leader. They are a peaceful people who embrace simplicity and prayerful reflection on God's presence in their life.

The means of final disposition is the decision of the family, and the Quakers respect any choice they make with caring for the human remains with respect and dignity. Some Quakers choose traditional burials, while others will opt for green burials. Cremation is permitted and in some Quaker Cemeteries in the United States, which are several hundred years old, only permit the interment of cremated remains, due to the limited space.

Memorial services held in the Meeting House are similar to that of a gathering of friends. After brief instructions by the clerk, the friends gathered will sit in a circle or semi-circle, facing each other. After a period of 40 minutes, or so, of silent prayer and reflection, the clerk will state: "Now is the time to share any message that may not have arisen during this meeting." At this time, people will share a thought about the deceased or maybe read a poem or spiritual verse. There is no formal order of worship. Some Society of Friends have more elaborate customs for memorial or funeral services but for the most part, this group embraces simplicity and prayerful reflection on the positive impact that the deceased life has made to the mourner.

The committal of the human remains, or cremated remains, are usually private with the family present witnessing the interment. Usually, the interment is done as the mourners witness the lowering of the casket or the burial of the cremated remains. No prayers are recited out loud and the mourners witness this event in silence.

Church of Christian Science

The Church of Christ, Scientist was established by Mary Baker Eddy in 1879, in Boston, Massachusetts. The premise of this religion is based on two holy texts of the faith: the Bible, and the *Science and Health with Key to the Scriptures* (written by Eddy). There are no formal rituals in this church although they do meet weekly for services and Readers read from both books. They believe in following Christ Jesus and his teachings including healing. Prayer is a daily, essential part of their practice. Solutions through a prayerful approach are found for illnesses and difficulties of all sorts. Practitioners are available to support individuals through spiritual treatment and prayer; however, there are no ordained ministers.

The human remains may be embalmed, however within the church teachings, a woman's remains should be prepared by a woman is possible. Public visitation is not the usual custom of this religious group, though they often hold funeral or memorial services. Funeral services are generally not held in the church. If the funeral services is held in the funeral home with the body present, the casket is usually closed. A Practitioner or Reader will often preside over the services and read from the Bible and from the *Science and Health with Key to the Scriptures* or other works by Mary Baker Eddy. The exact format is flexible and left to the family's discretion. The readings will vary and center around the immortal nature of man, "made in God's image and likeness," and death is only a phase which a person leaves the mortal dwelling while maintaining their immortal spiritual life. These types of services do have musical hymns played. The Lord's Prayer is often included, and the service is concluded with a benediction.

There are no prohibitions within the church regarding the means of final disposition and it is at the discretion of the family. Committal prayers, if any, are very brief.

Jehovah Witnesses

Jehovah Witnesses believe that Jehovah is God; Jesus is God's Son and that the Bible is the Word of God. This religious group believes in the literal interpretation of the Bible and is classified as a non-liturgical church. The church leadership are appointed Elders who are not paid and are addressed by their personal names.

Despite their beliefs against receiving blood transfusions as a form of medical intervention, they do not prohibit embalming as part of the preparation of the human remains. Customs regarding visitations are that of the personal preferences of the family and usually follow their historical funeral choices of past family members. Cremation is an acceptable means of final disposition.

Funeral services with the human remains present are permitted in Kingdom Hall (their sanctuary), however formal processions and recessions are not common practices. Prior to the services starting, the funeral directors will bring the casket to the front of the sanctuary for the services. Flowers are permitted on top of the closed casket during the services. The church Elder will read from scripture and provide a message for the family based on the readings. Prayers are also given during the services. The services are usually short in length. The playing and singing of hymns is usually customary during funerals.

Graveside services are usually private for family members only. Usually, the elder of the church does not say prayers at the grave. If burying cremated remains, some church members will bring the cremated remains to the cemetery and witness the interment by the groundskeeper.

The Church of Jesus Christ of Latter-day Saints*

Members of The Church of Jesus Christ of Latter-day Saints do not consider themselves to be Protestant, since they did not break away from another denomination based on doctrinal disputes. This is a non-liturgical church. Members of The Church of Jesus Christ of Latter-day Saints are a religious group that embrace concepts of Christianity as well as revelations received by their founder, Joseph Smith, and other modern-day prophets. While members embrace many Christian beliefs, they have their own distinct set of philosophies, values, and practices and the funeral director should be conscious and sensitive of them during arrangements and while conducting services at their church. One such belief is privacy during the grieving process.

In The Church of Jesus Christ of Latter-day Saints, the scriptures include the Bible, Book of Mormon, Doctrine and Covenants, and Pearl of Great Price. A congregation is called a Ward and smaller congregations are called a Branch. The ecclesiastical leader of a Ward is known as a **Bishop** (and should be addressed as such), and of a Branch, a **Branch President**. A group of wards in a geographical area constitutes a **Stake** and is led by a **Stake President**.

If the decedent has made **temple covenants**, they are to wear religious **garments** under their normal clothing to maintain a connection to their faith. If the decedent has gone through the temple, then they should be buried or cremated in garments and **temple clothing**. Generally, members of the family and/or ward will dress the decedent in the temple clothing. Accommodations should be made for the dressing team to have privacy while they dress the deceased. The remains should be placed on a dressing table, dressed in a hospital gown, and covered with a sheet, prior to the team's arrival. Some will allow the funeral director to put the garments on the deceased prior to the family or Ward members dressing the deceased in temple clothing. It is also permissible for the funeral home staff to casket the human remains after the dressing process is completed.

*Note: the terms *"Mormon"* and LDS are nicknames of this religion. The proper way to refer to this Church is by its official name, The Church of Jesus Christ of Latter-day Saints.

Ceremonial temple clothing is placed on the human remains as instructed in the endowment. The robe is placed on the right shoulder and tied with the drawstring at the left waistline. The [green] apron is secured around the waist. The sash is placed around the waist and tied in a bow over the left hip. A man's cap is usually placed beside his body until it is time to close the casket or container. The cap is then placed with the bow over the left ear. A woman's veil may be draped on the pillow at the back of her head. The veiling of a woman's face before burial or cremation is optional, as determined by the family." General Handbook, Church Policies and Guidelines, Temple Burial Clothing 38.5.8

Usually, earth burial is the common final disposition in this faith and green burials are allowed. Visitations may be held the night before the funeral and/or on the day of the funeral. Customarily, a private family prayer is held at the end of the visitation before the funeral service starts. Funeral services may be held at the funeral home, Church building, or at a home. Funeral services are not held in the temple. Funerals are religious services and should be a spiritual occasion.

Those serving in the Church do so as volunteers and members who take part in services for the deceased should not accept payment.

The **Relief Society** is a women's group in the Church designed to provide instruction to the adult female members of the church. They often coordinate the luncheon if one is held after the funeral. The **Relief Society Room** is one designated for the meeting of the Relief Society and is where the visitation is held before a funeral service. Members are a close-knit group whose major beliefs center around the family and family values.

The funeral services are under the direction of the Bishop of the Ward, and the funeral director should consult with him regarding when and where the casket should be placed in the chapel, as well as when the casket should exit the church. The casket is not opened in the chapel at any period before, during, or after the services. Pallbearers need to be briefed before the services commence and they usually sit with their family during the services. There is no formal procession or recession into the chapel, and the Bishop of the Ward will clarify how the casket will exit the church after the services have concluded.

Members of The Church of Jesus Christ of Latter-day Saints are usually buried as a means of final disposition. Entombment and cremation are also permitted. At the graveside, a member of the Church who holds the Melchizedek Priesthood says a prayer to dedicate the grave.

Other Religious Groups

Judaism – Can be broken down into 3 groups of believers:
- ➢ Orthodox (strict adherence to the rules and traditions of the faith);
- ➢ Conservative (adherent to the rules and traditions but accept some modern interpretations, such as dress attire in public);
- ➢ Reformed (embrace the traditions and theology of the faith but possess a liberal interpretation of the customs and rules).

In Judaism, God is referred to as Adonai, and the Father of the Hebrew people is Abraham. In Judaism, the first five books of the Bible are known as the Torah. Scrolls of these sacred writings are kept in an ark on the bimah (pronounced, BEE MA) and are used during religious services. The Talmud is a collection of rabbinic debates from the 2nd – 5th century on the teachings of the Torah. This religion is deep in religious traditions and symbolism and burying the dead is based on their understanding of sacred scriptures and traditions handed down for generations. The religious leader is known as a Rabbi and should be addressed as such, including their last name. Orthodox rabbis are male, and some Conservative groups do accept women as rabbis. In Reformed Judaism, the rabbi can be either male or female.

Funeral Rites: The strict Orthodox believers are known as Hassidic, and unless the funeral director is from this sect of believers, the Rabbi would probably prohibit a non-orthodox Jewish funeral director from handling or being a part of the final arrangements for the family. The Conservative appear to be not as strict with this rule, however there is still an element of not only an understanding of the customs and traditions of the faith but also an element of trust that requires the funeral director to conform to their ceremonial and sacred customs. People of Reformed faith adhere to most of the Jewish customs, however they are more accepting of variations and are open to liberal understandings of the faith. For example, most Conservative and all Orthodox Jewish religions condemn cremation as a means of final disposition. The Reformed Jewish believers may be more open to this practice, however this may vary from congregation-to-congregation. Before advising any clients on funeral services, the funeral director needs to understand and follow the rules of the congregation within their community.

Stemming from the early Hebrew belief in the Sheol (afterlife), there is importance placed on the maintenance of the dead human remains, and to not inflict unnecessary harm.

64

Therefore, cremation and embalming are prohibited in the Jewish faith. When a person dies, the Rabbi should be contacted, if they are not already aware of the death. The Jewish faith states that burials should be done by sundown or within 24 hours. However, nothing funeral and preparation related may be done on the **Sabbath/Shabbat** (sundown Friday to sundown Saturday). If the funeral home has mirrors, they should be covered with a cloth. This is a Jewish custom where during the mourning process, the bereaved are not concerned with their appearance, thus looking at themselves in a mirror is frowned upon.

The decedent will undergo the ritual washing process known as the **taharah** by the holy society of washers known as the **Chevra Kadisha**. These washers will be the same sex as the decedent, and those of the opposite sex are not permitted to be in the room. During the taharah the Chevra Kadisha team will recite prayers. Funeral prayers said before the funeral are known as Tehillim and are found in the book of Psalms. The Chevra Kadisha team will also shroud the decedent in the **Tachrichim**. Jewish deceased males are wrapped in a tallit during taharah. Once the human remains are shrouded, they are not to be viewed. The Chevra Kadisha will place the human remains in the Aron.*

In Orthodox rites, if the decedent died in a violent way, their bloodied clothing should also be placed in the Aron.

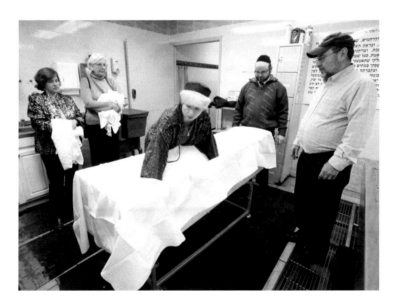

An **Aron** (Hebrew word for casket) is a traditional Jewish burial container that is made of unfinished wood, with no metal, and approved by a rabbi. The **Mogen David**, or Star of David, the 6-pointed star, should be placed at the top (and centered) of the foot end of the Aron. Israel is considered the homeland of the Jewish people, and thus Israeli earth or sand should be placed in the Aron under the head of the decedent. Pottery (representing the destruction of the Temple) and straw may also be placed in the Aron. The pottery is placed on the eyes, nose and mouth after the deceased is casketed. Usually, the bedding in an Aron is made of excelsior (or wood wool) and there are no metal fasteners holding the casket together. This casket is glued and doweled as a means of holding it together. During the time awaiting burial, a **Shomer** or watcher will sit with the human remains, to recite **tehillims,** and keep watch over the remains.

Funeral services may be held at the **synagogue** (religious institution) or the funeral home. The service will be run by the **Rabbi** (the religious leader) and may use a cantor for religious songs. During the service there will be prayers including the **Kaddish**, known as the Mourner's Prayer, and a eulogy (known as the **hesped**) may be given. The last prayer said during the service is known as **El Malei Rachamin**.

The funeral procession (known as the **levaya**) processes from the funeral service to the grave. The *levaya* may stop at the synagogue for prayers. In some traditions, if the funeral service was at the funeral home, the funeral procession will pass by the synagogue and come to a brief stop, in front of the open doors.

It is custom for the levaya to stops 7 times for prayers on the way to the grave. Once at the **grave** (known as the **kever****), the committal service and the **kevurah**** (burial) will take place. Traditionally only grave straps will be used for the kevurah instead of a modern lowering device. This is done to allow the family to perform one last act (that can never be repaid) for their loved ones. Family members will also help to fill in the dirt, sometimes even using the back of the shovel during the process, symbolizing how difficult it is to bury a loved one. Typically, the grave remains unmarked until a **matzevah** or memorial stone is placed at the end of the first year of death.

**One way to remember the difference between kever and kevurah, is both burial and kevurah both have "u", and kever and grave have the same number of letters.

Traditional Jewish garments which are also worn at funerals include the **Yamaka** (also known as Kippah and Yarmulke) which are skull caps worn by males, and the **tallith** which is a prayer shawl worn to maintain a connection to God.

As part of the mourning process, **kriah** is performed in which a tear is made in the clothing to symbolize grief. In more modern funerals, ribbons may be cut and pinned instead of the tearing of clothing. Orthodox males will with tear their clothing during this ritual

Once the burial has taken place the family will sit **shivah**, which is seven days of intense mourning practices. During shivah, the family should remain home to see visitors who come to express condolences. Throughout shivah, Orthodox people will stay in a state of uncomfortableness in which they will not work, shower, or use furniture cushions. After the seven days of shivah the family may return to their normal routines, however, they are to recite the Kaddish for the first thirty days after death, known as the period of **Sholoshim**. For the first year after the death the family will recite prayers daily and will participate in memorial services known as **Yizkor**, 4 times a year during Major Jewish Festivals/Holidays. The anniversary of death is known as the **Yahrzeit**. Usually, on the one-year anniversary of the death, the funeral director will arrange with the cemetery another ceremony which the family will gather, with the rabbi, and unveil the monument. The funeral director should assure that the final date of death has been engraved on the monument before this event and the monument unveiling cloth is in place. When visiting a grave, to pay respect to the dead, it is customary to leave a little stone on top of the monument.

Islam

In the Islamic faith, God is referred to as **Allah**, and **Mohammed** (Muhammad) is known as the prophet and founder of Islam. The holy text in Islam is the Koran (Qur'an).
Ideally, funeral rites should be before the next prayer or within 24 hours. However, funeral rites may not be done during sunrise, high noon, or sundown.

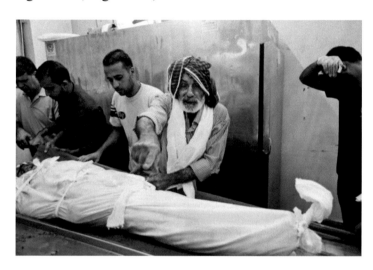

When a person dies the **Imam** (religious leader) should be contacted, if they have not been. The decedents' eyes should be closed, and prayers are recited. The Islamic faith prohibits embalming (with few exceptions) and cremation. The decedent will undergo ceremonial washing, called **Al-Ghusl** (Ghusl), in which a washing team of the same sex as the decedent will wash the body an odd number of times, with 3 being the minimum. The exception to the same sex rule is that family members may also participate. The decedent is then shrouded in a **Kafan**, which is comprised of 3 pieces for males, and 5 pieces for females. These Kafans are simple, white, without hems and should not be made of any silky material.

The decedent may be viewed before or after the washing but should not be unwrapped once they have been shrouded. Decedents may be placed in a casket or remain uncasketed, however, when they are casketed, they should not be viewed. The casket may be comprised of any material but should not have any images or symbols on it.

Islamic funeral services are known as the **Jinazah**. Jinazah can also refer to the funeral prayer. The Jinazah should be performed as soon as possible after preparation has taken place and may take place in the **Mosque** (Majid-the Islamic religious institution), funeral home, or cemetery (away from the burial site). During the Jinazah the Imam and congregation will stand at the head of a male decedent, and by the waist of a female decedent facing the **Quiblah** (the direction of prayer-facing Mecca, the birthplace of Mohammed and the holy city of the Islamic people). After the Jinazah the procession will occur from the place of the service to the place of burial.

Once at the grave, prayers will be said and the Shrouding ties should be loosened and the body should be placed in the grave on their right side facing the city of Mecca, or facing East (dependent on the direction of Mecca from the cemetery). If the decedent is casketed, the body may be positioned inside the casket on the right side, or they may be on their back with the head end towards the East (Mecca).
In some areas women are prohibited from attending the burial.

After the burial, the grave may be filled in above the surrounding area to create a mound and may be marked with a stone. It is customary for female relatives to visit the gravesite each Friday for the first 40 days after the burial and will bring palm leaves with cakes on it to distribute to the poor.

Buddhism

Buddhist funeral customs vary from denomination, culture and families, thus the funeral director should ask the family if there are any proper funeral etiquette customs that should be observed. Even though there are many denominations, the common values shared across all schools of Buddhism are meant to guide followers on their path towards enlightenment which involves practicing morality and meditation and acquiring wisdom. The goal for Buddhist believers is to reach *nirvana* and break the cycle of reincarnation so that the soul may be freed from the infinite rebirths it experiences.

Buddhists believe that the soul transmigrates from one body to the next in a cycle of life and death known as *samsara*. It is only when the soul achieves enlightenment that it can break away from the cycle and achieve nirvana. In addition, if a person has built up enough positive karma in life, they are believed to be more likely to benefit from positive karma in their next life. Thus, death for a Buddhist person is an opportunity to reflect on life in hopes that their next rebirth will provide them with a better life.

According to some beliefs, the body should not be touched or moved immediately after the death, because Buddhists believe that the soul does not leave the body as soon as the person passes away. Once a few hours have passed, it can be transported, washed, and prepared for cremation or burial.

In the Buddhist faith the **Bonze** is the Buddhist Monk that is the religious leader. The religious institution is known as the **Pagoda**. When someone is dying, bedside prayers and sutras should be recited to help the transition of the soul through its reincarnation in hopes of achieving **Nirvana**, the pure land of heavenly peace. Once death has occurred prayers (**Makura-gyo**) will continue to be said, and offerings, such as gold coins and rice, may be placed in the mouth of the decedent. Funeral preparations and the **service of casketing** the remains are typically done based on the *Book of Dates*, and the decedent will be washed and dressed.

The funeral service may include a visitation and may be held at the gravesite, funeral home, or other venue. A deceased altar should be created before the casket with photos of the deceased and items such as incenses, flowers, food, and candles. A Buddha altar should also be placed to the right of the decedent with images of the Buddha, and other items. The funeral service will be led by the Bonze and will include prayers and sutras such as **Gatha**, a Buddhist hymn used during funeral services. After the services, **Words of Appreciation** are given to thank congregation members for their presence.

Cremation is the preferred method of disposition as the Buddha was cremated on a pyre. The cremation should take place three days after the death. Generally, the family will witness the cremation and recite prayers. Customarily, the oldest male in the family will light the retort, symbolic for lighting the pyre in ancient times.

Within the Buddhist faith the bereaved will establish a shrine, known as **Kamidana-fuji**, for 35 days after the death has occurred. This ritual is performed to purify the home after the death has occurred. A picture, known as **Kakejiku** is hung in a place of honor and is meant to be a place where the soul of the deceased will eventually arrive. And finally, Buddhist will notify their neighbors that a death has occurred, and an Announcement will be placed on the front door of their home, signifying that the family are mourning the loss of a loved one.

Hinduism

Unlike other religions, Hinduism has no common doctrine or creed, and there is no founder. Since there are many branches of this religion, cultural traditions, death rituals will vary based on family origin in a particular region of India. The Hindu belief focuses on God being within each person, and the purpose of life is to gain awareness of the divine essence. This faith believes in reincarnation and the Hindu funeral rituals help each person through this transition process. The worship and rituals that are performed are designed to lead the soul towards the experience of Self or God. In their beliefs, the soul has no beginning or end, which means that the funeral is a ceremony to help the soul pass through to reincarnation.

After death occurs, the human remains are not removed from the house immediately. Some Hindu families will wash and prepare the deceased remains in the home as part of their mourning ritual. During this period of time, the remains will be washed in a bath of milk, honey ghee and yogurt. The deceased will be anointed with essential oils, sandalwood for men and turmeric for women. Most Hindu families in the United States will dress the remains in contemporary Indian clothing, however the traditional Indian death ritual utilizes a white sheet to shroud the dead. If the remains are waked in the funeral home, funeral attendees may place flowers and rice balls (known as *pinda*) around the remains. A lamp is placed near the head of the deceased and as a symbolism of cleansing, the remains will be sprinkled with water.

Hindu funerals are short in length, usually 30 minutes long and are conducted by a Hindu Priest, (known as a mukhagni).

The practice of embalming is not customary in this religion because cremation usually takes place within 24 – 48 hours from the time of death. A common practice is for the family to escort the human remains to the crematory. Once at the crematory, the human remains must enter the crematory feet-first. Mourners will be reciting prayers during the time their loved one is being cremated. Usually, the oldest male in the family will ignite the retort.

After the cremation process, the **shraddha ceremony** pays homage to the deceased person's ancestors and takes place over a 10-day period.

The cremated remains are usually scattered over a sacred body of water, such as the Ganges River in India, however alternate water sources that have significant meanings are also used. Funeral directors should caution and counsel the bereaved families not to scatter cremated remains in public waterway since this is a violation to Environmental Protection Agency (EPA) regulations.

Baha'i Faith

The Bahá'í religion believe in the unity of all religions, social justice and peace and harmony within the world. This religion originated in from the Islamic tradition by a Prophet known as the Bahá'u'lluáh. The Bahá'u'lluáh provided a series of divine messengers, which follower use as their guide towards spiritual enlightenment.

Their burial law states the body should be buried within a one-hour radius of the place of death. Believers do not believe in embalming, unless required by law, and cremation is forbidden. This rule has a physical and spiritual component, whereas the Bahá'u'lluáh taught that "allowing the body to return to the dust from which it came demonstrates the respectful Baha'i principle that the important life associated with the body is elsewhere, but that the physical temple was once a vehicle through which the soul could express itself" (Wood & Hain, 2020).

The rule prohibiting the cremation of human remains is rooted in their understanding of the afterlife. By consigning "…the body to the flames, it will pass immediately into the mineral kingdom and will be kept back from its natural journey through the chain of all created things" (Wood & Hain, 2020).

The funeral director should wash and dress the unembalmed human remains and place them in a wooden casket of the family choosing. A spiritual ring (as shown above) should be placed on the deceased right forefinger. There is no public visitation with the human remains present, however there is nothing in the church teaching that prohibit the family from paying their last respects or identifying the human remains for legal purposes.

The human remains should be buried within a 24–48 hour period of time, however if the human remains can be refrigerated, this time requirement can be extended. There is no clergy in this religion and the religious service is simplistic. The only requirement is the reading of the *Prayer of the Dead:*

The final requirement for Baha'i burial is entirely spiritual in nature—reciting the Prayer for the Dead revealed by Baha'u'llah. This special prayer is used only for adult Baha'is, and is recited by one believer while all presents remain standing:

> O my God! This is Thy servant and the son [if the departed is female, then "Thy handmaiden and the daughter"] of Thy servant who hath believed in Thee and in Thy signs, and set his face towards Thee, wholly detached from all except Thee. Thou art, verily, of those who show mercy the most merciful.
> Deal with him [her], O Thou Who forgivest the sins of men and concealest their faults, as beseemeth the heaven of Thy bounty and the ocean of Thy grace. Grant him [her] admission within the precincts of Thy transcendent mercy that was before the foundation of earth and heaven. There is no God but Thee, the Ever-Forgiving, the Most Generous. – Baha'u'llah, *Baha'i Prayers*, pp. 39-40.

> The one reciting the prayer then repeats six times the Baha'i greeting "Allah-u-Abha," and then repeats nineteen times each of the following verses:
> We all, verily, worship God.
> We all, verily, bow down before God.
> We all, verily, are devoted unto God.
> We all, verily, give praise unto God.
> We all, verily, yield thanks unto God.
> We all, verily, are patient in God.

The nine-pointed star is the Baha'i religious symbol and may be used on grave markers.

Amish and Mennonite Faith

The Amish and Mennonite faiths are part of the Anabaptist tradition, signifying "re-baptized." One of their core tenets is the belief in undergoing re-baptism into the faith during adolescence or early adulthood. Another foundational belief is the complete independence of church and state.

This conviction in re-baptism prompted the Anabaptists to separate from the Church of England and other Protestant denominations, leading to their exile and migration across Europe, eventually reaching the Americas. During this migration, they brought German and Dutch customs and languages to their communities in the Americas.

The Anabaptists eventually divided into what we now recognize as the Amish and Mennonite faiths. This schism resulted from various factors, with one significant point of contention being their differing views on shunning those who departed from the faith. The Amish are generally perceived as a more orthodox and traditional group compared to many Mennonite communities.

Both groups have followers categorized as "old-order" who adhere strictly to rules and traditions, as well as "new-order" followers who are typically less stringent. The hierarchy from most orthodox to most reformed (in a generalized sense) is as follows:
  ➢ Old-Order Amish
  ➢ New-Order Amish
  ➢ Old-Order Mennonite
  ➢ New-Order Mennonite

Amish

The Amish reside in communal areas referred to as districts. As the population of a community grows, it may divide into multiple districts. Bishops serve as the clergy for each district, overseeing church meetings where men and women participate separately. These services, conducted in various German or Dutch dialects, are known for their traditional length, spanning several hours. Ministers or deacons may accompany or assist the Bishop.

In the event of a death, the family has the option to prepare and keep the deceased in the house or barn for viewing. While embalming is allowed, restoration and cosmetics are not. Some families may opt for cremation. If embalming is chosen, the family may decide to wash the deceased beforehand. Amish tradition involves the use of plain wood coffins, usually crafted by the community. The Funeral Director dresses the deceased in undergarments and returns them to the family home for further preparation and services. Family members of the same sex dress the deceased in white attire (men: pants, vest, shirt; women: dress, cape, apron – typically worn on their wedding day).

Services typically occur within three days of the death and may take place in the family's home, a church (often a district member's house or a community building), and at the gravesite. Following the services, the coffin is transported in a hearse-buggy or another carriage to the cemetery. Amish cemeteries, where graves are dug by hand and only grave straps are used, are traditionally chosen. Attendees usually stay until the grave is filled in with dirt. After the burial, a funeral meal is hosted at the home.

Mennonite

While all Amish are considered Mennonite, not all Mennonites identify as Amish. Despite sharing a common Anabaptist origin, the Mennonites emerged as a distinct group by breaking away from the Amish. Mennonite beliefs and practices exhibit a spectrum of diversity, and their religious services, akin to other Protestant denominations, may vary significantly from one community to another.

Mennonite beliefs emphasize the principles of nonresistance, pacifism, and the separation of church and state. They often advocate for simplicity, humility, and community living. Unlike the Amish, Mennonites generally embrace modern conveniences and technology to varying degrees, reflecting the diversity within their communities.

In Mennonite services, there are similarities with other Protestant denominations. The structure and format of worship may differ between communities, ranging from more traditional to contemporary styles. Mennonite congregations often prioritize community engagement, social justice, and peacebuilding efforts.

When it comes to burial customs, Mennonites, like the Amish, hold distinctive practices. Funerals within Mennonite communities may involve traditional Christian funeral services, with variations depending on the specific congregation. Mennonites often use cemeteries that reflect a simplicity in design and gravestone inscriptions. Mennonite burial customs may include rituals such as a graveside service and the singing of hymns. The choice of burial plot, coffin, and attire for the deceased can vary among different Mennonite communities. While there may be general guidelines, the specifics often align with the preferences and traditions of the local congregation.

Fraternal Organizations

Fraternal comes from "frater" the Latin word for brother. Fraternal organizations are generally rooted in service to the community, although some fraternal organizations have ties to specific religions. If the decedent was a member of a fraternal organization, the chapter may wish to render their specific funeral honors and rites. These rites vary between fraternal organizations. These rites may take place at the religious institution, the funeral home, or the cemetery.

The Free and Accepted Masons

The Free and Accepted Masons originated from the craftsman guilds, or operative masonry. These were the men who build the churches and infrastructure, thus many of their symbol and rituals revolve would masonry building tools. As time progressed, these groups of men began to practice speculative masonry, using the symbols of the craftsmen as tools for self-improvement. As a member progresses through the ranks of this organization, they earn various degrees of rank. At the foundation of Masonry lies 'blue lodges.' This is where men are made into speculative masons and there are only 3 degrees; Apprentice, Fellowcraft, and Master. In addition to Masonic Lodges there are other branches of Masonry that a Mason can participate in. They could pursue the degrees of the Scottish Rite which culminates in the 32nd degree. A Mason could participate in the York Rite which culminates in one of the Masonic chivalric orders, the Knights Templar.

This secret society is rich in traditions and secret customs (most of which can be found on YouTube). A group of men form a lodge and are supervised by The Grand Lodge. The basic unit is a Lodge and is supervised by a Grand Lodge. The head of the Lodge is the Worshipful Master and there are other various officers within the ranks, each of which have specific duties. Speculative Masonry originated in the 1700s, and the words of that era need to be taken into context. 'Worshipful' in the context of that era means, "worthy of respect.' This is not a Christian organization, however they do utilize some Christian symbolisms and borrow heavily from the Old Testament. Some Protestant Churches will not permit a Mason service honoring one of their members, to be performed in the sanctuary. Masonic family of organizations, women of Masons can belong to the Order of the Eastern Star, Daughters of the Nile, or Order of the Beauceant and there are also some suborganizations for young children of Masons such as the Order of Rainbow for girls and DeMolay International for boys.

The order of a Masonic funeral is very straightforward. The Grand Lodge handling the services may have minor deviation from the prescribed script. Generally, the Worshipful Master guides the proceedings, and he starts with an introduction. This introduction discusses the custom of memorializing a Brother. He also states that the deceased has "reached the end of his toils."

After the introduction is complete, they play the funeral music. Mozart's solemn, instrumental pieces are popular choices, in part because Mozart was a Mason or Pleyel's Hymn, which was written by Ignatz Pleyel. After the musical interlude is over, the Sacred Roll pr Masonic Record is read. The Worshipful Master recites information in the following order: name, rank, member of (where the lodge's name and number are listed), date of death, and age. They list ages by years, months, and days.

After the Master reads aloud the deceased's entry in the Sacred Roll, a lengthy prayer follows. It serves as a tribute, full of wise reminders and verbiage that sound straight out of the Bible. This prayer revolves around reminders that "all material pursuits are vain." This prompts members to consider their own short lives. After the prayer is over, they introduce a chaplain.

After the chaplain prays and gives the audience prompts, music plays again. This prayer focuses on praise and comfort, which gives the mourners some sense of closure. After the music, the Worshipful Master declares the deceased ascended. They've gone to "the protection of the All-Seeing Eye and the smiles of Immutable Love." After this statement, the Worshipful Master displays a lambskin white apron. It's meant to serve as Mason's badge and uniform. The Master explains this within the service. It is a kindness to non-Masons and a reminder to those with aprons of their own.

One of the defining features of a Masonic funeral is the use of visual symbols. The apron is followed by the display of acacia. As a sprig of evergreen, it's meant to symbolize eternal faith that will never fade away.

This is followed by a eulogy. Depending on the loved one's preferences, the Worshipful Master can deliver it. Anyone can deliver the eulogy, though. After it's completed, the Worshipful Master extends condolences to those grieving.

After this, the Lodge says a special prayer for the "committal," which involves committing the Brother's soul to God. It can occur during the ceremony or graveside.

The chaplain quotes a famous Bible verse, known as the Aaronic Benediction, concluding the service.

Order of the Eastern Star

The Order of the Eastern Star is an organization within a local Mason Lodge whose membership consist of women of Masons. This organization honors their dead with a memorial service that centers around their symbolic emblem (as shown above). The Eastern Star emblem should be displayed at the head of the casket during visitation, at the funeral and graveside services. The service can take place in the funeral home, Chapter room, church or graveside.

This service is led by the Worthy Matron. Other Eastern Star officers will also participate in various parts of this ritual. During the service the Worthy Matron and other officers will have various color flowers represented on the five-point Eastern Star emblem.

Their membership badges are draped, and the officers stand in a specific order during the service. Words recited during this service reflect on the reality that within life there is death, and the deceased member of the order has lived a life within the principles and virtues of the Order. At various periods during the service, the Worthy Matron and other officers will explain the symbolism behind each of the colored flowers and a bouquet of colored flowers are left with the deceased.

Knights of Columbus

The Knights of Columbus is a fraternal and charitable organization founded by Father Michael J. McGivney in 1882 in New Haven, Connecticut. Established with the primary goal of providing financial aid to widows and orphans of deceased members, the organization has since evolved into one of the largest Catholic fraternal service organizations in the world. Inspired by the principles of charity, unity, fraternity, and patriotism, the Knights of Columbus engages its members in various charitable activities, community service, and social initiatives. Knights often work in unity to support local communities, promote Catholic values, and contribute to a variety of charitable causes. With a strong emphasis on faith and brotherhood, the Knights of Columbus continues to play a vital role in fostering a sense of community among its members while actively participating in charitable endeavors to make a positive impact on society.

The memorial service for a member of the Knights of Columbus is a solemn and dignified occasion, reflecting the organization's commitment to charity, unity, and fraternity. The ceremony typically takes place in a church or a venue that holds significance to the deceased and the Knights of Columbus community. The service is often marked by religious elements, such as prayers, hymns, and scripture readings, reflecting the Catholic faith that is central to the organization. Fellow Knights, dressed in their distinctive regalia, gather to pay tribute to their departed comrade, emphasizing the sense of fraternity and shared values that define the Knights of Columbus. Eulogies and speeches may highlight the individual's contributions to the community, charitable endeavors, and the impact they had within the Knights of Columbus brotherhood. The memorial service serves as a moment of reflection, mourning, and celebration of a life dedicated to service and the principles upheld by the Knights of Columbus.

Benevolent and Protective Order of Elks

The Benevolent and Protective Order of Elks, founded in New York City in 1868, stands as a distinguished fraternal organization committed to charity, community service, and promoting the principles of brotherly love and fidelity. Established by Charles A. Vivian and a group of actors, the Elks quickly expanded across the United States. The organization emphasizes benevolence through various charitable programs, scholarships, and community outreach initiatives. With a motto of "Elks Care, Elks Share," the Order strives to foster a sense of camaraderie and goodwill among its members while actively contributing to the welfare of society. The Elks' commitment to patriotism is evident through their support for veterans and military service members. Over the years, the Benevolent and Protective Order of Elks has played a crucial role in promoting philanthropy and community engagement, solidifying its place as a vital force for positive change since its inception.

The funeral service of a member of the Benevolent and Protective Order of Elks (BPOE) is a reverent and dignified occasion that reflects the organization's commitment to brotherhood, charity, and community service. The service typically takes place in a setting that holds significance for the departed member and the Elks community, often incorporating elements of ritual and tradition. Fellow Elks, dressed in their distinctive regalia with the emblems of their office, gather to pay respects to their departed comrade. The ceremony may include rituals that symbolize the principles upheld by the BPOE, such as the solemn ringing of the Elks Memorial Bell. Eulogies and speeches often highlight the individual's contributions to the Elks and the broader community, emphasizing their dedication to charitable endeavors and the principles of the organization. The funeral service becomes a moment of reflection, mourning, and celebration of a life lived in service to others, in accordance with the benevolent ideals cherished by the organization.

Independent Order of Odd Fellows

The Independent Order of Odd Fellows (IOOF), with its roots traced back to medieval trade guilds in Europe, stands as a fraternal organization dedicated to promoting fellowship, charity, and community service. Founded on the principles of friendship, love, and truth, the IOOF has evolved into an international organization fostering a sense of brotherhood and altruism. The order's commitment to aiding those in need is reflected in its charitable activities, mutual support systems, and community outreach initiatives.

The IOOF memorial services serve as a poignant and meaningful tribute to members who have passed away, embodying a harmonious blend of solemnity and celebration of a life committed to Odd Fellowship principles. These ceremonies are meticulously crafted to honor the departed individual's contributions to the IOOF community and their embodiment of the fellowship's values. Symbolic rituals and gestures form an integral part of these services, representing the profound principles that define Odd Fellowship. Such rituals may include the lighting of candles, symbolic presentations, or the laying of flowers, each holding a unique significance tied to the order's ethos. Eulogies and speeches delivered during the service weave together narratives that underscore the departed member's dedication to friendship, love, and truth—core tenets of the IOOF. As members gather to remember their comrade, the memorial service becomes a powerful expression of the enduring bonds of brotherhood within the Independent Order of Odd Fellows, providing solace, reflection, and a sense of continuity to those who continue to uphold the ideals of this venerable fraternal organization.

Rebekahs

Rebekahs, the female branch of the Independent Order of Odd Fellows (IOOF), holds a distinctive position in history as the first fraternity in the United States to embrace women as members. Founded on principles of fellowship, charity, and community service, Rebekahs draw inspiration from notable biblical women, and their beliefs are deeply rooted in the ethos of the Golden Rule—treating others as one wishes to be treated. The Rebekahs' memorial services for their members reflect the organization's commitment to honoring and celebrating lives dedicated to these principles. These services are characterized by a combination of reverence and a celebration of the individual's contributions to the Rebekahs and the broader community.

Symbolic rituals, reflective of the order's values, are incorporated into the ceremony. Eulogies and speeches pay homage to the departed member's embodiment of the ideals inspired by biblical women and the commitment to the Golden Rule. The Rebekahs' memorial service becomes a heartfelt tribute, highlighting the enduring legacy of sisterhood and benevolence within this historic fraternity.

B'nai B'rith International

B'nai B'rith International, a Jewish organization with a foundation in humanitarian aid, has been a prominent force in fostering Jewish identity, supporting charitable causes, and promoting global understanding. Notably, B'nai B'rith played a significant role in establishing the first Jewish Public Library in the United States, emphasizing the importance of education and cultural enrichment. When it comes to memorial services for its members, B'nai B'rith conducts ceremonies that encapsulate the organization's commitment to remembrance and community. These services often include prayers, rituals, and reflections on the individual's contributions to the Jewish community and humanitarian endeavors. Eulogies highlight the departed member's dedication to B'nai B'rith's principles, emphasizing their impact on fostering a sense of Jewish identity and contributing to the organization's legacy of philanthropy. The memorial service becomes a moment of collective remembrance, honoring the individual's commitment to the humanitarian mission and the enduring values upheld by B'nai B'rith International.

Funeral Directing Glossary

Acknowledgment cards – thank you cards.

Acolyte – an altar attendant.

Adaptive funeral rite – funeral rite that is adjusted to the needs and wants of those directly involved.

Aftercare – those appropriate and helpful acts of counseling, personal and/or written contact that come after the funeral.

Al-Ghusl (Ghusl) – practical and ceremonial washing of a deceased Muslim.

Alkaline hydrolysis – a process that uses water, alkaline chemicals, heat and sometimes pressure and agitation, to accelerate natural decomposition, leaving bone fragments.

Allah – in the Islam faith, the name for God.

Altar – an elevated place or structure on which sacrifices are offered or at which religious rites are performed; in the Christian faith, a table on which the Eucharist or Holy Communion is offered.

Alternative container – an unfinished wood box or other non-metal receptacle or enclosure, without ornamentation or a fixed interior lining, which is designed for the encasement of human remains and which is made of fiberboard, pressed-wood, composition materials (with or without an outside covering) or like materials.

Apostille – certification/legalization of a document for international use (under terms of the 1961 Hague Convention).

Archbishop – in the Roman Catholic faith, the head of an archdiocese.

Aron – Hebrew meaning container; a casket made entirely of wood with no metal parts.

Arrangement conference – the meeting between the funeral practitioner and the client family during which funeral arrangements are discussed, and may refer to pre-need or at-need situations.

At need – when a death has occurred.

Bishop – leader of multiple churches in a particular denomination; in the Roman Catholic faith, the head of a diocese; in the Latter-day Saints faith, Bishop of the Ward is leader of a single congregation.

Bonze – the title of the Buddhist priest. Dates – a term used in the Buddhist faith to describe a calendar that is used to determine an accurate time for casketing the deceased, services and disposition.

Brother – in the Roman Catholic faith, a man who is a member of a religious order without being ordained.

Brotherhood – relating to a social or religious organization.

Buddha altar – table or altar placed at a right angle to the deceased altar; contains an image of Buddha, incense, candles, flowers, and fruits.

Burial (Interment) – the act of placing the dead human body in the ground.

Burial-Transit Permit (Disposition Permit) – a legal document, issued by a governmental agency, authorizing transportation and/or disposition of a dead human body.

Calling hours - (Visitation / Visiting hours) – time set aside for friends and relatives to pay respect for the deceased prior to the funeral service.

Cantor – a religious singer who assists the clergy; one who assists the Rabbi in the Jewish faith; or one who assists the priest in the Eastern Orthodox faith.

Cardinal – in the Roman Catholic faith, Bishops who have the right to participate in a Papal election.

Cash Advance(s) – any item of service or merchandise described to a purchaser as a "cash advance," "accommodation," "cash disbursement," or similar term. A cash advance item is also any item obtained from a third party and paid for by the funeral provider on the purchaser's behalf. Cash advance items may include but are not limited to: cemetery or crematory services; pallbearers; public transportation; clergy honoraria; flowers; musicians or singers; nurses; obituary notices; gratuities and death certificates.

Casket – a rigid container which is designed for the encasement of human remains and which is usually constructed of wood, metal, fiberglass, plastic, or like material, and ornamented and lined with fabric.

Casketbearer (Pallbearer) – one who actively bears or carries the casket during the funeral service and at the committal service.

Cause of death – diseases, injuries, or complications that resulted in death.

Celebrant – a person who designs and officiates a personalized ceremony or rite; the officiant who celebrates the Mass in the Roman Catholic Church.

Cemetery – an area of ground set aside and dedicated for the final disposition of dead human remains.

Cemetery tent – a portable shelter employed to cover the grave area during the committal.

Certified copy of a death certificate – a legal copy of the original death certificate.

Chancel – the portion of the church surrounding the altar, usually enclosing the clergy; area behind the altar or communion rail.

Chapel – a building or designated area of a building in which services are conducted.

Chaplain – a person chosen to conduct religious exercises for the military, an institution or a fraternal organization.

Chevrah Kadisha – Hebrew meaning "Holy Society"; a group of men or women who care for the dead; they may be referred to by laymen as the "washers". In the past, they took care of all funeral arrangements and preparations for Jewish funerals.

Christian Burial Certificate – (Christian Burial Permit, Priest Lines) - a letter or form from a priest stating the eligibility of the deceased for burial in a Roman Catholic Cemetery.

Columbarium – a structure, room or space in a mausoleum or other building containing niches or recesses used to hold cremated remains.

Committal service – the portion of the funeral conducted at the place of disposition.

Common carrier – any carrier required by law to convey passengers or freight without refusal if the approved fare or charge is paid (airline, train, etc.).

Coroner – usually an elected officer without medical training whose chief duty is to investigate questionable deaths.

Cot – a portable stretcher commonly employed in a transfer vehicle for the moving of the deceased.

Cremated remains – the result of the reduction of a dead body to inorganic bone fragments by intense heat.

Cremation – the reduction of a dead human body to inorganic bone fragments by intense heat in a specifically designed retort or chamber.

Crematory – a furnace or retort for cremating dead human bodies; a building that houses a retort.

Cross – a Christian symbol without the corpus.

Crucifer/Crossbearer – one who carries the crucifix/cross during an ecclesiastical procession.

Crucifix – a cross with a figure or image representing the body of Christ (Corpus).

Cryonics – the freezing and storing of human remains for possible restoration of life in the future.

Crypt – a chamber in a mausoleum, of sufficient size, generally used to contain the casketed remains of a deceased person.

Deacon – a subordinate officer in a Christian church.

Death Certificate – a legal document containing vital statistics, disposition, and final medical information pertaining to the deceased.

Death Notice – a newspaper item publicizing the death of a person and giving service details. In some parts of the United States, can contain the same information as an obituary.

Deceased – a dead human body.

Deceased altar – table or altar placed before the casket with photos of the deceased, candles, oil lamps, incense vase, flowers, fruits, and food.

Department of Veterans Affairs or VA – a federal agency that administers benefits provided for veterans of the armed forces.

Diocese – in the Roman Catholic faith, a geographical grouping of parishes under the jurisdiction of a Bishop.

Direct Cremation – disposition of human remains by cremation, without formal viewing, visitation or ceremony with the deceased present.

Direct Disposition – any method of disposition of the human remains without formal viewing, visitation or ceremony with the deceased present.

Dismissal – procedures or invitation intended to facilitate an organized departure.

Disposition Permit – see Burial-Transit Permit.

Divine Liturgy – liturgical celebration of the Eucharist in Eastern Orthodox churches.

Ecclesiastic – pertaining to the church or clergy.

Elegy – song or poem expressing sorrow or lamentation for the dead.

Elder – governing officer of a church, often having pastoral or teaching functions; specific duties dependent upon various denominations.

El Malei Rachamin – in the Jewish faith, a memorial service; literally "God full of compassion"; usually the last prayer of the funeral service; sometimes referred to as the Malei.

Entombment – the placing of remains in a crypt in a mausoleum.

Epistle Side – the right side of the church as the congregation faces the altar from which readings and prayers are often proclaimed.

Epitaph – a commemorative inscription on a tomb or cemetery marker.

Escort – a leader(s) of the procession or guardian of the group, such as a military escort, police escort, etc.

Eucharist – the consecrated elements of Holy Communion.

Eucharistic Minister – layperson sanctioned to administer Holy Communion and other assigned tasks.

Eulogy – an oration praising an individual, usually after death.

Final Commendation – in the Roman Catholic faith, the ending portion of the Funeral Mass.

First call – when the funeral establishment receives notification of death.

First viewing (Preview) – a private time for the family to view the deceased before public visitation begins.

Forwarding remains – one of the categories required to be itemized on the GPL (if the funeral provider offers the service). This involves services of the funeral provider in the locale where death occurs and preparation for transfer to another funeral provider as selected by the family (consumer). Funeral Rule requires package pricing of this service with a description of the components included.

Foyer (Narthex, Vestibule) – the entry way into a church, funeral establishment or other public building; entrance hall.

Fraternal – relating to a social organization.

Funeral coach (Hearse) – specialty vehicle designed to transfer casketed remains.

Funeral liturgy (funeral mass) – name of the funeral service in the Roman Catholic Church; formerly called the Mass of Christian Burial.

Funeral procession – the movement of vehicles from the place of the funeral to the place of disposition.

Funeral rites – any funeral event performed.

Funeral service – the rites held at the time of disposition of human remains, with the deceased present.

Gatha – the first two and last two verses of a Buddhist hymn sung at the funeral service.

General Price List (GPL) – a printed list of goods and services offered for sale by funeral providers with retail prices. The GPL is considered the keystone of the Funeral Rule.

Genuflect – the act of bending the right knee as an indication of reverence or as an act of humility.

Ghusl – see Al-Ghusl.

Gospel Side – the left side of the church as the congregation faces the altar; a place for the reading of the Gospels and delivery of the homily by the minister.

Gratuity – gift or sum of money tendered (tip) for a service provided.

Grave – an excavation in the earth as a place for interment; interment space.

Graveside service – a ceremony or ritual, religious or otherwise, conducted at the grave.

Grave straps – webbing or similar material used for lowering the casket into the grave.

Green burial – disposition without the use of toxic chemicals or materials that are not readily biodegradable.

Green cemetery – a place of interment that bans the use of metal caskets, toxic embalming, and concrete vaults and may also require the use of aesthetically natural monuments.

Green funeral – deathcare that minimizes the use of energy in service offerings/products and that bans the use of toxic/hazardous materials.

Guaranteed contract – an agreement where the funeral establishment promises that the services and merchandise will be provided at the time of need for a sum not exceeding the original amount of the contract plus any accruals, regardless of the current prices associated with providing the services and merchandise at the time of the funeral.

Hearse – see Funeral coach.

Hesped – a eulogy or true evaluation of the deceased's life that is a part of a Jewish funeral service.

Holy Water – water blessed by a priest.

Home funeral – one that takes place within the residence of the deceased as was commonly done in the United States until the mid-20th century.

Honorarium – compensation or recognition for service performed.

Honorary casketbearers (Honorary pallbearers) – friends of the family or members of an organization or group who act as an escort or honor guard for the deceased. They do not carry the casket.

Humanistic funeral – a funeral rite that is in essence devoid of religious connotation.

Icon – in the Eastern Orthodox faith, a holy picture; usually mosaic or painted on wood.

Iconostasis (Iconostas, Iconostation) – the partition that extends across the front of an Eastern Orthodox Church separating the sanctuary from the solea.

Imam – in the Islam faith, the leader of the local congregation.

Immediate Burial – disposition of human remains by burial, without formal viewing, visitation or ceremony with the deceased present, except for a graveside service.

Informant – one who supplies vital statistics information about the deceased.

Initial notification of death – the first contact a funeral establishment receives regarding a death.

Inter – to bury in the ground.

Interment – see Burial.

Inurnment – placing cremated remains in an urn or placing cremated remains in a niche or grave.

Irrevocable contract - an agreement for future funeral services which cannot be terminated or canceled prior to the death of the beneficiary.

Islam – the religion of Muslims (Moslems) that began at the time of Mohammed; Muslims believe that Islam stands for purity, peace, submission to God's (Allah's) will, and obedience to his laws.

Jinazah – in the Islam faith the funeral or funeral prayer.

Kaddish – in the Jewish faith, a prayer recited for the deceased by the direct mourners (parents, siblings, spouse, and children) for the first time at the conclusion of the interment service. It is subsequently recited by children for parents at every service for eleven months and on yahrzeits. All other categories of mourners have the obligation to say the Kaddish for 30 days.

Kafan – burial garments utilized by Muslims.

Kin – one's blood relatives (legally, the surviving spouse is not kin).

Kingdom Hall – the worship facility for Jehovah's Witnesses.

Kippah - (Yamaka, Yarmulke) – in the Jewish faith, the skull cap worn by males at temple and funeral services.

Kneeler - (Prayer Rail, Prie Dieu) – a small bench placed in front of the casket or urn to allow a person to kneel for prayer.

Koran (Quran) – the holy book of the Islamic faith as revealed to Mohammed by the angel Gabriel.

Kriah – Hebrew term meaning rending or tearing; a symbol of grief; a tear in the upper corner of the garment or a tear on a symbolic ribbon which is worn by the survivors.

Last kiss – physical contact with the deceased and the Icon during the final pass by the casket.

Levaya – in the Jewish faith, the funeral procession.

Liturgical (Eucharist centered) worship – a prescribed order or form of worship specific to a particular denomination which will have the Eucharist or Holy Communion as its central element.

Lot – a subdivision in a cemetery which consists of several graves or interment spaces.

Lowering device – a mechanical device used to lower a casket into the ground.

Makura-gyo – traditionally, in the Buddhist faith, a bedside prayer which may be performed by the bonze just before funeral arrangements are made.

Manner of death – the mode of death, such as accident, homicide, natural, suicide, or unknown.

Masjid (Mosque) – local Islamic religious facility containing no icons, statutes, symbols, pews, chairs or musical instruments.

Mass – the liturgical celebration of the Eucharist in the Roman Catholic Church.

Mass card – of the written request for a Mass for a specific intention.

Mausoleum – a building containing crypts or vaults for entombment.

Mecca – the holiest city in the Islamic faith; Muslims are buried facing this city.

Medical Examiner – a forensically-trained physician who investigates questionable or unattended deaths (has replaced the coroner in some jurisdictions).

Memorial book (Register book) – a book signed by those attending a visitation or service.

Memorial folder (Service folder) – a pamphlet made available at the funeral service giving details about the deceased and the funeral arrangements.

Memorial gathering – a scheduled assembly of family and friends following a death without the deceased present.

Memorial park – a cemetery, or section of a cemetery, with only flush to the ground type markers.

Memorial service – funeral rites without the remains present.

Menorah – in the Jewish faith, a candelabrum with a central stem bearing seven candles; the oldest symbol in Judaism.

Military escort – military personnel assigned to accompany remains following an active-duty death.

Mogen David (Star of David) – in the Jewish faith, a hexagram formed by the combination of two triangles. May be called the Jewish Star. It symbolizes a new hope for the Jewish people.

Mohammed (Muhammad) – a prophet of the Islamic religion born in 571 C.E.; considered by Muslims to be God's messenger but he is not worshipped or considered divine.

Monsignor – an honorary title conferred upon a Roman Catholic priest.

Moslem (Muslim) – the name given to a member of the Islamic faith.

Mosque (Masjid) – see Masjid.

Mother Church – oldest original church from which other like-minded congregations have sprung.

Muslim (Moslem) – see Moslem.

Narthex (Foyer, Vestibule) – see Foyer.

National cemetery – cemetery created and maintained under an act of Congress for burial of veterans of military service and their eligible family members.

Natural organic reduction – the contained, accelerated decomposition of human remains.

Nave – the seating or auditorium section of a church.

Niche – a recess or space in a columbarium used for the permanent placing of cremated remains.

Nirvana – the Buddhist idea of heavenly peace or Pure Land.

Non-guaranteed contract – agreement in which the funeral establishment promises to apply the amount pre-paid plus any accruals to the balance due. However, the cost of the funeral will be based upon the current price for services and merchandise at the time death occurs.

Non-liturgical (scripture centered) worship – a form or order of worship which has the scriptures as its central element; the actual form or order of the worship service is left to the discretion of each individual church and/or minister.

Non-sectarian – not related to a specific religious group or organization.

Nun (Sister) – in the Roman Catholic faith, a woman who is a member of a religious order, especially one bound by vows of poverty, chastity, and obedience.

Obituary – traditionally, a news item concerning the death of a person which usually contains a biographical sketch. Can appear in media other than newspapers such as online sources and service programs. Is sometimes used interchangeably with death notice or funeral notice.

Officiant – one who conducts or leads a service or ceremony.

Outer burial container – any container designed for placement in the grave around the casket including containers commonly known as burial vaults, grave boxes, and grave liners.

Pagoda – the Buddhist place of worship.

Pall – a symbolic cloth placed over the casket.

Pallbearer (Casketbearer) – see Casketbearer.

Panachida – a rubric for the Eastern Orthodox funeral service.

Parastas (Parastasis) – the watch or all-night vigil over the deceased in the Eastern Orthodox community.

Paschal candle – in the Roman Catholic faith, a candle placed near the casket during the Funeral Mass that signifies the everlasting light of Christ.

Pastor – one having spiritual care over a number of people.

Perpetual care – an arrangement made by the cemetery whereby funds are set aside, the income from which is used to maintain the cemetery indefinitely.

Pope – the head of the Roman Catholic Church and the Bishop of Rome.

Practitioner - in the Church of Christ, Scientist, one authorized to read the lessons and scriptures.

Prayer card – a card with the name of the decedent and a prayer or verse, which may or may not include the dates of birth and death.

Prayer rail (Kneeler, Prie Dieu) – see Kneeler.

Pre-funded funeral arrangements – funeral arrangements made in advance of need that include provisions for funding or prepayment.

Pre-planned funeral arrangements – funeral arrangements made in advance of need that do not include provisions for funding or prepayment.

Preview – see First viewing.

Prie Dieu (Prayer rail, Kneeler) – see Kneeler.

Priest – a title conferred to clergy upon ordination in various religions.

Private carrier – those who transport only in particular instances and only for those they chose to contract with (e.g., funeral establishment vehicles and livery).

Procession/Processional – the movement, in an orderly fashion, at the beginning of a service.

Quran (Koran) – see Koran.

Rabbi – a teacher or ordained leader in the Jewish faith.

Reader – see Practitioner.

Receiving remains – one of the categories required to be itemized on the GPL (if the funeral provider offers the service). This involves services of the funeral provider after initial services have been provided by another firm at the locale of death. Funeral Rule requires package pricing of this service with a description of the components included.

Receiving vault – a structure designed for the temporary storage of bodies not to be immediately interred.

Recession/Recessional – the movement, in an orderly fashion, at the end of a service.

Register book (Memorial book) – see Memorial book.

Relief Society – a women's group of the Church of Jesus Christ of Latter-day Saints.

Relief Society Room – a room designated for the ladies of the Relief Society to meet. From a funeral standpoint, often the room where the casket is placed prior to the service.

Retort – the burning chamber in a crematory, also referred to as the cremator; the total mechanical unit for the cremation process.

Reverend – title used to address member of the clergy.

Revocable contract – agreement which may be terminated by the purchaser at any time prior to the death of the beneficiary with a refund of monies paid on the contract as prescribed by state law.

Rosary beads – a chain of adjoining beads and a crucifix used as an aid in the recitation of prayers.

Rosary prayers – a series of prayers in the Roman Catholic faith.

Rosary service – a service at which rosary prayers are recited.

Royal doors – doors in the center of the Iconostasis leading directly to the altar: only ordained clergy go through these doors; never cross on the solea in front of the Royal Doors.

Rubrics – in liturgical churches, stated directions in a prayer book or liturgical manual regarding the order of service as approved by the denomination.

Sacrament of the Sick – in the Roman Catholic faith, a sacrament given to those seriously ill or in danger of death to prepare their souls for eternity.

Sanctuary – the part of the church surrounding the altar, inside the chancel.

Scapular – in the Roman Catholic faith, a piece of cloth or a medal having religious significance usually worn around the neck.

Section – the largest subdivision of a cemetery.

Service folder – see Memorial Folder.

Service of Encasketing – in the Buddhist faith, a service performed as a part of casketing the deceased.

Sexton – the one who is in charge of the cemetery; the caretaker of a church.

Shabbat – the Jewish Sabbath; begins at sundown Friday and ends at sundown Saturday.

Shivah – in the Jewish faith, a seven (7) day mourning period.

Sholoshim – meaning 30 in the Jewish faith; the 30-day mourning period.

Shomer – in the Jewish faith, a watcher; one who sits with the deceased reading Psalms until burial.

Shroud – a cloth or garment in which a dead person is wrapped or dressed for burial.

Sign of the cross – a symbolic sign of the Cross, made with the right hand.

Sister (nun) – see Nun.

Social Security Administration – a branch of the U. S. Department of Health and Human Services which provides benefits for retirement, survivors and disability, and includes Supplemental Security Income (SSI) and Medicare.

Solea – in the Eastern Orthodox Church, the open area (sometimes raised) before the altar.
Star of David – see Mogen David.

Stake – a territorial grouping of the Church of Jesus Christ of Latter-day Saints made up of at least ten wards.

Survivor(s) – one who outlives another person or event.

Synagogue – a place of religious worship in the Jewish faith; may also be referred to as Temple or Shul.

Tachrichim – a hand-sewn white linen shroud in which the deceased members of the Jewish faith are dressed.

Taharah – in the Jewish faith, the ceremonial washing the deceased before the burial; a ritual purification or cleansing of the deceased which should be performed by the Chevra Kaddisha.

Tallith – a prayer shawl worn by Jewish males during the morning prayer service.

Tehillim – in the Jewish faith, prayers said before the funeral by a group of friends and the shomer. These prayers come from the book of Psalms.

Temple – a building dedicated to be the house of the Lord; a sacred structure on earth used for instruction by members of the Church of Jesus Christ of Latter-day Saints.

Temple clothing – garments worn by endowed members of the Latter-day Saints at the Temple and for burial.

Temple Ordinances – ceremonial instructions of the Latter-day Saints Church, given only within a Temple to worthy members of the sect.

Temporary container – a receptacle for cremated remains, usually made of cardboard, plastic, or similar materials designed to hold cremated remains until an urn, other permanent container is acquired, or other disposition is made.

Third party contracts – agreements which involve the funeral practitioner/funeral establishment because the family being served has contracted with someone else (a third party) for services or merchandise also available from the funeral establishment i.e., caskets, vaults, urns, pre-need insurance, etc.

Tomb – a general term designating those places suitable for the reception of a dead human body.

Transepts – wings of the main part of the church which may serve as small chapels for baptism, weddings, and even small funeral services.

Transfer of remains – see the moving of the dead human body form the place of death to the funeral establishment or other designated place.

Transfer vehicle – the automobile generally used for transporting the uncasketed dead human body from the place of death to the mortuary.

Trisagion – in the Eastern Orthodox faith, three short services or blessings that are part of the funeral rite.

Trust Account – account established by one individual to be held for the benefit of another (as a method of payment of funeral expenses); creates a fiduciary responsibility. Money paid to a funeral establishment for future services is placed in an account with the funeral establishment as trustee for the benefit of another.

Urn – permanent container for cremated remains meant for decorative or inurnment purposes.

Urn lowering device – a mechanical device used to lower an urn into the ground.

Vestibule (Foyer, Narthex) – see Foyer.

Vestments – ritual garments worn by the clergy.

Veteran – one who has served with the armed forces and who is no longer an active member of the armed forces.

Vigil (Vigil service, Wake Service) – a prayer or scripture service usually held at the funeral establishment the evening before the funeral.

Vigil lights – in the Roman Catholic faith, set of two candles that may be placed, one at the head and one at the foot of the casket, during the visitation period.

Visitation (Calling hours, Visiting hours) – see Calling hours.

Vital statistics – data concerning birth, marriage, divorce, sickness and death.

Wake – historically, a watch kept over the deceased; an all-night vigil.

Wake service (Vigil, Vigil service) – see Vigil.

Ward – group of Latter-day Saints members sharing familial, linguistic, or cultural characteristics.

Words of Appreciation – a brief expression of gratitude to the congregation for their presence at the Buddhist service.

Yahrzeit – in the Jewish faith, the anniversary of the death.

Yarmulke (Kippah, Yamaka) – see Kippah.

Yizkor – in the Jewish faith, a memorial service recited four times a year.

Domain II
Business Management

Small Business Management

Accounting

Types of Business Managements

Funeral Home Management

Technology

Small Business Management

Eighty-six percent of funeral homes in the United States are independently owned businesses and even though they may be incorporated for liability reasons, these businesses have many of the same characteristics of other small businesses that provide services as their main product. **Small business** is defined as a *business which is independently owned and operated and is dominant in its field of operation.* A unique characteristic of funeral homes, which use to be prevalent in the past, was the association owners had with local churches, which in turned branded a particular funeral home as the "Jewish or Protestant funeral home." Since the decline in religious participation in society, these types of associations are playing less of a role and the consumers are choosing funeral homes based on other factors, such as quality of services provided, the facilities and cost. These factors that influence consumers spending behaviors and loyalty to a funeral firm play a vital role in small business management.

Some of the common characteristics of a small business are:

Size	Small businesses are generally characterized by a relatively small number of employees. The size of a funeral home is based on the number of full-adult funerals handled by the firm annually.
Owner-Operated	Many small business funeral homes are owner-operated or family-owned, meaning that the owner or a family is actively involved in the day-to-day operations of the business.
Local Focus	The funeral firm usually serves families in a local or geographical regional market. They may be deeply connected to their communities and build relationships with local families.
Limitation of Resources	Independently owned funeral homes might have limited financial resources compared to larger corporations. This may impact their ability to invest in technology, marketing, or their ability to expansion in other markets.
Flexibility	Independent owned funeral homes can be more agile and flexible in responding to market changes. Corporate owned funeral homes may be more confined to corporate procedures and specific marketing actions that may work in one geographical market but not in another. Independent owners can quickly adapt to new trends to modify business strategies without navigating complex organizational structures.
Close Customer Relationships:	Independent firms often prioritize building close relationships with their customers. Personalized service and customer loyalty are crucial for their success.
Simple Organizational Structure	The organizational structure of a small funeral firm is often simpler compared to larger corporate owned organizations. Decision-making may be centralized, and there may be fewer layers of management. Less bureaucracy and formal procedures could streamline operations and make the decision-making process more conducive to change in operations.

These characteristics are generalizations, and there can be exceptions to them based on the history and longevity of the funeral firm.

Business

A **business** is *an organization that combines input of raw materials, capital, labor, and management skills to produce useful outputs of goods and services as to earn a profit.* The funeral business is a unique business, whereby when death occurs, the client-family contacts a funeral home and employes their services to properly dispose of the human remains in a respectful and dignified manner. The trained funeral professional possesses the knowledge, skills set, equipment and resources to accomplish this task in an organized and respectful manner. In addition, especially with the decline of in the consumers' affiliations with a religious organization, the funeral director is adopting additional roles as bereavement counselor and funeral celebrant.

Businesses typically fall into three major categories:

Manufacturing Business – *a business that makes finished goods from raw materials, by hand or machinery.* An example of a manufacturing business in the funeral industry would be a vault company. The vault company takes concrete, steel and other materials and fashions an outer enclosure that supports the weight of the earth and provides resistance to the earthly elements.

Merchandising Business – *a business that purchases finished goods for resale.* A retailer that sells finished goods is an example of a merchandising business.

Service Business – *a business that provides service as opposed to a product.* A funeral home is considered a service business. Even though a funeral home provides merchandise to the consumer, their main role is to plan, organize and direct the final disposition of the deceased, while giving comfort to the bereaved.

Entrepreneur

An **entrepreneur** *is someone who creates a business, assumes the liability and risk*, often marked by innovative ideas, and the ability to identify market opportunities. Their role is crucial in contributing to economic growth, generating employment, and fostering innovation. Entrepreneurs often initiate **startups** (*which are new business ventures that are started*), driven by innovations or new products, catalyzing these new ventures. Monitoring criteria for entrepreneurs involves both quantitative factors, such as employee numbers, sales figures, gross and net profits, and qualitative aspects, which vary based on business location and management styles. While quantitative criteria are number-based, qualitative criteria are more personalized, with the former generally holding greater importance in evaluating business performance.

Owning or starting a business necessitates a thorough analysis of business trends, financial market conditions, and the location's dynamics before committing financial capital. These considerations significantly influence the business model, impacting its longevity and future success. Economic competition comes in various forms, with funeral homes contending with each other for business. Additionally, businesses may depend on each other, creating complex interdependencies. For example, a funeral home relying on a specific casket company for supplies forms an interdependent relationship where changes in one business can ripple across others. This is evident in recent market trends where casket companies adapted to the growing preference for cremation by introducing ceremonial caskets and combustible cremation units.

Function of Management

Management *involves a set of functions that are essential for planning, organizing, directing, and controlling resources to achieve organizational goals. These functions, often referred to as the functions of management, provide a framework for effective and efficient operations within an organization. The classical management framework identified four key functions of management. These functions* are widely recognized and form the basis for understanding the managerial process. The functions of management are:

Planning: *Planning involves defining goals, establishing strategies, and developing plans to coordinate activities.*
Key Activities:
- ➢ Setting organizational objectives.
- ➢ Identifying tasks and activities required to achieve goals.
- ➢ Developing plans and allocating resources.
- ➢ Anticipating and preparing for potential challenges.

Organizing: *Organizing is the process of arranging resources and tasks to achieve organizational objectives.*
Key Activities:
- ➢ Structuring tasks and activities.
- ➢ Allocating resources (human, financial, and technological).
- ➢ Defining roles and responsibilities.
- ➢ Establishing relationships and communication channels.

Leading (Directing): *Leading involves influencing and guiding employees to achieve organizational goals.*
Key Activities:
- ➢ Motivating and inspiring individuals and teams.
- ➢ Communicating the vision and goals of the organization.
- ➢ Making decisions and resolving conflicts.
- ➢ Providing guidance and support to employees.

(Actuating): Motivation of all parties involved. Coordinating involves harmonizing and synchronizing activities to achieve organizational goals.
- ➢ Ensuring communication and collaboration among all team members.
- ➢ Aligning individual and team efforts with overall objectives.
- ➢ Balancing resources to optimize efficiency.
- ➢ Resolving conflicts and promoting a unified organizational effort.

Controlling (Evaluation): *Controlling is the process of monitoring, measuring, and adjusting activities to ensure they align with organizational goals.*

Key Activities:

> ➢ Establishing performance standards.
> ➢ Monitoring and measuring performance.
> ➢ Comparing actual performance to standards.
> ➢ Taking corrective action when necessary.

These functions are interrelated and often performed in an ongoing and iterative manner. Effective management requires a balance between these functions, and managers at different levels in an organization are typically responsible for different aspects of these functions. For example, top-level managers are more involved in planning and organizing, while middle managers focus on organizing and directing, and funeral directors are often engaged in directing and controlling.

Successful management involves adapting these functions to the specific needs and context of the organization. The functions provide a systematic approach to achieving organizational goals and ensuring that resources are used efficiently and effectively.

Legal Forms of Business Organizations

There are six legal forms of business organization:
Sole Proprietorship - *A business owned by one person, who bears unlimited liability for the enterprise:*

Advantages:
> ➢ Simplicity: Sole proprietorships are easy to set up and require minimal paperwork. There are fewer formalities compared to other business structures.
> ➢ Direct Control: The owner has complete control over decision-making and operations, allowing for quick and flexible responses to changes in the business environment.
> ➢ Tax Benefits: Profits and losses are reported on the owner's personal tax return, simplifying the tax process. Additionally, the business itself is not taxed separately.
> ➢ Costs: Operating costs are generally lower compared to other business structures. There are fewer regulatory and compliance requirements, reducing administrative burdens.
> ➢ Profit Motivation: The owner directly benefits from the success of the business. There are no partners or shareholders to share profits with.

Disadvantages:
> ➢ Unlimited Liability: The owner is personally responsible for all business debts and liabilities. In the event of financial problems, personal assets may be at risk.
> ➢ Limited Capital: Sole proprietorships may find it challenging to raise capital compared to larger business structures. Funding options are often limited to personal savings or loans.
> ➢ Limited Expertise: The owner must possess a diverse set of skills to manage various aspects of the business. This can be a disadvantage if the owner lacks expertise in certain areas.

- ➢ Business Continuity: The business is closely tied to the owner, and continuity may be affected by personal factors such as illness or death. It may also be challenging to sell or transfer the business.
- ➢ Limited Growth Potential: Sole proprietorships may face challenges in scaling and expanding due to limited resources and the potential lack of access to external funding.
- ➢ Perception: Some businesses may face challenges in terms of credibility and perception, as stakeholders, such as customers and suppliers, might view larger or more formal structures as more stable.

General Partnership – A *voluntary association of two or more people who have combined their resources to carry on as co-owners of a lawful enterprise for their joint profit. General partners are involved in the business management and actions, as well as they all assume liability.*

Advantages:
- ➢ Ease of Formation: General partnerships are relatively easy to form, with fewer formalities compared to other business structures. A written agreement is advisable but not always required.
- ➢ Shared Decision-Making: Partners share the responsibility of decision-making, which can lead to more diverse perspectives and ideas, potentially benefiting the business.
- ➢ Financial Resources: Partnerships can benefit from the financial contributions of each partner, providing more capital for the business. This can be advantageous for startups and small businesses.
- ➢ Taxation: Similar to a sole proprietorship, general partnerships are not subject to income tax themselves. Instead, profits and losses flow through to the individual partners, who report them on their personal tax returns.
- ➢ Flexibility: Partnerships offer flexibility in terms of structuring the business, profit-sharing, and management roles. This allows for customization based on the needs and preferences of the partners.

Disadvantages:
- ➢ Unlimited Liability: Each partner is personally responsible for the debts and liabilities of the business. This means that personal assets may be at risk if the business faces financial difficulties.
- ➢ Conflict of Interest: Differences in opinions, work ethic, or commitment among partners can lead to conflicts. Disagreements on business decisions, management styles, or the division of profits can be challenging to resolve.
- ➢ Shared Profits: While sharing profits can be an advantage, it may also be a disadvantage for some individuals who prefer to retain full control and enjoy all the benefits of business success, without the liabilities.
- ➢ Continuity Issues: Similar to a sole proprietorship, the continuity of a general partnership may be affected by events such as the withdrawal, death, or bankruptcy of a partner. It may be challenging to transfer ownership or sell a partnership interest. To avoid such challenges, when the partnership is formed, provisions within the partnership agreement should be made to address such issues.

- ➢ Limited Capital: While partnerships can provide more capital compared to sole proprietorships, they may still face limitations in raising funds compared to larger business structures.
- ➢ Legal Complexity: Though less formal than some business structures, partnerships may still involve legal complexities. A clear and comprehensive partnership agreement is extremely important to avoid potential disputes.

Limited Partnership – In addition to the definition of a partnership, *limited partners are solely investors that are not involved in the management or day-to-day operations of the business. Limited partners are solely financial investors.*

Advantages:
- ➢ Limited Liability for Limited Partners: One of the primary advantages is that limited partners have limited liability, meaning their personal assets are generally protected from the business's debts and liabilities. The extent of their liability is typically limited to their investment in the partnership.
- ➢ Investment Opportunities: Limited partnerships allow investors to contribute capital without taking an active role in management. This can be attractive for passive investors who want to participate in business ventures without being directly involved in day-to-day operations.
- ➢ Expertise and Management: Limited partnerships can benefit from the expertise and involvement of both general partners, who actively manage the business, and limited partners, who bring financial resources without the same level of responsibility.
- ➢ Taxation: Similar to general partnerships, limited partnerships are not taxed at the entity level. Profits and losses pass through to the individual partners, who report them on their personal tax returns.
- ➢ Flexible Management Structure: Limited partnerships offer flexibility in the distribution of management responsibilities. General partners typically handle day-to-day operations, while limited partners have a more passive role.

Disadvantages:
- ➢ Unlimited Liability for General Partners: General partners in a limited partnership have unlimited personal liability for the business's debts and obligations. This means their personal assets are at risk in the event of legal or financial troubles.
- ➢ Limited Control for Limited Partners: Limited partners generally has limited control over the management and decision-making processes of the business. They must rely on the general partners for operational decisions.
- ➢ Complex Formation: Establishing a limited partnership can be more complex than forming a sole proprietorship or general partnership. It often involves filing formal paperwork with the state, creating a partnership agreement, and complying with specific legal requirements.
- ➢ Potential for Conflict: Differences in management styles, decision-making, or financial expectations between general and limited partners

can lead to conflicts. Clear communication and a well-drafted partnership agreement are crucial to mitigating these issues.
- ➤ Transferability of Ownership: The transfer of ownership or selling a limited partnership interest may be restricted or more complex compared to other business structures, potentially impacting liquidity for investors.
- ➤ Limited Capital: While limited partnerships provide opportunities for passive investment, attracting limited partners may still be challenging, and the amount of capital raised may be limited compared to other business structures.

S Corporation - *An artificial being, invisible, intangible, and existing only in contemplation of law; an entity that has a distinct existence separate and apart from the existence of its individual members. A type of corporation that offers limited liability to its owners but is taxed by the federal government as a partnership.*

Advantages:
- ➤ Limited Liability: Shareholders in an S Corporation generally have limited personal liability for the company's debts and obligations. This means their personal assets are protected from business-related liabilities.
- ➤ Pass-Through Taxation: S Corporations enjoy pass-through taxation, where profits and losses are passed through to the individual shareholders' tax returns. The corporation itself is not taxed at the entity level, which can result in potential tax savings.
- ➤ Avoidance of Double Taxation: Unlike C Corporations, which are subject to double taxation (taxation at both the corporate and shareholder levels), S Corporations avoid this issue by passing income directly to shareholders.
- ➤ Tax Savings for Shareholders: Shareholders may be able to classify a portion of their income as dividends rather than salary, potentially reducing payroll taxes (e.g., Social Security and Medicare taxes).
- ➤ Attractive to Small Businesses: S Corporations are often suitable for smaller businesses, especially those that meet the eligibility requirements and want to avoid the double taxation associated with C Corporations.
- ➤ Transferability of Shares: Shares in an S Corporation can be easily transferred, making it relatively straightforward for shareholders to sell or transfer their ownership interests.

Disadvantages:
- ➤ Restrictions on Shareholders: S Corporations have restrictions on the number and types of shareholders they can have. For example, they cannot have more than 100 shareholders, and non-U.S. residents, certain trusts, and other entities are generally ineligible.
- ➤ Limited Classes of Stock: S Corporations can only have one class of stock, which limits the flexibility to offer different types of shares with varying rights and preferences.

- Taxable Fringe Benefits: Certain fringe benefits, such as health insurance, provided to shareholders owning more than 2% of the corporation may be treated as taxable income.
- Limited Capital Raising Options: Compared to C Corporations, S Corporations may face challenges in raising capital since they cannot issue multiple classes of stock and are subject to certain ownership restrictions.
- Risk of Termination of S Status: To maintain S Corporation status, certain eligibility requirements must be met. If these requirements are violated, the corporation may lose its S Corporation status and be subject to different tax treatment.
- Complexity in Compliance: While S Corporations offer tax advantages, they require careful compliance with IRS regulations and more complex record-keeping than simpler structures like sole proprietorships or partnerships.

C Corporation - *An artificial being, invisible, intangible, and existing only in contemplation of law; an entity that has a distinct existence separate and apart from the existence of its individual members. An ordinary corporation, taxed by the federal government as a separate legal entity.*

Advantages:
- Limited Liability: Shareholders in a C Corporation have limited personal liability for the company's debts and legal obligations. Personal assets are generally protected from business-related liabilities.
- Unlimited Number of Shareholders: C Corporations can have an unlimited number of shareholders, allowing for a broad base of investors and the ability to raise significant capital.
- Separate Legal Entity: The C Corporation is a distinct legal entity, which means it can enter into contracts, own assets, and incur liabilities on its own behalf. This separation can provide protection for shareholders.
- Perpetual Existence: A C Corporation has a perpetual existence, meaning the business can continue to exist even if ownership changes or key individuals leave the company.
- Ease of Transferability of Shares: Shares in a C Corporation can be easily transferred, providing liquidity for shareholders and making it easier to buy or sell ownership interests.
- Employee Benefits: C Corporations can offer a wide range of benefits to employees, including health and life insurance, retirement plans, and stock options.

Disadvantages:
- Double Taxation: C Corporations are subject to double taxation. The corporation itself is taxed on its profits, and then shareholders are taxed again on any dividends received. This can result in higher overall tax liability.
- Complexity: C Corporations are subject to more complex legal and regulatory requirements than simpler business structures. Compliance with corporate formalities, filing requirements, and ongoing administrative tasks can be time-consuming.

> Expensive to Establish and Maintain: The initial setup and ongoing maintenance of a C Corporation can be more expensive than other business structures, such as sole proprietorships or partnerships.

> Ownership and Control: The broad ownership structure may lead to a separation of ownership and control, with shareholders having limited influence on day-to-day operations. This can be a disadvantage for small, closely held businesses.

> Risk of Minority Shareholder Disputes: In larger C Corporations, minority shareholders may have limited influence on major decisions, potentially leading to disputes over control and decision-making.

> Complex Stock Issuance: Unlike S Corporations, C Corporations can issue multiple classes of stock with different voting rights and preferences. While this offers flexibility, it can also introduce complexity and potential conflicts among shareholders.

> Alternative Minimum Tax (AMT): C Corporations are subject to the Alternative Minimum Tax, which is an additional tax designed to prevent corporations from using certain tax incentives to eliminate their tax liability entirely.

Limited Liability Company (LLC) - *A form of business ownership which combines aspects of partnerships with the limited liability of a corporation; owners known as members.*

Advantages:

> Limited Liability: Members (owners) of an LLC enjoy limited personal liability for the company's debts and legal liabilities. In most cases, personal assets are protected from business-related obligations.

> Pass-Through Taxation: LLCs are typically treated as pass-through entities for tax purposes. Profits and losses are passed through to the individual members, who report them on their personal tax returns. This avoids the double taxation associated with C Corporations.

> Flexible Management: LLCs offer flexibility in management structure. Members can choose to manage the company themselves or designate a manager. This flexibility allows for customization based on the needs and preferences of the members.

> Ease of Formation: Forming an LLC is generally simpler and requires less paperwork compared to C Corporations. There is more flexibility in organizational structure and fewer ongoing formalities.

> No Ownership Restrictions: LLCs typically have fewer restrictions on ownership than S Corporations. There are no limitations on the number or types of members, and members can include individuals, other LLCs, corporations, or even foreign entities.

> Flexibility in Profit Distribution: Members have flexibility in how they distribute profits among themselves, providing versatility in structuring financial arrangements.

Disadvantages:

> Limited Capital Raising Options: While LLCs offer advantages in terms of flexibility and simplicity, they may face challenges in raising capital compared to C Corporations. The ability to issue different classes of stock is not available in an LLC.

> Potential Self-Employment Taxes: In some cases, members of an LLC may be subject to self-employment taxes on their share of the company's profits. This can be a disadvantage compared to certain corporate structures.

> State-Specific Regulations: LLC regulations can vary by state, and compliance requirements may differ. This can result in added complexity for LLCs operating in multiple states.

> Lack of Perpetual Existence: While LLCs offer more flexibility than certain business structures, they may lack perpetual existence. In some jurisdictions, the death, withdrawal, or bankruptcy of a member can trigger the dissolution of the LLC.

> Potential for Member Disputes: In the absence of a well-drafted operating agreement, disputes among members can be challenging to resolve. An operating agreement outlining roles, responsibilities, and dispute resolution mechanisms is crucial.

> Limited Stock Incentives: LLCs do not issue stock, which may limit the use of stock options and other equity-based incentives often used in corporations.

No matter which type of legal entity is formed for financial or business purposes, an attorney and certified public accountant should be consulted in order to select an entity that best meets the funeral home's long-term operational goals and objectives.

Business Plan

Creating a business plan is one of the most important documents an entrepreneur can do prior to establishing the business. This document serves as a foundation that provides direction for the business.

A business plan is a comprehensive document that serves as a roadmap for a business, outlining its strategy and structure. Four key components are crucial in developing an effective business plan. The Executive Summary provides a concise overview, summarizing essential aspects like the business concept, mission, and goals, acting as an introduction for potential investors or stakeholders. The Business Description delves into specifics such as the mission, vision, and values, outlining products or services, the target market, and the unique selling proposition that sets the business apart from competitors. The Market Analysis section evaluates the industry, market trends, and potential competitors, offering demographic information, a competitive landscape analysis, and insights into market needs and opportunities. Finally, the Financial Plan projects the business's financial health, encompassing income statements, balance sheets, and cash flow statements, providing a forecast of financial performance. This section may also outline funding requirements, anticipated returns, and financial milestones. Together, these components provide a holistic understanding of the business, assisting entrepreneurs and stakeholders in comprehending its purpose, market positioning, and financial trajectory.

Developing a thorough business plan involves considering numerous components, making it a foundational step in initiating and expanding a prosperous business. This plan offers a structured framework crucial for effective decision-making, aids in securing funding, and establishes the business on a solid foundation for sustained success in the long term.

Funding Sources

Funding a business can come from various sources, and the choice of funding depends on the specific needs and circumstances of the business. These are some of the possible sources for funding a business venture:

Working capital is a vital financial metric indicating a company's short-term financial health, calculated by deducting current liabilities from current assets. Current assets include cash, accounts receivable, and inventory, while current liabilities involve short-term obligations like accounts payable. Positive working capital signals the availability of resources for daily operations, facilitating timely payments and addressing unforeseen challenges. Efficient management of working capital is crucial for smooth business operations, supplier payments, and responsiveness to market demands, contributing to sustained growth and resilience.

Leveraging fixed assets as a funding source involves using long-term assets like real estate, machinery, and vehicles as collateral to secure business financing. This approach, known as asset-based financing, allows businesses to access capital while using assets to mitigate the lender's risk. Although it offers a valuable means of securing funds for expansion or strategic initiatives, businesses should carefully evaluate the terms, including interest rates and repayment terms, and consider the impact on their overall financial health and operational flexibility. Striking a balance between capital needs and prudent asset management is crucial for sustained growth and financial stability.

Utilizing **personal capital** as a funding source involves deploying personal financial resources, such as savings, investments, or assets, to support the establishment or growth of a business. This approach signals a direct commitment and financial stake from the entrepreneur or business owner, allowing for a swift and flexible injection of funds, especially in the early stages. While showcasing belief in the business concept and a willingness to take on personal financial risk, entrepreneurs must carefully assess the implications on their personal financial situation, aiming for a balance between personal investment and diversification of financial risk to ensure both business and personal financial sustainability.

Leveraging equity capital as a funding source involves obtaining investment from external parties in exchange for ownership stakes in a business, providing a substantial funding avenue without incurring debt. This method often includes investors like venture capitalists, angel investors, or crowdfunding platforms, who, in return for their investment, receive shares or ownership interests in the company. Commonly sought by startups and high-growth enterprises, equity capital enables access to expertise and mentorship from investors, though entrepreneurs must be prepared to cede some control and share potential profits. Establishing a fair valuation and negotiating favorable terms are crucial steps to attract equity investors and ensure a mutually beneficial partnership for long-term growth.

Debt equity, also known as mezzanine financing, is a hybrid funding source that blends features of both debt and equity. In this arrangement, businesses secure a loan with certain equity features, such as the lender's option to convert debt into equity under predefined conditions. Mezzanine financing serves as a middle ground between traditional debt and equity, providing businesses with flexible access to capital for growth initiatives, acquisitions, or capital-intensive projects. While it offers benefits of debt, such as interest tax deductions and lower costs compared to equity, it also entails elements of equity, including potential dilution of ownership. Debt equity is suitable for businesses seeking additional capital beyond traditional loans but aiming to retain more control over ownership compared to standard equity financing. Careful negotiation and structuring of terms are essential to align the interests of both the business and the lender in this unique funding approach.

These are some of the various forms of debt equity as well as their advantages and disadvantages:

Securing a loan from family and friends for a business opportunity can offer accessible initial capital, streamlining the borrowing process and minimizing bureaucratic hurdles. The advantages include the flexibility of terms, such as lower interest rates or extended repayment periods, fostering a supportive financial environment. However, entrepreneurs must carefully consider potential disadvantages and strike a balance between professionalism and personal relationships to prevent conflicts. Clear communication, a written agreement, and a commitment to financial responsibility are crucial, treating loans from family and friends with the same formality as those from financial institutions. Maintaining open dialogue is key to navigating financial transactions while preserving healthy relationships.

Opting for a **mortgage loan** to fund a business opportunity can be a strategic move, particularly when real estate is integral to the venture. Using property as collateral allows individuals to secure a mortgage with favorable interest rates and extended repayment terms, a relevant choice for businesses requiring a physical location like retail outlets or offices. While this method offers lower interest rates, potential tax benefits, and dual use of the property, entrepreneurs should carefully consider the risks, such as the potential loss of property in case of default, along with the stringent qualification criteria and time-consuming approval process.

For entrepreneurs seeking financing, **commercial** loans from banks and financial institutions are a common and strategic option. These loans provide capital for various purposes, including startup costs, equipment purchases, and operational expenses, without diluting ownership or involving personal assets. Despite the rigorous application process, successful approval of a commercial loan can establish a solid financial foundation for business growth. Entrepreneurs must carefully evaluate their financial needs, repayment capacity, and the impact of debt on their overall business strategy before committing to commercial loans.

Acquiring a **Small Business Administration (SBA)** (*the principle government agency concerned with the financing, operations, and management of small businesses*) **loan** to fund a business opportunity is a strategic move for entrepreneurs seeking financial support with favorable terms. The SBA, a U.S. government agency, partners with approved lenders to facilitate loans for small businesses, offering access to capital that may be challenging to secure otherwise. Renowned for competitive interest rates, extended repayment terms, and lower down payment requirements, SBA loans are an attractive choice for diverse business needs, from startup costs to expansion and equipment purchase. The SBA's involvement assures lenders, encouraging them to extend credit to small businesses that might not qualify for traditional loans. However, the application process is rigorous, necessitating a well-crafted business plan, financial documentation, and compliance with SBA eligibility criteria. A successful SBA loan application empowers entrepreneurs with a solid financial foundation and the backing of a government-supported lending program.

Securing funding from state and regional development commissions is a strategic avenue for entrepreneurs capitalizing on business opportunities. These commissions actively support economic growth by providing financial assistance, grants, and resources to businesses contributing to the local economy. Entrepreneurs benefit from specialized programs promoting job creation, innovation, and community development, gaining access to tailored funding solutions, mentorship, and networking opportunities. However, the application process demands a detailed business proposal highlighting the potential positive impact on the region's economic landscape, requiring careful alignment with the commission's objectives.

Engaging **venture capitalists (VCs)** to fund a business opportunity is a strategic move for rapid scaling. VCs, professional investors seeking substantial returns, inject capital into high-potential startups in exchange for equity. This funding is attractive for innovative businesses with high growth potential, providing access to substantial capital, expertise, mentorship, and industry connections. Successful collaboration with VCs demands a compelling business plan, a strong management team, and a shared vision, though it entails ceding control and ownership.

Engaging **angel investors** for early-stage financing is a transformative step for entrepreneurs. Angel investors provide capital to startups for equity or convertible debt, leveraging expertise and networks. Unlike traditional lenders, angel investors take risks on innovative ventures, offering valuable mentorship, strategic guidance, and business acumen. This investment form benefits early-stage businesses, helping them navigate challenges, refine business models, and accelerate growth, but requires relinquishing ownership and maintaining open communication for a mutually beneficial partnership.

Business Considerations

When establishing a new business, choosing a suitable physical location is critical for its success. The location serves as the face of the business, impacting its ability to attract customers, clients, and partners. Factors such as target demographics, industry requirements, and the overall business strategy must be considered. Thorough market research and analysis are essential to ensure the physical location is a strategic asset that enhances operational efficiency, brand image, and customer perception.

Ensuring customer accessibility is fundamental for business strategy and customer-centricity. The ease of customer access significantly influences their experience and satisfaction. Internal and external traffic flow, especially in the funeral industry, is crucial, considering factors like visitation and parking facilities. In the digital era, online accessibility, including user-friendly websites and mobile applications, is equally vital. Prioritizing accessibility demonstrates a commitment to inclusivity, contributing to brand loyalty and broadening market reach.

The design of a funeral home is critical for creating a comforting and dignified atmosphere for grieving families. Well-thought-out interior layouts, tasteful décor, and comfortable gathering spaces contribute to a serene environment. Modern designs often incorporate technology for multimedia presentations and virtual participation. The design directly impacts the ability to provide meaningful and supportive services to the community during difficult times.

When designing a funeral home, adherence to ADA regulations is paramount to ensure inclusivity. Compliance involves creating an environment that accommodates individuals with varying mobility and sensory needs, including wheelchair-accessible entrances, ramps, and restrooms. Incorporating these features underscores a commitment to providing a compassionate and accessible space for all community members.

When building or establishing a funeral home, zoning considerations play an important role. Zoning regulations dictate the types of activities allowed in specific areas, requiring compliance for necessary permits and approvals. Funeral homes are often subject to ordinances governing land use, building size, parking, and proximity to residential areas. Ensuring compliance is essential for harmonious integration into the community and preventing conflicts with neighbors or local authorities.

When establishing a funeral home, meticulous attention to OSHA regulations is essential, particularly for the embalming room's design. OSHA guidelines ensure the safety of workers involved in the embalming process, covering ventilation, lighting, eye-washing facilities, and safety training. Prioritizing compliance establishes the funeral home as a responsible institution that adheres to local, state, and federal regulations.

When establishing a funeral home, adherence to EPA regulations is crucial for the embalming room's design and operation. The EPA governs the handling, storage, and disposal of hazardous materials used in funeral practices. Compliance involves measures to prevent environmental contamination, proper waste disposal, and the use of eco-friendly embalming chemicals. Incorporating environmentally responsible practices aligns with EPA regulations and promotes community trust and environmental stewardship.

When establishing a funeral home, meticulous adherence to state licensing regulations is imperative. State licensing regulators govern various aspects, including licensing requirements for funeral directors and embalmers, facility standards, and procedures for handling human remains. Thorough research and ongoing compliance contribute to the legal standing and reputation of the funeral home, fostering transparency, integrity, and professionalism.

Market Analysis

When owning a business, keeping track of the current market by conducting a performance market analysis is the best way to understand the customer base and their spending trends. A **market** *is a group of potential customers that possess purchasing power and unsatisfied needs.* A **target market** is an audience/demographic that could potentially purchase a product or service.

Conducting a **market survey** is crucial for understanding customer needs and potential locations. Designing an effective survey involves considering demographic information, economic base, population and income trends, competition, social and business climates, and the business's location. Utilizing public data, such as Census information, can serve as a starting point for market analysis. Local Chambers of Commerce and internet sources also provide tailored information for specific areas, and funeral homes often collaborate with local Chambers for networking.

When identifying vendors to supply services, products, or materials, businesses must assess factors like quality of work, pricing, **economic order quantity (EOQ)**, options, delivery methods, purchasing terms, buyer assistance, customer service, and product liability insurance. Compiling a list of potential vendors and evaluating them based on business needs is essential.

Markup and markdown are used in pricing. Markup is the difference between *merchandise cost and selling price.* This is generally used by retailers to create a profit. An example is a funeral home that buys a casket from a warehouse for $500 and sells the same casket to a client family for $1500. They have used a 3X markup, meaning they multiply the wholesale price by 3 to create their sale price. **Markdown** is the *reduction of a product price,* generally, when a product is "on sale." A casket, for example, that has been in the funeral home for an extended period make be marked down so the product can be replaced with a different unit. Marking caskets up 2 or 3 times is an old pricing paradigm, considering the current consumer shift in the funeral market that uses cremation as a means of final disposition.

A new pricing strategy adopted by some funeral homes involves evenly distributing prices across the service cost rather than inflating prices merchandise. This approach places a greater emphasis on each consumer paying their fair share for services rendered, regardless of their chosen mode of final disposition. By avoiding inflated costs on specific items like caskets and vaults, this strategy aims to provide more transparency and fairness in pricing, ensuring that each client pays a reasonable and equitable amount for the overall funeral service.

Pricing Policies and Strategies

Establishing a solid pricing policy is crucial for the success of a funeral home. Unfortunately, pricing policies have been slow to change in the funeral industry, resulting in a lack of revenue opportunities for the funeral home. Traditionally, pricing services in merchandise has been predominately influenced on casket selection and when the market shifted towards cremation as a means of final disposition, the pricing policies and strategies failed to change with consumer's spending behaviors. This resistance to changing pricing policies is one cause for a negative cash flow in the funeral home operations.

The main factor to consider in establishing a pricing policy is to acknowledge the current trends in the funeral marketplace. On average, 60% of the consumers select cremation as a means of final disposition. In order to create positive cash flow in the funeral home, all consumers are responsible for covering the fixed and variable cost of running a funeral home. This cost is represented in the Basic Arrangement Fee on the General Price List. For example, if a funeral home services 185 families annually and the fixed and variable cost for doing business is $495,000, each family is responsible for covering the cost of operations. By dividing the cost of doing business by the number of families served annually, the Basic Arrangement Fee is determined: 495,000/185 = $2,675.00. *See FTC section for further explanation of how this figure is applied to a pricing strategy when calculating a General Price List.*

Developing a pricing policy requires a thoughtful analysis of internal and external factors. Regular reviews and adjustments are essential to ensure that pricing remains effective in achieving business objectives and responding to market dynamics.

Marketing

Marketing *is a process of planning and executing the development, pricing promotion and distribution of an organization's goods and services.* A church calendar with the funeral home name and contact information is one form of marketing, however the process of marketing and promoting quality funeral services is more complex and requires strategic planning. One of the primary objectives of a marketing plan is to build a brand for the funeral home. A **brand** *is a method of applying verbal or symbolic means to identify a product or a service. "Like a good neighbor, State Farm is there,"* is an example of a product brand for State Farm Insurance. Marketing involves a wide range of strategies aimed at promoting a product or service, building brand awareness, and ultimately driving sales. These are some common marketing strategies used in the funeral industry:

Word-of-Mouth Marketing: This is the primary marketing strategy in the funeral industry. Consumer satisfaction is the ultimate goal of a funeral home. Consumers become loyal to a firm based on their satisfaction with previous services. Likewise, dissatisfied clients tend to find other funeral providers, in addition to making negative comments in the community that could impact other people's perception of the business.

Influencer Marketing: Partnering with influencers or industry leaders to promote a brand. This is a concept that was more popular several years ago when people affiliated some funeral home's with a particular religious denomination.

Traditional Advertising: Traditional television and radio advertising is currently still an effective means of making the funeral home name known in a community. This could be pricey over a long period of time however market research has proven that the more a funeral home name is promoted on various media channels, the more the name recognition becomes synonymous to a brand of service. The key in this type of advertising is to identify the demographic of a target audience.

- ➤ Television and Radio Advertising: Broadcasting commercials to reach a wide audience.
- ➤ Print Advertising: Placing ads in newspapers, magazines, brochures, or other printed materials.
- ➤ Outdoor Advertising: Using billboards, posters, or signage in public spaces.

Digital Marketing: Digital advertising refers to the use of digital channels and platforms to promote products, services, or brands to a target audience. It has become an integral part of modern marketing strategies due to the widespread use of digital devices and the internet.

- ➤ Content Marketing: Creating and distributing valuable, relevant content to attract and engage a target audience.
- ➤ Search Engine Optimization (SEO): Optimizing online content to improve its visibility in search engine results.
- ➤ Social Media Marketing: Utilizing social media platforms to connect with and engage audiences.

Public Relations (PR): The best type of advertising that promotes a funeral home's values and ideals are events that publicize community involvement and promotion of a positive image of funeral services.

- ➤ **Media Relations**: Building relationships with journalists and media outlets to   secure positive coverage.
- ➤ **Press Releases:** Issuing statements or announcements to the media to generate publicity. Pre-written press releases are very powerful when promoting an event that will benefit the entire community, such as a Holiday Hope for the Bereaved ceremony or decorating veteran graves during Wreaths Across America annual event.
- ➤ **Event Sponsorship:** Associating a brand with a particular event or cause for visibility. Being a part of Mothers Against Drunk Driving (M.A.D.D.) Prom Night Reenactment builds awareness of the dangers of drinking and driving and promotes positive educational events that receive media attention.

Relationship Marketing: Relationship marketing is a marketing strategy focused on building and maintaining long-term relationships with customers. It goes beyond one-time transactions and aims to foster loyalty and customer retention by creating positive interactions and connections. The primary goal of relationship marketing is to develop a strong bond between the brand and the customer, leading to repeat business, customer advocacy, and a positive brand reputation.

Customer Relationship Management (CRM): Managing and nurturing relationships with existing customers to encourage loyalty and repeat business.
Email Marketing: Sending targeted and personalized messages to a specific audience.

Mail Marketing: Sending an anniversary card to the bereaved on either the birthday of the deceased or the one-year anniversary of their death, is one of the best ways to connect with the consumer, post-funeral.

Product Launch Strategies: Especially when a funeral home modifies their operations or building location, such an event builds excitement within the community. Remember, the primary product in funeral services is the services that the funeral home provides and the facilities that they use to provide such services.

Pre-launch Campaigns: Building anticipation and excitement before introducing a new product, such as a new funeral home location or partnership with a community organization.

Exclusive Offers: Providing special deals or early access to a select audience. When opening a new or remodeled funeral home, an event should be scheduled, and the public should be invited to preview the facilities.

Price and Promotion Strategies: Some funeral firms use this to advertise that their prices are the lowest in a geographical location. This type of marketing is often frowned upon in the funeral industry.

Discounts and Promotions: Offering limited-time discounts, promotions, or bundled deals. Not common in funeral services.

Dynamic Pricing: Adjusting prices based on market demand, competitor pricing, or other factors. While this pricing strategy is practiced in funeral directing, it is considered unethical.

Effective marketing often involves a combination of these strategies, tailored to the specific goals, target audience, and industry of a business. Successful marketing campaigns are typically well-planned, data-driven, and aligned with overall business goals and objectives. Especially in the funeral business, marketing needs to be tasteful, positive and non-offensive to the public.

Evaluating marketing strategies is a crucial process to determine their effectiveness, identify areas for improvement, and optimize future campaigns.

Establish clear objectives for your marketing strategy by defining specific, measurable, achievable, relevant, and time-bound (SMART) goals, such as increasing brand awareness or driving sales. Identify and establish key performance indicators (KPIs) aligned with your objectives, including metrics like conversion rates, customer acquisition costs, ROI, website traffic, social media engagement, and customer lifetime value. Utilize analytics tools such as Google Analytics, social media analytics, and email marketing tools for data collection and analysis to gain valuable insights into the performance of your marketing activities. Conduct ROI analysis to evaluate the cost-effectiveness of different strategies by comparing costs incurred against revenue generated or other desired outcomes. Additionally, gather customer feedback through surveys, reviews, and direct interactions to understand customer satisfaction, brand perception, and the impact of your marketing efforts on their decision-making process.

Accounting

General Accounting:

      Accounting is a *language of business employed to communicate financial information based upon collecting, analyzing, classification, recording, summarizing, reporting, and interpretation of financial data.* Like all successful businesses, accounting in funeral services is a vital part of day-to-day operations. The information recorded in a type of bookkeeping data system, such as QuickBooks, provides vital financial information to management, but also in many cases to a professional Certified Public Accountant (CPA). They then use that information to generate reports, analyze data, and to accurately complete and transmit required information to governmental authorities for official purposes, such as tax reporting. The accurate information also demonstrates the financial posture of the business to determine if the funeral home is profitable. This information is very valuable, especially when a business works with banks, investors and/or wishes to sell the business to another owner. In the latter instance, usually, a three-to-five-year analysis of the funeral home's Income Statements (revenues less expenses) and Balance Sheets (assets, liabilities and capital) are evaluated. In addition, a Cash Flow statement is created in order to provide a critical analytical measure known as EBITDA (**E**arnings **B**efore **I**nterest, **T**axes, **D**epreciation, and **A**mortization). This section of the review manual will discuss the basic concepts relating to accounting within the management of a funeral home.

      There are two basic accounting methods used in funeral homes for recording financial information: cash basis and accrual basis accounting. Bookkeeping for these methods is the same, however the way the information is reported to the government for tax purposes may be different.

Cash basis accounting is when r*evenue is recognized in the accounting records only when consideration is received and in which expenses are only recognized when they are actually paid.* Simply stated, revenue and expenses are not recognized until cash (or "consideration") has actually changed hands.

Accrual based accounting is when *expenses incurred (paid or not), and income earned (collected or not), are recorded each accounting period.* The accrual concept recognizes both revenue when it is earned and expenses in the period incurred, regardless if the cash has changed hands.

The difference between these two methods is that cash basis accounting is simpler and triggered by activity you might see in a checking account, such as checks written, and deposits made during a defined time frame. On the other hand, the accrual method is the most accurate measure of economics in a funeral home business and is more difficult (costly) to derive, with a focus on accounting period-based revenue and expenses. Determining what method is best for the funeral home is usually established by management and a CPA and is considered when filing tax returns with local, state and federal (i.e., Internal Revenue Service (IRS)) agencies. In funeral services, it is expected that large operations use accrual accounting while smaller, independent funeral homes likely use a cash basis accounting method. Each method has other advantages and disadvantages which need to be considered and managed within the organization.

Accounting is centered around one equation. There is an expanded version and a condensed version of the "Accounting Equation."

The condensed version is as follows:

Assets (+T-) = Liabilities (-T+) + Owner's Equity (-T+)

This equation simply means that the total Assets of the funeral home business equals the sum of the Liabilities plus the Owner's Equity. For example, if the liabilities (debts) of the funeral home are subtracted from the Assets (resources), what is left is the Owner's Equity (capital) in the business.

Assets are *property of monetary value that a business owns*. This includes tangible resources: cash, accounts receivables (a promise by a customer to pay a certain amount at a later date), equipment, vehicles, land, buildings; as well as intangible items: copywrites, patents, intellectual property, the name of the funeral home, goodwill etc. Assets are resources that have value. There are short-term assets and long-term assets: Short-term assets are items that can be converted into cash within one year or less, such as cash and accounts receivables (customer's obligations) that are paid to the funeral home for services rendered). Long-term assets are expected to last longer than a year, such as the funeral home vehicles, building(s), land, parking lot and office or embalming equipment.

Liabilities are *debts that a business may have* such as accounts payable, taxes and accrued expenses (in the case of accrual accounting). There are short-term liabilities, that will be paid off within a year, such as utility bills or casket invoices, and long-term liabilities, that are paid off over a longer period (greater than one year), such as a loan for a removal van or a mortgage on the funeral home property.

Owner's equity *is the amount of financial interest ("capital") an owner has in a business, calculated by how much assets exceed liabilities.* Owner's equity is comprised of the owner's initial capital investment in the funeral home business, plus the accumulated profits/(losses) that are retained in business, minus the cash or other assets that are withdrawn by the owner (sometimes known as "dividends").

Revenue in a funeral home comes from many sources. The primary source of revenue for a funeral home is from consumers after they select services and merchandise for a funeral or memorial service. *Expenses* represent the direct and indirect cost for doing business. These are debts that are incurred as legitimate business expenses that are required to provide the goods and services to the client, and can be recorded as direct costs: merchandise and services provided for resale direct to consumers, and; indirect costs: such as rent, depreciation, utilities, employee salaries, etc. used to run the business generally and not to a specific consumer.

In accounting terms, Revenue unpaid by a consumer is known as Accounts Receivables while incurred but unpaid Expenses are known as Accounts Payables. Receivables means money is coming into the funeral home at some future date from various sources while Payables means that funds will be paid out to others (vendors, employees, utilities etc.) to directly provide the goods and services for the customers as well as for indirect costs of running the business.

The accounting equation must always balance. In other words, the total value of assets must equal the combined value of liabilities and equity. This reflects the fundamental accounting principle of the conservation of accounting equations and ensures that a company's financial position is accurately represented.

When a business transaction occurs, it affects at least two accounts, and the accounting equation is used to maintain the balance. For example, if a company borrows money (incurring a liability), it must either receive an asset (cash) or use the funds to acquire an asset. Similarly, if a company generates revenue, it may increase assets (cash or accounts receivable) and equity (retained earnings).

The accounting equation is the foundation of double-entry accounting, a system that records each financial transaction with equal and opposite entries in at least two accounts to maintain the equation's balance.

T-Accounts

T accounts are a visual representation used in accounting to analyze and record transactions. They are called "T accounts" because they resemble the letter "T" and are used to illustrate the dual nature of accounting entries in a double-entry accounting system.

Here's what a T account looks like:

Accounts Receivables

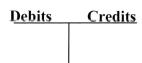

Debits   Credits

Here's an explanation of the different components:

Account Title: This is where the name of the specific account is written. It could be an asset, liability, equity, revenue, or expense account. For example, "Cash," "Accounts Receivable," "Sales," etc.

Debit and Credit sides: The left side of the T account is the debit side, and the right side is the credit side. In accounting, these terms do not always mean an increase or decrease; rather, they indicate the side of the account affected by a transaction.

Debit (left side): Increases assets, expenses, and withdrawals. Decreases liabilities, equity, and revenue.

Credit (right side): Increases liabilities, equity, and revenue. Decreases assets, expenses, and withdrawals.

Vertical Line: This line separates the debit and credit sides of the T account.

When a transaction occurs, accountants use T accounts to record how the transaction affects specific accounts. For example, let's say the funeral home receives $1,000 in cash from a customer for a monument sale. The entry in the Cash T account would look like this:

Cash

Debits	Credits
1000	

If the funeral home later uses $500 of that cash to pay for Monument Company expenses, the entry would be:

Cash

Debits	Credits
	500

This entry indicates that $500 has been subtracted from the Cash account (right side, which is the credit side).

On the other side of the equation, the Monument Company expense, the entry would be:

Monument Expense

Debits	Credits
500	

T accounts provide a simple and visual way to track and understand the flow of transactions in an accounting system. They are often used as a preliminary step before entries are transferred to the general ledger, which is a more formal record-keeping system in accounting.

1. Recording Transactions:

Debits and Credits: In double-entry accounting, each transaction affects at least two accounts. T accounts help illustrate these dual effects. For example, if a business makes a sale for cash, the Cash account would be debited (increased) on the left side, and the Sales account would be credited (increased) on the right side.

Balancing Entries: T accounts ensure that debits and credits are always in balance. The total of the debit side must equal the total of the credit side. This principle aligns with the fundamental accounting equation (Assets = Liabilities + Equity) and helps maintain the accuracy of financial records.

2. Types of Accounts:

- ➤ **Asset Accounts:** Debits increase asset accounts, and credits decrease them.
- ➤ **Liability Accounts:** Credits increase liability accounts, and debits decrease them.
- ➤ **Equity Accounts:** Credits increase equity accounts, and debits decrease them.
- ➤ **Revenue Accounts:** Credits increase revenue accounts, and debits decrease them.
- ➤ **Expense Accounts:** Debits increase expense accounts, and credits decrease them.

3. Normal Balances:

Understanding the normal balance for each type of account is crucial. Assets and expenses have a natural debit balance, while liabilities, equity, and revenues have a natural credit balance. T accounts help accountants visualize and apply these principles.

4. Posting to the General Ledger:

T accounts are often used as a preliminary step before entries are posted to the general ledger. The general ledger is a comprehensive record of all financial transactions for a business, organized by account.

5. Trial Balance:

The information from T accounts is used to create a trial balance, which is a list of all the accounts and their balances. The trial balance ensures that debits equal credits and serves as a preliminary check for errors before financial statements are prepared.

6. Closing Entries:

At the end of an accounting period, revenue and expense accounts are closed out to prepare for the next period. T accounts help visualize and understand the process of closing entries, ensuring that the financial records are ready for the new period.

7. Visual Representation:

T accounts offer a clear and concise visual representation of individual accounts, making it easier for accountants and stakeholders to understand the impact of transactions on specific accounts.

In summary, T accounts are a practical tool in accounting that facilitates the recording, analysis, and understanding of financial transactions. They serve as a bridge between the transaction level and the general ledger, helping maintain accuracy and consistency in financial reporting.

Expanded Accounting Equation

The expanded accounting equation is a modified version of the basic accounting equation, which is:

$$\text{Assets} = \text{Liabilities} + \text{Owner's Equity}$$

The basic equation reflects the fundamental accounting principle that the total assets of a business must be equal to the total of its liabilities and owner's equity. The expanded accounting equation takes into account additional elements to provide a more detailed view of a company's financial position.

The expanded equation is as follows:

$$\text{Assets} = \text{Liabilities} + \text{Owner's Equity} + \text{Revenues} - \text{Expenses} - \text{Dividends}$$

Here is a breakdown of each component:

➢ **Assets**: These are the economic resources owned or controlled by a business. Assets can include cash, accounts receivable, inventory, property, equipment, and other items of value.
➢ **Liabilities**: These are obligations or debts that the business owes to external parties. Examples include accounts payable, loans, and other liabilities.
➢ **Owner's Equity**: This represents the owner's claim on the assets of the business. It includes the owner's initial investment, retained earnings (accumulated profits not distributed as dividends), and other equity-related items.
➢ **Revenues**: These are the amounts earned by a business from its primary operations. Revenues increase owner's equity.
➢ **Expenses**: These are the costs incurred by a business in its efforts to generate revenue. Expenses decrease owner's equity.
➢ **Dividends**: This represents the distribution of profits to the owners (shareholders) of a corporation. Dividends reduce owner's equity.

The expanded accounting equation is a useful tool for understanding the relationships between various financial elements in a business. It shows how the different activities of a business, such as earning revenue, incurring expenses, and paying dividends, impact the overall financial position. By using this equation, accountants and financial analysts can gain insights into a company's performance and financial health.

An example of how the expanded accounting equation works:

Consider the Thomas Funeral Home Corporation. The company has the following financial transactions during a specific period:

- ➤ Thomas Funeral Home started with an initial investment of $100,000 from the owner.
- ➤ Generated $50,000 in revenue from its business operations.
- ➤ Incurred $30,000 in various expenses.
- ➤ Took out a loan of $20,000.
- ➤ Paid $5,000 in dividends to the shareholders.

This is how these transactions would apply to the expanded accounting equation:

$$Assets = Liabilities + Owner's\ Equity + Revenues - Expenses - Dividends$$

Initial Investment:
- ➤ Assets: +$100,000 (cash or bank balance increases)
- ➤ Owner's Equity: +$100,000 (owner's claim on the assets increases)
- ➤ Assets=$100,000+Liabilities+$100,000+Revenues−Expenses−DividendsAssets= $100,000+Liabilities+$100,000+Revenues−Expenses−Dividends
- ➤ Revenue Generation:
- ➤ Revenues: +$50,000 (business operations generate income)
- ➤ Assets=$150,000+Liabilities+$100,000+$50,000−Expenses−DividendsAssets = $150,000+Liabilities+$100,000+$50,000−Expenses−Dividends
- ➤ Expense Incurrence:
- ➤ Expenses: -$30,000 (costs incurred in business operations)

Assets=$120,000+Liabilities+$100,000+$50,000−$30,000−**DividendsAssets**=$120,000+ **Liabilities** ∣ $100,000 ∣ $50,000 $30,000 **Dividends**

Loan Acquisition:
  Liabilities: +$20,000 (company takes on debt)
  Assets=$140,000+$20,000+$100,000+$50,000−$30,000−**DividendsAssets**=$140,000+ $20,000+$100,000+$50,000−$30,000−Dividends

Dividend Payment:
Dividends: -$5,000 (distribution of profits to shareholders)

Assets=$135,000+$20,000+$100,000+$50,000−$30,000−$5,000

At this point, the equation reflects the Thomas Funeral Home after these transactions. The total assets equal the sum of liabilities, owner's equity, revenues, minus expenses, and minus dividends.

Cash Flow

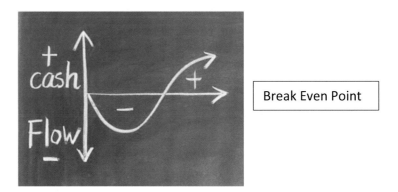

Break Even Point

In business, (including the funeral industry), **cash flow management** is one of the most important parts of providing quality services to consumers over time. As a matter of fact, one of the most common reasons for business failure is poor cash flow management. A funeral home that poorly manages resources coming into the firm and expenses going out, may experience a cash flow problem that could result in a temporary and/or permanent disruption in providing services and merchandise to consumers. For example, a funeral home that is experiencing a cash flow problem and is placed by its vendors on a Cash On Delivery (C.O.D.) status is a failing business that is not managing their assets and liabilities efficiently.

Poor cash flow management begins with how a firm manages their Accounts Receivables (AR). Successful funeral firms use policies and practices that strategically limit accounts receivables. That said, some states (such as New York) prohibit by law holding human remains for ransom until the funeral bill is paid in full. Firms with zero or low AR have strict credit policies that are in place. A industry-specific difficulty with AR is an old credit paradigm that extends 30-day credit for funeral expenses. This is further complicated by accommodation policies that allow consumers to place 'cash advance' items on their funeral bill. This is a adverse financial practice that has multiple negative business and cash flow ramifications for funeral home operators: 1) Adding 'Cash Advance' items (paid to third-party vendors, such as clergy, newspaper obituaries, musicians, florists, death-certificate fees, etc.) to a funeral contract gives a negative impression of the funeral expenses earned by the firm. In this example, the consumer perceives that the funeral expenses were $12,500.00 when in reality the total amount for funeral services and merchandise directly provided by the funeral home was less…only $9,500.00. Three thousand dollars were paid to third-party vendors. 2) Further, if a funeral home has 10 funerals a month and the average cash advance items paid to third-party vendors is $3,000 per funeral, this represents $30,000 in cash that could be used for paying expenses actually incurred by the funeral home within that month, and finally 3) large outstanding AR (greater than 30 days) that have cash advances as part of the outstanding balances, is placing a financial drain on the business because in addition to the cash needed for direct and day-to-day operating expenses not being collected, the firm paid those third parties the cash amounts out of its own pocket.

Funeral firms that have a positive cash flow have well defined credit policies and manage their AR as part of the initial transaction. Writing checks to third-party vendors as a 'cash advance' practice should be eliminated. This costs funeral homes time and money in accounting fees and follow-up with families to collect or refund inaccurate cost estimates. In addition, the practice restricts otherwise available cash necessary for the day-to-day operations. In practice, an exception to this policy for not writing checks to third-party vendors would be for pre-need accounts for funds that become available after a death occurs since the funeral home processes the necessary paperwork to secure those funds on behalf of the family.

In addition to the above challenges, some families will insist that the estate of the deceased should pay the funeral contract amount since funeral expenses are the first to be paid when the estate is settled. This is a negative cash flow challenge since some estates can take up to to a year to settle…for families where a will is being contested, this period of time could be even longer. Ideally, to free the business from the cash flow burden, a family member should pay the funeral expenses and when the estate is settled, they will be the first to be paid from the proceeds of the estate.

Outside of cash payments for goods and services, credit card payments can be a great way to improve cash flow and eliminate receivables. However, there will be a credit card processing fee against the business of between 2-4% of the amount being charged. Some funeral firms absorb this charge as a cost of doing business while others charge back this fee to the consumer. Cash advance charges should be avoided in these types of transactions.

Some funeral firms will take an Assignment of Proceeds from an insurance policy as another way to reduce receivables. However, this practice bears some risk with respect to enforced life insurance policies. There are some vendors in the funeral industry that will bear this risk and process these claims, however they do take a set percentage of the proceeds as an accommodation for their services.

Some consumers will ask for a discount if, for example, the account is paid-in-full with cash. In these instances, funeral businesses may provide these consumers with, say, a 2% discount. Of course, funds from this type of cash transaction need to be deposited into the funeral home bank account, as if the funds received were from a check or other form of payment. This practice should not be encouraged since it has a negative effect on business cash flow and the financial posture of the firm. In addition to being illegal from a tax perspective, owners who wish to sell will find their businesses undervalued in the future because of these unrecorded funds.

Funeral home credit policies need to be established and universal for all clients, in accordance with the Fair Credit Act.

Accounts Payables

Accounts Payables (AP) is a liability account used for short-term liabilities or charge accounts, usually due to be paid within 30 days. An important concept for managing payables is "2/10, net 30" early payment incentive. This is a discount that some companies offer to funeral homes if an invoice is paid quickly. "2/10, net 30" means that if the bill is paid within 10 days from the date of the invoice, the funeral home can subtract 2% of the total as a discount. If the bill is paid after the 10-day period, the entire amount is due in no more than 30 days.

For example: A casket company invoice totaling $25,000 and arrived at the funeral home on May 1. At the bottom of the invoice, it stated: "**2/10, net 30.**" The funeral director paid the bill on May 7.

How much did the funeral director pay?
   A. $22,500
   B. $23,500
   C. $24,500
   D. $25,000

Answer: The answer is **C**. Since the invoice was paid in its entirety within 10 days. Two percent of $25,000 is $500, thus $24,500 was paid to the casket company.

$$25,000 \text{ X } .02 = 24,500$$

If this was a monthly occurrence with the casket company, over the course of one year, over $6,000 would be saved by decreasing direct expenses for the firm which could help improve the profitability of the funeral home.

Net income is the difference between all Revenue earned during a specific period of time and the direct and indirect Expenses and income taxes which occurred during the same period of time. Before the net income can be calculated, the gross income should be established for analytical purposes. To determine the gross income, the cost of goods sold is subtracted from the total revenue. Gross Income does not consider operating ("indirect") or income tax expenses. However, **Net Income** takes into account operating and income tax expenses.

Example of Gross Income:

Funeral was...................................... $10,000.00
Cost of Good Sold
(casket, vault & sundries wholesale cost)......   - 4,500.00
              Gross Income .... $ 5,500.00

Example of Net Income

Funeral was.. $10,000.00
Cost of Good Sold
(casket, vault & sundries wholesale cost)......   - 4,500.00
Operating Expenses (employee salaries, etc)..   -2,500.00
Income taxes   -1,000.00

Net Income ....   <u>$ 2,000.00</u>

Cash Flow Statements are financial statements that explain where cash generated by a business is coming from and how those funds were used within a given period of time (i.e., month, a quarter or a year). There are three segments within a statement of cash flows:

Types of Cash Flow Segments	Elements of Each Segment
Cash Flow from Operating Activities	1. How much cash is being generated by the business enterprise. 2. Beginning with the Net Income, the operating expenses are added or subtracted from this amount. 3. This will determine if there is a positive or negative cash flow within the business.
Cash Flow from Investment Activities	1. This statement shows the impact to cash flow of any business investment activities that the company engages in during a given period of time. 2. Some of the factors that may influence these statements include the purchase or sale of land, buildings, vehicles, or other short/long term investments.
Cash Flow from Financing Activities	1. If a funeral home borrows or pays back money borrowed for operational expenses, loans or mortgages would be activities that would appear in this segment. 2. Capital transactions for money raised from and/or dividends paid to company investors

Income Statement

One vital piece of financial information is a profit/loss statement also known as an **Income Statement**. *This statement is a formal financial statement that presents the income, expenses, income taxes and net profit or loss for a given time period.* The income statement will include the **net sales** (*sales minus sales returns and allowances, minus sales discounts*), the direct costs of the items sold, the gross profit (*net sales minus the cost of goods sold*), and the business's overhead or operational expenses (utilities, repairs, maintenance, legal, accounting, depreciation, rent, mortgage interest, etc.). The Income Statement provides a snapshot of the funeral home's "bottom-line." The information on Income Statements can be analyzed to provide multiple key performance indicators for analysis to improve performance. One example would be to determine if the revenue to expense ratio is properly aligned. This analysis could result in the funeral operation adjusting their Basic Arrangement Fee to be more in alignment with the operating expense needs for the business.

Balance Sheet

A Balance Sheet *is a formal statement that illustrates the assets, liabilities, and owner's equity as of a specific date.* Recorded on a balance sheet are **current assets** (*cash or assets that will be converted to cash or used within a year*), **long-term assets** (*long-term investments, land, buildings, etc*), **current liabilities** (*debts that will be paid within the year*), **long-term liabilities** (*debts or amounts payable outside of a year*), and owner's equity. In short, a balance sheet is a list of everything that is owned, owed and invested in a firm. Usually, a balance sheet is completed at the end of the year. The balance Sheet will also disclose the depreciation of fixed and other long-term assets. Depreciation is meant to show the inherent decline in value of an assets due to wear and tear and/or the passage of time. This method is meant to match the initial cost of such assets against the revenue that the assets helped produce during its useful life. For example, an embalming machine that is purchased for $7,000 may be depreciated over a 7-year period, which would equal a $1,000 a year straight-line depreciation rate. This becomes a tax benefit for the funeral home business.

Important Terms	Definitions
Sales Journal	A book of original entry used for recording of sales of merchandise on credit only.
General Journal	A book of original entry in which business transactions are recorded in chronological order.
General Ledger	A book of accounts.
Chart of Accounts	A list of all account titles and the account numbers assigned to them
Debit (Dr.)	The left side of a standard account
Credit (Cr.)	The right side of a standard account
In Balance	A condition in which the total of the Debits and the total of the Credits are equal in an account
Trial Balance	A workpaper providing the equality of the debit and credit balance in a ledger
Summarizing	Brings accounting data together in a way that will further enhance its usefulness, usually by means of reports and statements, such as Cash Flow Statements and Balance Sheet
Profit Margin	Net income divided by net sales
Break-even analysis	Where total sales revenue equals total operating costs.

Thompson Funeral Home
Balance Sheet
As of December 31, 2023

ASSETS

Current Assets:

Cash and Cash Equivalents	$135,000	
Accounts Receivable	[amount]	
Inventory	[amount]	
Other Current Assets	[amount]	
Total Current Assets		[total]

Property, Plant & Equipment:

Land	[amount]	
Buildings	[amount]	
Equipment	[amount]	
Less: Accumulated Depreciation	[amount]	
Total Property, Plant & Equipment		[total]

Other Assets:

Intangible Assets	[amount]	
Investments	[amount]	
Other Assets	[amount]	
Total Other Assets		[total]

TOTAL ASSETS **[TOTAL]**

LIABILITIES

Current Liabilities:

Accounts Payable	[amount]	
Short-Term Loans	[amount]	
Accrued Liabilities	[amount]	
Total Current Liabilities		[total]

Long-Term Liabilities:

Long-Term Debt	[amount]	
Other Long-Term Liabilities	[amount]	
Total Long-Term Liabilities		[total]

TOTAL LIABILITIES [total]

OWNER'S EQUITY

Owner's Capital	$100,000	
Retained Earnings	[amount]	

TOTAL OWNER'S EQUITY [total]

TOTAL LIABILITIES & EQUITY **[TOTAL]**

Business Evaluation

As previously stated, recording accurate financial information is an essential part of managing a funeral home. In addition to having this information for governmental reasons, such as taxes, this financial information plays a vital role when valuing a funeral home for sale. The financial information of a Balance Sheet speaks to the financial posture of the business, whether it is solvent and/or has a positive net worth. When purchasing a funeral home, an analysis of all of the financial statements plays an important role in determining the value of the business and what is a fair price for the seller to sell and/or the buyer to pay for a funeral business. EBITDA (**E**arnings **B**efore **I**nterest, **T**axation, **D**epreciation and **A**mortization) is the industry standard for determining a fair market value for a funeral entity. Calculating EBITDA is a measure of cash flow and is an indicator of the company's overall financial performance and short-term operational efficiency. This analysis is usually completed by a CPA. Funeral homes usually are valued for sale at a multiple between 4.5 to 6.5 times their EBITDA, plus or minus other adjustments found during a deep analysis of financial results.

There are several factors to be considered when purchasing or acquiring a funeral home. Some of the factors to consider include:

There are many factors to consider when contemplating the decision to sell a funeral home:

1. Why is the business being sold?
2. Is the owner moving, retiring, or is the business in financial distress?
3. How much money is the business generating?
4. Is the business making a profit or losing money every month?
5. How much does the business cost to run?
6. Is the physical building in disrepair?
7. How much competition is present?
8. Is the business reliant on outside resources?
9. How many employees does the business have?
10. Are there issues within the employees?
11. Have there been issues regarding human resources (hiring, firing, discipline, etc.)?
12. What is your target audience?
13. Is the target audience still in need of your service/product/sales?
14. In terms of funeral home purchasing there are more specific questions that should be asked such as: how many preneed accounts does the business have?
15. How many locations are there?
16. Have the owners been legally compliant?
17. How are the buildings/rooms-specifically the prep room?
18. What are the current prices on the GPL?
19. How many other funeral homes are in the area?
20. What is the average background of current client-families and if the funeral home typically serves a specific population (i.e ethnic, religious, location)?

When purchasing a business there are many government regulations to keep in mind including:

1. **Americans with Disabilities Act** (*ADA- legislation that guarantees disabled people equal access to employment, and public places*),
2. **Zoning ordinances** (*formal codification of land use policies by local governments*),
3. **Occupational Safety and Health** (*OSHA-regulation and enforcement of safety and health matters*),
4. the **Environmental Protection Agency** (*EPA- environmental protection and enforcement*), and
5. **State Regulatory Agency**. The buyer needs to ensure that the business is unencumbered with complaints and in compliance with all regulations. Regular inspections should be completed on all business property to ensure that they are in working order and the business is in compliance with all regulations. This would include vehicles, ADA accessible ramps and elevators, buildings, prep rooms, and equipment.

A common misnomer is that a funeral home is exempt from various compliance because they are grandfathered in and exempt from the regulations. In many cases, the expiration or termination of a grandfather clause is explicitly stated within the legal or regulatory text that introduced the clause. It may specify a certain date, a triggering event, such as a remodeling project, or a condition that would lead to the expiration of the grandfathering provision.

For example, in zoning regulations, a grandfather clause might allow existing structures or land uses to continue even if they don't conform to new zoning requirements. The expiration of such a grandfather clause could be tied to specific conditions, such as a change in ownership or a significant alteration of the property. Before purchasing a funeral home with a grandfather clause attachment, legal and zoning requirements need to be explored.

The terms and conditions of the purchase need to be outlined in addition to any financial agreements and arrangements that are conditions to the sale. Some sellers will "hold some paper," meaning that the seller will take the risk of financing or holding all or part of the mortgage on the sale of the business. This is a risk, especially if the buyer has an unestablished managerial and financial investment in the business entity. Such a business should be approached with extreme caution.

Determining a fair and equitable price for the funeral home business can be based on a few factors. As explained above, the accounting principle EBITDA is usually used to calculate a purchase price of a business based on past performance. The **valuation** (*estimated of the worth or price of a company)* needs to consider both the tangible and intangible assets of the business. However, past performance is not indicative of sales, especially in the changing funeral market. These are **valuation of tangible assets** (*those assets that can be appraised by value or seen or touched*) that need to be considered when purchasing a funeral home:

➢ **Replacement value approach** – this is *an insurance concept in which the fair market price to purchase similar products in a similar condition is used to settle a claim.* This approach is important when determining how much insurance a funeral home should have to insure the financial investment, especially when a firm is encumbered with financial obligations that holds an indebtedness to others.

➢ **Earning valuation approach** – *a business valuation approach which centers on establishing the projected future income of a business typically over a 5-to-10-year period.* The *earnings value approach* is not a standard or widely recognized term in finance or valuation and should be approached with extreme caution in the funeral industry because trends in the business could greatly impact these financial projections.

➢ **Market value approach** – *an approach used in business valuation which determines value based upon previous sales of a similar business.* This was a common approach to valuing a funeral business in the past used primarily by the seller. The *market value approach* is a method used in business valuation to determine the value of a business or its assets based on comparable market transactions. This approach relies on the principle of comparing the subject company to similar businesses or assets that have been sold in the open market. The market value approach is particularly relevant in industries where comparable sales data is readily available. However, no two funeral homes or funeral businesses are the same because there are many factors that influence the value of such business.

➢ **Liquidations value approach** – the anticipated value of an asset that would be realized in case of liquidation of a business. The liquidation value approach is a method used in business valuation to estimate the value of a company's assets if they were to be sold in a liquidation scenario. This approach is particularly relevant in situations where the business is expected to be closed or sold in parts, and its assets are sold off. An example of this is common when a sole proprietor dies and leaves no successor to manage or run the day-to-day operations of the business. This places the funeral home at risk of being mismanaged and it could greatly impact the continued success of the operations.

These are **valuation of intangible assets** (*those assets that cannot be touched or grasped, such as goodwill, copyrights or trademarks*) that need to be considered when purchasing a funeral home:

➢ Goodwill – an intangible asset such as the name of the funeral home; also, an intangible asset which enables a business to earn a profit in excess of the normal rate of profit earned by other businesses of the same kind.
➢ Patents – *is a registered right of an inventor to make, use and sell an invention.* For example, the owner of a funeral home develops a piece of equipment that is used in the practice of funeral directing. A patent is obtained by the inventor that protects the invention from being pirated by other inventors.
➢ Copyrights

Payroll

A major category of costs in an operation, especially in labor-intensive funeral home businesses, is payroll accounting. Employees will want to be paid the rightful amount earned, and on a timely basis. Pay periods are typically tracked and paid weekly, bi-weekly, monthly, or as a stipend.

Employee earnings are usually determined at the time of employment. There are some fundamental rules that need to be followed when determining if an employee should be paid hourly or based on a set salary. Consult with a CPA with respect to all the qualifications for employees to be paid on a salary basis. The general rule is that an employee needs to be paid based on an hourly rate. If an agreed upon annual salary is $45K per year, the employee would receive approximately $865 per week before federal, state, and other deductions. Based on a 40-hour week, this translates to $21.65 per hour. If an employee works over 40 hours, they are entitled to overtime compensation which is calculated by time plus one-half or $21.65 + $10.82 = $32.47 per hour for overtime worked. These rules change slightly when compensation is paid on a bi-weekly basis.

One question that is frequently asked, "Is compensation time (a/k/a comp time) legal? The answer is, "that depends if all parties involved agree upon the terms of the comp time." Comp time cannot be forced on an employee and if a person works 45 hours, they should be compensated time plus one-half in compensation time for the five extra hours. This means the employee would be entitled to 7.5 hours of comp time off and this time should be taken within the payment cycle.

Staff who are salary-based employees are usually in management positions and have the ability to hire and terminate employees. Their salaries are not entitled to overtime compensation and usually their salaries are substantially higher than the average employee because of their position and responsibilities.

An employee's **gross pay** is the *income they have earned before any deductions are made*. The number of deductions on a paycheck will vary depending on the state and is based on what the employee has designated for withholdings on their federal **W-4 form** (*employees' withholding allowance certificate)* during their initial employment. The W-4 form can be changed at any time during their employment. On this form, the employee indicates the number of dependents they wish to declare and among other factors, this will determine the standard amount of tax withholdings per paycheck. Some people may opt to have extra money deducted for tax purposes.

W-4 forms are different from W-2 forms. **W-2 forms** are w*age and tax statements that are furnished at the end of each year for employees indicating their gross earnings, and total deductions over the year*. A W-2 form is the form used when calculating annual individual income that will be reported to the Internal Revenue Service (IRS).

One standard deduction on paychecks is the **Federal Insurance Contributions Act (F.I.C.A)**. *This is a federal act that requires employers and employees to pay taxes for federal social security and Medicare programs*. There may also be state income tax deductions if you reside in a state that has state tax. Other deductions that may be present on paychecks would be unemployment insurance, workers compensation premiums, insurance premiums, retirement contributions, donations, union dues, court settlements, and saving plans. This is an example of an Earnings Pay stub:

Earnings	rate	hours	this period	year to date
Regular	13.7100	67.00	918.57	21,459.46
Holiday Pay	13.7100	8.00	109.68	516.88
Ltd Imputed Inc			3.10	77.50
Overtime				745.11
Bereavement				329.04
Float Holiday				814.72
Sick Pay				491.20
Vacation Taken				1,629.44
Gross Pay			**$1,031.35**	26,063.35

Deductions	Statutory		this period	year to date
	Federal Income Tax		-26.65	769.76
	Social Security Tax		-29.20	741.67
	Medicare Tax		-10.08	256.05
	VA State Income Tax		-13.71	376.93
	Other			
	Checking 1		-406.78	10,599.32
	Dental		-19.40*	485.00
	Flex-Dep Care		-192.31*	4,807.75
	Flex-Medical		-57.69*	1,442.25
	Ltd Imputed		-3.10	77.50
	Medical		-66.78*	1,669.50
	401K Employee		-205.65*	4,837.62
	Net Pay		**$0.00**	

Employers also have contributions that need to be made regarding payroll taxes and deductions. These include F.I.C.A as well as the **Federal Unemployment Tax Act (F.U.T.A)** *which works to finance the administration costs of federal and state unemployment compensation programs*, and the **State Unemployment Tax Act (S.U.T.A)** which is *a tax to for state unemployment benefits*.

Mean, Median and Mode

Mean, median and mode are very important quantitative concepts that are helpful when analyzing financial performance including funeral service operations. Here is an example to demonstrate these concepts:

The funeral home sold the following caskets in the month of September:

Caskets Sold in September
1250
1875
2195
2250
2550
2550
3295

Mean is the average of all the casket sold. Add the caskets values together and divide it by the number of units sold. There were seven units sold in September.	$(1250+1875+2195+2250+2550+2550+3295) =$ $15,965/7 = \$2,280$
Median is the middle value in a series of numbers. Above there are 7 caskets sold and the middle value is **$2250**	What if the total number of caskets sold are an even number, such as 6 or 8 units? Take the middle numbers, add them together and divide by 2. 1250, 1875, 2195, 2250, 2550, 3295 $2195 + 2250 = 4,445/2 =$ **$2,223** This would be the median value
Mode is the most common occurrence in a series of numbers. The most common price of a casket sold above is $2550; it was sold twice in that month.	

Types of Managements in a Funeral Home

Risk Management

Risk management is the process of identifying, assessing, and mitigating or controlling potential risks that could affect the achievement of organizational objectives. A **risk** *is the probability or threat of damage, injury, liability, loss, or any other negative occurrence that is caused by external or internal factors*. Management of risks in a funeral home involves a systematic approach to understanding, evaluating, and responding to uncertainties and threats that may impact an organization's projects, operations, or overall business. These are some factors to consider:

1. **Risk Identification**: Identify and recognize potential risks that could affect the organization. This involves considering internal and external factors that may pose a threat.

Internal Risk Factors	Types of Risk Factors	Description of Risk Factors
Are factors that are present within the funeral home business.	Employee Competency	Example: Insufficient training and lack of experience among staff members can pose a risk to the quality of services provided to the consumers, including embalming procedures and funeral arrangements.
	Facility Maintenance	Example: Poor maintenance of the funeral home facilities, such as aging infrastructure or inadequate storage conditions, can compromise the overall presentation and service quality.
	Compliance and Regulation	Example: Failure to adhere to regulatory requirements and industry standards for handling and processing deceased individuals, such as proper licensing and documentation, can lead to legal issues.
	Ethical Concerns	Example: Ethical lapses in dealing with grieving families, such as misinformation or mishandling of remains, can damage the funeral home's reputation and lead to legal consequences.
	Client Confidentiality	Example: Inadequate measures to protect client information and maintain confidentiality can lead to breaches of privacy, impacting the trust between the funeral home and the families it serves.
	Health and Safety Practices	Example: Inadequate training on health and safety protocols, particularly in handling potentially infectious materials, can pose risks to the well-being of staff members, their family and clients.

Extrinsic Risk Factors	Types of Risk Factors	Description of Risk Factors
Are related to the business environment, economy and regulations.	Economic Conditions	Example: Economic downturns affecting the community may lead to reduced demand for high-cost funeral services, impacting the funeral home's revenue.
	Competitive Landscape	Example: Increased competition from other funeral homes or alternative funeral service providers may lead to pricing pressures and the need for the funeral home to differentiate itself.
	Natural Disasters	Example: Natural disasters like floods, earthquakes, or hurricanes can damage facilities, disrupt services, and impact the ability to carry out funeral arrangements.
	Public Perception and Image	Example: Negative media coverage or public perceptions related to incidents like mishandling of remains or ethical concerns can damage the funeral home's reputation and trust in the community.
	Legal and Regulatory Changes	Example: Changes in laws and regulations related to funeral services may require the funeral home to adapt its practices, documentation, or facilities to remain in compliance
	Technological Advances	Example: Rapid technological changes in the industry, such as new embalming techniques or online funeral planning services, may require the funeral home to invest in training and equipment updates to stay competitive

2. **The main objective in controlling risk** in a funeral home is to be able to identify the potential risk before an event happens. Clear communication channels are set up to share information about risks within the funeral establishment, with regular reporting on the status of identified risks, mitigation efforts, and emerging threats. Crisis management plans and procedures are developed to respond to and manage crises effectively, including communication plans, escalation procedures, and actions to minimize the impact. Risk management is integrated into the funeral home's decision-making processes, ensuring that risk considerations are taken into account in strategic, operational, and project-related decisions. Compliance with relevant laws, regulations, and industry standards is ensured, and a risk-aware culture needs to be fostered within the funeral home, where employees actively contribute to risk identification and mitigation efforts. Risks related to data security and the use of technology are addressed, including protection against cyber threats and ensuring the resilience of critical systems. Additionally, environmental, social, and governance (ESG) factors that could impact the funeral home, such as environmental sustainability, social responsibility, and governance practices, are considered in the risk management process.

Scenario

The following is an application of the above risk management concepts: A funeral director went to the hospital to remove Mr. Albert Thompson. The security guard had the funeral director sign the logbook and he opened the cooler door. The funeral director went into the cooler, verified the tag on the

129

body pouch and removed the remains. The funeral director brought the remains back to the funeral home and placed them in the cooler. After making arrangements, acquiring the necessary paperwork, the funeral director brought Mr. Thompson to the crematory. Two days later the hospital contacted the funeral director. There was an error made and the human remains were mislabeled by the nurse, prior to bringing Mr. Thompson to the morgue. Two people died at the same time, one person was African American, and the other was Caucasian. The nurse put the wrong tags on both sets of remains. The error was caught when the second funeral director made the removal and noticed that the person was the wrong race. Who was to blame?

- ➤ The nurse was at fault because she put the wrong tags on the wrong human remains.
- ➤ The hospital was at fault because they did not have an internal system to ensure that the human remains were the proper human remains being released.
- ➤ The family was at fault because they did not identify the human remains prior to cremation.
- ➤ The funeral director was at fault because he did not:
    1. Properly identify the human remains at the hospital prior to leaving the morgue.
    2. Provide the family with an opportunity to identify the human remains prior to cremation
    3. Compare the wrist band to the toe tag and
    4. Checking for a pacemaker and jewelry could have prevented this incident from happening because the funeral director could have identified the decease was of the wrong race.

In litigation cases, expert witnesses usually point out the number of missed opportunities for this type of negligence to occur. To manage the risk in the future, the funeral director implemented the following procedures prior to cremation:

1. Before human remains are removed from an institution, the wristband and toe tag are verified with the tag on the body pouch.
2. No human remains are taken to the crematory unless a family member or designee identifies the human remains.
3. The person who made the identification signs a release that indicates that have identified their loved one.
4. Before human remains are taken to the crematory, the remains are checked for jewelry, pacemaker or any other personal belongings.
5. The funeral director documents his findings on a form.

Risk management is rooted in controls, policies and procedures. In risk management, there are various strategies to deal with identified risks. These strategies are often categorized as risk controls and can be classified into four types: eliminate, minimize, shift, and absorb. Each strategy addresses risks in a different way.

Risk Insurance

Insurance *is the equitable transfer of the risk of a loss, from one entity to another in exchange for payment. It is a form of risk management primarily used to hedge against the risk of a contingent, uncertain loss.* There are different types of risk insurance, and each covers the funeral home from an unforeseen loss:

Life Insurance:
Purpose: Provides financial protection to beneficiaries in the event of the policyholder's death. There are different types, and each have their advantages and disadvantages:

Term Life Insurance:
Advantages:
Affordability: Term life insurance tends to be more affordable than permanent life insurance, making it accessible for individuals on a tight budget.
Simple and Transparent: The structure of term life insurance is straightforward, making it easy to understand. It provides coverage for a specified term without any cash value component.
Flexibility: Policyholders can often choose the term length based on their needs, such as 10, 20, or 30 years.
Disadvantages:
No Cash Value: Term life insurance does not accumulate cash value over time, and if the policyholder outlives the term, there is no return on the premiums paid.
Premiums Increase with Renewal: If the policyholder wants to renew the coverage after the initial term, premiums typically increase, and they may become cost-prohibitive.

Whole Life Insurance:
Advantages:
Lifetime Coverage: Whole life insurance provides coverage for the entire lifetime of the insured as long as premiums are paid.
Cash Value Accumulation: It builds cash value over time, which can be accessed or borrowed against during the policyholder's lifetime.
Level Premiums: Premiums remain level throughout the life of the policy, providing stability and predictability.
Disadvantages:
Higher Premiums: Whole life insurance tends to have higher premiums compared to term life insurance.
Limited Investment Options: The cash value component usually has a guaranteed interest rate, limiting the policyholder's ability to participate in market returns.

Universal Life Insurance:
Advantages:
Flexibility: Universal life insurance offers flexibility in premium payments and death benefits, allowing policyholders to adjust their coverage and premiums based on changing needs.

Cash Value Growth: The cash value component has the potential to grow based on market performance, providing an opportunity for increased returns.
Adjustable Death Benefit: Policyholders can often adjust the death benefit amount, offering more control over the policy.

Disadvantages:

Complexity: Universal life insurance policies can be complex, with various options and features that may be difficult for some individuals to understand.
Interest Rate Risk: If the policy's cash value is tied to the performance of financial markets, there is a risk of lower returns during economic downturns.

Variable Life Insurance:

Advantages:

Investment Opportunities: Variable life insurance allows policyholders to invest the cash value in a variety of sub-accounts, similar to mutual funds, potentially providing higher returns.
Adjustable Death Benefit: Like universal life insurance, variable life insurance policies often offer an adjustable death benefit.

Disadvantages:

Investment Risk: The cash value is subject to market fluctuations, so there is a risk of lower returns or even losses.
Complexity and Fees: Variable life insurance policies can be complex, and there may be fees associated with investment management, reducing overall returns.
Minimum Premiums: Policyholders may need to pay minimum premiums even if the investments underperform.

Other Types of Insurances

Health Insurance: Purpose: Covers medical expenses and provides financial protection for healthcare-related costs.
Types: Individual health insurance, group health insurance, Medicare, Medicaid, and supplemental health insurance.

Property Insurance: Purpose: Protects against financial loss due to damage or loss of physical property.
Types: Homeowners insurance, renters insurance, commercial property insurance, and flood insurance.

Automotive Insurance: Purpose: Provides coverage for damage to or loss of vehicles, as well as liability protection for injuries and property damage caused by the insured driver.
Types: Liability insurance, collision insurance, comprehensive insurance, and uninsured/underinsured motorist coverage.

Business Interruption Insurance: *Insurance that protects companies during the period necessary to restore property damage by an insured peril. Coverage for lost income and other expenses related to recovery.* Purpose: Covers various risks associated with business operations, including property damage, liability, and business interruption.

Types: Commercial property insurance, general liability insurance, professional liability insurance, and business interruption insurance.

Liability Insurance: Purpose: Protects individuals or businesses from legal claims and financial losses resulting from third-party injuries or property damage. Aso know as malpractice insurance.

Types: General liability insurance, professional liability insurance (errors and omissions), and product liability insurance.

Disability Insurance: Purpose: Replaces a portion of an individual's income if they become disabled and are unable to work.

Types: Short-term disability insurance and long-term disability insurance.

Income Protection Insurance: Purpose: Provides financial support in the form of regular income payments in the event of the policyholder's inability to work due to illness or injury.

Types: Disability insurance, critical illness insurance, and income protection insurance.

Cyber Insurance: Purpose: Offers protection against losses and liabilities arising from cyber threats, such as data breaches, ransomware attacks, and other cybercrimes.

Types: Cyber liability insurance and data breach insurance.

Workers' Compensation: *Coverage that provided benefits to employees injured at work.*

Workers' compensation programs are established by laws in most countries and states to ensure that employees receive necessary medical care and financial support when they suffer work-related injuries or illnesses. The key purposes of workers' compensation are as follows:

Medical Care: Purpose: To ensure that employees receive prompt and appropriate medical treatment for injuries or illnesses resulting from their work. Implementation: Workers' compensation covers medical expenses, including hospital visits, surgeries, medications, rehabilitation, and other necessary treatments.

Wage Replacement: Purpose: To compensate employees for a portion of their lost wages due to work-related injuries or illnesses that result in temporary or permanent disability.
Implementation: Workers' compensation provides a percentage of the injured employee's average weekly wage during the period of disability.

Disability Benefits: Purpose: To provide financial assistance to employees who suffer from temporary or permanent disabilities as a result of workplace injuries or illnesses.

Implementation: Disability benefits are designed to replace a portion of the employee's income during the period of disability. The degree of disability determines the amount and duration of benefits.

Vocational Rehabilitation: Purpose: To assist injured or disabled employees in returning to the workforce by providing rehabilitation services, vocational training, or job placement assistance. Implementation: Workers' compensation may cover vocational rehabilitation services to help employees transition back to work after recovering from injuries.

Death Benefits: Purpose: To provide financial support to the dependents of employees who die as a result of work-related injuries or illnesses. Implementation: Workers' compensation includes death benefits, such as funeral expenses and financial support for surviving spouses and dependents.

Legal Protections: Purpose: To establish a no-fault system that protects both employers and employees. Employees are generally entitled to benefits regardless of who is at fault for the injury, while employers are protected from certain lawsuits by employees. Implementation: Workers' compensation laws often provide immunity to employers from civil lawsuits related to workplace injuries, limiting legal actions to the workers' compensation system.

Prevention of Litigation: Purpose: To reduce the number of workplace injury lawsuits by establishing a streamlined process for addressing injuries and illnesses through the workers' compensation system. Implementation: Workers' compensation is designed to provide a quicker and more predictable resolution for injured workers without the need for lengthy legal battles.

Workers' compensation benefits are typically funded by employers through insurance premiums or self-insurance programs. The system is intended to strike a balance between protecting the rights of injured workers and providing employers with a framework that helps manage and control the financial impact of workplace injuries.

Human Resource Management

Human Resource Management *is a process of acquiring, training, developing, motivation and appraising a sufficient quantity of qualified employees to perform necessary activities; developing activities and an organization climate conducive to maximizing efficiency and worker satisfaction.* Human Resource Management (HRM) involves various processes related to managing an organization's workforce effectively. Job analysis, job description, and job specification are integral components of HRM that help in defining and managing job roles within the organization.

Job Analysis: *is the process of determining the critical components of a job for the purposes of selecting, training, and rewarding personnel.* Job analysis is the process of systematically gathering, documenting, and analyzing information about a job. It involves collecting data about the duties, tasks, and requirements of a particular job. The purpose of a job analysis is to:

> ➢ Identify the essential functions of a job.
> ➢ Understand the skills, knowledge, and abilities required for the job.
> ➢ Establish a basis for performance appraisals, training, and compensation.

Job Description: *a document that lists the major responsibilities and tasks of the job.* This written document provides a detailed overview of a specific job, including its title, duties, responsibilities, reporting relationships, working conditions, and qualifications. The purpose of a job description is to:

> ➢ Communicate the expectations and requirements of a job to employees.
> ➢ Assist in recruitment and selection by outlining the skills and qualifications needed.
> ➢ Serve as a basis for employee performance evaluations.

Job Specification: Job specification *is a statement that outlines the qualifications, skills, knowledge, and personal characteristics a jobholder must possess to perform effectively.* It provides details about the qualifications a candidate should possess to perform the job successfully. The purpose of job specifications is to:

> ➢ Guide the recruitment and selection process by specifying the criteria for candidate evaluation.
> ➢ Assist in matching candidate qualifications to job requirements.
> ➢ Ensure that employees are well-suited for their roles, contributing to overall job performance.

Human Resources Management and Federal Legislation

Human Resources (HR) professionals play a critical role in ensuring that organizations comply with various federal legislations governing the workplace. Several key federal laws impact HR practices and staying informed about these laws is essential to fostering a fair and legal work environment. Here are some significant federal legislations that HR professionals commonly deal with:

Title VII of the Civil Rights Act of 1964: *This law prohibits discrimination based on race, color, religion, sex, or national origin in employment practices.* HR professionals must ensure fair hiring practices, prevent workplace discrimination, and address harassment issues.

The Equal Employment Opportunity Act (EEOA) is not a standalone piece of legislation. Instead, it is often used interchangeably or in reference to Title VII of the Civil Rights Act of 1964. The EEOA is sometimes mentioned in discussions about the broader framework of equal employment opportunity, but it's important to recognize that Title VII is the specific law that addresses these issues. This is an overview of Title VII of the Civil Rights Act of 1964:

Key Provisions:
- ➢ Prohibits discriminatory practices in hiring, promotion, compensation, and other employment-related activities.
- ➢ Establishes the Equal Employment Opportunity Commission (EEOC) to enforce and oversee compliance with Title VII.
- ➢ Requires employers to reasonably accommodate employees' religious practices unless doing so would cause undue hardship.
- ➢ Addresses issues of sexual harassment in the workplace.

Equal Employment Opportunity Commission (EEOC): The EEOC is a federal agency responsible for enforcing federal laws related to workplace discrimination. The EEOC investigates and resolves complaints of discrimination, provides guidance to employers and employees, and works to prevent discrimination through education and outreach.
Title VII is a cornerstone of U.S. labor law, and it laid the foundation for subsequent legislation aimed at promoting equal employment opportunity. Over time, additional laws were enacted to address discrimination on other grounds, such as age, disability, and genetic information, further expanding the scope of equal employment.

Age Discrimination in Employment Act (ADEA): *This law prohibits age discrimination against employees who are 40 years old or older.* HR professionals need to prevent age-related discrimination and ensure fair treatment of older employees.

Equal Pay Act of 1963: *This law requires employers to pay employees of the opposite sex equally for equal work.* HR professionals need to ensure that compensation practices comply with equal pay standards and address any disparities.

Americans with Disabilities Act (ADA): *This law prohibits discrimination against qualified individuals with disabilities in employment, public services, and accommodations. This law guarantees disable people equal access to employment, as well as access to public places.* HR professionals must provide reasonable accommodations and ensure a non-discriminatory workplace for individuals with disabilities.

Family and Medical Leave Act (FMLA): *This law provides eligible employees with up to 12 weeks of unpaid, job-protected leave for childbirth, certain family, or medical reasons.* HR professionals must administer FMLA leave requests, maintain compliance, and ensure that employees' rights are protected.

Fair Labor Standards Act (FLSA): *This law established minimum wage, overtime pay eligibility, recordkeeping, and child labor standards. This federal legislation outlaws discrimination practices in pay. The law requires employers to pay a minimum wage to employees, and to pay a minimum of one and one-half times the regular rate for any hours beyond forty hours worked in a week.* HR professionals need to ensure compliance with wage and hour laws, including overtime eligibility and accurate recordkeeping.

Occupational Safety and Health Act (OSHA): *This law regulates and enforces the workplace to ensures safe and health matters for most United States Employees. An Individual state OSHA agency may supersede the U.S. Department of Labor OSHA regulations.* HR professionals must facilitate workplace safety, compliance with OSHA regulations, and proper reporting of workplace injuries.

Immigration Reform and Control Act (IRCA): *This law requires employers to verify the identity and employment eligibility of their employees by checking either U.S. citizenship or aliens authorized status to work in the United States.* HR professionals must comply with employment verification requirements and I-9 documentation.

These federal legislations significantly influence HR policies, procedures, and decision-making within organizations. HR professionals must stay updated on changes to labor laws, ensure compliance, and effectively communicate these regulations to employees and management. Non-compliance with federal laws can result in legal consequences, financial penalties, and damage to an organization's reputation.

Employment application: *A record of statements made at the time the applicant first seeks employment.* The employment application process refers to the series of steps that both employers and job seekers go through to facilitate hiring. The process typically includes several key stages, from creating a job opening to making a job offer.

Both the employer and candidate need to communicate effectively throughout the process. This may take different forms and in the beginning of the process, the candidate should ask the perspective employer if texting is an option. If so, parameters should be established. For example, "if I have a quick question, like did you receive my documents, may I text you?" Candidates should not overuse texting. Part of the evaluation process in funeral services is to ensure that the perspective employee has the ability to articulate effectively in person and on the phone. Employers should provide clear information about the job and application process, while candidates should present themselves professionally and be transparent about their qualifications and expectations. The goal is to create a positive experience for both parties and ensure a smooth transition for the new employee into the funeral home.

Job Opening and Position Identification	Identify the need for a new position or a replacement.
Job Posting	(person in charge of hiring new employees) to create a detailed job description, including responsibilities, qualifications, and any other relevant details.
Advertise the job	Using various trade journals
Application Submission	The job seekers should submit applications, resumes, and cover letters in response to the job posting. The employer will review and screen applications to shortlist candidates based on the job requirements.
Initial Screening	The employer will conduct initial screenings, which may involve phone or video interviews to assess candidates' qualifications, experience, and interest in the position.

Formal Interviews	The employer will establish and conduct in-person or virtual interviews to further evaluate candidates. Multiple rounds of interviews may be conducted. The candidate should prepare for interviews, showcase relevant skills, and experience, and ask questions about the position and company.
Assessment and Testing	An employer may require assessments or tests (such as the Myers Briggs Personality Test) to evaluate specific skills, knowledge, or personality traits relevant to the job. (*See Psychology section p.457*)
Reference & Background Checks	The employer have the right to contact the candidate's professional references to verify their work history, skills, and qualifications. This may also include criminal history and employment verification, to ensure the accuracy of the candidate's information.
Job Offer	The employer will extend a job offer to the selected candidate, including details such as salary, benefits, start date, and any other relevant terms. In some situations, if the candidate is not a proper fit for the funeral home, the employer should have the common curtesy to contact the candidate and inform them of their decision. The candidates should review the job offer, negotiate any conditions of employment if necessary, and formally accept or decline the offer.

Hiring

Once the employee has been hired, a medical physical should be conducted to ensure that the employee is physically able to perform the job. The employer is required to pay for such an examination and any test that are conducted relating to the employment. **Bona-fide occupational qualifications (BFOQ)** *is a qualification that is absolutely necessary for the job; it is an allowed and approved reason for discrimination.* For example, as a transporter for a funeral home, a person is required to lift 50 lbs. During the medical physical examination, it was discovered that the person hired had several herniated disks in his back and lifting over five pounds would not be medically advisable. The person can be terminated because of his medical condition.

Upon selecting a candidate, the employer will extend a job offer encompassing details like salary, benefits, start date, and other pertinent terms. In cases where the candidate is not deemed suitable for the funeral home, the employer should courteously communicate this decision to the candidate. Subsequently, candidates are advised to thoroughly review the job offer, negotiate any employment conditions if needed, and formally indicate their acceptance or rejection of the offer.

Federal Forms
Form I-9, Employment Eligibility Verification: Verifies the identity and employment eligibility of employees. The employers must complete Form I-9 for every new hire within three days of the employee's start date. The employee must provide various forms of identification to prove US citizenship or legal alien status.

https://www.uscis.gov/sites/default/files/document/forms/i-9.pdf

W-4, Employee's Withholding Certificate: Determines the amount of federal income tax to withhold from an employee's paycheck. Employees must complete Form W-4 upon hiring and update it as needed. This form requires them to declare the number of dependents the employee wishes to claim. Declaring the number of dependents will impact the amount of state and federal deductions that are subtracted from their weekly or bi-weekly income.

https://www.irs.gov/pub/irs-pdf/fw4.pdf

New Hire Reporting: Enables states to collect information on newly hired employees for child support enforcement. Employers must report new hires to the appropriate state agency within a specified timeframe.

State Labor Law Posters: Informs employees of their rights under state labor laws. Employers must display state labor law posters in a visible location in the workplace.

State-Specific Family and Medical Leave Act (FMLA) Forms: Some states have their own family and medical leave laws with specific forms for requesting and processing leave.

It's essential for employers to be aware of federal and state-specific hiring requirements, including any updates or changes to forms and regulations. Staying informed helps ensure compliance with the law and fosters a positive and legally sound hiring process. Funeral home employers are encouraged to consult with legal professionals or human resources specialists to address specific requirements in their jurisdiction and industry.

Talent management: *is a process used by human resource departments to locate, hire, train and retain the best qualified employees.* The funeral industry faces a notable shortage of qualified employees, partially stemming from a lack of positive working environments that foster employee motivation and skill development. Successful talent management is integral to organizational agility, innovation, and competitiveness, necessitating collaboration among HR professionals, managers, and organizational leaders to align talent strategies with business objectives. Organizations can cultivate a dynamic and resilient workforce, driving sustained success, by investing in the development and engagement of employees.

Financial Management

Financial management in a funeral home entail overseeing its financial activities and resources for sustained health and viability. Funeral home operators must navigate budgeting, accounting, pricing strategies, and financial planning to effectively manage various aspects. Some funeral homes employ specific accounting systems, especially large corporate-owned establishments with integrated systems managing multiple locations and extensive accounting data. Conversely, smaller and medium-sized firms often utilize business financial software like QuickBooks for compliance with state and federal regulations and profitability management. To determine the appropriate financial software, particularly for generating essential tax-related financial reports, a certified public accountant (CPA) is recommended.

Financial management is all about establishing priorities and planning how to effectively spend the financial capital that is generated from the business. Here are key considerations for financial management in a funeral home:

Budgeting and Planning	Develop a comprehensive budget that includes both fixed and variable costs, such as facility maintenance, staff salaries, utilities, supplies, and other operational expenses. Plan for capital expenditures, such as facility improvements or upgrades to funeral vehicles. Consider revenue projections based on historical data and market trends.
Pricing Strategies	Establish clear and transparent pricing for funeral services, merchandise, and related offerings. Consider competitive pricing while ensuring that prices cover the costs and contribute to profitability. Review pricing periodically to adjust for changes in costs or market conditions.
Cash Flow Management	Monitor cash flow closely to ensure that the funeral home has sufficient liquidity to meet its financial obligations. Implement effective invoicing and payment collection processes. Establish policies for handling pre-need and at-need payments.
Financial Reporting:	Utilize accounting software to maintain precise and current financial records, regularly generating statements such as income statements, balance sheets, and cash flow statements to analyze the business's financial performance and identify areas for improvement.
Tax Compliance	Ensure compliance with tax regulations relevant to funeral home operations. Working with a qualified accountant or tax professional to optimize tax planning and reporting. Keep abreast of changes in tax laws that may impact on the funeral home's financial obligations.
Risk Management & Insurance:	Assess and manage financial risks, including potential liabilities and insurance needs. Maintain appropriate insurance coverage for the business, employees, and assets. Establish contingency plans for unforeseen events that may impact operations.
Investment Management	If applicable, manage any investments held by the funeral home wisely to generate returns. Diversify investments to mitigate risks and optimize long-term financial growth.
Regulatory Compliance	Comply with industry-specific regulations governing funeral services. Stay informed about any changes in regulations that may affect financial management practices.
Employee Compensation and Benefits	Establish fair and competitive compensation packages for employees. Budget for employee benefits, including health insurance, retirement plans, and other perks.
Customer Financing Options:	Consider offering financing options or pre-need plans to customers. Communicate financing terms clearly and ensure compliance with applicable regulations.

Implementing Technology	Harness technology and automation tools to streamline financial management tasks, encompassing invoicing, payroll processing, and financial reporting, while utilizing technology to manage data pertaining to Pre-Need records in trust accounts or insurance funds.
Continuing Education	Best practices in financial management for funeral homes by attending workshops, seminars, or conferences that offer opportunities to enhance financial management skills.

Effective financial management is critical for the long-term success and sustainability of a funeral home. By implementing sound financial practices, funeral home operators can navigate challenges, optimize resources, and provide meaningful and respectful services to families while maintaining a financially viable business.

Inventory Management

Inventory or merchandise *is the goods or stock of goods which have been sold or used up during a period of time.* These items in a funeral home include but are not limited to, caskets and sundries (small items in the funeral home that are provided to the family) items, such as, prayer cards, memorial folders, casket crosses, temporary grave markers, memorial videos, etc. Part of inventory management is to monitor the **Inventory turnover,** *the number of times the average inventory has been sold or used up during a given period.* An accounting principle used when purchasing such items for resale in the funeral home is **Economic Order Quantity** (EOQ) which is, *the quantity to be purchased which minimizes the total cost* which in turn will maximize profitability for the funeral firm. For example, at the beginning of the year the funeral home will make a good faith estimate on how many (and what types) memorial folders to buy for the year. Replenishing this supply may allow the funeral home to receive a discount when ordering in large quantities. This discount can be absorbed as a profit when selling that particular type of folder. However, if when purchasing these items, not enough folders are purchased and supply is running low and a particular folder, needs to be overnight expressed shipped, the excessive cost will erode the profit margin for that item, thus creating a potential for negative cash flow.

Part of inventory management is identifying the types of items that will sell within a one-year period of time. Ideally, at the end of the year, most of the inventory should be depleted, and reordering should take place in the first week in January, after the annual in-house inventory audit has been completed, for accounting purposes. The **Age of Inventory** *measures the average time required to sell inventory.* A way to track the sale of inventory is to keep a log record on top of each inventory item, thus when an item is used, the date and quantity used should be recorded. Items that haven't sold in a few years should be withdrawn from the stock and replaced with different items. Items that have been discarded because of errors made during printing should also be recorded, and accounted for on the annual report. This could decrease the COGS for a particular item.

A concept that some merchandise companies have been offering is package box sundries that all matches. Such a box that includes: register book, memorial folders, thank you cards, book markers.

FEATURES:
- Memorial Register Book
- Memorial Service Folders (100)
- Acknowledgement Cards (50)
- Laminated Bookmark
- Writing Instrument
- Lapel Pin
- Healing Help Pamphlet
- Blooming Memorial Heart
- Floral Card Envelope
- Acknowledgement Etiquette Card
- Set of Catholic Pages

Photo provided by: The Messenger Co.

Selecting Vendors for the Funeral Home

Ideally, a funeral home should have a select few vendors. Having too many vendors could affect the EOQ, thus affecting the bottom line for merchandise. Selecting the right vendor is a critical decision for a business, as it directly impacts the quality of products or services, costs, and overall operational efficiency. Here are several factors to consider when choosing a vendor:

Quality of Products/Services	Identify and assess potential risks associated with a vendor, considering factors like geopolitical risks, regulatory changes, or reliance on a single supplier for critical components. When evaluating a casket company, unknown vendors may lack guarantees on product quality, while major suppliers ensure and stand behind their products with quality guarantees. This comprehensive risk assessment aids in informed decision-making for vendor selection.
Purchasing Terms	Evaluate the overall cost of the products or services, including not only the purchase price but also any additional fees, shipping costs, and potential hidden charges. Compare costs among different vendors. Some vendors, such as a casket company, will provide the funeral home with substantial savings at the end of the year if the monthly invoices were paid on time and there is an exclusivity in using them as a supplier

Competitive Pricing	Some funeral homes place an emphasis on pricing the services they provide and charge the wholesale cost for the product plus a nominal mark-up fee. Such pricing could have a positive approach to cash flow in two ways: 1) the consumer will select better merchandise because the cost will appear reasonable and 2) Every client will be paying their appropriate share for the services they will be receiving. Old pricing paradigms that place the bulk of profitability on the people who purchase caskets, penalize the consumers for selecting traditional funerals.
Product & Services Options	Providing consumers with product options is a crucial aspect of marketing and sales. Offering a variety of choices caters to different preferences and needs, enhances customer satisfaction, and can lead to increased sales. Knowing the customer's needs is an important part of providing product options. For example, if the consumer chooses cremation as a means of final disposition, this does not mean that they would like the direct cremation option. The funeral director should ask, "will that be before or after the visitation and funeral services?" If a funeral home provides the consumer with a wide variety of options for funeral goods and services, this will provide the consumer with such products and services that will facilitate their personal, emotional and psychological needs in dealing with the complexity of the death of their loved one.
Consignment Options	This is a concept that is not used as often in the funeral home due to selection showroom that have cutaway models or funeral homes that use lithographs or kiosk as a way of presenting merchandise items. This concept was usually established between a casket company and a funeral home. The casket company would provide a showroom with several caskets, on consignment, and when the funeral home ordered the casket for their customer, they would rotate the inventory and replace the model selected with the model delivered. This was a very consumer friendly policy for small funeral homes who could not afford a large inventory of caskets.
Customer Service	Evaluate the vendor's approach to customer service. Building a strong, collaborative relationship with a vendor can lead to better cooperation and problem resolution. A vendor needs to be responsive to any concerns that the funeral home might have regarding the product being purchased for resale. Poor customer service will result in the funeral director's inability to provide a premium and quality product to their clients.
Product Liability Insurance (Risk Management):	Identify and assess potential risks associated with a vendor, including geopolitical risks, regulatory changes, or dependence on a single supplier for critical components. For instance, when evaluating a casket company, unknown vendors may lack guarantees on product quality, whereas major suppliers ensure and stand behind their products with quality guarantees. **Product liability insurance** *is insurance that protects a firm against claims that its product caused bodily injury or property damage to the user.*

Contract Terms and Conditions	Carefully review contract terms and conditions, including warranties, payment terms, delivery schedules, and any clauses related to penalties or termination.
Scalability and Flexibility	Assess the vendor's ability to scale up or down based on your business needs. Look for flexibility in adapting to changes in order quantities or specifications.

By thoroughly considering these factors, businesses can make informed decisions when selecting vendors, ultimately contributing to the success of their operations and supply chain.

Market Management

Marketing management in a funeral home involves creating and implementing strategies to attract and retain clients, build brand awareness, and provide compassionate and supportive services to grieving families. In an industry where sensitivity and empathy are paramount, effective marketing can help a funeral home establish a positive reputation, differentiate itself from competitors, and foster lasting relationships with the community. These are some of the key considerations for marketing management in a funeral home:

Brand Positioning	Define the funeral home's unique value proposition and position in the market. Communicate the brand message consistently across all marketing channels.
Target Audience Identification	Understand the demographics, psychographics, and needs of the target audience. Tailor marketing messages and services to resonate with specific segments of the community.
Online Presence	Develop and maintain a professional and informative website. Utilize social media platforms to share educational content, community involvement, and testimonials. Implement search engine optimization (SEO) strategies to enhance online visibility.
Content Marketing	Create and share valuable and relevant content, such as blog posts, articles, and videos, to educate the community about funeral-related topics. Provide resources for grieving families, including grief support materials
Community Engagement	Establish relationships with local churches, hospitals, hospices, and community organizations. Sponsor or participate in community events, workshops, and educational programs. Support charitable initiatives and community outreach.
Funeral Home Facilities and Services Showcase	Showcase the funeral home's facilities, amenities, and service offerings through brochures, videos, and virtual tours. Highlight unique aspects that differentiate the funeral home from competitors.
Customer Testimonials	Encourage satisfied families to share testimonials about their experiences. Use testimonials in marketing materials, on the website, and in social media to build trust and credibility.
Professional Networks	Build relationships with local clergy, celebrants, and other professionals involved in end-of-life services. Collaborate with local businesses, such as florists or memorial product providers, to enhance service offerings.
Event Marketing	Host open houses, educational seminars, or workshops to engage with the community. Create awareness through press releases, local media coverage, and community calendars.
Online Reviews Management	Encourage satisfied clients to leave positive reviews on online platforms. Respond promptly and professionally to any negative reviews to demonstrate commitment to customer satisfaction.

Crisis Communication Planning	Develop a crisis communication plan to address unexpected situations or negative publicity. Train staff in how to handle sensitive situations and communicate effectively with the public.
Measuring and Analyzing Results	Use analytics tools to measure the effectiveness of marketing efforts. Track key performance indicators (KPIs) such as website traffic, social media engagement, and lead generation.
Continuous Improvement	Seek feedback from families and the community to identify areas for improvement. Continuously refine and adapt marketing strategies based on changing community needs and industry trends. Customer surveys are the best way to evaluate and monitor how the consumer is valuing the services that the funeral home provides.

In the funeral home industry, ethical and compassionate communication is crucial. Marketing efforts should focus on building trust, providing valuable information, and offering support to families during difficult times. Effective marketing management contributes to the funeral home's overall success and its ability to serve the community with empathy and professionalism.

Facilities Management

Facilities management in a funeral home involves overseeing and maintaining the physical spaces, equipment, and amenities to create a comfortable, respectful, and supportive environment for grieving families. Effective facilities management ensures that the funeral home is well-maintained, complies with regulatory standards, and provides a dignified setting for memorial services and other ceremonies. These are some of the key considerations for facilities management in a funeral home:

Funeral Home Design and Layout	Plan and design the funeral home layout to accommodate various functions, including visitations, memorial services, and family gatherings. Ensure that the design promotes a calm and comforting atmosphere for families and guests.
Building Maintenance	Regularly inspect and maintain the building structure, including roofing, plumbing, electrical systems, and HVAC (heating, ventilation, and air conditioning) systems. Address any repairs promptly to maintain a safe and comfortable environment.
Landscaping and Exterior Presentation	Maintain well-kept landscaping, including lawns, gardens, and exterior features. Ensure that the exterior of the funeral home presents a clean and welcoming appearance.
Amenities and Furnishings	Select and maintain appropriate furnishings and amenities, such as seating arrangements, caskets, urns, and memorial displays. Ensure that furnishings are clean, well-maintained, and meet the expectations of families.
Accessibility and ADA Compliance	Ensure that the funeral home is accessible to individuals with disabilities, complying with the Americans with Disabilities Act (ADA). Provide amenities such as ramps, handrails, and accessible restrooms
Technology Integration	Implement and maintain audiovisual equipment for presentations, music, and video tributes. Ensure that technology systems, including sound and lighting, are functional and enhance the overall experience.

Safety and Security	Establish and enforce safety protocols for staff and visitors. Install security measures, including surveillance cameras, to protect the premises.
Environmental Considerations	Implement eco-friendly practices, such as energy-efficient lighting and waste management. Consider sustainable options for landscaping and building materials.
Compliance with Regulations	Stay informed about local, state, and federal regulations related to funeral home facilities. Comply with licensing requirements, fire code, zoning regulations, and health and safety standards, i.e. OSHA.
Cleaning and Hygiene	Implement a regular cleaning schedule to maintain a clean and sanitary environment. Pay special attention to restrooms, chapel areas, and public spaces.
Waste Management	Implement proper waste disposal procedures, especially for biomedical waste. Comply with regulations regarding the disposal of embalming fluids and other waste products.
Vehicle maintenance	Implementing a regular cleaning schedule to maintain and clean the vehicles to ensure their readiness when needed. This includes maintaining annual inspections, routine maintenance, such as oil changes and service maintenance, and making sure the vehicle is always fuel to capacity.
Emergency Preparedness	Develop and regularly update emergency response plans for situations such as natural disasters or power outages. Train staff on emergency procedures to ensure the safety of everyone on the premises. Ensuring that exit lights are in working order and annually inspected.
Family Rooms and Reception Areas	Create comfortable and well-equipped family rooms for private consultations. Consider providing reception areas for families to gather and share memories.
Collaboration with Vendors	Build relationships with vendors for maintenance services, landscaping, and other facility-related needs. Ensure that vendors adhere to the funeral home's standards and values.

Effective facilities management in a funeral home contributes to the overall reputation of the business, providing a space that honors the deceased and supports grieving families during a challenging time. Regular maintenance, attention to detail, and a commitment to creating a compassionate environment are essential aspects of successful facilities management in the funeral industry.

Office Management

Office management *is the administration and supervision of office duties, functions, and equipment.* In a funeral home, this involves overseeing administrative tasks, maintaining organized records, managing communication, and ensuring efficient day-to-day operations. In a funeral home setting, effective office management is crucial for providing support to grieving families, coordinating services, and handling various administrative responsibilities. There always needs to be someone in charge of maintaining the records in the funeral home, in addition to being able to coordinate key personnel for various situations as they do arise. These are some of the key considerations for office management in a funeral home:

Reception and Communication	Greet visitors and families with sensitivity and empathy. Manage phone calls, emails, and inquiries promptly and professionally.

	Provide accurate and compassionate information to families regarding funeral services.
Appointment Scheduling	Coordinate and schedule appointments for families to make funeral arrangements. Use a centralized scheduling system to avoid conflicts and ensure efficiency.
Documentation and Record Keeping:	Maintain organized and accurate records of all funeral arrangements, contracts, and client information. Ensure compliance with legal requirements for record-keeping and documentation.
Payment Processing	Handle financial transactions, including receiving payments for services. Provide clear and transparent information about payment history and communicating with management regarding the age of account information.
Data Entry and Management	Input and manage data related to clients, services, and financial transactions. Use funeral home management software to streamline data entry and retrieval.
Coordination with Other Key Personnel	Collaborate with others, such as maintenance personnel, (trade) embalmers, and funeral directors, to ensure seamless coordination of services. Communicate effectively to meet the needs of families and adhere to timelines.
Inventory Management	Monitor and manage inventory levels of merchandise, such as caskets, urns, and memorial items. Implement systems for tracking and restocking inventory as needed.
Office Supplies and Equipment	Ensure that the office is well-equipped with necessary supplies, including stationery, forms, and office equipment. Schedule regular maintenance for office equipment.
Confidentiality and Privacy with Client Information:	Emphasize the importance of confidentiality and privacy when handling client information. Adhering to privacy policies and compliance with confidentiality regulations regarding client information will ensure that information is secure and only available to the appropriate personnel. This also includes cyber security and data protection.
At-Need Recordkeeping	Using a data management system to maintain accurate first call information, embalming reports, arrangement forms, completed and signed Statements of Goods and Services, Final Billing Statements, Releases/receipts forms/authorizations/disclaimers, death certificate and burial transit permit.
Pre-Need Recordkeeping	Using a data management system to maintain accurate case files for pre-funded and pre-arranged clients, maintaining copies of all financial transactions, and complying with regulatory agencies regarding pre-need matters.
Professional Development	Provide ongoing training and professional development opportunities for office staff. Stay informed about industry trends and changes in regulations related to office management. Maintaining continuing education records for licensing requirements.
Technology Integration	Use technology to streamline office processes, including funeral home management software, accounting systems, and communication tools. Training staff in the effective use of technology to enhance productivity plays a key role in using this software as a means of effective communications and continuity.

Family Services and Follow-Up	Offer additional support services to families, such as grief counseling resources and memorialization options. Conducting follow-up calls or surveys to gather feedback and ensure client satisfaction is one way to maintain consumer loyalty and future referrals.
Crisis Management	Develop protocols for handling unexpected situations or crises. Training staff on how to respond to sensitive or emotional situations with professionalism and empathy. During the Covid-19 Pandemic, this was a very important part of office management.
Professional Image	Maintain a professional and compassionate demeanor in all interactions with families, visitors, and colleagues. Uphold the funeral home's reputation through excellent customer service and attention to detail.

Effective office management in a funeral home contributes to the overall success of the business by ensuring that administrative tasks are handled efficiently and with sensitivity. By providing support to families during their difficult times, the office management team plays a vital role in creating a positive and respectful experience for grieving families.

Disaster Management

One area lacking in most funeral homes is a disaster management plan. This fact became very evident during the Covid-19 Pandemic when some areas in the country suddenly became inundated with a large number of deaths, and very few key personnel trained in disaster management to handle and maintain the proper care for the dead and their families. A **disaster** *is a sudden misfortune, resulting in the loss of life and/or property*. This becomes an **emergency** situation, *an unforeseen combination of circumstances that result in a need for immediate action*. In addition to not being prepared with a disaster management plan, few funeral homes had a contingency plan that kept the business operations moving forward in the absence of key personnel.

Disaster management policies and procedures for a funeral home are crucial to ensure the safety of staff, clients, and visitors, as well as to maintain the integrity of the funeral home's operations during unforeseen events. These policies should cover a range of potential disasters, including natural disasters, accidents, pandemics, or other emergencies. These are some of the key elements to consider when developing disaster management policies and procedures for a funeral home:

Emergency Response Team	Designate and train an emergency response team responsible for implementing disaster management procedures. Clearly outline the roles and responsibilities of each team member. Establish a chain of command for effective communication.
Emergency Contact Information	Maintain an updated list of emergency contact information for all staff members. Include contact details for local emergency services, utility providers, and other relevant entities.

Evacuation Plan	Develop and communicate a clear evacuation plan for the funeral home. Identify primary and secondary evacuation routes. Conduct regular drills to ensure that staff are familiar with evacuation procedures. Create an alternate site for the funeral home to continue operations. The site should be equipped with updated computer systems, access to client files and necessary supplies to maintain office management.
Communication Protocols	Establish communication protocols for both internal and external communication during a disaster. Designate a central point of contact for information dissemination. Ensure that all staff members know how to receive emergency alerts and updates.
Client and Family Communication	Develop guidelines for communicating with clients and families during a disaster. Establish alternative methods for communicating funeral arrangements and updates. This may include the use of ZOOM meetings and recorded arrangement conferences.
Security Measures	Implement security measures to protect the premises during a disaster. Develop procedures for securing valuable items, records, and equipment. Only authorized personnel should be allowed in secured areas. Privacy and confidentiality must be maintained at all times to protect the funeral home from liability and to ensure dignity and respect for the dead.
Emergency Supplies	Maintain emergency embalming and funeral home supplies. A funeral home should maintain a one year rotated supply of cremation containers and embalming supplies, excluding gloves. Only a six-month supply of gloves should be maintained and at the beginning of an emergency situation, an immediate inventory should be taken and the emergency funeral home supplies should be replenished to one year levels. Back up emergency generators and stabilized high octane fuel should be a part of these supplies.
Backup Systems for Operations	Establish backup systems for critical operations, including data backup for electronic records. Identify an alternate location for conducting essential operations if the funeral home is temporarily unusable.
Collaboration with Authorities	Establish relationships with local emergency services, law enforcement, and other relevant authorities. Coordinate disaster management plans with local agencies to ensure a cohesive response.
Training and Drills	Become a part of disaster management drills in your local community. Conduct regular training sessions for staff on disaster management procedures. At the very least, every 3 months, check and refill your inventory to 1 year levels, rotating the funeral home stock.
Documentation and Reporting	Develop a system for documenting incidents and reporting them to relevant authorities. Keep detailed records of any damage to property, injuries, or other significant events. Document all personal effects received with the deceased and return personal items to the family after these items have been decontaminated.
Post-Disaster Recovery	Develop a plan for post-disaster recovery and restoration of normal operations. Identify resources and contacts for rebuilding and repairs. This should also include de-briefing of personnel. Some emergency situations could cause psychological harm to personnel and a policy needs to be in place so that the mental and emotional welfare is delt with professionally and within a reasonable amount of time.

Regular Review and Updates	Conduct regular reviews of disaster management policies and procedures to ensure their relevance and effectiveness. Update the plans based on lessons learned from drills and actual events. Don't create this plan in a vacuum. Work with local and state disaster management teams to ensure continuity and connectiveness of services.

Become Involved with DMORT: DMORT stands for **Disaster Mortuary Operational Response Team**. DMORT is a federal program that falls under the National Disaster Medical System (NDMS), which is part of the U.S. Department of Health and Human Services (HHS). The primary purpose of DMORT is to provide mortuary and forensic services during mass fatality incidents and disasters. In a disaster situation a Rapid Response DMORT teams are composed of volunteers with expertise in mortuary affairs, forensic pathology, anthropology, dental forensics, and related fields. These teams can be quickly mobilized to respond to mass fatality incidents, such as natural disasters, transportation accidents, or public health emergencies. DMORT teams assist in the management and processing of human remains in the aftermath of a disaster. Their tasks may include establishing temporary morgue facilities, conducting victim identification, coordinating the transportation of remains, and providing mortuary services to ensure the respectful handling of the deceased.

By implementing comprehensive disaster management policies and procedures, a funeral home can minimize the impact of unforeseen events, protect the well-being of individuals on the premises, and ensure the continued provision of essential services during challenging times. Regular training and communication are critical components of an effective disaster management plan.

Small Business Management
(with Accounting) Glossary

Accounting – a language of business employed to communicate financial information based upon analyzing, recording, classification, summarization, reporting, and interpretation of financial data.

Accounting equation – Assets equal Liabilities plus Owner's Equity.

Accounts payable – an unwritten promise to pay creditors for property, such as merchandise, supplies, or equipment, purchased on credit, or for services received on credit.

Accounts receivable – an unwritten promise by a customer to pay, at a later date, for goods sold or services rendered.

Accrual accounting – recording in each fiscal period applicable expenses, whether paid or not, and income earned, whether collected or not.

Accrued expense – an expense incurred in operating a business during an accounting period, but not yet paid.

Accrued income – income actually earned during an accounting period but which will not be received until a future period.

Acquisition – a company inherited or bought.

Advertising – the art of making the public aware of the services or commodities that the business has for sale.

Age of accounts receivable – measures the average time required to collect receivables.

Age Discrimination in Employment Act – federal legislation that requires employer to treat applicants and employees equally regardless of age.

Age of inventory – measures the average time required to sell inventory.

Amortization – the paying off of a debt in regular installments over a period of time.

Americans with Disabilities Act (ADA) – legislation that guarantees disabled people equal access to employment, as well as access to public places.

Angel investors – private investors who are willing to supply financing for new or risky small venture start-ups.

Assets – property of monetary value owned by a business.

Bad debts – accounts receivable that are uncollectable.

Balance sheet (statement of financial position; statement financial condition) – a formal financial statement illustrating the assets, liabilities, and owner's equity of a business as of a specific date.

Bona Fide Occupational Qualification (BFOQ) – a qualification absolutely necessary for the job; it is an allowed and approved reason for discrimination.

Book value – the cost of a fixed asset less its accumulated depreciation.

Branding – a method of applying verbal or symbolic means to identify a product or service.

Break-even analysis – the point at which total sales revenue equals total operating costs; determined by formula or chart.

Business – an organization that combines inputs of raw materials, capital, labor, and management skills to produce useful outputs of goods and services to earn a profit.

Business interruption insurance – insurance that protects companies during the period necessary to restore property damaged by an insured peril. Coverage pays for lost income and other expenses related to recovery.

Business plan – a summary of how a business owner, manager, or entrepreneur intends to organize the business endeavor and implement the activities necessary for the venture to succeed.

Business policies – fundamental statements that serve as guides to management practice. Corporation – an ordinary corporation, taxed by the federal government as a separate legal entity.

Cash basis accounting – an accounting practice in which revenue is not recognized in the accounting records until received and in which expenses are not recognized until paid.

Cash discounts – discounts from quoted prices as an inducement for prompt payment of invoices.

Cash flow – the amount of cash a company generates and uses during a period.

Cash Flow Statement – a financial report showing a firm's sources of cash as well as its uses of cash.

Casualty insurance – insurance that provides monetary benefits to a business that has experienced an unforeseen peril, such as flood, fire, etc.

Census of Business – source of market data that explain where certain businesses are located.

Census of Housing – source of market data that keep track of new home sales by region or the construction of new houses by region and specific area.

Census of Manufacturing – source of market data that explains where certain manufacturers are located.

Census of Population – a source of market data that compiles population statistics with regard to distribution of population by region, area, etc.

Chamber of Commerce – an association of businesspeople who attempt to protect and promote commercial interests in a community.

Civil Rights Act – federal legislation that prohibits discrimination on the basis of race, color, religion, sex, pregnancy, or natural origin.

Closed end credit (installment credit) – balance of costly goods paid for in small monthly (fractional) payments over a period of time.

Competition – the practice of trying to obtain something being sought by others under similar circumstances at the same time.

Consumer credit – a type of credit granted by retailers used by individuals or families for satisfaction of their own wants.

Controlling (evaluating) – the process of measuring organizational and individual performance with predetermined standards or expected results.

Copyright – the registered right of a creator to reproduce, publish, and sell the work that is the product of the intelligence and skill of that person.

Corporation – an artificial being, invisible, intangible, and existing only in contemplation of law; an entity that has a distinct existence separate and apart from the existence of its individual members.

Cost of Goods Sold – The cost of producing or acquiring goods or services to be sold by a firm

Credit –
(1) the right side of a standard account;
(2) an agreement that payment for a product or service will be made at some later date.

Current asset – cash of other assets that will be converted into cash or consumed within one year.

Current liabilities – debts of a business that are generally paid within one year.

Current ratio – current assets divided by current liabilities.

Debt equity – any borrowed or loaned capital invested in the business that must be repaid to creditors.

Debit – the left side of a standard account.

Demographics – the statistical study of human populations with respect to their size, density, distribution, composition, and income.

Depreciation – the loss in value of a fixed asset due to wear and tear and the passage of time; or, a method of matching the cost of a fixed asset against the revenues that the fixed asset will help produce during its useful life.

Drawing account (owner withdrawals) – a separate owner's equity account in which withdrawals of cash or other assets by the owner for personal use are recorded.

Earnings valuation approach – a business valuation approach that centers on estimating the projected future income of the business, typically over a 5 to 10-year period.

Earnings before interest, taxation, depreciation, and amortization (EBITDA) – a firm's profits after subtracting cost of goods sold and cash operating expenses, but before subtracting interest expense, taxes, depreciation, and amortization.

Economic base – the wealth produced in or near a community that provides employment and income to the local population.

Economic Order Quantity (EOQ) – the quantity to be purchased that minimizes total costs.

Employee – one who is under the control and direction of an employer with regard to the performance of employment.

Employment application – a record of statements made at the time the applicant first seeks employment.

Entrepreneur – one who organizes, manages, and assumes the risk of a business firm or venture.

Environmental Protection Agency (EPA) – a governmental agency with regulatory and enforcement authority on environment protection.

Equal Employment Opportunity Act – federal legislation designed to eliminate employment discrimination based on race, color, religion, sex, or national origin.

Equal Pay Act – federal legislation which prohibits discrimination on account of sex in the payment of wages by employers engaging in commerce or in the production of goods for commerce.

Expenses – A decrease in assets, other than withdrawals by the owner, which result from efforts to produce revenues.

Factoring – a method to obtain cash for business operations before payments are received from customers by selling off accounts receivable to a third party.

Fair Labor Standards Act (Wage and Hour Law) – federal legislation that outlaws discriminatory practices in pay; requires employers to pay a minimum wage to employees, and to pay a minimum of one and one-half times the regular rate for any hours beyond forty worked in a week.

Family and Medical Leave Act (FMLA) – federal legislation that ensures employees of unpaid leave for childbirth and other family needs.

Federal Insurance Contributions Act/ F.I.C.A
– a federal act that requires most employers and employees to pay taxes to support the federal Social Security program and Medicare program.

Federal Unemployment Tax Act/F.U.T.A. – a federal act imposed upon each employer for financing the administrations costs of the federal and state unemployment compensation programs.

Fixed asset (capital) – long-term capital invested in the small business; also, funds invested in such long-term assets as land, building, machinery, furniture, fixtures, other equipment, not to be converted to cash within one year.

Fixed expenses – a cost that, for a given period of time and range of activity, called the relevant range, does not change in total, but becomes progressively smaller on a per unit basis as volume increases; these expenses do not increase with increased business, nor do they decrease with declining business activity.

General journal – a book of original entry in which any business transaction is recorded in chronological order.

General ledger – the book of accounts.

Goodwill – an intangible asset such as the name of a funeral home; also, an intangible asset that enables a business to earn a profit in excess of the normal rate of profit earned by other businesses of the same kind.

Gross pay (gross earnings) – income before any deductions have been made.

Gross profit (gross margin) – net sales minus the cost of goods sold.

Human Resource Management (Personnel Management) – process of acquiring, training, developing, motivating and appraising a sufficient quantity of qualified employees to perform necessary activities; developing activities and an organizational climate conducive to maximum efficiency and worker satisfaction.

Immigration Reform Act – federal legislation requiring employers to check job applicants' papers to be sure they are either U.S. citizens or undocumented individuals authorized to work in the U.S.

Income statement (profit and loss statement; statement of operations; operating statement) – a formal financial statement that presents the income, expenses, and resulting net profit or net loss for a given period.

Income tax – a tax levied on the earnings of individuals and businesses by federal, state, and local governments.

Independent contractor – a person who agrees to perform a service for a fee and is not subject to the control of those for whom the service is performed.

Innovation – the introduction of something new; a new idea, method or device.

Insurance – the equitable transfer of the risk of a loss from one entity to another in exchange for payment. It is a form of risk management primarily used to hedge against the risk of a contingent, uncertain loss.

Intangible assets – those assets that cannot be touched or grasped (examples include patents, copyrights and goodwill).

Interest – money paid for the use of money.

Inventory (merchandise) – those goods or stock of goods held for resale at a profit.

Inventory turnover – the number of times the average inventory has been sold or used up during a period.

Invoice – a source document showing quantity, description, prices of items, total amount of purchase and the terms of payment.

Job analysis – the process of determining the critical components of a job for purposes of selecting, training, and rewarding personnel.

Job description – a document that lists the major responsibilities and tasks of the job.

Job specification – a document that lists the knowledge, skills, abilities, and personal characteristics a job holder must possess to perform effectively.

Key-person life insurance – life insurance that protects a firm against losses due to the death of a key employee.

Leading (Actuating, Directing) – the process of guiding or supervising the activities of an organization to achieve plans and objectives.

Liabilities – any debts that a business owes.

Limited Liability Company (LLC) – a form of business ownership that combines aspects of partnerships with the limited liability of a corporation; owners known as members.

Liquidation value approach – the anticipated value of an asset that would be realized in case of liquidation of the business.

Long-term liabilities (fixed liabilities) – liabilities not due and payable within one year.

Management – the art and science of motivating people toward the achievement of a goal.

Manufacturing business – a business that makes finished goods from raw materials by hand or machinery.

Markdown – a reduction of selling price below the original selling price.

Market – a group of potential customers possessing purchasing power and unsatisfied needs.

Marketing management – the process of planning and executing the development, pricing, promotion, and distribution of an organization's goods or services.

Marketing – the process of planning and executing the development, pricing, promotion, and distribution of an organization's goods/services.

Market survey – a study used by a business to determine where the potential customers are located.

Market value approach – an approach used in business valuation that determines value based upon previous sales of similar businesses.

Markup – the difference between merchandise cost and selling price.

Merchandising business – a business that purchases finished goods for resale.

Motivating – the process of energizing, channeling and sustaining people's behavior.

Net earnings (net pay; take home pay) – gross pay less payroll deductions; an employee's take home pay.

Net income (net profit) – the difference between gross profit and expenses when gross profit is larger.

Net loss – the difference between gross profit and expenses when expenses are larger.

Net sales – sales minus sales returns and allowances minus sales discounts.

Occupational Safety and Health Act (OSHA) – Federal legislation that created the governmental agency with the responsibility for regulation and enforcement of safety and health matters for most United States employees; an individual state OSHA agency may supersede the U.S. Department of Labor OSHA regulations.

Open-end Credit (revolving account) – a line of credit that may be used over and over again up to a certain borrowing limit.

Operating expense (overhead expense) – Costs related to marketing and selling a firm's product or service, general and administrative expenses and depreciation.

Operating ratios – a comparison of profit and expense items in the income statement expressed as a percentage of sales income; the operating ratios can be compared to the industry standards in regard to measuring the possible growth of the business.

Organizing – the process of assigning tasks, allocating resources, and coordinating the activities of individuals and groups to implement plans.

Owner's equity (capital; net worth) – the amount by which the total assets exceed the total liabilities of a business; an owner's financial interest in a business.

Partnership – the voluntary association of two or more people who have combined their resources to carry on as co-owners of a lawful enterprise for their joint profit.

Patent – the registered right of an inventor to make, use, and sell an invention.

Planning – the process of setting performance objectives and determining what actions should be taken to accomplish them.

Pricing policy – factors which influence prices.

Product liability insurance – insurance that protects a firm against claims that its product caused bodily injury or property damage to the user.

Ratio analysis – quantitative evaluation of information contained in a company's financial statements (i.e., balance sheet, income statement and cash flow statement, etc.) to determine the overall financial strength of a business.

Recruitment – the process of forming a pool of qualified applicants for tasks that need to be filled.

Replacement value approach – an insurance concept in which the fair market price to purchase similar products in similar condition is used to settle claims.

Resume – written summary of one's personal, educational, and professional achievements.

Retail sales tax – a tax imposed on tangible personal property sold at retail.

Revenue (income) – an inflow of assets as a result of selling a product or providing a service.

Risk – a probability or threat of damage, injury, liability, loss, or any other negative occurrence caused by external or internal vulnerabilities.

Risk management – a process for identifying, assessing, and prioritizing certain kinds of events happening to or having an impact on a business with the intent to reduce or eliminate the risk.

S Corporation – a type of corporation that offers limited liability to its owners but is taxed by the federal government as a partnership.

Salary – generally considered to be compensation for managerial or administrative services, expressed in terms of a month or year.

Self-insurance – a form of risk management whereby a part of the firm's earnings is earmarked as a contingency fund for possible future losses, specifically for individual loss categories, such as property, medical, or worker's compensation.

Service business – a business that provides a service as opposed to a product.

Small business – a business independently owned and operated and is not dominant in its field of operations.

Small Business Administration (SBA) – the principal government agency concerned with the financing, operation, and management of small businesses.

Sole proprietorship – business owned by one person, who bears unlimited liability for the enterprise.

Startups – new business ventures started from the beginning.

Strategic plan – a document designed to communicate the organization's goals for the future.

State Unemployment Tax Act (S.U.T.A.) – a tax levied in most states to raise funds to pay unemployment benefits.

Talent management – a process used by human resource departments to locate, hire, train, and retain the best qualified employees.

Tangible assets – assets that can be appraised by value or seen or touched.

Trademark – an intangible asset that is a distinct name, sign, or symbol that the federal government grants exclusive rights to use for a specified period of time.

Transaction – any activity of a business enterprise that involves the exchange of values.

Transaction analysis – the effect of business activities on the accounting elements.

Useful Life – the estimated determinable life of a fixed asset.

Valuation – estimate of the worth or price of a company.

Variable expense – a cost that is uniform per unit, but fluctuates in direct proportion to change in the related total activity or volume.

Venture capitalist – anyone who invests in, or financially sponsors, a new business.

Vietnam Era Veterans Readjustment Act – outlaws discrimination in employment against Vietnam Era veterans.

W-2 form – Wage and Tax Statement; a report furnished by the employer for each employee indicating gross earnings and deductions.

W-4 form – Employees' Withholding Allowance Certificate.

Wage – a form of compensation usually for skilled and unskilled labor, expressed in terms of hours, weeks, or pieces completed.

Workers' compensation insurance – coverage that provides benefits to employees injured at work.

Working capital (circulating capital) – the difference between current assets and current liabilities.

Zoning ordinance – the formal codification of land use policies by a unit of local government with the goal to establish permitted uses for land and to distinguish between different types of uses which may be incompatible.

Funeral Service Management

Management refers to the systematic coordination and oversight of organizational resources, people, and processes to achieve specific goals and objectives. It involves planning, organizing, leading, and controlling various elements within an entity to ensure efficiency, effectiveness, and the successful attainment of predetermined targets. Managers play an important role in decision-making, resource allocation, and fostering a conducive work environment. Effective management requires a combination of leadership skills, strategic thinking, and the ability to adapt to dynamic circumstances. It encompasses a wide range of functions, including setting objectives, allocating resources, motivating and guiding employees, and monitoring performance. Whether in business, non-profit organizations, or government entities, successful management is integral to the accomplishment of organizational missions and the sustained growth and viability of an enterprise.

Effective funeral home management is crucial for ensuring the seamless and compassionate delivery of funeral services, which are deeply rooted in cultural, emotional, and ceremonial significance. Funeral home managers play an important role in orchestrating a range of functions, from coordinating memorial services and handling legal documentation to overseeing staff and maintaining facilities. The sensitive nature of the funeral industry demands skilled management to navigate intricate details and address the unique needs of grieving families. Efficient management contributes to a well-organized operation, creating an environment of trust and support during a difficult time. Financial viability, compliance with regulations, and the ability to adapt to evolving industry trends are also essential considerations for funeral home managers. Ultimately, effective funeral home management is integral to upholding the integrity of the funeral service profession, and fostering a reputation of empathy, professionalism, and reliability within the community it serves.

Establishing Goals and Objectives

Goals and objectives are related concepts but differ in terms of scope, specificity, and time frame. Goals are broad, overarching statements that express the overall aspirations and desired outcomes of an organization or individual. They provide a general direction and purpose, often reflecting long-term achievements. Objectives, on the other hand, are more specific, measurable, and time-bound. They are concrete steps and targets set to accomplish the broader goals. While goals focus on the destination, objectives are the actionable steps and milestones along the journey. For example, a business goal might be to become a market leader, while the corresponding objective could involve achieving a specific percentage increase in market share within the next year. In essence, goals provide the overarching vision, and objectives break down that vision into manageable, measurable and achievable steps.

Long-term and short-term goals serve distinct purposes in guiding individual or organizational planning and decision-making. Long-term goals encompass broad aspirations and accomplishments set over an extended period, often spanning several years. These goals provide a strategic vision and overarching direction, shaping the overall trajectory of an entity. In contrast, short-term goals are more immediate, focusing on specific, achievable outcomes within a shorter timeframe, typically ranging from weeks to a year. Short-term goals act as steppingstones toward fulfilling long-term objectives and contribute to the incremental progress necessary for sustained success. Balancing both types of goals is crucial for effective planning, ensuring that immediate actions align with the broader, strategic vision. Long-term goals provide purpose and vision, while short-term goals offer a practical roadmap for day-to-day operations, fostering a dynamic and goal-oriented approach to personal or organizational development.

For example, Thompson Funeral Home wishes to become the market leader in their community. The funeral home must strategically align both long-term and short-term goals. Long-term goals might include establishing a reputation for compassionate and personalized funeral services, investing in state-of-the-art facilities, and building strong community relationships. These overarching objectives provide a visionary direction for the funeral home. Short-term goals, on the other hand, could involve targeted marketing campaigns, enhancing online presence, and expanding service offerings to meet immediate community needs. These short-term goals act as tactical steps to incrementally build brand visibility, customer trust, and service excellence. By consistently achieving short-term goals, the funeral home contributes to the realization of its long-term vision, positioning itself as a trusted and leading provider of funeral services in the community. This strategic combination of long-term and short-term goals allows the funeral home to navigate the dynamic landscape of the funeral service industry while steadily advancing towards market leadership.

The **primary goals in managing a funeral home** revolve around providing compassionate and high-quality funeral services while maintaining operational efficiency and sustainability. Key objectives for funeral home management include:

1. **Properly Caring for the Deceased:** The primary goal in managing a funeral home is to compassionately care for the deceased, ensuring respectful and dignified handling of remains throughout the entire funeral process. This includes providing a range of funeral services, guiding families through the decision-making process, and creating a serene and comforting environment for mourning. Through this commitment to caring for the deceased, funeral home management strives to offer solace, support, and a meaningful farewell to grieving families during their difficult times. *Nihil nisi optima cura et misericordia pro vivis et mortuis.* "Nothing but the best care and compassion for the living and the dead."

2. **Fulfilling Client-Family Needs:** Prioritizing customer satisfaction by delivering exceptional service, addressing client needs with sensitivity, and maintaining open communication fosters trust and loyalty within the community. Fulfilling client-family needs in funeral services is paramount, involving attentive listening, empathetic guidance, and providing a range of personalized options to meet their unique preferences and cultural considerations. Funeral home services aim to create a supportive and compassionate environment, ensuring that each family's wishes are honored with sensitivity and professionalism.

3. **Promoting Funeral Services:** Promoting funeral services within the community is essential for raising awareness about available options, fostering trust, and establishing the funeral home as a reliable resource during times of loss. Through community engagement and outreach, funeral homes can share information about their services, pre-planning options, and grief support resources, ensuring that families are informed and prepared. This proactive approach not only strengthens the funeral home's relationship with the community but also contributes to a more open and informed dialogue surrounding how to cope with the complexity of death and the grieving process.

4. **Operational Efficiency:** Efficient management of resources, including staff, facilities, and equipment, is crucial for the smooth functioning of the funeral home. Streamlining processes and maintaining a well-organized operation contribute to overall effectiveness. Efficient funeral home managers play a crucial role in fulfilling the needs of their staff by providing clear communication, fostering a supportive work environment, and addressing professional development opportunities. Through effective leadership and management practices, funeral home managers contribute to a cohesive and skilled team capable of meeting the sensitive and diverse needs of grieving families with empathy and professionalism.

5. **Creating and Maintaining a Viable Business:** Creating and maintaining a viable funeral business requires a strategic combination of compassionate service delivery, prudent financial management, and community engagement. By consistently providing high-quality and personalized funeral services, managing operational costs effectively, and actively participating in the community, funeral businesses can establish a reputable presence and build lasting relationships. Ongoing adaptation to industry trends, technological advancements, and a commitment to ethical and transparent practices contribute to the long-term viability and success of the funeral business.

By aligning these primary goals, funeral home management can create an environment that not only meets the diverse needs of grieving families but also establishes the funeral home as a trusted and integral part of the community.

The **secondary goals in managing a funeral home** complement the primary objectives and contribute to the overall success and growth of the business. These secondary goals may include:

1. **Financial Management:** Achieving financial viability and sustainability is a core goal. This involves prudent financial management, including budgeting, cost control, and strategic financial planning to weather economic challenges and maintain the long-term stability of the funeral home.

2. **Reasonable Return on Investment:** Ensuring a reasonable return on the initial investment is paramount for the success and sustainability of any business, including a funeral home. By carefully managing costs, optimizing operational efficiency, and consistently delivering high-quality services, funeral home management can create a

financially sound foundation that honors both the fiduciary responsibility to investors and the commitment to providing compassionate and empathetic services.

3. **Investing in Capital Improvements**: Investing in capital improvements in the funeral home is essential for maintaining a modern, dignified, and efficient environment that meets the evolving needs of grieving families. Renovating facilities, upgrading technology, and enhancing amenities not only contribute to operational excellence but also reinforces the funeral home's commitment to providing a compassionate and contemporary funeral service experience.

4. **Optimizing Talent and Human Resource Management**: Human capital is one of the most valuable resources in the funeral home. It is critical for cultivating a skilled and compassionate team capable of delivering sensitive compassionate services. By focusing on effective recruitment, continuous training, and creating a supportive work culture, funeral home management can ensure that their staff is well-equipped to meet the diverse needs of grieving families with professionalism and empathy. Effective funeral home management should invest in the ongoing professional development of staff members, including funeral directors, embalmers and support personnel. This will ensure a high level of expertise and service excellence, contributing to the overall reputation of the funeral home.

By pursuing these secondary goals, funeral home management cannot only enhance the overall business but also position the funeral home as a forward-thinking and responsive institution within the community and the broader funeral service industry.

In the context of funeral services, management plays a multifaceted role in ensuring the seamless and compassionate delivery of death and bereavement care. The primary function is to oversee the entire spectrum of funeral operations, from coordinating funeral arrangements and managing staff to maintaining facilities and adhering to regulatory requirements. Strategic planning is crucial, involving the development of long-term goals that align with the funeral home's mission of providing dignified and respectful services to grieving families. Managers must optimize talent and human resources, ensuring that funeral directors and support staff are well-trained, empathetic, and capable of addressing the diverse needs of clients. Financial management becomes integral, balancing the cost-effective operation of the funeral home with the provision of quality services. Marketing and community engagement are vital functions, promoting the funeral home's offerings, nurturing relationships within the community, and establishing trust. Moreover, crisis management skills are essential, enabling funeral home managers to navigate sensitive situations with empathy and professionalism. Ultimately, the comprehensive function of management in funeral services involves creating an environment that supports both the grieving families seeking compassionate services and the dedicated staff committed to fulfilling the funeral home's mission.

Responsibilities of the Funeral Home Manager

The responsibilities of a funeral home manager are diverse and encompass various aspects of funeral service operations. A responsible funeral home manager demonstrates a commitment to ethical and transparent practices, ensuring the highest standards of service for grieving families. They prioritize regulatory compliance, staying abreast of industry changes and legal requirements to maintain the funeral home's integrity. Additionally, a responsible manager fosters a compassionate and supportive work culture, promoting ongoing staff training, professional development, and a dedication to meeting the diverse needs of clients with empathy and professionalism. These are some of the responsibilities of a funeral home manager:

1. **Staff Management**: Overseeing funeral directors, embalmers, administrative staff, and support personnel, ensuring they are well-trained, motivated, and capable of providing compassionate and professional services, is key to the success of the funeral home. A funeral home manager providing leadership serves as a guiding force, setting a tone of empathy, professionalism, and dedication within the team. They inspire staff by exemplifying a commitment to compassionate service and maintaining the highest ethical standards. Through effective communication, strategic decision-making, and a focus on continuous improvement, the funeral home manager leads by example, creating an environment that prioritizes both the well-being of the grieving families served and the professional development of the staff.

2. **Encouraging Employee Participation**: Encouraging employee participation in the funeral home is vital for fostering a collaborative and engaged work environment. A proactive funeral home manager encourages staff input on service enhancements, operational improvements, and community engagement initiatives, valuing the diverse perspectives of the team. By providing opportunities for professional development, recognizing contributions, and promoting a culture of open communication, the manager empowers employees to actively contribute to the funeral home's success and the satisfaction of the families they serve.

3. **Understanding Human Relations**: Handling sensitive and emotional situations with tact, empathy, and professionalism, guiding both staff and clients through challenging moments with care and understanding. Understanding human relations is crucial for a funeral home manager as it involves navigating the complexities of grief, emotions, and diverse cultural backgrounds when interacting with grieving families. A manager adept in human relations can build empathetic connections with clients, ensuring they feel supported and respected during a challenging time, while also fostering a compassionate work environment for the funeral home staff.

4. **Creating a Viable and Workable Environment**: Creating a viable working environment in the funeral home requires a multifaceted approach. First and foremost, fostering a culture of compassion and sensitivity is essential, recognizing the unique challenges that arise in the funeral service industry. Implementing ongoing training programs and professional development opportunities ensures that staff members are equipped with the skills and knowledge needed to navigate the delicate nature of their work. Providing a

supportive work-life balance, acknowledging achievements, and promoting a sense of teamwork contribute to a positive and sustainable atmosphere, encouraging staff commitment and ensuring the funeral home operates smoothly.

5. **Communicating Effectively**: Communicating effectively is integral to funeral home operations, involving clear and empathetic interactions with grieving families to understand their needs and preferences. Funeral home staff must also collaborate seamlessly, ensuring that everyone is informed about service details, scheduling, and any specific requirements. Additionally, effective communication extends to community outreach, marketing efforts, and maintaining a transparent dialogue with regulatory authorities to uphold ethical standards and compliance in the funeral service industry. This may require embracing and integrating new technological advancements in funeral service operations, including digital record-keeping, online web-based tools, and virtual service options.

6. **Regulatory Compliance:** Ensuring adherence to local, state, and federal regulations governing the funeral service industry, including licensing requirements, health and safety standards, and environmental considerations, need to be one of the primary administrative duties of the funeral home manager. Ensuring that employees understand and are properly trained on laws and regulations relating to funeral services is paramount for legal compliance and ethical practices. Managers must provide comprehensive training programs that cover local, state, and federal regulations governing funeral service operations, including licensing requirements, health and safety standards, and documentation procedures. Continuing educational courses are essential to keep staff abreast of any changes in regulations, fostering a well-informed and compliant team within the funeral home.

7. **Financial Management:** Budgeting, financial planning, and cost control to ensure the funeral home's financial stability, sustainability, and the ability to provide quality services within specified price ranges. Financial management is crucial in the funeral home to ensure the sustainable operation of the business, maintain affordability for grieving families, and uphold the highest standards of service by efficiently allocating resources and managing costs.

The funeral home manager plays an important role in creating an environment that supports both the grieving families served by the funeral home and the professional and compassionate staff dedicated to fulfilling the institution's mission.

Servant Leadership

Servant leadership traces its origins to the philosophical and spiritual teachings of ancient cultures and thinkers. The concept is deeply rooted in the teachings of great historical figures such as Laozi and Confucius in China, who emphasized the idea of leaders serving their followers and prioritizing the well-being of the community. In the Western world, the term gained prominence in the 20th century through the writings of Robert K. Greenleaf, a management expert who coined the term "servant leadership" in his influential essay, "The

Servant as Leader," published in 1970. Greenleaf drew inspiration from literature, including Hermann Hesse's "Journey to the East," which portrayed a servant leader guiding a group on a spiritual quest. The concept gained traction in subsequent decades, influencing leadership theories and practices across various sectors, emphasizing a shift from traditional hierarchical models to a more empathetic and service-oriented approach. Today, servant leadership continues to be a significant leadership philosophy, emphasizing humility, empathy, and a commitment to serving the needs of others as the foundation for effective and ethical leadership.

Hermann Hesse's "Journey to the East" is a short story that unfolds as a reflective and allegorical narrative, exploring themes of self-discovery, spirituality, and the nature of leadership. The story is recounted by the protagonist, H.H., who reflects on his involvement with a mysterious and spiritual organization known as the League. The League embarks on a symbolic journey toward the East, signifying the pursuit of higher knowledge, enlightenment, and self-realization. The protagonist introduces the reader to the central figure of the journey, Leo, a seemingly humble servant who unexpectedly emerges as a charismatic and revered leader within the League.

As the League progresses on its journey, Leo embodies the qualities of a servant leader—selflessness, humility, and dedication to the collective well-being of the group. However, the narrative takes a transformative turn when Leo mysteriously disappears, causing the League to disband and leaving H.H. in a state of disillusionment. The disappearance of Leo serves as a pivotal moment, prompting H.H. to reflect on the nature of leadership, the complexities of human relationships, and the pursuit of personal and spiritual truths.

Hesse's work is often interpreted as an allegory, with Leo symbolizing the archetype of the servant leader and the journey representing the metaphorical quest for meaning and enlightenment. The short story delves into the challenges of maintaining faith and purpose, the impact of individual actions on the collective, and the interconnectedness of leadership and self-discovery.

"Journey to the East" is a profound exploration of the human condition, inviting readers to contemplate the complexities of their own journeys, the nature of leadership, and the significance of spiritual and personal quests in the pursuit of a more meaningful existence. The short story continues to resonate for its philosophical depth, allegorical richness, and timeless insights into the complexities of human experience.

Servant leadership holds importance in the context of funeral services, where empathy, compassion, and a deep commitment to serving others are paramount. In the funeral industry, leaders adopting a servant leadership approach prioritize the needs of grieving families and their staff, fostering an environment of understanding and support. A servant leader in funeral services is attuned to the emotional nuances of their clientele, offering guidance with sensitivity, facilitating healing, and ensuring that the bereaved feel genuinely cared for during the grieving process. This leadership style also extends to the funeral home staff, emphasizing their professional and personal development, creating a cohesive team that collaboratively works towards the shared goal of providing dignified and compassionate services. Ultimately, servant leadership in funeral services embodies a profound dedication to the well-being of others during a challenging and sensitive period, making it a fitting approach for those guiding individuals through the complexities of grief and loss. These are some of the key components of Servant Leadership in funeral services:

1. **Listening:** In the realm of funeral services, the concept of servant leadership finds expression through active and empathetic listening. A servant leader in this context recognizes the profound importance of listening to grieving families and understanding their unique needs, concerns, and preferences. By fostering a culture of attentive listening, funeral service providers can offer personalized support, creating a sacred space for families to express their emotions and share memories of their loved ones. This practice goes beyond the transactional aspects of the industry, demonstrating a genuine commitment to serving and comforting others during a challenging time. Through empathetic listening, servant leaders in funeral services not only gain insight into the specific requirements of each family but also build trust, fostering a compassionate and supportive environment for both clients and staff.

2. **Empathy:** Empathy is the ability to understand and share the feelings of another, putting oneself in someone else's shoes to comprehend their emotions and experiences with sensitivity and compassion. It involves not only recognizing the emotions of others but also responding in a way that acknowledges and validates their feelings. In funeral services, empathy is a cornerstone of servant leadership, embodying the understanding and shared feelings that are vital in supporting grieving families. A servant leader in the funeral industry approaches their role with a deep sense of empathy, recognizing the unique and delicate emotions associated with loss. By empathizing with the bereaved, understanding their grief, and providing compassionate support, a servant leader fosters a comforting environment that goes beyond the logistical aspects of funeral services, creating a meaningful and healing experience for those navigating the challenging journey of loss.

3. **Awareness:** In the context of funeral services, awareness in servant leadership extends beyond logistical considerations to a profound understanding of the emotional and cultural dynamics surrounding death and bereavement. A servant leader in the funeral industry possesses a heightened awareness of the diverse needs and sensitivities of grieving families, recognizing the significance of rituals, traditions, and individual preferences. This awareness translates into a proactive approach, ensuring that funeral services are tailored to honor the deceased in a manner that aligns with the cultural and emotional context of the bereaved. By cultivating such awareness, a servant leader contributes to a more meaningful and supportive funeral service experience, demonstrating a commitment to both the specific needs of each family and the broader cultural nuances that shape the grieving process.

4. **Conceptual Thinking**: In funeral services, conceptual thinking within the framework of servant leadership involves the ability to envision and implement innovative approaches that transcend traditional practices. A servant leader in the funeral industry engages in conceptual thinking by considering evolving societal attitudes towards death, embracing technological advancements, and anticipating changing preferences in funeral rituals.

This approach extends beyond the immediate needs of grieving families to envision the broader landscape of the funeral service industry, encouraging creative solutions that cater to a diverse and evolving clientele. By fostering a culture of conceptual thinking, servant leaders in funeral services ensure adaptability, relevance, and a forward-thinking approach that meets the evolving expectations of the community and facilitates meaningful and personalized grieving experiences.

5. **Foresight:** Foresight in the context of servant leadership within funeral services involves a forward-thinking and anticipatory approach to meeting the evolving needs of grieving families and adapting to industry changes. A servant leader with foresight envisions the future landscape of funeral services, considering cultural shifts, technological advancements, and changing preferences in commemorative practices. By proactively anticipating these changes, a servant leader ensures that the funeral home is prepared to offer innovative and relevant services, creating an environment that not only honors the traditions of the past but also embraces the possibilities of the future. Foresight in servant leadership within funeral services is essential for maintaining the funeral home's significance within the community and consistently providing meaningful and forward-looking professional experiences.

A funeral director has one primary role as a servant leader, that is, "to take the death event and help the bereaved connect to their own grieving experience." In this profound role of a funeral director, the principles of servant leadership are exemplified through a commitment to helping individuals navigate their unique grieving experiences. A servant leader in the funeral industry understands that the process extends beyond the logistics of the death event; it involves fostering a compassionate and empathetic environment where individuals can connect with their emotions and memories. By prioritizing the needs of grieving families and providing support tailored to their individual experiences, the funeral director, as a servant leader, facilitates a healing journey. This approach embodies the essence of servant leadership, emphasizing empathy, active listening, and a dedication to guiding individuals through the complexities of their grief with understanding and compassion.

Caring for the Dead

Standard of care *is specific procedures to be followed to ensure that all essential details are addressed in a manner that the reasonably prudent funeral director would follow under the same or similar circumstance.* Additionally, the standard of care establishes a benchmark for ethical and professional conduct, guiding funeral directors to adhere to industry best practices and legal requirements. By consistently implementing specific procedures, funeral service providers uphold a commitment to transparency, integrity, and the responsible stewardship of public health and safety in every aspect of their services. When funeral directors experience litigation, most of the time such legal action is a result from a breach of the standard of care.

Establishing a standard of care for the deceased is a multifaceted commitment within the funeral services industry. Initially, it involves ensuring meticulous attention to the deceased's physical presentation, including embalming, dressing, and preparation for viewings or ceremonies. Protecting public health and safety is an integral component of the standard of care for the deceased as part of these preparations. Adhering to rigorous hygiene practices, proper embalming procedures, and compliance with health regulations and OSHA standards, not only honors the deceased but also ensures the well-being of funeral home staff, grieving families, and the broader community. This standard extends to creating a serene and dignified environment within the funeral home facilities, emphasizing cleanliness, organization, and aesthetic considerations. A commitment to emotional care is equally crucial, requiring funeral service providers to cultivate an atmosphere of empathy and sensitivity, offering bereaved families the space and support to grieve. Adherence to local, state, and federal regulations governing the funeral industry is paramount, encompassing proper documentation, legal compliance, and ethical practices.

Standardized procedures for communication with grieving families, such as clear and transparent service explanations, facilitate trust and provide families with the information needed to make informed decisions. A commitment to continuous training and professional development for staff ensures that the standard of care remains current and aligned with industry best practices. By fostering an atmosphere of respect and compassion, funeral service providers uphold a standard of care that not only honors the deceased but also supports the emotional well-being of those mourning their loss. Overall, the establishment and maintenance of a comprehensive standard of care for the deceased are foundational to the mission of funeral services, reflecting a commitment to excellence, empathy, and the highest standards of service provision.

The responsibility of the funeral director to ensure dignity and respect for the deceased is paramount and extends throughout every stage of the funeral process. Upholding the highest standards of professionalism and empathy, the funeral director plays a crucial role in safeguarding the deceased's dignity, ensuring that all actions, from preparation to ceremony, honor the individual's memory and provide solace to grieving families.

The funeral director bears the responsibility of safeguarding the personal information of the deceased and their families, upholding strict confidentiality standards. Ensuring the privacy and security of sensitive details, such as financial information and personal records, not only respects the wishes of the bereaved but also maintains the trust and integrity of the funeral service profession.

The funeral director holds the responsibility of safeguarding the personal property of the deceased and their families, ensuring it is handled with utmost care and respect. By implementing secure procedures for the storage and return of personal belongings, funeral directors contribute to a sense of trust and security for grieving families during a vulnerable time.

Caring for the Client Family

The relationship between the funeral director and the client family is built on a foundation of empathy, trust, and respect. Funeral directors understand the delicate nature of their role and strive to provide compassionate support while guiding families through the grieving process. Open communication is crucial, as funeral directors must listen attentively to the wishes and preferences of the client family, offering personalized services that honor the memory of the deceased. Additionally, funeral directors actively engage with the community, participating in local events and establishing connections that foster a sense of trust and reliability, ensuring the funeral home remains a respected and integral part of the community fabric.

A funeral director bears a legal obligation to the consumer that encompasses transparent communications, fair business practices, and adherence to applicable laws and regulations. This obligation includes providing accurate pricing information, offering itemized service options, and obtaining informed consent for all services rendered. Funeral directors must navigate the legal landscape to ensure compliance with consumer protection laws, addressing the rights and needs of consumers while maintaining the highest standards of integrity and professionalism in the funeral service industry. Due to the sensitive nature of dealing with people's emotions and feelings, the funeral director must be aware of the legal ramifications for emotional distress.

Funeral directors can be held liable for causing emotional distress in bereaved families if their actions demonstrate negligence, intentional infliction of emotional distress, or a breach of duty. This liability may arise from mishandling the deceased, providing misleading information, or engaging in behavior that exacerbates the grief of the family. Funeral directors must exercise a high standard of care and sensitivity to avoid legal repercussions and ensure that their actions do not contribute to emotional distress during the grieving process.

A funeral director's ethical responsibility encompasses maintaining the highest standards of integrity, honesty, and transparency in all interactions with client families. Upholding confidentiality and privacy is paramount, ensuring that personal information and sensitive details are handled with the utmost discretion and respect. Ethical funeral directors prioritize the well-being of the bereaved, offering compassionate guidance and support while honoring the wishes and cultural preferences of diverse client families. They refrain from engaging in exploitative or deceptive practices, providing clear and accurate information about pricing, services, and available options. Additionally, ethical funeral directors actively engage in continuing education, staying abreast of industry developments and ethical considerations to enhance their professional competence and better serve the needs of grieving families.

Funeral services possess profound psychosocial value by providing a structured and culturally embedded sacred space for individuals to express grief, find solace, and commemorate the life of the deceased. These rituals offer a meaningful framework for the bereaved to process their emotions, fostering a sense of closure and facilitating the beginning of the healing journey. Additionally, funeral services contribute to the creation of a supportive community network, as attendees come together to share memories, offer condolences, and provide comfort to one another. The psychosocial impact of funeral services extends beyond the immediate mourning period, helping individuals navigate the complexities of loss, reaffirming the importance of community support, and promoting a sense of connection and shared humanity in the face of mortality. In the current climate of increasing anti-social behaviors, funeral services play a crucial role in providing a structured and compassionate space for communities to come together, fostering a sense of unity and shared grief. These gatherings not only offer solace to grieving families but also serve as a powerful counterforce to anti-social trends, emphasizing the importance of collective support, empathy, and human connection during challenging times.

The value of educating the community on topics such as funeralization, grief education, ways to memorialize, and funeral options is immeasurable. By providing accessible and comprehensive information, communities can make informed decisions about how to deal with death and grief which inevitably foster a proactive and empowered approach to funeral arrangements. Grief education helps individuals navigate the complex emotions associated with loss, breaking down stigma and promoting open conversations about bereavement. Moreover, understanding various ways to memorialize and diverse funeral options allows for a more personalized and culturally sensitive approach to commemorating the lives of loved ones, contributing to a more compassionate and supportive community response during times of grief. Overall, community education in these areas not only demystifies the funeral process but also promotes a healthier and more informed relationship with death, encouraging a culture that values empathy, understanding, and thoughtful at-need choices when caring for the dead.

Inclusive services for the total community, such as the Holiday Hope for the Bereaved Services during the holidays, exemplify a commitment to supporting individuals from all walks of life through the challenging terrain of grief. These services recognize that the holiday season can intensify feelings of loss and isolation, and thus they aim to create a welcoming and inclusive space for everyone, irrespective of cultural or religious backgrounds. By acknowledging and addressing the specific needs of the bereaved during this time, inclusive services contribute to a sense of community and understanding. Offering support during holidays exemplifies a compassionate approach to funeral services that extends beyond traditional practices, fostering a sense of unity, shared experiences, and healing for individuals navigating the complexities of grief.

Developing a Positive Workplace Environment

Developing a positive workplace environment in the funeral home is essential for fostering a culture of compassion, professionalism, and support among staff. This begins with effective leadership that values open communication, recognizes individual contributions, and promotes a sense of camaraderie. Encouraging ongoing training and professional development creates a team that feels confident and competent in their roles. Emphasizing work-life balance and acknowledging the emotional toll of the profession ensures that staff members are equipped to provide empathetic and high-quality services. A positive workplace environment in the funeral home not only boosts morale among employees but also contributes to a compassionate and comforting atmosphere for grieving families, reinforcing the funeral home's commitment to exemplary service and care.

A negative workplace environment in the funeral home can have profound effects on both staff and the quality of services provided. It may lead to diminished morale, increased stress, and a lack of motivation among employees, ultimately impacting their ability to offer empathetic and compassionate support to grieving families. The emotional demands of the job coupled with a negative work atmosphere can contribute to burnout, affecting the overall well-being of funeral home staff. Additionally, a negative workplace environment may tarnish the reputation of the funeral home, potentially diminishing trust from the community and impacting the business's long-term success. Recognizing the potential consequences, it is crucial for funeral homes to prioritize creating a positive and supportive work environment to ensure the well-being of their staff and the delivery of high-quality services to those in need.

The importance of human relations among the staff in the funeral home cannot be overstated, as it directly impacts on the quality of service provided and the overall well-being of both employees and grieving families. Effective human relations foster a supportive work environment, encouraging open communication, trust, and collaboration among team members. This, in turn, enhances the staff's ability to handle the emotional challenges associated with their roles, promoting resilience and preventing burnout. Positive human relations contribute to a cohesive team, where individuals respect each other's unique skills and perspectives, leading to increased efficiency and a more seamless coordination of funeral services. A strong sense of camaraderie among staff members creates a compassionate atmosphere, which is essential for providing empathetic support to grieving families. By prioritizing human relations, funeral homes can cultivate a workplace culture that values diversity, inclusivity, and mutual understanding, ensuring that the emotional and professional needs of both staff and clients are met with sensitivity and care.

Motivational Theorists

Maslow's "Hierarchy of Needs Theory"

Maslow's Hierarchy of Needs, proposed by psychologist Abraham Maslow in the mid-20th century, was developed as a framework to understand human motivation and behavior. Influenced by his studies in psychology and observations of exemplary individuals, Maslow categorized human needs into a hierarchical structure. The theory posits that individuals strive to fulfill basic physiological needs, safety, social belongingness, esteem, and, ultimately, self-actualization, with each level building upon the foundation of the preceding one to describe the progression of human development and motivation.

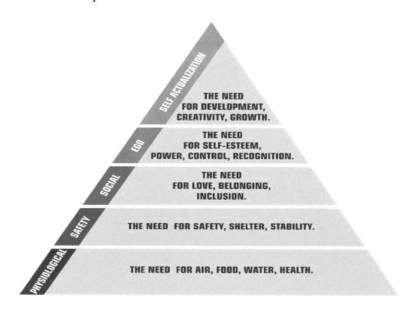

https://www.youtube.com/watch?v=P6PEf9WtEvs&t=9s

The hierarchy is structured as a pyramid, with five distinct levels representing different categories of human needs. At the base are the physiological needs, such as food, water, shelter, and sleep, which are fundamental for survival. Once these basic needs are satisfied, individuals move on to the second level, addressing safety and security concerns, including personal safety, financial stability, and a stable environment. The third level focuses on social needs, encompassing the desire for interpersonal relationships, love, and a sense of belonging within a community or family.

Moving higher up the pyramid, the fourth level pertains to esteem needs, involving the desire for self-esteem, recognition, and a sense of accomplishment. Finally, at the pinnacle of the hierarchy is the concept of self-actualization, where individuals seek personal growth, fulfillment of their potential, and a deeper understanding of themselves. Importantly, Maslow proposed that individuals typically progress through these levels in a sequential manner, with each higher need becoming prominent only after the lower ones are sufficiently satisfied.

Maslow's Hierarchy of Needs has been influential in various fields, including psychology, education, and management, as it provides a framework for understanding human motivation and guiding strategies for personal and organizational development. It emphasizes the importance of addressing basic needs before higher-level aspirations, offering insights into the complexities of human behavior and the pursuit of self-fulfillment.

In the context of the funeral home workplace, Maslow's Hierarchy of Needs provides valuable insights into the dynamics of staff motivation, well-being, and job satisfaction. Beginning with the physiological needs, funeral professionals must have a safe and comfortable work environment, access to necessary resources, and reasonable working hours to ensure their basic survival requirements are met. Safety needs are addressed by implementing clear protocols for handling deceased individuals, maintaining proper hygiene, and ensuring the emotional well-being of staff who routinely face grief and loss as part of their occupational responsibilities.

Moving to the social needs level, creating a supportive and collaborative team environment within the funeral workplace is crucial. Staff members who feel a sense of camaraderie, belonging, and mutual support are better equipped to navigate the emotionally demanding aspects of their roles. Esteem needs in the funeral workplace involve recognizing and valuing the contributions of each team member, providing opportunities for professional development, and fostering a culture that appreciates the significance of their work in the community.

At the highest level of Maslow's Hierarchy, self-actualization in the funeral workplace can be achieved by offering avenues for personal and professional growth. Encouraging staff members to pursue continuing education, mentoring, and exploring innovative approaches to funeral services can lead to a more fulfilling and purposeful work experience. By applying Maslow's Hierarchy of Needs in the funeral workplace, managers can better understand the motivations of their staff and create an environment that supports their holistic well-being, ultimately enhancing the quality of service provided to grieving families.

Herzberg "Two Factor Theory"

Herzberg's Two-Factor Theory, also known as the Motivation-Hygiene Theory, was developed by psychologist Frederick Herzberg in the 1950s. The theory emerged from Herzberg's extensive research on job satisfaction and dissatisfaction, wherein he conducted interviews with hundreds of professionals to identify factors that influenced their attitudes toward work. Herzberg proposed that there are two sets of factors affecting workplace motivation: motivators (or satisfiers), which contribute to job satisfaction and are intrinsic to the work itself, and hygiene factors (or dissatisfiers), which, when absent or insufficient, lead to job dissatisfaction but do not necessarily contribute to motivation when present.

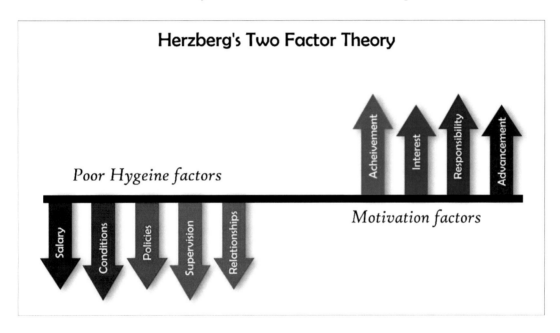

https://www.youtube.com/watch?v=UB2wiubO0fM&t=4s

Herzberg's Two-Factor Theory is a seminal concept in the field of organizational psychology, offering insights into the factors that influence employee motivation and job satisfaction. The theory posits that there are two distinct categories of factors impacting the workplace: hygiene factors and motivators. Hygiene factors encompass elements that, when adequate, prevent job dissatisfaction but do not inherently motivate. These factors include salary, working conditions, company policies, interpersonal relationships, and job security.

Contrastingly, motivators are intrinsic to the job itself and directly contribute to job satisfaction and motivation. Examples of motivators include recognition, achievement, responsibility, advancement opportunities, and the nature of the work. Herzberg argued that improving hygiene factors may only eliminate dissatisfaction, but it does not create motivation. True motivation comes from the presence of motivators, which stimulate a sense of achievement and personal growth. The theory suggests that organizations should strive to provide a work environment where both hygiene factors and motivators are adequately addressed to foster a positive and motivating atmosphere.

Herzberg conducted extensive research using the critical incident technique, interviewing employees to identify specific instances that led to satisfaction or dissatisfaction. The findings revealed that hygiene factors played a role in preventing dissatisfaction, while motivators were key to enhancing job satisfaction. The Two-Factor Theory has practical implications for employee management, as it emphasizes the importance of understanding the dual nature of employee needs. Managers are encouraged to go beyond merely addressing basic hygiene factors and actively cultivate motivators to stimulate long-term employee engagement and satisfaction. The theory also underscores the significance of recognizing individual differences in what motivates employees, highlighting the dynamic and subjective nature of job satisfaction. Herzberg's Two-Factor Theory remains influential in shaping organizational strategies for employee motivation and underscores the need for a comprehensive approach that considers both hygiene and motivational factors in the workplace.

In the funeral home workplace, Herzberg's Two-Factor Theory can be applied to understand and improve employee motivation and job satisfaction. Firstly, hygiene factors such as working conditions and physical facilities play a crucial role. Maintaining a clean, well-equipped, and respectful environment is essential to prevent dissatisfaction among employees dealing with sensitive and emotionally challenging situations.

Salary is another hygiene factor that needs careful consideration in the funeral home setting. Fair compensation is essential to ensure employees feel secure and valued, preventing dissatisfaction. Company policies, including those related to ethical practices and empathetic client interactions, contribute to a positive work environment.

Motivators in the funeral home workplace may include opportunities for personal growth and professional development. Employees who are given the chance to enhance their skills, attend training sessions, or take on additional responsibilities may experience higher job satisfaction. Recognition for their empathetic and compassionate service to grieving families is also a powerful motivator, fostering a sense of achievement and pride.

Responsibility in handling various aspects of funeral arrangements and services can be a motivator, as it provides employees with a sense of purpose and autonomy in their roles. Advancement opportunities within the funeral home, such as promotions to higher positions or specialized roles, can further contribute to employee motivation and job satisfaction.

In summary, applying Herzberg's Two-Factor Theory in a funeral home workplace involves addressing hygiene factors to prevent dissatisfaction and incorporating motivators that promote a sense of purpose, growth, and recognition within the unique context of providing compassionate and respectful funeral services.

McGregor's "Theory X and Theory Y"

Douglas McGregor's Theory X and Theory Y originated from his work and observations on management and human behavior in organizations. McGregor was a social psychologist and management theorist who introduced these two contrasting sets of assumptions about employee motivation and management styles in his book "The Human Side of Enterprise," published in 1960.

Theory X represents a traditional and pessimistic view of human nature and work. According to Theory X, people are inherently lazy, dislike work, lack ambition, and prefer to be directed and controlled. Managers who adhere to Theory X assumptions often use authoritarian and controlling leadership styles, believing that employees need constant supervision to ensure productivity.

On the other hand, Theory Y presents a more positive and modern view of human nature and work. According to Theory Y, people are not inherently lazy; rather, work is seen as a natural and necessary part of life. Theory Y assumes that individuals are capable of self-motivation, enjoy taking responsibility, and can be creative in solving organizational problems. Managers following Theory Y assumptions adopt a participative and collaborative leadership style, trusting and empowering their employees.

McGregor's intent was to challenge traditional management beliefs and encourage a more enlightened and humanistic approach to managing people. His work significantly influenced management and organizational behavior theories, contributing to the development of more participatory and employee-centered management styles in modern organizations. The Theory X and Theory Y framework remains relevant in discussions about leadership and management practices, serving as a foundation for understanding different managerial attitudes towards employee motivation and behavior.

In the context of a funeral home workplace, McGregor's Theory X and Theory Y can provide insights into different managerial approaches and assumptions about employee motivation:

1. Theory X Perspective on Funeral Home Employees: Theory X assumptions may lead some managers to believe that funeral home employees inherently dislike work and require constant supervision. This perspective might result in a more controlling management style, with managers closely monitoring and directing all aspects of funeral service operations.

2. Hygiene Factors and Control in Theory X: Funeral home managers adhering to Theory X might focus on hygiene factors such as strict adherence to policies and procedures, closely overseeing employee activities to ensure compliance with established protocols for handling grieving families and conducting funeral services.

3. Compensation and Incentives in Theory X: From a Theory X standpoint, managers may view financial incentives as crucial for motivating funeral home staff. Salary, benefits, and other tangible rewards might be emphasized to encourage employees to meet performance expectations.

4. Theory Y Perspective on Employee Intrinsic Motivation: Alternatively, a Theory Y perspective in a funeral home workplace recognizes that employees may find meaning and satisfaction in providing compassionate services to grieving families. Managers may believe that employees can be intrinsically motivated to perform well without constant supervision.

5. Recognition and Involvement in Theory Y: Theory Y managers in a funeral home setting may prioritize recognizing employees for their empathy and professionalism. They might involve staff in decision-making processes, allowing them to contribute ideas and suggestions for improving services.

6. Empowerment and Responsibility in Theory Y: Adopting a Theory Y approach, funeral home managers may empower employees by delegating responsibilities related to funeral arrangements and client interactions. This approach assumes that employees can handle tasks autonomously and take ownership of their roles.

7. Professional Growth Opportunities in Theory Y: Managers embracing Theory Y might provide opportunities for professional growth and skill development within the funeral home. Training programs, workshops, and mentorship initiatives could be implemented to support employees' personal and career growth.

8. Team Collaboration and Communication in Theory Y: Theory Y managers may emphasize open communication and collaboration among funeral home staff, recognizing the importance of teamwork in providing seamless and compassionate services to grieving families.

9. Balancing Control and Autonomy: An effective funeral home manager might blend elements of both Theory X and Theory Y, recognizing the need for certain controls while also fostering an environment that encourages employee autonomy and engagement.

10. Impact on Organizational Culture: Ultimately, whether Theory X or Theory Y prevails in the funeral home workplace the organizational culture will be impacted depending on the leadership style of the manager. Theory Y principles may contribute to a more positive and empowering work environment, enhancing employee satisfaction and the quality of services provided to grieving families.

Theory X and Theory Y are important management concepts in funeral home management as they provide a framework for understanding and addressing divergent assumptions about employee motivation. By recognizing the inherent beliefs that shape managerial approaches, funeral home leaders can tailor their management styles to create a more compassionate and effective work environment, ultimately influencing the quality of services provided to grieving families.

https://www.youtube.com/watch?v=kQp9zFHgimU

Ouchi "Theory Z"

William Ouchi introduced Theory Z in his 1981 book, *Theory Z: How American Business Can Meet the Japanese Challenge.* The theory emerged as a response to the success of Japanese companies, particularly in the post-World War II era, and aimed to blend Japanese and American management practices to enhance organizational effectiveness and employee satisfaction. Ouchi's Theory Z combines elements of American and Japanese management philosophies. It posits that a hybrid approach, incorporating the best aspects of both cultures, can result in a more successful and adaptive organizational structure. Central to Theory Z is the notion of a strong company culture built on trust, collaboration, and employee involvement in decision-making processes.

The basic concepts of Theory Z include long-term employment, where employees are viewed as valuable assets and are expected to remain with the company for extended periods. Lifetime employment fosters a sense of loyalty and commitment among workers. The theory also emphasizes collective decision-making, with a focus on consensus and group harmony. Employees are encouraged to participate in organizational decision-making, creating a sense of ownership and shared responsibility.

Additionally, Theory Z highlights the importance of holistic concern for employees' well-being, not only in the workplace but also in their personal lives. Companies following Theory Z often provide comprehensive employee benefits, including social support and a family-like atmosphere within the organization. Work-life balance is a key element, recognizing that employees' personal and professional lives are interconnected.

Quality circles, a concept borrowed from Japanese management practices, are another aspect of Theory Z. These are small groups of employees who voluntarily meet to discuss and solve work-related issues, contributing to continuous improvement and employee engagement. Ouchi's Theory Z represents an attempt to integrate the best practices of both Eastern and Western management styles, fostering a cooperative and adaptive organizational culture.

Critics of Theory Z argue that it may present an overly idealistic and impractical view of organizational management. They contend that the theory's emphasis on long-term employment and lifetime commitment to a single organization may not align with the realities of a dynamic and competitive business environment where job mobility is prevalent. Additionally, skeptics question whether the collectivist decision-making approach advocated by Theory Z is universally applicable, as it might hinder agility and responsiveness in rapidly changing industries.

Critics also argue that the emphasis on consensus and group harmony may stifle innovation and individual creativity within organizations. The theory's focus on employee well-being and benefits may be seen as economically unsustainable for some businesses, particularly in times of financial strain. Furthermore, the transplanting of Japanese management practices into Western cultures may face challenges due to differences in societal values, work ethics, and labor laws, raising questions about the practicality of implementing Theory Z in diverse organizational contexts. Ouchi's Theory Z is impractical in American culture because it attempts to transplant Japanese management practices, which are deeply rooted in different ethical and social demands, potentially clashing with the individualistic and dynamic nature of American organizational and social values.

The primary goal of motivation in the workplace is to inspire employees to give their best effort, perform at their highest potential, and actively contribute to the achievement of organizational objectives. Effective workplace motivation aims to create a positive and engaging environment that fosters job satisfaction, employee well-being, and a sense of fulfillment in one's work. Ultimately, by promoting motivation, organizations seek to enhance productivity, employee retention, and overall success.

Motivation in the funeral home environment is essential for cultivating a compassionate and dedicated workforce, as employees navigate emotionally challenging situations while providing support to grieving families. Recognizing the significance of their roles, motivation can be fostered by acknowledging employees for their empathy, providing opportunities for professional growth, and maintaining a supportive organizational culture that honors the meaningful nature of their work.

Developing Professional Associations

Developing professional relationships in the funeral industry is crucial for creating a supportive and collaborative environment. Building connections with funeral colleagues involves open communication, mutual respect, and a willingness to share knowledge and experiences. Attending industry conferences and workshops provides valuable opportunities to network, exchange insights, and stay updated on best practices within the profession.

Engaging with professional funeral organizations, such as the National Funeral Directors Association (NFDA), National Funeral Director and Morticians Association (NFDMA), or International Cemetery, Cremation and Funeral Association (ICCFA), also state and local funeral directors associations, fosters a sense of community and offers resources for ongoing education and professional development. Collaborating with industry peers through these organizations can lead to the exchange of innovative ideas and the establishment of a network that can prove invaluable in times of need.

In addition to industry connections, developing professional relationships with community organizations is essential for a funeral director. Establishing partnerships with local churches, grief support groups, and hospice organizations can enhance the funeral home's outreach and contribute to a holistic approach to bereavement care. Attending community events, volunteering, and actively participating in local initiatives can strengthen ties with various organizations and position the funeral home as a compassionate and integral part of the community.

Effective communication skills are paramount in building and maintaining professional relationships. Responding promptly to inquiries, demonstrating empathy, and ensuring transparency in all interactions contribute to a positive professional reputation. Collaboration with colleagues, funeral organizations, and community groups not only enriches the funeral director's skill set but also enhances the overall quality of funeral services provided to families in need.

Allied Professional within the Community

Developing professional relationships with allied community professionals is crucial for funeral directors, as it enhances the overall support network available to grieving families. Collaborating with clergy members, such as pastors, priests, or spiritual leaders, ensures a seamless integration of religious or cultural elements into funeral services. Building strong ties with medical professionals, including hospice staff and healthcare providers, facilitates smooth coordination in cases involving terminal illnesses and bereavement care.

Legal professionals, such as estate planning attorneys, can be valuable allies in providing comprehensive guidance to families regarding wills, estates, and other legal matters. Establishing connections with grief counselors and therapists contributes to a holistic approach to bereavement care, offering families additional resources to navigate the emotional challenges of loss.

Funeral directors can also benefit from relationships with local florists, caterers, and event planners, ensuring the availability of seamless logistical support for funeral-related events. Collaborating with transportation services and local authorities helps streamline the process of obtaining necessary permits and coordinating funeral processions.

Community outreach initiatives, such as participating in health fairs or educational events, provide opportunities to connect with allied professionals and reinforce the funeral home's role as a valuable resource in times of need. Regular communication, whether through networking events or professional forums, fosters a sense of mutual understanding and respect among various community professionals.

By actively engaging with allied community professionals, funeral directors not only broaden their support network but also contribute to a comprehensive and compassionate ecosystem that enhances the overall funeral experience for grieving families. These relationships underscore the funeral home's commitment to providing holistic and personalized care during the difficult time of loss.

Technology

Computers have revolutionized the practice of funeral directing. Computerization in business offers numerous advantages that contribute to increased efficiency, productivity, accuracy, and overall competitiveness. Here are some key advantages:

➢ **Automation of Tasks:** Computers can automate repetitive and time-consuming tasks, reducing the need for manual intervention. This leads to increased efficiency and allows employees to focus on more complex and strategic aspects of their work. If information is accurately entered into a funeral home data management system, multiple forms needed to serve the client can be generated in a short period of time.

➢ **Improved Accuracy:** Automated processes are less prone to human error. Computers can perform calculations, data entry, and other tasks with a high degree of accuracy, reducing the risk of mistakes that can occur in manual processes. Utilizing a laptop during the arrangements to enter the information in as part of the conference allows the funeral director and family an opportunity to verify the information for accuracy prior to the end of the arrangements.

➢ **Data Storage and Retrieval:** Computers enable the efficient storage, organization, and retrieval of vast amounts of data. Electronic databases and storage systems provide quick access to information, enhancing decision-making processes. With cloud-based software, client information can be accessed, by using other electronic devices that are also connected to the cloud, such as a sell phone of tablet.

➢ **Enhanced Communication:** Computerization facilitates communication within and outside the organization. Emails, instant messaging, video conferencing, and collaborative tools improve communication efficiency and effectiveness. Especially in the funeral industry when multiple people need access to information, computerization facilitates better communication among the staff.

➢ **Increased Productivity:** With streamlined processes and reduced manual intervention, businesses can accomplish tasks more quickly. This often leads to increased productivity as employees can focus on value-added activities, such as personalizing the funeral services or networking in the community.

➢ **Cost Savings:** While the initial investment in computer systems and software can be significant, the long-term cost savings can outweigh the initial expenses. Automation and efficiency improvements often lead to reduced operational costs over time.

➤ **Corporate Connectivity:** Computers enable businesses to connect globally. Through the internet, companies can reach customers and partners worldwide, expanding their market reach and opportunities for collaboration. This principle is utilized in larger corporate firms to streamline financial and purchasing trends in various marketplaces around the world and between various branch locations in a geographical location.

➤ **Data Analysis and Reporting:** Advanced computing capabilities allow businesses to analyze large sets of data to gain insights into trends, customer behavior, funeral director sales information and market conditions. This data-driven decision-making contributes to strategic planning within the funeral home.

➤ **Adaptability to Change:** Businesses can easily adapt to changes in the market, regulations, or internal processes through the use of flexible computer systems. Software updates and modifications can be implemented to address evolving needs.

➤ **Employee Collaboration:** Collaboration tools and platforms enable employees to work together seamlessly, whether they are in the same location or working between various funeral home locations. This promotes teamwork and knowledge sharing and better communication to increase client satisfaction.

Information Processing Cycle

The information processing cycle, also known as the data processing cycle or simply the processing cycle, is a sequence of steps or stages through which data is input, processed, stored, and output. It is a fundamental concept in computer science and information systems. The cycle typically involves the following four stages:

1. **Input:** *The process of entering data into the computer system. Input is also the information that is entered into a computer from an outside source for processing.* In this stage, raw data is collected and entered the computer system. Input devices, such as keyboards, a mouse, scanners, and sensors, are used to capture data and feed it into the computer for processing. The data may come from various sources, including users, sensors, or other systems.

2. **Processing:** *The rearrangement and refining of raw data into a form suitable for future use.* Once the data is input, the computer's central processing unit (CPU) processes the information. Processing involves manipulating, analyzing, and transforming the data based on predefined algorithms and instructions. This stage is where the actual computation or data manipulation occurs to produce meaningful results.

3. **Storage:** *Processed data and results are stored in the computer's memory or storage devices for future use.* Storage can be temporary (e.g., RAM) or more permanent (e.g., hard drives or solid-state drives). Storing data allows for quick retrieval and reuse, enabling the computer to access and work with information even after the initial processing.

4. **Output:** *The act of returning data to the user in some form or transferring data from a primary storage device to a secondary device.* The final stage involves presenting the processed data or information to users or other systems. Output devices, such as monitors, printers, or speakers, are used to display or communicate the results. Output can take various forms, including reports, visual displays, or digital files, depending on the nature of the processed information and the intended audience.

These four stages collectively form a continuous cycle, as the output from one cycle can become the input for the next. The information processing cycle is fundamental to the operation of computers and information systems, and it occurs rapidly and continuously as users interact with technology. There are often additional stages and considerations within each of the main stages of the information processing cycle, such as data validation, error checking, and feedback mechanisms. The efficiency and accuracy of the information processing cycle are crucial for the effective functioning of computer systems and the successful execution of various tasks and applications.

Selecting a computer system for a funeral home or personal use involves careful consideration of many factors to ensure that the chosen system meets specific requirements and objectives of what applications will best meet the business' needs. The funeral home will need to select **hardware** *(the physical equipment or device which makes up a computer, including all peripherals. Everything except programs or instructions in the computer system)* and **software** *(a set of instructions that directs the computer's operations)* designed to accomplish a data processing function.

1. Determination of need and wants for the funeral home:
   a. Identify what task the computer should perform (i.e. processing information on various forms, recordkeeping, communication information among the staff members, etc.)
   b. Determine how the data is to be entered into the computer.
   c. Determine the format of the output of the data.
   d. Determine storage needs and access to the cloud.
2. Software determination:
   a. Select software that will perform desired tasks and produce desired outputs.
   b. Determine the availability of software technical support.
3. Hardware determination:
   a. Identify the hardware requirements to support software selections
   b. Include provision for upgrading to the hardware.
   c. Determine the availability of service and support from the manufacturer.

Implementing technology is one of the most important functions of office management and the type of computer systems selected, in addition to the software to manage the data, will reduce the amount of time to generate the necessary forms. In addition, the management of information by using technology will increase funeral home productivity and efficiency. The technology selected for the funeral home should be able to:

1. Accurately record financial transactions so that the data can be utilized by a CPA for tax purposes.
2. Manage case information to be in compliance with governmental regulations.
3. Record and tract information regarding the types of funeral business is being conducted to determine trends in the marketplace.
4. Manage merchandise and services utilizing by various vendors and organizations.
5. Facilitate marketing and memorialization to better serve the client-families.

With all equipment in a funeral home, proper training is required by the vender, in-house training, and continuing education opportunities. Utilizing software to maximum efficiency requires a "learning curve," however when mastered, technology should save the funeral home in labor cost, time and accuracy. Eliminating or minimizing human error with the use of technology is a cost savings that could improve a funeral home's profitability at the end of the year.

Implementing technology also needs to have a set of policies and procedures in place to protect personal and business information from unauthorized personnel and the public. These policies and procedures should be a part of the employee handbook and reviewed and the beginning of a person's employment and periodically, to ensure confidentiality and proper conduct when using technology in the workplace. Establishing clear and comprehensive policies for using technology in the workplace is essential to ensure a secure, efficient, and productive work environment. These policies help guide employees in the proper use of technology resources and protect the organization from potential risks. Here are some key areas to consider when developing technology usage policies:

1. **Acceptable Use Policy (AUP):** Clearly outline the acceptable uses of technology resources within the workplace. Specify the permitted and prohibited activities related to internet usage, email communication, social media, and other technology tools. Contracting a computer virus could corrupt the data system and cost the funeral home thousands of dollars in recovery fees.

2. **Data Security and Confidentiality**: Emphasize the importance of safeguarding sensitive information. Establish guidelines for handling confidential data, encryption practices, and password management. Specify the consequences of unauthorized access or disclosure of confidential information. Some funeral home store photographs, copies of documents like DD214 or a birth certificate, or even fingerprints (for memorialization purposes).

3. **Bring Your Own Device (BYOD) Policy:** If applicable, create guidelines for employees who use their personal devices for work purposes. Define the security measures required for BYOD, such as device encryption, password protection, and remote wiping capabilities. NOT RECOMMENDED!

4. **Network Security:** Outline the protocols and security measures to protect the organization's network. Address issues such as unauthorized access, use of virtual private networks (VPNs), and guidelines for connecting to public Wi-Fi networks.

5. **Software and Application Usage:** Specify the types of software and applications that employees are authorized to install and use on company devices. Address licensing agreements, updates, and restrictions on downloading or installing unauthorized software.

6. **Email Usage Policy:** Establish guidelines for the appropriate use of email, including rules for personal use, handling sensitive information, and avoiding phishing scams. Encourage professional and respectful communication in business emails.

7. **Social Media Policy:** Clearly define the company's stance on social media use during working hours. Specify expectations regarding employee representation of the company on social media platforms and provide guidelines for responsible social media behavior. Some funeral homes use social media platforms as marketing tools, however a policy needs to be in place to prevent offensive or potentially improper conduct (this includes personal social media communications). Proper netiquette.

8. **Remote Work and Telecommuting Policies:** If applicable, outline policies related to remote work, including expectations for connectivity, data security, and communication protocols. Define the tools and technology that can be used for remote work.

9. **Equipment and Device Usage:** Detail guidelines for the use and care of company-owned equipment, such as computers, laptops, mobile devices, and other technology assets. Specify rules for reporting damage, loss, or theft of equipment.

10. **Monitoring and Privacy:** Clearly communicate the organization's stance on monitoring technology usage. Specify any monitoring practices in place, such as network monitoring, and address employee privacy concerns.

11. **Incident Reporting Procedures:** Establish a clear process for reporting technology-related incidents, security breaches, or any suspicious activities. Ensure that employees are aware of how to report incidents promptly and confidentially.

12. **Training and Awareness:** Provide regular training on technology policies and best practices. Ensure that employees are aware of potential risks and understand their role in maintaining a secure technological environment.

13. **Compliance with Laws and Regulations:** Ensure that technology policies align with applicable laws and regulations, such as data protection and privacy laws. Regularly review and update policies to remain in compliance with legal requirements.

14. **Consequences for Violations:** Clearly outline the consequences for violating technology policies. This may include disciplinary actions, up to and including termination, depending on the severity of the violation.

15. **Continuous Policy Review:** Regularly review and update technology policies to reflect changes in technology, industry best practices, and the evolving needs of the organization. Ensure that employees are informed of any policy updates.

When crafting technology policies, it's crucial to involve all parties involved in funeral home operations. Additionally, policies should be communicated effectively to all employees, and training sessions can be conducted to reinforce understanding and compliance.

FUNERAL SERVICE MANAGEMENT – GLOSSARY

Actuating (directing, leading) – the process of guiding and/or supervising the activities of an organization to achieve plans and objectives.

Advertising – the art of making the public aware of the services or commodities that a business has for sale.

Aftercare (post-funeral counseling) – a means of supplying support after a death has occurred.

Business plan – a summary of how a business owner, manager, or entrepreneur intends to organize the business endeavor and implement the activities necessary for the venture to succeed.

Controlling (evaluating) – the process of measuring organizational and individual performance with predetermined standards or expected results.

Critical incident stress debriefing – a process intended to prevent or limit the development of post-traumatic stress in people exposed to critical incidents.

Directing – (see Actuating)

Disaster – a sudden misfortune, resulting in the loss of life and/or property.

Emergency – an unforeseen combination of circumstances that result in a need for immediate action.

Ergonomics - study of workplace design; the study of how a workplace and the equipment used therein can best be designed for comfort, efficiency, safety, and productivity.

Evaluating – (see Controlling)

Facilities management –the monitoring and maintaining of the funeral establishment, physical plant, workspace and funeral equipment.

Financial management – the utilization and monitoring of assets, revenue, expenditures and capital.

Funeral service management – the administration of a funeral service enterprise, the activities of which encompass marketing, office, human resources, facilities, and financial management.

Goals – broad statements about what an organization wants to achieve; developed in the strategic planning process; they form the basic plan or direction toward which decisions and activities are focused. (Goals are motivational in nature and are usually stated in broad, general terms without reference to a time period).

Human relations – motivating people in organizations to develop teamwork, which effectively fulfills their needs and achieves organizational objectives.

Human Resource Management (Personnel Management) – the process of acquiring, training, developing, motivating, and appraising a sufficient quantity of qualified employees to perform necessary activities; developing activities and an organizational climate conducive to maximum efficiency and worker satisfaction.

Leading – (see Actuating)

Marketing management – the process of planning and executing the development, pricing, promotion, and distribution of an organization's goods and/or services.

Motivating – the process of energizing, channeling and sustaining people's behavior.

Objectives – specific statement of ends, the achievement of which are to be completed within a specific time period. (Objectives are used in the management control process and provide a quantitative and time framework to the organization's goals. Objectives are intended to be accomplished by a specific date and are stated in terms, preferably in such a way that there is some measurable basis for determining the extent to which they have been achieved).

Office management – the supervision of administrative duties, functions and equipment.

Organizing – the process of assigning tasks, allocating resources, and coordinating the activities of individuals and groups to implement plans.

Personnel management – (see Human resource management)

Planning – the process of setting performance objectives and determining what actions should be taken to accomplish them.

Post-funeral counseling – (see Aftercare)

Servant Leadership –a form of leadership that begins with the natural feeling that one wants to serve others first which is a conscious choice that brings one to aspire to lead.

Standards of care – specific procedures to be followed to ensure that all essential details are addressed in the manner that the reasonably prudent funeral director would follow under the same or similar circumstances.

Talent management – a process used by human resource departments to locate, hire, train and retain the best qualified employees.

Third party merchandise sales – in the funeral service context, sales of funeral goods to consumers by sellers other than a funeral establishment.

Total quality management (TQM) – the efforts of all members of an organization directed to ensure that quality in the production of goods and services is achieved.

Vicarious trauma – cumulative transformative effect upon the professional working with survivors of traumatic life events; individual exposure to traumatic events through first-hand account or narrative of an event.

Domain III
Regulatory Compliance

Business Law

Ethics

Funeral Service Law

Federal Trade Commission (FTC) Regulations

Occupational Health and Safety Commission (OSHA)

Business Law

The American legal system is comprised of a group of local, state and federal laws, proscribed under State and Federal Constitutions, that may vary from state-to-state. The federal and state legal system handle both civil and criminal matters and, depending on the type of legal issue, different courts handle different matters. Under the Tenth Amendment of the United States Constitution, issues not specifically persevered as 'federal,' are left to the States to handle. For example, the federal courts handle issues like immigration and bankruptcy, while state courts handle issues such as divorces and child custody. These are civil issues, however state laws towards divorce may vary and the bankruptcy laws remain universal between states. **Law** is a *governmental rule prescribing conduct and carrying a penalty for violation.* Laws may be restrictive or permissive in nature and prohibit and command certain behaviors and actions. These rules of civil conduct determine what is right and outlines what type of behaviors are prohibited in society. In the event that a person has a disagreement with a law and they feel that their civil liberties have been violated, and after exhausting lower court rulings on the matter, a final appeal to the United States Supreme Court can be made to determine if the Constitutional rights of the person has been violated.

There are four main sources for laws in the United States:
1. **Constitutional Law** - Constitutional law refers to the body of legal principles and rules derived from a country's constitution, defining the structure of government, delineating the powers of its branches, and protecting the rights and liberties of individuals. It serves as the foundation for the legal framework within a nation and guides the interpretation and application of laws in accordance with the constitution.
2. **Statutory Law** – A group of laws enacted by the federal and state that regulate specific act.
   a. **Federal statute:** A federal statute initiates as a bill voted upon by Congress; upon approval, it proceeds to the President of the United States for signing. If signed, it transforms into law, but if challenged as unconstitutional, the US Supreme Court has the authority to overturn it. In the event of a presidential veto, the bill can return to Congress, and with a two-thirds majority approval in both Houses, it can override the veto and become law.
   b. **State statutes:** In a comparable process, the state legislature initiates the creation of a law. The final decision rests with the governor of the state, who holds the authority to either approve or veto the legislation.
   c. **Municipal ordinance**: These are municipal rules applicable solely within the jurisdiction of a specific community. For instance, obtaining a building permit is necessary to place an unanchored 12'x12' shed on a homeowner's property. Such ordinances may vary in neighboring communities.
   d. **Administrative Laws**: Rules and regulations, as well as orders and decisions, are mandates established by state agencies tasked with enforcing specific directives. The administrative regulation governs the conduct of those responsive to the agency.

1) **Federal Administrative Laws**:
   a) **Federal Trade Commission (FTC)** – In the funeral industry, the FTC oversees the profession through the Funeral Rule. This regulation safeguards consumers by granting them the right to choose the funeral goods and services they wish to purchase, offering access to detailed, itemized price information before making decisions, and preventing misrepresentation, unfair, and deceptive practices in the sale of funeral goods and services.
   b) **Occupational Health and Safety Act of 1970** – OSHA. The Occupational Health and Safety Administration is a federal agency responsible for protecting employees from workplace health and safety hazards. OSHA mandates standards that require compliance by the employers.

2) **State Administrative Law** - Funeral **Regulatory Agencies,** have the ability to:

   a) Funeral Regulatory Agencies within the state supervise and enforce regulations on funeral services to guarantee adherence to legal standards and ethical practices.
   b) They set standards for appropriate conduct for funeral directors and embalmers.
   c) These agencies define licensing requirements for funeral homes, funeral directors, and embalmers.
   d) They establish proper business standards for the funeral industry within the state.
   e) Additionally, they formulate rules and regulations governing cemetery and crematory operations within the state.

3) **Police Powers - Police** power generally refers to the fundamental ability of a government to enact laws to coerce its citizenry to engage in conduct deemed 'good' societally. Almost all laws are exercised through this inherent power. State and Federal agencies are granted limited police powers to enforce their regulations, but police powers should not be a stand-alone here unless identifying the basis of the power exercised by legislative bodies and the created agencies. They have the ability to:

   a) Enforces regulatory standards for proper conduct of funeral directors and embalmers.
   b) Enforces licensing requirement for funeral homes, funeral directors and embalmer.
   c) Enforces proper business standards for the funeral industry within the state.

d) Enforces, oversees and monitor cemetery and crematory compliance within the state.

Application of concepts: In New York State, for example, the state legislature passed the Public Health Laws (PHL), a segment of laws which were designed to address the medical and scientific fields, including the practice of funeral directing. The Public Health Commissioner, as well as the local designee County Public Health Directors and Boards, are the administrative powers that oversee the PHL are being followed, The Bureau of Funeral Directing is a designated agency from the State Public Health Commissioner to implement the regulations and licensing of the funeral homes and funeral directors. In the event that a funeral director violates the regulations, a stipulation is issued and the funeral director can either pay the violation or request a public hearing. Once a particular legal issue has been resolved by a court, a precedent or principle has been established which may control future decisions by the courts of the same or lower jurisdiction. If the funeral director is found guilty of the violation, the matter is turned over to the State Attorney General or local district attorney who has the constitutionally granted police power to enforce the penalties and decision from the administrative adjudication.

4) **Case Law** - Case Law refers to the legal principles established through judicial decisions in specific cases, occurring at both state and federal levels. **Stare decisis** is defined as *the principle that the decision of a higher court should serve as a guide or precedent and control that decision of a similar case in the future.*

The judicial system in the United States is hierarchical and depending on the type of civil or criminal matter being tried, will determine which trial court will hear the case. The majority of cases are either resolved outside of the court system or settled at the state or federal level, by inferior courts. In either the state or federal level, there are three levels of adjudication the matter can be heard, however to get to the higher court system, there are certain criteria that need to be met in order for the higher court to hear the case. If a party disagrees with the decision from the lower court, the appeal process can be used to argue why they feel their rights have been violated during the proceedings with such challenges usually based upon a procedural error that occurred during the trial.

Federal Courts

U.S. District Courts

U.S. Courts of Appeals

U.S. Supreme Court

State Courts

State Trial Courts

State Appellate Courts

State Supreme Courts

At the **Federal level**, the court system has three levels:

1. U.S. District Court (94 courts across the country)
2. U.S. Circuit Court of Appeals (13 courts across the country) and finally
3. the U.S. Supreme Court (which only hears cases dealing with cases that invoke a Federal or Constitutional infringement issues). The U.S Supreme Court is the highest court in the land, and they choose annually a very select few number of cases that deal with Constitutional law and that are a violation of person's civil rights or civil liberties.

Generally, at the **State level**, the court system is similar to the Federal system. It also has three levels:

1. State Trial Courts
2. State Appellate Courts and
3. State Supreme Court. On very rare occasions, there are a very few numbers of cases that are referred to the U.S. Supreme Court after this system of appeals have been exhausted.

At the State and Federal levels, there are also specialty courts: At the Federal level, the Bankruptcy Court handles Chapter 7 and Chapter 11 of the Bankruptcy code. Also handle Chapter 13, which is useful for privately-owned and operated funeral home directors as it is a plan of reorganization with debt consolidation for payoff in typically no more than 5 years. and; The U.S. Court of Federal Claims, addresses grievances against the government dealing with financial issues, usually tax issues. The State also has specialty courts; Probate Court, which is a branch of the Surrogate Court, is the court that deals with wills and estates upon the death of an individual and; domestic relations court, i.e. Family Court.

The American Court system is based on an evolution of various systems of laws. **Common law** is *a body of law derived from judicial decisions, rather than from statutes or constitutions.* With the exception of Louisiana, which follows Napoleonic Code of justice instead of Common law, Common law is the foundation for the legal system in America. The basic principle in the legal system is there are a minimum of two sides to every legal issue. In civil cases, there is a **Plaintiff or Petitioner,** a party who initiates a civil action, and a **Defendant or Respondent,** a party against whom legal action is brought. When a **crime** (an offense which is injurious to society as a whole) has been committed, legal action is brought against the person in the name of the citizenry, embodied by a prosecutor. The plaintiff is the prosecutor and acts as the plaintiff on behalf of the citizens or state and the defendant is the party being accused of violating the law [eg. People v Penepent 2006 NY Slip Op 51324(U) [12 Misc 3d 1180(A)]. In this case, a traffic violation, the criminal act was considered an unclassified **misdemeanor** (*a less serious crime punishable by fine and/or imprisonment of less than one year*) and was punished with a fine. However, more serious crimes, such a stealing pre-need funds, may be considered a **felony** (*a serious criminal offense punishable by imprisonment for more than one year or death*).

Civil court procedures begin with a **complaint or petition** – *a document which initiates a civil lawsuit.* The court then issues a summons - *a notice given to a defendant, attaching the complaint and stating a time frame in which to respond.* The defendant then **answers** the summons - *official document responding to the plaintiff's complaint.* Both sides have a period of time to acquire information regarding the matter in dispute. This is known as **discovery** - *the formal and informal exchange of information between sides in a lawsuit.* In some cases, such as small claims, both sides meet with an arbitrator to see if the matter can be resolved outside of a hearing before a judge. If the issue cannot be resolved, the case goes to **trial court,** *the court which conducts the original trial of a case*, where a judge, and sometimes a jury for peers, will adjudicate the matter. Once the case is concluded, the judge will render their opinion, known as a judgment - the decision of the court. Finally, the decision by the court will render an **execution**, which is *the carrying out or completion of some task*, in which the plaintiff or defendant will have to do something or pay an amount to resolve the matter.

Civil law deals with behavior that constitutes an injury to an individual or other private party, such as a corporation.

The four main types of civil law are:
1. Contract Law
2. Property Law
3. Family Relations
4. Negligence (a/k/a Torts) civil wrongs causing physical injury or injury to property.

Contracts

A **contract** is a *legally enforceable agreement* between two or more competent persons (or entities). In order for a contract to be valid, all three of these components must be in place:

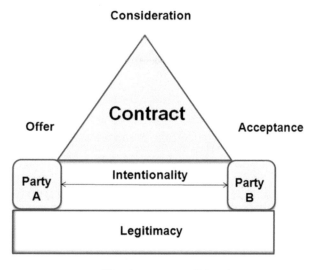

The Contractual Triangle

Valid contract has all for elements must be present:

1. Offer and Acceptance/Contractual Capacity
2. Considerations
3. Legal Purpose

If any one of these components are missing, the contract is void or voidable.

Application of Concept: Mrs. Thompson's husband dies and employs the Blackwell Funeral Home to take care of the arrangements. During the arrangements, Mrs. Thompson discusses they type of services she wishes for her husband. The funeral director creates a Statement of Goods and Services which itemizes the services she selected. The Statement of Goods and Services Selected is a valid contract because all four components of a contract have been fulfilled:

1. Mrs. Thompson requested that Blackwell Funeral Home take care of the funeral arrangements for her husband. The funeral director provided different options and she selected the services for her husband. The funeral director agreed to perform the services selected for an agreed upon fee. This is an Offer and Acceptance.
2. The Blackwell Funeral Home and it's staff performed the necessary services and provided the merchandise selected during the arrangements. These are examples of considerations.

3. Mrs. Thomson is of legal age, and she was mentally capable to make such a decision.

4. Blackwell Funeral Home and its agents are legally licensed by the state to provide funeral goods and services to the public and there is nothing illegal in making funeral arrangements with a licensed funeral home.

A contract is a legally binding agreement between two or more parties that creates obligations enforceable by law. To be valid, a contract typically requires certain essential elements, and the absence of any of these elements may render the contract unenforceable.

The first essential element is an offer. An offer is a clear expression of the intent to enter into a contract, outlining the terms and conditions. It must be communicated to the offeree, the party to whom the offer is made. A valid offer must have a lawful purpose. The subject matter and the terms of the contract must not violate the law or public policy. Contracts involving illegal activities or those against public interest are generally unenforceable. These elements collectively contribute to the formation of a valid and enforceable contract, providing a framework for parties to enter into agreements with confidence in the legal consequences of their commitments.

Consideration is the second critical element. It refers to something of value exchanged between the parties, such as money, goods, services, or a promise to do or refrain from doing something. Without consideration, a contract may lack mutuality and be unenforceable. Legal capacity is a part of this element, ensuring that the parties entering into the contract have the mental competency and legal ability to do so. Minors, individuals under the influence of drugs or alcohol, and those lacking mental capacity may not have the legal capacity to enter a contract.

The final element is acceptance, where the offeree agrees to the terms of the offer. Acceptance must be unequivocal and communicated to the offeror to create a binding agreement. It remains possible to establish the essential term of acceptance based upon the actions of the parties even if no document has been signed by both parties but the action, still, must be unequivocal demonstrating reliance upon the promises and obligations of the agreement.

Valid, Void, Voidable, Unenforceable and Breach of Contract

A **valid contract** is one that meets all the essential elements required by law, including an offer, acceptance, consideration, legal capacity, and a lawful purpose. It is legally binding and enforceable by the parties involved. Conversely, a void contract is considered null and void from its inception. It lacks one or more essential elements, such as legality or capacity, making it unenforceable. Essentially, it is as if the contract never existed.

A **voidable contract**, on the other hand, is initially valid but contains a defect that allows one party to void the contract if they choose. This might be due to fraud, duress, undue influence, or a lack of capacity. The party with the power to void the contract can either affirm it or choose to void it based on the circumstances. Voidable contracts are enforceable unless the party with the power to void exercises that right.

A **void contract** is a legal agreement that lacks one or more essential elements, making it null and void from its inception. For instance, a contract to perform an illegal act, like selling stolen goods, is considered void and unenforceable.

An **unenforceable** contract is a legal agreement that cannot be enforced in a court of law due to the violation of certain legal principles or requirements, even though it may initially appear valid. For example, a contract based on an illegal purpose, such as a contract to engage in unlawful activities, is typically deemed unenforceable.

A **breach of contract** occurs when one party fails to perform its obligations under a valid contract without a legal excuse. This can involve a failure to deliver goods, provide services, or fulfill any other agreed-upon terms. A breach can be material or minor, and the non-breaching party may seek remedies such as damages, specific performance, or cancellation of the contract. The innocent party is entitled to compensation for losses resulting from the breach.

In summary, a valid contract is legally enforceable, a void contract is null and void, a voidable contract can be voided by one party, and a breach of contract occurs when one party fails to fulfill its obligations, leading to potential legal remedies for the non-breaching party.

Classifications of a Contract

An **expressed contract** is a formal agreement where the parties clearly articulate the terms, either orally or in writing, leaving no ambiguity regarding their intentions. The terms are explicitly stated and agreed upon by the parties involved, creating a legally binding relationship.

An **oral contract** is a verbal agreement between parties that is not documented in writing. Despite its informal nature, an oral contract can be legally binding if it satisfies the essential elements of a contract, including an offer, acceptance, consideration, and an intention to create a legal relationship. For example, if a person verbally agrees to sell their bicycle to another person for a specified price, and the second person accepts, this oral agreement may be legally enforceable as a contract if the necessary elements are present and there has been partial performance by the parties.

A **written contract** is a legally binding agreement between two or more parties that is documented in written form, specifying the terms, conditions, and obligations of the parties involved. The agreement serves as a tangible record, providing clarity and evidence of the mutual understanding between the parties. The **Statute of Frauds, an old English Statute incorporated into American Jurisprudence and adopted statutorily in most states (NYS included),** is a legal doctrine that *requires certain contracts to be in writing to be enforceable.* These statutes stipulate that certain types of contracts must be in writing to be enforceable in court.

The Statute of Frauds typically requires written documentation for contracts related to real estate transactions, agreements that cannot be performed within one year, promises to pay the debt of another (suretyship agreements), contracts for the sale of goods over a specified monetary amount, and agreements in consideration of marriage. The purpose of this statute is to prevent fraudulent claims and misunderstandings by ensuring a reliable record of important agreements. By requiring written documentation, the law aims to reduce the potential for false allegations and enhance the credibility of contractual arrangements.

These written requirements are crucial when dealing with significant and potentially contentious agreements, as they offer a clear and tangible record that can be presented in court if disputes arise. For example, a real estate contract involving the sale of a property, a loan agreement with a repayment period extending beyond a year, or a promise to assume another person's debt must be in writing to be legally enforceable. The writing requirement can take various forms, including formal contracts, letters, emails, or other documents that sufficiently capture the key terms of the agreement. In essence, the Statute of Frauds serves as a safeguard, promoting transparency and reliability in contractual relationships.

Bilateral, Unilateral, Executed, and Executory Contract
A **bilateral contract** is an agreement in which both parties make promises to each other. For example, in a purchase agreement, the buyer promises to pay a certain amount, and the seller promises to deliver the specified goods or services. A Statement of Goods and Services Selected, in the funeral industry, is an example of a bilateral contract.

On the other hand, a **unilateral contract** involves a promise from one party in exchange for the performance of a specified act by the other party. A classic example is a reward offer, where the offeror promises a reward in return for the performance of a specific act, like finding a lost item.

An **executed contract** is one where both parties have fulfilled their contractual obligations. For instance, when a person pays for a product in a retail store, both the buyer (who pays) and the seller (who provides the product) have fulfilled their obligations, and the contract is executed.

In contrast, an **executory contract** is a contract where one or both parties have not yet fulfilled their obligations. For example, if you sign a lease agreement to rent an apartment, and you have not yet moved in, the contract is executory until both parties fulfill their respective promises.

In summary, a bilateral contract involves promises from both parties, a unilateral contract involves a promise in exchange for an act, an executed contract is one that has been fully performed, and an executory contract is one where performance is yet to be completed.

Defenses to Enforcement

Several defenses can be raised to challenge the enforcement of a legal contract. **Lack of capacity** is a defense that arises when one or more parties lack the mental or legal capacity to enter into a contract, such as minors or individuals with diminished mental capacity. **Duress** occurs when one party is forced into the contract under threat of harm, making the agreement voidable. Fraud or misrepresentation is a defense where one party intentionally provides false information to induce the other party to enter into the contract. **Undue influence** involves one party exerting excessive pressure on another, undermining their ability to make independent decisions.

Misrepresentation is a defense to the enforcement of a legal contract when one party intentionally provides false information or conceals material facts to induce the other party to enter into the contract. If the misled party can demonstrate that they relied on the misrepresented information and suffered harm as a result, the contract may be voidable due to the misrepresentation.

Illegality is a defense arising when the subject matter or purpose of the contract violates the law or public policy. **Mistake or errors,** whether mutual or unilateral, can be a defense if there is an error in understanding the terms of the contract. The **Statute of limitations** is a defense based on the expiration of the legally allowable time for bringing a lawsuit to enforce the contract. **Impossibility of performance** arises when circumstances beyond the control of the parties make it impossible to fulfill the contract.

Unconscionability is a defense based on the unfairness or oppression of contract terms, particularly if one party takes advantage of the other's vulnerability. **Ambiguity or vagueness** in the contract terms can also be a defense if the parties have different interpretations. **Failure of**

consideration arises when one party fails to deliver what was promised in the contract. **Public policy** can be a defense if enforcing the contract would go against societal interests.

Waiver and estoppel are defenses based on the principle that a party cannot enforce a contractual right if they have waived or are estopped from asserting it due to their conduct. **Illegitimate contracts**, such as those formed through bribery or extortion, are unenforceable. Finally, **frustration of purpose** can be a defense if unforeseen events make the contract's purpose impractical or impossible to achieve. These defenses provide parties with legal grounds to challenge the enforcement of a contract in various situations.

Contract Completion

In contract law, the remedy for a breach of contract can vary depending on the nature and extent of the breach. **Performance** is the ideal remedy, where the breaching party fulfills their contractual obligations as agreed. When a breach is not total but still hinders the contract's purpose, **substantial performance** may be accepted, allowing the breaching party to rectify minor deficiencies. If the breach is fundamental and goes to the heart of the contract, it constitutes a **material or mutual breach**, giving the innocent party the right to terminate the contract and seek damages for the losses suffered. Courts may order specific performance, compelling the breaching party to fulfill their obligations, or award compensatory damages to the innocent party to cover the financial harm resulting from the breach. The appropriate remedy is determined by the circumstances surrounding the breach and the desired outcome of the innocent party.

In contractual relationships, parties may seek various remedies by mutual agreement to address changing circumstances or unforeseen issues. One such remedy is the **mutual agreement to cancel the contract,** where both parties consent to terminate the agreement without legal consequences. **Novation** is another approach, involving the substitution of a new party with the consent of all original parties, releasing the exiting party from their obligations. **Accord and satisfaction** occur when the parties agree to settle a disputed claim by substituting a new performance or payment. These remedies, grounded in mutual understanding and consent, provide flexibility for parties to adapt to evolving situations and resolve disputes amicably without resorting to legal proceedings.

When a party to a contract faces **bankruptcy**, the remedy for the affected party often lies in the bankruptcy proceedings. Bankruptcy may result in the reorganization of the debtor's assets and liabilities, potentially affecting the terms and fulfillment of existing contracts. In the case of an **alteration of a written contract** without the consent of all parties, the innocent party may seek remedies through legal action, as such alterations can render the contract voidable. **Impossibility of performance,** arising from unforeseen events or circumstances beyond a party's control, may lead to the discharge of contractual obligations. For instance, natural disasters like earthquakes or floods, government actions such as sudden regulatory changes, or the death or incapacity of a key individual essential to the contract could render performance impossible and warrant legal consideration for discharge or modification of the contract. The affected party can seek remedies such as the termination of the contract, compensatory damages, or renegotiation. Each situation demands a nuanced approach, considering the specific details and legal implications associated with bankruptcy, contract alteration, or impossibility of performance.

Termination of a Contract & Remedies for Breach of Contract

Termination of a contract can occur through various means, including mutual agreement, performance, impossibility of performance, frustration of purpose, or a material breach by one of the parties. **Mutual agreement** for termination happens when both parties consent to end the contract, releasing each other from further obligations. occurs when the parties fulfill their contractual obligations, leading to the natural conclusion of the agreement. **Impossibility of performance** arises when external factors beyond the parties' control make it objectively impossible to carry out the contract, rendering it void.

Frustration of purpose occurs when unforeseen events make the contract's purpose impractical or impossible to achieve, justifying termination. A **material breach,** where one party fails to fulfill a significant contractual obligation, provides the innocent party with grounds for termination. **Remedies for breach of contract** include damages, which aim to compensate the non-breaching party for losses incurred due to the breach. **Compensatory damages** cover direct losses resulting from the breach, while **consequential damages** address indirect or special losses foreseeable at the time of contract formation. Statutory damages are fixed by law based upon the specific occurrence of an event and are designed to allow a plaintiff to establish a recovery amount where the full extent of their injury is difficult to ascertain.

Liquidated damages, predetermined amounts agreed upon in the contract, serve as compensation for specific breaches. **Restitution** is a remedy where the non-breaching party seeks to recover any benefits conferred on the breaching party. **Specific performance** compels the breaching party to fulfill the contractual obligations as agreed. **Rescission** allows the innocent party to cancel the contract and return to the pre-contract state if the breach is material. **Reformation** is a remedy to correct errors or ambiguities in the contract to reflect the parties' true intentions.

Nominal damages are symbolic amounts awarded when no actual loss is suffered but a legal right is violated. **Punitive damages,** though rare in contract law, may be awarded to punish the breaching party for egregious conduct. **Equitable remedies**, such as injunctions, prevent the breaching party from engaging in certain actions or require specific actions to prevent irreparable harm. The choice of remedy depends on the nature and extent of the breach, aiming to restore the non-breaching party to the position they would have been in if the contract had been properly performed.

Assignments, Delegations and Third-Party Contacts

Assignment, delegation, and third-party contracts are distinct concepts within contract law. **Assignments** occurs when one party, known as the assignor, transfers their rights and benefits under a contract to another party, known as the assignee. The original party, the obligor, must still perform their obligations to the assignee. **Delegations**, on the other hand, involves transferring one's duties or obligations under a contract to a third party, known as the delegatee, who becomes responsible for fulfilling those duties.

Assignments and delegations are often governed by the terms of the contract itself or require the consent of the other party. **Third-party contracts** involve a scenario where a third party, not initially part of the contract, gains rights or incurs obligations. This can happen through assignment or through a specific provision in the contract granting rights to a third party. The rights and obligations of the third party in a third-party contract are typically contingent on the intention of the original parties and the terms of the contract. Properly understanding and managing assignments, delegations, and third-party contracts are crucial aspects of contract law, ensuring clarity and enforceability in complex business arrangements.

Pre-Need and At-Need Funeral Contracts

Understanding the elements of a contract is crucial when creating both at-need and pre-need funeral contracts, as it establishes the legal framework for these agreements. First, clarity in identifying the parties involved, such as the funeral service provider and the client or purchaser, is essential. Second, specifying the considerations, which often involves the cost of funeral services and associated merchandise, ensures mutual understanding of the financial obligations. The terms of the contract, including the scope of services, merchandise details, and any agreed-upon funeral arrangements, need to be clearly articulated. Additionally, the duration or time frame for the performance of the contract, whether immediate or for future pre-need services, must be stated.

Ensuring the capacity of the parties, especially in pre-need contracts, safeguards against potential legal challenges. The contract should account for potential contingencies or changes, providing flexibility for adjustments when necessary. Compliance with applicable laws and regulations, including those specific to the funeral industry, is imperative to avoid legal complications. Incorporating ethical considerations and adherence to industry standards in the contract reinforces trust and integrity. Finally, the signature of both parties signifies mutual consent, making the contract legally binding. Overall, a comprehensive understanding of contract elements is vital to creating transparent, enforceable, and ethically sound at-need and pre-need funeral contracts.

SALES

Uniform Commercial Code

The **Uniform Commercial Code (UCC)** *is a model act that includes provisions concerning certain sales of goods and negotiable instruments.* Specifically, the UCC applies to transactions involving tangible personal property, providing a standardized set of rules and principles to facilitate consistency and fairness in commercial dealings. It establishes guidelines for the formation and enforcement of contracts, warranties, and remedies related to the sale of goods. However, the UCC does not extend its application to real property transactions, which involve immovable assets such as land and buildings. Additionally, it does not govern transactions related to intangible personal property, such as intellectual property or financial instruments. Moreover, the *UCC has limited applicability* to service contracts, *as its primary focus is on the sale of goods* rather than the provision of services. This legal framework serves to streamline commercial transactions involving tangible personal property while leaving other areas of law to regulate distinct aspects of the broader business landscape.

Commercial transactions, sales, and financial contracts are all governed by the Uniform Commercial Code (UCC) in addition to general contract law. It encompasses various types of contracts, including those related to real property, services, intangible assets, and transactions not explicitly governed by the UCC.

UCC Terminology

> **Sale** – *the transfer of title to goods from the seller to the buyer for considerations.*
> **Contract** – *a legally enforceable agreement.*
> **Price** – *the consideration stipulated by a contract, generally expressed in money.*
> **Goods** – *movable tangible personal property.*

Under the Uniform Commercial Code, a **sale** refers *to the transfer of title to goods from the seller to the buyer in exchange for consideration.* A **contract**, as defined by the UCC, is a *legally enforceable agreement governing the terms of the sale or other commercial transactions.* The **price**, a critical element, represents *the consideration stipulated in the contract, usually expressed in monetary terms.* Finally, **goods**, in the context of the UCC, *encompass movable tangible personal property*, emphasizing the legal framework's focus on regulating transactions involving physical, exchangeable assets rather than services or intangible property. This precise terminology provides clarity and standardization in commercial transactions governed by the UCC, promoting consistency and fair dealings in the sale of goods.

Existing goods	*goods which are, at the time of the contract, in existence and owned by the seller.*
Future goods	*goods not in existence or not yet owned by the seller at the time the contract was created.*
Identified goods	*the goods specified by the buyer and seller.*
Title	*ownership; evidence of ownership of property*

An **existing goods** refer to *items that are currently in existence and owned by the seller* at the time of the contract. **Future goods**, on the other hand, *are those items that do not yet exist and are not identified or are not owned by the seller when the contract is formed*. **Identified goods** in the context of the UCC are *those goods explicitly specified by both the buyer and the seller within the terms of the agreement*. This classification system is crucial in delineating the nature and status of the goods involved in a commercial transaction, ensuring precision and clarity in the contractual relationship between the parties.

The acceptance of goods by a buyer, as defined in the Uniform Commercial Code, involves two key elements: First, it requires **the passing of title**, *signifying the transfer of ownership from the seller to the buyer*. Second, acceptance occurs when the buyer signifies the intent to retain the goods. This can manifest through actions like taking possession or making statements that imply satisfaction with the received goods. However, the UCC provides the buyer with the option of revoking acceptance or rejecting the goods under certain circumstances, such as the discovery of defects or nonconformities. For example, if a buyer purchases a batch of electronic devices, title passes upon delivery, but acceptance occurs when the buyer, after inspecting the devices, expresses contentment and retains possession. If later discovering a defect, the buyer may choose to revoke acceptance or reject the goods, triggering the applicable remedies under the UCC.

The Uniform Commercial Code applies to the funeral business in the context of transactions involving the sale of tangible goods, such as caskets or urns. When funeral homes engage in the sale of merchandise, the UCC governs the contractual aspects, including terms, conditions, and warranties. However, it's essential for funeral businesses to also consider industry-specific regulations, ethical standards, and other legal frameworks that may apply to the unique aspects of funeral services.

Transfer of Title & Risk and Loss

The transfer of title and risk of loss are crucial concepts in the realm of commercial transactions, especially in the sale of goods. The transfer of title refers to the passing of ownership rights from the seller to the buyer. This is often accompanied by the physical transfer of possession, but it is not solely contingent on possession. The risk of loss, on the other hand, determines which party bears the responsibility for any damage or loss to the goods during transit. The rules governing the transfer of title and risk of loss are often outlined in the sales contract and may be influenced by various factors, including the delivery terms specified in the agreement.

In the context of a Bill of Lading (BOL) and a Bill of Sale, these documents play distinct roles in the transfer of goods. A **Bill of Lading** is *the contract existing between the consignor and the carrier*. It serves as both a receipt and a contract of carriage, detailing the quantity, condition, and destination of the goods. The transfer of a Bill of Lading can represent the transfer of title and may impact the risk of loss. Conversely, a **Bill of Sale** is *a legal document that conveys or is evidence of title to tangible personal property*. It serves as a comprehensive record of the transaction, providing details about the parties involved, the goods sold, and the terms of the sale. In the funeral industry, a Bill of Sale may be used to document the transfer of ownership for a pre-purchased burial plot from a cemetery to an individual purchaser. Both documents play essential roles in facilitating and documenting the transfer of goods in commercial transactions.

Warranties

Under the Uniform Commercial Code (UCC), the warranty of title is a guarantee provided by the seller to the buyer that the goods being sold are free from any third-party claims or legal encumbrances. Essentially, it ensures that the seller has legal ownership and the right to transfer ownership of the goods. If the buyer discovers a breach of the warranty of title, they may have legal recourse against the seller.

The warranty against infringement, also known as the warranty against infringement of intellectual property rights, is a promise made by the seller that the sale of the goods will not infringe upon any intellectual property rights of third parties. This warranty typically covers patents, trademarks, copyrights, or other intellectual proprietary rights associated with the goods. If the buyer discovers that the goods infringe on someone else's intellectual property rights, they may have a legal claim against the seller for breach of warranty. Both warranties play a crucial role in providing assurance to buyers regarding the legal status and non-infringement of the goods being sold under a commercial transaction.

Expressed warranties are explicit promises or guarantees made by the seller regarding the quality, condition, or performance of the goods. These promises can be communicated through statements, affirmations, or descriptions of the goods made by the seller. On the other hand, implied warranties are not explicitly stated by the seller but are automatically imposed by statutory law which are invoked by the circumstances of the sale.

One common implied warranty is the warranty of merchantability, which applies to all sellers, but particularly to **merchant sellers**. It assures the consumers that the goods sold are fit for their ordinary purpose and meet the standard expectations of similar goods in the market. Another implied warranty is the **warranty of fitness** for a particular purpose, which arises when the seller knows or has reason to know that the buyer is relying on their expertise to provide goods suitable for a specific purpose. If the goods fail to meet this purpose, the seller may be in breach of warranty.

Additionally, warranties can arise from circumstances or usage of trade, meaning that certain standards or expectations are established by the industry or trade practices. If the goods deviate from these customary standards and practices, the seller may be in breach of warranty. Understanding these various warranties is crucial for both buyers and sellers to ensure fair and lawful commercial transactions.

In the funeral industry, a casket warranty serves as an example of how warranties apply to the sale of goods, providing assurances to both funeral homes and consumers. An **expressed warranty** in this context could involve the casket company explicitly stating that the casket is made of certain materials, and is free from defects, and will be suitable for use during the funeral service.

Implied warranties also play a role, such as the **warranty of merchantability**. This assures that the casket, being a product offered by a funeral home (a merchant seller), is reasonably fit for its ordinary purpose, which is to serve as a dignified container for human remains. The **warranty of fitness** for a particular purpose might come into play if the funeral director is aware that the buyer has specific requirements, such as wanting a casket suitable for a burial with certain environmental considerations, i.e. biodegradable.

If the casket fails to meet the standards described in the warranty or deviates from the implied expectations, the funeral home and the casket company may be held responsible for breach of warranty. These warranty considerations ensure transparency and consumer protection in the funeral industry, allowing individuals to make informed decisions and have confidence in the quality of the goods they are purchasing for their loved one's funeral services.

Consumer Protection

Consumer protection in the funeral industry is crucial for ensuring transparency, fairness, and ethical practices, given the emotional and vulnerable state of bereaved individuals making funeral-related decisions. Regulations and safeguards help prevent exploitation, deceptive practices, and ensure that consumers receive accurate information, fair pricing, and the quality of services they deserve during a challenging time.

Usury fee typically refers to the illegal or unethical practice of charging excessively high interest rates on loans. The term *usury fee*, **in the funeral industry**, in this context, refers *to the practice of charging consumers an excessively high amount of interest on unpaid account receivable invoices.* However, it's important to clarify that the customary interest fee charged on such outstanding or delinquent accounts should adhere to the interest rates prescribed by law, which is known as statutory interest.

Statutory interest is *the legally established rate of interest that can be charged on overdue debts or unpaid invoices.* It is often set by government regulations or statutes and serves as a fair and standardized measure to prevent usury or excessive interest charges. The specific statutory interest rate can vary depending on the jurisdiction and the type of debt involved. In the funeral industry, adhering to statutory interest rates ensures that the charges for unpaid accounts remain within legal and ethical boundaries, promoting fair and transparent business practices while protecting consumers from exploitative fees.

Regulatory agencies, such as the Federal Trade Commission (FTC) and state funeral regulatory agencies, play a crucial role in safeguarding consumer interests within the funeral industry. The FTC, for instance, enforces the Funeral Rule, which mandates funeral providers to provide clear, itemized pricing information and affords consumers the right to select only the goods and services they desire. State funeral regulatory agencies oversee compliance with local laws, ensuring funeral homes adhere to ethical standards, maintain transparent business practices, and protect consumers from deceptive practices or excessive fees. These agencies set and enforce regulations that promote fair dealing, honest disclosure, and reasonable pricing, fostering an environment where consumers can make informed decisions during a vulnerable time while holding funeral providers accountable for maintaining the highest standards of integrity and service.

Bailments & Possession

Bailor	A party who gives up possession, but not the title, of personal property in a bailment.
Bailee	A party who acquires possession, but not the title, of personal property in a bailment.
Bailment	the transfer of possession, but not title, of personal property under agreement.
Actual Possession of Human Remains	occurs when an individual physically holds or has immediate control over the deceased, such as a funeral director overseeing preparations or transportation.
Constructive Possession of Human Remains	involves having legal authority or control over the disposition decisions, even if the person with such authority is not physically present with the deceased, such as a next-of-kin or designated legal representative.

A bailment is a legal relationship where one person (the bailor) delivers personal property to another person (the bailee) for a specific purpose, with the understanding that the property will be returned or disposed of as agreed upon. The bailor retains ownership of the property during the bailment. In an ordinary bailment, the bailee has a duty to exercise ordinary care in safeguarding the property. For example, in the context of bailment, if a widow entrusts her husband's watch to a funeral director, to be placed on the deceased during the funeral service, a bailment is created. The funeral director, as the bailee, has a duty to exercise ordinary care in safeguarding the watch, ensuring its return to the widow, the bailor, after the service is completed.

The duty of ordinary care in a bailment requires the bailee to take reasonable steps to protect and preserve the property while it is in their possession. This includes keeping the property in a safe and secure location, preventing damage or loss. The bailee must also use the property only for the agreed-upon purpose and not exceed the scope of the bailment without the bailor's consent. If the bailee fails to exercise ordinary care and the property is damaged or lost, they may be held liable for any resulting harm to the bailor.

Furthermore, the bailee is generally not allowed to use the property for their benefit unless such use is explicitly permitted by the terms of the bailment. The bailment relationship may be terminated once the agreed-upon purpose is fulfilled, and the property is returned to the bailor or disposed of according to the terms of the agreement. Overall, a bailment is a legal mechanism that balances the interests of both parties involved in the temporary transfer of personal property, but not title.

The distinction between actual possession and constructive possession of human remains lies in the physical and legal aspects of control. Actual possession occurs when a person physically holds or has immediate control over the human remains, such as a funeral director overseeing the preparation or transportation of the deceased. On the other hand, constructive possession involves legal control, where a person may not have physical contact with the remains but possesses the legal authority or right to control decisions regarding their disposition. For instance, a next-of-kin or a designated legal representative may have constructive possession by virtue of their authority to make decisions about funeral arrangements and the final resting place of the deceased. Understanding these concepts is crucial in delineating responsibilities and rights in the context of handling and caring for human remains.

When human remains are in transit on a common carrier, such as on an airplane, the distinction between actual and constructive possession becomes important. Actual possession occurs when a funeral director or an authorized representative physically accompanies the remains during transportation, ensuring immediate oversight and control. In contrast, constructive possession arises when the legal authority and responsibility for the remains rest with an individual who may not be physically present during transit. This could include a next-of-kin, legal representative, or designated person who possesses the legal right to make decisions regarding the disposition of the human remains while they are in transit. Understanding the nuances of actual and constructive possession in such scenarios is essential for navigating the legal and ethical responsibilities associated with the transportation and care of human remains. Example:

> Mrs. Thompson's husband died. She has actual possession of Mr. Thompson's remains.
> She assigns the Joyovich Funeral Home to take physical possession of Mr. Thompson's remains and prepare them to be sent, via common carrier, to Ohio for burial. Mr. Joyovich now has actual custody while Mrs. Thompson has constructive custody.
> Mr. Joyovich takes Mr. Thompson to the airport and ships his remains to Ohio. The airline now has the actual possession of Mr. Thompson, while Mr. Joyovich retains constructive possession of his remains.
> Once in Ohio, the Greenleaf Funeral Home takes actual possession of Mr. Thompson while Mr. Joyovich retains constructive possession of his remains.
> Mrs. Thompson meets with a Greenleaf funeral director and plans and organizes the burial arrangements of Mr. Thompson. Mrs. Thompson has constructive possession of her husband's remains, while Mr. Greenleaf has actual possession of Mr. Thompson.

In the context of handling human remains, actual possession occurs when an individual physically oversees their care, while constructive possession entails legal authority over disposition decisions, allowing a designated representative, like a next-of-kin or funeral director, to have control even when not physically present.

Negotiable Instruments

Maker	the party who executes a promissory note.
Payee	the party to whom a negotiable instrument is made payable.
Drawer	the person who executes any draft.
Drawee	the person, a company or financial institution ordered to pay a draft.

Draft Check	*a written order by one person directing another to pay a sum of money to a third person.*
Certified Check	*a check for which the bank assures that the drawer has sufficient funds to make payment.*
Cashier's Check	*a check drawn on a bank's own funds and by a responsible bank official.*

A **negotiable instrument** is *a signed document that promises payment to a specified person or assignee drawn in a special form which can be transferred as substitute for money or as an instrument of credit.* The **maker**, often an individual or entity, is *the party who executes a promissory note*, essentially committing to pay a specific sum of money. The **payee**, on the other hand, is the intended recipient to whom the negotiable instrument is made payable, holding the right to receive the funds specified in the document. The **drawer** is the person responsible for executing any draft, which is essentially a written order directing another party, known as the **drawee**, to pay a certain sum of money to a third person. A **promissory note** is *a negotiable instrument containing a promise to pay.*

In the realm of negotiable instruments, specific types of checks further illustrate these concepts. A **certified check**, for instance, involves the bank assuring that the drawer, the individual creating the check, possesses sufficient funds to cover the specified payment. Conversely, a **cashier's check** is a form of negotiable instrument drawn on the issuing bank's own funds and signed by a responsible bank official, providing a secure and reliable method of payment. These roles and terms within negotiable instruments create a framework for financial transactions, ensuring clarity and legal validity in the exchange of funds between parties.

When death occurs, financial institutions may temporarily freeze the deceased individual's funds as a precautionary measure to prevent fraud or mishandling of the person's assets. Some funeral homes may require payments in the form of cashier checks or certified checks due to the precautionary measures taken by these financial institutions. The freezing of the deceased individual's funds for security reasons can lead to delays or restrictions on accessing traditional forms of payment like personal checks. Funeral homes, seeking to ensure secure and immediate transactions, may opt for cashier checks or certified checks, which offer a guarantee of funds. This practice helps streamline the payment process during a sensitive time, minimizing potential complications arising from the temporary freezing of the deceased person's financial assets.

A Certificate of Deposit (CDs) can be utilized by funeral homes as a financial instrument to secure pre-need funds for future funeral expenses. When an individual enters into a pre-need funeral arrangement, they may choose to set aside funds in the form of a CD. In this context, the CD serves as an acknowledgment by a bank of the receipt of money, representing the funds designated for future funeral expenses. The individual and the funeral home agree on the terms of the CD, including the amount deposited, the maturity date, and any applicable interest.

By using CDs for pre-need funds, funeral homes can ensure that the designated funds are safely stored and potentially accrue interest over time. The interest earned is used to offset the rate of inflation when funeral expenses increase. The terms of the CD provide a clear agreement on when the funds will be available for use, aligning with the individual's pre-arranged funeral plan. This approach offers financial security and stability for both the funeral home and the individual, providing a reliable means to cover future funeral expenses while potentially gaining some return on the invested funds through interest earned on the CD.

Employment

Employer liability refers to the legal responsibility of an employer for the actions or negligence of its employees during the course of employment. There are two main types of employer liability: vicarious liability and direct liability, each of which are premised on notions of Agency Law.

Vicarious Liability: Vicarious liability, also known as "*respondeat superior*," holds an employer accountable for the actions of its employees while they are acting within the scope of their employment. Even if the employer did not directly participate in or endorse the employee's actions, they can be held liable for the employee's wrongful conduct or negligence. This doctrine is based on the idea that the employer benefits from the work and services of the employee and, therefore, should bear the responsibility for any harm caused by the employee in the course of their duties.

Direct Liability: Direct liability arises when an employer is held personally responsible for its own actions or negligence, independent of the actions of its employees. This can occur when the employer's policies, practices, or decisions directly contribute to an employee's harmful conduct. For example, if an employer fails to provide proper training, creates an unsafe work environment, or ignores complaints of harassment, they may be directly liable for resulting harm to employees.

Understanding various forms of employer liabilities are essential in determining legal responsibility and ensuring a safe and fair working environment. Both vicarious and direct liability considerations play a crucial role in employment law and legal actions related to workplace issues.

Employees vs Independent Contractors

The primary difference between an employee and an independent contractor in the funeral business, such as a trade embalmer, lies in the nature of their working relationship and the degree of control exercised by the employer.

Employee: An employee is typically hired under an employment contract, either oral or written, which establishes an ongoing relationship between the individual and the funeral home. Employees often work regular hours determined by the employer, and they may be subject to the employer's control over work methods, schedules, and other aspects of their job. Employers are responsible for withholding taxes, providing benefits, and adhering to labor laws, such as minimum wage and overtime regulations, for their employees.

Independent Contractor (e.g. Trade Embalmer): An independent contractor is generally engaged for a specific project or period and operates as a separate business entity. Independent contractors have more autonomy in their work, including the ability to set their own schedules and use their preferred methods to accomplish the task at hand. Contractors are responsible for their own taxes, insurance, and benefits, and they are not entitled to the same employment protections and benefits as employees.

In the funeral business, a trade embalmer may be hired as an independent contractor for specific embalming services. This arrangement allows funeral homes flexibility in utilizing specialized services without the ongoing obligations associated with traditional employment. However, misclassifying workers can have legal consequences, so it's crucial for employers to properly classify individuals based on the nature of their working relationship.

Agency in Employment

Agency in Employment: Agency in employment refers to the legal relationship in which one party (the principal) authorizes another party (the agent) to act on its behalf in dealings with third parties. In the context of employment, the employer is the principal, and the employee is the agent. This agency relationship is established when the employer delegates tasks or responsibilities to the employee as part of their job duties. The employee, as an agent, is expected to perform these tasks in the best interest of the employer and within the scope of their employment.

Authority and Duties: The agency relationship in employment entails the delegation of authority and the acceptance of certain duties. The employer grants the employee the authority to act on its behalf in various capacities, such as representing the company in negotiations, making decisions, or interacting with clients for making and performing funeral arrangements. The employee, in turn, has the duty to carry out these delegated tasks with diligence, loyalty, and adherence to the employer's instructions. The concept of agency extends to the actions of employees, creating legal implications for both the employer and the employee based on the principle of *respondeat superior,* which holds the employer responsible for the actions of its agents within the scope of employment.

Liabilities and Responsibilities: Agency in employment involves legal and ethical responsibilities for both parties. Employers are liable for the actions of their employees carried out within the scope of employment, and employees are accountable for fulfilling their delegated duties. This relationship creates a mutual obligation of trust and good faith. The employer must provide a safe working environment, fair compensation, and adherence to employment laws. On the other hand, employees are expected to act in the best interest of the employer, maintain confidentiality, and avoid conflicts of interest. Understanding and managing the agency relationship is fundamental for establishing a productive and legally compliant employment arrangement.

In the context of employee termination, agency refers to the legal principle that holds employers responsible for the actions of their agents, specifically employees, carried out within the scope of their employment. When an employer terminates an employee, it must be mindful of the potential legal implications arising from the agency relationship. The employer is responsible for ensuring that the termination process adheres to employment laws, company policies, and ethical standards. Misconduct during termination, such as wrongful dismissal or discrimination, can lead to legal consequences for the employer due to the agency relationship, reinforcing the need for employers to act responsibly and within the bounds of the law when ending the employment of an agent, i.e., an employee.

Property

Real property refers to land and any permanent structures or improvements attached to it, such as buildings, houses, trees, minerals, and other assets affixed to the land. It encompasses physical and tangible assets associated with a specific piece of land and typically includes the rights to use, lease, or sell the property. Real property is distinguished from personal property, which includes movable items not permanently affixed to the land. The ownership and transfer of real property are often governed by real property laws, and the property's value can be influenced by factors such as location, size, and the condition of structures on the land.

Real property ownership can be held in different forms, each with its own legal implications. Here are three common ways real property can be held:

Joint Tenancy	In joint tenancy, two or more individuals own the property together. Each joint tenant has an equal and undivided interest in the entire property. One key feature of joint tenancy is the right of survivorship, meaning that if one joint tenant passes away, their interest automatically transfers to the surviving joint tenants. This ensures that the property avoids probate and seamlessly passes to the surviving co-owners.
Tenancy in Common	Tenancy in common allows multiple individuals to own a property together, but unlike joint tenancy, the ownership shares need not be equal. Each tenant in common has a distinct, individually transferable ownership interest. Additionally, there is no right of survivorship in tenancy in common, meaning that if one tenant passes away, their interest becomes part of their estate and is not automatically transferred to the other co-owners.
Tenancy by the Entireties	Tenancy by the entireties is a form of ownership reserved for married couples. It combines elements of joint tenancy and tenancy in common but adds a crucial feature: the right of survivorship. If one spouse passes away, the surviving spouse automatically inherits the deceased spouse's interest in the property. Tenancy by the entireties offers certain legal protections for the property from the individual debts of one spouse.

These methods of holding real property have different legal implications and should be chosen based on the specific needs and preferences of the property owners.

The **transfer of real property** encompasses several essential steps. Initially, the current owner, referred to as the grantor, initiates the process by drafting a legal document known as a Purchase and Sales Agreement. This agreement must provide a precise description of the property and identify the grantee, the intended recipient. Both parties must sign this document in the presence of a notary public to ensure its legal validity. Subsequently, the signed and notarized Purchase and Sales Agreement serves as the contract of sale of real property. Once the considerations of this contract have been met, a deed is issued and recorded with the Clerk in the jurisdiction associated with the property. Depending on the deed type employed, the transfer may include warranties or covenants related to the property's title. Additionally, any existing mortgages or liens on the property may require attention during the transfer process. Overall, the execution and recording of a deed are crucial for a valid and legally recognized real property transfer.

An **abstract of title** is a summary or history of the legal documents and records related to a property's ownership and potential encumbrances, such as liens or easements. It is important prior to the transfer of real property as it provides a comprehensive overview, allowing the buyer and other interested parties to assess the property's title history, verify ownership, and identify any potential issues that may affect the transfer of ownership. The older the property, the longer the abstract of title is likely to be. Some states have established a minimum number of years for which an abstract must look back through the records in order for it to be considered valid.

Title insurance is crucial for protecting property buyers and lenders against potential legal and financial risks associated with the property's title. It provides coverage for unknown or undisclosed issues, such as liens, encumbrances, or defects in the title, ensuring a secure and unclouded ownership transfer.

Insurance

Policy	A legal contract between an individual or entity and an insurance company outlining the terms, conditions, and coverage details of the insurance agreement.
Premium	The amount of money an individual or entity pays to an insurance company in exchange for insurance coverage, usually paid on a regular basis.
Underwriter	A professional who assesses risks and determines the terms and pricing of insurance policies on behalf of an insurance company.
Agent	An individual who represents an insurance company, selling and servicing insurance policies to clients.
Broker	An intermediary who works independently, assisting clients in finding and purchasing insurance policies from various insurance companies.
Insurer	The insurance company that issues the insurance policy and assumes the financial risk covered by the policy.
Insuree	The individual or entity covered by an insurance policy, also referred to as the policyholder or insured.
Beneficiary	The person or entity designated to receive the benefits of an insurance policy, typically in the event of the insuree's death or a specified event.
Policy Lapse	The termination of an insurance policy due to the insuree's failure to pay the required premiums, resulting in a loss of coverage.

An **insurance policy** is a legal contract between an individual or entity (the insuree or policyholder) and an insurance company (the insurer), outlining the terms and conditions of coverage. The **policy** details the agreed-upon protections and benefits, specifying the risks covered, exclusions, and the duration of coverage. The insuree pays a periodic fee, known as a premium, to the insurer in exchange for the coverage provided. The **underwriter**, employed by the insurer, assesses the risk associated with insuring the insuree and determines the appropriate premium and policy terms. An agent, representing the insurer, may sell the policy directly to the insuree, while a broker, operating independently, helps the insuree find suitable coverage from various insurance companies. The insuree is the party covered by the policy, and in the event of a covered loss, the beneficiary, designated by the insuree, receives the benefits outlined in the policy. Failure to pay the required premiums may result in a policy lapse, leading to the termination of coverage.

Types of Policies

Term Life Policy: Term life insurance provides coverage for a specific period, known as the term, such as 10, 20, or 30 years. If the insured individual passes away during the term, the policy pays out a death benefit to the beneficiaries. Term policies do not accumulate cash value and are generally more affordable, making them suitable for individuals seeking temporary coverage.

The contestability clause in an insurance policy allows the insurer to investigate and challenge the validity of the policy within a specific period, often the first two years, in case of material misrepresentation by the policyholder. The suicide clause provision stipulates that if the insured person dies by suicide within a certain timeframe after the policy is issued, typically within the first two years, the death benefit may be limited or excluded, safeguarding the insurer against intentional self-harm.

Whole Life Policy: Whole life insurance offers lifelong coverage, and as long as the premiums are paid, it accumulates cash value over time. Premiums for whole life policies remain constant throughout the policyholder's life, and a portion of the premium contributes to the cash value component. Policyholders can access the cash value through loans or withdrawals, and the death benefit is paid to beneficiaries tax-free.

Universal Life Policy: Universal life insurance is a flexible policy that allows policyholders to adjust the death benefit and premium payments. It consists of two components: a death benefit and a cash value account. Policyholders can allocate premiums and adjust the death benefit based on their changing needs. The cash value component earns interest at a variable or guaranteed rate and can be used to pay premiums or increase the death benefit. Universal life provides a level of flexibility not found in other types of life insurance policies.

Accidental Life Policy: Accident life insurance, also known as accidental death and dismemberment (AD&D) insurance, is a specialized policy designed to provide coverage in the event of death or specific injuries resulting from accidents. Unlike traditional life insurance, which covers a broad range of causes of death, *accident life insurance focuses specifically on accidental fatalities or injuries*. If the policyholder dies due to a covered accident or experiences specified injuries such as the loss of limbs, eyesight, or hearing, the policy pays out a benefit to the designated beneficiaries. This type of insurance is often chosen as a supplementary coverage to traditional life insurance, offering additional financial protection against the unexpected and helping to alleviate the financial burden associated with accidental events.

Assignment of Proceeds for a Life Insurance: A funeral director can accept an insurance assignment of proceeds by working closely with the deceased's family and the insurance company. When a policyholder designates the funeral director as the beneficiary or assigns the policy to cover funeral expenses, the funeral director communicates with the insurance company to verify the policy details and coverage. Upon the insured's death, the insurance proceeds are then directly assigned to the funeral home to cover the costs of the funeral services. Any remaining balance from the insurance policy will be directed to the beneficiary. However, caution is needed when dealing with accidental death policies for such assignments. While accidental death policies specifically cover fatalities resulting from accidents, they often have stringent criteria and exclusions. Funeral directors must carefully review the terms of the policy to ensure that the cause of death aligns with the policy's definition of an accident to avoid complications and delays in receiving the insurance proceeds for covering funeral expenses. It's essential for funeral directors to communicate transparently with the family, guiding them through the process and ensuring that the insurance assignment aligns with the policy's terms.

Business Law - Glossary

Acceptance - an agreement to an offer resulting in a contract.

Accord and satisfaction - an agreement made and executed in fulfillment of the rights one has from a previous contract.

Agent - the party appointed by the principal to enter into a contract with a third-party on behalf of the principal.

Answer – official document responding to the plaintiff's complaint.

Antitrust law - laws which seek to promote competition among businesses.

Apparent authority - the rights an agent is believed to have by third parties because of the principal's behavior.

Appeal – request to a higher court to review a lower court's decision.

Appellate courts - courts that hear cases appealed from a lower court.

Assignee – a third-party to whom rights in a contract are assigned.

Assignment - a means whereby one party in a contract conveys rights to another, who is not a party to the original contract.

Assignor - the party assigning rights in a contract to a third-party.

Authority – power to act for someone else.

Bailee - the party who acquires possession, but not the title, of another's personal property, under agreement.

Bailment - the transfer of possession, but not the title of another's personal property, under agreement.

Bailor - the party who gives up possession, but not the title, of personal property in a bailment.

Beneficiary – recipient of the proceeds of a life insurance policy.

Bilateral contract - a legally enforceable agreement which consists of mutual promises to perform future acts.

Bill of lading - the contract existing between the consignor and the carrier.

Bill of sale - a document that conveys or evidences title to tangible personal property.

Board of directors - a body of persons elected by the stockholders to define and establish corporate policy.

Breach of contract - failure or refusal to perform contractual obligations.

Business law - rules of conduct for the performance of business transactions.

Cashier's check – 1) a check drawn on a bank's own funds and signed by a responsible bank official. 2) a check for which the bank assures that the drawer has sufficient funds to make payment.

Check - an order by a depositor to the bank to pay a sum of money to a payee.

Civil law - the body of law concerned with private or personal rights.

Close (closely held) corporation – a corporation in which outstanding shares of stock and managerial control are held by a limited number of stockholders and is not publicly traded.

Common law - the body of law derived from judicial decisions, rather than from statutes or constitutions.

Compensatory damages - an award paid to the injured party to cover the exact amount of their loss, but no more.

Complaint - the document which initiates a civil lawsuit.

Consideration - the bargained-for exchange in a contract.

Consignee - one who receives goods shipped by common carrier.

Consignor - one who ships goods by common carrier.

Contract - a legally enforceable agreement.

Contract to sell – an agreement to sell goods at a future time.

Contractual capacity - the legal ability to enter into a contract.

Corporation - a business entity created by statute and owned by stockholders.

Counteroffer - a change to an original offer that rejects that offer and becomes a new offer.

Creditor beneficiary - a third-party beneficiary owed a debt by a party to a contract.

Crime - an offense which is injurious to society as a whole.

Criminal law - laws dealing with crimes and the punishment of wrongdoers.

Damages - money that a wrongdoer must pay as the result of a legal action.

Deed – document conveying title to real property.

Defendant - the party against whom legal action is brought.

Delegation - transfer of contractual duties to a third-party.

Disaffirmance - election to avoid a voidable contract.

Discharge - any method by which a legal duty is extinguished.

Discovery – the formal and informal exchange of information between sides in a lawsuit.

Domestic corporation – a business organization that operates in the state that granted the charter.

Donee beneficiary - a third-party beneficiary to whom no legal duty is owed and performance is a gift.

Drawee - the person, company or financial institution ordered to pay a check.

Drawer - the person who executes any check.

Duress - removing one's free will and obtaining consent by means of a threat.

Employee - a person hired to perform work that is directed and controlled by the employer.

Employer - the party who hires employees to do certain work.

Executed contract - a legally enforceable agreement in which the terms have been fulfilled.

Execution - the carrying out or completion of some task.

Executory contract - a legally enforceable agreement in which the terms have not been completely executed or fulfilled.

Existing goods - goods which are, at the time of the contract, in existence and owned by the seller.

Express authority - rights of an agent stated in the agreement creating the agency.

Express contract – an agreement in which the parties communicate their intentions either verbally or in writing.

Express warranty - the actual and definite statement of a seller, either verbally or in writing, at the time of the sale.

Federal Trade Commission (FTC) – an agency of federal government to promote free and fair competition by prevention of trade restraints, price fixing, false advertising and other unfair methods of competition.

Felony - serious criminal offense punishable by imprisonment for more than one year or death.

Fiduciary - a person in relationship of trust and confidence.

Fixture – objects permanently attached to real property.

FOB Destination - a sales contract term where title and risk of loss passes to the buyer when the goods are delivered to the buyer.

FOB Shipment - a sales contract term where risk of loss passes to the buyer when the goods are delivered to the shipper and transportation arrangements are made.

Foreign corporation – a corporation that operates in a state other than where it is chartered.

Fraud - inducing another to contract as a result of an intentionally or recklessly false statement of a material fact.

Future goods - goods not in existence or not yet owned by the seller at the time the contract was created.

General agent - one who is given broad authority to conduct the principal's business.

General partner - individual actively and openly engaged in the business and held to everyone as a partner.

Goods - movable tangible personal property

Identified goods - the goods specified by the buyer and seller.

Implied authority - an agent's authority to do things in order to carry out express authority.

Implied contract – a legally enforceable agreement in which the terms are set by acts or conduct of the parties rather than expressed verbally or in writing.

Implied warranties - protections imposed by law, arising automatically because the sale has been made.

Independent contractor - one who contracts to do jobs and is controlled only by the contract as to how performance is to be rendered.

Injunction - a judicial order or decree forbidding certain conduct.

Intangible personal property - personal property that lacks a physical presence.

Judgment - a decision of a court.

Law - governmental rule prescribing conduct and carrying a penalty for violation.

Limited liability company (LLC) –a business organization that features liability protection and pass-through taxation.

Limited partner - partner whose liability for the firm's debts is limited to the amount of their investment.

Liquidated damages – reasonable damages stipulated in a contract to be paid in the event of a breach.

Mailbox Rule- a mailed acceptance to an offer is effective when posted.

Merchant - a person who deals in goods of the kind or otherwise by occupation purports to have knowledge or skill peculiar to the practices or goods involved in the transaction.

Minor - those persons under legal age; for most states, the standard is under the age of eighteen.

Misdemeanor - a less serious crime punishable by fine and/or imprisonment of less than one year.

Misrepresentation – false statement of a material fact.

Necessaries - items required for living at a reasonable standard (i.e. food, clothing, and shelter).

Negligence - failure to exercise reasonable care.

Negotiable instrument - a writing drawn in a special form which can be transferred as a substitute for money or as an instrument of credit.

Negotiation - the act of transferring ownership of a negotiable instrument to another party.

Nominal damages - small amount awarded when there is a technical breach but no injury.

Offer - a proposal to make a contract.

Offeree - the party to whom an offer is made.

Offeror - the party who initiates or makes an offer.

Ordinance - law enacted by a local unit of government.

Partnership - the voluntary association of two or more people as co-owners of a business.

Payee - the party to whom a negotiable instrument is made payable.

Personal property – movable and tangible property.

Plaintiff - the party who initiates a civil action.

Pre-existing duty rule - no consideration is given for a contract modification if a party is under a pre-existing duty to perform.
Price - the consideration stipulated by contract, generally expressed in money.

Principal - a party who appoints another to serve as an agent.

Private corporation - a corporation formed to carry out some non-governmental function.

Promissory estoppel - an equitable doctrine and substitute for consideration that prevents the promisor from revoking the promise when the promisee justifiably relies to their detriment.

Promissory note - a negotiable instrument containing a promise to pay.

Public corporation - a corporation formed to carry out government functions.

Punitive damages - an award paid to the plaintiff in order to punish the defendant.

Quasi contract – a contract created or implied by law to prevent unjust enrichment.

Ratification - approving an act which was executed without authority; electing to be bound by a voidable contract.

Real property - land and those objects permanently attached to land.

Rescission - to set aside or cancel a contract.

Rejection - refusal to accept.

Revocation - cancellation of an instrument by the maker or drawer; rescinding an offer.

Sale - the transfer of title to goods from the seller to the buyer for consideration.

Secret partner - a partner who is active but unknown to the public.

Service contract - a contract whose subject matter predominantly involves services.

Shareholders (stockholders) - those having title to one or more shares of stock in a corporation; combined, they represent ownership of the corporation.

Silent partner - an individual who takes no active part in the management of a partnership, but has capital invested in the business.

Sole proprietorship - a business owned by one person, who is personally subject to claims of creditors.

Special agent - one authorized by the principal to execute specific act(s).

Specific performance - a remedy by which the court requires the breaching party to perform the contract.

Stare decisis - the principle that the decision of a higher court should serve as a guide or precedent and control the decision of a similar case in the future.

Statute of Frauds - law requiring certain contracts be in writing to be enforceable.

Statute of Limitations - a law that restricts the period of time within which an action may be brought to court.

Statutes - laws which are enacted by legislative bodies.

Stockholders – see shareholders

Subchapter S corporation – business organization in which shareholders are taxed as a partnership (no double taxation) without losing corporation status.

Summons - a notice given to a defendant, attaching the complaint and stating a time frame in which to respond.

Term life policy – contract whereby insurer assumes risk of death of insured for a specific time with no cash surrender value.

Third-party beneficiary - person not party to a contract, but whom parties intended to benefit.

Title – ownership; evidence of ownership of property.

Tort - a private or civil wrong against a person or their property, other than by breach of contract, for which there may be action for damages.

Trial court - court which conducts the original trial of a case.

Undue influence - improper influence that is asserted by one dominant person over another, without the threat of harm.

Unenforceable contract - an agreement which at the current time is not enforceable by law.

Uniform Commercial Code (UCC) - model act that includes provisions concerning certain sales of goods and negotiable instruments.

Unilateral contract - a contract formed when an act is done in consideration for a promise.

Universal life policy – an insurance product combining features of both whole life and term life policies.

Usurious - exceeding the maximum rate of interest which may be charged on loans.

Valid contract - a contract which is legally enforceable.

Void contract - an agreement of no legal effect.

Voidable contract - a contract which would be an enforceable agreement, but due to circumstances may be set aside by one of the parties.

Warranties - guarantees made by a seller that an article, good or service will conform to a certain standard or will operate in a certain manner.

Whole life policy – insurance that covers an insured for life and accumulates cash surrender value.

ETHICS

Ethics and ethical conduct play a major role in funeral services. This basic premise derives from the fact that the funeral professional is serving the members of a bereaved family and has been entrusted with the human remains of their deceased loved one. While dealing with family members in crisis, the funeral director realizes that the decision-making process of these clients may be impaired. The funeral practitioner needs to possess a strong set of ethics and a student in funeral service education needs to develop the same set of standards. This section will discuss the importance of ethics in the funeral profession and proper conduct that exemplifies professional behavior that is expected by society from a funeral director. Proper training in ethics will help funeral service personnel in understanding the need to establish trust and build rapport with the families.

ETHICS

Ethics is *a branch of philosophy dealing with values relating to human conduct, with respect to the rightness and wrongness of certain actions and to the goodness and badness of the motives and ends of such actions.*

Ethics, also known as philosophical ethics, ethical theory, moral theory, and moral philosophy, is a branch of philosophy that involves systematizing, defending and recommending concepts of right and wrong conduct, often addressing disputes of moral diversity. This term comes from the Greek word *ethos*, which means "character." Philosophical ethics investigates what is the best way for humans to live, and what kinds of actions are right or wrong in particular circumstances.

Applied Ethics:

Applied ethics is a discipline of philosophy that attempts to apply ethical theory to real-life situations. The discipline has many specialized fields, such as funeral directing ethics, public service ethics and business ethics.

Applied ethics is used in some aspects of determining public policy, as well as by individuals facing difficult decisions. The sort of questions addressed by applied ethics include: "Is getting an abortion immoral?" "Is euthanasia immoral?" "Do animals have rights as well?" and "Do individuals have the right of self-determination?"

A more specific question could be: "If someone else has a better life than I do, is it then moral to sacrifice myself for them if needed?" Without these questions, there is no clear fulcrum on which to balance law, politics, and the practice of arbitration – in fact, no common assumptions of all participants – so the ability to formulate the questions are prior to rights balancing. But not all questions studied in applied ethics concern public policy. For example, making ethical judgments regarding questions such as "Is lying always wrong?" and, "If not, when is it permissible?" is made prior to any etiquette.

Business ethics:

Business ethics (or corporate ethics) is a form of applied ethics or professional ethics that examines ethical principles and moral or ethical problems that arise in a business environment. It applies to all aspects of business conduct and is relevant to the conduct of individuals and entire organizations.

Business ethics is defined as *a branch of philosophy dealing with values relating to human conduct as it applies to business transactions.* This ethical framework comprises normative and descriptive aspects. In its application as a corporate practice and a specialized career, the emphasis is predominantly normative. Academics seeking to comprehend business conduct utilize descriptive methods. The variety and volume of ethical issues in business stem from the interplay between profit-maximizing behavior and considerations beyond the economic realm. Governments use laws and regulations to point business behavior in what they perceive to be beneficial directions. Most Funeral Directors Associations have some sort of written statement that outlines proper business practices for funeral directors. For example, in 2009, the New York State Funeral Directors Association adopted a Code of Ethics that outlined proper conduct for their members to follow as funeral practitioners.

These codes of ethics addressed five important areas of conduct as professionals:

- ➢ Service to Families,
- ➢ Care of the Decedent,
- ➢ Obligations to the Public,
- ➢ Obligations to the Government and
- ➢ Obligations to Professional Organizations such as NYSFDA.

A **Code of Ethics** *is a declaration or public statement of professional standards of right and wrong conduct.*

The term **moral** is synonymous with," ethical." *Morals refers to the customs, values, and standards of practice of a group, age, or theory, and intended to be timeless.* Morals are the principles that guide a person's behavior within society. These standards of behavior are based on personal judgment, upbringing, societal norms, and values that are developed over time. A person who does not steal or cheat others may be a person with "good moral character." This moral character continues in funeral directing when a funeral director invests the consumer's pre-need funds in accordance with the laws governing funeral directing. An example of a person with poor moral character would be a person who steals pre-need money for their own personal use. When the consumer entrusts the funeral director with pre-need funds, they are entrusting the funeral director to:

1. Reserve these funds in accordance with the guideline established within the profession and
2. Provide the services at a future date.

Morals play a vital role in the practice of funeral directing and embalming, guiding ethical decisions that prioritize the dignity and respect for the deceased. Funeral directors must adhere to moral principles to ensure that the embalming process is conducted with professionalism, sensitivity, and a commitment to preserving the deceased person's appearance and integrity. Upholding high moral standards in embalming contributes to the overall trust and confidence that grieving families place in funeral directors to handle their loved ones with the utmost care and reverence.

Development of Ethics

Philosophy - *the set of values, ideas and opinions of an individual or group and what they believe they know about what they hold to be true.*

Philosophy encompasses the set of values, ideas, and opinions that shape the worldview of an individual or group. It serves as the intellectual foundation that guides decision-making, moral reasoning, and the overall perspective on life. Within philosophy, individuals or groups articulate what they believe to be true about fundamental questions related to existence, knowledge, morality, and the nature of reality. Philosophy represents a dynamic and reflective process through which individuals construct a coherent framework for understanding the world and their place within it.

In society, the philosophy surrounding death is diverse and often influenced by cultural, religious, and personal beliefs. Some cultures view death as a natural part of the life cycle, a transition to another existence, or a reunion with spiritual forces. Others may perceive death as a solemn event, prompting contemplation on the meaning of life and the ethical considerations surrounding mortality. The philosophy of death in society reflects a complex interplay of cultural narratives, religious doctrines, and individual perspectives, contributing to varied attitudes and rituals surrounding the inevitable and universal human experience of death.

Religion - a culturally entrenched pattern of behavior made up of:

> *(1) sacred beliefs,*
> *(2) emotional feelings accompanying the beliefs, and*
> *(3) overt conduct presumably implementing the beliefs and feelings.*

Religion is a culturally entrenched pattern of behavior that encompasses sacred beliefs, emotional feelings associated with those beliefs, and overt conduct meant to implement those beliefs and feelings. First, sacred beliefs are the core tenets and principles that form the foundation of a religious system. These beliefs often involve ideas about the divine, the purpose of existence, and the nature of the human condition. Emotional feelings associated with religious beliefs on the other hand, involve the deep and often intense sentiments individuals experience in connection to their faith, including reverence, awe, joy, or fear.

Overt conduct refers to the observable behaviors and rituals individuals undertake to express and uphold their religious beliefs. This can include practices such as prayer, worship, rites of passage, and adherence to moral or ethical codes. The culturally entrenched nature of religion means that these patterns of behavior are deeply embedded in the traditions, values, and practices of a particular community or society. Religious rituals and ceremonies often serve as a communal expression of shared beliefs, fostering a sense of belonging and identity among adherents. The symbolic and ritualistic aspects of religion play a significant role in reinforcing and transmitting sacred beliefs across generations.

Religious behavior is dynamic and adaptive, evolving over time to meet the changing needs and circumstances of a society. The interplay between sacred beliefs, emotional feelings, and overt conduct creates a comprehensive framework that guides individuals in their understanding of the sacred, shapes their emotional responses, and directs their actions in alignment with their religious worldview. In short, religion is a multifaceted phenomenon deeply ingrained in culture, encompassing a complex interplay of beliefs, emotions, and behaviors that provide individuals with a framework for understanding the sacred and navigating their place in the world.

Values - *beliefs that are held, both consciously and unconsciously, in high esteem*

In funeral directing, values are paramount as they shape the ethical considerations and decisions made during the delicate process of caring for the deceased and supporting grieving families. Funeral directors, guided by their values, prioritize compassion, empathy, and the utmost respect for the deceased and their loved ones. Whether consciously or unconsciously, these values influence every aspect of funeral directing, ensuring a dignified and considerate approach to the profound responsibilities involved in the profession.

Code of Ethics - *a declaration or public statement of professional standards of right and wrong.*

Ethics evolve over a person's lifetime, and these are some of the elements that shape a code of ethics:

a. **Historical (Golden Rule)** - a rule of ethical conduct found in some form in most major religions usually phrased, **"Do unto others as you would have them do unto you"** (Christianity). "What is hateful to you, do not do to your neighbor" (Judaism). "Not one of you truly believes until you wish from others what you wish for yourself" (Islam). "Treat not others in ways that you yourself would find hurtful" (Buddhism).

b. **Personal ethics** - those standards and values that are right for the individual - vary from person-to-person. Some personal ethics are developed by religious upbringing or by being a part of an organization when growing up, such as the Boy Scouts of America, Girl Scouts, or 4-H.

c. **Situational ethics** - *moral principles that vary with circumstances.* An example of situational ethics is the consideration of truth-telling in end-of-life care, where a healthcare professional might choose to withhold information about a terminal diagnosis from a patient if revealing it would cause severe distress, opting for a more compassionate approach based on the specific circumstances and the well-being of the individual involved. Situational ethics recognizes that moral principles can be flexible and contingent on the context, allowing for decisions that prioritize the greater good or minimize harm in specific situations.

      d. **Business ethics** - *that branch of philosophy dealing with values relating to human conduct as it applies to business transactions.* An example of business ethics in funeral directing is transparent pricing and clear communication with grieving families about the costs associated with funeral services. Adhering to business ethics principles ensures that funeral directors prioritize honesty, integrity, and fair practices, fostering trust with clients during a vulnerable and emotionally charged time.

A code of ethics serves as a foundational guide that shapes the conduct of a funeral director, fostering a commitment to professional standards and moral principles. With a clear code of ethics in place, a funeral director is equipped to navigate complex situations with integrity and empathy, placing the needs and wishes of grieving families at the forefront. By adhering to a code of ethics, a funeral director not only builds trust within the community but also establishes a reputation for providing compassionate, respectful, and ethical services in the practice of funeral directing.

Kohlberg's Stages of "Moral" or "Ethical" Development:

Psychologist Lawrence Kohlberg's formulated theory of moral development, inspired by the work of Jean Piaget, outlines stages through which individuals progress in their understanding of morality. Divided into three main levels, each comprising two stages, the theory spans childhood to adulthood. At the pre-conventional level, individuals follow self-interest and adhere to rules to avoid punishment or gain rewards. In the conventional level, moral development is influenced by societal norms and the desire for social approval, while at the post-conventional level, individuals develop an abstract and principled understanding of morality based on universal ethical principles, transcending specific laws. Kohlberg's theory provides a framework for understanding how moral reasoning evolves, emphasizing that moral development is a continuous process influenced by cognitive and social factors.

1. **Pre-moral** - *a stage of moral development in which the individual is characterized as not understanding the rules or feeling a sense of obligation to them.* In the pre-moral stage of moral development, individuals exhibit a lack of comprehension regarding moral rules and do not feel a sense of obligation towards them. At this early stage, ethical considerations and a deeper understanding of right and wrong are yet to fully develop, reflecting a basic level of moral awareness in which individuals may not recognize or adhere to societal norms and expectations.

2. **Pre-conventional** - *a stage of moral development in which moral reasoning is based on reward and punishment from those in authority.* In the pre-conventional stage of moral development, individuals rely on a simplistic form of moral reasoning centered around the anticipation of rewards and punishments from authority figures. At this

stage, moral decisions are guided by a self-centered perspective, where individuals weigh the consequences of their actions in terms of personal gain or avoidance of punishment rather than a more nuanced understanding of ethical principles.

3. **Conventional** - *a stage of moral development in which the expectations of the social group (family, community, or nation) are supported and maintained.* In the conventional stage of moral development, individuals prioritize the expectations and norms of their social groups, such as family, community, or nation, as the basis for ethical decision-making. Moral reasoning at this stage is largely influenced by a desire to conform to societal expectations and maintain social harmony, reflecting a recognition of the importance of adhering to established norms and values within the larger community.

4. **Post-conventional** - *a stage of moral development in which the individual considers universal moral principles which supersede the authority of the group.* In the post-conventional stage of moral development, individuals move beyond conformity to societal norms and instead consider universal moral principles that transcend the authority of any specific group. At this advanced stage, ethical decisions are guided by a personal commitment to principles of justice, fairness, and individual rights, reflecting a mature and independent moral reasoning that may challenge established societal norms for the sake of higher ethical values.

Heinz Dilemma

The Heinz dilemma is a moral thought experiment also crafted by Kohlberg to assess moral reasoning and development. In this scenario, a man named Heinz faces a moral quandary when his wife is terminally ill, and he cannot afford the costly medicine that could save her life. The dilemma revolves around Heinz's decision to either steal the medication or abide by the law and allow his wife to die. Kohlberg used this scenario to study how individuals' approach and resolve moral conflicts, particularly examining the reasoning behind their decisions.

The Heinz dilemma is structured to prompt individuals to consider the conflicting moral principles of preserving life versus respecting property rights and adhering to the law. Responses to the dilemma are categorized into stages of moral development. In the pre-conventional stage, individuals may focus on avoiding punishment or gaining rewards. In the conventional stage, they consider societal norms and expectations, weighing the importance of following the law. The post-conventional stage involves a more abstract and principled approach, with individuals emphasizing universal ethical principles over specific laws.

The Heinz dilemma is not designed to provide a definitive answer but rather to explore the moral reasoning behind different responses. Kohlberg argued that as individuals progress through stages of moral development, their reasoning becomes more sophisticated and guided by higher-level ethical principles. This thought experiment has been widely used in educational and psychological settings to stimulate discussions about ethics, morality, and the factors influencing ethical decision-making.

Gilligan's Theory on Moral Development

Carol Gilligan's theory of moral development, often seen as a critique of Lawrence Kohlberg's work, emphasizes the importance of relationships and care ethics in understanding morality, particularly in the context of female development. Gilligan argued that Kohlberg's original theory focused predominantly on justice-based reasoning but did not adequately consider the perspectives of women. According to Gilligan, women tend to approach moral dilemmas with a greater emphasis on care, compassion, and the interconnectedness of relationships.

Gilligan proposed three levels of moral development: the pre-conventional, conventional, and post-conventional, such as Kohlberg's stages. However, she suggested a different set of criteria for assessing moral reasoning:

1. In the pre-conventional level of moral development, individuals prioritize personal needs and the avoidance of harm. Moral reasoning at this stage is primarily guided by self-interest, where individuals make decisions based on the consequences for their own well-being, seeking to maximize personal gain and minimize potential harm or punishment.

2. The conventional level is characterized by an orientation toward interpersonal relationships and societal expectations. The conventional level of moral development is marked by an increased focus on interpersonal relationships and adherence to societal expectations. Individuals at this stage exhibit a strong desire to conform to established norms, seeking approval from others, and valuing social harmony. Moral decisions are often guided by the perceived expectations of family, peers, and society, reflecting a concern for maintaining positive relationships and upholding shared values within the community.

3. The post-conventional level involves an appreciation of the complexities of moral issues, considering multiple perspectives and adopting principles that prioritize care and justice. In the post-conventional level of moral development, individuals demonstrate an advanced understanding of moral issues, acknowledging their complexity and considering multiple perspectives. At this stage, individuals adopt principles that prioritize both care and justice, recognizing the interplay between personal relationships and broader ethical considerations. Moral decisions are guided by an internalized set of principles that transcend societal norms, emphasizing a commitment to fairness, individual rights, and the well-being of others.

Gilligan's theory challenges the universality of Kohlberg's stages, asserting that women may follow a distinct developmental trajectory shaped by a moral orientation grounded in care and relationships. Gilligan's emphasis on the importance of caring relationships and the recognition of diverse moral perspectives has influenced discussions on gender and morality, enriching the understanding of moral development beyond the framework originally proposed by Kohlberg. Her work has contributed significantly to the broader exploration of ethical reasoning and the multifaceted nature of moral development.

Differences between Ethics and Law:

Ethics and law are distinct concepts, although they share some commonalities. First, ethics refers to a system of moral principles that guide individuals or a group's behavior, emphasizing what is considered right or wrong based on values and beliefs. In contrast, law represents a set of rules established by a governing authority to regulate conduct within a society, with non-compliance often resulting in legal consequences.

Second, ethics is subjective and varies among individuals, cultures, and belief systems, allowing for a broader range of perspectives on what is morally acceptable. Law, on the other hand, is objective and enforced uniformly within a jurisdiction, providing a standardized framework for acceptable behavior.

Furthermore, ethics may involve principles that go beyond legal requirements, allowing individuals to make morally sound decisions even in situations where the law may be silent or insufficient. While law sets a minimum standard of behavior for a society, ethical considerations often encourage individuals to strive for a higher moral standard.

In summary, while *ethics and law both address human conduct, ethics is a broader subjective concept rooted in moral principles, whereas law is a specific, objective set of rules mandated by a governing authority with legal consequences for non-compliance.*

Ethics	Laws
Imposed Internally - Ethics is imposed internally as a set of moral principles and values that guide an individual's behavior, reflecting their internalized beliefs about what is right or wrong. Unlike law, which is enforced by external governing authorities, ethics operates as an internal compass that influences personal choices and conduct based on individual or cultural values.	**Imposed Externally** - Laws are imposed externally by governing authorities to regulate the behavior of individuals within a society. They represent a set of rules that are mandated by external entities and are enforced through legal mechanisms, with consequences for non-compliance.
Concerned with Motives - Ethics is concerned with motives as it delves into the underlying intentions and moral reasoning behind individuals' actions. It focuses on the intrinsic values, principles, and motivations that guide behavior, emphasizing the moral quality of actions beyond their outward consequences.	**Concerned with Overt Acts of Conduct** - Laws are concerned with overt acts of conduct as they primarily address observable behaviors and actions within a society. Unlike ethics, which delves into the motives and moral reasoning behind actions, laws focus on regulating and, if necessary, penalizing external conduct to maintain order and uphold societal norms.

Ethics	Laws
Concerned with the Interest of the Individual in Society - Ethics is concerned with the interests of the individual in society in regard to the moral principles that guide behavior for the greater good and well-being of the community. It involves considering how individual actions impact others and the broader societal context, emphasizing a balance between personal interests and the welfare of the collective.	**Concern with the Interest of Society as a Whole – Laws** are concerned with the interest of society as a whole, aiming to regulate behavior and maintain order for the collective benefit. They are designed to uphold the broader societal norms, values, and well-being, often at the expense of individual interests when necessary for the greater good.

Sometimes ethics and laws may be different. For example: Legally, the law states that human remains must be transported in a vehicle where the remains are obscured from public view. For most funeral directors, this means that the removal vehicle has tinted windows so the view of the deceased on a removal cot is obscured from public view.

The funeral director's van breaks down, so he goes to the hospital with his pick-up truck that has a tonneau cover and makes a removal. As he was loading the human remains into the back of the truck, a patient on the third floor was outraged and snapped a picture. The dilemma is: 1) did the funeral director break the law and 2) is it ethical for a funeral director to use a pick-up truck to make a removal? While the funeral director complied with the law and the human remains were obscured from public view, ethically, society was outraged because the perception of caring for the human remains appeared compromised. A pick-up truck is not perceived by society as being a suitable vehicle for transporting human remains. This underscores the importance of aligning with societal expectations and ethical standards in the sensitive field of funeral services.

Ethics and laws serve as distinct frameworks for guiding human behavior, with differences in their origin, scope, and enforcement mechanisms. Ethics, rooted in personal beliefs, cultural values, and philosophical principles, is a subjective and internalized system of moral guidelines. It extends beyond legal requirements, encompassing a broader range of considerations such as motives and individual values. In contrast, laws are externally imposed, objective rules established by governing authorities to regulate conduct within a society. They focus primarily on overt behaviors and actions, with formal enforcement mechanisms through the legal system, involving penalties for non-compliance. While ethics are flexible and adaptable, accommodating diverse perspectives, laws are more rigid, requiring a formal legal process for modification. Despite these differences, both ethics and laws play crucial roles in shaping behavior, contributing to social cohesion, and addressing individual and societal needs, with areas of overlap where legal requirements may align with ethical considerations.

In the above dilemma, did the funeral director break the law and was his behavior ethically wrong? To answer this question is an example of the complexity of understanding these two concepts.

Individual Ethics

Individual ethics refers to the personal moral principles, values, and beliefs that guide an individual's behavior and decision-making. These ethical foundations are shaped by a variety of factors, including cultural upbringing, religious beliefs, life experiences, and personal reflections. They serve as the internal compass that influences how individuals navigate moral dilemmas and make choices aligned with their own sense of right and wrong.

Individual ethics can significantly impact professional ethics, as one's personal values often influence their approach to ethical considerations in the workplace. The alignment between individual and professional ethics is crucial for maintaining integrity and ethical conduct in a professional setting. When an individual's personal ethics are consistent with the ethical standards of their profession, it fosters a sense of authenticity, trustworthiness, and a commitment to upholding ethical principles in both personal and professional realms. However, conflicts may arise when there is a disconnect between individual and professional ethics, highlighting the importance of self-awareness and ethical reflection to navigate these complexities effectively.

Personal Standards

1. **Culture** - *consists of abstract patterns (e.g., the rules, ideas, beliefs shared by members of society) of and for living and dying, which are learned directly or indirectly.* Culture is comprised of abstract patterns such as rules, ideas, and beliefs that are shared by members of society, influencing how individuals understand and navigate the concepts of living and dying. These cultural patterns are learned through direct or indirect means, shaping the collective perspectives and behaviors surrounding life and death within a particular community or society.

2. **Theism** - *a belief in a god or gods.* Non-Theism (**atheism**) - a belief in no god or gods. Theism involves a belief in one or more gods, emphasizing a divine presence or higher power, while non-theism, often represented by atheism, is characterized by a lack of belief in any god or gods. The key contrast lies in the affirmation of a deity's existence in theism and the absence of such belief in non-theism, reflecting differing perspectives on the divine within these two philosophical attitudes.

3. **Citizenship** - the character of an individual viewed as a member of society. Citizenship *is seen as behavior in terms of the duties, obligations and functions of an individual as a citizen and member of a particular society.* The character of an individual viewed as a member of society encompasses their role as a citizen, defined by their behavior in terms of duties, obligations, and functions within a specific social context. Citizenship, in this context, goes beyond legal status and implies an active engagement with the responsibilities associated with being a member of a particular society, emphasizing contributions and participation in the collective well-being.

Personal standards consist of:

a. Honesty - *having a sense of honor, upright and fair dealing - truthful.*
b. Integrity - *fidelity to the highest degree of honesty and moral principles.*
c. Morality - *a standard of living by the highest degree of honesty and integrity set by customs and values.*

Honesty, integrity, and morality are intertwined concepts that share a foundation in ethical behavior, yet they differ in their scope and application. Honesty involves having a sense of honor, upright conduct, and truthful communication, emphasizing transparency and fairness in one's dealings. Integrity takes honesty to its peak, incorporating fidelity not only to truthfulness but also to the highest moral principles. On the other hand, morality represents a broader standard of living guided by the highest degrees of honesty and integrity, as set by the customs and values of a particular society. ***While honesty and integrity focus on individual conduct, morality extends to societal expectations, reflecting a collective adherence to shared customs and values.*** In essence, while honesty and integrity are personal virtues, morality encapsulates a communal adherence to ethical standards rooted in honesty and integrity.

4. **Family relationships** - Family relationships play an important role in shaping personal standards by influencing an individual's values, beliefs, and moral framework. From an early age, individuals observe and absorb the behaviors, attitudes, and ethical principles modeled by their family members. The family serves as a primary socialization agent, imparting cultural and societal norms that contribute to the formation of personal standards.

Positive family relationships characterized by open communication, trust, and mutual respect can foster a sense of empathy, responsibility, and integrity in individuals. These qualities often become integral components of their personal standards. Conversely, negative family dynamics or exposure to unhealthy behaviors may lead individuals to consciously reject certain standards, adapt alternative values, or strive to break negative cycles.

Family relationships also shape personal standards through the transmission of intergenerational knowledge and traditions. Cultural, religious, and ethical values passed down within families contribute to the establishment of personal standards that align with familial and societal expectations. Ultimately, family serves as a foundational influence on an individual's moral compass, significantly contributing to the development of their personal standards and guiding principles.

Professionalism

Professionalism is of paramount importance in funeral directing as it directly impacts the quality of service provided to grieving families and the overall reputation of the funeral industry. Funeral directors are entrusted with a sensitive and profound responsibility to guide families through one of life's most challenging experiences – the loss of a loved one. Maintaining a high level of professionalism ensures that funeral directors approach their duties with compassion, empathy, and the utmost respect for the deceased and their grieving family members.

Professionalism in funeral directing also establishes and maintains trust within the community. Families rely on funeral directors to handle the logistical, legal, and emotional aspects of funeral services with competence and integrity. By upholding professional standards, funeral directors contribute to the establishment of a supportive and dignified environment during a difficult time. Professionalism is not only a commitment to ethical conduct and proficiency but also a demonstration of understanding and compassion, essential qualities that elevate the funeral director's role beyond a mere service provider to a trusted source of solace and guidance for those mourning the loss of a loved one.

Funeral directors have an obligation to uphold:

1. Service to the community
2. Welfare of the profession
3. Honesty – *acting with a sense of honor and fairness in all dealings.*

A funeral director's obligations extend beyond the immediate responsibilities of arranging and conducting funeral services. The obligations are deeply rooted in principles that prioritize service to the community, the welfare of the profession, and unwavering honesty. First, **service to the community** implies a commitment to providing compassionate support to grieving families and offering guidance through the emotional and logistical aspects of the funeral process. Second, the **welfare of the profession** demands a dedication to upholding the highest standards of practice, contributing to the credibility and trustworthiness of the funeral industry. Third, **honesty** is integral, requiring a sense of honor and fairness in all dealings, from transparent communication with families about costs and services to ethical business practices.

A funeral director's responsibility to the community involves fostering an environment of empathy, understanding, and dignity during a difficult time. Simultaneously, contributing to the welfare of the profession ensures the longevity and positive reputation of funeral services, establishing them as a vital and respected part of society. Upholding honesty reflects not only ethical conduct but also establishes the foundation for trust and integrity in all professional interactions, further solidifying the funeral director's role as a trusted guide for individuals and communities in their moments of grief and loss.

Integrity - *fidelity to the highest moral standards* of fairness and truth in all professional relationships. Integrity is characterized by fidelity to the highest moral standards, emphasizing a commitment to fairness and truth in all professional relationships. It involves a steadfast adherence to ethical principles and a consistent demonstration of honesty, even in challenging situations. In professional contexts, individuals with integrity are trusted for their reliability, transparency, and unwavering dedication to upholding moral values.

Integrity is demonstrated by a person's 'word' or personal commitment. If a person's word can't be trusted, the person lacks integrity. A funeral director's word holds significant weight as it serves as a foundation for building trust with grieving families. Clear and honest communication, coupled with integrity in honoring commitments and promises, establishes the funeral director as a reliable and trustworthy guide during a sensitive and challenging time.

Sources of Ethics

Sources of Personal Ethics	Sources of Professional Ethics
Culture – Culture plays an important role in shaping personal ethics by influencing an individual's values, beliefs, and moral perspectives through the shared customs, traditions, and societal norms of their cultural background.	**Model of Codes of Conduct** – Model codes of conduct in the funeral profession are typically derived from a combination of input from national and international funeral associations, state and local regulations, religious and cultural practices, legal frameworks, funeral service education programs, and industry publications, collectively shaping ethical standards and best practices for funeral directors.
Religion – Religion contributes to personal ethics by providing a moral framework, guiding individuals' beliefs, values, and behaviors based on the teachings and principles of their faith.	**Education** – Education serves as a fundamental source of professional ethics in the funeral profession, instilling ethical principles, codes of conduct, and a commitment to compassionate and respectful practices within future funeral directors through formal training programs and coursework.
Community – Community is an integral aspect of personal ethics as it shapes individual values and behaviors through shared norms, collective expectations, and the social fabric that influences one's sense of responsibility and moral conduct.	**Formal Academics** – Complying with funeral industry standards learned in formal mortuary science education serves as a foundational source of professional ethics in the funeral profession, ensuring that funeral directors adhere to established norms, ethical guidelines, and best practices to maintain integrity and uphold the highest standards of service.
Family & Relationships – Family and relationships are intrinsic to personal ethics, influencing individual values and behaviors through the shared values, role modeling, and interpersonal dynamics within the familial and relational context.	**Field Training – Residencies or Internships** During a funeral director's internship, the employer becomes the primary source and model for proper professional conduct, offering practical insights, guidance, and firsthand examples of ethical practices in the funeral industry.
Career – A career such as funeral directing becomes part of personal ethics as it involves aligning professional responsibilities with one's moral principles, reflecting a commitment to compassion, integrity, and ethical conduct in providing support to grieving families.	**Continuing Education** – Continuing education is a crucial source of professional ethics for funeral directors as it enables them to stay abreast of evolving industry standards, legal regulations, and ethical considerations, fostering a commitment to ongoing learning and the highest standards of service
Public Organizations – Involvement in public organizations such as the Elks Lodge or Masons becomes part of personal ethics by reflecting an individual's commitment to community service, charitable activities, and upholding the shared values and principles promoted by these organizations.	**Regulations and Legal Compliance** – Regulations and legal compliance in funeral directing serve as a foundational source of professional ethics, ensuring funeral directors uphold the law, adhere to ethical standards, and prioritize the well-being and legal rights of grieving families and the deceased.

Ethics in Funeral Services

When facilitating a client-family relationship in the funeral profession, confidentiality emerges as an utmost priority. **Confidentiality** is defined as - *to hold certain information in trust and not disclosing it without proper authorization or authority.* Grieving families entrust funeral directors with sensitive and personal information about their deceased loved ones, as well as details regarding financial matters and family dynamics. Respecting and safeguarding this confidential information not only upholds the trust placed in the funeral director but also preserves the dignity and privacy of the grieving family during a profoundly vulnerable time. The commitment to confidentiality not only aligns with ethical standards but also underscores the funeral director's professionalism and compassion, demonstrating a genuine understanding of the delicate nature of the information shared during the funeral arrangement process.

Knowledge and Factual Information

During the funeral arrangements, providing client-families with knowledgeable and factual representation is an essential aspect of ethical funeral directing. First, in terms of disposition options, funeral directors must educate families about various choices such as burial, cremation, or donation, ensuring they understand the implications, costs, and cultural considerations associated with each option. Second, with service options, funeral directors should present a comprehensive range of funeral services, guiding families through the planning process and ensuring they make informed decisions about ceremonies, rituals, and memorialization. Additionally, offering detailed information on merchandise options, including caskets, urns, and other funeral-related products, helps families make choices that align with their preferences and budget.

Financial transparency is paramount, and funeral directors must provide clear, itemized pricing, complying with state and FTC regulations, discuss payment options, and address any financial concerns to avoid misunderstandings or undue stress during an already challenging time. Furthermore, educating client-families about custody and trusteeship considerations concerning personal effects and human remains helps them make decisions about handling belongings and ensuring the deceased's wishes are respected. In essence, knowledgeable and factual representation empowers client-families to make well-informed choices, fostering transparency, trust, and ethical conduct in the funeral profession.

Respect and Equity in Funeral Services

Providing equitable professional funeral service to all is essential in upholding principles of fairness, respect, and inclusivity within the community. Acknowledging the diverse social groups, including race and ethnicity, religious diversity, lifestyle, gender roles, personal preferences, medical circumstances, socioeconomical status, culture, and veteran status, underscores the importance of treating every individual and family with equal dignity and consideration. Recognizing and respecting these aspects ensures that funeral services are tailored to meet the unique needs and preferences of each group, fostering a sense of cultural competence and sensitivity. By embracing equity in funeral services, funeral professionals contribute to a compassionate and inclusive community environment, where individuals from various backgrounds can navigate the mourning process with understanding, dignity, and a sense of belonging. This approach not only reflects ethical standards but also strengthens the bond between funeral service providers and the diverse communities they serve. Ultimately, equitable funeral services uphold ethical standards and contribute to creating a more compassionate and understanding community.

Ethics in Regard to the Deceased

Safeguarding information is crucial in funeral services both legally and professionally to ensure compliance with privacy laws, maintaining the confidentiality of sensitive details about the deceased and their family. Professionally, it fosters trust with clients, upholding ethical standards by respecting their privacy during a vulnerable time and reinforcing the funeral director's commitment to dignified and responsible handling of personal information.

Informed Consent	Upholding confidentiality and privacy ethics involves obtaining informed consent from the deceased's family before sharing any information or images for educational or other purposes.
Safeguarding Personal Information	Funeral directors must safeguard personal information of the deceased, including medical records and other sensitive details, respecting the family's privacy and adhering to legal requirements.
Secure Handling of Personal Effects	Ethical practices dictate the secure handling of personal effects, ensuring that the deceased's belongings are treated with utmost confidentiality and security and returned to the family without compromise.
Respecting Cultural Sensitivities	Consideration of cultural sensitivities is vital in maintaining confidentiality. Funeral directors should be aware of and respect any cultural practices that may affect the handling of information or personal effects.
Confidentiality in Cause of Death	Ethical guidelines necessitate discretion in disclosing the cause of death, sharing this information only with those entitled to it and with the family's explicit consent.
Limiting Access to Information	Access to confidential information should be restricted to authorized personnel only, with funeral directors and staff adhering to strict protocols to prevent unauthorized disclosure.
Securing Electronic Data	In the digital age, funeral directors must employ secure measures to protect electronic data related to the deceased, ensuring that sensitive information is not vulnerable to unauthorized access or breaches.
Educating Staff on Confidentiality	Funeral home staff should be educated on the importance of confidentiality and privacy ethics, understanding the significance of respecting the deceased's information and maintaining the trust of grieving families.
Transparency in Privacy Policies	Funeral homes should have transparent privacy policies in place, clearly communicating to families how their loved one's information will be handled, shared, and protected during and after the funeral process

Professional Funeral Directing Procedures

Professional procedures in funeral services encompass a set of ethical guidelines and meticulous practices that underscore the industry's commitment to upholding the highest standards. Care and concern for the dignity of the deceased is at the forefront of these procedures, with funeral directors ensuring that every step is taken to preserve the respect and integrity of the individual who has died. This extends from the moment the deceased is received into the funeral home's care to the final presentation during services.

Thoroughness in the preparation of the deceased is a hallmark of professional funeral services. Funeral directors meticulously attend to every detail, including embalming, dressing, and grooming, to present the deceased in a dignified and peaceful manner. This thoroughness reflects the industry's dedication to providing a serene and respectful environment for grieving families. The adherence to professional procedures is evident in the comprehensive documentation and administrative processes involved in funeral services, ensuring legal requirements are met and facilitating a seamless experience for the bereaved.

Beyond legal compliance, professional procedures encompass compassionate communication with grieving families, guiding them through the decision-making process with empathy and understanding. Attention to detail is evident in the organization of funeral services, from coordinating transportation to orchestrating ceremonies, creating an environment that allows families to focus on remembrance and healing. The commitment to professional procedures is not only a testament to the funeral industry's integrity but also a reflection of its role as a source of solace and support during one of life's most challenging moments.

ETHICS WITHIN FUNERAL SERVICE OPERATION

Human Resource Management

Ethical professional conduct in the employer and employee relationship is fundamental to fostering a healthy and productive work environment. Employers are responsible for upholding fair employment practices, ensuring that hiring, promotion, and compensation decisions are made without discrimination and based on merit. Transparency in communication and providing clear expectations and guidelines for employees promotes a sense of trust and accountability. Ethical conduct also involves respecting employees' privacy, safeguarding confidential information, and creating a workplace that values diversity and inclusion. Fair compensation, reasonable working hours, and access to opportunities for professional development contribute to ethical employer-employee relations. Additionally, employers must provide a safe and respectful workplace, addressing any concerns or grievances promptly and impartially. Ethical professional conduct strengthens the employer-employee relationship, fostering a culture of integrity, mutual respect, and collaboration for the benefit of both the organization and its workforce.

Addressing harassment and bullying concerns in the funeral home is imperative to maintain a professional and respectful work environment. Funeral directors must be vigilant in preventing and addressing any form of harassment or bullying among and of staff. Establishing clear policies that explicitly condemn such behavior and providing comprehensive training on workplace conduct is crucial. Additionally, fostering an open communication culture where employees feel safe reporting incidents and seeking support helps create a workplace that upholds the dignity and well-being of every team member.

Proper hiring practices are the cornerstone of professionalism in a funeral home, ensuring that individuals with the right skills, values, and dedication to ethical conduct become integral members of the team. Thorough training programs contribute to professionalism by equipping staff with the necessary expertise, enhancing their ability to provide compassionate and efficient services to grieving families. Continuing education is a significant part of maintaining professionalism, as it keeps funeral directors updated on industry advancements, evolving regulations, and ethical standards, fostering a commitment to excellence. Collectively, these practices not only elevate the professionalism of the funeral home staff but also contribute to the establishment of good business practices, enhancing the reputation and success of the funeral home in the community.

The funeral director should treat interns and apprentices as valuable members of the team, providing them with opportunities to engage in meaningful tasks and learn essential skills rather than relegating them to menial assignments. By fostering a supportive and inclusive environment, the funeral director helps interns and apprentices develop professionally and contributes to a positive and collaborative workplace culture.

The importance of safe working conditions in a funeral home cannot be overstated, and compliance with OSHA regulations, including rigorous monitoring, is essential. Prioritizing a safe workplace not only protects the well-being of funeral home staff, but also ensures that the funeral director meets legal requirements, fostering a work environment that values the health and safety of everyone involved in the funeral service.

Personal appearance is a critical aspect of conveying a positive image of funeral service, as funeral directors often serve as the public face of the profession. Maintaining a professional and well-groomed appearance not only reflects personal pride but also communicates a sense of respect for the solemn nature of the work. By dressing appropriately and presenting themselves in a dignified manner, funeral directors instill confidence in grieving families and contribute to a positive perception of the funeral service industry. A polished personal appearance is integral to establishing trust, professionalism, and empathy, reinforcing the funeral director's role as a compassionate and reliable guide during difficult times.

Allowing Unlicensed Personnel

Allowing unlicensed personnel to conduct activities reserved for licensed funeral director/embalmer is both illegal and unethical for several reasons. First, it violates state and local regulations that require specific licensing for tasks related to funeral directing and embalming. This jeopardizes the legal standing of the funeral home and puts it at risk of facing legal consequences. Second, it undermines the professional standards set by licensing boards to ensure the competency, knowledge, and ethical conduct of those in the funeral service industry. Third, it compromises the quality of services provided to grieving families, as unlicensed personnel lack the necessary expertise and training. Finally, such actions erode public trust in the funeral profession, as it goes against the ethical obligation of transparency and adherence to established standards of care. Unlicensed activities in the funeral home should be documented and reported to the funeral directing regulatory agency. Not reporting unlicensed activities may render the licensed professional complicit in the activity, leading to potential consequences such as the loss of one's professional license and exposure to criminal penalties.

Accuracy and Confidentiality of Records

Accuracy and confidentiality in funeral information are integral to the funeral business for several crucial reasons. First, providing accurate details about funeral services, costs, and procedures is essential to establishing trust with client-families, ensuring transparency, and facilitating informed decision-making during a sensitive and challenging time. Second, maintaining confidentiality of personal and sensitive information, including medical details and family circumstances, is a legal and ethical imperative. Upholding confidentiality safeguards the privacy and dignity of the deceased and their loved ones, reinforcing the funeral director's commitment to ethical practices. Inaccuracies or breaches of confidentiality can not only lead to legal repercussions but can also erode the reputation of the funeral home. Accuracy and confidentiality play an important role in preserving the integrity and professionalism of the funeral business.

Compliance with the Federal & State Laws, Rules and Regulations

Compliance with federal and state laws, rules, and regulations is very important in the funeral home for several compelling reasons. These are some of the ethical reasons for complying with state and federal regulations in the funeral home business:

Legal Standing	Compliance with federal and state laws is essential for the funeral home to maintain its legal standing and operating license, ensuring it can continue to provide funeral services within the bounds of the law.
Consumer Protection	Adhering to regulations safeguards the rights and interests of client-families, providing legal frameworks that ensure fair business practices, transparent service offerings, and protection against potential exploitation of client-families.
Financial Integrity	Compliance is crucial for the accurate and ethical handling of financial transactions, preventing fraudulent practices and ensuring the financial integrity of the funeral home.
Workplace Safety	Adherence to health and safety regulations, including those outlined by OSHA, is vital to maintaining a secure work environment for staff, minimizing risks, and preventing potential liabilities.
Dignified Treatment of the Deceased	Compliance ensures ethical embalming and disposition practices, guaranteeing the proper and respectful treatment of the deceased, aligning with legal and ethical standards.
Transparency and Trust	Compliance fosters a culture of transparency and trust with client-families, who rely on the funeral home to guide them through legal processes and uphold their rights with integrity.
Accurate Record-Keeping	Adhering to regulations includes accurate record-keeping, meeting legal requirements and maintaining the integrity of the funeral home's operations, including financial and client records.
Ethical Marketing	Compliance promotes ethical marketing practices, avoiding false advertising or deceptive practices that could mislead consumers and ensuring that services are accurately represented.
Tax Obligations	Compliance is crucial for tax purposes, ensuring the funeral home meets its financial obligations, reports income and expenses accurately, and operates within the bounds of tax laws.
Employee Rights	Adherence to employment laws guarantees fair treatment of staff, preventing issues related to discrimination, harassment, or unfair labor practices, and creating a positive workplace environment.
Environmental Regulations	The funeral home's commitment to environmental responsibility includes proper waste disposal and embalming fluid handling.

Finally, compliance serves to protect the reputation and goodwill of the funeral home, reinforcing its standing as a trusted and law-abiding institution within the community. In essence, compliance with federal and state laws is a multifaceted imperative that not only ensures legal standing but also upholds ethical standards, safeguards the interests of client-families, and maintains the professionalism and integrity of the funeral home.

Aftercare Services

Aftercare services provided by a funeral home serve as a continuing obligation to support the bereavement needs of families beyond the immediate funeral service. This ongoing support through offering resources, counseling, and assistance to help client-families navigate the challenging journey of mourning, acknowledges the profound and lasting impact of grief. However, it is crucial that aftercare services are approached with the sole intention of providing genuine support and not be used as a platform for the solicitation of pre-need arrangements under the pretense of aftercare. Mixing aftercare services with pre-need solicitation can compromise the trust and vulnerability of grieving families, potentially leading to ethical concerns and undermining the compassionate foundation upon which aftercare services should be built. Maintaining the integrity of aftercare services ensures that families receive genuine and dedicated support without any ulterior motives, fostering a relationship of trust and genuine care during a difficult time.

Professional Referrals

Ethical concerns arise in professional referrals within the funeral industry, particularly concerning conflicts of interest and the potential for referral fees. The first concern involves funeral homes striking deals with agencies for referrals of potential clients, creating a conflict of interest that compromises the impartiality and objectivity of the referral process. Such arrangements may prioritize financial gains over the best interests of grieving families, eroding trust in the profession. The second concern involves the solicitation of referral fees or kickbacks from professional ally agencies, it's illegal in some jurisdictions and it could raise ethical issues related to transparency and fairness. Accepting fees for referrals can lead to biased recommendations and undermine the primary commitment to providing genuine and unbiased assistance to clients in their time of need. To maintain the ethical integrity of professional referrals, funeral homes should prioritize the well-being of client-families above financial incentives, ensuring that referrals are made in the best interest of those seeking support during a difficult time.

PUBLICITY AND PROMOTIONAL PROCEDURES

Dealing with the Media

When dealing with the media, a funeral director should exercise utmost discretion and provide factual information. Transparency is crucial in communicating details related to funeral services, ensuring that the public receives accurate and reliable information. Factual information not only establishes trust with the community but also upholds the funeral director's commitment to ethical communication. Simultaneously, discretion in the release of information is paramount in respecting the privacy and sensitivity of grieving families. By striking a balance between transparency and discretion, funeral directors can navigate media interactions ethically, fostering a positive public image and demonstrating compassion and professionalism during times of grief.

Publicity

Advertising within the funeral industry should adhere to the highest standards of accuracy and avoid deceptive practices such as Bait-and-Switching, which violates FTC regulations. **Bait-and-switching** *is a deceptive marketing practice where a business advertises a product or service at an enticing price but then substitutes it with a different, often inferior, option when consumers express interest.* Accurate representations in advertising are essential to provide the public with truthful and transparent information about the funeral services offered. Misleading tactics, such as Bait-and-Switching, where advertised services differ substantially from what is actually provided, not only erode consumer trust but also breach federal regulations designed to protect consumers from deceptive business practices. Funeral directors must prioritize accurate and clear representations in their advertising to maintain ethical standards, foster trust with client-families, and ensure compliance with regulatory guidelines set forth by the FTC and the Funeral Rule.

Advertising by the funeral home should be approached with utmost sensitivity, ensuring that it is tasteful and respects the dignity of human life and the bereaved family. This requires a careful balance between promoting services and acknowledging the solemnity of the occasion. Ethical advertising in the funeral industry avoids sensationalism and focuses on conveying information in a compassionate and empathetic manner. By prioritizing the principles of dignity and respect, funeral homes can build trust with the community and demonstrate their commitment to providing meaningful and considerate services during times of grief.

Pricing comparison, while not illegal, may be considered borderline unethical when used in a manner that is misleading or manipulative. If a business employs pricing comparisons to deceive consumers or unfairly disparage competitors without presenting accurate and relevant information, it can be deemed unethical. In the context of funeral services, using pricing comparison tactics that lack transparency or exploit the vulnerability of grieving families would be considered unethical. This could also violate both expressed and implied warranties. It's crucial to ensure that any pricing comparisons are conducted honestly, with full disclosure of relevant details, to maintain ethical standards and foster trust within the community.

Social Media

Social media can serve as both an asset and a liability for funeral homes, depending on how it is managed. As an asset, social media provides funeral homes with a powerful platform to connect with the community, share information about services, and offer support to grieving families. It allows for meaningful engagement, fostering relationships and establishing trust. However, social media can also be a liability if not handled carefully. Inappropriate posts, negative reviews, or the sharing of sensitive information can harm the funeral home's reputation. Striking the right balance between using social media as a valuable communication tool and avoiding potential pitfalls is crucial for funeral homes to leverage its benefits while mitigating any risks.

Social media can be a valuable tool for funeral homes when used ethically and responsibly. First, funeral homes should only post authorized information, ensuring that the content shared is accurate, respectful, and aligns with the wishes of the bereaved families. This helps in maintaining transparency and trust within the community. Second, funeral homes must craft appropriate responses to public comments, addressing queries, expressions of sympathy, or concerns with empathy and professionalism. This engagement fosters positive relationships and demonstrates the funeral home's commitment to communication. Finally, monitoring public comments is essential to protect the bereaved from personal attacks or inappropriate discussions. By actively moderating and removing any offensive content, funeral homes can create a safe and supportive online environment for grieving families. Overall, utilizing social media responsibly allows funeral homes to provide valuable information, engage with the community, and offer support during sensitive times.

Funeral home personnel using personal social media need to be attentive to various considerations. First, their social media presence serves as a representation of funeral services, making it essential to maintain an appropriate image. Some aspects of personal lives may need to be kept private to uphold the dignity of the profession. Second, personnel should be mindful of the appropriate use of company resources and time when accessing social media during work hours. Excessive personal use can impact productivity and reflect negatively on the funeral home. Third, authorized release of work-related information is crucial to prevent the dissemination of sensitive or confidential details that could compromise the integrity of funeral services or breach client confidentiality. Personal social media use should align with the ethical standards and professionalism expected in the funeral industry. Striking a balance between personal expression and professional responsibilities is vital in upholding the reputation and trust associated with funeral services.

PRE-NEED ETHICS

Pre-Planned Funeral Arrangements

When making pre-planned funeral arrangements, funeral directors have a profound ethical obligation to ensure that the wishes of the individual are understood, respected, and accurately documented. This process involves active listening to the oral expressions of the client's preferences and concerns. It is incumbent upon the funeral director to meticulously document these oral wishes, translating them into a written plan that serves as a legally binding agreement. The importance of oral and written wishes lies in their role in a guiding document, ensuring that the funeral service aligns with the individual's values and desires. Ethically, funeral directors must prioritize transparency and clarity in presenting various options, providing informed guidance without imposing undue influence.

Respecting the autonomy of the individual is very important, and any conflicts of interest or financial incentives should be transparently disclosed. Funeral directors should also emphasize the importance of communication with family members and encourage discussions about the pre-planned arrangements to prevent potential disputes in the future. The ethical obligation extends to safeguarding the individual's financial investments, ensuring that funds are securely managed and allocated according to the pre-planned agreement. Ultimately, the ethical conduct of funeral directors in pre-planned arrangements rest on their commitment to preserving the dignity of the deceased, honoring their wishes, and providing peace of mind for both the individual and their bereaved loved ones.

Maintaining pre-need records and other information is crucial for several reasons. First, it upholds the principle of privacy, ensuring that sensitive details about individuals' pre-arranged funeral plans are securely stored and accessible only to authorized personnel. Second, a robust system of security safeguards these records from unauthorized access, protecting the confidentiality of the pre-need arrangements and preventing potential breaches. Especially when pre-need information is stored digitally, cybersecurity is another critical factor that needs to be considered to protect the confidentiality and integrity of sensitive records. Third, providing copies of these records to clients (families) and/or their authorized representatives is essential for transparency and accountability, allowing individuals to review and confirm that their wishes have been accurately documented. This transparency builds trust and empowers clients to ensure that their pre-need plans align with their expectations.

Additionally, maintaining comprehensive pre-need records is crucial for legal compliance, helping funeral homes adhere to regulations governing the funeral service industry. Each state has standards regulating how pre-needs funds need to be kept in trust for future use. Compliance with the regulations is both a legal and moral obligation of the funeral director. By prioritizing privacy, security, and transparency, funeral directors demonstrate their commitment to ethical conduct and the responsible management of pre-need arrangements.

A funeral director bears a fiduciary responsibility to the client when managing pre-funded funeral arrangements. This encompasses the careful determination of funding methods, which may include establishing trusts, utilizing insurance policies, or making other prudent investments that safeguard the consumer's funds. Risky or uninsured deposits should be avoided because this may put the client's funds at risk. The funeral director must assess and recommend funding options that align with the client's preferences and financial goals while prioritizing the protection of their funds. Whatever method of securing these funds is determined, compliance to regulations is essential. Additionally, transparent disclosures play a significant role in fulfilling this fiduciary duty. The funeral director must provide comprehensive information about the chosen funding method, including any associated fees, risks, and benefits. By navigating these aspects ethically and with full transparency, the funeral director upholds their fiduciary responsibility, ensuring that the client's pre-funded funeral arrangements are both financially sound and aligned with their wishes.

Pre-funded funeral arrangements involve both financial and professional considerations, with specific attention to ethical issues. In terms of professional issues, concerns may arise regarding commissions, referrals, and the substitution of merchandise. First, the acceptance of commissions raises ethical questions as funeral directors must prioritize the client's best interests over financial incentives, avoiding any conflicts of interest that could compromise the objectivity of their recommendations. Some states prohibit commissions for establishing pre-need accounts.

Second, referrals to other service providers or the acceptance of referral fees should be avoided because this may potentially be misconstrued as undue influence. Finally, the substitution of merchandise, if permitted, should be handled with utmost transparency and in adherence to the client's wishes, ensuring that any changes align with ethical business practices and client expectations.

In the event a casket, for example, is no longer available when the at-need arises, the funeral director should disclose to the family that the casket being provided is a substitute. A reason for the substitution should also be given. If possible, the casket should be similar in color, style, material and price point. Maintaining a high standard of professionalism in these areas is crucial to preserving the integrity of pre-funded funeral arrangements and building trust with clients.

Post – Funeral Needs Ethics

Aftercare services provided by funeral homes extend beyond the funeral itself, encompassing post-funeral follow-up as a demonstration of genuine concern for the welfare of the bereaved. This thoughtful engagement involves checking in on the grieving family, offering support, and addressing any needs that may arise after the funeral service. It serves as a testament to the funeral home's commitment to providing holistic care during the entire grieving process. Importantly, during aftercare services, the solicitation of pre-need arrangements is strictly prohibited. This ethical stance prioritizes the emotional well-being of the bereaved over any potential business interests, ensuring that aftercare remains a genuine and supportive service rather than a platform for sales or marketing activities. By upholding these principles, funeral homes strengthen their relationships with client-families and demonstrate a sincere dedication to compassionate care beyond the immediate funeral event.

Promoting Professionalism in the Community

A funeral director holds a multifaceted obligation to develop relationships among funeral practitioners, fostering a cohesive and professional community. Promoting understanding and cooperation is essential for creating a supportive network within the industry, allowing practitioners to collaborate effectively. Second, the funeral director should actively work towards developing a professional image, both individually and collectively, contributing to the overall positive perception of the funeral service profession. The sharing of information and ideas among practitioners enhances knowledge, skills, and industry practices, contributing to the continuous improvement of services. A funeral director should also be involved in professional associations, as it provides a platform for networking, education, and the exchange of best practices.

Funeral directors should develop a willingness to share personnel and equipment when necessary. Written agreements regarding risk of loss while in use by the party to whom the lending has occurred are recommended. This reflects a spirit of collaboration and unity within the funeral service community. Avoiding gossip and negative statements is vital for maintaining a positive and respectful professional environment, promoting trust and camaraderie. The funeral director's commitment to ethical communication reinforces a culture of professionalism. Overall, these tenets underscore the importance of a funeral director's role in building and sustaining strong relationships within the funeral service industry, contributing to a united and reputable professional community.

Relationships with Allied Professionals

Relationships with allied professionals are crucial for a funeral director as they contribute to a seamless and comprehensive service for grieving families. Collaborating with allied professionals, such as clergy, florists, and grief counselors, ensures a holistic support system for the bereaved. These relationships enhance the funeral director's ability to provide well-rounded care, creating a network of support that extends beyond the immediate funeral service.

These are some examples of allied professionals:

a.   Medical
b.   Clergy
c.   Legal
d.   Florists
e.   Cemetery - Superintendents and Sextons
f.   Crematory operators
g.   Monument dealers
h.   Insurance agents
i.   Government and public agencies - Federal, State, Local, Law Enforcement
j.   Military
k   Third party vendors
l.   Hospice
m.   Organ and tissue recovery organizations

Responsibility to Report Ethical Violations

The responsibility to report ethical violations is a crucial aspect of maintaining integrity within the funeral service profession. Personally, individuals who witness ethical violations should feel compelled to report such behavior, as it upholds their commitment to ethical standards and ensures accountability. Internally, within the funeral home, staff members should have clear channels for reporting ethical concerns to the management or appropriate authorities. This internal reporting mechanism is essential for addressing issues promptly and fostering a culture of transparency and ethical conduct. Externally, funeral professionals have a responsibility to report ethical violations to external regulatory bodies or industry associations, contributing to the overall accountability of the profession and helping maintain public trust. Upholding these reporting responsibilities at personal, internal, and external levels is integral to preserving the ethical standards of the funeral service industry. Separately, it is often a requisite to avoid complicity in unethical or illegal activity.

Addressing Ethical Conflicts

Addressing ethical conflicts as part of standard operating procedures is essential for maintaining ethical standards within a funeral home. First, it provides a structured framework to resolve conflicts between coworkers, ensuring a harmonious work environment. Second, having protocols in place helps navigate and resolve conflicts between employees and employers when they arise, fostering a fair and respectful workplace. Third, addressing ethical conflicts between the establishment and client-families is crucial for upholding the trust and integrity of the funeral industry. Standard operating procedures provide clear guidelines for ethical decision-making, facilitating the resolution of conflicts in a manner that aligns with industry standards and the welfare of all parties involved. This proactive approach contributes to a professional and ethical culture within the funeral home, ultimately benefiting both the staff and the clients served.

ETHICS GLOSSARY

Business Ethics – that branch of philosophy dealing with values relating to human conduct as it applies to business transactions.

Citizenship – the character of an individual viewed as a member of society, behavior in terms of the duties, obligations and functions of a citizen.

Code of Ethics – a declaration or public statement of professional standards of right and wrong conduct.

Confidentiality – to hold certain information in trust and not disclose without proper authorization or authority.

Conventional stage – (Kohlberg) a stage of moral development in which the expectations of the social group (family, community, and nation) are supported and maintained.

Culture – consists of abstract patterns (the rules, ideas, beliefs shared by members of society) of and for living and dying, which are learned directly or indirectly.

Ethics – that branch of philosophy dealing with values relating to human conduct, with respect to the rightness and wrongness of certain actions and to the goodness and badness of the motives and ends of such actions (Webster).

Ethnicity – the cultural heritage or identity of a group, based on factors such as language or country of origin.

Golden Rule – a rule of ethical conduct found in some form in most major religions usually phrased as, "Do unto others as you would have them do unto you."

Honesty – having a sense of honor; upright and fair dealing.

Integrity – fidelity to moral principles.

Law – rules that govern society.

Moral – (synonymous with "ethical") Refers to the customs, values, and standards of practice of a group, age, or theory and intended to be timeless.

Motives – something, as a reason or desire, acting as a spur to action.

Non-theistic – a philosophy that does not focus on the worship of a god or gods (atheism).

Philosophy – the set of values, ideas and opinions of an individual or group.

Post-Conventional stage – (Kohlberg) a stage of moral development in which the individual considers universal moral principles which supersede the authority of the group.

Pre-Conventional stage – (Kohlberg) a stage of moral development in which moral reasoning is based on reward and punishment from those in authority.

Pre-Moral stage – (Kohlberg) a stage of moral development in which the individual is characterized as not understanding the rules or feeling a sense of obligation to them. Looking to experience only that which is good or pleasant or to avoid that which is painful.

Religion – a culturally entrenched pattern of behavior made up of: (1) sacred beliefs, (2) emotional feelings accompanying the beliefs, and (3) overt conduct presumably implementing the beliefs and feelings.

Situational Ethics – Moral principles that vary with circumstances.

Theism – a belief in a god or gods.

Values – beliefs that are held in high esteem.

Funeral Service (Mortuary) Law

Funeral law, also known as mortuary law, encompasses the legal regulations and requirements that govern the funeral and burial industry, ensuring ethical practices and protecting the rights of both funeral service providers and the bereaved. These laws vary from state-to-state and cover a range of topics, including the handling, preparation, and transportation of deceased individuals. Funeral law often addresses issues related to the sale of funeral goods and services, including pricing transparency and consumer protection.

Funeral homeowners, funeral directors, and embalmers must adhere to specific licensing and certification requirements outlined in mortuary law, which may include educational qualifications, apprenticeship/residency periods, and continuing education. The legislation also dictates the proper disposal of human remains, outlining procedures for cremation, burial, or other disposition methods.

Funeral service law is designed to safeguard public health by establishing standards for sanitation and infection control within funeral homes. Additionally, these laws may address the proper documentation and recordkeeping practices related to the handling and transportation of deceased individuals, ensuring accountability and traceability in the funeral service industry. In essence, mortuary law serves as a comprehensive framework that governs the ethical, professional, and legal aspects of funeral services, aiming to uphold the dignity of the deceased and protect the interests of both funeral service providers and the bereaved families they serve.

Human Remains and What Constitutes Death

Cadaver	*a dead human body intended solely for scientific study and dissection.*
Corpse (dead human body)	*the body of a dead human being, deprived of life, but not yet entirely disintegrated.*
Cremated remains	*the final product remaining after completion of the entire cremation/pulverization process. Within the profession, the product is never referred to as "cremains or ashes."*

Dead human remains, commonly referred to as a person's body after death, encompass the physical remnants of an individual who has ceased to be alive. This includes the body's various biological components, such as bones, tissues, and organs. The term is often used in legal and medical contexts to describe the postmortem state of an individual. A **dead human body**, also known as a **corpse**, is defined as, *the body of a dead human being, deprived of life, but not yet entirely disintegrated.* Clinical death and brain death are distinct concepts that refer to different states of physiological functioning. Clinical death is often associated with the cessation of heartbeat and breathing, indicating the stoppage of vital bodily functions. In contrast, brain death refers to the irreversible loss of all cerebral and brainstem activities, including the absence of reflexes and responses, while other bodily functions, such as heartbeat and respiration, may be sustained through artificial life support. While clinical death can sometimes be reversible with prompt medical intervention, brain death is considered irreversible and legally defines the point at which an individual is deemed legally and medically deceased.

Following death, the handling, disposal, and treatment of dead human remains are guided by cultural, religious, and legal considerations. The respectful and dignified treatment of dead human remains is a universal principle, and legal frameworks typically dictate who holds the rights and responsibilities for making decisions regarding the disposition of the deceased. The understanding and management of dead human remains involves a complex interplay of ethical, cultural, and legal considerations that vary across societies and jurisdictions.

Property rights for dead human remains are typically governed by legal statutes, and the specifics can vary by jurisdiction. In many cases, the right to control the disposition of a deceased person's remains is granted to a specific individual, often designated in a legal document such as a will, or it may fall to the next-of-kin. State laws commonly outline a hierarchy of individuals with the authority to make decisions regarding the deceased. This is a sample of the At-Need Right to Control Final Disposition:

> Person designated in written instrument;
> Spouse;
> Domestic Partner;
> Any Child 18 or Older;
> Either Parent;
> Any Brother or Sister 18 or Older;
> Authorized Guardian;

Person 18 or Older now Eligible to Receive an Estate Distribution, in the following order:
> Grandchildren;
> Great-Grandchildren;
> Nieces and Nephews;
> Grand-nieces and Grand-nephews;
> Grandparents;
> Aunts and Uncles;
> First Cousins;
> Great-Grandchildren of Grandparents;
> Second Cousins;
> Fiduciary;
>> Close friend or other relative who is reasonably familiar with the decedent's wishes, including his or her religious or moral beliefs, when no one higher on the list is available, willing, or competent to act;
>> Public administrator (or the same official in a county not having a public administrator);
>> or, anyone willing to act on behalf of the decedent who completes the "At-Need Written Statement" form.

Funeral directors and mortuary professionals are granted custodial rights over the physical possession of the remains during the embalming, preparation, and funeral service processes. However, these professionals do not typically hold property rights over the remains;

rather, they act as custodians working under the legal authority granted to the family or designated individuals. (*See Actual and Constructive Possession p.207*)

Historically, under early English law, the dead human remains fell under the exclusive control of the Church. During this period, there was no property theory applicable, as the church-maintained ownership, leaving no room for individual property rights. However, as the church's control diminished, courts began recognizing a property theory that granted rights to the surviving spouse and next-of-kin. This acknowledgment allowed them the right to take possession of the body for the purpose of arranging its disposition. This is also known as the Right of Sepulcher in most states.

The currently accepted **quasi-property theory** diverges from a commercial understanding of property. This is *the accepted theory of the legal status of a dead human body; rights associated with the body are as if it were property for the purpose of disposition only.* Instead, the law endows the next of kin with a bundle of rights concerning the deceased body. This includes the survivor's right to take possession of the body for disposition, authorize the use of body parts within legal boundaries, exclude others from possessing the body, and determine the body's disposal—all within the specified scope of these rights. While not framed as traditional property ownership, this quasi-property theory establishes a legal framework governing the rights associated with the deceased body.

In addition to the rights mentioned earlier, the quasi-property theory extends to grant the next-of-kin the legal authority to determine the method of disposition for the human remains. This encompasses various options, allowing the survivor to make decisions regarding burial, cremation, alkaline hydrolysis, or body donation. The flexibility in choosing the method of disposition reflects a recognition of the deeply personal and cultural aspects involved in honoring the deceased. This legal right ensures that the next-of-kin has the autonomy to align the method of disposition with the wishes of the deceased or the cultural and religious practices important to the family, further acknowledging the importance of respectful and individualized final arrangements.

Within the Uniform Anatomical Gift Act (UAGA), a "part" is comprehensively defined to encompass a wide range of components, including organs, tissues, eyes, bones, arteries, blood, other fluids, and any other distinct portion of a human body intended for transplantation. Following the removal of such body parts, conducted with due consideration to avoid unnecessary mutilation, the custody of the remaining body rests with the individual who holds the right to control the final disposition. This legal provision emphasizes the importance of respecting the wishes and decisions of the person authorized to determine the ultimate fate of the deceased. By clearly outlining the custodial arrangement, the UAGA ensures a balance between facilitating organ and tissue donation for medical purposes and upholding the rights of individuals and their designated decision-makers in handling the human remains with care and dignity.

In the context of the Uniform Anatomical Gift Act (UAGA), funeral directors play a crucial role in facilitating the wishes of individuals regarding organ and tissue donation. They collaborate with families and relevant authorities to ensure the respectful and lawful execution of anatomical gifts while providing support and guidance during the complex process of organ donation and final disposition. The funeral director and embalmer must adhere to precise protocols throughout and after the embalming process to guarantee that the donated human remains are restored to a dignified and presentable condition. Their goal is to achieve a state of repose for the deceased, ensuring there is no visible evidence of the procedures employed to procure the donated tissues while upholding the highest standards of professionalism and respect.

The term "mutilation" refers to any alteration or change made to a deceased human body after death, excluding natural causes. This holds significant importance for funeral directors, as embalming, being a form of alteration, changes the human remains from its natural state at death. Therefore, it is crucial for funeral directors to seek permission from the next-of-kin before embalming the human remains. Furthermore, a licensed embalmer with the necessary skills and experience has the authority to prepare the human remains for public viewing through embalming, effectively slowing down the natural decomposition process, provided they have obtained permission from the next-of-kin prior to the embalming process.

Scenario:
The funeral director obtained consent from the next-of-kin to embalm his mother, with specific instructions not to apply any cosmetics due to the deceased's aversion to make-up. The embalming process, however, involved fluids with active dyes that rendered a natural appearance to the deceased, eliminating the need for make-up. When the son saw his mother, he was upset and requested the removal of what he perceived as make-up. This situation could potentially be considered a tort, as the funeral director failed to inform the next-of-kin about the active dyes in the embalming fluid, denying the son the opportunity to make an informed decision regarding embalming based on this information.

Final Disposition

Funeral directors bear a crucial responsibility to adhere to the wishes of the next-of-kin when making decisions regarding the preparation and presentation of the deceased. This obligation stems from the fiduciary relationship established between the funeral director and the bereaved family, emphasizing the importance of trust and transparency. The funeral director is ethically and professionally bound to communicate effectively with the next-of-kin, ensuring that their preferences and cultural or religious traditions are respected. This includes discussing aspects such as embalming, cosmetics, and other funeral procedures in alignment with the family's desires. The standard of care expected in the funeral profession necessitates a commitment to providing compassionate and personalized services while upholding the ethical principles that govern the industry.

Moreover, community standards play a foundational role in guiding funeral directors to navigate the diverse expectations and practices within different cultural and religious groups. Understanding and acknowledging these community standards are essential for a funeral director to provide culturally sensitive and respectful services. When religious or cultural traditions are involved, funeral directors must be well-versed in the specific requirements and customs associated with each community. Sensitivity to diverse beliefs and practices not only upholds the dignity of the deceased but also ensures that the bereaved family feels supported during a challenging time. By integrating community standards into their practices, funeral directors contribute to the overall well-being and satisfaction of the families they serve, reinforcing the trust placed in them during times of grief.

In addition to the funeral director's obligation to honor the wishes of the next-of-kin and adhere to community standards, there are broader considerations that come into play. Balancing the individual wishes of the family, the desires of the survivors, and the public's best interest requires a nuanced approach. While respecting the autonomy of the family and the deceased's wishes is paramount, funeral directors must also be mindful of legal and ethical responsibilities. In cases where the family's requests may conflict with public health and safety regulations or legal requirements, funeral directors may need to delicately navigate these challenges. Communicating openly with the family about any limitations imposed by external factors ensures transparency and helps manage expectations. Striking a balance between personalized services and adherence to broader regulations is essential to maintain the funeral profession's integrity and ensure that the public's welfare is safeguarded. Funeral directors, in their role as trusted professionals, play a crucial role in guiding families through these considerations and finding solutions that align with ethical, legal, and cultural expectations.

Funeral directors bear the responsibility of upholding both state regulations governing the funeral industry and local ordinances that impact funeral home operations. This dual obligation ensures legal compliance at both the broader state level and within the specific community where the funeral home operates, contributing to ethical and lawful practices in the profession.

Right to Control Final Disposition

As stated above, there is a hierarchical authoritative structure that needs to be followed when making funeral arrangements with the next-of-kin. Having the right to make the final disposition for the dead pertains to the legal authority granted to individuals, usually the next-of-kin, to make decisions regarding the handling and disposal of a deceased person's remains. This right is often outlined by laws and regulations, designating who holds the primary authority for such decisions. On the other hand, the duty to make the final disposition implies a moral or ethical responsibility to carry out the necessary arrangements for the deceased, ensuring a dignified and respectful conclusion. While the right is a legal entitlement, the duty emphasizes a broader sense of obligation and ethical commitment to fulfilling the responsibilities associated with final disposition.

The General Common Law rule of priority in final disposition typically designates the surviving spouse as the primary decision-maker regarding the handling of a deceased person's remains. In some states, this may extend to domestic partners as well. However, the effect of divorce or legal separation can alter this priority. In cases of divorce, the former spouse may lose the right to make decisions about the final disposition, unless specified otherwise in legal documents. Separation or estrangement, without a formal legal process, may still leave the surviving spouse with the authority, highlighting the nuances and complexities within the Common Law framework regarding final disposition.

The term **next-of-kin** refers to *one's relatives collectively; referring to blood relationship (legally, the surviving spouse is not a kin).* In legal terms, the concept of next-of-kin is often linked to blood relationships, encompassing family members such as parents, siblings, and children. It excludes the surviving spouse, despite their close relationship with the deceased. This distinction is crucial in various legal contexts, including those related to the disposition of a deceased person's remains, where specific individuals are granted, priority based on their status as next-of-kin.

Sample Questions: 1. **Who is the immediate kin to the deceased?**
    a. The spouse
    b. The son over the age of 18
    c. The parents
    d. The siblings

Answer is B. The son over the age of 18 is a blood relative of the deceased. A spouse is only related by marriage, not through blood relations.

2. **Who has the legal authority to make the funeral arrangements?**
    a. The spouse
    b. The son over the age of 18
    c. The parents
    d. The siblings

Answer is A. The spouse has the legal authority to control the final disposition.

The are two fundamentally different questions because Question 1 is asking about kinship and Question 2 is asking about the legal right of the person who has the legal rights control the final disposition of the deceased.

Other Factors that could Affect the General Rule to Control Final Disposition

Several factors can influence the general rule determining who has the right to control final disposition. When individuals **make pre-arrangements** before their death, these agreements become legally binding contracts, and their wishes must be honored, often superseding other claims. Additionally, a properly **executed Will** can serve as a testament to the deceased's preferences for their final arrangements. In some cases, **a formal written instrument**, such as an Appointment of Agent form to Control Final Disposition, can designate a specific person with the authority to make decisions regarding the deceased's remains, trumping the hierarchical authority.

Furthermore, the legal concept of next-of-kin plays a significant role. Traditionally, the surviving spouse holds priority as next-of-kin, but specific statutes may vary by jurisdiction. Issues related to family dynamics, such as divorce or estrangement, can complicate matters. In the absence of clear legal directives, disagreements among family members may arise, leading to disputes over the right to control final disposition.

Religious and cultural considerations also impact these decisions, as certain traditions prescribe specific rituals or burial practices. If the deceased had expressed religious or cultural preferences, these may carry legal weight in determining final disposition.

It's essential to recognize that state laws play a crucial role in shaping these rights, and individuals should be aware of and comply with state regulations. Ultimately, understanding and respecting the deceased's wishes, whether documented in pre-arrangements, a Will, or other legal instruments, ensures a more seamless and respectful final disposition process.

In certain states, domestic partnerships are recognized as equal to spousal relationships, offering similar rights and considerations, particularly in the absence of a formal marriage. The specific qualifications for establishing a domestic partnership are typically outlined in state laws, and funeral directors must adhere to these guidelines when dealing with matters of final disposition. It's essential to note that common law marriages, though once more prevalent, are now rare and not acknowledged in most states. Therefore, funeral directors should be well-versed in state regulations to appropriately address the legal standing and rights associated with domestic partnerships when navigating issues related to final disposition.

In the presence of a restraining order against a spouse or next-of-kin, the individual subjected to the order may forfeit their rights to control the final disposition of the deceased. Legal restrictions imposed by such orders can significantly impact the decision-making authority traditionally afforded to these individuals. Funeral directors must exercise diligence in recognizing and adhering to these legal constraints when dealing with the final disposition of the deceased. As state statutes undergo modifications pertaining to the regulation of the right to control final disposition, it is imperative for funeral directors to stay informed and ensure compliance with evolving laws.

The next-of-kin holds the legal authority to transfer custody of the deceased to a funeral practitioner, entrusting them with the responsibility to oversee the final disposition. This decision significantly influences the course of the final disposition process, allowing the funeral practitioner to carry out the deceased's wishes, or any pre-arrangements made, ensuring a respectful and appropriate conclusion to the individual's journey. The collaboration between the next-of-kin and the funeral practitioner plays a crucial role in honoring the deceased's preferences and contributing to a meaningful and dignified farewell.

Dispute Resolution

In navigating a dispute where half the family prefers traditional burial while the other half leans towards cremation, the funeral director must delicately facilitate communication and mediate a compromise. It is essential to foster an open dialogue, allowing each faction to express their sentiments and concerns regarding their preferred method of disposition. The funeral director can offer alternative solutions that may satisfy both parties, such as organizing separate memorial services or incorporating elements of both burial and cremation into a unified ceremony. Maintaining sensitivity to the family's emotions and cultural considerations is paramount, and the funeral director's role extends beyond logistical coordination to ensuring that the final arrangements resonate with the diverse wishes and beliefs within the family.

Despite efforts to mediate and find common ground, persistent disagreements among family members regarding the preferred method of disposition may necessitate legal intervention. If the funeral director is unable to facilitate a mutually exclusive resolution that satisfies all parties involved, it is advisable to recommend seeking legal guidance to address the impasse. The family should be directed to seek legal counsel and rectify this matter in the courts. The remedy from the courts is the funeral director's directive to follow for the final disposition wishes. Funeral directors typically refrain from taking sides in family disputes, recognizing the potential legal repercussions and liabilities associated with such involvement. Referring the matter to the courts ensures an impartial and legal resolution, protecting the funeral home and director from potential litigation and allowing the legal system to adjudicate the matter objectively.

Liability for Funeral Expenses

In the funeral profession, there are two primary types of expressed legal contracts: at-need and pre-funded preneed contracts. An at-need contract is initiated when a death has occurred, and the family or legal representative engages the funeral services on an immediate basis. This contract itemizes the specific services and merchandise chosen for the deceased and the associated costs. On the other hand, pre-funded preneed contracts are established in advance, allowing individuals to plan and fund their funeral arrangements before the need arises. These contracts provide a detailed agreement between the individual and the funeral home, specifying the desired services, merchandise, and associated costs. The pre-funded aspect ensures that the funds are set aside and designated for the prearranged funeral, offering both financial security and peace of mind for the individual and their family.

Either contract is a legally enforceable agreement. This contract serves as a safeguard for both parties involved, providing a clear framework for the funeral director's duties and the client's expectations. The fiduciary responsibility assumed by the funeral director underscores the trust bestowed upon them to act in the best interests of the deceased and their family. This duty encompasses not only the fulfillment of contractual obligations but also the exercise of professional judgment and ethical decision-making to navigate the sensitive and emotional nature of funeral arrangements, ensuring a compassionate and dignified service.

The funeral director bears the responsibility to fulfill the terms outlined in both at-need and pre-funded preneed contracts. For at-need contracts, immediate arrangements and services are carried out according to the agreement reached with the family or legal representative. In the case of pre-funded preneed contracts, the funeral director must ensure that the predetermined services and merchandise are provided when the time comes, and the funds allocated for these arrangements are appropriately managed and preserved until needed. This dual responsibility underscores the importance of professionalism and ethical conduct in the funeral director's role, ensuring the wishes of the deceased and their family are respected and executed as agreed upon in the contracts.

The consequences of failing to fulfill the terms of the contract extend beyond legal ramifications and potential disciplinary action; it can profoundly impact the grieving family, exacerbating their distress during an already difficult time. Recognizing and upholding the contractual obligations is fundamental to maintaining the trust and integrity that are integral to the funeral director's professional role in providing meaningful and respectful services.

Upon the funeral director completing the agreed-upon goods and services as specified in the contract, the family is required to fulfill their financial obligations promptly. Timely payment not only ensures the funeral home's financial stability but also reflects a mutual understanding and respect for the contractual arrangement. Failure to meet this obligation can strain the professional relationship, potentially leading to legal measures for the collection of outstanding fees. Therefore, adherence to the terms of the contract, both in the provision of services and the fulfillment of payment, contributes to the overall integrity and ethical standards of the funeral profession.

An implied contract in the funeral profession may arise when parties conduct themselves in a way that implies mutual consent, even without explicit verbal or written agreement. A quasi-contract, on the other hand, is a legal remedy used when there is an obligation to prevent unjust enrichment. This may come into play if a family benefits from a funeral service but hasn't entered into a formal contract. Additionally, funeral contracts are subject to state statutes that dictate specific regulations and requirements governing funeral service agreements. Adherence to these statutes is crucial for funeral directors to ensure legal compliance and uphold the ethical standards of the profession. Understanding the nuances of implied, quasi, and explicitly stated contracts, within the framework of state laws, is essential for funeral professionals to fulfill their responsibilities effectively.

In New York State, once a funeral director takes possession of human remains, there is a legal obligation to fulfill the final disposition, irrespective of the family's financial capability to cover the services. This implies that if there are concerns about the family's ability to pay, the funeral director should temporarily halt the removal of the deceased until transparent financial arrangements are established. This practice ensures that the funeral director acts in accordance with legal obligations and promotes ethical considerations in providing funeral services.

Funeral Home is the First to be Paid

In some cases, families opt to utilize the deceased's estate to cover funeral expenses, a practice that was more prevalent in the past. Funeral expenses are prioritized as primary payments within the estate, preceding other debts. However, this approach can present challenges, especially in contested estates, leading to prolonged delays in receiving payment for services. Such delays can significantly impact the funeral home's cash flow, creating financial strain in meeting other obligations. To address this, a prudent funeral director may request payment directly from the responsible party at the time of need, furnishing them with a paid receipt. This action shifts the payment priority to the payer, irrespective of the terms outlined in the will or the absence of such legal documentation, thereby safeguarding the funeral home's financial stability. The payer now becomes the priority for payment from the estate, regardless of the terms of the will.

In situations where the estate is insolvent, meaning that the deceased's estate lacks sufficient assets to cover its liabilities, the funeral home faces limitations in claiming payment from the estate. In such instances, the responsibility for payment shifts to the individual(s) who signed the contract for the funeral services. This shift can pose challenges and hardships, potentially leading to litigation against the family member(s) who assumed financial responsibility for the funeral arrangements. Managing these complexities requires a careful examination of the estate's financial status and a clear understanding of the legal obligations outlined in the contract. Funeral directors must approach these scenarios with sensitivity and legal expertise to address potential challenges that may arise in the payment process.

When a funeral director encounters challenges in receiving payment for services rendered, there are instances where litigation may be necessary. If the claim is less than $5,000, the funeral director can pursue legal action in Small Claims Court, which is designed to handle relatively minor disputes efficiently. This amount cap may vary in some jurisdictions. In these cases, the funeral director initiates a lawsuit against the individual who signed the funeral contract, seeking to recover the outstanding amount. Small Claims Court provides a streamlined and cost-effective avenue for resolving disputes of lower financial magnitude, allowing funeral directors to address unpaid bills and seek redress for their services without the complexities associated with larger legal proceedings. It's essential for funeral directors to be aware of the legal thresholds for Small Claims Court and to navigate the process judiciously to secure payment for their services.

When funeral claims exceed the $5,000 threshold, seeking legal counsel becomes imperative due to the increased complexity of the proceedings and the necessity for comprehensive legal documentation. In such cases, funeral directors need to enlist the support of an attorney to comply with the intricacies of the legal system and pursue a financial remedy effectively. Legal professionals can guide funeral directors through the formalities of initiating a lawsuit, presenting evidence, and advocating for their claim in a court of law. This assistance is crucial in ensuring that the funeral director's rights are protected, and the legal process is followed accurately, increasing the likelihood of a successful resolution and the recovery of the outstanding amount for the services provided. Note: The funeral director needs to be mindful of the statutes of limitations governing such claims, as these legal time constraints may vary by jurisdiction and can impact the timing and success of pursuing remedies for outstanding payments.

Funeral Service Practitioners and Funeral Service Law

Funeral service practitioners must adhere to high standards of professional conduct and ethical behavior, exercising due diligence in all facets of their profession. This involves taking reasonable and prudent actions when providing care and support to bereaved families, ensuring sensitivity and empathy in their interactions. In addition, human remains must be treated with unwavering respect and dignity throughout the entire process, adhering to industry-specific standards of care. It is imperative to strictly follow established and accepted procedures and formalities within the industry, avoiding any deviation from these norms. Deviating from the industry specific established standards within the profession, especially if it results in emotional distress for the bereaved, has the potential to lead to legal action. Practitioners must recognize the profound impact of their actions on grieving families and exercise the utmost care to prevent any unnecessary distress or legal repercussions.

To meet these standards, funeral service practitioners establish, maintain, and follow prescribed standards of care, which are acquired through rigorous education in mortuary science programs. These standards are further enforced through the implementation of policies and procedures within the funeral home, fostering a culture of excellence and accountability.

Recognizing the dynamic and evolving nature of funeral service law, practitioners understand the importance of ongoing training and education to stay informed about legal compliance at the local, state, and federal levels. This commitment to continuous learning is crucial for risk management, as it allows practitioners to navigate legal complexities, mitigate potential liabilities, and uphold the highest standards of professionalism.

Effective communication is paramount in achieving legal compliance, and funeral service practitioners must communicate clearly and transparently with families, colleagues, and regulatory authorities. This includes providing accurate information about services, pricing, and legal requirements, fostering trust and transparency in the funeral service process.

Furthermore, funeral service practitioners play a crucial role in ensuring that their operations align with ethical and legal standards, such as those related to consumer protection, privacy, and occupational health and safety regulations. By upholding these principles, practitioners contribute to the overall integrity and reputation of the funeral service profession.

Documentation

Accurate documentation is a cornerstone of risk management in the funeral service profession. Thorough and precise records serve as a vital safeguard for practitioners, providing a comprehensive account of their actions and decisions. In the event of any issues or disputes, these documented records become invaluable evidence that can help demonstrate the practitioner's adherence to established protocols and standards of care. In the age of technology, funeral service practitioners should leverage digital tools and software to enhance documentation practices. Electronic records and digital communication platforms not only streamline documentation processes but also provide secure and accessible storage, ensuring the preservation of accurate records for both immediate and future needs. Precise documentation not only safeguards the practitioner from potential litigation but also contributes to transparency and accountability, fostering trust with the bereaved families and regulatory authorities. Therefore, practitioners must prioritize meticulous record-keeping to enhance their risk management practices and maintain the integrity of their professional conduct.

Accurate documentation of various aspects, such as an inventory of personal property, written authorizations, copies of legal documents prescribed by state law, embalming reports, releases, and inspection reports of third-party crematory vendors, are crucial as standard operating procedures in the funeral service profession for several reasons. First, maintaining an inventory of personal property ensures transparency and accountability in handling personal belongings of the deceased, preventing disputes and loss of valuable items. Written authorizations and legal documents are essential for compliance with state regulations and safeguarding the funeral service practitioner against legal challenges. Embalming reports provide a detailed record of the embalming process, ensuring adherence to industry specific standards for preservation care. Releases and inspection reports of third-party crematory vendors are crucial for verifying the proper handling and disposition of remains, minimizing the risk of errors or complications. Overall, these documented procedures contribute to professionalism, legal compliance, and effective risk management within the funeral service industry.

Torts Involving the Human Remains

Torts may arise in the funeral service profession when handling human remains, particularly if there is a violation of the consumer's rights. These legal wrongs can encompass various issues, such as negligence, intentional infliction of emotional distress, or breaches of contract, leading to harm or distress for the bereaved family. For instance, failure to adhere to agreed-upon services, mishandling of remains, or inadequate communication can give rise to legal claims. Therefore, it is imperative for funeral service practitioners to exercise due diligence, adhere to ethical standards, and communicate transparently with the bereaved families to mitigate the risk of potential tort claims related to the handling of human remains.

Before commencing with the embalming process, oral permission must be obtained when it is necessary for public visitation. In response to consumer inquiries about the cost of embalming, the funeral director is obligated to provide a copy of the General Price List to the consumer before disclosing the associated costs. Within the funeral arrangement conference, the family should sign a formal statement consenting to authorize embalming, and the document should explicitly state the reason for the embalming procedure. Additionally, this reason should be disclosed on the Itemized Statement of Goods and Services Selected for transparency in the funeral service arrangements.

Taking unauthorized photographs, fingerprints, or biological blood samples is strictly prohibited, and obtaining consent with permission is mandatory before engaging in such activities. This measure ensures respect for the deceased and upholds ethical standards in handling sensitive information and materials related to the deceased individual.

During the COVID-19 pandemic, there was a significant increase in cases where burial occurred without the presence of the next-of-kin. Proper documentation and clear communication were crucial in dealing with these situations. Funeral service practitioners had to ensure that all legal requirements were met, and effective communication channels were established to keep the family informed and involved in the decision-making process, even if they couldn't be physically present.

The right to privacy and confidentiality is paramount in the funeral service profession, particularly when dealing with high-profile cases. The right to privacy has several federal and state statutes that govern the release of images of the likeness of an individual. If the funeral home permits distribution or publishing of a likeness, without consent of the next-of-kin, the funeral home could face a separate cause of action under the privacy acts that are applicable. Funeral service practitioners must exercise discretion and sensitivity when communicating information to the community, ensuring that they respect the privacy of the deceased and their bereaved family. Upholding confidentiality fosters trust and professionalism, safeguarding the dignity of the deceased and maintaining the integrity of the funeral service profession. Information should be safeguarded and selectively shared only with individuals whom the family deems necessary to have access to such details.

Failing to adhere to the wishes of the party with the right to control the final disposition can lead to legal consequences for the funeral director, potentially resulting in litigation. It is crucial for funeral practitioners to communicate effectively, document directives, and implement the chosen disposition method in alignment with the legal and ethical obligations. Non-compliance may not only harm the funeral home's reputation but also create emotional distress for the grieving family, emphasizing the importance of honoring the deceased's final wishes.

When a hospital or healthcare facility withholds or mislabels human remains, it can lead to significant emotional distress for the grieving family and potential legal consequences. To prevent this potential liability, the funeral director should ensure, prior to leaving the health care institution, that the toe tag, wristband, and tag on the body pouch all match. Funeral directors should communicate effectively with healthcare providers, ensuring the prompt release and accurate identification of the deceased. Failure to address such issues promptly may result in violations of the family's rights and could lead to legal actions against the facility and/or funeral director. In cremation cases, it is essential for the next-of-kin or their designated agent to confirm the identity of the human remains before the cremation process. Visual identification should be conducted, and a document should be signed to officially verify the identification of the deceased. While not mandated by law in most states, adopting these procedures serves to reduce the potential for cremating the wrong human remains, thus reducing the potential for future litigation.

Public officials, including coroners and medical examiners, may act beyond the scope of immunity in matters related to death investigations. While they generally enjoy certain legal protections, engaging in gross negligence or intentional misconduct can potentially expose them to legal liability. Public officials must adhere to established protocols, exercise due diligence, and act within the bounds of the law to minimize the risk of legal consequences in death-related matters.

Inappropriate interment, such as burying human remains in the wrong grave, is a serious violation that can lead to emotional distress for the bereaved family and legal consequences for the funeral service provider. This error undermines the sacred and respectful nature of burial practices and can result in significant harm to the grieving process. Funeral directors must exercise utmost care and precision to avoid such mistakes, ensuring that human remains are interred in the designated and properly prepared gravesite. To prevent the error of inappropriate interment, the funeral director should facilitate a meeting between the family and cemetery personnel before the committal. This pre-committal meeting is crucial to ensure that the correct grave is opened for the deceased, allowing the family to verify the location and avoid any errors in the burial process. Clear communication and coordination between the funeral director and the cemetery staff at this stage are essential to uphold the dignity of the deceased and provide peace of mind to the grieving family.

The right of possession implies that upon receiving the human remains, they should be in the same condition as at the time of death. This means that the funeral director has a duty to handle the remains with the utmost care, preserving their dignity and integrity. Leaving the deceased in a hot removal van, thereby accelerating the stages of decomposition and putrefaction, serves as an example of such a violation. Any alteration or change to the body, beyond what is necessary for legal and sanitary reasons, would be a violation of this right. Funeral directors must adhere to industry standards and ethical practices to fulfill their obligation to the bereaved family and respect the deceased.

Mutilation

Mutilation of human remains in funeral directing is the alteration or modification of a deceased person's body from its natural state at the time of death. There are several situations where a funeral director can become liable, such as unauthorized alterations during embalming, failure to follow the family's wishes, or negligence in handling the deceased, leading to visible changes that deviate from their natural condition. These actions can result in legal consequences and potential claims against the funeral director and the funeral home.

Unauthorized or negligent embalming and/or restorations refer to actions taken by a funeral director that are not in accordance with the wishes of the deceased or their next-of-kin. This could include altering the body's appearance without proper authorization, applying cosmetics or restorations against the family's explicit instructions, or performing embalming procedures without consent. Such actions may lead to significant emotional distress for the family and can be considered a violation of the duty to exercise reasonable care in handling human remains. Funeral directors engaging in unauthorized or negligent embalming may face legal consequences and potential liability for damages.

Unauthorized trimming or removal of a deceased person's moustache, beard, or facial hair can be a sensitive matter as it may alter the individual's recognizable features. Such actions could impact the deceased's identity, especially if certain facial hair features were distinctive and recognizable by loved ones. Funeral directors should exercise caution and obtain proper authorization from the next-of-kin before making any changes to the deceased's appearance.

Unauthorized removal of tissue, organs, and medical devices from a deceased person is strictly prohibited unless explicit, written permission is obtained from the family before any such procedures. This ensures that the family's wishes regarding the handling of the deceased's body are respected and followed. Funeral directors/embalmer should adhere to legal and ethical standards, obtaining proper authorization to avoid potential legal consequences and emotional distress for the bereaved family. In addition, an embalmer must operate within the boundaries defined by their license and refrain from removing any tissue or medical device unless they have received appropriate training for such procedures.

Performing procedures beyond the scope of a standard embalming or deviating from industry-accepted practices is strictly prohibited. Funeral directors and embalmers must adhere to ethical and legal standards, ensuring that their actions align with industry norms. Unauthorized or unconventional procedures may lead to legal consequences and compromise the integrity of the human remains, potentially causing distress for the bereaved family.

Unauthorized (private) autopsies, involving the retrieval of tissue samples or other forms of dissection, require proper authorization before being conducted. It is essential for the funeral director or embalmer to ensure that the necessary legal permissions have been obtained before authorizing any agency to conduct autopsy-related activities. Performing such procedures without proper authorization can result in serious legal consequences and potential liabilities for the funeral professional.

In the funeral profession, the right of a public official, whether it be a coroner/medical examiner, law enforcement officer, or health official, exists to conduct post-mortem examinations. However, it is crucial for these officials to obtain proper authorization from the family before proceeding with such examinations. If the family refuses consent, legal intervention may be required, potentially causing delays in the funeral proceedings. Funeral directors play a crucial role in effectively communicating with families about the potential legal implications, guiding them through the process, and ensuring that their wishes are respected while adhering to legal requirements. Open communication is key to facilitate these sensitive situations and minimizing disruptions to the funeral services.

Performing any unauthorized procedures on human remains is strictly prohibited to ensure compliance with ethical standards, legal regulations, and industry norms in the funeral profession. This prohibition also helps maintain the integrity of the funeral profession and mitigates potential legal and ethical consequences associated with unauthorized actions on human remains. In addition, such prohibitions serve to uphold the dignity and respect owed to the deceased and their families.

Other Funeral Service-Related Torts

Controlling a funeral procession requires the funeral director to exercise reasonable caution. Whenever feasible, it is advisable to enlist a police or motorcade escort to enhance the visibility of the slow-moving funeral procession. All vehicles in the procession should activate their four-way hazards and headlights. Some type of signage should be affixed to all cars indicating a funeral procession. The lead car and hearse ought to be equipped with oscillating headlights, four-way flashers, and a purple strobe light atop the vehicle, serving as a clear signal to motorists. The funeral director bears the responsibility of driving below the speed limit, maintaining vigilance for potential hazards or conditions that could disrupt the funeral procession. This comprehensive approach ensures the safety and smooth flow of the funeral cortege.

Liability within the context of a funeral procession involves the responsibility of drivers for their own torts. Funeral processions often have restrictions in place to ensure a smooth and orderly flow, but individual drivers remain accountable for any legal violations or wrongdoing. In cases of negligence, such as failure to adhere to traffic regulations or causing an accident, drivers within the funeral procession may face liability for their actions.

In instances where **volunteer drivers**, such as a friend designated by the family, are involved in transporting the bereaved to the church and cemetery during a funeral, it's essential to clarify that these drivers are not agents of the funeral service provider. The funeral director holds no control or liability over the actions of such drivers. However, if the funeral director observes any indication that the driver may pose potential harm to the grieving family due to an inability to drive safely, it is the responsibility of the funeral director to advise the family and recommend an alternative driver. This ensures the safety and well-being of the bereaved during the funeral procession.

When funeral homes employ agent drivers as part of their services, the funeral service practitioner assumes control and liability for any driving infractions committed by these drivers. This is particularly crucial in the context of **livery**, *where automotive equipment is made available for hire*. In such cases, if the funeral service practitioner holds out these cars and drivers as their own, they are personally liable. To mitigate potential risks and protect the funeral firm from liability, it is advisable for funeral homes engaged in livery and related businesses to establish a separate legal entity complete with its own liability insurances. This separation helps ensure clarity and safeguard the funeral home from potential legal consequences.

Funeral Firm	*The legal name of the funeral home registered with a governing agency.*
Funeral Establishment	*A facility used in the care and preparations of human remains for final disposition*
Invitee	*One who has been invited to the property by the landowner; person(s) coming to the funeral home for the purpose of attending funerals, viewing the remains, or engaging in funeral directed services.*
Trespasser	*One who intentionally or without consent or privilege enters onto another's property.*

The distinction between a funeral firm and a funeral establishment lies in their definitions and roles within the funeral industry. The **funeral firm** refers to the legal name of the funeral home as registered with a governing agency, embodying the entity responsible for providing funeral services. On the other hand, a **funeral establishment** represents the physical facility used for the care and preparation of human remains, ensuring they are appropriately handled before their final disposition. While the funeral firm encompasses the entire business entity, the funeral establishment specifically denotes the operational space dedicated to the practical aspects of funeral services, highlighting the dual aspects of legal registration and physical infrastructure in the funeral industry.

When a family organizes funeral arrangements and extends public invitations for people to gather in mourning, attendees are lawfully permitted on the premises as part of the contractual agreement with the family. However, family dynamics often lead to requests that certain individuals not be admitted due to estrangement. The only effective means of restricting access to a public gathering is to make the visitation and funeral private, with the family holding the responsibility to extend invitations as they see fit. Funeral directors should counsel families to approach extreme measures of restriction with caution, recognizing that everyone has the right to grieve the loss and participate in the mourning process. Balancing the family's wishes with the respectful acknowledgment of others' right to mourn is crucial in facilitating these sensitive situations.

The funeral provider assumes potential liability when conducting services in their facilities, requiring a commitment to maintaining a hazard-free and safe environment for attendees. Hazards such as uneven sidewalks, broken furniture, obstructed exits, and throw rugs pose risks and can lead to liability issues.

When services are held in churches, funeral directors must exercise a reasonable amount of care to ensure the safety of attendees, with consideration for well-lit hallways, stairwells, and properly maintained sidewalks in winter conditions. Although the responsibility for illumination and maintenance lies with the church, funeral personnel should be vigilant about potential hazards and advise families, accordingly, exploring alternative entry points if necessary. Additionally, at cemeteries with uneven grounds, funeral providers should assist individuals with difficulty walking to ensure their safety during the proceedings. This proactive approach helps mitigate potential liabilities and provides a safer environment for all involved in the funeral services.

Mental Anguish

Intentional infliction of in the context of funeral services involves deliberate and outrageous acts that cause significant mental harm to the deceased or the bereaved. This may include malicious actions or intentional misconduct by funeral service providers, such as mishandling or desecration of the deceased's remains, disrespectful behavior during the funeral service, or intentional infliction of emotional pain on grieving family members. This conduct is so egregious to "shock the moral conscience." In such cases, individuals may pursue legal action against the funeral service provider for intentional infliction of emotional distress.

On the other hand, negligent infliction of emotional distress occurs when funeral service providers act negligently, resulting in emotional harm to the bereaved. This may involve careless actions that lead to distressing consequences, such as mishandling the deceased's remains, providing incorrect information, or failing to fulfill contractual obligations. Negligent acts that cause emotional harm can result in legal claims, with the bereaved seeking compensation for the emotional distress experienced due to the funeral service provider's negligence. Both intentional and negligent infliction of emotional distress underscore the importance of funeral service providers exercising due care and professionalism to avoid causing harm to grieving families during the delicate process of funeral arrangements and services.

In some jurisdictions, establishing mental anguish as a result of intentional or negligent infliction may require a physical impact or injury. This means that there must be a direct connection between the wrongful actions of the funeral service provider and an organic consequence that results in emotional distress for the bereaved. Additionally, a claim for intentional or negligent infliction of emotional distress may be framed as a breach of a personal service contract. When funeral service providers fail to meet the standards of care and professionalism outlined in their contract with the bereaved family, resulting in emotional harm, it can be considered a breach of the personal service contract, opening the door for legal remedies. This reinforces the importance of funeral service providers upholding the terms of their contracts and acting with utmost care and sensitivity to avoid causing harm to grieving individuals during the funeral process.

Complying with Local Ordinances

Funeral establishments are subject to various legal considerations to ensure compliance with zoning ordinances, special use permits, building codes, and deed restrictions, commonly known as restrictive covenants. Zoning ordinances dictate the specific zones within which funeral homes can operate, taking into account the character of the surrounding area. Special use permits may be required in certain zones, allowing the funeral establishment to operate within defined parameters. Building codes ensure that the physical structure of the funeral home adheres to safety and construction standards, and deed restrictions, or restrictive covenants, outline limitations on the use of the property as specified in legal documents. Adhering to these regulations is crucial for funeral establishments to operate lawfully and maintain a harmonious presence within the community they serve.

Nuisance in fact	*acts, occupations or structures which are not nuisances per se, but may become nuisances by reason of the location or manner in which it is operated.*
Nuisance per se	*acts, occupations or structures which are nuisances at all times and under all circumstances; it may be prejudicial to public morals, dangerous to life, or injurious to public rights.*

Nuisance in fact and nuisance per se are two legal concepts related to the category of nuisance, but they differ in their elements and application. **Nuisance in fact**, also known as private nuisance, occurs when there is an unreasonable interference with another individual's use and enjoyment of their land. It is a subjective standard, relying on the impact on a particular person or property rather than a broader community perspective. In the context of funeral services, an example of nuisance in fact could be excessive noise or disturbances caused by funeral activities that unreasonably disrupt the neighboring properties, affecting the residents' peaceful enjoyment of their homes.

On the other hand, **nuisance per se**, or public nuisance, involves conduct that is inherently harmful to the public welfare or violates a statute or regulation. It doesn't require proof of specific harm to an individual but rather focuses on the act itself. In the context of funeral services, a violation of environmental regulations, such as improper disposal of embalming fluids or hazardous materials, could be considered a nuisance per se as it poses a threat to public health and safety.

In summary, while nuisance in fact is more about the impact on specific individuals, nuisance per se is concerned with activities that are inherently harmful or violate laws or regulations, affecting the broader public.

Administrative Laws or Regulations Impacting the Funeral Establishment

Occupational Safety and Health Administration (OSHA), Environmental Protection Agency (EPA), and the Americans with Disabilities Act (ADA) are federal administrative agencies that enforce laws and regulations impacting funeral establishments. OSHA regulates workplace safety and health, ensuring that funeral homes provide a safe environment for their employees. Funeral establishments must comply with OSHA standards regarding the handling of hazardous chemicals, such as embalming fluids, and provide appropriate personal protective equipment for employees. Failure to adhere to OSHA regulations can result in penalties and citations.

The EPA oversees environmental regulations, and funeral establishments must comply with rules related to the proper disposal of hazardous materials in municipalities without sewage treatment facilities or a municipal water supply. For example, funeral homes need to adhere to guidelines for the handling and disposal of embalming fluids to prevent environmental contamination. This may include, but is not limited to, a separate storage tank for hazardous and biological material as a byproduct from the embalming process. Violations of EPA regulations may lead to fines and legal consequences for the funeral firm.

The ADA ensures equal opportunities and accessibility for individuals with disabilities. Funeral establishments must comply with ADA requirements to provide accessible facilities and services for people with disabilities. This may include wheelchair ramps, accessible restrooms, and accommodating service arrangements. Failure to adhere to ADA regulations can result in legal actions and penalties, emphasizing the importance of ensuring that funeral services are accessible to everyone.

State and Local Standards

State and local standards play a crucial role in regulating funeral establishments, ensuring public health and safety, and maintaining ethical practices within the industry. Health codes, established at the state and local levels, dictate the sanitary conditions and health practices within funeral homes. These codes may cover the handling of human remains, infection control measures, and the proper disposal of biohazardous materials like embalming fluids. Regular inspections, often conducted annually, help ensure that funeral homes comply with health codes and maintain a safe environment for both staff and the public.

Fire and safety standards are another integral aspect of state and local regulations governing funeral establishments. These standards are designed to mitigate fire hazards and promote overall safety within funeral home premises. Inspections may focus on fire exits, emergency evacuation plans, and the proper storage of flammable materials. Compliance with fire and safety standards helps prevent accidents and ensures the protection of both funeral home personnel and visitors.

State regulatory guidelines also address the physical infrastructure of funeral homes, requiring fixed locations that adhere to zoning laws and building codes. Adequate licensed personnel are essential for the proper functioning of funeral establishments, ensuring that trained professionals handle various aspects of funeral services. Access to rolling stock, such as hearses and other funeral vehicles, is typically regulated to guarantee reliable transportation for the deceased. Additionally, preparation rooms within funeral homes must be adequately equipped and meet specific state guidelines to maintain the highest standards of care for the deceased. Overall, adherence to state and local standards is crucial for the ethical, legal, and safe operation of funeral establishments.

Funeral homes that engage in multi-use operations, encompassing services such as cemeteries, crematories, and reception facilities, should consider establishing separate business entities for liability purposes. The primary reason for this separation is to compartmentalize potential risks and liabilities associated with each distinct operation. For instance, the risks associated with cemetery management, including grounds maintenance and perpetual care, may differ significantly from those related to the operation of a crematory or reception facility. By creating separate legal entities for each operation, funeral homes can shield themselves from potential cross-liabilities, limiting exposure to legal issues arising in one area of the business from affecting the others. This legal strategy enhances the overall risk management framework, protecting the financial interests and reputation of the funeral home in the event of legal challenges or unforeseen issues in any specific facet of its operations.

Covenant Not to Compete

Covenants not to compete, also known as non-compete agreements, are contractual clauses that restrict one party, typically an employee or a business owner, from engaging in certain competitive activities, often within a specified geographical area and for a defined period after the termination of the business relationship. In the context of purchasing a funeral business, these covenants may be included in the sale agreement to protect the buyer's interests. Such agreements are considered reasonable and valid when they are directly related to the protection of legitimate business interests, such as client relationships, goodwill, and trade secrets.

These agreements are subject to legal scrutiny, and their enforceability depends on certain criteria. Courts generally recognize the validity of non-compete clauses if they are part of a broader contract for the sale of a funeral business. However, these covenants cannot be overly restrictive, unreasonably limiting the seller's ability to pursue their livelihood. Additionally, they must adhere to the principle of reasonableness concerning the duration, geographical scope, and the nature of the prohibited activities. If a covenant not to compete is found to be overly broad or violates public policy, a court may deem it unenforceable.

The primary purpose of a covenant not to compete in the context of a funeral business sale is to safeguard the buyer's investment by preventing the seller from establishing a competing business in close proximity or soliciting the business's clientele. While these agreements are meant to protect the buyer, they must strike a fair balance, ensuring that the seller is not unduly restricted from pursuing lawful business opportunities after the sale. Therefore, careful drafting and consideration of the specific circumstances are crucial to create an enforceable and equitable non-compete agreement in the funeral industry.

In determining the enforceability of non-compete agreements in the funeral industry, it is imperative that the terms are not only reasonable but also comply with state guidelines. The length of time during which the restriction applies, the geographical distance it covers, and the specific scope of prohibited activities must align with state regulations and be reasonable in the context of the funeral business. State laws vary, and some jurisdictions may have specific requirements regarding the permissible duration and geographic extent of non-compete clauses. Striking the right balance between protecting the buyer's legitimate interests and allowing the seller the freedom to pursue their livelihood is crucial for creating a non-compete agreement that stands up to legal scrutiny and serves the interests of both parties involved.

Employment contracts within the funeral industry often incorporate non-compete clauses to safeguard the owner's interests and preserve trade secrets. While the concept of trade secrets may not be as straightforward as in some other industries, funeral homes may have proprietary methods, unique service offerings, or specialized knowledge in caring for the deceased that they seek to protect. Non-compete clauses serve to prevent employees from using such confidential information to the detriment of the former employer.

On April 23, 2024, the Federal Trade Commission voted in a special meeting to adopt the "Non-Compete Clause Rule," barring most employee non-competes with retroactive effect, except for existing provisions for senior executives. The rule will also prohibit future non-compete agreements, including those for senior executives, with few exceptions. Despite facing legal challenges, including a lawsuit led by business groups arguing that the FTC lacks authority to regulate "unfair methods of competition," the rule could potentially affect up to one-fifth of American workers, including funeral professionals. Dissenting commissioners raised concerns about the rule's legality and its potential impact on existing contracts and state laws. As legal battles unfold, funeral homes are advised to adhere closely to state and local laws regarding non-competes and seek legal counsel to safeguard their interests. The possibility that non-compete clauses are going to be permitted in funeral home employment moving forward, based on this recent decision, is highly unlikely.

Consider this perspective: When employers address both the financial and personal growth requirements of their employees, and foster a non-hostile working atmosphere, the inclusion of non-compete clauses may become unnecessary. Funeral home employees don't leave their places of employment; they leave poor management and an uninviting/hostile work environments.

Pre-Need Funeral Contracts

Pre-planned Funeral Arrangements	Funeral arrangements made in advance of need that do not include provisions for funding or prepayment.
Pre-funded Funeral Arrangements	Funeral arrangements made in advance of need that include provisions for funding or prepayment.
Revocable Contracts	Agreement which may be terminated by the purchaser at any time prior to the death of the beneficiary with a refund of the monies paid on the contract as prescribed by state law.
Irrevocable Contracts	An agreement for future funeral services which cannot be terminated or canceled prior to the death of the beneficiary.

Guaranteed Contracts	An agreement whereby the funeral home promises that the services and merchandise will be provided at the time of need (in the future) for a sum not exceeding the original amount of the aforementioned contract plus any accruals, regardless of the current prices associated with providing the services and merchandise at the time of the funeral.
Non-guaranteed Contracts	Agreement in which the funeral home promises to apply the amount pre-paid plus any accruals to the balance due. However, the cost of the funeral will be based upon the current price for the services and merchandise at the time the services are provided.
Trust Accounts	An account established by one individual to be held for the benefit of another (as a method of payment of funeral expenses); creates a fiduciary responsibility. Money paid to a funeral home for future services is placed in an account with the funeral home as trustee for the benefit of another.

Distinguishing between pre-planned and pre-funded funeral arrangements is crucial in understanding the various aspects of funeral preplanning. **Pre-planned funeral arrangements** refer to decisions made in advance of the need for funeral services, encompassing choices related to the type of service, casket, burial or cremation, and other relevant details. However, pre-planned arrangements do not involve any provisions for funding or prepayment; they primarily focus on documenting the individual's preferences and ensuring that those wishes are known to family members or the designated executor.

On the other hand, **pre-funded funeral arrangements** go beyond preplanning by including provisions for financing or prepayment. In addition to detailing the desired funeral services, a pre-funded plan involves setting aside funds or purchasing insurance to cover the anticipated costs of those services. This financial aspect aims to alleviate the burden on the family during a challenging time and ensures that the predetermined arrangements are financially secured. Understanding the distinctions between these two types of arrangements is essential for individuals contemplating end-of-life planning and wanting to make informed decisions about both the logistical and financial aspects of their funeral services.

Creating a pre-funded funeral account with a funeral home offers several advantages for individuals planning for their end-of-life arrangements. One key benefit is financial security, as the funds set aside in the account are specifically designated to cover future funeral expenses. This can provide peace of mind to both the individual and their loved ones, knowing that the financial aspects of the funeral are already taken care of. Additionally, pre-funded funeral accounts often offer the flexibility to lock in current prices for services and merchandise, protecting against potential future price increases. This not only ensures cost predictability but also helps in managing the overall expenses associated with funeral arrangements. Overall, a pre-funded funeral account streamlines the planning process, minimizes financial strain on survivors, and allows individuals to make personalized choices without concerns about the economic implications for their loved ones.

Guaranteed Contracts and Non-guaranteed Contracts represent two distinct approaches to pre-funded funeral arrangements, each with its own set of implications. In a **Guaranteed Contract**, the funeral home commits to providing the specified services and merchandise in the future at a cost not exceeding the original contracted amount plus any accrued interest. This arrangement shields individuals from potential price increases in funeral services and ensures that the agreed-upon services will be delivered without additional financial burden on the family. The funeral home assumes the responsibility of honoring the agreed-upon terms, offering financial security to the pre-planning individual and their loved ones.

Non-guaranteed Contracts, in contrast, involve an agreement where the funeral home commits to applying the pre-paid amount plus any accrued interest to the future balance due. However, the actual cost of the funeral is determined by the prevailing prices for services and merchandise at the time of need. This means that the family may be subject to paying any additional costs resulting from price inflation between the time of pre-planning and the time of the funeral. While this approach allows for flexibility and potential adjustments based on current prices, it introduces uncertainty regarding the total financial commitment required when the services are eventually rendered. Choosing between these contract types depends on individual preferences and priorities, balancing the desire for cost predictability against potential flexibility in service selection.

Many funeral homes adopt a hybrid approach when establishing pre-funded funeral contracts, combining elements of both Guaranteed and Non-guaranteed Contracts. Internal costs, such as services and merchandise directly provided by the funeral home, are often guaranteed to shield pre-planning individuals and their families from potential price fluctuations. However, external charges, known as cash advance charges, are typically treated as non-guaranteed. These charges, associated with third-party vendors, are external to the funeral home's control, making it challenging to predict or fix the costs over time. This strategic blend allows funeral homes to offer financial security for certain aspects of the funeral services while acknowledging the unpredictable nature of external charges, ensuring transparency and flexibility in the pre-funded funeral arrangements.

Example:

As an illustration, Mrs. Thompson allocates $10,000 for her funeral arrangements, with $8,000 designated for services and merchandise, and $2,000 allocated for cash advance charges. This distribution implies that 80% of the reserved funds cover services and merchandise, while the remaining 20% is assigned to cash advance charges. Over the duration, the pre-funded trust account accrues $1,000 in interest. Applying the same percentage breakdown, 80% of the interest, amounting to $800, is allotted for services and merchandise, while the remaining 20%, or $200, is designated for cash advance charges.

Pre-Funded Contract	Total Amount	Percentage	Interest Accrued	Available At-Need	At-Need Cost	Deficit
Initial Deposit	$10,000	100%	$1000	$11,000	$12,000	<$1000>
Services & Merchandise	$8,000	80%	$ 800	$ 8,800	$ 9,500	< $700>
Cash Advance Charges	$2,000	20%	$ 200	$ 2,200	$ 2,500	< $300>

Mrs. Thompson died, and her funeral expenses total $12,000, with $9,500 allocated for services and merchandise and $2,500 for cash advance charges. Utilizing the previously determined percentage allocations: 80% of the $1,000 interest, or $800, is applied to cover services and merchandise, and the remaining 20%, equivalent to $200, is assigned to offset cash advance charges.

This results in a $1,000 shortfall for the funeral home, encompassing both service and merchandise costs and cash advance charges. Employing the Guaranteed Prefunded Contract approach would entail the funeral home absorbing the entire $1,000 deficit for both services and merchandise as well as cash advance charges. Although the funeral home could opt to write off the $700 as a financial loss or discount, the remaining $300 designated for cash advance charges to third-party vendors would adversely affect the funeral home's overall profitability.

In the hybrid approach for Prefunded Contracts, the funeral home would still account for the $700 as a financial loss or discount. However, the non-guaranteed aspect of the contract, specifically the cash advances, would become the financial responsibility of the next-of-kin. Consequently, they would be required to cover the additional $300 in fees to third-party vendors. This represents the most financially prudent business move when dealing with pre-funded contracts, eliminating the financial burden on the funeral home to absorb fees independent from funeral home operations. Particularly in large funeral homes that handle several thousand dollars annually in prefunded pre-need accounts, this approach would significantly impact the company's cash flow.

Revocable Pre-Funded Accounts

A revocable pre-funded pre-need funeral account is an arrangement where individuals set aside funds for their future funeral expenses, allowing them to plan and ensure that their wishes are met after death. One essential element of such an account is its revocability, meaning that the account holder retains the right to modify or cancel the arrangement at any time. This flexibility provides individuals with the option to adjust their plans based on changing circumstances or preferences, offering a degree of control over their financial decisions.

Another crucial aspect is the pre-funding component, involving the allocation of funds for funeral services, merchandise, and potentially cash advance charges. The funds are typically placed in a trust or insurance policy, ensuring that the designated amount is available when needed. This pre-funding aspect helps protect against rising funeral costs, providing financial security for both the account holder and their loved ones. If there are surplus funds after covering the funeral expenses, typically, these remaining funds are returned to the estate of the deceased for redistribution in accordance with the stipulations outlined in the will.

Moreover, a well-structured revocable pre-funded pre-need funeral account should include clear terms and conditions, specifying how the funds will be utilized and the funeral services covered. Transparent communication between the account holder and the funeral home is paramount to ensure that expectations are met. Overall, a revocable pre-funded pre-need funeral account offers individuals the peace of mind that their end-of-life wishes will be honored while allowing for flexibility in financial planning.

Irrevocable Trust Accounts

Establishing an irrevocable pre-funded funeral account involves specific elements and qualifications, particularly for individuals who qualify for public assistance, DSS (Department of Social Services), SSI (Supplemental Security Income) benefits, or those in a 'spend-down mode' of their assets. The primary purpose of these accounts is to assist individuals with limited financial resources in setting aside funds for their funeral expenses while ensuring that these funds are protected and used exclusively for this purpose.

To qualify for this type of account, individuals often work with financial and legal professionals to create a legally binding and irrevocable trust agreement. The trust agreement outlines the specific terms and conditions governing the use of funds and designates the funeral expenses as the sole purpose for which the funds can be utilized. These funds are considered portable, meaning they can be transferred from one funeral home to another if the beneficiary relocates, providing flexibility to the account holder. In such instances, the funds must be directly transferred to the alternative funeral home, accompanied by the condition that an irrevocable account is to be established utilizing these funds.

However, it's crucial to note that any surplus funds remaining in the irrevocable pre-funded funeral account after covering the funeral expenses become the property of the governmental agency that financially supported the individual before their death. This condition ensures that the funds set aside for funeral expenses do not impact the individual's eligibility for public assistance, and any excess surplus reverts to the entity responsible for the individual's financial support during their lifetime. Irrevocable pre-funded funeral accounts serve as a valuable resource for individuals in need, offering a means to plan for funeral costs while adhering to the regulations governing public assistance programs.

Scenario

Upon Mrs. Thompson's death, the family gathered to arrange her funeral. She had pre-funded her wishes for a traditional service, including calling hours and a funeral at the local United Methodist Church, with burial beside her late husband in Pleasant Grove Cemetery. However, a division emerged within the family, with half inclined to honor Mrs. Thompson's predetermined wishes, while the other half leaned towards foregoing services, opting for cremation as the chosen method of final disposition, with plans to inter the cremated remains atop her husband's grave.

A mistake often made in the funeral industry is the inclination of some funeral directors to modify the terms of preneed contracts to align with the preferences of the grieving family. It's essential to underscore that preneed and pre-funded funeral contracts are legally binding agreements that must be upheld, regardless of the family's inclination to modify the funeral services and arrangements. This becomes particularly crucial in families experiencing internal conflicts, where disagreements may arise regarding the predetermined terms of the prearrangements. In such instances, strict adherence to the wishes outlined by the deceased becomes imperative. In situations where there's an anticipated chance of family opposition to the purchaser's preferences, it is advisable to implement a Designated Agent agreement. This measure ensures that the buyer's wishes are honored and adhered to as intended.

Deviating from or altering these arrangements constitutes a breach of the contractual obligations assumed by the funeral director in relation to the deceased, thereby exposing the funeral home to potential legal repercussions in the form of future litigations. Funeral professionals need to approach these situations with sensitivity, emphasizing the legal and ethical obligations associated with preneed contracts as part of risk management.

Setting Pre-Need Funds Aside for Future Use

To secure preneed funds for future use, a prudent approach involves depositing these funds into a secure financial instrument, like FDIC-insured accounts or Certificates of Deposit (CDs), registered in the name of the purchaser along with their social security number. This financial segregation ensures that preneed funds remain distinct from the funeral home's operational funds, establishing a clear delineation of assets. Co-mingling of funds can also lead to criminal charges of fraud or larceny. The decision to earmark these funds in the purchaser's name is driven by the tax implications associated with the annual interest accrued. In the case of revocable accounts, it becomes the purchaser's responsibility to fulfill tax obligations on the earned interest. In contrast, those who opt for irrevocable trust accounts often fall below the income tax filing threshold, providing a tax advantage. Any deviation from these practices, such as funeral directors utilizing pre-need funds for personal use or commingling them with funeral home funds, constitutes a breach of state laws governing pre-need accounts. Such violations not only expose the funeral home and its director to potential litigation but also erode the sacred trust established between the funeral director and their clients.

Funeral professionals are entrusted with a solemn duty to uphold the integrity of preneed funds and maintain unwavering fidelity to legal standards. This commitment goes beyond financial prudence; it speaks to the ethical foundation of the funeral industry, where transparency, accountability, and the sanctity of the client-funeral director relationship must be safeguarded at all costs. Any deviation from these principles jeopardizes the reputation of the funeral home, eroding the trust that families place in their chosen funeral director during times of grief and vulnerability.

Using Insurance to Fund Funeral Accounts

Funeral insurance and burial insurance, often used interchangeably, have nuanced differences. Funeral insurance typically refers to a broader coverage that extends beyond funeral expenses alone, including additional costs related to end-of-life arrangements. On the other hand, burial insurance is more specific, focusing primarily on covering funeral costs and related expenses. The advantages of using insurance as a funding vehicle for funeral expenses lie in the financial security it provides to the insured's beneficiaries. In the event of the policyholder's demise, the insurance payout can be utilized to cover funeral costs, relieving the family of immediate financial burdens. Additionally, these insurance policies often offer flexibility in terms of coverage amounts, allowing individuals to tailor their plans according to their anticipated funeral expenses.

However, there are disadvantages to relying solely on insurance for funeral funding. One limitation is that insurance policies may have waiting periods before the full benefits become available, leaving families in a vulnerable position during the initial period after a loved one's passing. Another consideration is the potential for premiums to increase over time, impacting the affordability of the insurance. Moreover, insurance may not be an option in some states due to regulatory constraints. Strict adherence to state regulations is imperative, necessitating proper licensing for insurance agents involved in selling funeral insurance policies.

The use of funeral and burial insurance requires a thorough understanding of the specific policies, terms, and regulatory frameworks in place. Families should carefully assess the advantages and disadvantages of insurance options, considering their unique financial circumstances and the regulations governing such policies in their state. From a consumer perspective, burial insurance may not be the most user-friendly option. If, for any reason, the policyholder fails to make premium payments, the policy could lapse, leading to a forfeiture of funds accumulated over time. On the contrary, individuals contributing monthly payments to a pre-need burial fund enjoy a more protective structure. Even if they miss a scheduled payment or two, their funds remain safeguarded within the account and are not subject to stringent restrictions. This flexibility in pre-need burial funds offers a more resilient and forgiving approach for individuals managing their financial commitments. A well-informed decision ensures that the intended financial support for funeral expenses remains a reliable and effective strategy.

FTC Compliance with Pre-Need

Compliance with state and Federal Trade Commission (FTC) guidelines is crucial for funeral homes when managing pre-funded pre-need accounts. State regulations vary, and funeral directors must adhere to specific guidelines outlined by state authorities to ensure the proper handling of pre-need funds. These guidelines often cover the establishment, management, and reporting of pre-funded accounts, emphasizing transparency and accountability.

In addition to state regulations, the FTC's door-to-door rule plays a significant role in pre-need sales. This rule ensures that consumers have the right to cancel a contract made at their home, workplace, or dormitory within three days of signing. Funeral directors engaged in door-to-door sales of pre-funded pre-need plans must provide consumers with a written cancellation notice and a form for canceling the contract. Some states, such as New York, prohibit door-to-door sales of pre-need sales. Adherence to these guidelines is crucial to maintaining ethical practices, protecting consumers' rights, and avoiding potential legal issues for funeral service providers.

Probate

Will	an instrument executed with required formality, by an individual making disposition of their property to take effect upon their death.
Nuncupative Will	oral will declared or dictated by testator during last illness before appropriate witnesses to dispose of personal property and afterwards reduced to writing (not valid in all states).
Holograph Will	a will written entirely by the hand of the testator.
Codicil	an addition or amendment of a last will and testament executed with the same formality of the will.
Per Capita	the method of dividing an estate by which an equal share is given to each of a number of persons, all of whom stand in equal degree of kindred to the decedent.
Per Stirpes	the method of proportionately dividing an estate between beneficiaries according to their deceased ancestor's share.
Escheat	forfeiture of a decedent's property to the state in the absence of heirs.
Executor	A male appointed by a testator to carry out the terms of their will.
Executrix	A female appointed by a testator to carry out the terms of their will.
Administrator	A male legally appointed by the courts to manage and dispose of the estate of a person who dies intestate, without a will.
Administratrix	A female legally appointed by the courts toto manage and dispose of the estate of a person who dies intestate, without a will.
Testator	A person who makes and executes a last will and testament.
Letters of Testamentary	A document issued by Probate Court that permits the executor/executrix of an estate to act on behalf of a person who died with a will.
Letters of Administration	A document issued by Probate Court authorizing an administer/administratrix the authority to settle the final affairs of a person who died intestate.

Probate Court System

Probate Court is a legal forum tasked with overseeing the administration and distribution of a deceased person's estate, ensuring that their assets are properly managed and dispersed according to the law. The probate process involves validating the deceased individual's will, if one exists, or determining the rightful distribution of assets through intestate succession if there is no will. Typically, the court appoints an executor or personal representative to handle the estate affairs, settle outstanding debts, and distribute assets to heirs and beneficiaries. The probate process is designed to provide a structured and legal framework for the fair resolution of a deceased person's financial and legal matters, offering a transparent and accountable approach to estate settlement.

A **will** is a legal document that outlines an individual's wishes regarding the distribution of their assets and the care of any dependents upon their death. It typically names an executor, who is responsible for ensuring the terms of the will are carried out. To create a valid will, one must be of sound mind and follow specific legal requirements, such as having witnesses present during the signing.

Nuncupative wills, also known as oral wills, are verbal declarations made by a testator in the presence of witnesses. These are often limited to specific circumstances, such as imminent peril of death, and their validity varies by jurisdiction. Some states do not honor nuncupative wills. **Holograph wills** are handwritten by the testator and are recognized in some regions even if they lack witnesses. A **codicil**, on the other hand, is a legal document that modifies, amends, or revokes provisions in an existing will without rewriting the entire document. It allows individuals to make updates or changes to their will without creating an entirely new one, providing flexibility in estate planning.

The **court proceeding that validates a will** is known as probate. Probate is the legal process through which a court determines the authenticity and legality of a deceased person's will. During probate, the court reviews the document, verifies its authenticity, and ensures that it meets all legal requirements. The court also oversees the distribution of the deceased person's assets as outlined in the will, paying off debts and taxes before distributing the remaining estate to the beneficiaries. The funeral expenses are the first to be paid from an estate, in addition to back taxes.

A **will can be contested** for various reasons, leading to disputes during the probate process. Some common grounds for contesting a will include allegations of undue influence, lack of testamentary capacity, fraud, or the existence of a more recent and valid will. Undue influence implies that someone pressured or manipulated the testator into making decisions against their own free will. Lack of testamentary capacity means that the testator was not mentally competent or of sound mind when creating the will. Fraud involves deceptive practices that might have influenced the testator's decisions. Disputes can arise when family members or beneficiaries believe that the will does not accurately reflect the testator's true intentions or that it is not legally valid.

The designation of an executor or administratrix holds significant importance within the probate procedure. An executor, specified in the will of the deceased, assumes the crucial role of overseeing and dispersing the estate in accordance with the stipulations outlined in the will. In the case of a female appointed for this role, she is referred to as an executrix. **Letters of testamentary**, legal documents granted by the court, confer the necessary authority upon the executor to fulfill their responsibilities. These letters serve as official recognition of the executor's status and furnish proof to financial institutions and other entities regarding their legal empowerment.

In cases where there is no will or the appointed executor is unable or unwilling to fulfill their duties, the **court may appoint an administrator or administratrix**. A letter of administration is then issued by the court, providing legal authority to the administrator to manage and distribute the estate. In the case of a female appointed by the courts for this role, she is referred to and as an administratrix. When a person dies intestate, meaning without a valid will, the court may appoint an administrator or administratrix to handle the distribution of assets according to the laws of intestate succession, which typically prioritize spouses, children, or other close relatives as beneficiaries. The administrator ensures that the estate is distributed fairly and in accordance with applicable laws when no specific instructions are provided by a will.

Specific Form and Terms

For a **will to be considered valid**, it typically needs to conform to specific legal requirements. First, the document must be in writing and signed by the testator, the person making the will, or by someone else in their presence and at their direction. Additionally, the testator's signature must be witnessed by at least two competent individuals who also sign the document in the testator's presence. These witnesses are typically required to be disinterested parties, meaning they do not stand to inherit from the will. Some jurisdictions may have additional requirements, such as notarization or the inclusion of certain language to express the testator's intent clearly.

Now, let's delve into the comparison and contrast of the terms "**per stirpes**" and "**per capita**" in the context of inheritance. Both are Latin terms used to determine how an estate is distributed among descendants. Per stirpes means "by branch" and involves distributing the estate among different branches of the family, typically through the deceased person's children. Each branch receives an equal share, regardless of the number of individuals in that branch. On the other hand, per capita means "by head" and involves distributing the estate equally among all living descendants, regardless of the family branch. In per capita distribution, each individual receives an equal share, promoting equality among all heirs. The key distinction lies in whether the distribution is based on family branches (per stirpes) or individuals (per capita), highlighting the nuanced approaches to inheritance planning and reflecting the diverse preferences and circumstances that may arise in estate distribution scenarios.

In addition to the last will and testament, several other legal documents may be created simultaneously to ensure comprehensive estate planning. A common companion document is a living will, which outlines an individual's preferences for medical treatments and decisions in case they become incapacitated. A durable power of attorney appoints someone to make financial and legal decisions on behalf of the individual if they are unable to do so themselves. A healthcare proxy designates a person to make medical decisions in case the individual is unable to communicate their wishes. A revocable & irrevocable living trust is another option that allows for the seamless transfer of assets without going through probate. Additionally, individuals may create a letter of instruction, providing guidance on personal and financial matters for their heirs. These supplementary legal documents work in conjunction with a will to create a comprehensive and clear plan for the management of one's affairs during both life and after death.

Distribution of Assets

The administration of an estate involves the systematic and legal management of a deceased person's assets by a personal representative, often appointed in the deceased's will or by the court. The personal representative, commonly referred to as an executor or administrator, plays a crucial role in executing the deceased's wishes, settling debts, and distributing remaining assets to heirs or beneficiaries. One of the initial duties involves taking an inventory of the deceased person's assets to determine the overall value of the probate estate. This inventory includes a comprehensive list of real estate, bank accounts, investments, personal property, and other assets. The valuation process is essential for calculating the estate's worth and addressing financial obligations, such as debts and taxes, before distributing the remaining assets.

In the context of secured claims and liens, these represent legal interests or financial obligations tied to specific assets within the estate. Real estate mortgage and personal property liens may be attached to assets to secure debts owed by the deceased. When calculating the value of the probate estate, these secured claims are deducted from the overall value to determine the net value available for distribution among heirs or beneficiaries. Real estate mortgages, for instance, involve loans secured by the deceased's real property, and the outstanding balance is subtracted from the property's value. Similarly, personal property may be subject to liens, and the amount owed is subtracted from the overall value of that particular asset. Addressing secured claims and liens is a critical step in the probate process to ensure an accurate and fair distribution of the remaining estate assets.

An insolvent estate refers to a situation in probate where the deceased person's debts surpass the total value of their assets. In such cases, the estate lacks sufficient funds to cover all outstanding debts and obligations, leaving creditors with unresolved claims. When confronted with an insolvent estate, the probate process typically involves a specific order of priority in settling debts, with secured creditors taking precedence over unsecured creditors. The assets are then distributed among creditors in proportion to their respective claims. In situations of insolvency, heirs or beneficiaries may not receive the full value of their inheritance, highlighting the importance of estate planning and financial management to mitigate the risk of an insolvent estate.

Escheat is a legal concept that comes into play when an individual dies without a will (intestate) or without any identifiable heirs to inherit their property. In such cases, the deceased person's assets, including real estate, bank accounts, and other possessions, may revert to the state through the process of escheat. The rationale behind escheat is to prevent property from remaining ownerless or abandoned, ensuring that assets are ultimately put to use for public benefit rather than being left in a state of legal limbo. Laws governing escheat vary by jurisdiction, and the conditions under which property escheats to the state are typically outlined in statutes. While the concept serves a practical purpose in preventing the indefinite abandonment of assets, it underscores the importance of estate planning to designate heirs and beneficiaries, as without such arrangements, the state may step in to claim the unclaimed property.

Misconduct or Unethical Professional Behavior

In funeral services, adherence to ethical standards and professional conduct is of paramount importance. Across the United States, states have implemented specific statutes, rules, and regulations to define and govern what constitutes misconduct or unprofessional behavior for individuals working in the funeral profession. These guidelines may vary from state-to-state, they are designed to ensure the integrity of funeral services, protect the interests of bereaved families, and maintain the reputation of the industry. The careful explanation of acceptable practices and ethical standards serves as a framework for funeral professionals to uphold the highest standards of service and compassion while maintaining the delicate responsibilities associated with death care and serving the bereaved. The adherence to state-mandated rules becomes a cornerstone in preserving the trust and dignity essential to the funeral profession.

Prohibited Conduct

The prohibition of specific behaviors in the funeral industry is grounded in ethical considerations, legal obligations, and the fundamental principles of respect for the deceased and their grieving families. One such prohibited behavior is the removal of human remains without expressed authority from the next-of-kin. This safeguard ensures that the family's wishes are respected, and their legal rights to make decisions regarding the disposition of their loved one's remains are upheld. Unauthorized removal can lead to emotional distress for the family and erode trust in funeral professionals, emphasizing the need for explicit consent and communication to maintain the integrity of the funeral process.

Embalming without the oral or written permission of the family is another prohibited act. Embalming is a significant aspect of funeral practices, and obtaining consent is crucial for ethical reasons and legal compliance. Families have the right to decide how their loved ones are treated after death, and unauthorized embalming infringes upon that right. Conducting a funeral or disposing of remains without proper authority is also expressly prohibited. Such actions can result in legal consequences, as they undermine the legal frameworks established to ensure that funeral services are carried out in accordance with the wishes and rights of the deceased and their families.

Furthermore, mutilation in the preparation or restoration of human remains is strictly forbidden. This prohibition stems from a commitment to treating the deceased with dignity and preserving their physical integrity as much as possible. Acts like removing the deceased's teeth, even at the family's request, violate ethical standards and are actions outside the scope of a funeral director's license. Failure to surrender or dispose of remains upon the family's request and engaging in illegal acts or violations of licensing laws are additional prohibitions designed to maintain the trust and professionalism within the funeral industry, ultimately prioritizing the rights and wishes of grieving families.

Qualifications for Funeral Service Practitioner License

Specific Requirements by Law

Licensing within the profession for funeral directors and embalmers is a regulated process governed by state-specific legal requirements. These regulations, while varying from state-to-state, commonly include prerequisites such as meeting a legal age requirement, holding citizenship or legal residency status, and demonstrating good moral and legal character. These criteria aim to ensure that individuals entering the funeral profession possess the foundational qualities necessary to uphold the ethical and legal standards associated with this sensitive field. Professional education is another key aspect of licensure, with most states requiring completion of a mortuary science program accredited by the American Board of Funeral Service Education (ABFSE). This educational component ensures that aspiring funeral directors and embalmers acquire the necessary theoretical knowledge and practical skills to provide competent and compassionate service to bereaved families.

A crucial step in the licensure process involves practical experience through a residency, internship, or apprenticeship within a funeral home, typically conducted on a full-time basis and within the jurisdiction of the state. This hands-on training ensures that individuals are well acquainted with the day-to-day operations of a funeral home and are prepared to handle the diverse challenges that may arise in the profession.

To assess basic competency, many states mandate the completion of a state or national board exam. The National Board Exam in Funeral Services, administered by the International Conference of Funeral Service Examination Boards, is currently one of the most widely recognized examinations in the field. This exam evaluates candidates on a range of topics, including funeral service arts, sciences, and regulatory compliance.

Finally, to gauge knowledge of state-specific laws governing the practice of funeral directing, most states require candidates to pass a final mortuary jurisprudence exam. This examination ensures that licensed professionals are well-versed in the legal framework that governs their practice within a particular state, reinforcing the commitment to ethical, legal, and professional conduct in the funeral services industry.

Revocation of Suspension of License

The revocation or suspension of a funeral director's license can occur for various reasons, primarily tied to professional misconduct and unethical behavior that violate the state laws governing the practice of funeral directing and embalming. Instances of such misconduct may include breaches of ethical standards, violation of legal regulations, or actions that undermine the integrity of the funeral service profession.

One specific reason for license revocation or suspension is the fraudulent acquisition of a license or credentials, including altering documents verifying educational qualifications. Making false statements or engaging in false representation to obtain a license also falls within this category. Aiding and abetting the false identity of a licensed funeral director or embalmer is considered a serious offense, warranting regulatory action, and possibly criminal litigation.

Another set of grounds for disciplinary action includes being convicted of a criminal act involving a felony or moral turpitude or being deemed unfit for licensure due to reasons such as substance abuse or insanity. These factors are considered significant indicators of an individual's ability to responsibly carry out the duties associated with the funeral services profession.

Refusal to surrender human remains when requested by the family, holding remains hostage for payment, or performing services outside the authorized limits are additional actions that may lead to the revocation or suspension of a funeral director's license. Such behaviors not only violate ethical standards but also compromise the trust and well-being of the bereaved families involved.

Finally, willful false statements on death certificates or other legal documents, untrustworthiness in financial matters, including the misappropriation of pre-funded pre-need funds, and failure to fulfill continuing education requirements are all factors that can contribute to the disciplinary measures taken against a funeral director. These regulations and consequences aim to maintain the highest standards of professionalism, ethics, and integrity within the funeral services industry. Again, such violations are criminal offences.

Complaint Against Funeral Directors

When a funeral director is alleged to have violated a state regulation overseeing the practice of funeral directing and a written complaint is filed by a consumer, a comprehensive investigation is initiated by the regulatory agency. The focal point of this inquiry is to scrutinize the alleged violations and assess their legitimacy. In response to the charges, the funeral director is required to provide a timely and substantive reply, detailing their perspective and offering any pertinent evidence. A funeral director should seek legal counsel during this phase to ensure a thorough understanding of the legal implications and to prepare a robust defense. Saying the wrong thing without advice from counsel could incriminate them in their defense of the regulations.

Should the regulatory agency decide that the matter warrants further examination, it may proceed to a formal hearing. In this scenario, the funeral director may be issued a subpoena, requiring their attendance at a hearing, signaling the seriousness of the accusations. The hearing serves as a platform for presenting evidence, witness testimonies, and legal arguments to adjudicate the alleged violations. Legal representation remains crucial at this stage to navigate the complexities of the hearing process and to advocate for the funeral director's rights and best interests.

The adjudication process aims to reach a fair and just resolution, considering the evidence presented and the applicable legal standards. The outcome may include disciplinary actions such as license suspension, revocation, or imposition of fines, depending on the severity of the violations. Overall, this structured regulatory process is designed to uphold the integrity of the funeral profession, ensuring accountability for practitioners, and safeguarding the interests and trust of the bereaved families they serve.

FUNERAL SERVICE LAW – GLOSSARY

Abatement – a proportional reduction of a devise when estate assets are not sufficient to pay it in full.

Actual custody – the physical possession of the dead human body or other property.

Ademption – the extinction or withdrawal of a devise because decedent did not own the named property at the time of death.

Administrative agency – a governmental body created by legislation empowered to make and enforce rules and regulations.

Administrative law – the rules and regulations created by Federal and State administrative agencies (e.g., OSHA, FTC, state board rules and regulations).

Agent driver – those drivers under the directions and control of the funeral establishment which is liable for the driver's negligent actions.

Americans with Disabilities Act (ADA) – a federal statute prohibiting discrimination against the disabled in employment, public transportation, telecommunications services, and public accommodations and services.

Apprenticeship (internship/resident training) – the process by which a person engages in learning the practice of funeral directing and/or embalming under instruction, direction or personal supervision of a duly licensed funeral director and/or embalmer.

Bailee – a person who receives personal property from another as a bailment.

Bailment – a delivery of personal property by one person (the bailor) to another (the bailee) who holds the property for a certain purpose under an express or implied-in-fact contract.

Bailor – a person who delivers personal property to another as a bailment.

Body parts – organs, tissues, eyes, bones, arteries, blood, other fluids and other portions of a human body.

Brain death – total and irreversible cessation of brain function as indicated by a flat EEG reading.

Building code – laws, ordinances and government regulations setting forth requirements for construction, maintenance, operation, occupancy, use or appearance of buildings.

Burial (interment/inhumement) – the act of placing the dead human body in the ground.

Cadaver – a dead human body intended solely for scientific study and dissection.

Case law – appellate court decisions based on custom and usage and prior decisions

Cemetery – an area of ground set aside and dedicated for the final disposition of dead human bodies.

Codicil – an addition or amendment of a last will and testament executed with the same formality of the will.

Common carrier – any carrier required by law to convey passengers or freight without refusal if the approved fare or charge is paid (e.g., airline, train, etc.).

Constitution – the fundamental law that establishes the government, limits what government can and cannot do and states the underlying principles to which the government will conform.

Contract – a legally enforceable agreement.

Contract carrier – provides transportation for compensation only to those with whom it desires to do business (e.g., livery service)

Constructive custody – the situation whereby one party has a right to acquire actual custody/possession of the dead body although another party has actual physical possession.

Coroner – a public officer whose duty it is to investigate cause of death when the question of accident, suicide, or homicide may be evident or where there was no doctor in attendance (see also medical examiner).

Corpse (dead human body) – the body of a dead human being, deprived of life, but not yet entirely disintegrated.

Cremated remains – the final product remaining after completion of the entire cremation/pulverization process. The biproduct should never be referred to as "cremains or ashes."

Cremation – the reduction of a dead human body to inorganic bone fragments by intense heat in a specifically designed retort or chamber.

Crematory – the location of the retort/cremation chamber which will perform the cremation process.

Crime – an action against society as a whole in violation of constitution, statues, or ordinances, e.g., treason, felony, misdemeanor.

Custodian – status associated with funeral service practitioner/funeral establishment who becomes legal protector of dead human body from time of removal until final disposition.

Dead human body – (see corpse)

Death – the cessation of life; permanent cessations of all vital functions and signs. (See additional definitions in Embalming Outline, PHT 6)

Degree of kindred – relationship of decedent to blood relatives.

Devise – a gift of real or personal property by will.

Devisee – the person who receives a devise.

Disinterment (exhumation) – the removal of a human remains from previous location of final disposition.

Due diligence – the attention reasonably expected from, and ordinarily exercised by, a person who seeks to satisfy a legal requirement or to discharge an obligation.

Durable power of attorney – a power of attorney that remains in effect after the disability or incapacity of the principal (see also power of attorney).

Embalmer – a person, properly licensed, who disinfects, preserves, and/or restores a dead human body.

Eminent domain – the inherent power of a government to take private property for public use. In the U.S. just compensation to the property owner(s) is required.

Entombment – the placing of remains in a crypt in a mausoleum.

Environmental Protection Agency (EPA) – a governmental agency with environmental protection regulatory and enforcement authority.

Escheat – forfeiture of a decedent's property to the state in the absence of heirs.

Escrow account – in funeral service, a vehicle used to hold monies paid on prefunded contracts and beyond the control of the funeral director.

Estate – the property and debts of a deceased person, both real and/or personal.

Estrangement – the physical and/or emotional separation for a period of time showing the lack of affection, trust and regard.

Exhumation – see Disinterment.

Federal Trade Commission (FTC) – an agency of federal government to promote free and fair competition by prevention of trade restraints, price fixing, false advertising and other unfair methods of competition.

Final disposition – the conclusive performance of services with respect to the dead human body by one of the legally recognized methods.

Funeral director (funeral service practitioner) – a person properly licensed, engaged in, or conducting, or holding himself/herself out as being engaged in preparing, other than by embalming, for the burial or disposition of dead human bodies.

Funeral establishment – a facility used in the care and preparation for the funeral and/or final disposition of dead human bodies.

Funeral service law (mortuary law/mortuary jurisprudence) – that branch of law which relates to matters concerned with the disposal of the dead and regulation of funeral directors/embalmers and funeral establishments.

Funeral service practitioner – see Funeral director.

General power of attorney – a written instrument granting the agent broad powers to act for the principal.

Gross negligent act – the intentional failure or the reckless disregard of the consequences with respect to conduct affecting the life or property of another.

Guaranteed contract – an agreement whereby the funeral home promises that the services and merchandise will be provided at the time of need (in the future) for a sum not exceeding the original amount of the aforementioned contract plus any accruals, regardless of the current prices associated with providing the services and merchandise at the time of the funeral.

Guardian – a person appointed by the court to administer the affairs of another person who is incompetent by virtue of age or legal disability.

Heir – one who inherits or is entitled to receive property by laws of intestacy.

Holographic will – a will written entirely by the hand of the testator.

Inheritance – the estate which passes from the decedent to heirs.

Inhumement (burial/interment) – see Burial.

Insolvent estate – the condition of the estate of a deceased person which is unable to pay the debts of the decedent and/or the estate.

Interment – the act of placing the dead human body in the ground.

Internship – see Apprenticeship.

Interstate – between two or more states.

Intestate – the state or condition of dying without having made a will; intestacy.

Intestate succession – the method used to distribute property owned by a person who dies without a valid will.

Intrastate – within a state.

Inventory – listing and valuation of a decedent's assets by personal representative of the estate.

Invitee – one who has been invited on the property by the landowner; persons coming to a funeral home for the purpose of attending funerals, viewing remains, or engaging the funeral director's services are some examples.

Irrevocable contract – an agreement for future funeral services which cannot be terminated or canceled prior to the death of the beneficiary.

Kin – one's relatives collectively; referring to blood relationship (legally, the surviving spouse is not a kin).

Law – those rules of conduct commanding what is right and prohibiting what is wrong.

Liability – responsibility for actions and/or other debts; the quality or state of being legally obligated or accountable.

Lien – a claim or charge against real or personal property for payment of some debt (there can be no lien against a dead human body for it is not property).

Livery – automotive equipment made available for hire.

Living will – a document which governs the withholding or withdrawal of life-sustaining treatment from an individual in the event of an incurable or irreversible condition that will cause death within a relatively short time, and which becomes effective when such person is no longer able to make decisions regarding his/her medical treatment.

Malpractice – failure to perform a professional service with the ability and care generally exercised by others in the profession.

Medical examiner – a forensically-trained physician whose duty it is to investigate questionable or unattended deaths (has replaced the coroner in many states); (see also coroner)

Mental anguish – a condition which may result from an outrageous intentional or grossly negligent act and may be accompanied by physical injury.

Morgue – a place where dead human remains are kept until identified and/or released for final disposition.

Mortgage – a secured loan on a parcel of real property.

Moral turpitude – an act showing inherent baseness or vileness of principle or action; shameful wickedness; depravity.

Mortuary law – see Funeral service law.

Mutilation – any altering or change made to a dead human body from the time of death, other than by natural causes.

Negligence – failure to exercise reasonable care.

Non-guaranteed contract – agreement in which the funeral home promises to apply the amount pre-paid plus any accruals to the balance due. However, the cost of the funeral will be based upon the current price for the services and merchandise at the time the services are provided.

Nuisance - a landowner's use of property which interferes with the public or another landowner's use of his property.

Nuisance in fact – acts, occupations or structures which are not nuisances per se, but may become nuisances by reason of the location or manner in which it is operated.

Nuisance per se – acts, occupations or structures which are nuisances at all times and under all circumstances; it may be prejudicial to public morals, dangerous to life, or injurious to public rights.

Nuncupative will – oral will declared or dictated by testator during last illness before appropriate witnesses to dispose of personal property and afterwards reduced to writing (not valid in all states).

Occupational Safety and Health Administration (OSHA) – a governmental agency with the responsibility for regulation and enforcement of safety and health matters for most employees.

Ordinance – a law passed by a local municipal governing body (e.g., zoning, building, safety, etc.).

Outrageous act – an act with complete disregard for proper conduct which transcends the bounds of common decency.

Per capita – the method of dividing an estate by which an equal share is given to each of a number of persons, all of whom stand in equal degree of kindred to the decedent.

Personal representative – person who is appointed by the court to represent and administer the estate of deceased persons.

Per stirpes – the method of proportionately dividing an estate between beneficiaries according to their deceased ancestor's share.

Police power – the inherent power of a government to make reasonable laws to protect the safety, health, morals and general welfare of its citizens.

Power of attorney – an instrument granting someone authority to act as agent or attorney-in-fact for the principal; an ordinary power of attorney is revocable and automatically terminates upon the death or incapacity of the principal.

Preferred claim – a claim which is accorded a priority, advantage or privilege.

Pre-funded funeral arrangements – funeral arrangements made in advance of need that include provisions for funding or prepayment.

Preparation room – that portion or location in a funeral establishment specifically designed and equipped for embalming and otherwise preparing dead human bodies.

Pre-planned funeral arrangements – funeral arrangements made in advance of need that do not include provisions for funding or prepayment.

Priority – the order in which claims will be paid when there are insufficient assets to pay all of the claims, or the order in which certain classes of people have the right to make decisions concerning the disposition of the dead body.

Private carrier – those who transport only in particular instances and only for those they choose to contract with (e.g., funeral home vehicles and livery)

Private cemetery – a cemetery owned by a private enterprise such as a corporation for profit, a non-profit corporation, partnership, sole owners, religious orders, etc.

Probate – the process of administering the estate and determining the validity of a will.

Probate court – a court having jurisdiction over estates.

Probate estate – the property and debts of a decedent that is subject to administration by the personal representative of an estate.

Public cemetery – a cemetery owned by a governmental unit (federal, state or municipal).

Quasi-property theory – the accepted theory of the legal status of a dead human body; rights associated with the body are as if it were property for the purpose of disposition only.

Reciprocity – the relationship existing between two states whereby each extends some privileges of licensure to licensees of the other state.

Replevin – an action to recover possession of wrongfully withheld personal property.

Resident training – see Apprenticeship.

Restrictive covenant – provision in a deed limiting the use of real property and prohibiting certain uses.

Revocable contract – agreement which may be terminated by the purchaser at any time prior to the death of the beneficiary with a refund of the monies paid on the contract as prescribed by state law.

Revocation – the omission or cancellation of an instrument, act, license or promise.

Rules and regulations – laws created by an administrative agency within its jurisdiction.

Secured claim – a debt which is supported by a pledge, mortgage or lien on assets belonging to the debtor.

Solvent estate – an estate in which the assets exceed the liabilities.

Springing power of attorney – a written instrument authorizing one person to act as an agent for another effective only upon a certain event occurring.

Stare decisis – a policy of courts to stand by a decision and apply it to future cases where the facts are substantially the same.

Statute – a law enacted by a legislative body

Testate – the condition of leaving a will at death.

Testator – a person who makes a valid will.

 Third party contracts – agreements which are incident to providing services and merchandise other than by the funeral establishment i.e. caskets, vaults, urns, cremation services, etc.

Tort – a private or civil wrong against a person or his or her property, other than by breach of contract, for which there may be action for damages.

Trespasser – one who intentionally and without consent or privilege enters another's property.

Trust Account – account established by one individual to be held for the benefit of another (as a method of payment of funeral expenses); creates a fiduciary responsibility. Money paid to a funeral home for future services is placed in an account with the funeral home as trustee for the benefit of another.

Trustee – one who holds title to property or another position of trust to a beneficiary.

Uniform Anatomical Gift Act (UAGA) – a law permitting competent persons or others to give gifts of all or any part of the body to take effect upon death.

Uniform Probate Code – a model law intended to achieve uniformity in probate proceedings throughout the U.S.

Unsecured claim – a claim which is not supported by a pledge, mortgage or lien on other assets.

Vital statistics – the registration, preparation, transcription, collection, compilation and preservation of data pertaining to births, adoptions, deaths, stillbirths, marital status, etc.

Volunteer driver – those drivers not under the control of the funeral director.

Will – an instrument executed with required formality, by persons making disposition of their property to take effect upon their death.

Zoning ordinance – a law passed by a local unit of government which regulates and prescribes the land use planning.

Federal Trade Commission and the Funeral Rule

Brief History of the Federal Trade Commission

The Federal Trade Commission (FTC) was established in 1914 as a response to growing concerns about unfair business practices and anticompetitive behavior in the United States. The agency was created with the enactment of the Federal Trade Commission Act, signed into law by President Woodrow Wilson. The primary objective of the FTC is to promote fair and competitive business practices, prevent anticompetitive behavior, and protect consumers from deceptive or unfair trade practices. Over the years, the FTC has evolved to address emerging challenges in the marketplace, including issues related to consumer privacy, data security, and the regulation of advertising and marketing practices. Today, the FTC plays a vital role in enforcing laws that safeguard consumers and maintain fair competition in the marketplace, making it a cornerstone of consumer protection and antitrust regulation in the United States.

The Sherman Antitrust Act of 1890 and the Clayton Antitrust Act of 1914 played significant roles in influencing the creation of the Federal Trade Commission (FTC). The Sherman Antitrust Act was the first federal legislation designed to curb anticompetitive practices and prevent monopolies. It declared illegal any contract, combination, or conspiracy in restraint of trade, and it aimed to promote fair competition in the marketplace.

However, the Sherman Act lacked specific mechanisms for enforcement and detailed guidelines for businesses to follow. In response to this, the Clayton Antitrust Act was enacted, providing more comprehensive provisions to address antitrust issues. The Clayton Act included provisions that prohibited certain anticompetitive practices, such as price discrimination and exclusive dealing.

The need for a specialized agency to enforce antitrust laws and address unfair methods of competition became apparent. The FTC was established to prevent unfair methods of competition and unfair or deceptive acts or practices in commerce. It was designed to complement the existing antitrust laws by providing a dedicated body to enforce and regulate competition, investigate anticompetitive practices, and promote consumer protection. The creation of the FTC was a response to the evolving challenges in the business landscape, providing a more proactive and specialized approach to antitrust enforcement.

In the history of funeral directing, this industry went unchecked by the FTC until 1963 when Jessica Midford wrote the New York Times Best Sellers book, *The American Way of Death*. This book was an exposé that critically examined the funeral industry and their practices in the United States. Mitford investigated and exposed various practices within the industry, including high costs, exploitation of grieving families, and the commercialization of death, sparking significant public discourse and contributing to reforms in the funeral service sector.

Prior to FTC funeral regulations, the funeral industry in the United States used unit pricing as a means for charging the consumer for goods and services selected by the family at the time of death. Families would select a casket and whatever casket they selected, that was the cost for not only the casket but also the services and other merchandise for the funeral services. For example, the consumer would select a solid oak casket for $2,350.00 and that would include: the use of the funeral home for three days of calling hours and the funeral services, use of the hearse, lead car, pallbearers' car, sundries, and graveside service. This package deal, while all inclusive, was the same price for a consumer who only selected a graveside service with use of the lead car, hearse and graveside service. Midford's book exposed this, and other unfair business practices in the funeral industry.

The funeral industry was on the brink of FTC regulation in the 1960s, but the tragic event of President John F. Kennedy's assassination on November 22, 1963, shifted public attention and mourning to a national scale, largely facilitated by television. In the four days following Kennedy's death, the world witnessed a grieving nation burying a global leader, portraying funeral directors as participants in a noble profession, earning them the moniker of a "good monopoly." It wasn't until the mid-1970s that the FTC re-evaluated the industry's business practices, prompting reforms and the establishment of modern-day regulations.

The Federal Trade Commission (FTC) regulates funeral services through the Funeral Rule, enacted in 1984. This rule ensures that funeral homes provide consumers with clear and comprehensive information about funeral costs and services. The FTC requires funeral homes to provide a General Price List (GPL) that outlines itemized charges for various services and merchandise. Funeral directors must also disclose information about the availability of caskets for direct purchase and cannot refuse to use a casket purchased elsewhere. The Funeral Rule (also known as: Trade Regulation Rule for Funeral Industry Practices) prohibits deceptive or unfair practices, ensuring that consumers have the right to select only the services and goods they desire. Additionally, funeral homes must provide a Casket Price List and Outer Burial Container Price List for items that may be required, and they are not allowed to misrepresent legal, crematory, or cemetery requirements. The FTC's regulation of funeral services aims to empower consumers, promote transparency, and prevent unfair or deceptive practices within the funeral industry. As emerging consumer buying habits and trends take place in the funeral profession, the FTC institutes new regulations that address these changes in consumer spending.

The Funeral Rule:

The primary purposes of the Funeral Rule are threefold:

1. to give consumers the right to select those funeral goods and services which they wish to purchase;
2. to provide consumers access to detailed, itemized price information prior to purchase decisions; and
3. to prevent misrepresentations and other unfair and deceptive practices in the sale of funeral goods and services.

The Funeral Rule seeks to obtain its objectives by requiring funeral directors to distribute the consumers a series of price lists and documents at various stages of funeral arrangements. These stages are known as "triggering events." These lists must contain itemized prices of the various components of a funeral. Also included in the lists are mandatory printed disclosures informing consumers of the practical and legal necessity of certain funeral goods and services.

A **funeral provider**, as defined by the FTC, encompasses *any individual, partnership, or corporation engaged in the sale or offering for sale of funeral goods and services to the public.* This broad classification includes entities involved in facilitating funeral arrangements, providing caskets or urns, conducting embalming services, coordinating viewings or memorial services, and offering various funeral-related merchandise. The definition reflects the diverse range of entities involved in the funeral industry, emphasizing that anyone involved in the sale or provision of funeral goods and services is subject to the regulations and standards outlined by the Federal Trade Commission. The overarching goal is to ensure transparency, fair practices, and consumer protection within the funeral service sector.

Types of Price Lists

The Funeral Rule outlines several types of price lists that funeral providers must make available to consumers:

1. **General Price List (GPL)** *is a printed or typewritten list of goods and services offered for sale by a funeral provider with retail prices. The GPL is considered the keystone of the Funeral Rule.* The GPL is a comprehensive list of the prices for all the funeral goods and services offered by the funeral home. It must be provided to consumers who inquire about pricing, at various triggering events, enabling them to make informed decisions. Only the GPL is required, under the Funeral Rule, to be given to the consumer for their retention.

2. **Casket Price List** *is a printed or typewritten list of the casket and alternative containers normally offered for sale by the funeral provider which does not require special ordering. CPL must include retail price and enough descriptive information to enable consumers to identify the merchandise.* This list itemizes the prices of caskets available for purchase and must be provided to consumers prior to the selection of a casket or when they inquire about casket prices. It allows consumers to select a casket that suits their preferences and budget.

3. **Outer Burial Container Price List** *is defined as any container which is designed for placement in the grave around the casket including, but not limited to, container commonly known as burial vaults, grave boxes, and grave liners.* Similar to the casket price list, this document details the prices of outer burial containers. It must be given to consumers who ask about the cost of these containers, providing transparency in pricing. This document must be presented to the consumer prior to discussing outer burial container selection.

4. **Alternative Price Lists** *is a price lists which may be prepared for use in certain limited situations such as children/infants, for government agencies to provide for indigent persons, for agreements with religious groups, burial or memorial societies for members of their group.* This type of price list refers to a supplementary document that funeral providers may use in addition to the General Price List (GPL) when discussing prices

with consumers. This document should also be presented with the GPL prior to discussing such specified services or merchandise.

These price lists are essential components of the Funeral Rule, ensuring that consumers have access to clear and detailed information about the costs associated with funeral goods and services. Funeral providers must provide these lists upon request, allowing consumers to make well-informed and financially sound decisions during a difficult time.

Price Disclosure, Distribution and Triggering Events

A **triggering event** *is classified as an occurrence of situation that requires certain action (i.e.) the triggering event for giving out the GPL is face-to-face meeting.* A triggering event for the Federal Trade Commission (FTC) occurs when a consumer initiates contact with a funeral home to inquire about funeral goods and services or when the funeral home starts discussing prices with the consumer. This prompts the obligation for the funeral home to provide the General Price List (GPL), Casket Price List, and Outer Burial Container Price List before discussing specific funeral arrangements. The triggering event is crucial in ensuring that consumers receive transparent information about pricing and options during funeral-related discussions.

Telephone Inquiries

Telephone price disclosure a *funeral provider must give consumers who call accurate information from the price lists and answer questions about offerings and prices with readily available information.*

Funeral providers must provide accurate information from their General Price List, Casket Price List, and Outer Burial Container Price List to consumers who telephone their place of business inquiring about prices or offerings. They are also obligated to respond to any other questions regarding their services and prices with readily available information that reasonably addresses the inquiry. Callers cannot be compelled to provide their names, addresses, or phone numbers before receiving the requested information, although they may be asked to identify themselves. Funeral providers are still required to answer questions even if callers choose not to disclose personal information. Additionally, consumers cannot be mandated to visit the funeral home in person to obtain price information.

Funeral providers have the option to utilize an answering machine or answering service to record incoming calls. However, they are required to respond to questions from callers on an individual basis. The funeral service provider is obligated to provide the requested information when consumers call during those hours. Alternatively, they can use an answering machine or answering service to collect consumers' names and phone numbers, allowing them to return calls at their earliest convenience.

A funeral service provider may assign an employee to answer phones, addressing easier questions about offerings and prices by consulting the printed price lists and referring more complex inquiries to the responsible personnel. If the primary contact person, i.e. funeral director, is unavailable, the designated employee is permitted to take messages for later follow-up. The funeral service provider is not obligated to provide price and other information after business hours if it is not their regular practice to do so. They have the discretion to inform consumers calling during non-business hours that the information will be provided during regular business hours. However, if a consumer contacts the funeral service provider after hours inquiring about an at-need situation, and it is customary for the provider to make funeral arrangements during non-business hours, they should furnish the requested price or other information.

Does the funeral provider need to mail or email a copy of the GPL to the consumer, upon request? According to the funeral rule, the funeral provider is not required to mail or email a copy of the GPL to the consumer.

Consumer Inquiry

In addition to phone disclosure, if the consumer comes into the funeral home and requests a copy of the GPL, the funeral director is obligated to provided them with a copy for their retention. Even if the funeral provider's competitor comes in the funeral home and request a copy of the GPL, the funeral provider is required under the Funeral Rule to provide them with a copy of the GPL.

Federal law supersedes state law unless state law is stricter than federal law. In the five boroughs of New York City, local laws governing funeral directing require the GPL to be on display and available to the consumer within close proximity to the main entrance. While this is not a regulation under the Funeral Rule, in the five boroughs of NYC, this rule needs to be followed.

Engaging in a Death Related Activity

When engaging in a death-related activity, such as a home removal, funeral providers are required to provide consumers with the General Price List (GPL) upon inquiry about pricing. The GPL is a comprehensive document that itemizes the costs associated with various funeral services and merchandise offerings. Furnishing the GPL during death-related activities ensures transparency and empowers consumers to make informed decisions about the services they wish to select. This practice aligns with state and federal regulations and standards in the funeral service industry, emphasizing the importance of clear and accessible pricing information to promote fair business practices and protect consumer rights during times of bereavement.

Example:
During a home removal the funeral director asks Mrs. Thompson what type of services she would like for her husband. She replies, "I would like a church service with burial in Calvary Cemetery. The funeral director then asks, "Mrs. Thompson, may I have your permission to embalm Mr. Thompson?" She then inquires about the cost for embalming. This is a triggering event, in which the funeral director needs to *hand* her a copy of the GPL prior to explaining the pricing for the service of embalming.

"Mrs. Thompson you asked me how much embalming cost. In order to be in compliance with state and federal regulations, I must present you with a copy of our General Price List, which list all the goods and services we provide at the Joyovich Funeral Home. You asked me how much it cost for an embalming and as indicated in our GPL, the cost is $895.00. Do I have your permission to embalm Mr. Thompson?"

The GPL must be given to Mrs. Thompson for her retention and another GPL needs to be given to her at the Arrangement Conference, even though she received a copy the night before. The Funeral Rule indicates that a funeral service provider must have on their possession, a copy of their current GPL whenever engaging in a funeral related function.

If Mrs. Thompson approaches a funeral director in the grocery store and inquiries about funeral pricing, is the funeral director required to provide her with the GPL? No, because shopping is not considered a funeral related activity.

Before Discussing Funeral Goods and Services

Under the Funeral Rule, funeral providers are required to provide consumers with a copy of the General Price List (GPL) before discussing specific funeral goods and services. This practice ensures transparency and empowers consumers by giving them detailed information about the costs associated with various funeral options, allowing them to make informed decisions without being influenced by specific product details prior to understanding the overall pricing structure. The GPL serves as a crucial document that outlines the pricing for the entire range of funeral services offered by the funeral home, promoting fair business practices and protecting consumers during a vulnerable and emotional time.

A recent amendment to this section of the Funeral Rule mandates that funeral providers, whose arrangement room is integrated with the selection room (characterized by a conference table in the center and merchandise displayed around the room), must provide consumers with the GPL, Casket Price List, and Outer Burial Container Price List before entering the room. To adhere to this requirement, funeral directors should have an arrangement folder containing these price lists enclosed when greeting the consumer in the funeral home, before proceeding to the arrangement room. Following appropriate greetings, the funeral director should articulate the FTC requirement in a professional manner.

Example of Dialog:

> "Mrs. Thompson, before we enter the arrangement room, in order to be in compliance with state and federal regulations, I must present you with the arrangement folder that has a copy of the General Price List, Casket Price List, and Outer Burial Container Price List. When we discuss merchandise selection, we will be using these documents." Mrs. Thompson should at that moment take into her possession the arrangement folder.

Prior to discussing specific funeral goods and services with a consumer, funeral providers are mandated by the Funeral Rule to present the GPL, Casket Price List, and Outer Burial Container Price List. This requirement ensures transparency and empowers consumers by providing detailed information on the costs associated with various funeral options. By presenting these price lists upfront, funeral providers enable consumers to make informed decisions about the services they wish to acquire without being influenced by detailed product discussions. It promotes fair business practices, protects consumer rights, and fosters an environment where individuals can navigate funeral arrangements with a clear understanding of the associated financial implications.

Misrepresentation

Under the Funeral Rule, misrepresentation is strictly prohibited to ensure transparency and protect consumers from deceptive practices within the funeral service industry. Funeral providers are required to provide accurate and clear information to consumers, and any form of misrepresentation is considered a violation of the rule. Key aspects of misrepresentation under the Funeral Rule include:

➤ **Accurate Information:** Funeral homes must accurately represent the goods and services they offer, as well as their prices. Any false or misleading information is not allowed.

➤ **Itemization of Costs:** The General Price List (GPL) must clearly itemize the costs associated with various goods and services. This prevents misrepresentation of bundled services or unclear pricing.

➤ **Casket Price Lists:** Funeral homes must provide a separate Casket Price List that includes the retail prices of individual caskets. This ensures that consumers are fully informed about their casket options without any misrepresentation.

➤ **Outer Burial Container Price Lists:** Similarly, funeral homes must provide a separate Outer Burial Container Price List with retail prices for outer burial containers.

➤ **No Requirement for Unnecessary Services:** Funeral homes cannot misrepresent or imply that certain goods or services are required by law if they are not. Consumers have the right to choose the services they want without unnecessary pressure or misinformation.

➤ **No Requirement for Embalming:** The Funeral Rule explicitly forbids any misrepresentations concerning the mandatory nature of embalming. Additionally, a violation occurs if the funeral director neglects to communicate to the consumer that, by law, embalming is not obligatory except in specific circumstances. By including the necessary disclosure about embalming on the General Price List (GPL), the funeral director fulfills the obligation to provide accurate information to the consumer regarding the necessity of embalming.

Violating the Funeral Rule also involves disseminating incorrect information to consumers, asserting that embalming is a practical necessity in particular scenarios, including direct cremation, immediate burial, and situations where refrigeration is available without viewing and with a closed casket. Such misrepresentation is expressly prohibited by the regulations.

By prohibiting misrepresentation, the Funeral Rule aims to empower consumers with accurate information, allowing them to make informed decisions during a difficult and vulnerable time. Violations of the rule can result in legal consequences for funeral providers.

Caskets for Direct Cremation - The Funeral Rule prohibits a funeral director from stating that state or local law mandates a casket for direct cremation. Furthermore, if a funeral home provides direct cremation services, it must have alternative containers accessible for consumers opting for direct cremation. **Alternative container** *is defined as an unfinished wood box or other non-metal receptacle or enclosure, without ornamentation or a fixed interior lining, which is designed for the encasement of human remains and which is made of fiberboard, pressed-wood, composition materials (with or without an outside covering) or like materials.*

Requirements for Outer Burial Containers - Violating the Funeral Rule includes making false claims that outer burial containers are legally required when they are not. Furthermore, failing to proactively inform consumers that state law does not mandate outer burial containers is also a violation. This obligation is fulfilled by including the mandatory disclosure on the Outer Burial Container Price List.

Legal and Cemetery Requirements - The Funeral Rule also prohibits misrepresentations about cemetery rules regarding outer burial containers, emphasizing the need for funeral directors to stay informed about local cemetery regulations. The rule encompasses a broad prohibition against any misrepresentation about legal or cemetery requirements, and funeral directors must disclose any such requirements on the Statement of Funeral Goods and Services Selected.

Preservative and Protective Claims - Funeral directors are not allowed to claim to consumers that funeral goods (such as an outer burial container) or service (such as embalming) will indefinitely delay the natural decomposition of human remains. While the Rule permits funeral directors to explain that embalming offers temporary preservation to the body, it expressly forbids any assertions that embalming or other services will preserve the body for an extended or indefinite period.

The Funeral Rule also prohibits funeral directors from making deceptive claims about the protective features of caskets and vaults. Any assertions about the ability of caskets and vaults to shield the body from substances at the graveside should only be made if they can be substantiated. In addition, an outer burial container does not serve to protect the casket and human remains, instead, its purpose is to support the weight of the earth and resist the elements.

Cash Advance Items – *are any item of service or merchandise described to a purchaser as a "cash advance," "accommodation," "cash disbursement," or similar term. A cash advance item is also any item obtained from a third party and paid for by the funeral provider on the purchaser's behalf. Cash advance items may include but are not limited to: cemetery or crematory services; pallbearers; public transportation; clergy honoraria; flowers; musicians or* *singers; nurses; obituary notices; gratuities and death certificates.* Violating the Funeral Rule includes marking up cash advance items or receiving undisclosed commissions, rebates, or discounts not passed on to the consumer. It is a violation to claim to the consumer that the charge represents the same amount the funeral home paid for these items if there's a markup. Additionally, consumers must be informed about which specific cash advance items have been marked up, and the funeral director is required to identify these items on the Statement.

Requirement of "Funeral Goods and "Services"

Funeral goods are defined as, *goods which are sold or offered for sale directly to the public for use in connection with funeral services.* **Funeral services** *are defined as any services which may be used to: (1) care for and prepare deceased human bodies for burial, cremation or other final disposition; and (2) arrange, supervise or conduct the funeral ceremony or the final disposition of deceased human bodies.*

The Federal Trade Commission mandates specific requirements for funeral providers to ensure transparency and fairness in the provision of goods and services to consumers. Funeral homes are obligated to provide accurate and itemized pricing information through the General Price List (GPL), which includes details about basic services, embalming, viewing, funeral ceremonies, and other related offerings. Furthermore, the Funeral Rule prohibits misrepresentations regarding legal requirements, such as embalming or the necessity of certain funeral products. The FTC aims to empower consumers with the necessary information to make informed decisions during a challenging time, promoting fairness and ethical conduct within the funeral industry.

Tying Arrangements

Tying arrangements, (*exist when a seller requires the purchase of unwanted items/services in order to obtain the desired item/service*) Occurs when a seller conditions the acquisition of a desired good or service on the compulsory purchase of an unwanted item. To illustrate, if a funeral director insists on providing funeral services only upon the consumer's agreement to buy a casket exclusively from the funeral home, this constitutes a tying arrangement, thus violating the Funeral Rule. This prohibition ensures that consumers have the freedom to make independent choices regarding the specific goods and services they wish to acquire during funeral arrangements, preventing undue pressure or coercion by funeral providers. The Funeral Rule seeks to uphold consumer rights and foster a fair marketplace within the funeral industry by prohibiting such tying arrangements that limit consumers' choices.

The Funeral Rule explicitly prohibits tying arrangements, except under the following three circumstances:

1. **Non-Declinable Basic Service Fee**: The fee for the Basic Services of Funeral Director and Staff may be non-declinable, meaning that consumers are required to pay this charge as a condition of receiving funeral services. Other fees may be declinable unless they meet one of the exceptions allowed.

2. **Legal Requirements**: If state or local law mandates the purchase of a funeral good or service, funeral directors may tie the acquisition of that specific good or service to the provision of funeral services. For instance, if state law necessitates embalming for contagious disease cases, funeral directors may require embalming for all contagious disease cases as a condition of providing funeral services.

3. **Impossible, Impractical, or Excessively Burdensome**: The Funeral Rule acknowledges that funeral directors are not obligated to honor a request for a combination of goods and services that would be deemed "impossible, impractical, or excessively burdensome" to provide. While the initial judgment lies with the funeral director, the final determination would be made by the Federal Trade Commission (FTC) if a Rule violation is alleged.

One exception to the tying arrangement prohibition involves the practical necessity of embalming. For instance, a funeral director may decline a family's request for the public viewing of an unembalmed body, citing practical necessity. Public sensitivity to viewing an unembalmed body may make it offensive to some individuals, and in such cases, embalming is commonly acknowledged as a practical necessity. Conversely, if the family requests a brief viewing of an unembalmed body exclusively for family members and for identification purposes, the funeral director cannot reject this specific request.

Pricing Methods

Itemization is Required

Under the Funeral Rule, itemization requirements play a crucial role in ensuring transparency and consumer protection within funeral services. **Itemization** is a method of price quotation by which each unit of service and/or merchandise is priced separately.

Funeral providers are obligated to present consumers with a detailed General Price List (GPL) that itemizes the costs associated with various funeral goods and services. This itemization must encompass charges for professional services, facilities, equipment, and other related expenses. Additionally, funeral homes must provide itemized lists for caskets and outer burial containers, enabling consumers to make informed decisions by understanding the specific costs involved. These requirements aim to prevent deceptive practices, empower consumers with clear pricing information, and foster an environment of trust during the emotionally challenging process of making funeral arrangements. The itemization provisions under the Funeral Rule contribute to a fair and open marketplace where consumers have the necessary information to make choices aligned with their preferences and budget.

Package Pricing (Optional): Under FTC regulations, funeral providers are allowed to offer package pricing options to consumers, encompassing various funeral goods and services at a bundled rate. This approach provides consumers with a convenient and potentially cost-effective way to select the necessary elements for a funeral service. However, it is crucial for funeral directors to maintain transparency in their pricing and clearly outline the specific items and services included in each package. The Funeral Rule mandates that consumers have the option to decline any goods or services not desired, ensuring that they can make informed choices based on their individual preferences and budget considerations within the package pricing framework.

Some states, like New York, package pricing his prohibited except for four packages: Direct Cremation, Direct Burial, Forwarding of Remains and Receiving Remains. When creating these packages, the package price cannot exceed the price of each service, if itemized individually. Discounting is permitted under FTC regulations for package pricing, however financially, this practice will directly impact the funeral home's bottom line and cash flow.

General Price List:

The Funeral Rule places significant emphasis on the General Price List (GPL), considering it a cornerstone for fostering transparency and informed decision-making in funeral service transactions. This crucial document is provided to consumers before any commitment is made to funeral arrangements, serving as a comprehensive and itemized guide to the array of goods and services offered by the funeral home. By offering a detailed breakdown of costs, the GPL empowers consumers to make well-informed choices tailored to their preferences and financial considerations. Its role extends beyond a mere list, embodying the commitment to openness within the funeral industry. The GPL exemplifies a commitment to ethical business practices, ensuring that consumers have a clear understanding of the financial aspects associated with the services and merchandise available, fostering trust and transparency in funeral service transactions.

Introductory Matters

On the General Price List, the funeral home must place its ***name, address, telephone number, and in some states the funeral home registration number, in addition to the words "General Price List" and the effective date*** of the General Price List.

Itemization of Sixteen (16) Goods and Services

To safeguard consumers' right to make individual choices, the Federal Trade Commission has identified 16 distinct funeral goods and services that must be individually priced on the General Price List (GPL). Funeral homes are obligated to list these items and services only if they are available for purchase. For instance, if a funeral home opts not to provide direct cremation, it may be excluded from the GPL. Funeral homes commonly offer additional goods and services beyond the mandated sixteen, and although not mandatory, it is advisable for proper business transparency to include all offered goods and services on the GPL.

There are sixteen (16) goods and services that must be separately itemized on the General Price List (GPL) under the Funeral Rule:

1. **Basic Services of Funeral Director and Staff**: This includes the non-declinable fee for the funeral director's professional services and staff coordination. This also known as the **Non-declinable Service Fee** which is the *basic services is the only fee which the consumer cannot decline (unless state or local law requires otherwise). Funeral provider should recover expenses for services, facilities or unallocated overhead in this charge.*

2. **Embalming**: The cost associated with the preservation process of the deceased's body, known as embalming.

3. **Other Preparation of the Body**: Charges related to additional preparations such as dressing, cosmetology, or restorative art.

4. **Services and Facilities for Viewing**: Fees for using the funeral home's services and facilities for viewing or visitation.

5. **Services and Facilities for Funeral Ceremony**: Costs for using the funeral home's services and facilities during the actual funeral ceremony. **Funeral ceremony** is defined as *service commemorating the deceased with the body present.*

6. **Services and Facilities for Memorial Services**: Charges for using the funeral home's services and facilities for a memorial service. **Memorial Service** is defined as a *ceremony commemorating the deceased without the body present.*

7. **Service and Equipment for Graveside Service**: Fees associated with services and equipment provided for a graveside service. **Graveside service** is defined as a ceremony commemorating the deceased at place of final disposition.

8. **Transfer of Remains to Funeral Home**: The cost of transporting the deceased from the place of death to the funeral home. **Transfer of Remains** – *(also referred to as removal) one of the specified items required on the GPL; defined as the moving of the dead human body from the place of death to the funeral home or other designated place.*

9. **Hearse**: Charges related to the use of a hearse for transporting the deceased to the burial site.

10. **Limousine**: Fees associated with the use of a limousine for transportation during funeral events.

11. **Casket Price Range**: This itemizes the range of prices for caskets offered by the funeral home.

12. **Outer Burial Container Price Range**: The range of prices for outer burial containers, if selected.

13. **Forwarding of Remains**: Charges for sending the deceased's remains to another funeral home. **Forwarding of Remains** - *one of the 16 items specified required on the GPL (if the funeral provider offers the service). This involves services of the funeral provider in the locale where death occurs and preparation for transfer to another funeral provider as selected by the family (consumer). The Funeral Rule requires package pricing of this service with a description of the components included.*

14. **Receiving Remains**: Fees for receiving the deceased's remains from another funeral home. **Receiving Remains** - *one of the specified items required on the GPL (if the funeral provider offers the service). This involves services of the funeral provider after initial services have been provided by another firm at the locale of death. Funeral Rule requires package pricing of this service with a description of the components included.*

15. **Direct Cremation:** Charges for direct cremation without any additional ceremonies. **Direct cremation** is defined as the *disposition of human remains by cremation without formal viewing, visitation, or ceremony with the body present.*

16. **Immediate Burial**: The cost associated with immediate burial without any ceremonies. **Immediate burial** is defined as the *disposition of human remains by burial, without formal viewing, visitation, or ceremony with the body present, except for a graveside service.*

These individual itemizations ensure that consumers receive detailed and transparent information about the specific costs associated with each service and item offered by the funeral home.

Mandatory Disclosures

There are six (6) distinct mandatory disclosures that must be prominently featured on the General Price List (GPL). Funeral directors are expressly forbidden from altering or modifying these mandatory disclosures, and they must be presented on the GPL exactly as provided in the sample embedded to this section. Furthermore, it is imperative that these mandatory disclosures be printed in a clear and conspicuous manner, ensuring they are not in smaller type than other printed materials on the GPL. This commitment to visibility and clarity aligns with the Funeral Rule's emphasis on transparency and consumer empowerment.

The **six mandatory disclosures** include:

Choice of Goods and Services: This disclosure underscores the consumer's right to select individual goods and services, allowing for personalized funeral arrangements.

> **The goods and services shown below are those we can provide to our customers. You may choose only the items you desire. However, any funeral arrangements you select will include a charge for our basic services and overhead. If legal or other requirements mean you must buy any items you did not specifically ask for, we will explain the reason in writing on the statement we provide describing the funeral goods and services you selected.**

Non-Declinable Service Fee: Highlighting the fee for Basic Services of Funeral Director and Staff and Overhead, this disclosure clarifies its non-declinable nature.

> **Our services include: conducting the arrangements conference; planning the funeral; consulting with family and clergy; shelter of remains; preparing and filing of necessary notices; obtaining necessary authorizations and permits; coordinating with the cemetery, crematory, or other third parties. In addition, this fee includes a proportionate share of our basic overhead costs.**

> **This fee for our basic services and overhead will be added to the total cost of the funeral arrangements you select. (This fee is already included in our charges for direct cremations, immediate burials, and forwarding or receiving remains.)**

Embalming Disclosure: Informed by the practical necessity of embalming, this disclosure ensures consumers are aware of their options.

> **[Except in certain special cases]*[1] [E]mbalming is not required by law. Embalming may be necessary, however, if you select certain funeral arrangements, such as a funeral with viewing. If you do not want embalming, you usually have the right to choose an arrangement, such as direct cremation or immediate burial, that does not require you to pay for it.**

Availability of Casket Price Lists: This disclosure emphasizes the consumer's right to access and review specific pricing information for caskets.

> **A complete price list will be provided at the funeral home.**

---

*[1] Delete "[Except in certain special cases]" if state law does not require embalming.

Availability of Outer Burial Container Price Lists: Similar to the casket disclosure, this informs consumers about their right to access price information for outer burial containers.

A complete price list will be provided at the funeral home.

Alternative Containers for Direct Cremation: This disclosure underscores the availability and options for alternative containers when opting for direct cremation, aligning with consumer choice and transparency principles.

> **Our charge for a direct cremation (without ceremony) includes: basic services of funeral director and staff; a proportionate share of overhead costs; removal of remains; transportation to crematory; necessary authorizations [and cremation]. *[2]**

> **If you want to arrange a direct cremation, you can use an alternative container. Alternative containers encase the body and can be made of materials like fiberboard or composition materials (with or without an outside covering). The containers we provide are a fiberboard container or an unfinished wood box.**

Package Funerals

Funeral homes are obligated to itemize funeral goods and services, but they have the flexibility to present package selections, in most states. Essentially, the funeral home can curate various packages of goods and services and assign a single price to them. Furthermore, if desired, these packages can be offered at a discounted rate compared to the itemized pricing. For instance, while a traditional funeral, when itemized, might cost $9,000, the funeral home could create a package that includes the same goods and services, offering it at a discounted package price of $8,500. It is crucial to note that package pricing must be presented in addition to, and not instead of, itemized pricing.

Casket Price List

If the General Price List (GPL) does not include the retail prices of the caskets offered by the funeral home, a separate Casket Price List (CPL) must be created. This list is notably simpler than the GPL, as it does not require mandatory disclosures. The Casket Price List (CPL) should contain:

1. Introduction: It must include the name and location of the funeral home, the designation "Casket Price List," and the effective date of the Casket Price List.

---

*[2] Delete "[and cremation]" if you bill cremation as a cash advance item.

2. Casket and Alternative Container Listings: All caskets and alternative containers available for sale or as part of the funeral home's regular offerings must be listed on the Casket Price List, along with their respective retail prices. Caskets requiring special ordering are exempt from inclusion. There are no stipulations on the order in which the caskets and containers are listed, nor are there specific requirements for the types of caskets to be stocked. However, if the funeral home offers direct cremation, it must make an alternative container or an unfinished wooden box readily available.

In detailing the caskets and alternative containers, the funeral home should provide concise descriptions of the exterior construction and interior lining. For metal caskets, the gauge of the metal should be indicated. Any prominent exterior trimming or coloring should be noted on the Casket Price List. There is no obligation to identify manufacturers, model names, or model numbers, under the FTC regulations, however some states do require the casket and model number to be identical to that on the shipping invoice.

Distribution of Casket Price List

The presentation of the Casket Price List to consumers is mandated at the initiation of a face-to-face discussion concerning the offerings detailed on the list or their corresponding prices. The Funeral Rule explicitly specifies that, at a minimum, the list must be provided to the consumer before the funeral director showcases casket models. Unlike the General Price List, the Casket Price List is not required to be handed over to consumers for their continued possession. Funeral directors have the option to request the return of the list after displaying the caskets.

Furthermore, the Funeral Rule permits the preparation of the Casket Price List in alternative formats such as binders, notebooks, brochures, and charts, offering flexibility in how this essential information is presented to consumers.

Outer Burial Container Price List

The Outer Burial Container Price List shares similar requirements with the Casket Price List.

1. **Introduction:** The top of the price list must include the name of the funeral home, the words "Outer Burial Container Price List," and the effective date.

2. **Outer Burial Container Listings:** All containers regularly offered by the funeral home should be included on the Outer Burial Container Price List. Containers that require special ordering are exempt from listing. If a funeral home does not provide outer burial containers, there is no obligation to prepare an Outer Burial Container Price List.

3. **Mandatory Disclosures:** The disclosure communicates to consumers that outer burial containers are not generally mandated by law, although specific cemeteries may enforce such requirements. This disclosure can be placed anywhere on the Outer Burial Container Price List.

Distribution of Outer Burial Container Price List

Whenever the topic of outer burial containers arises, the funeral director must provide the Outer Burial Container Price List to the consumer. Similar to the Casket Price List, this list should be given to consumers before the funeral director showcases any displays or models. Unlike the General Price List, the Outer Burial Container Price List is not required to be given for retention. Furthermore, funeral homes have the flexibility to use alternative formats such as brochures, notebooks, and charts in place of a printed Outer Burial Container Price List.

Statement of Funeral Goods and Services Selected

Itemized Listings

Statement of Funeral Goods and Services Selected is an *itemized written statement provided for retention to each person who arranges a funeral or other disposition. It must include the goods and services selected and prices paid for each, itemization of cash advance items and the total cost.*

The primary purpose of the Statement of Funeral Goods and Services Selected ("Statement") is to furnish consumers with a detailed breakdown of their acquisitions at the conclusion of the funeral arrangement conference. To achieve this, the items listed on the Statement must correspond with those on the GPL. In other words, every distinct good and service selected by the consumer from the GPL must be individually identified and outlined on the Statement, along with the specific price for each item. It is inappropriate to merge separate automotive charges, for instance, under a single fee on the Statement.

If a consumer opts for a package funeral, the funeral director should include the package purchase on the Statement, along with the corresponding package price. Additionally, each individual good and service encompassed in the package should be itemized on the Statement. While it is not obligatory for the funeral director to separately specify the price of each item within the package, it is crucial for the consumer to have a detailed listing of each component.

In addition to the goods and services obtained from the funeral home, the Statement should also enumerate any cash advance items acquired through the funeral home. If the precise price of a cash advance item is unknown, the funeral director should provide a reasonable estimate of the item's cost on the Statement.

Mandatory Disclosures – There are two and possibly three mandatory disclosures that funeral homes must make on the Statement of Funeral Goods and Services Selected:

Listing of Legal and Other Requirements

The Statement must include the mandatory disclosure, informing consumers that they will only be billed for the items they choose or those that are mandatory. This required disclosure can be placed anywhere on the Statement, although many funeral homes opt to position it at the top. In conjunction with this disclosure, the Funeral Rule stipulates that the funeral home must also detail on the Statement any legal, cemetery, or crematory requirements that mandate the consumer to purchase a specific good or service.

For instance, if state law necessitates embalming or if the cemetery enforces a regulation specifying the use of outer burial containers, the funeral director is obligated to include these requirements on the Statement.

Example of the disclosure:
Vault as selected per family and required under cemetery requirements.
Urn as selected per family.

Embalming Approval

The Statement is required to include the mandatory disclosure detailing the embalming requirements for consumers. This disclosure can be placed anywhere on the Statement. Moreover, there is an associated requirement that necessitates the funeral director to specify on the Statement the rationale behind the decision to embalm. Common reasons include obtaining family consent, facilitating interstate transportation of remains, or enabling public visitation.

Example of this disclosure:
Embalming as selected per family and necessary for public visitation.

Marked-up Cash Advances –

If a funeral home imposes an additional fee on a cash advance item or retains a rebate, commission, or discount from the supplier without passing it on to the consumer, it is considered a mark-up on the cash advance. The Funeral Rule mandates that funeral homes clearly identify on the Statement those specific cash advance items that have incurred a mark-up. The required mandatory disclosure, indicating the identification of marked-up cash advance items, is placed at the bottom of the cash advance listings on the first page of the sample Statement. Some states prohibit the mark-up of cash advanced items.

In some states, like New York, the Statement of Goods and Services is divided into three sections:
A. Services and Merchandise
B. Additional Services and Merchandise
C. Cash Advance Items

In this particular case, Section B has a mandatory disclosure at the top of the section that indicates:

The price in this section includes a charge for our services in buying these items.

Note: If the funeral home doesn't mark-up any cash advance items, there is no obligation to include this disclosure on the Statement. Additionally, the funeral home is not required to specify the dollar amount of the mark-up; rather, it must only indicate the cash advance items that have been marked up. This disclosure must be presented immediately alongside the listing of cash advance items.

In some states, like New York, marking up cash advanced items is prohibited, thus compliance with state regulations supersedes this regulation.

Distribution of Statement

The Statement should be presented at the conclusion of the funeral arrangements, providing a comprehensive overview with all details filled out, including the total funeral cost. The funeral director should review all charges with the consumer prior to asking for signatures. Although not mandatory under FTC regulation, obtaining signatures on the Statement is advisable as it can serve as the funeral contract. Failure to obtain the consumer's signature on the Statement places the funeral home at legal risk as it lacks evidence that the listed goods and services were indeed selected at the time of the arrangements. In cases where arrangements are made via telephone or video chat, while not mandated by the Rule, a recording should be made for quality and legal purposes. The funeral home should promptly mail the completed Statement to the consumer when such alternative conference arrangements have been made.

Additional Information Under the Funeral Rule

Embalming Requirements

A fee for embalming may be charged only under the following three circumstances:

1. When state or local law mandates embalming in specific circumstances, irrespective of the family's preferences. In such instances, the funeral home must explicitly indicate on the detailed Statement of Funeral Goods and Services Selected that embalming was conducted due to a legal requirement and provide a brief explanation of that requirement.

    Note: Federal law does not necessitate embalming in any situation; requirements are determined solely by state laws.

2. The funeral director has obtained prior approval for embalming from a family member or another authorized person, and it is crucial to note that the Funeral Rule does not define who qualifies as an "authorized person" for such approval, as it varies

based on state or local law. Express permission for embalming must be explicitly sought and obtained; implied consent is not acceptable.

For example, if a family expresses a desire for a viewing before burial and asks the funeral director to "prepare" the deceased, the funeral director must specifically request permission to embalm and receive explicit consent before proceeding. To secure the family's express consent, the funeral director must both explicitly seek and obtain permission and refrain from misrepresenting when embalming is required.

In the absence of a written requirement by the Funeral Rule, some states may mandate written authorization. On the Statement of Funeral Goods and Services Selected, the funeral director is obligated to explain why a fee for embalming was charged. If the family requested the service, this can be stated as the reason. However, if the funeral director communicated that embalming is required for a specific reason (e.g., viewing or legal necessity), the Statement should specify this reason rather than a general "family consent." Simply noting "family consent" does not convey the specific rationale behind embalming; it only indicates that the family has granted permission.

3. In the given situation, the funeral director faces a scenario where several conditions must be met:

> **Exigent circumstances** in the context of funeral services refer to situations where a funeral director faces exceptional and time-sensitive challenges in obtaining necessary authorization for embalming. To invoke the exigent circumstances exception, three conditions must be met: first, despite exercising due diligence, the funeral director is unable to contact a family member or authorized person; second, there is no reason to believe the family opposes embalming; and third, after performing the embalming, the funeral director informs the family that no fee will be charged if they choose a non-embalming funeral. However, if the family selects a funeral that requires embalming, a fee will be applied. This exception recognizes the need for flexibility when immediate action is crucial, ensuring that the funeral director can proceed with embalming while keeping the family informed and providing options based on the specific funeral services chosen.

Note: Mandatory disclosure regarding embalming on the itemized Statement ensures that consumers are informed that they are not obligated to pay for embalming if prior approval was not obtained.

Retention of Documents

Funeral directors must adhere to the Funeral Rule's stipulation to ***preserve all price lists for a duration of one year from the last distribution date***. For example, if a funeral home updates its price list on January 1, 2023, it is obligated to retain the preceding list until January 1, 2024. Similarly, a duplicate of the Statement of Funeral Goods and Services Selected should be kept for one year from the date of the arrangement conference. Once this one-year timeframe expires, funeral directors are permitted, under the Funeral Rule, to discard outdated price lists and previous statements. Some states may enforce longer document retention periods than those outlined in the Funeral Rule. If state law requirements supersede federal law requirements, state regulations must be followed.

Third – Party Merchandise

Third party merchandise – *funeral goods consumer purchase from a source other than the price list/funeral provider.* The Federal Trade Commission (FTC) mandates transparency and consumer protection in the funeral industry, especially concerning third-party merchandise. Funeral homes are required to clearly disclose to consumers whether the prices for caskets and outer burial containers include third-party charges or if those charges are separate. This ensures that consumers are fully informed about the costs associated with funeral goods and services, promoting fair business practices. The FTC's regulations aim to prevent any potential deceptive practices related to third-party merchandise and contribute to a more transparent and accountable funeral service industry.

Casket handling fees – a *charge, fee or surcharge applied to consumers who purchase their casket elsewhere from a source other than the price list/funeral provider.* The FTC explicitly forbids funeral homes from imposing a handling fee when consumers provide their own third-party caskets. Moreover, recent regulations from the FTC prohibit funeral providers from mandating the consumer's presence during the delivery of the casket to the funeral home. Additionally, charging for the disposal of packing or shipping materials related to the casket is also deemed impermissible under these regulations, reinforcing the commitment to fair and transparent practices within the funeral industry. These guidelines aim to protect consumers from unnecessary fees and ensure greater clarity in the funeral service transaction process.

Enforcement:

Failure to comply with the Funeral Rule established by the Federal Trade Commission (FTC) can result in significant fines and penalties. The FTC has the authority to impose civil penalties of up to $43,280 per violation, as of 2023. These penalties apply to funeral homes found in violation of the rule, and the total amount is calculated based on the number of infractions committed. Additionally, the FTC may pursue legal action against non-compliant funeral homes. Apart from monetary penalties, funeral homes may face cease and desist orders, requiring them to rectify their practices and adhere to the Funeral Rule. The severity of the penalties underscores the FTC's commitment to ensuring transparency, honesty, and fair business practices within the funeral industry. Funeral homes are strongly advised to stay informed about the Funeral Rule's requirements and diligently follow its guidelines to avoid legal consequences.

FEDERAL TRADE COMMISSION GLOSSARY

Alternative container - unfinished wood box or other non-metal receptacle or enclosure, without ornamentation or a fixed interior lining, which is designed for the encasement of human remains and which is made of fiberboard, pressed-wood, composition materials (with or without an outside covering) or like materials. [16 CFR 453.1(a)]

Alternative Price Lists - price lists which may be prepared for use in certain limited situations such as children/infants, for government agencies to provide for indigent persons, for agreements with religious groups, burial or memorial societies for members of their group.

Cash Advance items - any item of service or merchandise described to a purchaser as a "cash advance," "accommodation," "cash disbursement," or similar term. A cash advance item is also any item obtained from a third party and paid for by the funeral provider on the purchaser's behalf. Cash advance items may include, but are not limited to: cemetery or crematory services; pallbearers; public transportation; clergy honoraria; flowers; musicians or singers; nurses; obituary notices; gratuities and death certificates. [16 CFR 453.1(b)]

Casket - rigid container which is designed for the encasement of human remains and which is usually constructed of wood, metal, fiberglass, plastic, or like material, and ornamented and lined with fabric. [16 CFR 453.1(c)]

Casket handling fees - charge, fee or surcharge applied to consumers who purchase their casket elsewhere from a source other than the price list/funeral provider.

Casket Price List (CPL) - printed or typewritten list of the casket and alternative containers normally offered for sale by the funeral provider which does not require special ordering. CPL must include retail price and enough descriptive information to enable consumers to identify the merchandise.

Commission - refers to the Federal Trade Commission. [16 CFR 453.1(d)]

Cremation - heating process which incinerates human remains. [16 CFR 453.1(e)]

Crematory - any person, partnership or corporation that performs cremation and sells funeral goods. [16 CFR 453.1(f)]

Direct cremation - disposition of human remains by cremation without formal viewing, visitation, or ceremony with the body present. [16 CFR 453(g)]

Effective date - date that the specific price list was put into use.

Exigent circumstances - situation requiring immediate action or urgency; FTC recognizes that funeral provider might embalm without permission. (See NFDA FTC Amended Funeral Rule Compliance Manual and 453.5(a)(3) for examples)

Federal Trade Commission (FTC) - agency of federal government created in 1914 to promote free and fair competition by prevention of trade restraints, price fixing, false advertising and other unfair methods of competition.

Forwarding of Remains - one of the 16 items specified required on the GPL (if the funeral provider offers the service). This involves services of the funeral provider in the locale where death occurs and preparation for transfer to another funeral provider as selected by the family (consumer). Funeral Rule requires package pricing of this service with a description of the components included.

Free items - none of the 16 specified items required to be separately itemized on the GPL can be listed as free or no charge. Items not required by the rule can be listed as free.

Funeral ceremony - service commemorating the deceased with the body present. (16 CFR 453.1(m)

Funeral goods - goods which are sold or offered for sale directly to the public for use in connection with funeral services [16 CFR 453.1(h)].

Funeral provider - any person, partnership or corporation that sells or offers to sell funeral goods and funeral services to the public. [16 CFR 453.1(i)]

Funeral services - any services which may be used to: (1) care for and prepare deceased human bodies for burial, cremation or other final disposition; and (2) arrange, supervise or conduct the funeral ceremony or the final disposition of deceased human bodies. [16 CFR 453.1(j)]

General Price List (GPL) - printed or typewritten list of goods and services offered for sale by a funeral provider with retail prices. GPL is considered the keystone of the Funeral Rule.

Graveside service - ceremony commemorating the deceased at place of final disposition.

Immediate burial - disposition of human remains by burial, without formal viewing, visitation, or ceremony with the body present, except for a graveside service. [16 37 CFR 453.1(k)]

Itemization - method of price quotation by which each unit of service and/or merchandise is priced separately.

Mandatory disclosures - statements required by the Rule which cannot be modified or edited and must appear in a clear and conspicuous manner.

Memorial Service - ceremony commemorating the deceased without the body present. [16 CFR 453.1(l))

Non-declinable Service Fee - basic services is the only fee which the consumer cannot decline (unless state or local law requires otherwise). Funeral provider should recover expenses for services, facilities or unallocated overhead in this charge.

Outer burial container - any container which is designed for placement in the grave around the casket including, but not limited to, container commonly known as burial vaults, grave boxes, and grave liners.

Outer Burial Container Price List (OBC PL) - printed or typewritten list of outer burial containers normally offered for sale by the funeral provider which does not require special ordering. OBC PL must include retail price and enough descriptive information to enable consumers to identify the merchandise.

Package pricing - use of a single dollar amount to identify the charge for a group or bundle of goods and/or services.

Person - any individual, partnership, corporation, association, government or governmental subdivision or agency, or other entity. [16 CFR 453.1(o)]

Receiving Remains - one of the specified items required on the GPL (if the funeral provider offers the service). This involves services of the funeral provider after initial services have been provided by another firm at the locale of death. Funeral Rule requires package pricing of this service with a description of the components included.

Services of Funeral Director and Staff - basic services, not to be included in prices of other categories in Section 453.2(b)(4), that are furnished by a funeral provider in arranging any funeral, such as conducting the arrangements conference, planning the funeral, obtaining necessary permits, and placing obituary notices. [16 CFR 30 453.1(p)]

Statement of Funeral Goods and Services Selected - itemized written statement provided for retention to each person who arranges a funeral or other disposition. It must include the goods and services selected and prices paid for each, itemization of cash advance items and the total cost.

Telephone price disclosure - funeral provider must give consumers who call accurate information from the price lists and answer questions about offerings and prices with readily available information.

Third party merchandise – funeral goods consumer purchase from a source other than the price list/funeral provider.

Transfer of Remains – (also referred to as removal) one of the specified items required on the GPL; defined as the moving of the dead human body from the place of death to the funeral home or other designated place.

Triggering event - occurrence of situation that requires certain action (i.e.) the triggering event for giving out the GPL is face-to-face meeting.

Tying arrangements - exist when a seller requires the purchase of unwanted items/services in order to obtain the desired item/service.

Viewing – (calling hours, visitation, visiting hours, wake) time set aside for friends and relatives to pay respect for the deceased prior to the funeral service.

The Occupational Safety and Health Act of 1970 – OSHA

1. The Background and Function of OSHA

    a. **Application** - In 1970, Congress enacted the Occupational Safety and Health Act. That Act created the Occupational Safety and Health Administration ("OSHA") within the Department of Labor. OSHA has been charged with the responsibility to protect the nation's employees by implementing new safety and health programs, providing research into occupational safety, instituting a recordkeeping system and reporting to track job related injuries and illness, establish training programs, and develop and enforce mandatory job safety and health standards.

    In general, OSHA extends to all employers in the 50 states, the District of Columbia and all other territories under federal government jurisdiction. Coverage is provided directly by federal OSHA or through an OSHA-approved state program. Approximately half of the states conduct OSHA-approved state programs - these are typically referred to as "state-plan-states." New York, for example, is a state-plan-state.

    Any person or business that is engaged in business and has employees are subject to the OSHA standards. However, OSHA does not cover self-employed persons. Therefore, if a funeral home is a sole proprietorship with the owner serving as the only employee, the funeral home would not be subject to OSHA requirements. However, if the funeral home has one employee, then they would be subject to the standards.

    b. **Enforcement** - To enforce the standards, OSHA is authorized under the Act to conduct workplace inspections. OSHA compliance officers will conduct the inspection. Typically, such inspections can be triggered by fatal accidents on the job site, employee complaints, or random inspections of any industry that OSHA is targeting. Following the inspection, the OSHA officer will conduct a closing conference with the employer to discuss all unsafe or unhealthful conditions observed on the inspection. At this time, all apparent violations for which a citation may be issued are discussed. The compliance officer will submit a report to the OSHA state director with a recommendation as to proposed penalties.

    The state director may issue citations and propose penalties for those citations. When issued a citation or notice of a proposed penalty an employer may request an informal meeting with the OSHA state director to discuss the case. If the employer does not contest the citation, the employer must correct the cited hazard by the prescribed date.

    c. **General Duty Clause** - The OSHA law states that each employer has a "general duty" to furnish each of its employees with a place of employment free from recognized hazards that are causing or likely to cause death or serious physical harm to employees as well as comply with specific occupational safety and health standards promulgated under the Occupational Safety and Health Act. The General Duty Clause, however, will not apply if there is specific safety and health standard or regulation dealing with the hazard.

    This "General Duty" covers "recognized hazards" which are dangers recognized by the employer's industry or industry in general, by the employer, or by common sense, regardless of whether the condition is covered by a specific safety or health standard or regulation. The compliance issue then becomes whether the employer knew of or could have known of the hazardous condition with reasonable diligence.

Specific standards include the safety and health standards contained under the OSHA General Industry Standard for all industries, found at 29 C.F.R. 1910 in the Code of Federal Regulations, and, for construction, under the Construction Standard, found at 29 C.F.R. 1926 in the Code of Federal Regulations.

d. Inspections

An inspection begins with the arrival of a compliance officer and an opening conference at which time the inspector will present identification, advise the employer of the reason for the visit, and outline the scope of the inspection. Subsequent to this conference, all required safety and health records will be reviewed, including: OSHA forms 300 (LOG of Work-Related Injuries and Illnesses for the worksite), 300A (Yearly Summary of Work-Related Injuries and Illnesses), and 301 (Report of Occupational Injuries and Illnesses that are Recordable). These records may be kept on a computer if a computer can produce equivalent forms when needed.

Types of OSHA Inspections:

- **Routine/Program** - General Compliance Inspection - Sometimes, based on data obtained from a state's Workers' Compensation Commission, through an Employer's First Report of Injury, the entire worksite could be inspected from basement to ceiling.

- **Target Inspection** - This is an inspection directed to employers who are deemed or perceived to have a potential exposure for their employees to a specific occupational safety and health hazard. This can take the form of a Local Emphasis Program or a National Emphasis Program. Working with Formaldehyde could be a target.

- **Complaint Inspection** - This is an inspection based on a complaint filed, usually by an employee, with OSHA alleging a specific safety or health hazard or hazards or violations of enacted rules, regulations or standards. The employee has the right to remain anonymous.

- Employees are **protected from retaliation** for raising workplace health and safety concerns and for reporting work-related injuries and illnesses. Section 11(c) of the Occupational Safety and Health Act of 1970 (OSH Act) prohibits employers from retaliating against employees for exercising a variety of rights guaranteed under the OSH Act, such as filing a safety or health complaint with OSHA, raising a health and safety concern with their employers, participating in an OSHA inspection, or reporting a work-related injury or illness.

- **Accident Inspection** - This is an inspection done usually because of a serious accident. The scope of the inspection will be narrow and be generally limited to the accident site. The focus of the inspection will be whether or not a law, standard or regulation was violated during the accident occurrence, but additional violations found, that may not relate to the accident itself, can and will be cited.

- **Follow-Up Inspection** - This occurs at the site of a prior violation and is conducted to verify that the required hazard abatement has been made within the prescribed time given in the prior issued citation.

e. A recordable occupational injury or illness is an occupational injury or illness that results in a fatality, a lost workday, restricted work, or a non-fatal case without a lost workday that requires:

      1) transferring the employee to another job;
      2) termination of employment;
      3) medical treatment other than first aid; or
      4) involving loss of consciousness or restriction of work or motion.

Contagious diseases are considered work-related and recordable if the employee is infected at work. A pre-existing injury or illness that is significantly aggravated by the work environment is also recordable, and injuries and illnesses that occur when an employee is on work-related travel status, and engaged in work activities, are recordable.

A *few low-hazard industries, such as funeral service,* designated by standard industrial classification (SIC) number (SIC Code 726), are NOT required to maintain OSHA forms 300, 300A and 301, **unless** the specific employer has been ordered to do so. *Small employers with ten or fewer employees at any time during the calendar year are also exempt from these recordkeeping requirements, unless otherwise required to maintain them.*

During an inspection, the inspector has a right to interview employees privately and without the presence of management or the employer. The inspector also has the right to interview management privately and without the presence of an employee representative.

During an inspection, the inspector will take photographs, make any necessary measurements, and, in a case involving a health issue, may do environmental testing. An OSHA inspector does not, however, have the right to take identifiable photographs of remains.

At the close of the inspection, the inspector will hold a separate closing conference for the employer and its representative, and with the employees and their representatives. The purpose of this conference is to advise of potential violations found, which will then be submitted to the inspector's supervisor for a final determination as to whether or not a citation penalty will be issued.

f. Penalties and Fines - If a penalty is issued, a serious violation can carry a civil penalty of not more than $14,502.00 for each violation in which there is a substantial probability that death or serious physical harm could occur. An other-than-serious violation also carries a maximum civil penalty of up to $14,402.00 for each violation. No penalties are issued for other-than-serious violations unless there are ten or more citations.

Other penalties than can be assessed include a civil penalty of not more than $145,027.00 for each violation deemed to be a willful or repeated violation, with a minimum required penalty of not less than $14,402.00 for each willful violation.

If the willful violation causes death to an employee, there is a provision for a criminal fine of not more than $10,000.00 or imprisonment of not more than six (6) months. If the conviction is for a second offense, the criminal penalty is punishment of a fine of not more than $20,000.00 or by imprisonment of not more than one (1) year, or both.

Failure to correct a violation carries a civil penalty of not more than $14,502.00 per day for each day during which the violation continues. Making a false statement carries a maximum criminal fine of not more than $20,000.00 or imprisonment of not more than one year, or both, for falsifying representations or certifications on any application, record, report, plan or other document filed or required to be maintained. Violations of any posting requirements carry a civil penalty of up to $7,000.00 for each separate violation.

2. THE HAZARD COMMUNICATION STANDARD (29 C.F.R. 1910.1200)

a. **Purpose** - The purpose of the Hazard Communication Standard is to assure that hazards of all chemicals are evaluated, whether produced or imported, and that the information concerning their hazard is transmitted to employers and employees through a comprehensive written **Hazard Communication Program** and through the development and update of **Safety Data Sheets (SDS)** by chemical manufacturers and importers of each hazardous chemical they produce or import, at no cost to the purchasing employer. *The employer is required to maintain an up to date 16-section Safety Data Sheet (SDS)* for each hazardous chemical in the workplace. Note that Material Safety Data Sheets (MSDS) are outdated and not aligned with current Globally Harmonized System (GHS) standards.

b. **The Hazard Communication Program** - The Hazard Communication Program must be written, maintained at each workplace, and contain information indicating how the criteria that are part of the Hazard Communication Standard will be met for labels and other forms of warnings, the Safety Data Sheets, and for employee information and training.

The written Hazard Communication Program must also include a list of the hazardous chemicals known to be present, using an identity that is referenced on the appropriate Safety Data Sheet, and describe the methods used to inform employees of the hazards of non-routine tasks and the hazards associated with chemicals contained in unlabeled or improperly labeled containers in their work area. Additional requirements may be needed for state specific regulations, including the Chemical Information List.

A **Safety Data Sheet** is not required for consumer products used in the work area, if the use results in a duration and frequency of exposure which is not greater than what could reasonable be experienced by consumers when the product is used by the purpose intended.

The best funeral home practice is to keep two sets of Safety Data Sheets, one set in the prep-room with the chemicals and the other in an office. In the event of a chemical spill or emergency exposure incident, safety information about the chemical needs to be readily available. Digital copies of the SDS can also be retained on a funeral home computer. Employees need to be aware how to access this digital information in an emergency situation.

c. **Labeling** - The employer must ensure that each container of hazardous chemicals is marked with the product identifier, supplier identification, signal words (DANGER or WARNING), hazard statement, precautionary statements, and appropriate hazard pictograms. Portable containers of hazardous chemicals, that are transferred from labeled containers, do not have to be labeled <u>if</u> they are intended *only* for the immediate use of the employee who performs the transfer.

d. **Training** - Employers must provide employees with training on the hazardous chemicals in the workplace at the time of initial assignment and whenever a new physical or health hazard is introduced. The employees must be informed of the requirements of the Hazard Communication Standard, any operations in their work areas where hazardous chemicals are present, and the location and availability of the written Hazard Communication Program, the prepared list of hazardous chemicals, and the applicable Safety Data Sheets.

The training must also include methods and observations that may be used to detect the presence or release of hazardous chemicals in the work area, the physical and health hazards of the chemicals in the work area, the measures that can be taken by employees to protect themselves from these hazards, and the details of the Hazard Communication Program.

The employer should maintain training records to verify that the required training has been completed. These records should include the date of the training, the trainer's name and credentials, the name of the employee involved in the training, and, most importantly, a clear statement of the subject of the training given.

3. THE FORMALDEHYDE STANDARD (29 C.F.R. 1910.1048)

This section is very important for the National Board Exam.

a. **Purpose and Scope** - This Standard requires an employer to identify <u>all</u> employees who may be exposed at or above the **Action Level (AL)** or the **Short-Term Exposure Limit (STEL)** and accurately determine the exposure of each employee so identified.

Important Formaldehyde Exposure Limits:

Permissible Exposure Limit	**PEL**	0.75 ppm
Action Level	**AL**	0.50 ppm
Short-term exposure limit	**STEL**	2.00ppm (for 15 minutes, not be exceeded more than 4x per day)
Time weighted average	**TWA**	8-hour workday
Immediate danger to life and health	**IDLH**	20.00ppm

The Formaldehyde Standard applies to all occupational exposure to formaldehyde. It requires each employer to sample and verify that no employee is exposed to an **air borne concentration of formaldehyde which exceeds the permissible exposure limit (PEL) of 0.75 parts formaldehyde per million parts (0.75 ppm) of air, as an eight-hour time weighted average (TWA), or an airborne concentration exceeding 2 parts formaldehyde per million parts (2.0 ppm) of air, as a fifteen-minute short-term exposure limit (STEL).**

Documentation of this sampling must be maintained with the employer's records and must be made available, upon request, to the employee, to an employee representative, and to an OSHA inspector.

Sampling must be performed during a preparation and must be <u>repeated</u> every time there is a change in production, equipment, processes, personnel, or control measures that may result in a new or additional exposure.

Employees shown to be at or above the **Action Level (AL) of 0.5 ppm, as an eight-hour time weighted average**, by the initial monitoring must be re-monitored at least every six months, or, **if above the STEL of 2.0 ppm as a 15-minute short-term exposure limit, at least once per year** *until* **the results from two (2) consecutive sampling periods, taken at least seven days apart, show that the employee exposure is below the Action Level and the STEL.**

If employee exposure is over the TWA or the STEL, the employer must develop and implement a **written plan** to reduce employee exposure to or below the TWA or the STEL and give written notice to the employee. The written notice must contain a description of the corrective action being taken to decrease exposure.

b. **Regulated Areas** - Regulated areas are those areas where the concentration of airborne formaldehyde exceeds the TWA or the STEL. The Formaldehyde Standard requires that all entrances and access ways to the regulated areas must be posted with signs stating:

"Danger: Formaldehyde. Irritant and Potential Cancer Hazard. Authorized Personnel Only."

   c.   **Methods of Compliance** - Engineering controls and work practice controls must be implemented if necessary to reduce or maintain exposure at or below the AL and the STEL limits. If not adequate, they must be supplemented by the use of Personal Protective Equipment.

Engineering controls: those items designed for safety, such as a sharps container or fume hood.

Work practice controls: tasks we complete to keep us safe, such as placing sharps into the sharp's container, or washing hands.

   Respirators must be used in an emergency, which is defined as an occurrence that results in an uncontrolled release of a significant amount of formaldehyde. The term significant is NOT defined in the Standard. An example of a significant release:
   In a plastics factory where formaldehyde is available at full strength (37% by weight as formalin) in 55-gallon drums and often moved around on a forklift 4 or 5 drums at one time. If the drums should fall and split open causing a spill in an area where unprotected workers are, this would be significant. In the funeral home setting, it would be nearly impossible to have a release that would be considered significant. One 16 oz. bottle of 32 index fluid becoming broken or spilling its contents would not be significant.

   Respirator usage, if required, mandates an employer to implement a **respirator protection program,** including respirator fit tests consistent with the Respiratory Protection Standard which is described in OSHA Respiratory Protection Standard, 29 C.F.R. 1910.134.

   d. **Personal Protective Equipment** - The employer must provide Personal Protective Equipment and clothing to employees at no cost and enforce their usage.
   Potential eye and skin contact with liquids containing *one percent (1%)* or more formaldehyde requires the use of personal protective clothing, goggles and face shield.
   Containers for contaminated clothing or equipment must have signs stating:

   "Danger: Formaldehyde-Contaminated Clothing or Equipment.
   Avoid Inhalation and Skin Contact."

   e. **Housekeeping and Emergencies** - Quick drench showers must be provided when there is a possibility of a splash of the solution containing *one percent* or greater formaldehyde.
   Eyewash facilities must be provided if there is any possibility that an employee's eyes may be splashed with solutions containing 0.1 percent or greater formaldehyde.
   Leaks and spills must be cleaned promptly by trained employees wearing Personal Protective Equipment.

   f. **Medical Surveillance** - *A medical surveillance program is required for all employees exposed to concentrations of formaldehyde at or exceeding the Action Level of 0.5 ppm, as an eight-hour time weighted average, or the short-term exposure limit (STEL) of two parts formaldehyde per million (2.0 ppm) of air as a 15-minute short-term exposure limit.*

Medical surveillance must be made available for any employee who develops signs and symptoms of overexposure to formaldehyde and for all employees exposed to formaldehyde in emergencies consistent with the requirements of the Formaldehyde Standard.

Results of medical examinations and tests are to be retained consistent with the provisions of the Access to Employee Exposure and Medical Record Standard, 29 C.F.R. 1910.1020. **That OSHA Standard requires retention for the duration of employment plus thirty (30) years.** *This is very important and could be on the NBEs.*

g. **Medical Removal** - An employee, based on a physician's examination and recommendation regarding employment restrictions or removal from current formaldehyde exposure, must be transferred to a position having no or significantly less exposure to formaldehyde.

The transfer must be to comparable work for which the employee is qualified or can be trained in a short period (up to six months), or where formaldehyde exposure is at least below the Action Level of 0.5 ppm.

The employee's pre-removal current earnings, seniority and benefits are to be maintained during the transfer to other employment. If no other employment is available, earnings, seniority and other benefits are to be maintained until a determination is made that the employee can return to the original job, or until a determination is made that the employee can NOT return to the workplace with formaldehyde exposure, or for six (6) months, whichever comes first.

h. **Hazard Communication** - All mixtures or solutions of formaldehyde greater than 0.1% formaldehyde and materials capable of releasing formaldehyde into the air under reasonable foreseeable conditions of use, at concentrations reaching or exceeding 0.1 ppm, are subject to the Formaldehyde Standard Hazard Communication Requirements that include, at a minimum, specific health hazards of cancer, irritation and sensitization of the skin and respiratory system, eye and throat irritation, and acute toxicity.

An employer in compliance with the Formaldehyde Standard does not need a separate written hazard communication program for formaldehyde as long as formaldehyde is included in the hazard communication program. If the employer is not in compliance with the Formaldehyde Standard, as would be the case where there is an overexposure, the employer is required to develop, implement and maintain a separate written hazard communication program for formaldehyde exposure that, at a minimum, describes the requirements for labeling, Safety Data Sheets, other forms of warning, and the requirements for employee information and training to be met.

Formaldehyde labelling must comply with the requirements of the Hazard Communication Standard, 29 C.F.R. 1910.1200.

i. **Training** - Where objective data demonstrates that employees are not exposed to formaldehyde at 0.1 ppm, training is NOT required, other than that required by the Hazard Communication Standard, 29 C.F.R. 1910.1200. All employees who are assigned to workplaces where there is an exposure to formaldehyde at or above 0.1 ppm must be trained at the time of initial assignment and whenever a new exposure to formaldehyde is introduced into the work area. Training must be repeated at least annually.

Required training must include, among other things, the use and understanding of the contents of Safety Data Sheets, medical surveillance, health hazards, safe work practices, Personal Protective Equipment, spills, and emergencies.

A record of employee training should be maintained to verify that the training has been completed as required and include the date the training was given, the employees trained, the identity of the trainer, and the contents of the training.

j. **Recordkeeping** - If the employer determines that NO monitoring is required under this Standard, the employer must maintain a record of the objective data relied upon to make this determination.

If an employer determines that monitoring is required under this Standard, the employer must establish and maintain an accurate record of all measurements taken to monitor employee exposure to formaldehyde. This record must include the date of measurement, the operation being monitored, methods of sampling and analysis, and evidence of their accuracy and precision, the number, duration time, and results of samples taken, and the types of protective devices worn. The report must also include the names, job classifications, social security numbers, and exposure estimates of employees whose exposure is represented by the actual monitoring results.

Records must be maintained of all sampling and monitoring of employee exposure to formaldehyde, medical surveillance, and respiratory fit testing.

Exposure records must be kept for thirty (30) years, and medical records for length of employment plus thirty (30) years consistent with OSHA Standard 1910.1020, Access to Employee Exposure and Medical Records.

Respiratory fit testing records must be maintained, *if respirators are required*, until they are replaced by a more recent record.

4. THE BLOODBORNE PATHOGEN STANDARD 29 C.F.R. 1910.1030

a. **Purpose and Scope** - The Bloodborne Pathogen Standard applies to all occupational exposure to blood or other potentially infectious material (OPIM) and mandates the use of Universal Precautions, the treatment of all human remains as being infectious. Each employer with one or more employees with occupational exposure must have a written Exposure Control Plan (ECP) to eliminate or minimize employee exposure and survey the job site, by job classification, to determine the actual exposure to employees, as well as evaluate all tasks and procedures where exposure can occur.

A **bloodborne pathogen** is defined as a pathogenic micro-organism present in human blood that can cause disease in humans. These pathogens include, but are not limited to, Hepatitis B Virus (HBV) and Human Immunodeficiency Virus (HIV).

Occupational exposure under the Bloodborne Pathogen Standard is defined as reasonable anticipated skin, eye, mucous membrane, or parenteral contact with blood or other potentially infectious materials that results from performance of an employee's duties.

As defined by the Standard, *other potentially infectious materials* include semen, vaginal secretions, cerebrospinal fluid, synovial fluid, pleural fluid, pericardial fluid, peritoneal fluid, amniotic fluid, saliva and dental prostheses, any bodily fluid that is physically contaminated with blood, bodily fluids in situations where it is difficult or impossible to differentiate between body fluids and any unfixed tissue or organ (other than intact skin) from a human (living or dead).

b. **Exposure Control Plan** - The required written **Exposure Control Plan (ECP)** must include, as part of its elements, an exposure determination of the worksite, a schedule and method of implementation for engineering and work practice controls, the required Hepatitis B vaccination and post-exposure evaluation and follow-up, communication of hazards to employees, recordkeeping, and the procedures for evaluating circumstances of exposure incidents.

The written Exposure Control Plan (ECP) must be accessible to employees and reviewed and updated at *least annually* and wherever necessary to reflect new or modified tasks or procedures that effect occupational exposure, and new and revised employee positions with occupational exposure.

An employer, at least *annually*, must also consider the selection and implementation of appropriate effective, commercially available, safer control devices for *sharps injury protection*. The employer must solicit non-managerial employees, who are potentially exposed to injuries from contaminated sharps, for their input to identify, evaluate, and select effective sharps injury protection devices. This consideration should be documented and include the date of consideration, the device or control being considered, the name of the employer providing input, the decision reached, and the basis of the decision.

1) **Universal Precautions** - When, under circumstances in which differentiation between body fluid types is difficult or impossible, *all* human blood, certain human body fluids, and any unfixed tissue or organ (other than intact skin) must be considered potentially infectious.

2) **Engineering and Workplace Controls** - Engineering and workplace controls must first be used to eliminate or minimize employee exposure. If occupational exposure remains after the implementation of these controls, personal protective equipment must be used. Readily accessible hand washing facilities must be provided. When this is not feasible, either an appropriate antiseptic hand cleaner in conjunction with clean cloth/paper towels or antiseptic towelette to be followed as soon as feasible by washing with soap and running water. Employees must wash their hands immediately, after removal of gloves or other personal protective equipment. Mucous membranes must be flushed with water immediately following contact of such body areas with blood or other potentially infectious materials. See Microbiology section for Microorganism Control Practices (pp. 270-272).

3)   **Contaminated Needles and Sharps** - Contaminated needles and sharps must not be bent, recapped or removed unless the employer can demonstrate that no alternative was feasible or that such action is required by a specific medical or dental procedure. Shearing or breaking of contaminated needles is prohibited. Contaminated reusable sharps must be placed in appropriate containers until properly re-processed. These containers must be puncture-resistant, labeled or color coded as to content and hazard, leak-proof on the sides and bottom and stored and processed in such a way that employees are not required to reach into the container where the sharps have been placed.

4) **Prohibitions** - Eating, drinking, smoking, applying cosmetics or lip balm, and handling contact lenses in work areas are prohibited where there is a reasonable likelihood of occupational exposure. Food and drink must not be placed or stored near blood or other potentially infectious materials. All procedures must be performed in such a manner as to minimize splashing, spraying, spattering, and generation of droplets.

5) **Personal Protective Equipment** - *Personal protective equipment must be used and must be provided to employees at **NO cost to the employee.*** This includes gloves, gowns, laboratory coats, face shields or masks, and eye protection that does not permit blood or other potentially infectious material to be passed through or reach an employee's work clothes, street clothes, undergarments, skin, eyes, mouth or other mucous membranes under normal conditions of use and duration of time that the personal protective equipment will be used.

   The personal protective equipment must be cleaned, laundered, disposed of, repaired or replaced at no cost to the employee. The employer must also ensure the workplace is maintained in a clean and sanitary condition and implement appropriate written schedules for cleaning and decontamination.

6) **Housekeeping** - Contaminated sharps must be immediately discarded in containers that are closable, puncture-resistant, leak-proof on sides and bottom, and labeled or color-coded in accordance with the Bloodborne Pathogen Standard. All contaminated work surfaces must be decontaminated after completion of procedures, immediately when surfaces are overly contaminated, after any spill, and after or at the end of the work shift if the surface becomes contaminated since the last cleaning. Disposal of all regulated waste must comply with all applicable state and federal regulations.

7) **Warning Labels** - The Bloodborne Pathogen Standard requires that warning labels be placed on containers of regulated waste, refrigerators and freezers containing blood or other potentially infectious materials and other containers used to store, transport, or ship blood or other potentially infectious materials. The labels must include this Legend: **"BIOHAZARD"** and the Biohazard symbol. Red bags or red containers may be substituted for labels.

8) **Vaccination** - The Bloodborne Pathogen Standard requires that the **Hepatitis B vaccine** and vaccination series be made available to all employees who have occupational exposure. It also requires that all medical evaluations and procedures, including the Hepatitis B vaccine, booster doses, vaccination series and post-exposure evaluation and follow-up, must be made available at ***no cost to the employee***, at a reasonable time and place and be performed by or be under the supervision of a licensed physician or other licensed health care professional, as well as be provided according to current U.S. Public Health Service recommendations.

The Hepatitis B vaccination itself must be made available to employees after they have received the appropriate training and within ten (10) days of their initial assignment to a position with occupational exposure unless the employee has previously received the complete Hepatitis B vaccination series, antibody testing has revealed that the employee is immune, or the vaccination is contraindicated for medical reasons. An employee who declines to accept the vaccination must sign and date a **mandatory Hepatitis B Vaccination Declination** which must be presented to the employee exactly as written in the regulation.

9) **Post-Exposure Follow Up -** In a case of a exposure incident, the Standard requires post-evaluation follow-up to include documentation of the route of exposure and circumstances under which the exposure occurred, identification and documentation of the source individual, unless this is unfeasible or prohibited by state or local law, the testing of the source individual's blood as soon as possible after the incident, after any required consent is obtained, to determine HBV and HIV infection, unless the source individual is already known to be infected, post-exposure counseling and prophylaxis follow-up at no cost to the employee in accordance with current Centers for Disease Control and Prevention (CDC) Guidelines for Hepatitis B, Hepatitis C, and HIV.

10) **Training -** The Bloodborne Pathogen Standard has specific training requirements that include giving a copy of the Standard itself and an explanation of its contents to the employee. The employee must also be given an explanation of the epidemiology and symptoms of bloodborne diseases, the modes of transmission of bloodborne pathogens, explanation of the employer's required written **Exposure Control Plan**, and the means by which the employee may obtain a copy of the Plan.

The employee must be given, under the training program, an explanation of the appropriate methods for recognizing tasks and other activities that may involve exposure to blood or other potentially infectious materials, and explanation of the use, limitations and methods that would prevent or reduce exposure, including appropriate engineering controls, work practices and personal protective equipment and information on the proper use, location, removal, handling, decontamination, disposal of appropriate personal protective equipment.

The employee must be given information on the Hepatitis B vaccine, information on the appropriate action to take and the person to contact in an emergency involving blood or other potentially infectious materials and an explanation of procedures to follow if an exposure incident does occur, including the method of reporting the incident and the medical follow-up that will be made available.

The employee must also be given information on post-exposure evaluation and follow-up that the employer is required to provide to the employee following an exposure incident, must be trained in the use and recognition of the signs and labels and/or color-coding required by the Bloodborne Pathogen Standard and be given an opportunity for questions and answers with the person conducting the training who must be knowledgeable in the subject matter.

11) **Recordkeeping** - Training records, under the Bloodborne Pathogen Standard, must be kept for *three (3) years* from the date in which the training occurred and include the dates of the training sessions, the contents or summary of the training sessions, names and qualifications of the person conducting the training and names and job titles of all persons attending the sessions. These records will be reviewed by OSHA inspectors and must be available for examination and copying by the employee.

There is also a requirement, *unless* the employer is specifically *exempt* from maintaining the otherwise required OSHA log of injuries and illnesses, due to the employer's standard industrial code (SIC) classification as a low-hazard industry, to establish a *Sharps Injury Log* that describes the type and brand of device involved in an exposure incident, the department or work area in which the exposure incident occurred and an explanation of how the incident occurred. No special form is required, but the Sharps Injury Log must be recorded and maintained to protect the confidentiality of an injured employee and be maintained for the same period of time as the OSHA log of injuries and illnesses.

5. PERSONAL PROTECTIVE EQUIPMENT STANDARDS 29 C.F.R. 1910.132, 133, 135, 136, 137 AND 138

a. **General** - Personal protective equipment must be provided, used and maintained in a sanitary and reliable condition whenever it is necessary by reason of hazards of processes or environment, chemical hazards, radiological hazards, or mechanical irritants encountered in a manner that may cause impairment or injury in the function of any part of the body through absorption, inhalation, or physical contact.

Personal protective equipment may include personal protective equipment for the eyes, face, head and extremities, protective clothing, respiratory devices and protective shields and barriers. Employers are responsible to ensure the use, adequacy, proper maintenance and sanitation of personal protective equipment, even if the employees provide their own personal protective equipment.

b. **Workplace Assessment** - The employer is required to assess the workplace to determine if hazards are present or likely to be present that require the use of personal protective equipment. If they are present, the employer must explain to the employees when personal protective equipment is to be used and ensure that each affected employee uses properly fitted personal protective equipment that will protect the employee form the identified hazard. Any equipment that is defective or damaged shall not be used, and all equipment must be specifically designed to be used with the specific hazard encountered. Respiratory protection is covered under a separate Standard, which is 1910.134.

The Standard requires an employee to verify that the required workplace hazard assessment has been performed through a *written certification* that documents the assessment and identifies the workplace evaluated, the person certifying that the evaluation has been performed and the dates of the assessment.

c. **Training** - The Standard requires an employer to provide training sufficient to inform employees of when personal protective equipment is necessary, what type of personal protective equipment is necessary, how to properly wear personal protective equipment, the limitations of personal protective equipment and the proper care, maintenance, useful life and disposal of personal protective equipment *before* employees can be allowed to perform work requiring the use of personal protective equipment.

Re-training is necessary when changes in the workplace or in the type of personal protective equipment to be used makes the previous training obsolete or when an employer demonstrates that the employee does not have the required understanding or skill to properly use the required personal protective equipment. The employer must keep a *written certification* that contains the name of each employee trained, dates of the training and the subject matter of the training.

29 C.F.R. 1910.133 contains the specific requirements for eye protection, 29 C.F.R. 1910.135 contains the specific requirements for head protection, 29 C.F.R. 1910.136 contains the specific requirements for foot protection, 29 C.F.R. 1910.137 contains the requirements for electrical protective equipment, and 29 C.F.R. 1910.138 contains the specific requirements for hand protection.

6. THE RESPIRATORY PROTECTION STANDARD 29 C.F.R. 1910.134

a. **General** - The Respiratory Protection Standard requires that when effective engineering controls are not feasible to control occupational injury or disease caused by breathing contaminated air, an employer *must* provide respirators suitable for the intended purpose. Contaminated air may include potentially harmful levels of hazardous gases or vapors and/or potential respiratory hazards such as dust, mist, fumes, sprays, or airborne particles, as well as airborne biologic hazards.

As of July 1, 2004, OSHA will apply the general Respiratory Protection Standard, 29 C.F.R. 1910.134, to respiratory protection against *Tuberculosis.*

b. **Respiratory Protection Program (a/k/a The Program)** - The Standard requires that when respirators are necessary to protect the health of employees or whenever respirators are required by an employer, the employer must establish and maintain a written Respiratory Protection Program with required worksite procedures for required respiratory use in routine and foreseeable emergency situations.

The Program must be *worksite specific* and be updated as necessary to reflect changes in workplace conditions that affect respiratory use. The written Respiratory Protection Program must include procedures for selecting respirators, *medical evaluation of employees required to us respirators,* fit test procedures for tight fitting respirators, procedures for proper use of respirators in routine and foreseeable emergency situations and procedures and schedules for cleaning, disinfecting, storing, inspecting, repairing, discarding or otherwise marinating respirators. The Program must also contain procedures to ensure adequate air quality, quantity and flow of breathing air into atmosphere supplying respirators, if this type of respirator is in use.

Employees must be trained in the respiratory hazards to which they are potentially exposed, during routine and emergency situations and in the proper use of respirators, including putting them on or removing them, and limitations in their use and their maintenance. The Program must also contain procedures for regularly evaluating the effectiveness of the Program.

When a written Respiratory Protection Program is required, the employer must designate a Program Administrator, qualified by appropriate training or experience commensurate with the complexity of the written Respiratory Protection Program to administer or oversee the Program and to conduct required evaluations of Program effectiveness. All respirators under the Program shall be provided, along with required training and medical evaluations, at no cost to the employee.

1) **Voluntary Respirator Usage** - If respiratory protection is not required, but employees voluntarily choose to use their own or employer-provided respiratory protection, even when such protection is not mandated, the employer is NOT required to have a full Respiratory Protection Program as indicated, but must still ensure that the employees are medically able to use the respirators, ensure that respirators are properly cleaned, stored and maintained and provide voluntary respirator usage with the information contained in 29 C.F.R. 1910.134, Appendix D, which provides information for employees using respirators when such respirators are not required under the Respiratory Protection Standard.

2) **Respiratory Selection** - Respirator selection, when a respirator is required, must be based on the employer's evaluation of the respiratory hazards to which the employee is exposed and workplace and user factors that affect respiratory performance and reliability. The respirators that are selected must be NIOSH (National Institute for Occupational Safety and Health) certified and used in compliance with the conditions of their certifications. The employer's evaluation of the respiratory hazard must include a reasonable estimate of the employee exposure to respiratory hazards and an identification of a contaminant, chemical state and physical form. If employee exposure cannot be identified or reasonably estimated, the employer must consider the atmosphere to be immediately dangerous to life or health. The employer shall select a respiratory appropriate for the level of hazard identified. The respiratory hazards to be considered include *biological,* as well as *chemical hazards.*

3) **Fit Testing** - The requirements for fit testing are specific and contained in Appendix A to the Respiratory Protection Standard, 29 C.F.R. 1910.134. Before any required use, the employee must be fit tested on the same make, model, style and size of the respirator that will be used. Fit testing can be performed, for the employer, by an outside industrial hygienist or qualified health care professional and must include a qualitative or quantitative fit test as described by the Respiratory Protection Standard in Appendix A. Fit testing must be done prior to initial use, whenever a different face piece is used, at least annually thereafter and whenever there is a change in the employee's facial appearance/physical condition that warrants additional testing.

c. **Medical Evaluation** - The requirement for a medical evaluation is to determine the employee's physical ability to use a respirator *before* the employee is fit tested or required to use or allowed to voluntarily use a respirator in the workplace. This evaluation, which must be performed by a physician or other licensed health care professional, is necessary since a respirator does present a restriction on an individual's respiratory system and may be medically contraindicated for the individual.

The evaluation includes a medical questionnaire to be administered confidentially and the employee must be provided the opportunity to discuss the questionnaire and the examination results with the physician or other licensed health care professional. The employer must provide the physician or other licensed health care professional information about the actual type and weight of the respirator to be used, the duration and the frequency of the respiratory use, the expected physical work effort, and additional information as to any additional personal protective clothing or equipment to be worn and the temperature and humidity extremes that may be accounted *before* the physician makes a recommendation as to the employee's ability to use the respirator.

The medical recommendation regarding the employee's ability to use the respirator must be written and must contain any limitations in respirator usage related to the medical condition of the employee or the workplace conditions and contain a specific, clear determination as to whether the employee is medically able to use a respirator, the need for any follow-up medical evaluations and a statement that physician or licensed health care professional has provided the employee with a copy of the written recommendations.

d. **Training** - Employees who are required to use respirators must receive comprehensive and understandable training in their usage at least annually and more often if necessary. This training must include why a respirator is necessary and how improper fit, usage, or maintenance can compromise the protective effect of the respirator. The employee must also be trained in the limitations and capacities of the respirator being used, how to use the respirator effectively in emergency situations, including situations in which the respirator malfunctions and how to inspect, put on, remove, use, and check the seals of the respirator.

The training must also include procedures for maintenance and storage and the recognition of the medical science and symptoms that may limit or prevent effective use of the respirator, along with the general requirements of the Respiratory Protection Standard. Training must be given prior to requiring the employee to use the respirator in the workplace with retraining administered annually and when there are changes in the workplace or type of respirator that render previous training obsolete. Retraining must also be done when there are changes in the workplace or the type of respirator that render previous training obsolete, or whenever the employee's usage of the respirator indicates that retraining is required.

While the Respiratory Protection Standard does not require employers to keep training records, this should be done as a matter of practice to verify that training has been completed as required, the date of the training, the scope of the training, the employee being trained, and the identity of the trainer.

7. AIR CONTAMINANTS 29 C.F.R. 1910.1000

This Standard contains tables that list chemicals and the exposure limits for each substance stated as a ceiling value or as an 8-hour time-weighted average. To achieve compliance, administrative or engineering controls must first be determined and implemented wherever feasible. When administrative or engineering controls are not feasible to achieve full compliance, personal protective equipment must be used to keep employee exposure to the listed air contaminants within the limits prescribed by 29 C.F.R. 1910.1000.

Whenever respirators are to be used, their usage shall comply with the Respiratory Protection Standard 29 C.F.R. 1910.134.

8. QUICK DRENCH SHOWERS AND EYE WASHES 29 C.F.R. 1910.1048(i)(2)(3) and 1910.151

OSHA Standard 1910.1519(c) specifically requires that where the eyes or body of any person may be exposed to injurious corrosive materials, suitable facilities for quick drenching or flushing of the eyes and body shall be provided within the work area and available for <u>immediate</u> use should an employee get splashed with an injurious corrosive/destructive material. A shower or eye wash station that is located in another room, that would require an employee to pass through a door or to move more than a few steps, would not be in compliance with the requirements of this Standard.

To ensure that the equipment is operating properly and available for immediate emergency use, and employer must also, on a regular basis, test the unit's operation and should document this test to prove it was done.

In addition, under the specific OSHA Formaldehyde Standard, 29 C.F.R. 1910.1048(i)(2)(3), there is a requirement that states: "If employees' skin may become splashed with solutions containing 0.1% or greater Formaldehyde, the employer shall provide conveniently located quick drench showers and ensure that affected employees use these facilities immediately. If there is any possibility that an employee's eyes may be splashed with solutions containing 0.1% or greater Formaldehyde, the employer shall provide acceptable eye wash facilities within the immediate work area for emergency use."
Hands-free eye wash stations are the best option.

9. NEW FOR OSHA AS OF JANUARY 1, 2015
    a. As of January 1, 2015, all employers must report to OSHA:
- All work-related fatalities with 8 hours.
- All work-related inpatient hospitalizations, all amputations and all losses of an eye with 24 hours.

    b. The OSHA revised recordkeeping rule includes two key changes:
- First, the rule updates the list of industries that are exempt from the requirement to routinely keep OSHA injury and illness records, due to relatively low occupational injury and illness rates.
- Second, the rule expands the list of severe work-related injuries that all covered employers must report to OSHA.

    c. State-Plan State Regulations:

There are 27 states and U.S. territories that have their own OSHA-approved occupational safety and health programs called State Plans. State Plans are required to have standards that are at least as effective as OSHA's.

All State Plans have recordkeeping and reporting requirements in place. These requirements are at least equivalent to OSHA's previous reporting requirements for fatalities and catastrophes. In addition, several states have different or additional requirements that may already be in line with OSHA's revision.

All State Plans have begun reviewing their current reporting and recordkeeping requirements to determine how they compare to OSHA's new reporting requirements.

    d. Hazard Communication:

The Hazard Communication Standard (HCS) is now aligned with the Globally Harmonized System (GHS) of Classification and Labeling of Chemicals. This update to the Hazard Communication Standard (HCS) will provide a common and coherent approach to classifying chemicals and communicating hazard information on labels and safety data sheets (SDS). The revised standard will improve the quality and consistency of hazard information in the workplace, making it safer for workers by providing easily understandable information on appropriate handling and safe use of hazardous chemicals. This update will also help reduce trade barriers and result in productivity improvements for American businesses that regularly handle, store, and use hazardous chemicals while providing cost savings for American businesses that periodically update safety data sheets and labels for chemicals covered under the hazard communication standard.

List of OSHA Acronyms

ACGIH – American Conference of Governmental Industrial Hygienists
AL – Action Level
E.P.A. – Environmental Protection Agency
F.T.C. – Federal Trade Commission
G.H.S. – Globally Harmonized System
HBV – Hepatitis B Virus
HCHO – Formaldehyde
H.C.S. – Hazardous Communication Standard
NIOSH – National Institute for Occupational Safety and Health
OPIM – Other Potentially Infectious Material
OSHA – Occupational Safety and Health Act OR Administration
P.E.L. – Permissible/Prolonged exposure limit
pH – Potential of Hydrogen
P.P.E. – Personal Protective Equipment
ppm – Parts Per Million
S.D.S. – Safety Data Sheet
STEL – Short-term exposure limit
T.W.A. – Time-weighted average

Glossary for OSHA

Action level/A.L. (exposure limits) - Concentration of 0.5 ppm of formaldehyde calculated as an 8-hour T.W.A. concentration as defined by OSHA.

Biohazard - biological agent or situation that constitutes a hazard to humans.

Biohazardous waste - any potentially infective, contaminated waste that constitutes a hazard to humans in the workplace.

Bloodborne pathogen - microorganism present in human blood that can cause disease in humans.

Bloodborne Pathogen Standard - OSHA mandate (29 CFR 1910.1030) regulating the employee's exposure to blood and other body fluids.

Drench shower - OSHA-required safety device for a release of a copious amount of water in a short time.

Eyewash station - OSHA-required emergency safety device providing a steady stream of water for flushing the eye.

Formaldehyde/HCHO - colorless, strong-smelling gas that when used in solution is a powerful preservative and disinfectant; a known carcinogen.

Formaldehyde Standard - OSHA (29 CFR 1910.1048) regulation limiting the amount of occupational exposure to formaldehyde.

Hazard Communication Standard - (29 CFR 1910.1200) OSHA regulation that deals with identifying and limiting exposure to hazardous chemicals within the workplace.

Hazardous material - agent exposing one to risk.

Hepatitis B virus/HBV - infectious bloodborne virus.

Occupational exposure - reasonably anticipated skin, eye, mucous membrane, or parenteral, contact with blood or other potentially infectious materials that may result from the performance of a worker's duties.

Permissible exposure limit (PEL) - 0.75 ppm of formaldehyde present over an 8-hour time weighted average.

Short term exposure limit (STEL) - 2 ppm of formaldehyde present over a 15-minute time weighted average.

Domain IV
Cemeteries & Crematories

Cemeteries

Crematories

Cemeteries

Cemeteries serve as sacred grounds, providing a final resting place for departed loved ones and a space for reflection, remembrance, and memorialization. Interment, the act of laying to rest human remains within the cemetery grounds, is a deeply symbolic and culturally significant practice that varies across different traditions and belief systems. Cemeteries, with their rows of gravestones and carefully tended landscapes, represent a physical connection between the living and the deceased. They can offer solace to grieving families and provide a tangible link to the memories of those who have passed away. The interment process involves careful rituals and procedures, from the opening of the grave to the placement of the casket or urn. This act not only honors the deceased but also contributes to the communal aspect of mourning, as friends and family come together to pay their respects. In essence, cemeteries and the interment process play a vital role in the cultural, spiritual, and emotional aspects of the human experience, offering a place of eternal rest and a tangible connection to the continuity of life and memory.

A cemetery is not considered a nuisance per se due to the recognition of its essential and lawful purpose within society. Zoning ordinances play a crucial role in determining where and how different types of land uses, including cemeteries, can be established. Zoning regulations help ensure that how land is used is compatible with the surrounding community and its intended purpose. In the case of cemeteries, zoning ordinances provide guidelines for their location, size, design, and other factors to prevent conflicts with adjacent land uses and to maintain the overall harmony of the community. By adhering to zoning regulations, cemetery planners can mitigate potential issues related to traffic, aesthetics, and environmental impact, contributing to the peaceful coexistence of cemeteries with residential, commercial, or industrial areas. Recognizing and respecting these zoning ordinances ensures that cemeteries can fulfill their vital societal role while minimizing any adverse effects on the surrounding community.

The question of zoning becomes crucial when considering the burial of human remains in a person's backyard. Many communities prohibit such practices, primarily due to zoning regulations that govern land use and property development. Beyond the legal aspects, funeral directors often discourage this approach as personal properties can change hands over time through sales or inheritances, potentially limiting access to the gravesite for family members. To address this concern, if the burial of human remains is to occur on private property, it is advisable to amend the property deed with an easement. This legal provision grants family members the right to access the property, ensuring they retain the ability to pay their respects to the deceased buried on the premises. Such considerations emphasize the importance of thoughtful planning and legal arrangements when contemplating nontraditional burial practices on private land.

Types of Cemeteries

There are various types of cemeteries, each with its distinct ownership and purpose. Public cemeteries are typically operated by a cemetery board and serve as communal resting places open to the general public. Private or family-owned cemeteries are often exclusive to a particular family; these resting places usually restrict or specify who has burial rights. Religious cemeteries are affiliated with specific faiths, adhering to religious customs and traditions in the interment process. Municipal cemeteries, run by local governments, provide a final resting place for residents, and contribute to overall civic planning. Finally, national cemeteries are designated for veterans and their spouses, symbolizing a collective acknowledgment of the service and sacrifice of military personnel. Each type of cemetery reflects a unique blend of community, tradition, and purpose, catering to diverse needs and preferences in the perpetual commemoration of the departed.

In cemeteries, regardless of their type, an organized and systematic layout is employed to facilitate the location of graves. This numeric structure ensures that each burial site is precisely identified. A single grave is commonly referred to as a plot, and a group of plots forms a lot. Several lots make up a block, and multiple blocks constitute a particular section. Several sections create a cemetery. This structured system helps visitors navigate the grounds efficiently and locate specific burial sites using a standardized method. For instance, an address like Lot 5, Grave 2, Block 6, Section 3 provides a precise and easily interpretable reference point for finding a particular grave within the larger cemetery, contributing to the overall order and accessibility of these sacred spaces.

National cemeteries hold a special significance as hallowed grounds dedicated to honoring the service and sacrifice of military veterans and their spouses. Managed by the government, these cemeteries, such as Arlington National Cemetery in the United States, serve as solemn resting places for those who have served in the U.S. Armed Forces. The meticulously maintained landscapes and uniform rows of white headstones symbolize a collective tribute to the nation's heroes. National cemeteries often feature prominent memorials, reflecting a deep sense of national gratitude and remembrance. The meticulous care taken in the interment process, coupled with the ceremonial traditions observed during military funerals, adds a profound layer of reverence to these sacred sites. National cemeteries stand as reminders of the sacrifices made in service to the country and provide a place of perpetual honor for those who have defended the country's freedoms.

Some cemeteries pay a distinct and honorable tribute to veterans by designating special sections within their grounds exclusively for those who have served in the military. Although these sections may not be directly governed by federal authorities, they hold a special status as designated spaces acknowledged by the county or specific organizations. These dedicated areas adhere to unique requirements, often necessitating proof of military service, such as the presentation of a DD214 form. By establishing these exclusive sections, cemeteries demonstrate a profound commitment to recognizing and preserving the legacy of those who have bravely served their country, ensuring that their final resting places stand as enduring symbols of valor and sacrifice.

Requirements for Burial

When a consumer acquires a cemetery plot, it is common for the purchase to encompass more than one plot, collectively referred to as a lot. Upon acquiring a deed for the lot, the owner is granted certain entitlements and rights. Unlike property deeds for residential homes, for example, where owners have broader autonomy over their land, cemetery deeds come with specific restrictions and guidelines that lot owners must adhere to as a condition of the purchase. Lot owners don't own the property, they possess the right to be buried on the site.

At the time of purchase, a copy of these regulations is typically provided to the lot owner, detailing various specifications. These may include guidelines on the type of monument or grave marking permissible on the site. In memorial cemeteries, for example, where all grave markings are lawn-level and flush to the ground, the rules may allow only either a lawn-level granite or bronze marker. Some regulations may be intricately detailed, requiring lot owners to obtain approval from the cemetery before purchasing or installing a marker or headstone.

In addition to the right of burial, lot owners in cemeteries often enjoy additional privileges. One fundamental right is the right to be memorialized, allowing lot owners to mark the grave with a headstone or monument, providing a lasting tribute to their departed loved ones. In public cemeteries overseen by a cemetery board, lot owners may further exercise their democratic rights. This includes the right to vote at lot owner meetings, typically convened annually, where important decisions regarding cemetery management and policies are discussed. Moreover, lot owners in these public cemeteries may have the opportunity to hold office on the Cemetery Board, contributing to the governance and decision-making processes that shape the future and character of the cemetery. These rights extend beyond the act of burial, fostering a sense of ownership and community engagement within the cemetery's broader framework.

In the scenario where a husband and wife jointly purchase six plots, the deed is typically issued in both parties' names, establishing them as joint owners with equal and regular lot owner rights. As joint owners, they share the entitlements associated with the cemetery plot, ensuring their joint involvement in decisions related to the burial site. However, if the deed is registered in the name of only one spouse, the surviving spouse retains the right of burial as long as there is available space. In the absence of specific instructions in a will, the ownership of the plot descends to the children. In this case, all the children become joint lot owners, collectively inheriting the rights and responsibilities associated with the burial site.

Separately, the **right of consanguinity** highlights the importance of familial relationships in matters related to cemetery plots. In instances where a deceased individual has not designated a specific heir or beneficiary for the burial plot in their will, consanguinity comes into play. This legal principle recognizes the rights of blood relatives, often prioritizing the closest living relatives, such as children or siblings, as rightful successors to the burial plot. The right of consanguinity ensures that family ties are considered in determining the rightful inheritors of cemetery plots in the absence of explicit instructions from the deceased.

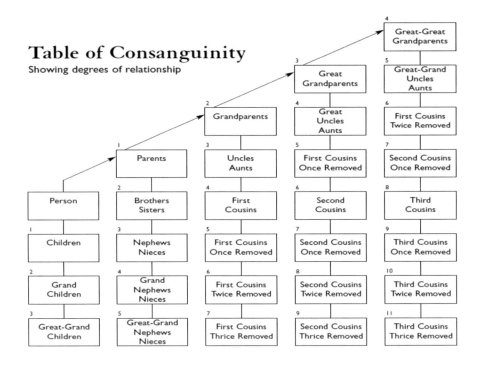

Table of Consanguinity
Showing degrees of relationship

In the above scenario, when both the husband and wife have died, leaving four unused burial plots, the inheritance of these plots typically passes to their four children. In this inheritance, each child is granted an equal right to all four plots, reflecting a fair and equitable distribution among the siblings. However, the practical utilization of these plots introduces a cooperative element among the siblings. Should one of the children express a desire to use one of the plots, the respectful implementation of such intentions necessitates the consensus of the other three siblings. The decision to use a specific plot becomes a collective one, requiring mutual agreement among the siblings to ensure harmony and unity in the use of the family burial space. This collaborative approach emphasizes the significance of communication and cooperation among family members, fostering a shared understanding and respect for everyone's wishes and rights within the context of the family's burial arrangements.

A cemetery retains the authority to decline a burial on a specific plot under various circumstances. One primary reason is nonpayment of the right of burial (grave), which encompasses the costs associated with reserving the burial space. Additionally, the refusal of interment services may be enforced if payment for the opening and closing fees is not received. Another factor leading to the denial of burial rights is nonpayment of authorized lot taxes, including perpetual care fees that contribute to the ongoing maintenance and upkeep of the cemetery. These measures ensure the financial sustainability of the cemetery while upholding its commitment to providing a dignified and well-maintained resting place for the dead.

Typically, cemeteries operate six days a week to accommodate families seeking burial services or visiting their loved ones' final resting places. While some cemeteries extend their availability to include weekends and holidays for added convenience, note that this service may come with additional overtime charges. The provision of weekend and holiday access reflects a commitment to meeting the diverse needs of families, ensuring flexibility for those who may prefer these days for burials or memorial visits. However, the associated overtime fees acknowledge the extra resources and personnel required to maintain operational efficiency during non-standard hours.

Some cemeteries feature a receiving vault as a practical solution when burial must be postponed due to inclement weather or other circumstances. These designated structures serve as temporary housing for casketed human remains awaiting final interment. While the availability of receiving vaults offers a valuable option for families facing delays, it's essential to be aware of specific requirements or restrictions imposed by some cemeteries. For instance, some cemeteries may mandate that human remains placed in these vaults undergo both pouching and embalming for long-term storage. Such regulations ensure proper preservation and hygiene during the temporary storage period, aligning with the cemetery's commitment to maintaining respectful and sanitary conditions for the deceased before their ultimate resting place is prepared.

Disinterment/Reinterment

Disinterment/reinterment, is a process involving the relocation of human remains, and requires specific procedures that must adhere to specific legal and ethical guidelines. In the field of funeral directing, a foundational principle emphasizes allowing the deceased to rest in peace after burial. Disturbing a grave is an exceptionally rare occurrence and is typically reserved for extraordinary circumstances in recognition of the sanctity and reverence associated with final resting places. When at all possible, a family should be counseled to let the deceased rest in peace, unless the reason for not moving the deceased will cause emotional or mental duress for the bereaved.

Scenario: A father with two daughters faced a distressing situation during the visitation for their mother, as the siblings quarreled over who would inherit their late mother's diamond ring after the funeral. Appalled by their behavior, the father sternly instructed the funeral director to inter his wife with the ring on her finger, forbidding removal under any circumstances. When the father died six months later, the daughters, seemingly more concerned about retrieving the ring than dealing with their father's funeral arrangements, approached the funeral director to disinter their mother and retrieve the ring. Honoring the father's explicit wishes, the funeral director, aware of the legal implications, advised the daughters to seek legal counsel and obtain court authorization for disinterment. Following legal advice and court proceedings, their request for disinterment was ultimately denied, reinforcing the importance of respecting the wishes of the deceased and legal protocols in such matters.

Disinterment and reinterment may be prompted by family wishes, particularly when there are changes in preferences or decisions. In some instances, families may choose to relocate their deceased loved ones to family plots or ancestral burial sites. A notable example of this is when, at the time of the individual's death, the family was unaware of an existing family grave in another cemetery. Discovering this family burial site later can lead to a decision to disinter and reinter the deceased to align with the family's desire for a more unified and meaningful resting place. This underscores the importance of accommodating evolving family preferences and ensuring that the final resting place aligns with a family's collective wishes.

Disinterment can become a necessity within the realm of investigation or legal requirements, particularly in cases involving forensic examinations, or exhumations related to criminal inquiries or legal disputes. Exhumation, defined as the process in which the coroner/medical examiner suspects foul play in the deceased's death and deems it necessary to examine the human remains to determine the cause of death, is a specific form of disinterment. This procedure is initiated to facilitate a comprehensive examination of human remains for evidentiary purposes or to address legal matters that demand meticulous scrutiny. The medical examiner/coroner usually obtains a court order to exhume human remains based on probable cause. This highlights the exceptional and specialized circumstances under which disinterment may be mandated, underscoring the intersection of funeral practices with the legal and investigative realms, particularly when there is a need for thorough examination and resolution in cases when the cause of death is suspicious or contested.

Disinterment may be deemed necessary in situations involving the correction of mistakes, particularly when a burial has been mistakenly conducted in the wrong plot within the cemetery. Recognizing the gravity of such errors, disinterment becomes a remedial measure to rectify the unintentional misplacement of human remains. This process ensures that the deceased is laid to rest in the intended and rightful location, addressing the inadvertent errors made during the initial burial. While disinterment is approached with utmost care and sensitivity, it serves as a means to uphold the integrity of the burial process and rectify any unintended deviations from the family's or cemetery's original intentions. Since this disinterment/reinterment is completed within the cemetery, the need to obtain a disinterment/reinterment permit with the municipality where the death occurred is not necessary. The only time a correction to the death certificate needs to be made and a new Burial Transit Permit needs to be issued, is when the human remains are leaving the confines of the cemetery.

Cemetery relocation is an intricate process triggered by urban development, environmental concerns, or other factors necessitating the closure or movement of existing burial grounds. The legal concept of **eminent domain** plays a crucial role in this process, empowering the government to acquire private property for public use and ensuring just compensation for property owners. In the context of cemetery relocation, eminent domain may be invoked to obtain the required land for urban development initiatives, such as the construction of roads or highways. For instance, the need to build a new roadway for the overall benefit of the community could prompt the use of eminent domain in cemetery relocation. This decision is guided by considerations of the broader public interest and the imperative of advancing urban development projects that benefit the greater community. The legal framework ensures fair compensation to property owners, including those managing cemeteries, while maintaining dignity and respect in relocating affected gravesites. Cemetery disinterment and reinterment involve a meticulous and respectful process of exhuming remains and burying them in a new location, adhering to legal and ethical standards. Government agencies or private developers spearheading cemetery relocation projects shoulder the responsibility of coordinating the process and addressing the concerns of affected families and communities. Balancing the needs of urban development with the sensitivity required in handling human remains emphasizes the significance of comprehensive planning, legal adherence, and compassionate communication throughout the cemetery relocation process. A funeral director should be assigned to supervise such projects.

Paperwork Necessary for Interment/Entombment/Inurnment

Before entering the cemetery for the final disposition of human remains, specific paperwork is required. In some instances, cemeteries may mandate that the next-of-kin or the person making arrangements identifies the grave before burial to ensure that the correct site is opened. There is a customary practice in some cultures for a husband and wife to be buried with the man on the right and the woman on the left, though this is a social custom rather than a strict rule. Another social convention involves placing the head of the deceased at the west end of the grave, although variations exist among cemeteries. As the funeral procession enters the cemetery, the funeral director must sign-in and present essential paperwork, including the Burial Transit Permit, Interment Authorization Form (or other form required by state law or cemetery requirements), and any required interment fees. Once these requirements have been fulfilled, the funeral procession may proceed to the grave.

The cemetery retains the right to deny burial for several reasons, including but not limited to: 1. Lack of proper paperwork, 2. Lack of payment, 3. Failure to follow cemetery policies and procedures, 4. If the interment poses a risk to cemetery personnel, ensuring that the sanctity and security of the burial grounds are upheld with meticulous care and adherence to established standards.

Burial/Entombment/Inurnment

Upon meeting cemetery entry requirements, the funeral procession stops at the gravesite, positioning the hearse at the end of the pathway leading to the grave. The funeral director consults with the cemetery sexton to determine the orientation of the grave, guiding whether the casket should be carried head or feet first. Pallbearers gather at the back of the hearse, and the funeral director provides instructions for the procession to the grave. The grave stands as a sacred space, and the funeral director assumes the crucial responsibility of upholding decorum and proper funeral etiquette throughout the journey to the final resting place and during the committal services. Carrying the deceased to the grave is a profound and sacred gesture, an act of reverence that can never truly be repaid. This solemn ritual symbolizes the highest form of honor and respect extended to the departed and their grieving family.

The funeral director, as a guiding presence in this delicate process, ensures that each step taken is marked by the dignity and solemnity befitting the gravity of the occasion. In navigating this sacred path, the funeral director plays a central role in creating an environment that fosters solace, reflection, and a fitting farewell to the departed soul.

Once at the grave, the vault or cemetery personnel take control of the casket, placing it on the lowering device. As the casket rolls onto the device, the funeral director instructs the pallbearers to release their hands. Once the casket is securely placed on the lowering device, the funeral director thanks the pallbearers for their service and assistance to the grave. The family is then seated in in front of the casket, with the clergy directed to the head end of the grave, marking the culmination of the solemn burial ceremony.

Upon conclusion of the committal prayers and if the deceased was in the U.S. Armed Forces, **military honors** are performed. Military honors at a gravesite are a dignified tribute bestowed upon veterans who have served their country with honor. The ceremony typically involves a carefully coordinated series of rituals performed by a military honor guard, comprising uniformed service members, usually from the branch of service in which the deceased served. One of the most recognizable elements is the playing of "Taps," a hauntingly beautiful bugle call that resonates across the cemetery, symbolizing both sorrow and gratitude. The folding and presentation of the American flag to the deceased veteran's next-of-kin is a solemn tradition, representing the nation's appreciation of the individual's sacrifice. Precision in the execution of these rituals is paramount, highlighting the respect and esteem with which the military honors its fallen comrades. The firing of a rifle volley, often known as the "21-gun salute," adds a final, thunderous tribute, echoing the profound impact of the veteran's service.

Beyond the symbolic gestures, military honors at a gravesite also convey a sense of unity, camaraderie, and shared commitment among those who have served. The meticulous choreography of each element in the ceremony is a testament to the military's dedication to honoring its own, providing a solemn yet powerful farewell that acknowledges the sacrifices made by the departed service member and offering solace to their grieving loved ones.

Upon the conclusion of the committal services, funeral personnel should assist people back to their cars. Risk management in funeral services is of paramount importance, particularly when assisting people who need help to and from the grave. Funeral directors must prioritize the safety and wellbeing of both their staff and the mourners, recognizing the potential physical and emotional challenges that may arise during the process. Assisting individuals who require support to reach the gravesite involves careful planning, communication, and coordination to minimize any potential risks, such as uneven terrain, inclement weather, or the emotional distress of grieving individuals. Ensuring a safe and secure environment not only upholds the integrity of the funeral service but also fosters an atmosphere of compassion and respect. By proactively identifying and addressing potential risks, funeral professionals contribute to a seamless and dignified experience, allowing mourners to focus on the grieving process without additional concerns about their physical wellbeing or the logistics of the burial ceremony.

Opting for entombment in a mausoleum crypt is a choice made by some families seeking an alternative to traditional burial. Within certain mausoleums, a chapel area is designated for the committal services, providing a serene and contemplative space for the final farewell. At the conclusion of these services, cemetery personnel carefully handle the transition of the deceased's casket. A unique practice involves scattering buckshot on the crypt floor, facilitating the smooth sliding of the casket into the chamber. For wooden caskets, an additional precaution is taken by placing the casket on a plastic tray or crypt vault to prevent potential leakage. Note: Some cemeteries may have casket or embalming requirements for human remains entombed in a mausoleum crypt.

The sealing process involves placing a plate over the opening of the crypt, secured with caulk to ensure a hermetic seal. The final touch involves the placement of a marble or granite faceplate over the front, completing the entombment process and providing a lasting, dignified memorial within the mausoleum.

Cremated remains offer families flexibility in choosing their final resting place, with options ranging from inurnment in a columbarium to interment in a grave. Families opting for ground interment face two choices: they can select a grave designated for the individual's cremated remains, or they may choose to inter them on top of a grave already occupied by another family member. However, in the latter case, certain restrictions may apply, and some cemeteries may impose an accommodations fee for multiple burials in a single grave. Additionally, specific requirements, such as using an urn or vault, might be mandated by the cemetery, with an urn vault serving to encase the urn and provide resistance against the elements.

Some families prefer the serene setting of a columbarium for the inurnment of cremated remains. The small chambers, known as niches, within the columbarium serve as a final resting place for urns. Some cemeteries have difficulty selling these spaces because it's a niche market (lol). Similar to traditional burials, families gather in the chapel for the committal prayer, followed by a meticulous process of sealing the urn within the chosen niche. This alternative provides families with a secure and respectful location to memorialize their loved ones while offering a range of choices to accommodate individual preferences.

In response to the evolving preferences in memorialization, some cemeteries now provide innovative alternatives, such as scattering gardens and ossuary options, for the final disposition of cremated remains. **Scattering gardens** offer a serene and tranquil setting where cremated remains are gently blended into the earth, creating a peaceful connection between the departed and nature. This option allows families to find solace in a natural environment, fostering a sense of continuity and interconnectedness. On the other hand, **ossuaries** provide a communal resting place, with cremated remains interred in a common grave vault. This choice appeals to those seeking a shared memorial space, where the essence of each individual contributes to the collective memory of the community. These contemporary alternatives reflect the changing landscape of funeral practices, accommodating diverse preferences and offering families unique ways to honor their loved ones' memories.

The primary responsibility of a funeral director extends beyond the logistics of handling the death event; it encompasses aiding individuals in connecting with their own grieving experiences. In the United States, where the average cremation rate stands at 60%, funeral directors face a growing concern related to unclaimed cremated remains. This challenge often arises when funeral directors neglect to plan, during the arrangement conference, appropriate resting spaces and ceremonies that facilitate closure for the bereaved. The grieving process persists as individuals adapt to the loss, highlighting the importance of providing meaningful and respectful options for the final disposition of cremated remains. Recognizing the cemetery as sacred ground, funeral directors play a crucial role in guiding families toward a place of solace, ensuring that their loved ones find a peaceful resting place, fostering a sense of comfort and tranquility amid the journey of grief.

Green Cemeteries

Green cemeteries, also known as natural or eco-friendly cemeteries, have emerged as environmentally conscious alternatives to conventional burial grounds. These cemeteries adhere to a set of regulations and requirements designed to minimize environmental impact and promote sustainable practices. Regulations often include restrictions on the use of embalming fluids and nonbiodegradable materials, advocating for biodegradable caskets or shrouds. Additionally, grave markers in green cemeteries are typically limited to natural and noninvasive options, such as native plants or flat stones, to preserve the natural aesthetics of the landscape.

The philosophy behind green cemeteries centers on creating burial spaces that contribute to environmental conservation and habitat preservation. The idea is to allow nature to reclaim the land, fostering biodiversity and maintaining a harmonious coexistence between the resting place of the departed and the natural ecosystem. By promoting sustainable burial practices, green cemeteries aim to minimize the ecological footprint associated with traditional burials and provide individuals with a choice that aligns with their environmental values.

Hybrid cemeteries represent a blending of traditional and green burial practices within the same cemetery grounds. In these cemeteries, a designated section adheres to the guidelines and burial objectives of green cemeteries, allowing individuals to choose environmentally friendly options while maintaining the overall structure and familiarity of a conventional cemetery. This approach accommodates a range of preferences within communities, offering families the opportunity to participate in eco-friendly burial practices while preserving the option for more conventional interments in adjacent sections of the cemetery. Hybrid cemeteries exemplify a thoughtful integration of environmentally conscious practices into the broader landscape of traditional burial grounds.

Cemetery Glossary

Block – Several lots together in a cemetery.

Burial (Interment) – the act of placing the dead human body in the ground.

Burial-Transit Permit (Disposition Permit) – a legal document, issued by a governmental agency, authorizing transportation and/or disposition of a dead human body.

Cemetery – an area of ground set aside and dedicated to the final disposition of dead human remains.

Cemetery tent – a portable shelter employed to cover the grave area during the committal.

Chart of Consanguinity - is used to determine the kinship of two individuals characterized by the sharing of common ancestor(s). In some countries, consanguinity is a common feature, and marriages among relatives occur widely, particularly in rural areas, the most prevalent being between first cousins.

Christian Burial Certificate – (Christian Burial Permit, Priest Lines) - a letter or form from a priest stating the eligibility of the deceased for burial in a Roman Catholic Cemetery.

Columbarium – a structure, room or space in a mausoleum or other building containing niches or recesses used to hold cremated remains.

Committal service – the portion of the funeral conducted at the place of disposition.

Coroner – usually an elected officer without medical training whose chief duty is to investigate questionable deaths.

Cremated remains – the result of the reduction of a dead body to inorganic bone fragments by intense heat.

Cremation – the reduction of a dead human body to inorganic bone fragments by intense heat in a specifically designed retort, or chamber.

Crematory – a furnace, or retort, for cremating dead human bodies; a building that houses a retort.

Direct Disposition – any method of disposition of the human remains without formal viewing, visitation or ceremony with the deceased present.

Disposition Permit – see Burial-Transit Permit.

Entombment – the placing of remains in a crypt in a mausoleum.

Funeral procession – the movement of vehicles from the place of the funeral to the place of disposition.

Grave – an excavation in the earth as a place for interment; interment space.

Graveside service – a ceremony or ritual, religious or otherwise, conducted at the grave.

Grave straps – webbing or similar material used for lowering the casket into the grave.

Green burial – disposition without the use of toxic chemicals or materials that are not readily biodegradable.

Green cemetery – a place of interment that bans the use of metal caskets, toxic embalming, and concrete vaults and may also require the use of aesthetically natural monuments.

Green funeral – death care that minimizes the use of energy in service offerings/products and that bans the use of toxic/hazardous materials.

Immediate Burial – disposition of human remains by burial, without formal viewing, visitation or ceremony with the deceased present, except for a graveside service.

Interment – see Burial.

Inurnment – placing cremated remains in an urn or placing cremated remains in a niche or grave.

Lot – Several plots owned by an individual or couple.

Mausoleum – a building containing crypts or vaults for entombment.

Medical Examiner – a forensically trained physician who investigates questionable or unattended deaths (the M.E. has replaced the coroner in some jurisdictions).

Niche – a recess or space in a columbarium used for the permanent placing of cremated remains.

Plot – is also known as a grave.

Receiving vault – a structure designed for the temporary storage of bodies not to be immediately interred.

Section – the largest subdivision of a cemetery.

Cremation

Cremation, a means of final disposition, *is the reduction of a dead human body to inorganic bone fragments by intense heat in a specially designed retort, or chamber.* The cremation process is irreversible. Its byproduct, after the completion of the entire cremation/pulverization process, is cremated remains. **Cremated remains** are never referred to as cremains or ashes; these are terms that lack reverence and respect for the human body.

Following the completion of the cremation process and the processing of large bone fragments in a cremulator, the resulting pulverized and unrecognizable cremated remains are placed in either a temporary or permanent urn. Subsequently, these cremated remains are either returned directly to the family or cared for according to the family's specified wishes. This section will elaborate on the legal responsibilities of the funeral director when managing families' requests for cremation. It will also outline the procedural processes established within the funeral industry for interacting with families who choose cremation as their preferred method of final disposition.

Legal Authorization

Obtaining proper authorization from the next-of-kin before cremating a loved one is of paramount importance in the funeral industry. Authorization ensures that the family's wishes are respected and that the legal and ethical considerations surrounding cremation are diligently followed. Authorization not only confirms the family's consent for the cremation process, it also safeguards the funeral director and the funeral home from potential legal issues. This step helps foster transparency and trust between the funeral director and the family, acknowledges the sensitive nature of the decision, and allows for open communication to address any concerns or questions that may arise during the process. Ultimately, receiving authorization from the next-of-kin is a crucial ethical practice that upholds the dignity of the deceased and honors the family's autonomy in making decisions about their loved one's final disposition.

Identification

The identification of human remains prior to the cremation process is of uppermost significance from both ethical and legal perspectives. Accurate identification ensures that the right individual is undergoing the cremation, respecting their wishes and those of their family. This serves as a crucial step in maintaining the integrity of legal procedures and documentation, preventing any potential mix-ups or errors that may lead to unintended consequences. This process upholds the dignity of the deceased, providing closure for families, and ensuring the appropriate treatment of the remains in accordance with cultural, religious, or personal preferences. In addition, identification also safeguards against any potential legal complications. Should a funeral director neglect to ensure the proper identification of human remains before cremation, they could potentially be liable for cremating an individual's loved one without the necessary authorization and authority. This failure to adhere to proper identification procedures can lead to legal consequences, as it infringes on the rights of the deceased and their family, raising concerns of unauthorized actions and potential emotional distress for those affected. In essence, the responsibility to secure proper identification before the cremation process is crucial to avoid legal ramifications and to uphold the ethical and legal standards associated with handling human remains. Overall, the identification of human remains before cremation is an indispensable measure that upholds ethical standards, legal requirements, and the emotional well-being of the bereaved.

Authorization

Authorization and a clear and thorough explanation of how the cremation process works are critical aspects of funeral and cremation services that aim to ensure transparency, respect the wishes of the deceased, and involve the appropriate individuals in the decision-making process.

Determining the Person(s) with the Right to Control Final Disposition: Before proceeding with cremation, it is essential to identify and obtain authorization from the person or people with the legal right to control the final disposition of the deceased. Typically involving close family members, the funeral director must seek their consent to proceed with the cremation.

The hierarchical order needs to be followed in the absence of a written instrument or clear instructions from the deceased, such as in a pre-need arrangement or will (*See the At-Need Right to Control Final Disposition p.250*). This comprehensive order ensures that there is a structured and legally recognized process for decision-making, considering various familial relationships and connections.

Impact of Deceased's Wishes: Understanding and respecting the wishes of the deceased is a fundamental part of the authorization process. If the deceased has expressed specific preferences or desires regarding their final disposition, such as choosing cremation over burial, it is crucial to honor these wishes. This ensures that the funeral and cremation services align with the individual's beliefs and choices. When there is documentation detailing the wishes of the deceased, these preferences must be adhered to, even in cases where they conflict with the desires of the next-of-kin.

Explain the Irreversible Nature of the Cremation Process: Full disclosure of the irreversible nature of the cremation process is essential for informed decision-making. The funeral director must be completely transparent, explaining as simply and clearly as possible that cremation involves the irreversible transformation of the body into cremated remains through intense heat. The family needs to comprehend the irreversible nature and finality of the process so they can make a fully informed decision regarding the disposition of their loved one's remains.

In many states, the requirement for *informed consent* necessitates a clear and detailed explanation on the cremation form. When going through the cremation authorization with the next-of-kin, it is essential to carefully examine the section on informed consent to ensure that they acknowledge and understand that the cremation process is irreversible by initialing the relevant section.

By addressing these three components – determining the appropriate decision-makers, honoring the deceased's wishes, and explaining the irreversible nature of cremation – funeral professionals ensure that families are well-informed, empowered to make decisions aligned with their values, and have a clear understanding of the process their loved one will undergo. This transparency fosters trust and follows ethical practices established within the funeral industry.

Removal of Implanted Pacemaker or Defibrillator

The removal of implanted devices, particularly those containing battery cells, such as pacemakers or defibrillators, is of utmost importance in the context of cremation. These devices, when subjected to intense heat during the cremation process, can pose significant risk of explosion, in effect turning into hand-grenades. The explosive response arises from the accumulation of pressure within the battery cells, triggered by the heat. Consequently, the cell can explode, leading to the creation of metal fragments that can become projectiles. The removal of these devices before cremation is crucial for several reasons:

1. Operator Safety: The safety of the crematory operator is paramount. If implanted devices with battery cells are not removed, the risk of explosion poses a direct threat to the well-being of the operator and anyone in the vicinity.
2. Crematory Integrity: The explosive nature of these devices can damage the crematory equipment. The force of an explosion could harm the retort, leading to costly repairs or, in extreme cases, rendering the equipment unusable.
3. Environmental Concerns: Explosions during cremation can result in the release of hazardous materials into the environment, posing risks to both the immediate surroundings and potentially affecting air quality.

To mitigate these risks, it is standard practice for funeral directors and crematory operators to identify and remove implanted devices with battery cells before proceeding with cremation. The funeral director could be found legally liable if an implanted device harms the crematory operator or the retort. This precautionary measure not only safeguards human lives, it also protects the integrity of the crematory equipment and prevents environmental damage. Proper communication with families about the importance of removing such devices is crucial to ensure a safe and respectful cremation process.

Before removing such devices, written authorization must be obtained from the authorizing agent. Once extracted, the device should be disposed of properly and not in a biohazard waste container, as this poses similar risks due to similar incineration processes. A recommended method of disposal is sending these devices back to the manufacturer or a refurbishing center. Alternative mail services, such as UPS or Federal Express, need to be used when sending these devices back to the manufacturer or refurbishing center. Sending such devices via United States Postal Services is prohibited by law.

Similarly, individuals with implanted **nuclear or radioactive materials cannot undergo cremation** unless these implants are first removed. Cremating such implants would violate U.S. Environmental Protection Agency (EPA) standards and knowingly doing so could expose the funeral home and funeral director to potential fines from the EPA. Proper disposal of such harmful waste requires the expertise of a trained medical professional, as funeral directors lack the necessary training for this task. If a medical professional declines to remove these implants, the funeral director must inform and guide the client on alternative final disposition options.

Documentation

Documenting personal effects during and after the removal process is of paramount importance for various reasons. This meticulous record-keeping serves as a crucial safeguard against any potential disputes, ensuring transparency and accountability in the handling of the deceased's belongings. Thorough documentation at the time of removal helps maintain the integrity of personal effects, allowing for their safe return to the bereaved family. Moreover, it provides a valuable resource for future reference, aiding in the resolution of any inquiries or concerns that may arise during the funeral and post-funeral processes. Additionally, this documentation plays a significant role in upholding ethical standards, reinforcing trust between the funeral service provider and the grieving family, and ultimately contributing to a respectful and organized handling of the deceased's personal effects.

Preparing Human Remains for Cremation

Preparing human remains for the cremation process is a meticulous and respectful procedure. Once the family or designated agent has identified the remains, the funeral director takes several important steps. First, the funeral director needs to palpate the chest area of the remains to check for and, if necessary, remove any subcutaneous electronic devices. Simultaneously, a careful examination is conducted to identify and document any jewelry or personal effects present on the individual. The documented personal effects are then returned to the next-of-kin. Only human remains are allowed to be in the cremation unit. Subsequently, the human remains are appropriately attired, with a hospital gown being the minimum attire if not dressed otherwise. Following a visual examination, the remains are carefully placed in the chosen cremation unit by the consumer. The container is then securely closed, with specific steps taken for alternative containers, such as using stretch wrap to secure the lid. To ensure proper identification, the deceased's last name and the name of the funeral home are marked at the top of the cremation unit. This comprehensive process not only adheres to ethical standards but also ensures a dignified and organized preparation for the cremation process.

Documents Needed for Cremation

The documentation required for the cremation process is essential to ensure legal compliance, authorization, and a smooth transition through the various stages of cremation. The following documents play key roles and need to be obtained and certified prior to the cremation process:

1. **Burial Transit Permit**: This is a crucial legal document that authorizes the transportation of the deceased from the place of death, to the funeral home, and to the place of final disposition. This permit is typically issued by the local registrar or health department after the death certificate has been filed, confirming that the human remains can be moved for final disposition.

2. **Authorization for Cremation:** Often signed by the next-of-kin or an authorized agent, this grants permission for the cremation process to proceed. This document outlines the individual's identity, the decision to cremate, and any specific instructions or wishes regarding the process.

3. **Customer Designation of Intention:** This is a document through which individuals articulate their intentions and preferences regarding the care of the cremated remains. It may include specific details about cremation, burial, or other preferences after the cremation process has been completed. While not always legally binding, it serves as a valuable in-house guide for the funeral director and family to bring proper delivery or disposition to the cremated remains.

4. **Coroner/Medical Examiner Permit to Cremate:** In cases where the death is under the jurisdiction of a coroner or medical examiner, a specific permit to cremate may be required. This document ensures that all necessary investigations have been conducted and that the human remains are cleared for cremation. It adds an additional layer of oversight to guarantee compliance with legal and health regulations.

These documents collectively form a comprehensive set of paperwork that address legal, regulatory, and personal aspects of the cremation process. Proper documentation is not only essential for legal compliance, it also facilitates effective communication between funeral homes, crematories, and the families involved, ensuring that the wishes of the deceased and their loved ones are respected and carried out appropriately.

Delivery to the Crematory

Most crematoriums require appointments to be scheduled for both the delivery of human remains and the cremation process. The funeral director plays a crucial role here by ensuring that all necessary paperwork is provided to the crematory operator along with the cremation fee at the time of delivery. The required paperwork typically includes documents such as the Authorization for Cremation, any permits from the county (i.e. Burial Transit Permit) where the death occurred and the coroner/medical examiner authorization, when applicable. If the crematory mandates additional paperwork, such as a Body Delivery Receipt, it is imperative for the funeral director to complete these documents before leaving the human remains at the facility. To maintain their dignity and integrity, the human remains should be secured in a designated area or refrigeration unit while awaiting the scheduled cremation. This careful and systematic approach ensures that all legal and procedural requirements are met, contributing to a respectful and well-organized cremation process.

The container used for housing human remains before cremation is typically supplied by the funeral home, chosen by the family, or mandated by applicable laws and regulations. When at all possible, the human remains should be identified (prior to the cremation) in the container selected by the family during the arrangement conference. Transporting human remains to the crematory on a removal cot is generally prohibited in most states, as it is considered undignified.

Instead, the use of an appropriate container ensures a respectful and dignified handling of the deceased, aligning with regulatory standards and cultural sensitivity. This careful consideration of container choice reflects the commitment to upholding the dignity of the deceased throughout the entire funeral process.

After the cremation process is finalized, the cremated remains are typically either sent back to the funeral home by the crematory or collected by funeral home personnel during subsequent deliveries. The crucial element in this process is its timely execution to align with the family's deadlines, especially for services intending to incorporate the presence of the cremated remains into a memorial or graveside ceremony. This ensures that the funeral home can seamlessly facilitate the family's preferences and meet the scheduled timeline for the commemorative services.

Cremated remains processed by the crematory must be accurately identified through the placement of a metallic tag on the cremation unit upon delivery to the facility. This sequentially ordered tag corresponds to the crematory's logbook and tracking system. The number on the tag serves as a permanent record, aligning with the identification number found on the temporary cremation container and cremation certificate. This meticulous identification system ensures consistency and traceability throughout the cremation process, maintaining a reliable record of the remains from start to finish.

Disposition of Cremated Remains

The disposition of cremated remains refers to the final handling or placement of the cremated remains following the cremation process. Families typically have several options for the disposition of cremated remains, including burial in a cemetery, placement in a columbarium or mausoleum, scattering in a designated area, or retaining the cremated remains in an urn kept at home. The chosen method often reflects personal, cultural, or religious preferences and is an important aspect of the funeral planning process.

Upon receiving the cremated remains from the crematory, the funeral home must handle the inurnment process with utmost care. The permanent urn, chosen by the family, should be prepared in a meticulous manner to prevent any markings or spillage of the cremated remains. A soft towel is recommended as a protective surface. After carefully opening the urn, the funeral home staff may insert a plastic bag inside the unit and transfer all the cremated remains into the permanent urn. During the closure process, it is crucial to use a zip tie to attach the metal ID tag to the cremated remains. This step plays a significant role in associating the cremated remains with the specific crematory and the entire cremation procedure. The urn is then closed, and any fine particles are wiped off before placing an identification label on the bottom of the urn. The prepared urn is then secured in a dignified place, awaiting final delivery to the family or to its designated resting place. This process reflects the attention to detail and respect required in handling cremated remains within the funeral profession.

If the cremated remains exceed the urn's 200 cubic inch capacity, it is advisable for the funeral director to promptly contact the client and discuss available options. This may involve a larger urn to accommodate all of the cremated remains or purchasing an additional smaller urn that matches the chosen one to accommodate the excess remains. Typically, regardless of the individual's size, normally, cremated remains fit within a standard urn; any excess remains are often related to the cremation container used during the cremation process. Clear communication and guidance from the funeral director ensure that the family is informed and involved in decisions related to the final placement of the cremated remains.

The extra cremated remains should never be discarded in an undignified manner. The respect and care shown during the entire process of handling and managing cremated remains, including any excess, are essential aspects of the funeral profession. Funeral directors uphold the dignity of the deceased and their remains, ensuring that every step of the process is conducted with sensitivity and reverence. Families are typically provided with options and guidance to make informed decisions about the final disposition of any excess remains, ensuring that the chosen course aligns with their preferences and cultural or religious beliefs.

The issue of unclaimed cremated remains in funeral homes is a growing concern within the funeral industry. Unclaimed remains can arise for various reasons, such as financial constraints, estranged family relationships, or lack of communication regarding the disposition of the cremated remains. Funeral homes face the challenge of determining appropriate protocols and ethical practices for handling unclaimed cremated remains, including potential options for respectful and dignified disposition in the absence of family involvement. This issue underscores the need for ongoing discussions within the industry to address the complexities surrounding unclaimed remains and to develop compassionate and thoughtful procedures for their proper handling.

If cremated remains remain unclaimed in the funeral home, and the regulatory timeframe for claiming them has expired, funeral directors may have the authority to dispose of them in a dignified and respectful, yet retrievable, manner. Options for handling unclaimed cremated remains may include burial in a mass grave alongside other unclaimed remains, or entombment. These practices prioritize a sense of dignity and respect even in the absence of familial involvement. The decision on how to handle unclaimed cremated remains often involves a balance between regulatory requirements, ethical considerations, and a commitment to treating the deceased with the utmost reverence.

Torts, Liabilities, and Negligence

Because cremation can pose unique challenges for funeral establishments and can create potential liabilities leading to tort claims, implementing **risk management practices** is essential to minimize exposure. This includes conducting thorough risk assessments of cremation processes, ensuring that staff are adequately trained, and implementing safety protocols to prevent accidents or errors.

Implementing secure **identification measures** is essential to prevent potential torts related to misidentification of remains. Funeral establishments should use reliable identification systems from intake to the final delivery of cremated remains. Clear and consistent identification procedures minimize the risk of legal liabilities associated with errors or mix-ups.

Proper documentation is a critical tool in minimizing liability exposure. Funeral establishments should maintain comprehensive records throughout the cremation process, documenting authorizations, identification procedures, and any specific instructions from the family. Detailed documentation serves as evidence of compliance with legal and ethical standards, reducing the risk of legal challenges. Funeral directors who experience legal issues with cremations usually deviate from accepted industry standards.

Proper **informed consent** procedures are also vital to minimize liability. Funeral establishments should thoroughly explain the irreversible nature of the cremation process to the next-of-kin and obtain their consent in writing. Failure to secure informed consent may result in legal challenges, making documentation of this process essential.

Documentation of the removal and disposal of implanted devices is also crucial to minimize legal risks. Funeral establishments should obtain written authorization for the removal of such devices, document the proper disposal method, and communicate the potential risks to the family. Thorough documentation ensures compliance with legal requirements and reduces the risk of liability.

Clear communication with the family regarding the cremation process is crucial to avoid potential legal issues. Funeral establishments should document all discussions with the next-of-kin, addressing their concerns, explaining procedures, and obtaining any necessary approvals. This documentation serves as a record of transparent communication, reducing the risk of misunderstandings or disputes. Clear policies for handling complicated family dynamics are essential to minimize legal liabilities. Funeral establishments should document all interactions, agreements, and any deviations from standard procedures. Detailed documentation helps establishments navigate potential legal challenges arising from family disputes or disagreements. In the event of complications or errors during the cremation process, prompt communication is key to minimizing legal liabilities. Funeral establishments should inform the affected parties, including the family, about the issue, its resolution, and any potential impact on the cremated remains. Transparent communication can mitigate legal repercussions.

Educating staff on legal requirements and industry standards is essential in minimizing legal liabilities. Funeral establishments should provide ongoing training to ensure that staff members are aware of and comply with relevant laws and regulations. A well-informed staff can reduce the risk of potential torts. Clear policies for handling complicated family dynamics are essential to minimize liability. Funeral establishments should document all interactions, agreements, and any deviations from standard procedures. Detailed documentation helps staff members navigate potential legal challenges arising from family disputes or disagreements.

When family members hold divergent opinions on choosing cremation as the final disposition, the funeral director assumes the role of a counselor, providing guidance on available options and apprising them of state-specific regulations governing the proper authorization for cremating human remains. State requirements vary; some mandate unanimous familial consent, while others require a 2/3 majority agreement. Importantly, the funeral director should refrain from involvement in the decision-making process. Once the family collectively opts for cremation, it is advisable for all members to endorse the authorization form. This procedural approach serves as a risk management policy, safeguarding the funeral director's interests by ensuring comprehensive consent and adherence to legal protocols.

Staying informed about changes in laws and regulations related to cremation is crucial for minimizing legal liabilities, and funeral establishments should regularly update their practices to align with evolving standards. Proactive measures reduce the risk of legal challenges related to noncompliance with current legal requirements.

Funeral establishments may face **potential liability for third-party cremator services**. Ensuring that the selected crematory follows industry standards, complies with legal regulations, and maintains appropriate insurance coverage is crucial. Funeral directors should conduct annual due **diligence in vetting and selecting crematories** to minimize the risk of liability associated with the actions or negligence of third-party providers.

Ensuring the appropriate handling of **excess cremated remains** is crucial to mitigate potential legal complications. A funeral director must meticulously record every attempt made to reach out to the family and ascertain their preferences for disposition. In instances where cremated remains are returned from the crematory in multiple temporary containers, the funeral director should promptly inform the family about the surplus. Additionally, the funeral director may recommend opting for a larger or companion urn, facilitating the consolidation of all cremated remains into a single vessel for a more unified and respectful disposition.

Clear documentation ensures compliance with regulations and reduces the risk of legal liabilities associated with unclaimed remains. The proper handling of **unclaimed cremated remains** requires clear policies and documentation. Funeral establishments should document efforts made to contact the family, any decisions made regarding disposition, and adherence to relevant regulations. If the funeral home chooses to dispose of unclaimed cremated remains, it should be done in a respectful and retrievable manner, documenting their location in either a cemetery plot or mausoleum crypt.

Compliance with environmental regulations is essential to reducing legal liability related to cremation. Funeral establishments must guarantee the correct disposal of devices containing battery cells and adhere to guidelines for environmentally responsible practices. Because they lack the required licensing, training, and expertise, funeral directors should avoid attempting the removal of radioactive or nuclear implants themselves. Moreover, they are not equipped to dispose of hazardous materials properly. Noncompliance with environmental regulations may lead to legal problems with the U.S. Environmental Protection Agency (EPA) or other regulatory agencies.

Funeral establishments should have legal professionals review their policies, procedures, and documentation practices to ensure compliance with relevant laws. Legal review contributes to a legally compliant environment, reducing the risk of potential torts.

FTC Requirements for Cremation

The Federal Trade Commission (FTC) imposes specific rules for funeral directors regarding cremation practices to ensure transparency and protect consumers. One key stipulation is that when a consumer opts for direct cremation – when a body is cremated shortly after passing without embalming, a viewing, or any kind of formal service – funeral directors cannot compel consumers to buy a casket. The FTC's mandate underscores the importance of offering consumers the freedom to make choices in accordance with their preferences and financial considerations.

Moreover, if funeral establishments provide direct cremation as an option, they must include this service on the General Price List (GPL) along with a comprehensive range of prices. The FTC specifies that the prices be itemized based on different scenarios: a) when consumers provide their own cremation container, b) when the funeral home supplies an alternative container, and c) when consumers choose an unfinished wooden box. This requirement ensures clarity and enables consumers to make informed decisions by understanding the associated costs of various elements involved in the cremation process.

In addition to these provisions, the FTC strictly prohibits the misrepresentation of caskets designated for cremation. Funeral directors must provide accurate information about the characteristics, materials, and functionalities of caskets offered for this purpose. This regulation aims to prevent deceptive practices and ensures that consumers are well informed when making choices related to cremation arrangements. By enforcing these requirements, the FTC seeks to uphold fair business practices within the funeral industry and protect the rights and interests of consumers during sensitive and often challenging times.

Procedures for Cremation

Cremating individuals with a larger body mass requires a careful and specific approach to mitigate potential risks. When cremating overweight individuals, it is essential to initiate the cremation process when the retort is cool to minimize the likelihood of a grease fire. Due to the higher adipose tissue content in individuals of larger body mass, slower combustion is necessary to prevent the rapid ignition of fats, which could lead to a grease fire within the retort. This precautionary measure ensures the safety of the crematory facility and underscores the importance of adhering to specialized procedures tailored to different body compositions. By taking these precautions, crematory operators prioritize safety and uphold the integrity of the cremation process for individuals of larger body mass. Finally, it is suitable to use a shipping container for people of larger size.

Maintaining the proper temperature within a retort is crucial for a successful and safe cremation process; the range is typically from 1400-1800 degrees Fahrenheit. However, it is imperative to adhere to specific guidelines regarding the materials allowed for cremation. Only human remains and their accompanying clothing are permissible. The human remains must be encased in a container suitable for cremation, preferably one that is combustible. While some crematories permit metal caskets, any zinc components must be removed to avoid violations of environmental regulations set by the U.S. Environmental Protection Agency (EPA). Wooden caskets are accepted, but it is essential to consider that while the wood burns, residual ash remnants may contribute to excess cremated remains, and multiple cremation containers. Ceremonial caskets offer a practical option for families who prefer a wooden casket for funeral services. These caskets facilitate a smooth transition by allowing the easy removal of an alternative cremation insert for the final cremation process.

Human remains should be placed in a designated body pouch explicitly designed for the cremation process. This is a precautionary measure, in the event that the human remains release any bodily fluids. The use of disaster pouches for cremation is prohibited, as they are not tailored for this purpose. Disaster pouches can emit black smoke during the cremation process, posing environmental issues and the possibility of citizen complaints due to the nuisance caused by the smoke.

Furthermore, the use of plastic or fiberglass caskets is strictly prohibited due to the release of toxins during the cremation process. This restriction aligns with environmental and safety concerns, emphasizing the importance of responsible and ethical practices in the handling of human remains. By adhering to these guidelines, crematories ensure the integrity of the cremation process while prioritizing environmental sensitivity and adherence to safety standards.

After the Cremation Process

Various avenues exist for families to memorialize and pay tribute to the life achievements of their departed loved ones. Funeral directors who express concerns about cremation affecting their profitability may overlook the potential for offering meaningful services or not adequately presenting options for honoring the accomplishments of the deceased. When a consumer expresses a preference for cremation as the final disposition, a funeral director's response should extend beyond logistical details, asking, "Will that be before or after the visitation or funeral services?" This approach emphasizes the importance of integrating cremation into a broader context of commemoration.

A funeral director's primary objective extends beyond the technical aspects of the funeral process: it involves guiding individuals through the grieving experience. Failing to provide families with options for memorialization and guidance on properly handling cremated remains post-cremation is a disservice, as it focuses solely on caring for the human remains without addressing the broader emotional needs of the client-family. Funeral directors are best positioned to facilitate a comprehensive grieving process by offering diverse memorialization choices and helping families navigate the proper disposition of cremated remains; this ensures more holistic and supportive approach to grief. Furthermore, funeral homes that have a problem with unclaimed cremated remains are failing to provide memorialization options that incorporate the cremated remains into a final committal ceremony that supports final commendations to the deceased.

A crucial aspect of funeral directing involves embracing creativity and reimagining traditional approaches to provide services that allow consumers to personalize the death event and connect it to their unique grieving experience. Some individuals who opt for cremation as their chosen method of final disposition may feel uncomfortable or resistant to viewing their loved ones in a traditional casket. A novel concept emerging in the funeral service industry is the use of a slumber room featuring a reposing bed, where the embalmed human remains lie as if peacefully asleep. After the funeral services, the deceased is transferred to a cremation unit, and the family accompanies them to the crematory, integrating this process into their mourning experience. Upon the return of the cremated remains to the funeral home, the family reconvenes for a ceremonial procession to the cemetery, using a hearse carrying an urn ark (housing the urn and cremated remains) for the inurnment ceremony. This shift toward ceremony and personalization marks the future of funerals in the United States, emphasizing the progressive funeral director's role in implementing innovative options for memorialization within the cremation process. Given the contemporary trend of consumers often lacking strong religious affiliations, funeral directors play a crucial role in crafting meaningful rituals and ceremonies that guide individuals through the grieving process and that foster a connection to their own unique experiences of loss.

In the author's perspective, the landscape of funeral directing in the United States is poised for a significant transformation within the next two decades. A dual model is expected to emerge: Socialized Funeral Directing, wherein local health departments oversee the disposal of human remains through methods such as alkaline hydrolysis; concurrently, there will be a private funeral home sector will offer inventive alternatives for the dignified care of the deceased that support the grieving process for the bereaved. This evolving landscape of funeral services foresees a dichotomy: one branch prioritizing streamlined practices managed by public health authorities with minimal connection to the grieving process, while the other accentuates private funeral homes' innovative options to enrich the personalized and meaningful aspects of the funeral experience.

Scattering of Cremated Remains

Scattering cremated remains in public waterways carries legal considerations to ensure compliance with regulations. The choice of the ocean as a final resting place generally requires cremated remains to be released a minimum of 3 nautical miles from the shoreline. This distance helps to maintain environmental integrity and prevent any potential issues related to public health. Additionally, it is advised to record the precise GPS coordinates of the scattering event and report them to the U.S. Environmental Protection Agency (EPA). This recording process helps maintain transparency and accountability, aligning with environmental regulations and ensuring adherence to the designated scattering areas.

Governmental restrictions also come into play when considering the scattering of cremated remains in public places and certain inland waterways. While the scattering of cremated remains may be permitted, specific guidelines and regulations must be followed. In some cases, local authorities may have restrictions or designated areas for such practices to prevent environmental impact or public disturbance. Families should be aware of these restrictions and seek proper permissions or information from relevant authorities before proceeding with the scattering of cremated remains. Being informed about the legal considerations ensures that the final act of remembrance aligns with both personal wishes and legal requirements, respecting both the integrity of public spaces and environmental regulations.

Scattering Gardens

Designated scattering gardens within cemeteries provide a serene and meaningful option for the final disposition of cremated remains. In these carefully designed spaces, the pulverized cremated remains are delicately spread and incorporated into the landscape, seamlessly blending with the natural elements. This intentional integration allows families to scatter the cremated remains of their loved ones in a designated and aesthetically pleasing area, fostering a connection with nature. A scattering garden often features landscaped surroundings, such as lush greenery, flowers, and peaceful pathways, creating a tranquil environment for reflection and remembrance. This approach not only honors the deceased but also offers a peaceful and harmonious setting for families to find solace and closure in the beauty of the natural surroundings.

Inurnments and Ossuaries

Some families will opt to bury the cremated remains on top of another family member's grave. While some cemeteries permit such inurnments, the specific restrictions can vary significantly from one cemetery to another. In addition to the standard opening and closing fees associated with the grave, the cemetery may impose a multi-use fee to facilitate this interment practice. Alternatively, some cemeteries offer columbarium options where consumers can purchase a niche to house the cremated remains. These niches are often customizable, allowing for personal engravings to memorialize the deceased.

Moreover, certain cemeteries provide an ossuary as an alternative for the communal placement of cremated remains. Functioning as a burial vault with a large PVC pipe attached, an ossuary allows for a unique interment process. When cremated remains are placed into the ossuary, the cap of the PVC is removed, and the remains are gently poured into the buried receptacle. This option provides a distinctive and communal way to honor the departed, offering families a choice in how they wish to preserve the memory of their loved ones within the cemetery grounds.

Mailing and Traveling with Cremated Remains

Mailing cremated remains, via the U.S. Postal Service (USPS), involves careful adherence to specific regulations and guidelines to ensure a secure and respectful transit. The USPS permits the shipment of cremated remains, provided they are packaged securely in a funeral urn or appropriate container. Additionally, the outer packaging must meet USPS specifications and include proper labeling to indicate the nature of the contents. It is essential to check with the USPS for specific requirements and to use services that prioritize the safe and dignified transportation of cremated remains. Families choosing this method should work closely with their funeral director to ensure that all legal and logistical aspects are appropriately addressed. Other delivery services are not recommended; they lack specific guidelines that treat cremated remains with respect and dignity, which could raise legal issues.

When carrying cremated remains through airport security, navigating Transportation Security Administration (TSA) protocols is crucial for a smooth and respectful process. Plastic or wood containers are advisable, as these materials are more compatible with X-ray equipment, minimizing the need for physical inspection. Alongside the urn, it is essential to have a Certificate of Cremation, providing documentation to verify the contents. To further facilitate the screening process, including a letter on funeral home stationery explicitly stating that the urn contains only the cremated remains of the deceased is recommended. These measures align with TSA regulations, ensuring a dignified and efficient process when individuals are traveling with the cremated remains of loved ones.

In conclusion, adhering to established protocols is paramount in avoiding potential legal or ethical issues in the realm of funeral services. By meticulously following the prescribed guidelines, funeral directors not only uphold industry standards but also prioritize the well-being of grieving families. Offering a range of options to families ensures that the funeral director effectively navigates the intricacies of the death event, facilitating a connection to the unique grieving experience of each family. This commitment to both professional protocols and personalized care underscores the importance of a holistic and empathetic approach to help families through the challenging process of saying farewell to their loved ones, no matter what means of final disposition they choose.

Photo provided by: D.M. Williams Funeral Home, Inc. Rochester, N.Y.

CREMATION – GLOSSARY

Alkaline hydrolysis – a process that uses water, alkaline chemicals, heat and sometimes 4 pressure and agitation, to accelerate natural decomposition, leaving bone fragments.

Alternative container – an unfinished wood box or other non-metal receptacle or enclosure, without ornamentation or a fixed interior lining, which is designed for the encasement of human remains and which is made of fiberboard, pressed-wood, composition materials (with or without an outside covering) or like materials.

Authorizing agent – the person(s) with the paramount right to authorize cremation and disposition

Casting (Scattering) – the release of cremated remains over land, through the air or over water.

Ceremonial (Rental) Casket – an exterior casket shell with a removable insert designed for cremation.

Columbarium – a structure, room or space containing niches or recesses used to hold cremated remains.

Commingling – combining the cremated remains of more than one person.

Corrugated container – a container used to hold human remains which is constructed out of a type of cardboard, which is made with a series of alternate folds and ridges.

Cremated remains – the final product remaining after completion of the entire cremation/pulverization process. The product is never referred to as "cremains".

Cremation – the reduction of a dead human body to inorganic bone fragments by intense heat in a specifically designed retort or chamber.

Cremation casket – a combustible, rigid, leak-resistant casket manufactured to be cremated.

Cremator – the mechanical unit used for the cremation process.

Crematory –the physical location of the cremator where the cremation process is performed.

Cremulator – A device used after the cremated process to pulverize bones into cremated remains.

Direct cremation – disposition of human remains by cremation, without formal viewing, visitation or ceremony with the body present. [16CFR 453(g)]

Due diligence – the attention reasonably expected from, and ordinarily exercised by, a person who seeks to satisfy a legal requirement or to discharge an obligation.

Identification – the verification of the deceased's identity through visual, photographic or other reliable means.

Indemnification – a legal agreement by one party to hold another party not liable for potential losses or damages.

Inurnment – the act of placing cremated remains in an urn; act of placing cremated remains in a niche or grave.

Memorial service – funeral rites without the body present.

Niche – a recess or space used for the permanent placement of cremated remains.

Opacity – Degree to which light is reduced when viewed through a smoke plume. Visible emissions. EPA identifies opacity testing methods; state opacity limits vary.

Ossuary – receptacle for communal placement of cremated remains.

Pouch – a leak resistant zippered bag designed to contain human remains and body fluids.

Processing/Pulverization – reduction of identifiable bone fragments after the completion of the cremation by manual or mechanical means and reducing to granulated particles.

Raking – placing cremated remains onto the ground and working into the soil or garden.

Refrigeration – a process of securely maintaining human remains at or above degrees 34 Fahrenheit.

Retort – See Cremator

Scattering – See Casting

Temporary Container – receptacle for cremated remains usually made of cardboard, plastic or similar materials intended to hold the cremated remains until an urn or other permanent container is acquired or other disposition is made.

Third Party Crematory – crematory operated by an entity other than the funeral home or funeral provider.

Witnessing cremation – family and friends who may be present for the initiation of the cremation process.

Domain V
Funeral Home Merchandise

Caskets

Vaults

Urns

Grave Markers

Accessories

Funeral Merchandising

Regardless of the method of disposition chosen there are applicable pieces of merchandise. These pieces of merchandise should be referred to and selected appropriately based on the desires and needs of the client family. It is vital that funeral directors are knowledgeable in all types of merchandise, as well as the pricing laws that affect them.

Caskets

Arguably one of the most well-known and sought-after pieces of merchandise from funeral homes are caskets.

First it is important to define the differences between casket and coffin. Although many people use the terms interchangeably, they refer to different pieces of merchandise. **Caskets** *are rigid containers which are designed for the encasement of human remains*, typically rectangular in shape. Caskets are generally made from wood, metal, or similar byproduct materials, with a fabric liner and design. **Coffins** *are anthropoid shaped*, or human shaped. They are wider at the elbows and narrower at the feet.

There are different categories of caskets that may be selected by the client family. They are as follows:

Types of Caskets	Description
Burial Caskets	Caskets intended for burial
Cremation casket	Caskets intended for cremation (made of combustible materials)
Rental or Ceremonial Caskets	Caskets that are used for viewing before cremation and have replaceable casket liners to be reused.
Environmentally friendly caskets	Made from environmentally friendly material such as bamboo or willow. 100% nontoxic and biodegradable.

Casket Shell Materials and Designs
Caskets may be constructed using various materials such as wood, metals, and fiberglass.

1. Measurements stated according to **inside dimensions** and vary between manufactures.
2. **Over-sizes or extra sizes**: Caskets that are oversize or larger than the average casket increase in size by two inches in width and three inches in length. An X after the size represents each step in increased size. **Standard size for metal** is 6'6" (78") by 24" wide and for **wood** 6'3" (75") x 22". **Outside dimension** for a standard casket is 7' (84") x 29".
   a. Width increases in increments of 2 inches.
   b. Each step increase in **width** is represented by an "X" (each "X" equals 2 inches).
   c. **Length** increased in increments of 3 inches.
   d. Oversize casket may require the use of an oversize vault and oversized grave plot.

Example: Here is an example of a poorly worded question.

A casket is described as 6-3 XX, on the invoice. What is the interior width of the casket?

     A. 24"
     B. 26"
     C. 28"
     D. 30"

Answer: At first glance, this question might be difficult to answer because it does not state if the casket is made of wood or metal. The answer could be either B. 26" if it was a wood casket or, C. 28" if it was a metal casket. This is definitely a question to be flagged on the NBEs. After closer look at the question 6-3 is describing the length of the casket, thus the two XX indicates that the interior is four inches larger than the standard size. 6-3 is describing a wood casket and the interior width of a wood casket is 22." Each X = 2 inches more, thus, the answer is **B. 26"**

3. **Infant and children's caskets:**
  a. Materials used are similar to, or the same as, adult caskets.
  b. Dimensions vary by manufacturer.
  c. Sizes increase in increments of 6 inches in length and 9" in height to a max length of 5' (60").
  d. Widths are made proportionately to the length.

Twenty- five percent of caskets sold in the United States are made from various woods. Wood caskets may be made from solid wood or engineered wood.

Wood caskets are made from either hardwood or softwood trees. Hardwood trees, or deciduous trees shed their leaves annually, are heavy, closed-grained, resistant, and typically more costly. Softwood trees, or coniferous trees are lighter, are cone and needle bearing, and typically less expensive.

Type of Hardwoods	Description
Mahogany	Most expensive, seen as the "most high end or best wood". It has a fine grain and is reddish brown in color.
Walnut	Dark brownish tone and the second most expensive casket.
Cherry	Closed grain. Heavy white wood usually stained red with a high gloss finish.
Oak	Strong and durable light wood.
Maple	Closed grained. Light, and typically stained in various colors.
Pecan	Rich brown color and moderate density wood grains
Birch	Closed grain. Heavy and durable white wood.
Poplar	White in color and easy to stain. Classified as a soft wood but is technically a deciduous tree.
Cottonwood, Tulip tree, Willow and Salix.	White in color and stains well. Again, classified as a soft wood but is technically hardwoods because they are a deciduous tree. Lower-level caskets and the construction usually uses a mixture of various woods comprising the casket.

MOST EXPENSIVE

Types of Softwoods	Description
Cedar	A distinctive reddish-brown hue. Popular in European caskets.
Spruce	A pale white to light yellow color and is sometimes used in casket construction
Pine	Knotty. Light color wood.

Caskets may also be made from engineered wood including laminates (sheets of different materials glued together with a thin covering), or wood by-products.

Laminate Caskets	Descriptions
Wood veneer	Gluing a thin layer of a high-end wood on top of lower end wood
Artificial laminate	Vinyl. Glued wood to either other wood, or wood by-products.
Wood by-product	Secondary wood scraps, glued together to create new wood material.
Corrugated fiberboard	Cardboard.
Composition board	Fiberboard, particle board, hardboard, pressed board. Bonded by waterproof glue.
Plywood	Thins sheets of wood glued so grains are at right angles to each other. Odd numbers of sheets used so grain will be the same on front and back.

Caskets may also be cloth covered in which a base wood is covered with cloth.

Cloth Covered	Description
Broadcloth	Twilled, napped, woolen or worsted fabric (cotton, silk, rayon) with smooth lustrous face and dense texture. May have soft semi-gloss finish.
Doeskin/moleskin	Heavy durable cotton fabric with a short (<1/8th"), thick, velvety nap on one side. May have suede-like appearance. May be smooth: no raised surface or embossed: ornament with raised work, designs raised above the surface.
Plush/ high pile	Woven cloth with a nap exceeding 1/8" thickness.

Wood caskets can also have different finishes. These finishes include unfinished wood (no stain or varnish), natural finished wood (stained color applied or unstained with an outer protective coating of varnish or polyurethane), painted wood, laminate wood, or cloth covered.

Unfinished	Bare wood	No stain or varnish
Natural finish	Polished (Gloss)	Surface made smooth and flossy by friction. Highly developed, finished, refined state, burnished.
Natural finish	Semi-gloss	Low luster finish
Natural finish	Flat (matte)	Free of gloss, dull, lusterless, no shine
Natural finish	Satin	Less luster than semi-gloss
Cloth covered	Smooth	Material has no raised surfaces.
Cloth covered	Embossed	Ornamented with raised work. Designs raised above the surface.

Metal Caskets

These metals are classified as Ferrous, any metal formed from iron, or non-ferrous, in which there is no iron.

Ferrous	Steel	A metal **alloy** (*solid solution containing metals*) consisting of iron and carbon. Soft and malleable. Measured in **U.S. Standard Gauge** (*thickness, number of sheets needed for 1" thickness*. Ex. A 16 gauge needs 16 sheets for 1" thickness- the higher the gauge the thinner the sheets)
Ferrous	Stainless Steel	400 series (martensitic): 12% chromium with almost 0% nickel. 300 series (austenitic): 18% chromium with 8% nickel.
Ferrous	Galvanized Steel	Steel coated with zinc to increase rust resistance.
Non-ferrous	Copper	Malleable, ductile, metallic. Reddish brown in color. May be Wrought (rolled into sheets). Copper deposit: a casket made from a core of copper metal to which copper ions are combined by an electrolytic process. Measured in **Brown and Sharpe Gauge** (*ounces per square foot – oz/ft^%2*). The more ounces, the thicker the metal. Ex. 48 oz/square foot copper is thicker than 32 oz.
Non-ferrous	Bronze	The premier alloy consists of 90% copper with 10% zinc or tin. May be Wrought (rolled into sheets) or Cast (melted and poured into a mold). Measured in Brown and Sharpe Gauge (ounces per square foot – oz/ft^2). The more ounces, the thicker the metal. Ex. 48 oz/square foot copper is thicker than 32 oz.

Metal caskets can also have different **Finishes and Designs**:

Brushed finish	Bare metal is scratched with abrasive material and finished until a smooth high gloss is obtained. Then it is filled with a sealer and buffed.
Plated finish	Base metal is coated by another metal via an electrolytic process.
Sprayed Finish	Painted
Sprayed Finish	Polished/gloss- high shine, clear coat varnish
Sprayed Finish	Crinkled/wrinkled- metal coated with substance that wrinkles as dries.
Sprayed Finish	Hammertone- small indentation appearance, as if hit with a hammer
Sprayed Finish	Matte/flat- no shine or gloss, no clear coat finish, no varnish

Other casket construction materials include:

Other material	Polymer	Similar to plastic, highly durable
Other material	Fiberglass	Fine filaments of glass embedded in resin.

These materials may also have various finishes and designs:

Wood grained	Simulates appearance of wood
Polished/gloss	Shined to high luster
Sprayed	Paint applied to surface via airbrush

Casket Closure

Depending on the material of the casket selected, the method of casket closure will be different. Caskets may be gasketed, non-gasketed, or hermetically sealed. It is important to know what type of closure each casket must be sure to appropriately close the casket during services, for the burial or entombment, or for shipping.

Gasketed caskets include a flat rubber material along the top body molding flange of the casket shell, and another rubber piece between the lids. They are comprised of a **gasket** (*single molded piece of rubber*), hinges, and locking mechanism to lock the cap to the body.

End lock	Slide bar into top body molding, key opening at end of casket
Side lock/front lock	Same lock as end lock, key opening is in the front
Lever lock	No key, flip lever
Threaded fasteners	Screw type fastener

Non-gasketed caskets

Latch closure	Simple latch secures the cap to the body after closure
Threaded fasteners	A screw type fastener. Used on hinged cap caskets
Chemical compounds	Epoxy and other cements are used. Butyl tape may be used.

Hermetically sealed caskets are airtight, impervious to external influence. *Seal created by fusion or soldering*, which is rarely utilized.

When sending human remains in a casket, via common carrier, metal units can be closed and locked, however the plug for the locking mechanism needs to be placed in the information envelope on top of the air tray box. Failure to do so will result in the caps collapsing when the plane reaches high altitudes.

Interior Designs and Materials:

Within the interior of the casket there are various materials and linings used to create the fabric designs and linings.

The **lining material** is the material that *comes in contact with the body* and may be made of crepe, satin, velvet, linen, or woven linen and twill.

Crepe	Thin crinkled cloth. Silk, rayon, cotton, wool.
Satin	Silk, rayon, nylon. Woven to create a smooth lustrous face and dull back.
Velvet	Silk, cotton, rayon. Fabric contains a nap (texture)
Linen	Made from flax. Used for its strength, coolness, and luster.

Backing materials *are not visible but provide strength and support for the lining material it is affixed to.* These materials include:

Fiberboard	Cardboard
Masselin	Pressed paper in sheet form. Upholstery material.
Plastic	Synthetic or natural organic material shaped when soft before hardening.

Padding material is used to *fill space between the backing material and the lining material.* These include cotton, polyethylene foam, shredded paper, spun polyester, or excelsior/wood wool (wood shavings).

The cap panel of the casket may have various lining material designs depending on the casket. These cap panels can generally be switched upon request. This is the design the family will see on the open portion of the casket. The designs include (or may be a combination of):

Shirred	Material is drawn and gathered in parallel fashion utilizing multiple needles.
Crushed	The lining material is on a metal form with weights added before being steamed. After steaming the material is attached to a backing material.
Tufted	Padding material is placed between the lining and backing materials. Stitching includes forming raised puffs. May be carriage or biscuit style.
Tailored	Tightly drawn without wrinkles.
Semi-tailored	Combination of tailored design with another style.
Specialty	Unique design – may be personalized with words or pictures.

Shell Designs

Elliptic	a casket having ends in the shape of a half circle.
Octagon	a casket having eight angles or corners and therefore has eight sides or body panels.
Flaring	a casket shell design in which the sides and ends of the casket body flare out from the bottom to the top; a casket shell design that is narrower and shorter at the bottom than at the top.
State casket; Vertical side square	casket in which the body panels are at a 90-degree angle to the bottom and the corners form 90-degree angles.
Urnside	a casket design in which the body panels display the shape of an urn.

Types of Casket Handles

Swing bar	a moveable casket handle with a hinged arm.
Stationary Handle	a non-moveable casket handle.
Bailing Handle	a single handle is which the lug, arm, and bar are combined in one unit.

The casket **selection room** is a separate space within a funeral home, designed to provide families with a thoughtful and comfortable environment to choose an appropriate casket for their departed loved ones. The recommended number of units plays a significant role in enhancing the overall experience. With a minimum of 12 caskets, there is sufficient variety to cater to different preferences and budgets. A maximum of 30 units allows for a diverse selection without overcrowding the display. Ideally, maintaining 22 units strikes a balance, ensuring that families have ample choices while also allowing for a spacious and organized layout. The careful arrangement of caskets is essential to enable consumers to move freely within the room, ensuring a seamless and respectful process as they make significant decisions during a challenging time.

Many funeral homes feature sectional displays strategically positioned within the arrangement room. Some establishments opt for lithographs assembled in booklet form, while others utilize interactive kiosks, allowing consumers to use technology for their merchandise selection. Whether utilizing physical units or alternative methods of presenting merchandise, it is essential for the funeral director to educate the consumer on the merchandise that aligns with their budget and meets their specific purchase needs.

Casket Parts

Parts of the Casket	Description
Roll, (Cove, Puff)	a component part of the casket interior which lines the rim (ogee) and surrounds the cap panel.
Gimp (fold)	a strip of metal, plastic, or cloth that is attached to the inside of the panel, covering the area at which point the roll (cove) is anchored.
Throw (Overthrow, Overlay)	the aesthetic covering for the foot cap or inner foot panel of the casket.
Apron (Skirt)	the lining attached to the undersurface of the foot panel of the casket and/or a component part of the throw (overlay) which extends downward into the body of the casket.
Extendover	the portion of the casket interior which extends over the top body molding (body ledge) for aesthetic value
Bed	the portion of the casket upon which the human remains are placed.
Mattress covering	interior cloth or material that covers the mattress or bedding of the casket.
Hinge Covering (Hinge skirt)	that portion of the casket interior covering the hinges that attach the casket cap to the casket body; usually extends from the roll and becomes a part of the body lining.
Pie (Fishtail)	the wedge-shaped portion of the cap (lid) at each end of a casket.
Cap (lid)	the upper portion of the casket shell, including the ogee, crown, pie, and header.
Head Panel	a component part of the casket interior which is inside the head portion of the cap; no distinction is made between the head panel and foot panel in full couch caskets.
Crown (swell)	the uppermost part of the casket cap.
Rim (Ogee)	the "S" shaped molding component of a casket cap.
Rim Flange (Ogee flange)	The turned under edge or horizontal portion of the casket rim which comes into contact with the gasket or body ledge flange (top body molding flange).
Body ledge (top body molding)	a molding along the uppermost edge of the body panels.
Body ledge flange (top body molding flange)	the horizontal portion of the top body molding (body ledge) where the gasket is placed on gasketed caskets.
Header flange	the turned under edge or horizontal portion of the header of the casket cap.
Lug (Ear)	the part of the casket handle attached to the casket body.
Arm	the part of the casket handle that attaches the bar to the lug (ear).
Bar	a part of the casket handle attached to the lug or arm and held by a casket bearer when moving and positioning a casket.
Tip	the decorative or ornamental part of the casket handle that covers the exposed ends of the bar.
Body Panels	compose the sides and ends of the casket shell.
Body Lining	material which drapes the inside perimeter of the body of the casket.
Bridge (header, cap filler)	Component part of the cap (lid) on half couch caskets that provides support at the point of the transverse cut.
Gasket channel	The channel found on the foot panel header of a half couch casket.
Base molding	molding along the lowermost edge of the body panels.

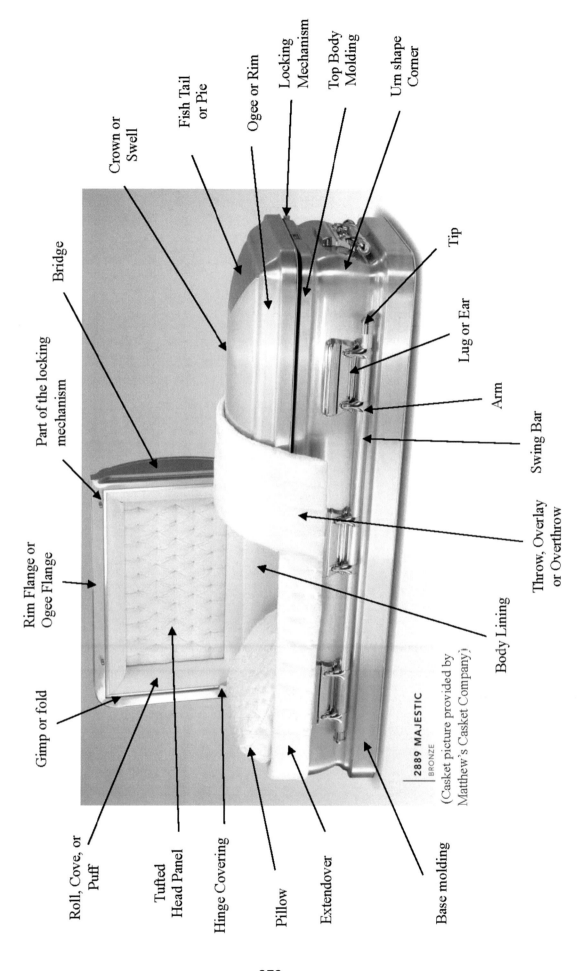

Crown or Swell

Fish Tail or Pie

Ogee or Rim

Locking Mechanism

Top Body Molding

Urn shape Corner

Bridge

Part of the locking mechanism

Tip

Lug or Ear

Arm

Swing Bar

Rim Flange or Ogee Flange

Throw, Overlay or Overthrow

Body Lining

Gimp or fold

Roll, Cove, or Puff

Tufted Head Panel

Hinge Covering

Pillow

Extendover

Base molding

2889 MAJESTIC
BRONZE
(Casket picture provided by Matthew's Casket Company)

373

Outer Burial Containers

Outer burial containers are any containers, which are designed for placement in the grave around the casket or urn. These include grave liners, grave boxes, and burial vaults.

Vaults *are outer enclosures that offer protection from the earth's weight, as well as possessing other features that resist the elements.*

    a.   Standard size concrete burial vaults are 30" x 86" inside dimension (measure caskets outside dimensions carefully and at the widest point – measure from arm-to-arm with a vault caliper. The lid and base of the vault has a tongue and groove mechanism that uses butyl tape to seal the vault.

    b.   Standard Precast Concrete burial vaults are 34" wide; 90" long; and 30" high, outside dimension.

    c.   Concrete Cremated Remains Urns or Urn Vaults are: 12" x 12" x 16" high, with 1.5" thick cover, 1.5" wall thickness and a Quick Clamp Design Top (butyl tape seal). Sizes may very depending on supplier.

    d.   Burial Plots (standard size) = 8" (96") X 3' (36") – hence the opening of the grave to accommodate the vault would be the entire grave! Some cemeteries have more generous grave sizes, i.e. 8'4"X 3'4" or 100" X 40".

Note: If you ever find yourself in an area where you are required to make the Cemetery Setup, you will need to know these outside dimensions. Typical you would dig the grave 8'x3' if using a vault and 7'7" X 30" for a burial with just a casket!

Unlike grave liners, vaults are made to resist the elements, such as rain and water. Vaults may be made from concrete, metal, or polymers/fiberglass. Concrete vaults may be reinforced with chicken wire or rebar; or may be lined with plastic (ABS material or polystyrene), metal (stainless steel, copper, bronze), or asphalt to plug pores and add to the protective features. **Metal vaults** may be made of steel, stainless steel, or copper utilizing the United States Standard Gauge. The typical metal vault is 10 or 12 gauge.

Vaults may be finished for protection against the elements, or with decorative features. Some vaults have words and photos on them for display during the services and burial. **Concrete vaults** have an asphalt coating, and steel vaults may be galvanized (coated with zinc to prevent rust) or painted. Decorative features such as embellishments may also be added.

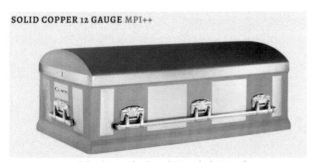
Clarke Air Seal Burial Vault

Doric Top Seal Burial Vault

Depending on the vault that is selected, the way it is closed and sealed may vary. The following closure methods are the most common:

Air seal	Utilizes air pressure created by placing the top of the vault on the bottom. This type of vault uses the Bell Principle to resist the elements from entering the vault. If the dome lid is placed securely on the base, and the vault is level in the grave, the unit creates a vacuum that resists water from entering the unit.
Double seal	Utilizes the air seal along with epoxy. This is not recommended because, if dirt or debris gets on the butyl tape, the dome will not properly seal on the base, causing a pathway for the elements to enter the vault.
Top seal	Utilizes an epoxy compound in conjunction with a tongue-in-groove closure

Vaults do not offer 100% protection against the elements. In some states, funeral directors are prohibited from using terminology that implies protective features of a burial vault.

Grave liners are less protective than vaults, and generally do not seal. These may be made of concrete, polymers, or wood (known as a rough box. Not common nor permitted in most cemeteries). Grave boxes are a type of grave liner consisting of a body, and a one- or two-piece lid. A concrete sectional is a grave liner that consists of 6-8 unfinished concrete slabs around the casket (Not common or permitted in most cemeteries).

Urn vaults allow for the placement of urns within the grave and have features similar to casket vaults. Urn vaults are made from metal, concrete or polymers.**

If the family desires, they may select a combination unit, in which the container is used as both the burial receptacle and the outer burial container.

Cremation Merchandise

Cremation is chosen as the final disposition method for around 60% of deaths in the United States. Despite the shift in disposition preferences, funeral directors play a crucial role in assisting consumers by offering diverse options to honor the life achievements of the deceased. To effectively care for the remains before, during, and after the cremation process, cremation merchandise is essential. Presenting consumers with these varied options ensures a more comprehensive and respectful approach to caring for their loved ones with dignity and respect.

If the deceased is having services before cremation, the family has the option to choose between a traditional wood burial casket, a cremation casket for the cremation process, or a ceremonial or rental casket used solely for the service. In the case of the latter, the human remains will be removed with the casket insert before cremation. Alternatively, if the family decides against purchasing a casket or having services, they can choose to buy an alternative container. An alternative container is an enclosure made of suitable combustible material, offering rigidity for ease of handling, ensuring the safety of the crematory operator, and providing appropriate covering for the remains. Alternative containers may be:

**Urn dimensions vary, be sure to check dimensions when ordering an urn vault.*

Corrugated container a/k/a Alternative Container	An enclosure for human remains in preparation for cremation. The container is composed of an appropriate combustible material; rigid enough for handling ease; assures the protection of the health and safety of the crematory operator as well as provide appropriate covering for the remains.
Unfinished wood box	Made of wood without ornamentation on the exterior
Particle board/plywood	Cremations units used made of wood byproducts.
Cremation pouch	Combustible bags are designed to meet EPA regulations with respect to emissions. Must states require the human remains to be brought to the crematory in a ridged container.

Once the cremation has been completed and the remains have been processed, the cremated remains, may be placed in a bag within a temporary container (cardboard or plastic) by the crematory. However, the family may want a specialized urn or other container to encase the cremated remains.

Urn sizes vary depending on the type selected. Standardized urns have an internal dimension that is usually 200 cubic inches. Urns may be a single capacity, in which they are designed for one set of cremated remains or double capacity, in which they are made for two sets (i.e., spouses). These are known as companion urns. Urns may also be designed specifically for infants and children (much smaller).

Urns may also come in various sizes including keepsake urns, in which only a portion of the cremated remains are enclosed. Miniature or keepsake urns are usually selected when consumers wish to retain a small portion of cremated remains. Cremated remains may also be encapsulated in objects, such as jewelry or other unique products.

Ocean Water Blue **Cloisonne Urns**

Urns may also be made of a range of materials including but not limited to wood, metal, marble, ceramic, plastic, glass, and cloisonne (enamel covered metal). These materials may also be of various colors, designs, and shapes. Urns may also be personalized and engraved if desired.

Urns may also be "green" or biodegradable. Various types of biodegradable urns exist to degrade in a selected manner, burial urns will degrade in soil and water urns will degrade in water (such as rock salt or paper). Scattering urns are designed for the spreading of cremated remains. Typically, they have a removable lid that allows for easy scattering. Along with the typical urns that most may be familiar with, a few newer options have entered the market.

Cremation jewelry is becoming increasingly popular. Cremation jewelry can include bracelets, rings, and necklaces. These items will vary in size, shape, design, material, and color depending on what is selected by the family. Thumbprint cremation items are also newer in the market. These are urns, jewelry, or other items that have the decedents thumbprint engraved onto them. Some manufacturers utilize ink and paper, and some have mobile phone apps that scan and populate a digital thumbprint.

Glass urns are also becoming popular. These glass urns may be orbs, paperweights, and other blown glass creations. These companies generally require the mailing of a miniscule amount of cremated remains to the artist, and once the pieces are completed, they will be returned to the family or the funeral home. This process can be lengthy depending on the pieces selected.

An even newer cremation trend is eternity diamonds. In which cremated remains are used in the creation of lab-grown diamonds. This process can be expensive depending on the size of the diamond desired and can take upwards of a year to be completed.

There are other creative ways that people are using cremated remains for including fireworks, artwork, and tattoos.

However, despite the many options available for cremated remains, the family may choose to select an item of personal value or meaning. This may be in the form of a family heirloom, a wine bottle, a homemade urn, or any other valuable container. These meaningful items can help to personalize cremation services, and direct cremation services that otherwise would not have any personalized touches.

Cemetery Merchandise

Burial

Cemeteries *are an area of ground set aside and dedicated for the disposition of human remains.*

A single grave is a **plot**. A family may purchase a family **lot**, which is a group of plots. Graves (plots) may be single depth, in which only one set of casketed remains may be placed or there may be a lawncrypt in which decedents are buried in grave liners stacked on top of each other. Depending on the cemetery, a plot may have the allotment of one casketed remains, plus one set of cremated remains, or two sets of cremated remains. These policies vary between cemeteries.

A cemetery may be a memorial park or may have a **memorial park** section in which *all headstones and markers are flush (flat) against the ground.* A cemetery may also have a scattering garden section designated for the spreading of cremated remains.

A cemetery may also be a "Green" cemetery in which they do not allow outer burial containers, carcinogenic embalming preparations, or non-biodegradable containers. Or a cemetery may be hybrid in which only a section is designated for "Green" burials. True green burial cemeteries will not have markers, or headstones, but instead use technology markers such as GPS coordinates.

Entombment

Some people decide that they want their remains to be entombed rather than buried under the earth. Mausoleums are above ground structures or buildings containing crypts (chambers for casketed remains) or niches (spaces for cremated remains) for the placement of human remains. Mausoleums may be public in which anyone can walk through them or private and locked for family only. Some mausoleums are small and contain only one set of remains, while others are larger and may contain multiple sets of remains.

Cremated remains may also be entombed. An ossuary is a receptacle for communal placement of remains. Ossuaries may be attached to cemeteries or mausoleum buildings. Columbariums (structures, rooms, spaces or niches, to hold cremated remains) may also be available. These columbariums may be individualized, or large enough for more than one person. They may also be religiously affiliated, public, or private.

Markers & Memorialization

Many families will choose to have the decedent's grave/burial spot marked. These markers allow for identification of whose remains have been buried or entombed and allow for families to come and memorialize their loved ones.

Each monument typically has a base, which is the lower, supporting portion of the monument that is against the ground, with the die or tablet on top which may be inscribed.

Markers, monuments, and headstones may be temporary or permanent and come in various shapes, sizes, materials (granite, bronze, marble, slate, etc.) and styles:

Upright Vertical Tablet	The die (the tablet or main part of the monument) is taller than is wide
Upright Horizontal Tablet	The die is wider than is tall. (as shown above)
Bench	A type of cemetery memorial consisting of a top piece supported by two standards; used to identify family burial plots or in conjunction with a family monument.
Flush	Flat or parallel with the ground
Bevel Top	Above ground, slanted top
Slant	Face has an angle greater than 45 degrees, but less than 90 degrees to the ground
Personalized/Custom	Customized shape or style

Slant   Beveled   Lawn Level (Flush)

Once the marker material, size, and style has been selected the next item to select is the **epitaph** (*inscription*) or embellishments desired. Inscriptions may have the decedent's name, birthdate, death date, or other words/phrases/sayings. Some may choose to have photos etched into the stones or other designs.

Families may also opt for a **cenotaph**, a *monument in memory of the decedent with human remains not present.*

Along with a formal marker, families may choose to plant flowers or add other accessories such as planters, figurines, flags, and lights to the gravesite to add a personal touch.
- *Each cemetery has its own restrictions and regulations for markers and gravesite items.*
- *See Funeral Directing section for information on Military Markers, p.38.*

Other Merchandise

There are various other items of merchandise that funeral directors should be knowledgeable about.

Shipping containers

When shipping a decedent to another funeral home via airplane, different containers may be utilized.

Air tray	A transfer container consisting of a wooden tray with a cardboard covering for the casket.
Combination tray	Any product designed or intended to be used together as both a casket and as a permanent burial receptacle.
Zeigler case or Metal case	A gasketed container, which can be used as an insert in a casket or as a separate shipping container. *Generally, is used as an insert for long time storage or in cases that present advanced trauma and decomposition*

Mortuary Bags

Mortuary bags vary in size, color, and reinforcement depending on what is selected. It is important that funeral homes have various sizes, and thicknesses of mortuary bags on hand.

Miscellaneous or Sundry Items

Sundies are the miscellaneous items provided or used to complement the services of a funeral director, i.e. register books, acknowledgment cards, memorial folders/programs, religious paraphernalia, flag case, etc. These may include personalization and memorialization items.

Some sundry items may include:

Register book	A book with information regarding the decedent and allows for messages and signing by friends and family.
Prayer cards	Cards with the name, birthdate, death date of the decedent along with a prayer, poem, or photo.
Temporary grave marker	A marker placed at the grave before a headstone or monument is purchased.
Acknowledgement cards	Thank you cards for the family to send to funeral attendees.
Tribute videos	Video compilations made with photos of the decedent
Religious paraphernalia	Crosses, crucifixes, Mogen David. Religious items used in services
Clothing	The funeral home may sell burial or cremation clothing.

Selling Merchandise

When selling merchandise, having a business plan is crucial. The business plan should include a market analysis to identify merchandising trends. Understanding whether the current funeral clients in the area prefer traditional burial merchandise or cremation merchandise is essential. Additionally, identifying the most popular types of caskets and urns is important. Once the firm has a clear idea of the items to keep and sell, the next step is deciding on distributors. Evaluating local casket, urn, and other merchandise distributors that offer the desired items is crucial. When making these decisions, factors such as cost, shipping, customer service, and availability should be considered. Working with reputable distributors that align with the business' budget and price points and can be easily contacted for any questions, are important factors to consider. Some families may choose funeral homes, goods, and services based on price alone. However, explaining the purpose of the funeral, and the value of the goods and services may assist families in understanding the price point of the firms' offerings.

Display

Effectively selling merchandise requires proper display and presentation. This can be achieved through physical showrooms where client families can explore and interact with the merchandise or virtual showrooms where families view items through a catalog on various devices. Regardless of the showcasing method, it is crucial for the funeral home to present merchandise alongside FTC pricing lists. The General Price List (GPL) should encompass price ranges for caskets and outer burial receptacles, with separate pricing lists provided as mandated. Ensuring that these price lists are regularly updated and accurate is essential to reflect the correct pricing for each merchandise option.

If the funeral home has a physical selection room, it is ideal that the room is on the main floor and easily accessible with ADA accommodations (ramps, railings, eye level merchandise) for client families. Physical selection rooms may have full sized merchandise available, or fractional displays, in which a section of the item (such as an endcap) is available to showcase the style, color, and material, but does not take up the space of the full-size item. If the firm has full size caskets on hand, they may utilize church trucks (wheeled collapsible support), biers (casket stand), or a casket rack to hold the caskets in place and allow for them to be moved.

Selection rooms should feature appropriate lighting that accurately reflects the atmosphere during services. Mismatched lighting between the selection room and wake room can create a different perception for client families, emphasizing the importance of consistency in lighting. The room's ambiance should be inviting and comforting, avoiding intimidation for client families. A warm and tasteful setup and decoration contribute to a positive atmosphere. For rooms displaying full-sized caskets, the recommended number ranges from 12 to 30 (optimal at 22), ensuring an ample yet manageable selection for families. Allocating 40-60 square feet per casket provides sufficient space, requiring a room of 600-900 square feet for a 15-casket display. Selection rooms may adopt a consecutive casket arrangement based on cost or group caskets by material or design. Additionally, having a demonstration casket setup can educate client families on the casket parts and construction, aiding them in their decision-making process.

Pricing

When it comes to pricing items all Federal Trade Commission (FTC), and State rules must be followed. The appropriate goods and services must be listed on the General Price List (GPL).

Funeral Homes must determine how they want to price their goods and services. Firms may choose a pricing strategy based on customer value (the buyers perceived value), cost (based on cost of production, distribution, and selling), or competition (basing it on other firm's prices). Merchandise may be marked up (priced) using a fixed value, percent, fixed dollar amount, or it may vary (graduated recovery).

Ex. The wholesale price on a pine casket from the distributor is $400.

Option 1: **Fixed multiple**
>   The funeral home decides they are going to markup merchandise using a factor of 5. This means that they will multiply the wholesale price by 5 (the times factor or multiple) to get the price. A casket with a wholesale cost of $400 with a multiple of 5 will have a price of $2000 ($400 x 5).

Option 2: **Percentage**
>   The funeral home markup based on a percentage; the wholesale cost will be multiplied by the percent value to obtain the amount that will be added to the wholesale cost.
>   A casket with a wholesale cost of $400 with a markup of 50% will set a price of $600. ($400 x 0.50= $200. $400 +$200 = $600).

Option 3: **Fixed dollar amount**
>   If the funeral home markup based on a fixed dollar amount, that amount will be added to the wholesale cost. A casket with a wholesale cost of $400 with a markup of $500 will have a sale price of $900. ($400 + $500= $900).

Whatever pricing method is selected should be analyzed through accounting to ensure effectiveness and profits are being met.

According to FTC regulations, funeral home goods and services may only be priced using itemization, in which each good and service must have its own price. It prohibits the use of **Package pricing** (single dollar amount for a group of goods and services), **unit pricing** (service and casket together), **bi-unit pricing** (the price of the services are separate from the casket), or **functional pricing** (charges are broken down into categories). The only "package" items that can exist would be for additional merchandise and sundry items. All itemized prices must be entered on the Itemized Statement of Goods and Services Selected, in which the family signs that they are not being charged for any items they are not receiving, and that they understand and accept the charges. Cash Advance items on the Statement of Goods and Services are third party vendors that require money, that the funeral home pays on the behalf of the family and are not marked up. Cash Advance items may include certified death certificates, clergy honorariums, cemetery opening fees, crematory fees, obituary fees, church fees, etc.

The Selection Process

Merchandise selection is an integral aspect of the arrangement conference (refer to Funeral Directing & FTC sections). During this phase of the arrangement conference, the funeral director should clarify the available options to the client family, whether utilizing an in-house physical showroom or a virtual showroom. Before proceeding to view the actual merchandise, it is essential to provide the client with the GPL, CPL, OBCPL and Urn Price List.*

Once the funeral director has prepared the client family to view the merchandise, the director may choose to remain in the selection room, to answer any questions the family may have about the merchandise (**direct selection room process**) or exit the room (**indirect selection room process**), allowing the family, time to browse and discuss without feeling pressured or overwhelmed.

After the family has made a selection, the funeral director should physically confirm the choice to ensure both parties are documenting the same item. The director should then accurately document the selection (preferably including a detailed photograph) in the decedent's file. The price of the selected merchandise should be recorded on the Itemized Statement of Goods and Services.

If the selected item is in a physical showroom, the item should be removed and labeled with the decedent's name. If the selected item is in a virtual catalog, the item should be promptly ordered, and the receipt and tracking information should be included in the file.

Payment

Along with deciding what merchandise to sell, it is important to determine how to sell, and how to accept payment. Some firms may accept cash, check, or credit cards, while some may only accept certain payment methods. Firms may also offer discounts on older items that have been in stock for a lengthy period of time.

Payment may also be received through a pre-funded burial account, life insurance policies, social services, or through other agencies. Accurate financial information for each case should be recorded and monitored. Including payment values, date of payments, person making the payment, and the payment method.

Best practice would include having price labels on the merchandise in the showroom in addition to the price lists for client convenience.

FUNERAL SERVICE MERCHANDISING – GLOSSARY

Air seal – a method of closure that utilizes the air pressure created by placing the dome of the vault onto the base of the vault, often called the diving bell principle.

Air tray – a transfer container consisting of a wooden tray with a cardboard covering for the casket.

Alternative container – An enclosure for human remains in preparation for cremation. The container is composed of an appropriate combustible material; rigid enough for handling ease; assures the protection of the health and safety of the crematory operator as well as provide appropriate covering for the remains.

Apron – the lining attached to the undersurface of the foot panel of the casket and/or a component part of the throw (overlay) which extends downward into the body of the casket.

Arm – the part of the casket handle that attaches the bar to the lug (ear).

Average (mean) – the sum of a group of numbers divided by the number of units.

Axed – (steeled, frosted) is a smooth non-polished finish for stone monuments and markers achieved by sandblasting a polished finish with steel shot or other abrasives.

Bail handle – a single handle is which the lug, arm, and bar are combined in one unit.

Bar – a part of the casket handle attached to the lug or arm and held by a casket bearer when moving and positioning a casket.

Base – the lower or supporting part of a monument. In some monuments, there may be a first, second, and third base.

Base molding – molding along the lowermost edge of the body panels.

Bed – the portion of the casket upon which the human remains are placed.

Bench – a type of cemetery memorial consisting of a top piece supported by two standards; used to identify family burial plots or in conjunction with a family monument.

Bevel top marker – a small headstone, set above ground, with a slanting top.

Bier – a stand on which a casket is placed for funeral service display.

Bi-unit pricing – a method of price quotation showing separately the price of the service to be rendered and the price of the casket.

Block – a subdivision of a cemetery containing several lots.

Body – the lower portion of the casket shell containing the top body molding, body panel, base molding, and casket bottom.

Body ledge (top body molding) – a molding along the uppermost edge of the body panels.

Body ledge flange (top body molding flange) – the horizontal portion of the top body molding (body ledge) where the gasket is placed on gasketed caskets.

Body lining – material which drapes the inside perimeter of the body of the casket.

Body panels – compose the sides and ends of the casket shell.

Bridge (header, cap filler) – Component part of the cap (lid) on half couch caskets that provides support at the point of the transverse cut.

Broadcloth – a twilled, napped, woolen or worsted fabric with a smooth lustrous face and dense texture; a fabric usually made of cotton, silk, or rayon woven in a plain or rib weave with a soft semi-gloss finish.

Bronze – a metal alloy consisting of 90% copper with tin and sometimes zinc comprising the other 10%.

Brushed finish – bare metal is scratched with an abrasive material and then finished until a smooth high gloss is obtained.

Burial casket – a casket for interring or entombing human remains.

Cap (lid) – the upper portion of the casket shell, including the ogee, crown, pie, and header.

Cap filler – see Bridge.

Cap panel – the focal part of the interior which fills the inside of the crown, sometimes bordered by the roll (cove); may be referred to as the panel.

Cash advance items – any item of service or merchandise obtained from a third party and paid for by the funeral provider on the purchaser's behalf.

Cash discount – Discounts from quoted prices as an inducement for prompt payment of invoices.

Casket – a rigid container designed for the encasement of human remains that is available in various shapes, other than anthropoidal.

Casket liner – a removable metal unit that is placed inside a wooden casket shell to provide protective qualities.

Casket rack – a device upon which caskets are placed, above the other, for display or storage.

Casket stand – the stand or support upon which a casket rests in the selection room.

Cast bronze – molten bronze poured into a mold and allowed to cool.

Cast hardware – production method in which molten metal is poured into a mold, allowed to cool.

Cemetery – an area of ground set aside and dedicated for the final disposition of human remains.

Cenotaph – a monument erected to the memory of the dead, with the human remains not present.

Ceremonial casket (rental casket) - a casket designed to be re-used for multiple funeral service events typically with a removable liner to facilitate the cremation or other disposition of human remains following funeral service events.

Church truck – a wheeled and collapsible stand for a casket.

Cloisonné – a crafted metal container with an applied enamel finish.

Coffin – a rigid container designed for the encasement of human remains that is anthropoidal in shape.

Columbarium – a structure, room, or space in a mausoleum or other building containing niches or recesses used to hold cremated remains.

Combination case (a.k.a. "combo case") – a transfer container for uncasketed human remains consisting of a particle board tray with a cardboard cover.

Combination unit – any product designed or intended to be used together as both a casket and as a permanent burial receptacle.

Competition based pricing – setting prices based on the competitor's strategies, prices, costs, and market offerings.

Composition board (particle board, pressed board, fiberboard, hardboard) – particles of wood bonded together with waterproof glue; the different types are distinguished by the size and shape of the particles of wood used.

Concrete sectional (sectional) – a grave liner consisting of six or eight slabs of unfinished concrete placed around the casket.

Consecutive method – placing caskets for selection in their order of increasing or decreasing value.

Consignment – to give to an agent to be cared for or sold and is not paid for until sold.

Copper – a malleable, ductile, metallic element having a characteristic reddish brown color; frequently used in construction of caskets, urns and vaults due to its non-corrosive qualities.

Copper deposit – a casket made from a core of copper metal to which copper ions are combined by an electrolytic process.

Corner – an optional part of casket hardware that is attached to the four corners of the body 9 panel.

Corrugated container – a container used to hold human remains constructed out of cardboard made with a series of alternate folds and ridges.

Cost based pricing – pricing based on the cost of producing, distributing, and selling the product plus a fair rate of return for effort and risk.

Couch crypt – a crypt in which the casket lies parallel to the face of the crypt.

Cove (roll, puffing) - a component part of the casket interior which lines the rim (ogee) and surrounds the cap panel.

Cremation casket – a casket manufactured with easily combustible materials for the cremation of human remains following funeral service events.

Cremation pouch – a non-rigid combustible cremation-friendly container for human remains.

Crepe – a thin crinkled cloth of silk, rayon, cotton, or wool.

Crinkled (wrinkled) finish – An exterior casket finish in which the metal is coated with a substance that wrinkles as it dries; most often found on less expensive caskets.

Crown (swell) – the uppermost part of the casket cap.

Crushed interior – a casket interior style created by placing the lining material on a metal form, then adding weights, and using steam to permanently maintain the style. Casket interior cloths are then attached to a suitable casket upholstery (backing material.

Crypt – a chamber in a mausoleum used to safeguard casketed human remains.

Customer value based pricing – setting prices based upon the buyers perceived value.

Demonstration group (educational group) – caskets utilized to educate the selecting party regarding casket construction.

Die (tablet) – main part of a monument, the upright portion above the base where the inscription is located.

Direct Cremation – a disposition of human remains by cremation without formal viewing, visitation, or ceremony.

Direct lighting – illumination directly shining on an object.

Direct selection room procedure – the method of selling merchandise whereby the funeral director remains in the selection room throughout the selection process.

Doeskin (moleskin) – a heavy durable cotton fabric with a short (1/8th 9 inch or less), thick, velvety nap on one side; woven cloth with a suede-like appearance.

Dome – the top of a metal air seal burial vault which entraps air as it is put in position; it also supports the weight of the earth above.

Domesticated – as related to animals, one that has been tamed and disciplined by human beings for personal companionship.

Double seal – a method of closure that utilizes the principle of the air seal in conjunction with an epoxy material at the junction of the dome and the base of a metal burial vault.

Ear (lug) – the part of the casket handle attached to the casket body.

Educational group – see demonstration group.

Elliptic – a casket having ends in the shape of a half circle.

Embossed – material having designs raised above the surface; frequently seen on cloth covered caskets.

Engineered wood – a range of derivative wood products, which are manufactured by binding together wood strands, particles, fibers, or veneers with adhesives to form composite materials. Sometimes referred to as composite wood or manufactured wood products.

Environmentally friendly (green, natural) – eco-friendly approach that utilizes products, services and merchandise that are free of toxic/hazardous materials, are biodegradable or that minimize use of energy.

Epitaph – an inscription placed on a monument to commemorate the deeds or qualities of the deceased.

Excelsior (wood wool) – wood that has been shredded into spaghetti-like strings.

Exclusivity discount – an agreement whereby a purchaser agrees to purchase goods or services from one seller, exclusive of all others, in exchange for a reduction in the per-unit cost for such goods or services.

Extendover – the portion of the casket interior which extends over the top body molding (body ledge) for aesthetic value.

Ferrous metal – any metal formed from iron (steel or stainless steel).

Fiberboard – see composition board.

Fiberglass – a material consisting of extremely fine filaments of glass embedded in various resins.

Fishtail (Pie) – the wedge-shaped portion of the cap (lid) at each end of a casket.

Fixed dollar amount – pricing method in which the same dollar amount is added to the wholesale cost of merchandise.

Fixed multiple – pricing method whereby the casket cost is multiplied by a constant factor.

Flaring square – a casket shell design in which the sides and ends of the casket body flare out from the bottom to the top; a casket shell design that is narrower and shorter at the bottom than at the top.

Flat finish (Matte finish) – a finish used on casket exteriors free of gloss; a dull, lusterless surface.

Fluorescent lighting – the illumination produced by a tubular electric discharge lamp; the fluorescence of phosphors coating the inside of a tube.

Flush marker – a headstone which is set parallel with the surrounding terrain.

Fold (gimp) – a strip of metal, plastic, or cloth that is attached to the inside of the panel, covering the area at which point the roll (cove) is anchored.

Foot panel – a component part of the casket interior, which is inside the foot cap.

Fractional display – use of portions of caskets in the selection room vs. full sized caskets.

Full Couch – a cap opening style in which the rim (ogee), crown, and pies are formed with a transverse cut in the cap, thereby forming a two-piece lid for the casket.

Functional pricing – a method of price quotation in which the charges are broken down into several major component parts such as professional services, facilities, automobile and merchandise.

Funeral ceremony – a service commemorating the deceased with the body present.

Galvanized – steel that has been coated with zinc for increased resistance to rust.

Gasket channel – The channel found on the foot panel header of a half couch casket.

Gauge – a thickness measurement of metals.

Gimp – see Fold.

Graduated recovery – a pricing method where the mark-up varies.

Grave – an excavation in the earth as a place for interment.

Grave box – an outer enclosure consisting of a body and a one or two-piece lid.

Grave liner – an outer enclosure, which offers protection from the earth load but without protection from the elements.

Graveside service – a ceremony commemorating the deceased at the place of final disposition.

Green (natural) – see Environmentally friendly.

Half couch – a cap opening style in which the rim (ogee), crown, and pies are formed with a transverse cut in the cap, thereby forming a two-piece lid for the casket.

Halogen lighting – a high intensity light source that produces a white light approximating natural daylight.

Hammertone finish – a sprayed finish that has the appearance of small indentations in the metal (as if struck by a ballpeen hammer); the indentations are in the paint and appear as the paint dries.

Hardboard – see Composition board.

Hardware – the handles, ornamental fixtures, and associated fittings attached to the casket shell.

Hardwood – any tough, heavy timber with a compact texture; any deciduous tree (any tree that loses its leaves annually).

Header – see Bridge.

Header flange – the turned under edge or horizontal portion of the header of the casket cap.

Head panel – a component part of the casket interior which is inside the head portion of the cap; no distinction is made between the head panel and foot panel in full couch caskets.

Hermetically sealed – airtight; impervious to external influence; completely sealed by fusion or soldering.

High gloss finish – a smooth, burnished, and polished finish used on casket exteriors; created by rubbing and polishing the surface to a finished or refined state.

Hinge cover (hinge skirt) – that portion of the casket interior covering the hinges that attach the casket cap to the casket body; usually extends from the roll and becomes a part of the body lining.

Hinge skirt – see Hinge cover.

Horizontal tablet – a type of cemetery monument in which the die is wider than it is tall.

Immediate burial – disposition of human remains by burial without formal viewing, visitation, or ceremony except for a graveside service.

Incandescent lighting – the illumination resulting from the glowing of a heated filament.

Indirect lighting – reflected illumination of an object.

388

Indirect selection room procedure – the method of selling merchandise whereby the funeral director does not stay in the selection room during the selection process.

Inner panels – functional or ornamental covering for the foot end of a full couch casket; may be available for the head end in some full couch casket models.

Itemization – the method of price quotation by which each unit of goods and services is priced separately.

Knee brace – hardware used to prop and hold a casket cap open for viewing.

Laminate – the process of bonding superimposed layers of different materials.

Lawn crypt – grave space where two or more persons may be buried in grave liners, which have been stacked one on top of the other with the first person who dies being buried in the deepest grave liner.

Ledger – a grave marker set parallel to the ground that covers a grave completely.

LED lighting – light emitting diode lighting; a semiconductor device that converts electricity into light; noted for its high energy savings and long-lasting durability.

Lid – see Cap.

Linen – a fabric made from flax; noted for its strength, coolness, and luster.

Lot – a subdivision of a cemetery which consists of several graves or interment spaces.

Lug – see Ear.

Marker – an object, usually of one piece, used to identify individual graves.

Markup – the difference between the cost of goods sold and the selling price.

Masselin – pressed paper in sheet form; used in casket construction as a backing (upholstery) material.

Matte finish – see Flat finish.

Mattress cover – interior cloth or material that covers the mattress or bedding of the casket.

Mausoleum – an above ground structure or building containing crypts or vaults for entombment of caskets; may also include niches for cremated remains.

Mean – see Average.

Median – a value in an ordered set of values which represents the midpoint, whereby there are an equal number of values above and below the midpoint value.

Memorial – a physical object designed for the purpose of remembering an individual, group, or event.

Memorial gathering – a scheduled assembly of family and friends following a death without the deceased present.

Memorial park – a cemetery or section of a cemetery with only flush to the ground type markers.

Memorial service – a ceremony commemorating the deceased without the body present.

Merchandising – the purchasing, pricing, display, and sale of goods and services.

Metal case (Ziegler case) – a gasketed container, which can be used as an insert in a casket or as a separate shipping container.

Mode – the value that occurs most frequently in a group of numbers.

Moleskin – see Doeskin.

Monolith – a single massive stone or rock, or a large piece of stone or rock, placed as a monument or marker in a cemetery or other place of remembrance.

Monument – a structure, usually of stone or metal, erected to commemorate the life, deeds, or career of a deceased person; derived from the Latin word meaning "to remind."

Natural (green) – see Environmentally friendly.

Natural lighting – illumination by the sun.

Niche – a recess or space in a columbarium used for the permanent placing of cremated remains.

Non-ferrous metal – any metal not formed from iron.

Octagon – a casket having eight angles or corners and therefore has eight sides or body panels.

Ogee (rim) – the "S" shaped molding component of a casket cap.

Ogee flange (rim flange) - the turned under edge or horizontal portion of the casket rim which comes into contact with the gasket or body ledge flange (top body molding flange).

Ossuary – receptacle for communal placement of cremated and/or skeletal remains.

Outer burial container – any container designed for placement in a grave to surround and safeguard a casket or urn, including burial vaults, grave boxes, and grave liners.

Overlay (overthrow, throw) - the aesthetic covering for the foot cap or inner foot panel of the casket.

Package pricing – A pricing method using a single dollar amount to identify the charge for a group or bundle of goods and/or services.

Particle board – see Composition board.

Pie – see Fishtail.

Plastic – synthetic or natural organic polymers shaped when soft and then hardened.

Plastic extrusion molding – a method of forming items by injecting molten plastic into a die.

Plated finish – the finish created when base metal is coated by another metal via an electrolytic process; often found on casket hardware; in casket construction identified by the term "deposit," as in "copper deposit."

Plush – a woven cloth with a nap exceeding 1/8th inch.

Plywood – thin sheets of wood glued together so the grains are at right angles to one another; an odd number of sheets will be used so the grain on the front and back will always run the same direction.

Polished - a smooth, glass-like appearance for stone monuments and markers achieved by running rough to fine grit diamond polishing wheels over the surface. The sun will often reflect off a polished granite surface.

Polymer – a compound, similar in appearance to plastic, that has a high molecular weight 2 creating an extremely durable substance.

Pouch – a leak resistant zippered bag designed to contain a dead human body and body fluids and is used mainly for the removal of dead human remains from the place of death.

Pressed board – see composition board.

Price quotation – method by which prices are explained to the consumer.

Priest casket (slip panel) - a casket opening style in which the cap or lid at the head of the casket is completely removed for the purpose of viewing; the remains may be viewed from either side of the casket.

Puffing (roll) – see Cove.

Quantity discount – an incentive or inducement for a purchaser that will reduce the per-unit cost for goods or services when purchases reach a larger number of quantities.

Range – the difference between the upper and lower limits of a series of numbers.

Rebate – the return of a portion of a payment.

Rental casket – see Ceremonial casket).

Rental casket insert – a cremation container designed to encase human remains while placed in the shell of a rental casket (ceremonial casket). This container includes all necessary material and bedding for a dignified viewing.

Rim – see Ogee.

Rim flange – see Ogee flange.

Rock pitch – a rough rock finish for stone monuments and markers created by splitting or breaking the stone to enhance the natural finish and give it a more structured and balanced appearance.

Roll (puffing) – see Cove.

Sales frequency – the number of times sales in a given price bracket occur over a fixed period of time.

Satin – a fabric woven to create a smooth lustrous face and dull back.

Satin finish – a low-luster finish used on casket exteriors that is smooth; with well defined, fine lines or striations.

Sawed – is a semi-smooth finish for stone monuments and markers created as a result of the stone being cut with a wire or diamond saw.

Scattering garden – a section in a cemetery set aside for the scattering of cremated remains.

Section – a subdivision of a cemetery containing several blocks.

Sectional – see Concrete sectional.

Semi-gloss finish – a medium luster finish used on casket exteriors.

Semi-tailored interior – a combination of a tailored interior with one or more other styles of interior for effect.

Shell – the basic exterior of a casket, including the cap (lid) upper portion and body lower portion.

Shirred interior – a style of casket interior in which the material is drawn or gathered in parallel fashion in a multiple needle head sewing process.

Shroud – a cloth or garment in which human remains are wrapped for burial.

Single hinged panel – a casket in which the cap is in two pieces. The rim (ogee) and foot panel is one piece, hinged to the top body molding; and the head panel is the second piece, hinged to the rim (ogee).

Slant marker – a cemetery marker that has a face and has an angle greater than 45 degrees but less than 90 degrees in relationship to the terrain.

Slip panel – see Priest casket.

Slip top – see Priest casket.

Softwood – wood from cone bearing or coniferous trees.

Solid wood – raw material used to manufacture products entirely from natural wood pieces that contain no wood by-products or composite wood derivatives.

Stainless steel – a rust-resistant metal alloy of steel, chromium, and sometimes nickel.

Stamped hardware – a hardware production method whereby the casket hardware sections are pressed out on a hydraulic press.

State casket (vertical side square) – casket in which the body panels are at a 90-degree angle to the bottom and the corners form 90-degree angles.

Stationary bar – a non-moveable casket handle.

Steel – a metal alloy consisting mainly of iron and carbon; used in caskets it is low in carbon which keeps it soft (mild) and malleable; commercial steel contains carbon in an amount up to 1.7% as an essential alloying constituent. May be referred to as carbon steel based upon the percentage of carbon in the alloy.

Stiffeners – elongated indentations that are pressed into the casket bottom and help to strengthen the casket shell.

Sundry items – the miscellaneous items provided or used to complement the services of a funeral director, i.e. register books, acknowledgment cards, memorial folders/programs, religious paraphernalia, flag case, etc.

Swell – see Crown.

Swing bar – a moveable casket handle with a hinged arm.

Tablet – see Die.

Tailored interior – a tightly drawn casket interior style.

Threaded fastener – a screw-type fastener.

Throw – see Overlay.

Tip – the decorative or ornamental part of the casket handle that covers the exposed ends of the bar.

Top body molding – see Body ledge.

Top body molding flange – see Body ledge flange.

Top seal – a method of closure that utilizes an epoxy compound in conjunction with tongue ingroove construction at the top edge and the lid of the vault.

Transfer container – an enclosure used for the protection of human remains during transportation.

Transverse gasket – a rubber gasket that seals the space between the head and foot caps on a split-cap or half-couch metal casket.

Tufted interior – a style of casket interior created by placing a padding material between a lining material and a backing material, with subsequent stitches taken, forming small raised puffs.

Unit pricing – a method of price quotation in which one price includes both service and casket.

Urn – a container for cremated remains.

Urnside – a casket design in which the body panels display the shape of an urn.

Vault – an outer enclosure which supports workload earth load and offers limited protection from most outside elements.

Velvet – a fabric of silk, cotton, and possibly rayon, with a nap typically found in higher quality caskets.

Vertical side – see State casket.

Vertical tablet – a type of cemetery monument in which the die is taller than it is wide.

Visitation (calling hours, visiting hours) – time set aside for friends and relatives to pay respect for the deceased.

Wood veneer – created by gluing a thin layer of wood of superior value or excellent grain to an inferior wood.

Wood wool – see Excelsior.

Wrinkled finish – see Crinkled finish.

Wrought bronze – bronze metal rolled into sheets.

Wrought copper – copper metal rolled into sheets.

Ziegler case – see metal case (represents a specific brand of metal case but in use have become synonymous terms).

Domain VI
Bereavement Counseling

Communications

Sociology in Funeral Services

Psychology in Funeral Services

Bereavement Counseling

Professional Communications

Effective communication skills are indispensable for a professional funeral director, forming the foundation of compassionate and supportive interactions with grieving families. This chapter will discuss the key components and elements essential to proper communication within the funeral director's role, skills that encompass active listening, empathy, and clarity in conveying information. A funeral director must navigate delicate conversations with sensitivity, understanding, and respect, providing families with the necessary information while acknowledging and addressing their emotional needs. Additionally, the ability to communicate clearly and transparently ensures that families comprehend the funeral process, which enables them to make informed decisions during a challenging time. This chapter will also delve into the nuances of communication strategies, recognizing the unique role they play in establishing trust, fostering connection, and guiding families through the intricate facets of funeral arrangements with professionalism and empathy.

Difference between Intrapersonal & Interpersonal Communication

Intrapersonal and interpersonal communications constitute distinct yet interconnected dimensions of human interaction. **Intrapersonal communication** involves an individual's internal dialogue, self-reflection, and thoughts, serving as a foundation for personal understanding and decision-making. Intrapersonal communication usually involves writing skills. On the other hand, **interpersonal communication** refers to interactions among individuals, encompassing verbal and nonverbal exchanges that build relationships, convey emotions, and share information. Interpersonal communication usually involves oral or verbal skills. While both intrapersonal and interpersonal communications involve self-awareness and expression, the former is solitary, occurring within one's mind, while the latter occurs during social interactions.

Expanding beyond individual and interpersonal realms, communication extends to small group, public, and mass communication. **Small group communication** involves interactions among a limited number of participants, fostering collaboration and mutual understanding, such as in the arrangement conference. **Public communication** involves one individual addressing a larger audience, such as a speaker delivering a presentation or a funeral director conducting a funeral. **Mass communication**, on the other hand, reaches a vast and diverse audience through channels like media, social media, broadcasting, or publications. Each type of communication shares the common goal of conveying information and facilitating understanding but differs in scale, context, and the number of participants involved.

Communication Model

The communication model comprises several interconnected elements that facilitate the exchange of information between individuals. The **sender**, originating the communication, encodes a message, which is the information intended for the **receiver**. **The channel** represents the medium through which the message is transmitted, be it verbal, written, or nonverbal. The receiver, on the other end, decodes the message, extracting meaning from what is communicated. However, external and internal noise can disrupt this process, with external noise stemming from the environment and internal noise arising from individual cognitive factors. **Feedback**, a crucial component, involves the receiver's response, completing the communication loop. Finally, the situational environment, encompassing physical, social, and cultural contexts, influences how the message is perceived and understood. Understanding and managing these elements are essential for effective communication, as they collectively shape the dynamics of information exchange in various interpersonal and organizational contexts.

In the study of language, the demographic context, rule-governed syntax, and semantics play important roles in understanding communication patterns. **Demographic context** considers the social and cultural characteristics of the individuals involved in communication, such as age, gender, education, and cultural background, influencing language choices and expressions. **Rule-governed syntax** delves into the structural organization of language, examining the grammatical rules and order that guide sentence formation. It encompasses the arrangement of words and phrases to convey meaning within a particular language system. **Semantics**, on the other hand, focuses on the study of meaning in language, exploring how words, symbols, and expressions convey intended messages. Together, these elements contribute to a comprehensive understanding of linguistic communication, acknowledging the influence of both social context and the formal structures that govern language use.

Attitude shaping, credibility, and self-esteem are interconnected aspects that significantly impact individual behavior and interactions. An **attitude shaper** is a force, whether external or internal, that influences and molds one's beliefs, opinions, and perspectives. **Credibility**, on the other hand, is built upon trust, expertise, and reliability, enhancing an individual's persuasive power in shaping attitudes and opinions. A person with high credibility is often perceived as more influential in guiding the attitudes of others. **Self-esteem**, the evaluation and perception of one's own worth, plays a crucial role in this dynamic, influencing how individuals respond to attitude shapers and assess the credibility of information. A person with higher self-esteem may be more resistant to external influences, critically evaluating attitude-shaping forces and credibility. The intricate interplay of these factors underscores the complexity of how attitudes are formed, shaped, and perceived within individual and social contexts.

Attitude reflectors encompass a spectrum of psychological factors that influence how individuals perceive and respond to various stimuli. A person's sense of power, or perceived control over their circumstances, can significantly shape their attitudes by influencing their level of confidence and assertiveness. The degree of interest an individual has in a particular subject or context also plays an important role, for higher interest often correlates with stronger attitudes and more significant engagement. Affiliation, reflecting the human tendency to connect with others and seek social belonging, can influence attitudes as individuals align their beliefs with those of their social groups. Attraction or interest in a particular subject matter further contributes to attitude formation because individuals are more likely to develop positive attitudes toward stimuli that captivate their attention or evoke positive emotions. Finally, a sense of responsibility can shape attitudes by influencing individuals to adopt perspectives that align with their perceived duties or moral obligations. Together, these attitude reflectors highlight the multifaceted nature of human attitudes, shaped by a combination of internal psychological factors and external influences within social and contextual frameworks.

Misinterpretation

The misinterpretation of verbal symbols often stems from the ambiguity inherent in language, in which equivocal, relative, and emotive terms can lead to confusion. **Equivocal terms**, having multiple meanings, can result in miscommunication when the intended meaning is unclear. **Relative terms**, dependent on context, may be interpreted differently by different individuals based on their subjective understanding. **Emotive terms**, laden with emotional connotations, can evoke varied responses based on personal experiences. Additionally, the distinction between denotation, the literal meaning of a word, and connotation, the emotional or cultural associations attached to it, can contribute to misinterpretations because individuals may ascribe different emotional nuances to the same term.

To better understand these concepts, consider the word "home." The denotation or literal meaning of "home" refers to a place where one lives, typically with their family or household. This is the straightforward dictionary definition of the term. However, the connotation or emotional/cultural associations attached to "home" can vary significantly among individuals. For some, "home" may evoke feelings of warmth, security, and comfort, associated with positive emotions. On the other hand, for someone who has experienced a difficult or troubled family life, "home" might carry more complex and possibly negative emotional connotations.

In a communication context, if someone uses the word "home" if everyone shares the same positive connotations, there could be a misinterpretation. For instance, in a discussion about childhood memories, one person might express a longing for "home," expecting others to relate to the positive feelings they associate with the term. However, someone with a different personal history may interpret the term "home" with less favorable emotions or even distress. This example illustrates how the distinction between denotation and connotation can contribute to misinterpretations, for individuals may indeed ascribe different emotional nuances to the same seemingly straightforward term.

In navigating effective communication, it is essential to be mindful of the potential misinterpretations stemming from these linguistic nuances and to strive for clarity to minimize ambiguity and foster shared understanding.

Euphemisms are linguistic devices employed to soften the impact of harsh or direct expressions, often used when discussing sensitive topics like death. While phrases like "passed away," "expired," or "gone" are commonly used euphemisms for "died," opting for the straightforward term acknowledges the reality of the situation without sugarcoating it. For instance, asking, "How did your husband die?" instead of using a euphemism like "How did your husband pass away?" may convey a sense of directness, promoting clear and honest communication. Embracing a more direct language approach can foster openness and authenticity in conversations about loss, helping individuals express and navigate their emotions more openly and candidly.

Avoiding **slang and jargon** in communication, especially when discussing topics as sensitive as death, is crucial for ensuring clarity and understanding. Using plain language and industry-specific terms, such as "cremated remains" instead of "ashes," helps maintain a level of respect and professionalism while minimizing potential confusion. Employing commonly used terms and colloquialisms fosters accessibility for a wider audience, ensuring that information is easily comprehensible to individuals from various backgrounds. For instance, using "obituary" instead of the formal term "obit" may resonate better with people because it aligns with everyday language, making the information more relatable and accessible during times of grief. This approach not only respects diverse linguistic capacities but also promotes open and empathetic communication, acknowledging the importance of clarity and sensitivity in discussions surrounding loss.

Nonverbal Cues

Nonverbal communication, often considered as influential as verbal expression, encompasses a spectrum of cues that convey significant meaning. The communicative value of nonverbal cues, such as facial expressions, gestures, and body language, plays a significant role in expressing emotions, attitudes, and relational dynamics. These cues provide insights into the nature of relationships, establishing a subtle yet powerful form of connection. However, nonverbal communication is inherently ambiguous, often requiring careful interpretation within the specific context. Understanding and decoding these cues appropriately is crucial for effective communication, for misinterpretations can lead to misunderstandings. Context appropriateness is essential in nonverbal communication, in which gestures or expressions may carry different meanings in various cultural or situational contexts. Being attuned to these nonverbal elements enhances the richness and depth of interpersonal interactions, allowing for a more nuanced and comprehensive understanding of the messages being conveyed.

When addressing individuals, particularly those who are bereaved, the significance of kinesics, or nonverbal communication, cannot be overstated. Facial expressions and eye contact convey empathy and sincerity, allowing for a more meaningful connection with those experiencing grief. Appropriate gestures, whether comforting touches or supportive movements, serve as a physical expression of empathy. Posture also plays a crucial role, with open and non-threatening body language fostering a sense of trust and comfort. Additionally, the tone and modulation of one's voice contribute to the overall communication experience because a soothing and empathetic voice can provide solace. Recognizing the impact of these nonverbal cues is essential when addressing individuals coping with loss, for they enhance the ability to convey genuine compassion and support, creating an environment that acknowledges and respects the emotions associated with grief.

Maintaining a conservative and **professional appearance** is paramount for a funeral director, given the nature of their role in facilitating funeral ceremonies and supporting grieving families. Dressing conservatively not only reflects a sense of respect for the solemnity of the occasion but also demonstrates a commitment to upholding traditional values associated with the funeral industry. A funeral director's appearance can significantly influence the perception of professionalism and competence because families often seek comfort in dealing with individuals who exude a sense of reliability and dignity. Being cognizant of physical appearance extends beyond attire to personal grooming and demeanor, reinforcing the importance of presenting a compassionate and composed presence during emotionally charged moments. By embodying a conservative and polished appearance, funeral directors can establish a sense of trust and reassurance, acknowledging the gravity of their responsibilities in guiding families through the delicate process of saying farewell to their loved ones.

Theory of Personal Space

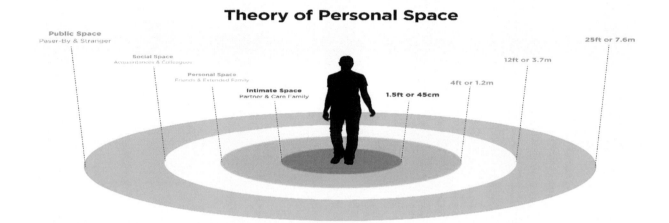

Proxemics, haptics, and chronemics are integral components of nonverbal communication, especially in the context of funeral directing. **Proxemics** refers to the study of spatial distances between individuals during interactions. In funeral settings, understanding proxemics helps funeral directors navigate the appropriate physical distance with grieving families, ensuring a balance between providing support and respecting personal space. **Haptics**, the study of touch communication, is crucial in expressing empathy and comfort. Funeral directors may use gentle touches, such as a supportive hand on the shoulder, to convey compassion to grieving individuals. **Chronemics** involves the perception and use of time, which is particularly relevant in funeral services where pacing, pauses, and the overall duration of interactions contribute to the communication process. Being mindful of the timing and duration of conversations and ceremonies is essential to facilitate a respectful and meaningful experience for grieving families.

In the delicate realm of funeral directing, misinterpretation of nonverbal symbols can occur, potentially impacting the communication dynamics. For example, misjudging proxemics may lead to unintentional intrusion into personal space, causing discomfort for grieving individuals. In haptics, a well-intentioned touch may be misinterpreted if not culturally or individually appropriate, potentially creating tension. For instance, although a comforting touch on the shoulder can express support, it might be deemed inappropriate if a male funeral director employs this gesture with a female individual of the Orthodox Jewish faith. In different cultural and religious contexts, such physical contact could be considered offensive, inappropriate, and culturally insensitive. Additionally, misunderstandings related to chronemics can arise if the pace of interactions is perceived as rushed or prolonged, impacting the emotional resonance of the funeral process. Funeral directors must be attuned to these nonverbal nuances to ensure that their gestures and interactions are received as intended during a time when clarity and sensitivity are paramount.

The Funeral Director and Active Listening

Active listening is a multifaceted process, particularly crucial for a funeral director engaged in sensitive and emotional conversations with grieving individuals. The first component, **hearing**, involves the reception of auditory stimuli, but it extends beyond mere sound detection to encompass a deliberate focus on the speaker's words. **Attending** involves concentrating on the speaker and their message, minimizing distractions to fully absorb the information being shared. **Acknowledging** is the act of responding to the speaker, offering verbal or nonverbal cues to convey engagement and understanding. **Understanding** goes beyond surface-level comprehension; it involves grasping the emotional nuances and underlying meanings of the communicated message. Finally, **remembering** is the capacity to retain and recall information, showcasing genuine investment in the speaker's words. For a funeral director, mastering these components of active listening is fundamental to providing empathetic and effective support during the delicate moments of bereavement.

In the role of a funeral director, **ineffective listening behaviors** can hinder the ability to provide meaningful support to grieving families. **Pseudo listening**, a common pitfall, involves feigning attention while mentally disengaged. An example might be nodding or making appropriate sounds without truly absorbing the speaker's words. **Conversation narcissism** occurs when a funeral director consistently redirects discussions back to their experiences rather than focusing on the bereaved individuals. **Defensive listening** involves perceiving remarks as personal attacks, hindering open communication. **Selective listening, or filtering hearing**, occurs when only specific aspects of a message are attended to, potentially leading to misunderstandings. **Ambushing** entails actively listening for opportunities to counter or challenge the speaker's statements, disrupting the empathetic flow of the conversation. **Insulated listening** involves disregarding specific topics, potentially overlooking crucial details relevant to the grieving process. Finally, **insensitive listening** occurs when a funeral director fails to consider the emotional implications of their responses, potentially causing unintentional distress to the bereaved. Recognizing and rectifying these ineffective listening behaviors is essential for providing the compassionate and supportive care that grieving families require.

The **self-concept**, the relatively stable perception individuals hold of themselves, significantly shapes communication dynamics. This development begins with social interactions and feedback from others, influencing how individuals perceive their abilities, values, and identities. **Reflective appraisal**, the process of internalizing judgments based on how others view us, further refines self-concept. The opinions of significant others, such as family, friends, or mentors, play a crucial role in shaping self-concept, as does the roles individuals assume in various contexts, like being a funeral director. The self-concept profoundly influences intrapersonal communication, impacting how individuals process information, make decisions, and navigate their internal thoughts and emotions. A **positive self-concept** can foster confidence and effective self-expression, while a **negative self-concept** may lead to self-doubt and hinder open communication with oneself. Understanding and managing self-concept is essential for fostering healthy intrapersonal communication, enabling individuals to navigate their inner dialogue with authenticity and resilience.

Various influences contribute to the shaping of one's self-concept, and among these, the **self-fulfilling prophecy** plays a significant role. This psychological phenomenon occurs when an individual's expectations about themselves influence their behavior in a way that aligns with those expectations. A positive self-concept can initiate a cycle of affirming behaviors, while negative self-concepts may perpetuate detrimental patterns. **Self-disclosure**, the act of revealing personal information to others, is another fundamental factor. Choosing what to disclose and to whom is influenced by one's self-concept, impacting the depth and authenticity of interpersonal relationships. Moreover, **self-esteem**, an individual's overall evaluation of their own worth, acts as a cornerstone in the construction of self-concept. Healthy self-esteem fosters a positive self-concept, facilitating confident self-expression and resilient intrapersonal communication. Conversely, low self-esteem may contribute to a negative self-concept, impeding communication with oneself and others. Navigating these intricate interplays requires a conscious understanding of these influences and a commitment to fostering a positive self-concept conducive to effective and authentic communication.

Interpersonal communication is marked by several distinctive characteristics, three of which are irreplaceability, self-disclosure, and interdependence. The concept of **irreplaceability** highlights the uniqueness of each interpersonal connection, emphasizing that individuals bring irreplicable qualities and experiences to their relationships. **Self-disclosure**, the intentional sharing of personal information, is vital for building trust and deepening connections. **Interdependence**, acknowledging the mutual influence between individuals in a relationship, highlights the shared responsibilities and interwoven destinies within interpersonal dynamics. In the realm of funeral directing, these characteristics are particularly poignant. Funeral directors, engaging in highly sensitive and emotionally charged interactions, recognize the irreplaceability of each person they encounter, tailoring their support to the unique needs of grieving families. Self-disclosure, done properly, can foster a sense of trust and empathy, allowing funeral directors to connect with clients on a more personal level. Additionally, the interdependence between funeral directors and bereaved families underscores the collaborative nature of creating meaningful and respectful ceremonies honoring the life accomplishments of the deceased or healing the rifts that may have occurred over time. These interpersonal communication characteristics are foundational in navigating the delicate dynamics of grief and loss within the funeral directing profession.

Soft Skills

Soft skills are *personal attributes that enable someone to interact effectively and harmoniously with other people.* These skills encompass both verbal and nonverbal considerations. Verbal communication, including tone, pitch, and choice of words, plays a significant role in conveying messages accurately and with empathy. A thoughtful and respectful tone fosters positive engagement, while clear and concise language enhances understanding. Nonverbal cues, such as body language, facial expressions, and gestures, are equally impactful. Maintaining appropriate eye contact demonstrates attentiveness, while open and welcoming body language contributes to an atmosphere of approachability. Soft skills also involve active listening, in which nonverbal cues like nodding or maintaining an engaged posture signal genuine interest and understanding. Overall, the integration of both verbal and nonverbal elements in communication is important for cultivating strong soft skills, enabling individuals to navigate social interactions with effectiveness.

Soft skills are characterized by a range of attributes that contribute to effective interpersonal interactions. **Empathy**, a cornerstone of strong soft skills, involves the ability to understand and share the feelings of others, fostering a sense of connection. **Communication skills**, encompassing both verbal and nonverbal elements, enable individuals to express themselves clearly and listen attentively. **Adaptability and flexibility** are key soft skills that allow individuals to navigate diverse situations with ease. **Collaboration and teamwork**, essential in various professional settings, especially funeral directing, require individuals to leverage their interpersonal skills to work harmoniously with others. **Time management and organizational skills** contribute to one's ability to handle tasks efficiently and meet deadlines, enhancing overall effectiveness. **Resilience**, the capacity to bounce back from setbacks, is another critical soft skill that promotes emotional intelligence and fortitude in challenging situations. Together, these characteristics define a well-rounded set of soft skills that empower individuals to interact successfully and foster positive relationships in both personal and professional spheres.

A **strong work ethic** and emotional intelligence are significant contributors to the effectiveness of soft skills. A robust work ethic, characterized by diligence, reliability, and a commitment to quality, ensures that individuals consistently deliver their best efforts in various tasks. Such diligence enhances the reliability and trustworthiness components of soft skills, creating a positive impact on professional relationships. **Emotional intelligence**, on the other hand, encompasses the ability to understand and manage one's own emotions while also empathizing with others. This trait significantly influences soft skills by fostering better communication, conflict resolution, and collaboration. Individuals with high emotional intelligence can navigate interpersonal dynamics with sensitivity, adapting their communication style to suit different situations and personalities. The combination of a strong work ethic and emotional intelligence strengthens the overall soft skills repertoire, enabling individuals to not only excel in their professional responsibilities but also to foster positive and harmonious relationships in diverse social and work settings.

Effective Communications

Improving interpersonal communications, particularly in the realms of climate and conflict resolution, requires a deliberate focus on fostering open, transparent, and constructive dialogue. Creating a positive communication climate involves cultivating an environment where individuals feel comfortable expressing their thoughts and emotions without fear of judgment. Encouraging active listening, acknowledging perspectives, and providing constructive feedback contribute to this positive climate. In **conflict resolution**, effective communications entail the skillful navigation of disagreements with empathy and respect. Using assertiveness and empathy allows individuals to express their needs and concerns while understanding those of others. Implementing conflict resolution strategies, such as finding common ground and seeking compromise, facilitates a more harmonious and productive interpersonal environment. This skill is extremely helpful in situations in which family members are at odds when determining the proper type of services that best corresponds with their bereavement needs. Continuous efforts to enhance interpersonal communication skills in both climate and conflict resolution contribute to healthier relationships, increased mutual understanding, and a more cooperative and supportive social or professional environment.

In the profession of funeral directing, good interpersonal communication is essential across various funeral functions. In the initial notification of death and transfer of human remains, conveying empathy, sensitivity, and clear information is crucial to support grieving families during an emotionally charged moment. During the arrangement conference, effective communication involves active listening to discern the wishes of the bereaved, providing information with clarity, and ensuring a collaborative decision-making process. In conducting services both as a funeral director and celebrant, effective interpersonal communication encompasses the ability to guide and comfort mourners, addressing their emotional needs with compassion while maintaining professionalism. Finally, in interactions with other professionals and colleagues, effective communication fosters seamless collaboration, ensuring a cohesive and supportive team environment. These communication skills, ranging from empathy and active listening to assertiveness and collaboration, are integral to the multifaceted role of a funeral director, contributing to a positive, respectful, and supportive experience for grieving families and colleagues alike.

Trust is a foundational element in interpersonal communications, acting as a catalyst for positive interactions and fostering a supportive environment. The benefits of trust in communications are multifaceted. First, it opens channels of communication, creating a space where individuals feel safe to express themselves openly and honestly, which, in turn, leads to increased awareness and understanding as information is shared transparently. Trust also plays a vital role in developing significant interpersonal relationships, for it cultivates a sense of reliability and dependability among individuals. Furthermore, trust establishes credibility, making communications more effective and influential.

Behaviors that develop trust are crucial in cultivating an atmosphere of openness and support. Consistency in actions and words builds trust, as individuals can rely on the predictability of behavior. **Active listening**, where one demonstrates genuine interest in others' perspectives, fosters trust by validating and respecting their experiences. Transparency and honesty in communication contribute to trust development, as individuals appreciate sincerity and forthrightness. Being responsive and reliable in fulfilling commitments builds a sense of dependability, further strengthening the foundation of trust. Overall, these behaviors collectively contribute to creating a trustworthy and supportive communication environment.

In the funeral service practice, the development of trust is extremely important to providing personal care for grieving families. Establishing an open line of communication is essential to understanding their unique needs, preferences, and cultural considerations during a highly emotional time. Funeral professionals who communicate openly and transparently create an environment where families feel heard, valued, and supported. By actively listening to their concerns and wishes, funeral directors can tailor their services to honor the deceased in a manner that resonates with the family, fostering trust in the funeral service process.

In cases where families harbor internal wounds and complex relationships with the deceased, active listening becomes even more crucial in the funeral service process. Funeral directors, through empathetic and attentive listening, can discern the intricacies of family dynamics, understanding the underlying emotions and histories at play. This level of engagement allows funeral professionals to offer tailored suggestions that not only honor the deceased but also address the family's unique healing needs. By acknowledging and navigating these complexities with sensitivity, funeral directors can help transform the funeral service into a therapeutic event, providing a platform for emotional catharsis and fostering a sense of closure for families dealing with intricate relationships and unresolved issues. This personalized approach not only contributes to the healing process but also solidifies trust in the funeral director's ability to navigate and address the specific challenges that may arise within families during the mourning process.

Moreover, trust is paramount when educating families on the importance of honoring the life accomplishments of the deceased as part of the healing process in the grief experience. **Open communication** allows funeral professionals to convey the significance of celebrating a person's life and achievements, offering meaningful ways to commemorate their legacy. By building trust through transparent discussions, funeral directors can guide families in crafting services that truly reflect the individual's life, contributing to a healing and cathartic experience for those mourning the loss. In the realm of aftercare, the commitment to open communication remains crucial. Trust is solidified when funeral professionals genuinely follow through, providing ongoing support and resources to help bereaved individuals navigate the complexities of their grief journey. This commitment to open communication ensures that the bereaved feel cared for, beyond the immediate funeral services, fostering lasting trust and a sense of ongoing support.

Elements of Groups

Group communication involves the exchange of information and ideas within a collective setting, and understanding the characteristics of groups is critical in navigating this dynamic. Groups typically possess shared goals, interdependence among members, and a sense of cohesion. **Roles** within a group structure define the various functions individuals assume, ranging from leadership roles to task-oriented responsibilities. However, **role-related problems** can arise, leading to challenges in group communication. **Role ambiguity**, in which the expectations of a role are unclear, can cause confusion and hinder effective collaboration. **Role conflict**, arising when expectations for a role are incompatible, may lead to tension within the group. Additionally, issues such as **role overload**, in which an individual is assigned excessive responsibilities, can impact group dynamics. Addressing these role-related challenges is essential for fostering cohesive and productive group communications.

Groups serve various purposes, and their types can be categorized based on distinct functions. **Learning groups** are designed to facilitate educational experiences, encouraging members to acquire new knowledge and skills collaboratively. **Growth groups** focus on personal development and self-improvement, providing a supportive environment for individuals to explore and enhance their emotional well-being. **Problem-solving groups** are geared towards addressing specific challenges or tasks, leveraging the collective wisdom and expertise of members to find effective solutions. **Social groups**, on the other hand, emphasize interpersonal connections and shared interests, fostering a sense of community and camaraderie. Each type of group serves a unique purpose, catering to different aspects of an individual's needs for learning, personal development, collaborative problem-solving, or social interaction.

Decision-making methods play a crucial role in the dynamics of group processes, and various approaches are employed to reach resolutions. **Expert opinion** involves relying on the insights and recommendations of individuals with specialized knowledge or experience in a particular domain. **Authority rules** delegates decision-making authority to a designated leader or figurehead within the group. **Majority control** emphasizes reaching decisions based on the preferences of the majority, allowing the largest faction to determine the course of action. In contrast, **minority control** involves giving decision-making power to a smaller, often specialized, subset of the group. **Consensus** seeks agreement from the entire group, requiring collective approval and alignment on the chosen decision. The effectiveness of these methods depends on the context, goals, and dynamics of the group because each approach brings its own advantages and potential challenges to the decision-making process.

Elements of Public Speaking

Public speaking is a nuanced skill that involves not only effective delivery but also strategic consideration of various elements. When choosing a topic, speakers should align their interests, expertise, and audience preferences. **Selecting a topic** that resonates with both the speaker's passion and the audience's interests enhances engagement and connection. **Analyzing** the speaking opportunity is crucial for tailoring the message appropriately. **Understanding the purpose of the speech**—whether it is to inform, persuade, or entertain—helps guide the content and delivery style. An **informative speech** aims to educate the audience on a specific topic, a **persuasive speech** seeks to influence attitudes or behaviors, and an **entertaining speech** should be captivating and enjoyable without crossing into offensive territory. Additionally, considering the audience's demographics, interests, and prior knowledge allows the speaker to craft a message both relevant and relatable. **Adapting the speech** to the occasion ensures that it fits the tone and expectations of the event, further enhancing the effectiveness of public speaking.

In the realm of public speaking, the purpose of the speech is an important factor that guides the content and delivery style. An informative speech serves to impart knowledge or convey facts on a particular subject, requiring clarity, accuracy, and organization. A persuasive speech, on the other hand, aims to sway the audience's opinions or encourage specific actions. It demands compelling arguments, evidence, and a persuasive tone. Entertaining speeches, while aiming to engage and amuse, must be carefully crafted to ensure appropriateness and avoid any offensive content. Understanding the audience is equally essential. Speakers need to tailor their message to align with the audience's preferences, knowledge level, and interests. Finally, considering the occasion ensures that the speech fits the context, tone, and expectations of the event, contributing to a successful and impactful public speaking experience.

Structuring a speech effectively involves a well-thought-out organization of ideas that guides the audience through a coherent flow of information. The **introduction** serves as the foundation, comprising the theme and strategies to engage the audience. The theme encapsulates the **main idea or message** the speaker aims to convey, providing a clear direction for the speech.

Engaging the audience is crucial in capturing their attention and creating a connection, which can be achieved through compelling anecdotes, thought-provoking questions, or relevant quotes, setting the stage for the rest of the speech. The **body of the speech** follows in which the main points are presented logically. The structure of the body can take various forms, such as organizing information based on time sequence, space sequence, or topic sequence. This arrangement ensures a coherent and easy-to-follow presentation, enhancing the audience's comprehension and retention of the content. Each main point should be supported by evidence, examples, or anecdotes to reinforce the speaker's message and maintain audience interest.

The **conclusion of the speech** is equally critical, providing a sense of closure and leaving a lasting impression. It should succinctly summarize the key points and reinforce the theme, emphasizing the main message in the audience's minds. A well-crafted conclusion can leave a powerful impact, whether it is a call to action in a persuasive speech, a reflection on the importance of the information in an informative speech, or a memorable closing statement in an entertaining speech. The overall structure of a speech, from the introduction through the body to the conclusion is essential for delivering a clear, organized, and impactful presentation that effectively communicates the speaker's message to the audience.

The aspects of delivery encompass both visual and auditory elements, collectively contributing to the effectiveness of a presentation or speech. **Visual aspects** involve non-verbal cues, body language, facial expressions, and the use of visual aids, which can significantly enhance the audience's understanding and engagement. Maintaining eye contact, appropriate gestures, and a confident posture are essential visual components that convey confidence and credibility. On the other hand, **auditory aspects** pertain to the speaker's vocal delivery, including tone, pitch, pace, and articulation. A well-modulated voice, clear enunciation, and strategic variations in tone can captivate the audience's attention, convey emotion, and emphasize key points. The harmonious integration of both visual and auditory aspects ensures a comprehensive and impactful delivery, fostering effective communication and connection with the audience.

The **types of speech delivery** play a crucial role in shaping the overall presentation and communication style. An **extemporaneous speech** involves delivering a prepared and organized message without memorization, relying on notes or an outline to guide the speaker. This approach allows for flexibility, adaptability to the audience's response, and a more natural, conversational tone. An **impromptu speech**, on the other hand, is delivered without prior preparation, often requiring the speaker to think on their feet and respond spontaneously to a given topic. While impromptu speeches can be challenging, they showcase the speaker's ability to communicate effectively in unforeseen situations.

Formal speeches can be delivered in different styles, such as scripted, memorized, or impromptu. In a **manuscript delivery**, the speaker reads the entire speech verbatim from a prepared script. This approach ensures precision and accuracy in conveying the intended message but may result in a less engaging delivery. A memorized speech involves committing the entire content to memory, allowing for a polished and rehearsed performance. However, memorization can sometimes lead to a robotic delivery, limiting the speaker's ability to connect with the audience. The choice of speech delivery type depends on the nature of the speech, the preferences of the speaker, and the desired impact on the audience, emphasizing the importance of adapting one's approach to suit the context and goals of the presentation.

Stage fright, also known as performance anxiety, is a common phenomenon characterized by nervousness or fear experienced by individuals when speaking or performing in front of an audience. **Facilitative apprehension** refers to a moderate level of anxiety that can enhance performance by heightening focus and alertness. In this context, the nervous energy acts as a positive force, leading to a dynamic and engaging presentation. On the other hand, **debilitative apprehension** is an overwhelming level of anxiety that hinders performance, causing physical and psychological distress. Excessive nervousness can lead to symptoms such as trembling, sweating, and impaired cognitive function, negatively impacting the speaker's ability to convey their message effectively. Recognizing and managing stage fright is crucial for speakers to harness the positive aspects of facilitative apprehension while mitigating the detrimental effects of debilitative apprehension, ultimately allowing for a more confident and successful public speaking experience.

The principles of effective public speaking find valuable application in funeral service practice across various settings. Community presentations play a vital role in fostering connections and disseminating information about funeral services, grief support, and pre-need planning. Funeral professionals participating in community presentations must employ engaging and empathetic communication to effectively address the concerns and questions of the audience. Similarly, preneed presentations, in which funeral plans are discussed before the need arises, require clear and compassionate communication to guide individuals and families through the sensitive process of making future arrangements.

Celebrant services, a distinctive aspect of modern funeral services, involve crafting and delivering personalized ceremonies that honor the life accomplishments of the deceased. Funeral celebrants rely on effective public speaking techniques to create a meaningful and comforting experience for grieving families. Community memorial services, continuing education sessions, and staff meetings within the funeral service practice also benefit from skilled public speaking. Whether commemorating lost lives, imparting knowledge to colleagues, or fostering team cohesion, funeral professionals must communicate with empathy, clarity, and professionalism to navigate these diverse settings successfully. The application of effective public speaking techniques in these contexts ensures that funeral service practitioners can provide the highest level of support, guidance, and comfort to grieving families and maintain the professional development of their teams.

Business Communications

Business communications are integral to various aspects of employment, starting with resume development and cover letters. A well-crafted resume and cover letter showcase a candidate's skills and qualifications effectively, demonstrating their ability to communicate professionally in writing. Business letters play a crucial role in formal communication within the workplace, from addressing concerns to conveying important information. Thank you notes, an often overlooked but essential aspect, demonstrate gratitude and professionalism. During interviews, both verbal and nonverbal communication skills are critical for creating a positive impression. Effective communication continues through employee evaluations, in which clear and constructive feedback is essential for professional growth and development. In the realm of employment, business communication is a multifaceted tool that influences various stages, ensuring effective interaction, collaboration, and success in the professional arena.

In the funeral industry, adept use of business communication is vital for individuals seeking positions within the field. Commencing with resume development and cover letters, a prospective funeral professional must skillfully articulate their qualifications and skills to showcase a strong written communication ability. This proficiency extends to business letters, a vital component for formal communication within funeral service settings, addressing concerns, or conveying critical information professionally. Demonstrating gratitude and professionalism through well-crafted thank you notes is equally essential, reflecting an appreciation for the opportunity and attention to detail. When participating in interviews, effective verbal and nonverbal communication skills become instrumental in creating a positive impression, conveying empathy and professionalism. The importance of clear and constructive communication persists through employee evaluations, in which feedback becomes a catalyst for continual professional growth and development within the funeral industry. In summary, adept business communication is an indispensable tool for those aspiring to secure positions in the funeral industry, influencing various stages of the application and employment process to ensure effective interaction, collaboration, and success in this unique and sensitive professional arena.

Effective communication is of utmost importance in a funeral home, particularly when responding to emails and text messages, managing social media and website postings, and obituary notices. In the sensitive context of the funeral industry, timely and compassionate responses to emails and text messages are crucial for providing support to grieving families and addressing their inquiries promptly. Properly managing social media and website postings is equally essential because these platforms serve as public-facing representations of the funeral home.

Maintaining a respectful and empathetic tone in online communication ensures that the funeral home is perceived as professional and considerate. Crafting emails and obituary notices requires meticulous attention to detail, for these messages carry significant emotional weight. Clear, compassionate, and accurate communication in these formats is vital to convey information about memorial services, obituary details, and other essential information while demonstrating empathy and understanding.

Consistency in communication throughout the organization is a key element for maintaining a cohesive and professional image. All staff members, from funeral directors to administrative personnel, should align in their communication style, ensuring a unified and reliable experience for clients. This consistency extends from in-person interactions to written communications, emphasizing the importance of a cohesive message across all touchpoints. **Effective internal communication** also plays a role in ensuring that everyone within the organization is well-informed and aligned in their approach, contributing to a seamless and professional experience for grieving families during their interactions with the funeral home.

When addressing **confidential information** in the communication process within a funeral home or similar setting, several crucial considerations come into play. First, protecting confidentiality and privacy is essential. Funeral professionals often handle sensitive information about deceased individuals and their families. Ensuring that this **information is safeguarded** from unauthorized access or disclosure is essential to maintain the trust of clients and adhere to ethical standards in the industry. **Timeliness** is another consideration, for the communication of confidential information should be managed promptly to meet the needs of grieving families and other stakeholders. Delays in conveying critical details, such as funeral arrangements or legal processes, can impact the overall experience and trustworthiness of the funeral home.

Additionally, the **manageability of confidential information** is a vital consideration. Funeral professionals must employ secure systems and practices to organize and store confidential data efficiently. Establishing permanent records, whether in electronic or physical form, aids in accountability and reference, ensuring accurate and consistent communication.

Using Technology in Communications

The use of **supporting materials** is integral to enhancing the clarity, relevance, and engagement of a speech or presentation. Multimedia, such as slideshows, videos, or interactive content, can bring depth and visual appeal to the message. These materials should be selected based on their relevance to the topic, ensuring they contribute to the audience's understanding and retention of information. They should also be clear and concise, avoiding information overload and maintaining the audience's focus. Appropriate size and formatting are crucial to prevent distraction and ensure the audience can easily comprehend the visuals without straining.

In the context of technology-assisted arrangements conferences and technology-mediated services like webcasting, incorporating multimedia elements becomes even more significant. Leveraging webcasting technology allows funeral professionals to extend their services beyond physical boundaries, providing a virtual platform for remote attendees to participate in memorial events. Visual aids, electronic media, and verbal aids play key roles in creating a comprehensive and emotionally resonant experience for both in-person and virtual participants. Visual aids, such as photo slideshows or video tributes, can evoke memories and emotions, while electronic media facilitates seamless communication and connection. Verbal aids, including well-crafted speeches or eulogies, serve to provide context, share stories, and offer comfort. The thoughtful integration of these supporting materials in technology-assisted funeral services ensures a meaningful and inclusive experience for all participants, regardless of their physical presence.

Professional etiquette, both verbal and nonverbal, is crucial when handling confidential information. Maintaining a respectful and empathetic demeanor in all interactions contributes to a positive and trustworthy relationship with clients and colleagues. Technology, including netiquette, plays a role in ensuring that digital communication is conducted professionally and securely (*see Technology section pp.180-185*). Compliance with business policies and organizational culture is integral to aligning communication practices with industry standards and expectations.

Moreover, legal considerations must be adhered to when managing confidential information. Funeral professionals must be aware of relevant laws and regulations governing the protection of personal information and privacy. Safeguarding digital identities is crucial because funeral homes increasingly use online platforms for communication and information sharing. Adhering to legal and ethical standards in the handling of confidential information not only protects the funeral home from legal consequences but also upholds the integrity and professionalism of the industry.

PROFESSIONAL COMMUNICATION SKILLS – GLOSSARY

Ambiguous – A disconfirming response with more than one meaning, leaving the other party unsure of the responder's position.

Articulation – The process of correctly pronouncing all the necessary parts of a word.

Ambushing – A style in which the receiver listens carefully to gather information to use in an attack on the speaker.

Artifact – A simple object or ornament representing significant cultural meaning.

Attending – The process of focusing on certain stimuli from the environment.

Channel – The medium through which a message passes from sender to receiver.

Climate – The emotional tone of a relationship as it is expressed in the messages that the partners send and receive.

Communication – The process of human beings responding to verbal/nonverbal behavior. Human survival skills are needed to maintain contact with the world.

Concise – To be clear and brief.

Connotation – The emotional associations of a term.

Consensus – Agreement among group members about a decision.

Credibility – The believability of a speaker or other source of information.

Chronemics – The study of how humans use and structure time.

Conversation narcissism – When one turns the attention of the conversation to oneself.

Critical listening – A style in which the goal is to evaluate the quality or accuracy of the speaker's remarks.

Debilitative apprehension – An intense level of anxiety about speaking before an audience resulting in poor performance.

Defensive listening – Taking innocent comments as personal attacks.

Denotation – The objective, emotion-free meaning of a term.

Emotional intelligence – An assortment of noncognitive skills, capabilities, and competencies that influence a person's ability to successfully cope with environmental demands and pressures; also known as EQ.

Empathy – The ability to perceive another's experience and communicate that perception back to the person.

Empathetic listening – A style in which the goal is to help the speaker solve a problem.

Environment – Physical location and personal history surrounding the communication.

Equivocal terms Words that have more than one dictionary meaning.

Euphemism – A pleasant term substituted for a more direct, less pleasant term.

Evaluative listening – A style in which the goal is to judge the quality or accuracy of speaker's remarks.

Extemporaneous speech – A presentation planned in advance but presented in a direct, conversational manner.

Facilitative apprehension – A moderate level of anxiety about speaking before an audience that helps improve the speaker's performance.

Faulty assumption – Incorrect perceptions that lead individuals to believe that they have heard the message before or that the message is too simple or too complex to understand.

Feedback – The discernible response of the receiver.

Haptics – How touch affects the communication process.

Impromptu speech – A presentation given without preparation.

Informational listening – A style by which one strives to understand another person or idea.

Insensitive listening – The failure to recognize the thoughts or feelings not directly expressed by a speaker, and instead accepting the speaker's words at face value.

Insulated listening – A style in which the receiver ignores undesirable information.

Interpersonal communication – A process in which the parties involved consider one another as unique individuals.

Intrapersonal communication – A process involving only one person, such as talking to oneself.

Jargon – Special words or expressions used by a particular profession or group and are difficult for others to understand.

Kinesics – The study of body movement, gestures, and posture.

Listening – The active process of receiving, constructing meaning from, and acknowledging verbal messages.

Manuscript speech – A presentation read word-for-word from a prepared text.

Mass Communication – The transmission of messages to large, usually widespread audiences.

Memorized speech – A presentation learned and delivered by rote without a written text.

Message – A person's words and actions.

Message overload – Excessive written or verbal information.

Monochronic – A nonverbal means of communication that emphasizes punctuality in beginning and completing a task.

Noise – A force that interferes with the process of communication.

Pitch – The highness or lowness of one's voice.

Polychronic – A nonverbal means of communication that emphasizes flexibility in beginning and completing tasks.

Proxemics – The study of how people and animals use space.

Pseudo listening – Pretending to be attentive.

Rate – The speed at which one speaks.

Receiver – The person who decodes the message.

Relative terms – Words that gain their meaning through comparison.

Selective listening – A style in which the receiver responds only to messages that interest them.

Self-concept – The set of perceptions each individual holds of themself.

Self-disclosure – The process of deliberately revealing information about oneself that is significant and that would not normally be known by others.

Self-esteem – The degree of regard a person holds for themself.

Self-fulfilling prophecy – A prediction or expectation of an event that makes the outcome more likely to occur than would otherwise.

Semantics – The study of meaning of words and phrases in language.

Sender – The person who encodes and delivers the message.

Slang – A type of language that consists of informal words or phrases.

Soft skills – Personal attributes that enable someone to interact effectively and harmoniously with other people.

Syntax – The arrangement of words in a sentence.

Theme – A complete sentence describing the central idea of a speech, usually found in the first paragraph.

Volume – The loudness of one's voice.

Sociology in Funeral Service

Background: A group of people who live in a specific geographical area, who interact with each other, and who share a common culture, is known as a "society." A group's shared practices, values and believes is referred to as the group's "culture." **Sociology,** therefore, *is the branch of social sciences that studies groups and group behavior in societies.*

Families and communities are commonly studied by sociologists to help explain how such groups are organized and operate, including what social rules are to be followed. A society's culture involves a group's whole way of life, from the most routine to the most important parts of group members' lives, including major life events like death.

Since the onset of the 20th and 21st century, funeral directors have worked in a social landscape that their predecessors would never have predicted. They are dealing with an American population and culture more mobile and individualistic than ever before; thus, their funeral choices can be quite unique. The following section describes some of the changes over the past 50 years that have greatly influenced the changing role of funeral services in society.

Still, some cultural universals remain. Please note that while there are certain universals, this text focuses primarily on American funeral rites. Readers are encouraged to work with their client families to be sensitive to their needs and wishes pertinent to their particular cultures. For example, while the religious customs outlined in the first section of this book will serve as a foundation for developing an understanding of social structures that some families identify with and believe in (e.g., for their spiritual understanding of the afterlife), it should not be assumed that all families follow the same customs.

The funeral rite is a social function that is culturally universal, even if the expression of various activities may vary from culture to culture. For example, an announcement of death, care of the deceased, the method selected for disposition, the ceremonies or rituals, and the memorialization of the deceased exist in different cultures but may appear quite different depending on the culture.

Societal changes have significantly guided and will always influence the expression of funeral rites. Today's funeral directors working with modern families observe these changes every day, changes that include the following:

> ➢ Changed and more open attitudes towards marriage and divorce. The adults in a family unit may not be legally married, and divorce may not be stigmatized.
> ➢ Delayed exposure to death because of increased longevity and mobility.
> ➢ Increased likelihood of dying outside of the home in institutions such as hospitals, nursing homes, or hospice care facilities, in which individuals are separated from their families at the time of passing. Families may thereby experience little, if any, daily confrontation with death, including a decline towards death (*"visible death"*).
> ➢ The placement of older family members in nursing homes, retirement villages and other institutions, resulting in increased isolation from other family members. The death of these older family members becomes more abstract to the survivors.

On a broader level, social factors need to be acknowledged that can often contribute and affect American funeral rites and rituals. Some of the social factors that may influence the decision-making process during the arrangement conference are the following:

➢ **Abuse Awareness:** Whether a family wishes to acknowledge these factors, death does occur as a result of domestic violence, or a family may be dealing with the complicated dynamics of grieving an abuser. Today's funeral directors must be sensitive to the needs and desires of the family members within the context of these family dynamics.

➢ **Cohabitants:** In current times, it has become more common and accepted for two unrelated adults to share living quarters and to create a family structure representing a traditional family unit, such as a nuclear family, but without being legally married. Some families do this for purely economic reasons, while others form such units because the stigma of living together is not as taboo as it was 30 years ago.

➢ **Demographics:** The U.S. Census reveals that the American population has become more diverse than ever before in history, with ethnic minorities becoming the majority in some cases.

➢ **Divorce:** More than half of American families experience divorce. Funeral etiquette, including how decisions are made in such situations, can be complex when ex-spouses and former significant others are involved, either as decision-makers or as the deceased.

➢ **Economic Factors:** Interestingly, poorer families have tended to spend the most on funerals. Not only do they spend the highest overall dollar amount, but also the highest percentage of their available funds. Often, a funeral is one of the largest and most significant events to occur in the lives of some of these families.

➢ **Educational level:** Families with higher levels of education have tended to spend less on funerals compared with less educated families.

➢ **Ethnicity:** As the United States Census demonstrates, the ethnic and racial make-up of Americans is changing significantly and now, for example, Latinos are the largest minority group in the United States.

➢ **Family Structure:** A family can embody patriarchal, matriarchal, or egalitarian structures, and these societal frameworks impact decision-making and authority within the family dynamics. The distribution of decision-making power and authority within a family has repercussions on the choices made in funeral practices as well. The prevailing structure influences who take charge of decisions related to funeral arrangements and establishes the dynamics that shape the overall funeral planning process.

➤ **Geographic Factors:** Where a family lives will influence funeral rites. However, even when someone moves away from their place of origin, the family's funeral practices will typically continue to be practiced.

➤ **Government Structures:** Federal, state, and local laws and regulations play a key part in funeral choices and must often be balanced with cultural and religious expectations. Such agencies are **bureaucratic** in nature. **Bureaucratization** *is the creation of a system that governs, through departments and subdivisions managed by sets of officials who follow inflexible routines.*

➤ **Religion:** The Roman Catholic Church currently serves the largest number of professed religious adherents, and the Southern Baptist Church is second. However, in modern times, formal religion has generally played a lesser role in funeral customs, even when the families identify with a certain denomination. Also, fewer people report being formally affiliated with a religion, and even though some people do currently identify with a particular denomination, church attendance has decreased significantly over the past 20 years. Less than 30% of Americans attend church (worship) regularly.

➤ **Same-Sex Partnerships:** Serving the LGBTQ+ community may have social and legal challenges, depending on the geographical location.

➤ **Social Stratification:** Social stratification describes how one's social status is ranked according to income level, prestige, or power. One may therefore be considered *"upper-class," "middle-class,"* or *"lower-class."* A **class** is *a social grouping in which members possess generally equivalent culturally valued attributes or similar economic resources/levels (e.g., higher, middle, lower socioeconomic "class") but differ from members of another class.*

Funeral service choices may be made to reflect one's status (*"status symbol"*). The lowest stratification has the least access to resources such as health care that could extend life expectancy. Perhaps it is not surprising that this stratification of Americans tends to experience the highest frequency of death.

Generational Differences: In the contemporary workplace, employers and employees are navigating interactions among various generations simultaneously, leading to potential challenges arising from differences in attitudes and behaviors. Similarly, within the realm of funeral services, there exists a need to identify and fulfill the values and wishes of diverse generations. Although each generation possesses distinct attributes, some fundamental characteristics identify them.

➤ **Matures (born 1909-1945)**
  1. In the Workplace:
     ➤ Loyal to employer, superior interpersonal skills
     ➤ Believe promotion and raises should come from job tenure
     ➤ Value timeliness and productivity

2. In the Marketplace:
   - ➢ Tend to have faith in nation's institutions, companies, and government
   - ➢ Demand quality and place it before speed or efficiency
   - ➢ Are loyal customers
   - ➢ Follow rules
   - ➢ Believe standard options for products are fine without any need to customize

➢ **Baby Boomers (born 1946-1964)**
   1. In the Workplace:
      - ➢ Evaluate self and others based on a work ethic measured by hours worked
      - ➢ Believe teamwork is critical to success and relationship building
      - ➢ Expect loyalty from co-workers

   2. In the Marketplace:
      - ➢ Believe technology brings with it as many problems as it does solutions
      - ➢ Want products and services to be customized and made personalized (e.g., custom caskets)
      - ➢ Generally believe in following rules
      - ➢ Want products and services that will indicate success to their peers (e.g., obviously costlier funeral products)
      - ➢ Tend to be loyal, cautious customers

➢ **Generation X (born 1965-1980)**
   1. In the Workplace:
      - ➢ Are independent
      - ➢ Want open communication regardless of position or tenure
      - ➢ Respect production over tenure
      - ➢ Value efficiency and control of their time

   2. In the Marketplace:
      - ➢ Embrace technology
      - ➢ Are individualistic
      - ➢ Are media savvy
      - ➢ Research products & services prior to purchase
      - ➢ Are skeptical and not swayed by trends

➢ **Millennials (born 1981-2000)**
   1. In the Workplace:
      - ➢ Seek open communication, positive feedback, and affirmation
      - ➢ Find it less difficult to work with someone of the mature generation
      - ➢ Search for a job that provides personal fulfillment.

2. In the Marketplace:
   - ➢ Do not want to be hurried
   - ➢ Are loyal customers
   - ➢ Want to be like peers but with a unique twist
   - ➢ Value companies that possess an altruistic attitude
   - ➢ Want value and service
   - ➢ Prioritize technology

➢ **Generation Z (born 2001-2015)**
   1. In the Workplace:
      - ➢ Seek diversity and inclusion
      - ➢ Motivated by individuality and creativity
      - ➢ Adept at and expect electronic communication
      - ➢ Prefer managers closer to their generational cohort
      - ➢ Expect formal training
      - ➢ Prioritize work schedule flexibility over compensation and benefits

   2. In the Marketplace:
      - ➢ Prioritize value and convenience
      - ➢ Use technology to find lower cost
      - ➢ Value experiences over products
      - ➢ Prefer personalization

➢ **Generation Alpha** (Born 2015 to present)
   1. Projected to be the largest generation in the world's history.
   2. Shaped by technological advances and social media.
   3. Grew up experiencing how the world reacted to global and societal crisis.'

Basic Terminology and Concepts Relating to Sociology & Funeral Services:

Term/ Concept	Definition	Example/ Context
Funeral	Rites with the human remains present.	Sometimes known as traditional services, these services usually include embalming, visitation hours, and funeral services, followed by burial.
Memorial service	Funeral rites without the human remains present.	Popular with people who choose cremation as a means of final disposition; these funeral rites may or may not have visitations, services with or without the cremains present and possibly inurnment of the cremated at a cemetery or in a columbarium.
Funeral rite	Any funeral event performed in a prescribed manner.	The funeral rite honors the dead while bringing closure for the family members and friends, which could be public or private.
Social function	An event that allows individuals to gather as a community for sharing a common purpose.	A funeral, memorial service, or repast after these events are all examples of a social function.

Term/Concept	Definition	Example of Term/Concept
Traditional funeral rite	A funeral rite that follows a prescribed ritual or ceremony dictated either by religious belief or social custom.	A Russian Orthodox funeral service is an example of a traditional funeral rite.
Non-traditional funeral rite	A funeral rite that deviates from the normal or prescribed circumstances or established custom.	Having a surfer's funeral off the coast and in the water at their favorite place to surf.
Adaptive funeral rite	A funeral rite adjusted to the needs and desires of the deceased and family members or has been altered to suit modern trends.	A celebrant, after meeting with a family, alters their funeral service to be less religious and more focused on the life accomplishments of the deceased instead.
Humanistic funeral rite	A funeral rite devoid of religious connotation.	Absolutely no mention of God and devoid of prayers for the dead. Usually poems and stories about the deceased are shared at these types of services.
Immediate disposition	Any disposition of human remains completely devoid of any form of funeral rite at the time of disposition.	A graveside service conducted without a visitation or funeral service prior to the burial. For example, the burial of an unidentified individual or in Potters Field may be a basic burial without funeral rites because not enough information about the deceased is available to create a meaningful rite and no significant others to the deceased have been identified or are available to provide instructions for funeral rites. The deceased also may not have left any instructions for disposition.

Cultural Influences on Caring for the Dead and Funeral Arrangements. These are terms that influence the American culture on caring for the dead:

Term/Concept	Definition	Example how it applies to death within society
Customs	Social behavior as directed by the traditions of the people.	In the Jewish tradition, it is customary to bury the dead within 24 hours from the time of death.
Norms	A group of beliefs about how members should behave in a given context.	The funeral director makes their presence known at a funeral but does not do anything to draw attention towards them and away from helping the bereaved grieve the loss of their loved one.
Mores	*Must* behaviors, the basic and important patterns of ideas and acts of a people that call for strong reactions from society if violated.	Care, respect, and dignity must be always given to the dead. If a funeral director mishandles human remains or demonstrates disrespect to the remains society will become outraged.

Term/Concept	Definition	Example how it applies to death within society
Taboos	A social prohibition of certain actions.	A bereaved spouse dating the deceased's sibling may be considered unacceptable or "weird" even if legal.
Folkways	Behaviors construed as somewhat less compulsive than mores of the same society, which do not call for a strong reaction from society if violated.	Norms of etiquette not very serious if broken like chewing gum during a funeral service. While such an act may be perceived by some as not proper etiquette, it can be overlooked by many.
Laws	Rules of action prescribed by an authority able to enforce them at will.	Stealing pre-need funds and using these funds for personal use rather than funeral needs of the consumer.
Rules	Specific procedures to be followed.	The rules of embalming. Specific procedural methods that must be followed on all embalming cases (e.g., receiving oral or written permission before beginning the embalming process).
Symbols	An object or act that represents a belief of idea.	The Star of David is a symbol of the Jewish faith, and the crucifix is the symbol of the Roman Catholic faith.

How are social behaviors learned? Most social behaviors are learned through enculturation (or socialization). Enculturation *is the method by which social values are internalized and learned.* The vast number of human interactions experienced over a person's lifetime, in addition to the cultural milieu in which the person is raised, shape and molds human development. Death is an element of enculturation that is part of a person's social development. The way a person responds to the death event is in part because social values are internalized and learned based on past experiences. These internalized social values give shape to a prescribed set of rituals that are expected when caring for the dead. **Direct learning** *is the acquiring of a culture by a person through deliberate instruction by other members of society, or formal learning.* Religious groups use direct learning to form a conceptual framework that supports their ideology. To be a full member of the religious group, learning the customs and rituals of the group gives shape to human behavior. **Indirect learning** *is a process by which a person learns norms within their culture by observation of others in their society.* Some death customs are not taught directly, but rather learned by watching older family members care for their dead with a prescribed set of rituals and behaviors. Some older generations practice certain funeral customs, not because of direct or indirect learning, but rather because of a **lifelong** entrenched set of understanding that "this is the way it is done." Of all the socialization skillsets, such observational learning has limited identifiable links to why the customs and rituals are performed. Finally, **diffusion** *is the process by which a cultural item spreads from group-to-group or from society-to-society.* An example of this socialization concept would be Jewish people placing a shovel full of dirt on the casket as part of the committal service. Some Christian groups use either sand or dirt and place it on the casket as part of their burial ritual.

The following are other sociological terms related to funeral services:

Term/Concept	Definition	Example how it applies to death within society
Class	A group that shares a common social status or standing based on factors such as income, education, occupation, or individual accomplishments.	The majority of people in the Unites States are middle class, middle income families.
Culture	The rules, ideas, and beliefs shared by members of a society of and for the living and the dying, which may be learned directly or indirectly.	The Catholic Church has a prescribed set of rules, customs, and rituals performed when burying the dead.
Subculture	A division or smaller identifiable unit of a culture having their own unique traits and customs.	The Knights of Columbus is a subculture within the Catholic Church that has their own way of honoring their members when they die.
Demographics	Quantitative data about a people that can be analyzed statistically (e.g., race, age, sex, socioeconomic status, religious affiliation, etc.).	The demographic of a funeral home has changed over the past 30 years. Though they served Ukrainian Orthodox people previously, now the neighborhood consists mostly of Latino Catholics.
Ethnocentrism	The emotional attitude that one's own race, nation, group, or culture is superior to all others.	The Ku Klux Klan is an example of an ethnocentric group.
Culture Shock	The feelings of disorientation, uncertainty, and even fear that people experience when they encounter unfamiliar cultural practices.	Attending a Buddhist burial service where various burial customs are performed, which are unlike the Christian burial customs a person learned while growing up.
Cultural Universal	Common traits and patterns found in all cultures.	While the specific details may differ, all cultures have some set of rituals and customs for caring for the dead with respect and dignity.
Cultural Relativism	The emotional attitude that all cultures are pertinent.	Making a negative judgment call of a custom or ritual based of one's own world view. Such cultural bias could affect the way the funeral director approaches a foreign culture, religious traditions, and customs.

The following are funeral specific terminology that are important concepts to know to understand how they are part of funeral customs in society:

Term/Concept	Definition	Example how it applies to death within society
Religion	A culturally entrenched pattern of behaviors made up of: 1) sacred beliefs, 2) emotional feelings accompanying the beliefs, and 3) overt conduct presumably implementing such beliefs and feelings.	The Catholic Church, for example, is a religion whose focus is the consecration of the Eucharist during spiritual events like baptism, weddings, and funerals. Their belief is that Jesus is truly present in the Eucharist, and by consuming Communion during the funeral service, he becomes part of their grieving experience.
Ceremony	An established or prescribed procedure for a religious or other rite. Considered a formal activity conducted for an important occasion (e.g., a wedding or a funeral). The ceremony includes all the rituals that mark the occasion.	A funeral could be classified as a type of ceremony.
Ritual	Similar to a ceremony. The ritual is the series of actions that make up the ceremony.	In baptism, pouring water over a person's head is the ritual that is a part of the ceremony.
Rite	An event performed in a prescribed manner.	The Rite of Christian Burial is the Catholic Church's prescribed manner of conducting a funeral.
Innovation	The process of introducing new ideas or objects to a culture through discovery or invention.	Displaying objects important to the deceased's life at the funeral home allows attendees more insight into who the deceased was and what they valued.

Participant Roles:

> Celebrating the life of the deceased has become more common as opposed to burying the dead.

> Family members are becoming less passive and much more actively involved in the funeral process.

> Regarding increased instances of clergy not present, increasing responsibility has been placed on the funeral director rather to provide solace and grief counseling to modern families.

> Some funeral directors have become trained celebrants so they can lead funeral and committal services.

> Modern funeral directors are now expected to be familiar with the use of technology to provide services such as digital death announcements and obituaries, video tributes, merchandise selection, streaming of rites, electronic guest books, video tributes, data management systems, and so on. Although there may be a concern about the deterioration of the human contact aspect of bereavement, modern technology has also enabled a greater ability for many to participate in funeral service, especially concerning family and friends who cannot travel from long distances.

As social trends change, so does the way the consumer selects merchandise and services to care for their loved ones, which are some of the factors that represent the shift in consumer's selection of services and merchandise:

Selection of Funeral Homes and Disposition Sites: The availability of modern transportation such as the automobile and air travel now enables families to travel farther distances to attend funerals and for remains to be shipped over great distances in less time. Additionally, mobility means families can travel to funeral services in different locations, thus giving them the ability to select services and sites by style, quality, and attractiveness rather than simple proximity. For example, some families will select green burials. However, the nearest natural cemetery could be 125 miles away. If this new means of final disposition is chosen, travel distance and cost associated with such a burial would be minor and enable a burial that represents a family's lifestyle and beliefs.

Preparation of human remains and social trends: There may be little or no preparation depending on the type of services chosen. For example, cremation has become a more popular disposition option, as has anatomical gift donation, for which minimal preparation of the human remains is required. However, most families, if provided options during the arrangement conference, will select some type of services that help in mourning the loss of their loved one while honoring their life accomplishments.

Casket selection: While earthen burial in a metal casket is still the top choice of final disposition, the casket may no longer be a major portion of funeral expenses. There has been a shift in the types of merchandise selected by the consumer. Some families who wish to have cremation as a means of final disposition would still like a visitation with a funeral service prior to cremation. They may select either a cremation casket or a ceremonial casket (rental casket). This shift in consumer spending has allowed some funeral providers to give consumers more options other than direct cremation with an alternative container.

Disposition Options: Most recently, cremation, body donations, entombment, "green" burials, natural organic reduction, and alkaline hydrolysis have increased. Some of these means of final disposition are pending legislative modifications in a number of states, before being implemented. Nevertheless, the new methods require the funeral director to redefine their business practices to accommodate the consumer's needs and method of final disposition.

Location of the Funeral: Rather than the traditional church or funeral home, selection of non-traditional facilities, including banquet halls, parks or organizational meeting places, such as the Elks or Moose Lodges has risen. The alternate location allows families to have food and drink alongside the services that honor their loved one. Some states have now permitted funeral homes to provide food and beverages during visitations and funerals. Again, the prudent funeral director needs to redefine their funeral practices and services to meet the social needs and trends of the consumer.

Modern Funerals

Funeral Rites: While funeral rites structured by religious traditions continue to be part of the chosen selections, newer funeral rites are now increasingly accepted and chosen including what follows:

> ➤ **Adaptive Funeral Rite:** *A funeral rite adjusted to the needs and wants of those directly involved; one which has been altered to suit the trends of the times.* For example, to include the values of an inter-faith family, a representative of each religion could speak on behalf of the deceased.
>
> ➤ **Humanistic Funeral Rite:** *A funeral rite generally devoid of religious connotation.* For example, a celebrant can provide a tribute to the deceased that includes stories and information provided by family and friends.
>
> ➤ **Immediate Disposition:** *Any disposition of human remains completely devoid of any form of funeral rite at the time of disposition.* Although the remains are still required to be treated respectfully, the deceased is simply buried, possibly because there is no identified relation to make decisions, and the deceased has not left instructions for disposition.

Fundamental Family Structures: To work appropriately with families, funeral service directors must understand their structure and the dynamics of how families function as a unit. More importantly, the funeral director must understand the role the deceased had in the family, and the impact that the death of a specific family member has had on the family. Upon the death of a family member, the funeral director must also recognize and respect the dynamics of authority in the family unit to assist with the decisions that must be made during the funeral arrangements.

Purpose of the Family: A family is considered a social unit with an obligation to care for other members included in the unit. Among the responsibilities a family has are to teach, to maintain order, to guide, and to motivate. When death occurs, the family unit's structure is disrupted. The funeral director could encounter internal dysfunctions that may surface as a result of the death while the family struggles to develop a new stable family unit without the deceased.

Types of Family Government: While the field of sociology recognizes 20-25 different forms of family structures, the following are the most commonly recognized:

> ➤ **Patriarchal:** *The father rules the family and power and property are typically passed to the oldest male child.*
>
> ➤ **Matriarchal:** *The mother rules the family, with a woman holding a position analogous to that of a patriarch.*
>
> ➤ **Egalitarian:** *Males and females have equal rights, duties, and governing power.*

Types of Family Structure

Extended (Joint) Family: *Membership within household includes the father and mother, all their children (except married daughters who live with their spouses), and their sons' wives and children (except married daughters who live with their spouses) living in one household.* An example of such a family structure are Amish families. Historically common characteristics may include the following:

- ➢ *Patriarchal government structure*: The father is considered the head of the family.
- ➢ *Agrarian (agricultural-based):* This family structure is more commonly based in rural, farm-based environments.
- ➢ *Economics:* This family structure is often extremely self-sufficient and less reliant on outside resources.
- ➢ *Religious function:* Religion is seen as central to the family structure and religious activities may be held at home.
- ➢ *Gender roles:* Women are generally expected to be subservient.
- ➢ *Restricted mobility:* Families can span several generations in the same location. Members of this family structure may not travel very far from home unless required to do so.
- ➢ *Impact of death on a member:* Depending on which member dies, the family government structure may be impacted, but with this form of family structure, the duties that the deceased may have had can be readily fulfilled by remaining family members.

Recently, there has been a movement away from the joint family structure because of social influences such as industrialization and urbanization. Industrialization offered family members employment outside of the family unit but coupled with the loss of artisanship skills resulted in increased dependence on outside resources for survival. Urbanization, or the movement of families to more populated cities, increased anonymity and bureaucratization, making it more difficult for funeral service directors to truly know each family as they might have as neighbors sharing a smaller community. Increased bureaucratization also made crafting funeral rites unique and reflective of a family more challenging.

- ➢ **Modified Extended Family:** *A nuclear family linked to another nuclear family.* Modified extended families are linked by*:*
    - *(a) nuclear families related by marriage, such as sisters with their respective husbands and children, or*
    - *(b) friendships.*

- ➢ **Nuclear Family:** *Membership within this type of family unit includes one man, one woman, and their children, if any.*
    - Historically common characteristics may include:
        - (a) Patriarchal, matriarchal or egalitarian government structure, with the power and prestige of membership not uniformly determinable.
        - (b) The income of the family unit in its economic structure, with both adults in the family unit possibly working outside of the home.
        - (c) The religious function, if any, being institution-based rather than home-based.

(d) The social and actual physical mobility of this family unit being relatively flexible. This family unit may be able to move from one social class level to another or from location to location more readily than other types of family structures.

(e) A significant impact on the family unit from the death of an adult member. For example, the death of the family breadwinner or of either spouse if both contribute financially, may cause great economic hardships on the remaining spouse. Additionally, the death of either mate leaves the remaining spouse to rear children alone (*"single-parent family"*) as well as entry to a new societal status as a widow or widower.

➤ **Blended Family:** *In this family unit, membership consists of one male and one female and the children from their previous marriages. This family unit may also include children from the present marriage.* This type of family unit is very prevalent in society, for divorce and remarriage are accepted forms of serial monogamy.

➤ **Multigenerational Household**: *This type of family unit can be similar to the extended (joint) family but may not be agriculturally based ("agrarian").*

➤ **Common-Law Marriage:** *A marriage recognized in some but not all jurisdictions and premised on the partners' perspective that they are married and their cohabitation status.* Common-Law marriages are not recognized in most states. Domestic partnerships are a similar type of family unit. Such arrangements share living quarters, household responsibilities and in some situations, child rearing.

How Family Affects the Funeral Rite

Family structure plays an important role in shaping the funeral rites, influencing the dynamics and decision-making within the grieving process. In patriarchal family structures, in which authority is typically vested in a male figure, funeral decisions may be centralized around this individual, impacting the choice of funeral rituals and the overall tone of the ceremony. Conversely, matriarchal family structures, in which a female holds significant authority, may see funeral planning decisions influenced by the preferences and values of the female head of the family. In egalitarian family structures, decisions are shared more evenly among family members, and funeral rites may be collaborative endeavors, reflecting a collective consensus.

Patriarchal Family Structure

In Indian culture, in which cremation is a common means of final disposition, a specific example of how patriarchal family structures influence funeral decisions can be observed in the role of the male head of the family, often the father or eldest son. In such families, the authority vested in the male figure can significantly impact the choice of funeral rituals and the overall tone of the ceremony. For instance, the patriarch may play a central role in deciding whether the funeral will follow traditional Hindu rites, including specific rituals, prayers, and offerings, or if it will incorporate more contemporary elements.

The patriarch's influence extends to decisions about the location of the cremation, the type of cremation ceremony, and the duration and nature of mourning rituals that follow. His preferences may also shape considerations related to the immersion of ashes in a sacred river or the scattering of ashes at a specific location. The patriarch's authority in determining the funeral process reflects not only cultural traditions but also the familial hierarchy. This centralized decision-making by the male figure impacts the entire family's experience during the funeral, for the rituals chosen and the overall tone of the ceremony are influenced by his leadership and cultural values. Funeral professionals working with families in this cultural context must be attuned to these dynamics to provide personalized and culturally sensitive services.

Matriarchal Family Structure

In many Native American culture, the matriarch often plays an integral role in the planning of funeral ceremonies, contributing to decisions that honor traditions and spiritual beliefs. For example, the matriarch may guide choices related to ceremonial practices such as smudging rituals, drumming ceremonies, or the inclusion of sacred elements like sage or sweetgrass. The choice between burial and cremation, as well as the selection of a burial site, may be influenced by the matriarch's connection to ancestral lands and cultural traditions. Furthermore, the matriarch may prioritize involving extended family and community members in the mourning process, emphasizing communal support and unity during the funeral rites. Understanding the matriarch's essential role is crucial for funeral professionals working with Native American families, ensuring that funeral ceremonies respect and align with the cultural significance and spiritual values that the matriarch holds within the community.

Egalitarian Family Structure

In egalitarian family structures, prevalent in American culture, funeral rights are typically influenced by shared decision-making among family members. For instance, when planning a funeral, decisions related to the choice between a traditional burial and cremation may be reached through collaborative discussions involving all family members. In egalitarian settings, various family members might contribute equally to decisions about the type of service, incorporating a mix of religious or secular elements that resonate with the diverse beliefs within the family. The egalitarian approach often extends to other aspects of the funeral, such as the selection of readings, music, and the design of the funeral or memorial service. In these families, the egalitarian ethos fosters an environment in which everyone's input is valued, ensuring that the funeral reflects a collective representation of the deceased's life and the shared values of the family. This inclusive decision-making process in egalitarian family structures contributes to a funeral that is meaningful and resonant for all involved.

Additionally, family structure can impact the level of involvement and support each family member provides during the funeral rite. The relationships among siblings, parents, and extended family members can shape the extent of emotional and practical assistance offered, affecting the overall experience and outcomes of the funeral process. Understanding the nuances of family dynamics is crucial for funeral directors to navigate and address the varying needs and expectations of each family structure, ensuring that funeral rites are conducted with sensitivity and respect for the unique family dynamics at play.

Changes in Culture and Social Mobility

Changes in culture and social mobility have together shaped a more diverse and dynamic society. As cultures evolve, the traditions and rituals associated with funerals undergo a parallel transformation, influenced by the increased interaction brought about by social mobility. This blending of cultures has fostered a pluralistic approach to funeral customs, allowing traditional religious rites to be modified or combined with secular elements to accommodate diverse belief systems. The accessibility to alternative funeral practices from various cultural traditions has expanded, providing individuals with a broader range of choices for their funeral arrangements. In this evolving landscape, the perception of funerals has shifted from somber events to celebrations of a person's life, marked by personalization and unique ways of remembering the deceased. Changing cultural norms have impacted decisions regarding burial versus cremation, and environmental considerations, such as green burials and eco-friendly cremations, have gained prominence.

Moreover, economic factors influenced by social mobility contribute to varying preferences in funeral expenditures. The rise of social media has introduced new avenues for memorialization, allowing people to share memories and attend virtual funeral services online. The breakdown of traditional family structures due to social mobility has affected the dynamics of funeral decision-making, prompting funeral professionals to be more adaptable and inclusive. As cultural diversity increases, individuals often prioritize creating meaningful experiences during funerals, moving away from strict adherence to cultural or religious norms. The decreasing stigma against discussing death has fostered open conversations about funeral preferences, and cultural and social shifts have given rise to the proactive trend of pre-planning funerals to align with individual wishes. Overall, these changes underscore a transformation in the funeral landscape, emphasizing individualization, inclusivity, and reflection of the diverse societies in which we live.

Contemporary Social Factors

Contemporary social factors exert significant influence on funeral rites, reflecting the evolving landscape of societal values and norms. Economics plays an important role as individuals and families, affected by financial considerations, make decisions about funeral arrangements. Social stratification and class dynamics contribute to varied funeral practices, with different socioeconomic groups often adopting distinct approaches. Geographic factors and neo-localism impact funeral arrangements as families, influenced by factors like relocation, may seek services that align with their new communities. Religion continues to be a crucial determinant, shaping funeral rituals and ceremonies in accordance with spiritual beliefs.

Government regulations also play a role, with legal frameworks affecting aspects of funeral planning such as burial practices and cemetery regulations. Educational levels can influence the extent of customization in funeral services, as individuals with higher levels of education may seek more personalized and unique arrangements. Ethnicity contributes to diverse funeral practices, as cultural traditions and customs play a significant role in shaping how individuals are memorialized.

The prevalence of divorce and dysfunctional family dynamics may introduce complexities in decision-making, potentially leading to varied preferences and conflicts in funeral arrangements. The recognition of same-sex partnerships has prompted a shift in funeral practices, with an increasing acknowledgment of diverse family structures and preferences. The rise of cohabitants as a familial unit introduces considerations for funeral professionals to navigate the dynamics of relationships outside traditional marriages.

Moreover, disposition options, such as cremation, burial, or eco-friendly alternatives reflect changing environmental concerns and individual preferences. These contemporary social factors collectively impact funeral arrangements by contributing to a more diverse, personalized, and inclusive landscape. Funeral professionals must navigate these complexities with sensitivity and adaptability to meet the unique needs and preferences of individuals and families in the modern social context.

Modern Trends and Shift in Funeralization

Over the past 50 years, the perception of modern American funeral rites has undergone a substantial transformation. Traditionally influenced by religious customs, contemporary practices now place less emphasis on strict conformity and more on celebrating the life accomplishments of the deceased. This shift reflects a broader societal move toward individualization and the recognition of diverse belief systems. The advent of the Covid-19 pandemic had a profound impact on societal funeral practices, imposing restrictions on gatherings, altering mourning rituals, and prompting creative adaptations in funeral planning.

The involvement and roles of family and friends during funerals have experienced significant changes due to the pandemic. Attendance limitations, social distancing measures, and health concerns have reshaped customary gestures of support, making it challenging for loved ones to participate in the mourning process as they once did.

The rise of virtual memorials and online attendance options has emerged as a response to these challenges, leveraging technology to bridge physical distances. However, as technology evolves, there is a growing concern about people becoming increasingly detached from the human experience. The convenience of virtual alternatives may inadvertently contribute to a decline in the appreciation for the significance of honoring the dead in traditional public services. The immersive and communal aspects of physically attending a funeral, sharing condolences, and collectively expressing grief may be compromised as individuals opt for digital interactions.

This detachment from the tangible and shared grieving process could potentially lead to a shift in social behavior, creating a society in which the value of public funeral services diminishes. Such a shift may contribute to complicated grief, as the absence of communal rituals and shared expressions of mourning may impact the healing process and individuals' ability to find solace and support in their grief journey. Balancing the convenience of technology with the essential human need for shared, physical experiences in times of loss becomes a critical consideration in the evolving landscape of funeral practices.

Additionally, the broader societal trend toward decreased social connections, exacerbated by factors like busy lifestyles and digital interactions, has further impacted funeral planning and services. Families may find themselves navigating funeral arrangements with less immediate community support, prompting a reevaluation of traditional practices. Funeral professionals have had to adapt to these evolving dynamics, incorporating more flexible and personalized approaches to meet the diverse needs of families in an era of changing social structures. Despite these shifts, the fundamental purpose of funerals remains paramount: to provide a meaningful and respectful farewell to the departed while navigating the nuanced complexities of contemporary society.

The Role of the Funeral Director in the Shift in Consumer Trends

The evolving cultural shift in consumer attitudes towards funeral services necessitates a transformative role for funeral directors, placing increased responsibilities on them to navigate this changing perception. Beyond traditional responsibilities, funeral directors are now expected to possess a deeper knowledge of social sciences, enabling them to comprehend the intricate dynamics of diverse family structures, evolving societal norms, and the psychological aspects of grief. As the emphasis on personalization and unique funeral practices grows, funeral directors are called upon to be not only service providers but also counselors, requiring a heightened ability to empathetically support the bereaved through their grief journey.

Cremation stands as a chosen means of final disposition. However, a prevalent misconception among funeral directors arises when consumers opt for cremation; some immediately presume a default to direct cremation without accompanying services. This misconception is exacerbated by certain funeral directors who inadvertently contribute to the detachment from the human experience in two significant ways. First, some neglect to have consumers identify their loved ones before the cremation process, disregarding the importance of both identification and the psychological significance this act holds for the bereaved. Ignoring this psychological function not only disconnects the bereaved from a critical part of the grieving process but also runs the risk of potential litigation if the wrong human remains are cremated.

Second, there is a failure among some funeral directors to offer ceremonial options that aid the grieving process. The lack of such options perpetuates the disconnection by not providing avenues for the bereaved to acknowledge the death event and connect meaningfully with their own grieving experience. The process of grieving is most effectively undertaken within a sociological setting where the mourning is shared openly. In this communal environment, friends and family members unite as a social unit to provide support and empathy to the bereaved. Simultaneously, they pay tribute to the life achievements of the deceased and the impactful contributions they made to the collective development of people's lives. In family situations marked by tumultuous relations with the deceased, funeral services have the potential to serve as an opportunity for healing and forgiveness. Despite strained relationships resulting from the actions of the departed, the funeral can become a cathartic moment for reconciliation and a chance to mend emotional wounds within the family.

This sociological approach to griefwork creates a sacred space where individuals can share their sorrow, find solace in communal support, and collectively honor the legacy of the departed. Addressing these aspects is crucial to ensuring that cremation, as a chosen disposition method, is accompanied by a thoughtful and supportive approach that acknowledges the emotional needs of those mourning the loss of a loved one.

Moreover, funeral directors are challenged to innovate and create new funeral practices that resonate with the changing cultural and social factors influencing funerals, which involves adapting traditional rituals to accommodate diverse beliefs, facilitating more celebratory and life-honoring ceremonies, and providing options that reflect the unique qualities of the deceased. The integration of technology is a critical aspect of this adaptation, for funeral directors must embrace digital platforms for virtual memorials, online attendance options, and innovative ways of memorializing the deceased in the digital realm.

A holistic approach to technology is essential, not just for the logistical aspects of funeral services but also for facilitating a meaningful connection to the grieving experience. Funeral directors are increasingly tasked with using technology to bridge physical distances, allowing families and friends to share their grief collectively. This shift requires funeral directors to be not only technologically adept but also attuned to the emotional and spiritual dimensions of the grieving process, ensuring that the use of technology enhances rather than diminishes the human connection in times of loss. In essence, the emerging role of the funeral director involves a multifaceted skill set that encompasses social sciences, counseling, innovative practices, and a holistic embrace of technology, all aimed at facilitating a meaningful and supportive journey through the grieving process for those they serve.

Sociology in Funeral Services Glossary

Adaptive funeral rite - A funeral rite adjusted to the needs and desires of the deceased and family members or which has been altered to suit modern trends.

Agrarian – Related to agriculture or being farm-based. Considered the original locale of the extended (joint) family structure.

Anonymity – When a person or entity's identity is unknown.

Blended family - Membership consists of one male and one female and the children from their previous marriages. May also include children from the present marriage.

Bureaucratization - Systems that governing, through numerous levels of departments and subdivisions in an inflexible manner. Not responsive to the needs of the individual.

Ceremony (ritual) - An established or prescribed procedure for a religious or other rite. Considered a formal activity conducted for an important occasion (e.g., a wedding, a funeral).

Class - A social grouping in which members possess generally equivalent culturally valued attributes or similar economic resources/levels (e.g., higher, middle, lower socioeconomic "class").

Cohabitants – Two unrelated adults sharing living quarters without being legally married.

Common-law marriage – A marriage recognized in some but not all jurisdictions and premised on the partners' perspective that they are married and their cohabitation status.

Contemporary - Living or happening in the same time period. Considered the present time.

Cultural assimilation – The process by which a group's language, culture, and so o becomes incorporated into another's.

Cultural relativism - The emotional attitude that all cultures are equal and pertinent.

Cultural universal - Common traits or patterns existing in all cultures. For example, all cultures deal with death.

Culture - Consists of abstract patterns of the rules, ideas, beliefs shared by members of society, including for living and dying, which are learned directly or indirectly.

Culture Shock – Experience of disorientation, uncertainty, and anxiety when encountering unfamiliar cultural practices.

Customs - Social behavior as dictated by the tradition of a people.

Demographic - Quantitative data about a people that can be analyzed statistically (e.g., race, age, sex, socioeconomic status, religious affiliation, etc.).

Diffusion – How a cultural process or concept spreads from group to group or from one society to another.

Direct learning – Formal teaching and learning.

Egalitarian - Males and females have equal rights, duties, and governing power.

Enculturation (AKA "socialization") - The method by which the social values are internalized (learned).

Ethnicity - Any of the basic divisions or groups of humankind, distinguished by customs, characteristics, language, and so on.

Ethnocentrism - The emotional attitude that one's own race, nation, group, or culture is superior to all others.

Extended (joint) family - Membership within household includes father and mother, all their children (except married daughters), and their son's wives and children (except married daughters).

Family of orientation - The family into which one is born.

Family of procreation - The family established by one's marriage and the production of children.

Folkways - Behaviors construed as somewhat less compulsive than mores of the same society, and do not call for a strong reaction from society if violated. Does not involve moral foundations.

Funeral - Rites with the body present.

Funeral rite - An all-inclusive term used to encompass all funerals or memorial services.

Funeralization - A process involving all activities associated with final disposition.

Hospice – a home or facility-based palliative care service for the terminally ill.

Humanistic funeral rite - A funeral rite devoid of religious connotation.

Immediate disposition - Any disposition of human remains without any form of funeral rite at the time of disposition.

Industrialization - The change from independent, multi-talented, self-sufficient family units to employment of family members in jobs outside the unit, increasing dependency on outside resources for their total needs.

Laws - Formal norms that protect particular social mores and are typically the most strictly enforced in comparison to folkways and other social mores. Considered rules of societal conduct of what is right and prohibiting and restricting what is wrong.

Matriarchal - The mother rules the family. A woman holding a position analogous to that of a patriarch.

Memorial service - Funeral rites with the body not present.

Mobility - The state or quality of being mobile; the ability to move from place to place readily, or to move from class to class, either up or down.

Modern - Of or characteristic of the present or recent times. Not ancient, and often used to designate *certain contemporary tendencies.*

Mores - Must-behaviors, or the social norms that demonstrate the moral and often religious expectations of a group (e.g., as related to the treatment of the dead) and call for a strong reaction from society if violated.

Multigenerational-household - Three or more generations of the same immediate family living in the same house, (e.g., grandparents, adult children and grandchildren). Similar to an extended (joint) family, but not necessarily existing in an agricultural ("agrarian") environment.

Neo-localism - The tendency of offspring to move away from the area in which they were born.

Non-traditional funeral rite - A funeral rite that deviates from the normal or prescribed circumstances or established custom.

Norms – A societal belief about how members should behave.

Nuclear family - Membership within household that includes one man, one woman, and their children, if any.

Patriarchal - The father rules the family and power and property are typically passed to the oldest male child.

Pre-literate society - A culture developed before the invention of writing, and hence, leaving no written record.

Primitive funeral rite - A funeral rite that may be construed as being identifiable with a pre-literate society.

Religion - A culturally entrenched pattern of behavior made up of:
    1) sacred beliefs,
    2) emotional feelings accompanying the beliefs, and
    3) overt conduct presumably implementing the beliefs and feelings.

Rite - Any event performed in a solemn and prescribed manner.

Rites of passage - Ceremonies centering on transition in life from one status to another (e.g., baptism, marriage, funerals).

Ritual (also see "ceremony") - An established or prescribed procedure for a religious or other rite. Considered a formal activity conducted for an important occasion (e.g., a wedding, a funeral).

Rules - Specified procedural methods.

Single-parent family - Membership consists of one adult, either male or female, and his/her children.

Social function - An event in which people come together to share in that event (e.g., a funeral).

Social stratification - Categorization of people by money, prestige and power. A ranking of social status (position) in groups such as upper, middle, and lower class.

Socialization (AKA "enculturation") - The method by which social values are internalized (learned).

Society - A group of people forming a single community with some interests in common.

Sociology - The science of social groups and human social interactions.

Step-family - The family one acquires when one enters a new marriage that already has children, with the *parent having been widowed or divorced.*

Subculture - A division or smaller identifiable unit of culture connected to that culture by common traits, but also having unique traits to itself (e.g., ethnicity, religion, language, geography, etc.).

Symbol - Anything such as a tangible object or an act to which socially created meaning is given.

Taboos – Must-behavior that dictates that the individual must abstain from certain acts dealing with death.

Traditional funeral rite - A funeral rite that follows a prescribed ritual or ceremony dictated either by religious belief or social custom.

Urbanization - The change from rural to urban in character.

Psychology of Funeral Directing

What is Psychology?

Psychology *is the scientific study of the mind and behavior, exploring both conscious and unconscious mental processes.* It is used to understand how individuals think, feel, and behave in various situations. Rooted in empirical research, psychology employs systematic methods to observe, measure, and analyze human behavior and mental processes. Psychologists aim to uncover underlying principles and mechanisms that influence individual and group behavior. The field encompasses diverse areas such as cognitive, developmental, social, and clinical psychology, each addressing specific aspects of human experience. Psychologists use various research methods, including experiments, surveys, and observations to gather data and draw conclusions. Understanding the influence of biological factors, social interactions, and cultural contexts is integral to psychological analysis. Psychological theories help explain human behavior and contribute to practical applications in fields like therapy, education, and organizational management. The interdisciplinary nature of psychology connects it to biology, sociology, and neuroscience, broadening its scope and impact on understanding the complexities of the human mind.

Schools of Psychological Thought

Structuralism: Developed by Wilhelm Wundt, structuralism was aimed to analyze the basic elements of consciousness through introspection. It focused on breaking down mental processes into elemental components to understand the structure of the human mind.

Functionalism: Originating with William James, functionalism emphasized the adaptive functions of consciousness and behavior in helping individuals interact with their environment. It explored the purpose and utility of mental processes.

Behaviorism: Pioneered by John B. Watson and later B.F. Skinner, behaviorism focused on observable behavior as a response to stimuli. It rejected the study of mental processes and consciousness, emphasizing the role of environmental factors in shaping behavior.

Gestalt: Gestalt psychology, led by Max Wertheimer, emphasized holistic perception and the idea that the mind organizes stimuli into a unified whole. It focused on studying how people perceive and interpret visual information.

Cognitive: Emerging in the mid-20th century, cognitive psychology, influenced by Jean Piaget and others, shifted the focus back to mental processes, including memory, problem-solving, and decision-making, to understand how people think and process information.

Psychoanalytic: Founded by Sigmund Freud, psychoanalytic theory delves into the unconscious mind, emphasizing the role of unconscious desires and conflicts in shaping behavior. It explores the impact of early childhood experiences on personality development.

Humanistic: Developed by Carl Rogers and Abraham Maslow, humanistic psychology emphasizes individual potential, personal growth, and the importance of self-actualization. It focuses on understanding subjective experiences and the pursuit of personal fulfillment.

Biological: Biological psychology explores the biological basis of behavior and mental processes, examining the role of the nervous system, neurotransmitters, and genetics in shaping psychological phenomena.

Physiological: The physiological perspective investigates the biological mechanisms underlying psychological processes in understanding how the brain, hormones, and bodily functions contribute to behavior and mental functions.

Sociocultural: Sociocultural psychology examines how cultural and social factors influence behavior and mental processes. It considers the impact of societal norms, cultural values, and social interactions on individual and group psychology.

The Understanding of the Mind

The various schools of psychology contribute distinct perspectives that collectively enhance our understanding of human behavior and the workings of the human mind. Structuralism, by breaking down consciousness into basic elements, laid the foundation for studying the mind's structure. Functionalism expanded this understanding by focusing on the adaptive functions of behavior, highlighting the purpose and utility of mental processes.

Behaviorism shifted the focus to observable behavior and environmental influences, providing insights into how external factors shape human actions. Gestalt psychology emphasized holistic perception, offering valuable insights into how individuals organize and interpret sensory information. The cognitive school, in turn, refocused on mental processes, shedding light on memory, problem-solving, and information processing.

Psychoanalytic theory delved into the unconscious mind, revealing the profound impact of unconscious desires and early experiences on behavior. Humanistic psychology added a positive perspective, emphasizing individual potential, personal growth, and the pursuit of self-actualization.

Biological psychology and physiological perspectives explore the biological basis of behavior, examining the role of the nervous system, genetics, and bodily functions. These perspectives reveal the intricate connections between physiological processes and psychological phenomena.

Sociocultural psychology expands understanding by considering cultural and social factors, highlighting the influence of societal norms, cultural values, and social interactions on behavior. The integration of these diverse schools provides a comprehensive framework for understanding the complexities of human behavior, acknowledging the interplay among biological, cognitive, emotional, and environmental factors in shaping the human experience. Each school contributes a unique lens, enriching the collective understanding of the intricacies of the human mind and behavior.

Specialty Areas in Psychology

> **Behavioral Psychology**: Specializing in observable behavior and its environmental influences; behavioral psychology informs interventions, therapies, and strategies for behavior modification; contributing practical insights into learning and behavioral change.

> **Clinical Psychology**: Focused on the assessment, diagnosis, and treatment of mental health disorders, clinical psychology plays a crucial role in providing therapeutic interventions, psychological assessments, and counseling services to individuals with psychological challenges.

> **Cognitive Psychology**: By investigating mental processes such as perception, memory, and problem-solving, cognitive psychology enhances our understanding of how individuals process information, aiding in the development of cognitive therapies, educational strategies, and interventions for cognitive disorders.

> **Counseling Psychology**: Specializing in helping individuals cope with life challenges and transitions, counseling psychology provides therapeutic support, guidance, and interventions to enhance mental well-being, making it integral to addressing everyday stressors and personal development.

> **Psychoanalysis:** Rooted in Freudian theory, psychoanalysis delves into the unconscious mind, contributing to in-depth explorations of unconscious conflicts and desires, providing a foundation for psychodynamic therapies and insight-oriented approaches.

> **Developmental Psychology**: Focusing on human growth and maturation across the lifespan, developmental psychology informs educational practices, parenting strategies, and interventions by examining how psychological processes evolve from infancy through old age.

Educational Psychology: Centering on understanding learning processes and educational systems, educational psychology contributes to effective teaching methods, curriculum development, and student assessment, guiding educational practices and policies.

Industrial Psychology: Applying industrial psychology in organizational settings, it enhances workplace efficiency, employee well-being, and organizational success by addressing issues related to personnel selection, training, leadership, and workplace dynamics.

Social Psychology: Investigating how individuals are influenced by social contexts and interactions, social psychology informs our understanding of group dynamics, prejudice, conformity, and interpersonal relationships, offering insights into societal behavior and societal change.

Diverse areas of specialization within psychology serve as essential pillars, playing significant roles in both facilitating and propelling the field forward. These distinct branches contribute significantly to the richness and expansiveness of the discipline, each offering unique insights and applications. By delving into specific aspects of human behavior, cognition, and development, these specializations collectively deepen our comprehension of the intricacies of the mind and behavior. Their individual contributions contribute to the overall growth of psychology, fostering a comprehensive understanding that spans a spectrum of phenomena and applications. In essence, the multifaceted nature of these specializations enhances the discipline's versatility, ensuring that psychology remains a dynamic and evolving field with relevance across diverse contexts and dimensions.

Various specialization areas in psychology play crucial roles in facilitating and advancing the field, contributing to its depth and breadth. **Behavioral psychology**, focusing on observable behavior, provides practical insights into learning, behavior modification, and behavioral therapies, aiding in practical applications like addiction treatment and behavioral interventions. **Clinical psychology**, specializing in mental health assessment and treatment, facilitates the understanding and management of psychological disorders, contributing to therapeutic approaches and interventions for individuals facing mental health challenges. **Cognitive psychology**, by investigating mental processes like memory and problem-solving, advances our understanding of how people think, informing cognitive therapies, educational strategies, and interventions for cognitive disorders.

Counseling psychology, dedicated to helping individuals cope with life challenges, facilitates personal development and mental well-being through therapeutic support and guidance. **Psychoanalysis**, rooted in Freudian theory, contributes to depth psychology and psychodynamic therapies, exploring unconscious conflicts and desires, influencing insight-oriented approaches. **Developmental psychology**, focusing on human growth across the lifespan, advances our understanding of psychological development, informing educational practices, parenting strategies, and interventions for various life stages. **Educational psychology** contributes to effective teaching methods, curriculum development, and student assessment, guiding educational practices and policies. **Industrial psychology**, applied in organizational settings, enhances workplace efficiency, employee well-being, and organizational success by addressing personnel selection, training, leadership, and workplace dynamics.

Social psychology, investigating how individuals are influenced by social contexts, contributes to our understanding of group dynamics, prejudice, conformity, and interpersonal relationships, offering insights into societal behavior and societal change. These specializations collectively advance the field by informing evidence-based practices and interventions across various domains. The interplay among these areas fosters interdisciplinary collaboration and a comprehensive understanding of the human mind and behavior. The continual advancement of these specialization areas ensures that psychology remains dynamic, relevant, and responsive to the evolving needs of individuals and society, fostering a holistic and nuanced understanding of the complexities of the human experience.

Types of Psychological Professionals

> **Psychologist:** Psychologists are professionals with advanced degrees in psychology who assess, diagnose, and treat various mental and emotional issues. They use a range of therapeutic approaches, conduct research, and may specialize in areas such as clinical, counseling, educational, or industrial-organizational psychology.
>
> **Psychiatrist:** Psychiatrists are medical doctors who specialize in mental health. They can diagnose and treat mental illnesses, often combining medication management with psychotherapy. Unlike psychologists, psychiatrists can prescribe medications due to their medical training.
>
> **Psychoanalyst:** Psychoanalysts are practitioners who employ psychoanalytic therapy, a method developed by Sigmund Freud. This approach explores unconscious processes and unresolved conflicts influencing behavior. Psychoanalysts engage clients in long-term, in-depth exploration to promote insight and emotional healing.
>
> **Psychotherapist:** Psychotherapists encompass a broad category of mental health professionals, including psychologists, counselors, and social workers. They employ various therapeutic approaches to address emotional and psychological challenges, offering support, guidance, and interventions to promote mental well-being.

Understanding these Professionals as they Apply to Grief Work

Psychological professionals, including psychologists, psychiatrists, psychoanalysts, and psychotherapists, play vital roles in addressing bereavement issues. **Psychologists**, with their expertise in understanding human behavior, can provide grief counseling, helping individuals navigate the emotional complexities of loss. **Psychiatrists**, as medical doctors, can assess and treat bereavement-related mental health disorders, offering medication management when necessary. **Psychoanalysts,** through the lens of psychoanalytic therapy, delve into unconscious processes, aiding clients in understanding unresolved conflicts related to loss.

Psychotherapists, encompassing various mental health professionals, offer diverse therapeutic approaches to support individuals in coping with grief, providing a safe space for expression and healing.

Psychologists specializing in grief and loss use targeted interventions and coping strategies, promoting healthy mourning. Psychiatrists contribute by addressing potential mental health issues exacerbated by bereavement, such as depression or anxiety. Psychoanalysts offer a deep exploration of the unconscious aspects of grief, fostering insight into unresolved emotions. Psychotherapists, drawing from various modalities, tailor their approaches to meet the unique needs of bereaved individuals, offering guidance through the mourning process. Collaboratively, these professionals contribute to the holistic care of those experiencing loss, addressing emotional, mental, and psychological aspects of bereavement.

Psychologists specializing in grief and loss employ evidence-based interventions to assist individuals in navigating the intricate emotions associated with bereavement. These professionals often use therapeutic techniques that focus on coping strategies, grief processing, and fostering resilience. Psychiatrists, having a medical background, play a crucial role in identifying and managing mental health conditions that may arise or intensify during the grieving process. They can prescribe medications when necessary to alleviate symptoms of depression, anxiety, or other disorders related to the loss.

Psychoanalysts contribute to the understanding of bereavement by delving into the unconscious mind, exploring the deeper layers of grief, and helping individuals gain insight into unresolved emotions and conflicts. This psychoanalytic approach allows for a more profound exploration of the emotional nuances surrounding loss. Psychotherapists, drawing from diverse therapeutic modalities such as cognitive-behavioral therapy, humanistic approaches, or mindfulness techniques, tailor their strategies to the specific needs of bereaved individuals. By offering personalized guidance and support, they assist in navigating the mourning process and fostering adaptive coping mechanisms.

In a collaborative effort, these professionals contribute to the holistic care of individuals experiencing loss, addressing the multidimensional aspects of bereavement. The integration of psychological, psychiatric, psychoanalytic, and therapeutic approaches ensures a comprehensive support system for those coping with grief, fostering healing on emotional, mental, and psychological levels. This multidisciplinary approach recognizes the uniqueness of each individual's grief experience and tailors interventions to provide effective and compassionate care throughout the bereavement journey.

Mental Health in Society

Mental health encompasses emotional, psychological, and social well-being, influencing how individuals think, feel, and act. It involves coping with stress, maintaining fulfilling relationships, and making choices that contribute to overall well-being. A positive mental health state contributes to resilience, productivity, and the ability to navigate life's challenges. Negative mental health refers to a state of emotional, psychological, or social well-being marked by challenges, distress, or disorders, significantly impacting one's ability to cope with stress, form healthy relationships, and engage effectively in daily life.

Prevalence refers to the frequency or proportion of cases of a particular condition within a population at a specific time. In the context of mental health, prevalence rates highlight the extent to which mental disorders exist within a given community or society. Understanding prevalence is crucial for public health planning, resource allocation, and the development of effective mental health interventions. For instance, if a study finds that 15% of a city's population experiences depression in a given year, that statistic represents the prevalence of depression in that community. This information is vital for policymakers, healthcare providers, and mental health advocates to allocate resources, design targeted interventions, and address the specific needs of the affected population.

Classification of disorders involves categorizing mental health conditions based on specific criteria, symptoms, and patterns. Systems like the Diagnostic and Statistical Manual of Mental Disorders (DSM-5) provide a framework for clinicians to diagnose and treat mental health disorders systematically. This classification aids in communication among professionals, ensuring a common understanding of various mental health conditions. For example, complicated grief, as defined by the DSM-5, involves persistent and pervasive grief reactions that extend beyond the expected timeframes following a loss, characterized by intense longing, preoccupation with the deceased, and difficulty accepting the death. An example could be a person experiencing debilitating grief for more than a year, accompanied by symptoms like overwhelming sadness, difficulty moving forward, and disruptions in daily functioning, indicating the persistence and complexity of the grieving process.

Stigma of mental illness refers to negative attitudes, beliefs, and stereotypes surrounding mental health conditions. Stigma can lead to discrimination, hindering individuals from seeking help and contributing to societal misconceptions. Addressing mental health stigma is crucial for fostering an environment where individuals feel comfortable seeking support, promoting early intervention, and challenging societal perceptions about mental health. Reducing stigma is an essential step toward building a more compassionate and understanding society that supports mental health and well-being. The funeral director plays a crucial role in reducing the stigma of mental health when referring clients to psychological professionals by fostering an open and empathetic environment that encourages seeking mental health support. Through compassionate communication and destigmatizing discussions about grief and mental well-being, funeral directors contribute to creating a supportive pathway for clients to address their emotional needs with psychological professionals.

Social Behaviors as it Relates to Funeral Directing

Social behavior in the context of funeral directing refers to the observable actions and interactions of individuals involved in the funeral process. Funeral directors engage in social behaviors when facilitating mourning rituals, providing support to grieving families, and coordinating with various professionals involved in the funeral service. Their ability to navigate social dynamics and communicate effectively is vital in creating a supportive and safe grieving environment for the bereaved, ensuring the seamless execution of funeral proceedings.

Social comparison becomes relevant in funeral directing as funeral directors may compare their approach and services to industry standards or the practices of other funeral homes. This comparison can drive continuous improvement, encouraging funeral directors to adopt best practices and innovative strategies to better meet the needs of the bereaved. Additionally, clients may engage in social comparison when selecting a funeral director, assessing the reputation and services of different funeral homes to make informed choices during a vulnerable time.

Social perception plays a significant role in funeral directing, influencing how funeral directors interpret the emotional needs of grieving individuals and families. Funeral directors must accurately perceive and understand the unique dynamics of each family they serve, recognizing cultural nuances, individual preferences, and varying coping mechanisms. Sensitivity to social cues and an understanding of the diverse ways people express grief are essential components of effective social perception in the funeral directing profession. Furthermore, social perception guides funeral directors in tailoring their approach to communication and support, ensuring a personalized and empathetic response to the unique social and emotional context of each funeral service.

Social perception of funeral services from a societal standpoint is deeply influenced by cultural norms, religious beliefs, and societal expectations surrounding death and grieving. The way a community perceives funeral practices reflects its collective values and traditions, shaping the rituals and ceremonies associated with death. Societal attitudes towards funeral services may dictate the preferred funeral customs, such as burial or cremation, elaborate ceremonies or more subdued gatherings. Additionally, societal perception influences the role of funeral directors, who are expected to navigate and respect these cultural nuances while providing support and guidance to bereaved families. The level of formality, the duration of mourning, and the emphasis on communal grieving are all aspects influenced by social perception, creating a shared understanding of how grief is expressed and processed within a particular society. The acceptance or rejection of modern funeral practices, such as green burials or virtual memorials, further reflects the evolving social perception of death and funeral services. Ultimately, social perception plays a foundational role in shaping the collective response to loss, highlighting the intricate interplay between individual mourning and the broader societal context.

Social Influences

Social influence is a pervasive factor in shaping societal attitudes towards death and dying. Cultural norms and religious beliefs, often influenced by influential figures and community leaders, guide how societies view and approach death. The media, through its portrayal of death-related topics, can shape public perceptions, influencing societal attitudes and beliefs about death issues. Persuasive communication from healthcare professionals, religious leaders, and even funeral directors can impact societal perspectives on death, encouraging certain attitudes or approaches to bereavement.

Prejudice and discrimination in the context of death and dying can be influenced by social dynamics surrounding cultural practices and beliefs. Prejudice may manifest in biased attitudes towards specific death rituals or mourning practices associated with certain cultural or ethnic groups. Discrimination, in this context, can involve unequal treatment in death care, funeral services, or memorialization based on cultural differences. Social influence plays a significant role in either perpetuating such biases or promoting inclusivity and understanding in death-related practices.

Ethnic variations in societal attitudes towards death and dying are deeply influenced by social and cultural factors. Different ethnic groups may have unique death rituals, mourning traditions, and beliefs about the afterlife. Social influence can impact how these ethnic variations are accepted or marginalized within a society. The interplay among cultural norms, societal expectations, and individual preferences shapes the narrative surrounding ethnic diversity in death practices. Socially influenced attitudes towards ethnic variations in death and dying can affect how these practices are respected, integrated into mainstream funeral services, or, conversely, how they face discrimination and marginalization. Recognizing and addressing the impact of social influence is crucial for fostering cultural sensitivity and promoting equitable treatment in death experiences across diverse ethnic groups.

How a Group Processes Death

The way a group processes death significantly influences the collective approach to funeral arrangements and memorial services. Social facilitation, where individuals perform better in the presence of a group, enhances the emotional and practical support provided to the bereaved during the mourning process. The attraction to groups contributes to the willingness of individuals to actively participate in caring for the dead, creating a sense of shared responsibility and a collaborative spirit. Leadership within the group guides and organizes the caring process, ensuring that decisions align with cultural practices and the wishes of the deceased, while the development of group norms shapes the collective approach and decisions related to funeral customs and post-mortem rituals.

Social facilitation is a group process that influences caring for the dead by amplifying individual efforts when undertaken in a group context. In funeral services, the presence of a group—comprising family, friends, and community—can enhance the emotional and practical support provided to the bereaved. The collective effort in arranging funeral rituals and memorial services can be facilitated by the shared goal of honoring the deceased, creating a supportive environment for mourning.

Social facilitation is exemplified in the context of funeral services in which the collective presence of a group, encompassing family, friends, and community members, plays a foundational role in caring for the dead. In this group process, individual efforts are amplified, for the shared goal of honoring the deceased creates a supportive environment for mourning. The emotional and practical support provided by the group enhances the overall funeral experience, allowing individuals to draw strength from one another and collaboratively arrange funeral rituals and memorial services. The collective effort, guided by the shared objective, not only facilitates the practical aspects of caring for the dead but also fosters a sense of communal support, acknowledging the significance of coming together during a time of grief.

Attraction to groups significantly impacts how individuals engage in caring for the dead. The emotional and social bonds within a group contribute to the willingness of individuals to actively participate in funeral arrangements and provide comfort to grieving families. The sense of belonging to a group fosters a collaborative spirit, enhancing the overall care and support offered during the grieving process.

Leadership within the group plays an important role in guiding and organizing the caring process for the dead. A designated leader, such as a funeral director, clergy, or a family member, can provide direction, allocate tasks, and ensure that the group's efforts align with the wishes and cultural practices associated with the deceased. Effective leadership contributes to the smooth coordination of funeral services and the creation of a meaningful and respectful farewell.

Development of group norms shapes the collective approach to caring for the dead. Shared beliefs, values, and cultural norms within the group influence decisions regarding funeral customs, burial or cremation preferences, and the overall tone of memorialization. Group norms provide a framework for how individuals within the group contribute to the care of the dead, creating a cohesive and harmonious approach that respects the diversity of opinions and preferences.

Group decisions in caring for the dead involve collaborative choices regarding funeral arrangements, memorial services, and post-mortem rituals. The decision-making process within the group considers the input of various members, balancing individual desires with collective traditions. This collaborative decision-making fosters a sense of shared responsibility and ensures that caring for the dead reflects the collective wishes and values of the group.

The presence of dissension within a group can disrupt the group decision-making process and complicate funeral arrangements. Conflicting opinions or divergent perspectives make the decision process challenging among group members regarding aspects of funeral planning, such as burial preferences, memorial services, or post-mortem rituals. Dissension may lead to delays, increased stress, and difficulty in reaching a consensus on crucial matters, which can hinder the smooth coordination of funeral arrangements and may result in tensions within the group, creating additional emotional strain for the bereaved. Effective communication and conflict resolution strategies become essential to navigate dissension, ensuring that the group can collaboratively make decisions that align with the wishes of the deceased and meet the diverse needs of those involved in the funeral process.

The counseling role of the funeral director is a crucial aspect of their profession, influencing various dimensions of the funeral process. Beyond logistical coordination, funeral directors often serve as grief counselors, providing emotional support to grieving families. Their empathetic communication and active listening skills help guide families through the complexities of mourning, facilitating a healthy grieving process. By offering a compassionate and understanding presence, funeral directors contribute to the emotional well-being of the bereaved, helping them navigate the challenges of loss. This counseling role extends to assisting families in making decisions about funeral arrangements, ensuring that the services align with the emotional needs and preferences of the grieving individuals. Overall, the funeral director's counseling role plays a critical part in fostering a supportive and empathetic environment during a time of profound loss.

In addition to their multifaceted counseling role, funeral directors maintain a crucial sense of neutrality when confronted with family disputes during funeral arrangements. Recognizing the potential for tension and emotional strain within families, the funeral director strives to bring a sense of calm to the proceedings. Amidst disagreements or conflicting opinions, the funeral director focuses on the overarching objective of providing the utmost respect and dignity for the deceased. Their neutral stance allows them to navigate familial dynamics delicately, ensuring that the funeral arrangements proceed smoothly without exacerbating existing tensions. By fostering a positive and calm environment of understanding and empathy, the funeral director plays an anchoring role in guiding families through challenging moments, upholding a commitment to the overall emotional well-being and dignity of those mourning the loss of a loved one. If the funeral director becomes involved in negative family dynamics, funeral arrangements will be complicated further, which can intensify shared negative emotions, and potentially hinder the process of creating a respectful and supportive environment for grieving and mourning the loss of the dead.

Emotional Intelligence

Emotional intelligence refers to the ability to recognize, understand, manage, and effectively use one's own emotions and those of others. In the context of grieving, emotional intelligence plays a vital role in navigating the complexity of death and the emotions associated with loss. A person with high emotional intelligence, for example, may be able to identify and comprehend their own feelings of grief and sorrow, as well as empathize with the emotions of others who are mourning. This awareness and understanding contribute to more effective communication and support during the grieving process. *Emotional intelligence allows individuals to express and process their emotions in a healthy manner, fostering resilience and aiding in the gradual healing that comes with grieving.* Moreover, funeral directors, as compassionate professionals assisting bereaved families, benefit from emotional intelligence by sensitively responding to the diverse emotional needs of those they serve, creating an atmosphere of empathy and support during times of profound loss.

Perceiving emotions is the foundational aspect of emotional intelligence, involving the ability to recognize and accurately interpret both one's own emotions and the emotions of others. This skill enables individuals to navigate and respond effectively to the emotional responses in various situations, including those associated with grieving and loss.

In the funeral profession, perceiving emotions is crucial for funeral directors who interact with bereaved families. Consider a situation in which a family is making arrangements for a loved one who has died unexpectedly. The funeral director must be attuned to the emotions expressed by family members, ranging from shock and disbelief to profound or exacerbated grief. Perceiving these emotions allows the funeral director to approach the situation with sensitivity, acknowledging the family's unique emotional state and providing support tailored to their needs.

For example, if family members appear overwhelmed and hesitant during the arrangement process, a funeral director with high emotional intelligence would recognize their distress and adjust their communication style accordingly. They may offer additional time for decision-making, provide reassurance, and express empathy to create a supportive environment. On the other hand, if family members seem more composed and express a desire for specific funeral customs, the funeral director would perceive these emotions and guide the arrangements in accordance with their wishes.

By perceiving emotions effectively, funeral directors can navigate the delicate landscape of grief, offering compassionate and personalized support and the proper service that connects a grief experience to the death event. This foundational aspect of emotional intelligence enhances the overall funeral experience for bereaved families, fostering a connection based on empathy and understanding during a challenging time.

Using emotions involves the strategic application of emotions to facilitate problem-solving, decision-making, and interpersonal interactions. Individuals with high emotional intelligence leverage their emotional awareness to enhance communication, build relationships, and navigate the complexities of grief constructively.

Using emotions in the grieving situation involves a strategic application of emotional intelligence to provide empathetic and supportive care. The following are examples of how funeral professionals leverage emotions effectively:

1. **Empathy in Communication:** Funeral directors with high emotional intelligence use empathy to connect with grieving families. They express genuine understanding of the family's pain, validating their emotions and creating a compassionate and sacred space for open communication.

2. **Compassion in Decision-Making:** Understanding the emotional context, funeral directors can guide families in decision-making by offering options aligned with their emotional needs. For example, suggesting personalized funeral rituals that reflect the deceased's personality can bring comfort and a sense of connection.

3. **Building Trust through Emotional Support:** Funeral professionals use their emotional awareness to build trust with grieving families. By demonstrating genuine care and concern, they create a supportive environment where families feel comfortable sharing their emotions and concerns.

4. **Respectful Handling of Cultural Sensitivities:** Recognizing the diverse emotional expressions tied to cultural practices, funeral directors navigate the complexities of grief by respecting and incorporating cultural sensitivities into funeral arrangements, which ensures that the grieving process is in harmony with the family's emotional and cultural context.

5. **Creating a Healing Atmosphere**: Funeral directors may use emotions to create a healing atmosphere during funeral services. Incorporating elements that evoke positive memories and honor the life accomplishments of the deceased can help ease the emotional burden on the grieving family.

   Through the strategic use of emotions, funeral directors could curate strained or complex relationships with the deceased. This deliberate approach can offer a supportive environment that fosters understanding, reconciliation, and emotional healing for individuals grappling with the complexities of their relationships during the mourning process.

6. **Providing Comfort through Rituals**: Funeral professionals can use emotions strategically by suggesting comforting rituals, such as a memorial ceremony or a moment of reflection, to help families express and process their emotions collectively.

By strategically using emotions, funeral directors contribute to a constructive grieving process, fostering connections and providing meaningful support tailored to the unique emotional needs of each bereaved family.

Understanding emotions delves more deeply into the cognitive aspect of emotional intelligence, requiring individuals to comprehend the nuances and intricacies of different emotions. This understanding helps in discerning the root causes of emotional responses, fostering empathy and facilitating a more holistic approach to supporting others in their grieving process.

Understanding emotions represents a profound aspect of emotional intelligence, involving a cognitive exploration into the intricate realm of human feelings. It goes beyond surface-level recognition, necessitating a deeper comprehension of the nuances and intricacies inherent in various emotional states. Funeral professionals with a high degree of understanding emotions are adept at discerning the root causes behind the emotional responses exhibited by grieving individuals. They engage in empathetic listening and observe non-verbal cues to unravel the layers of sorrow, anger, or sadness that may manifest during the funeral arrangement process.

This nuanced understanding enables funeral directors to foster empathy, as they connect emotionally with bereaved families on a deeper level. By recognizing and comprehending the underlying emotions, funeral professionals can tailor their support to address the unique needs and concerns of grieving individuals. For instance, if a family member expresses anger, an emotionally intelligent funeral director would probe further to understand the source of that emotion, whether it be frustration with the circumstances of the death or a manifestation of deeper unresolved issues.

Understanding emotions is important in guiding funeral directors toward a more holistic approach to supporting others in their grieving process. It allows them to provide not only logistical assistance but also emotional support that aligns with the specific emotional dynamics of each family. This depth of understanding contributes to the creation of a funeral experience that acknowledges the complexity of grief, fostering a compassionate and healing environment where individuals feel truly seen and supported during their journey of loss.

Managing emotions is the proactive regulation of one's own emotions and the ability to influence the emotional experiences of others. In the context of grieving, effective emotion management allows individuals to cope with the intense feelings associated with loss, fostering resilience and promoting a healthier emotional environment for both themselves and those around them.

Managing emotions is a proactive and essential component of emotional intelligence, involving the deliberate regulation of one's own emotions and the skill to impact the emotional experiences of others. In the context of grieving, effective emotion management becomes a powerful tool for individuals to navigate the intense and often overwhelming feelings associated with loss. Funeral professionals, equipped with high emotional intelligence, demonstrate adept emotion management as they guide bereaved families through the funeral process. By maintaining composure, offering a comforting presence, and expressing empathy, funeral directors contribute to fostering resilience in those grappling with grief. This proactive approach to emotion management not only supports individuals in coping with their own emotions but also creates a healthier emotional environment for the broader grieving community. The ability to regulate emotions in a constructive manner enables funeral professionals to facilitate a funeral experience that honors the deceased, acknowledges the complexity of grief, and ultimately promotes healing within the community of mourners.

In conclusion, emotional intelligence encompasses a multifaceted set of skills that enable individuals to perceive, use, understand, and manage emotions. Applied to the context of grieving, these aspects of emotional intelligence contribute to more compassionate and effective support during times of loss, both for oneself and for those navigating the challenging journey of grief.

Bereavement Counseling in Funeral Services

Background: Psychology plays a key role in the response to death and to funeral services.

Funeral Service Psychology is the study of human behavior and mental processes as related to funeral services.

What is Grief? Grief is considered **an emotion or set of emotions due to a loss, in this case, a death**. Other key concepts involved in the process of grief include the following:

> **Bereavement:** the act or event of separation or loss that results in the experience of grief. This experience is an emotion to grief; the "event" of a loss or death.
> **Mourning:** an outward expression of grief. Mourning is an adjustment process that involves grief or sorrow over a period of time and helps in the reorganization of an individual's life following the loss or death of a loved one, and is considered a "process" of adjustment following such a loss.

What Are the Needs of the Bereaved? The bereaved moves to a "new normal," which includes tasks such as the following:

> Confirming the reality of the loss
> Establishing stability and security after the loss
> Receiving emotional support (which can begin before the actual loss)
> Expressing emotions (feelings that include grief, created by chemical changes in the brain and accompanied by bodily changes)
> Modifying emotional ties to the deceased
> Providing a basis for building new interpersonal relationships.

The Purposes and Values of the Funeral in Processing Grief: The funeral is considered an organized, flexible, purposeful, group-centered, time-limited response to death, and is expected to reflect reverence, dignity and respect. In relation to processing grief, the funeral provides the following:

> Showing respect for the deceased and for the deceased's friends and family
> Providing a face-to-face confrontation with the death, which makes the death real and helps the bereaved accept that death has occurred
> Meeting theological, psychological, and sociological needs of the mourners
> Providing a socially accepted environment to mourn
> Providing an opportunity to reflect upon the memories of the deceased
> Gaining emotional support through sharing and using a social support network to establish emotional stability (e.g., joy expressed is joy increased; grief shared is grief diminished; opportunity to express and receive love and support)
> Expressing grief and providing an opportunity to bid farewell through this ritual.

Theories of Grief

I.   **Lindemann:** Psychiatrist Erich Lindemann conducted a historic study of bereavement after a 1942 fire at Boston's Cocoanut Grove Nightclub, that until 9/11 was considered the second-deadliest single-building fire in the United States. Lindemann's work tremendously influenced how the medical community understood grief and contributed to the restructuring of mental health treatment, the development of crisis theory, and a greater understanding of trauma.

Before Lindemann, there was little understanding of somatic (bodily) distress, hostile reactions, guilt, changes in conduct patterns, and even hallucinations survivors exhibited, which Lindemann termed "grief syndrome." The role of the psychiatrist was to assist the survivors to engage in "grief work," which assisted in helping develop new social patterns and ways of going on without the deceased.

Grief work *is defined as a set of tasks that must be completed for successful mourning to take place.*

II. **Bowlby and Parkes:** Edward John Bowlby, a British psychologist and psychiatrist who specialized in child development, theorized that humans are born with the need to form close emotional bonds with caregivers ("attachment theory") and early bonding was critical to healthy functioning. Bowlby suggested that grief is an instinctive and universal response to separation, and that the stronger the attachment, the greater the level of grief that can occur if such bonds are threatened or broken.

Bowlby and fellow psychologist Parkes proposed a **4-stage model of grief** that ultimately led to the development of a new circumstance. *These stages include shock-numbness, yearning-searching, disorganization-despair, and reorganization.*

Attachment theory *is the theory describing a tendency to make strong affectional bonds with others coming from the need for security and safety.*

III. **Kubler-Ross:** Swiss psychiatrist Elisabeth Kübler-Ross described **5 stages of grief** *(DABDA).* When a person is told that they are dying, various stages of emotions occur and these stages happen at different times during the dying process. The patient becomes overwhelmed with emotions. Kübler-Ross outlines the five stages:

   Denial – *the defense mechanism by which a person is unable or refuses to see things as they are because such facts are threatening to the self.* The initial response is often feelings of disbelief and refusal to accept the event is really happening. This defense mechanism facilitates and numbs the intensity of the reality of the pending death experience.

452

Anger – *a strong feeling of displeasure and usually of antagonism.* For a dying patient, anger may be considered a defense mechanism, whereas it could be masking some of the emotions and pain that the person is harboring. Anger could mask itself in feelings of bitterness and resentment, either towards oneself or others. Anger could be an obstacle; however, once these feelings subside, a person is able to think more rationally about the emotions and pain being suppressed.

Bargaining – dying makes a person feel helpless and vulnerable. Humans, by their very nature, seek control, and bargaining is a stage of grief in which the individual attempts to regain control over the situation. People who are religious will often attempt to make a deal with a higher power (God) for healing or relief from the grief and pain they are experiencing.

Depression – *a state of despondency marked by feelings of powerlessness and hopelessness.* Of all the stages of grief, depression could be the most difficult. This stage may appear as a quiet one in which the person turns inward towards isolation in an attempt to fully cope with the reality of the imminent death. Feelings of being foggy, heavy, or confused are all associated with depression, and a mental health therapist could help the person work through these thoughts.

Acceptance – the understanding that death is a part of the life cycle, and the person accepts the reality of this event in their life. Some people who accept the good days with the bad, have come to a sense of resolution that death is a part of the life cycle.

These stages are not linear, and not all people will necessarily experience any or all of them. However, these stages have been commonly observed among the bereaved.

Kübler-Ross also offered the concept of **anticipatory grief** – *grief in anticipation of death or loss.* During the stage of bargaining, the death is anticipated but has not yet occurred. However, the individual anticipating the eventual death of a loved one may experience a type of grief, nonetheless. Anticipatory grieving may begin as soon as someone realizes that a loss will ultimately occur or after a while when the signs of impending loss are too obvious to ignore. While some may find that anticipatory grief better prepares them for the eventual loss, others may still feel the shock of loss vividly – both are considered normal reactions.

IV.   **Worden:** Psychologist William Worden proposed that mourners should actively engage with 4 tasks of "healthy grieving," which are as follows:

1. **Accepting the reality of the loss:** A bereaved person may possess the intellectual awareness of someone's passing, yet disbelief can persist until engagement in tasks that compel an acknowledgment of the death, such as contacting the funeral home or participating in the funeral services. It is

through these actions that the individual starts to confront the reality of the situation.

2. **Experiencing the pain of grief:** While everyone experiences pain, it is impossible for anyone to truly experience someone else's pain. Grief is a multifaceted experience that one feels emotionally, spiritually, cognitively, and even physically, which is natural! "Healthy grieving" means to be able to experience the safe expression of all the grief reactions.

3. **Adjusting to an environment with the deceased missing:** Various types of adjustments are part of the grieving process. "External" adjustments may involve shouldering different responsibilities and acquiring new skills, such as managing family finances previously handled by the deceased. On the other hand, "spiritual" adjustments may encompass questioning the meaning and purpose of life, along with one's belief system.

4. **Finding an enduring connection with the deceased while embarking on a new life without them:** Ultimately, a balance is achieved. The bereaved person continues to remember the deceased, but they are able to live a productive and meaningful life.

V. **Freud:** In 1917, Sigmund Freud published **Mourning and Melancholia**, a paper discussing psychological responses to loss. He theorized that there were two types of responses to loss, "mourning" and "melancholia." While both are responses to grief, "mourning" was considered healthier, necessary, more time-limited, and even "transforming." However, "melancholia" was considered chronic, unconscious, and detrimental.

According to Freud, a person in "mourning" feels the pain of a loss in an external way. The world around them may feel changed and worse because of an individual's loss, but the individual allows themselves to experience the feelings of loss. Ultimately, there is an acceptance of the loss and the individual is able to move on, even though their world has been irrevocably changed.

However, Freud believed that a person experiencing "melancholia" feels the pain of loss internally, within the unconscious. Therefore, the significance of the loss is not as apparent to the griever, although of course, the pain may be felt. As with other experiences that Freud believed could be too difficult for an individual to accept, the grief is pushed to the unconscious, where the conscious mind cannot process it. Instead of processing the grief and "putting it in its proper place" then as in the mourning process, the pain is instead directed towards the self in "melancholia."

A grief counselor or therapist can be very helpful in providing an opportunity for the bereaved to verbalize and test their feelings of grief to experience a healthy grief.

Grief and the Family System: Psychologist William Worden postulates that the functional position (or "role") of the deceased in a family can affect the severity and experience of grief of the remaining family members. The family system's functional equilibrium (or "homeostasis") has been disturbed and the individuals' affect (feelings and their expression) are changed.

An emotionally well-integrated, "healthy" family will be better equipped to support its members in bereavement, even of a significant family member, perhaps not needing outside assistance to do so. However, a less-integrated family may have more difficulty. Such a family may not necessarily demonstrate significant grief reactions at the time of death, but then show physical or emotional symptoms or even social misbehavior at a later time.

In some circumstances, the value that a family places on emotions and their expression may allow or hinder individual members from expressing them or from expressing negative feelings, thus impacting the individual from reaching grief resolution.

A Special Circumstance – Children and Death (Rabbi Earl Grollman, PhD):

Some reactions may be influenced by how death is explained to the child. As a funeral director, parents will ask how to best explain death to a child. Grollman explains how to best explain death and dying to a child:

1. **Birth to 3 years old:** Children are not considered able to comprehend death.

2. **Three to five years old:** Children do not tend to comprehend the finality of death and may consider death as a "long sleep" or "taking a long journey." They do not understand that they will not see the deceased again.

3. **Five to nine years old:** Children may understand that death is final but may not accept that it happens to everyone eventually. They may depict death as a type of character (e.g., a "bogeyman").

4. **Nine years old and above:** Children are able to understand that death is final and inevitable.

Children Attending Funerals: A personal decision on the part of the family, but a funeral is considered an important occasion in the life of the family. A child may be offered the opportunity to attend the funeral, to pay last respects, and to express love and devotion. Young children may become restless, and families may need to plan to take them home after a short visit and to have quiet activities (e.g., coloring books and crayons) at hand.

What Can Be Said to Children: It may be appropriate to share personal religious convictions or to offer analogies such as with the death of a pet or flower or to encourage children to express their emotions. They should be wary of expressing philosophical perspectives. Speaking in concrete terms (e.g., "living things die") may be appropriate. They should always consult with the family.

What is NOT Recommended when explaining Death to Children:

➢ Lying to "soften the blow" or with the best intentions, including fantasy scenarios, fairy tales and the like.

➢ Offering platitudes, especially if people do not believe them themselves! Examples: "Everything happens for a reason." "They're in a better place now." Children will struggle to find out what good reason there could be for the loved one dying and wonder why staying with them was not considered "good enough" that the loved one had to go to a "better place."

➢ Saying that the deceased has "gone on a long trip," for the child may then expect the deceased to return.

➢ Saying that the deceased has "gone to sleep or their rest." The child may develop a fear of sleeping!

➢ Saying that the deceased is now in heaven. The child's family can communicate their own beliefs. Using heaven can also could make the child develop a fear that heaven and the afterlife are places that take their loved one away from them.

➢ Being careless about indicating that illness led to the death. Again, the child's family may prefer to handle this scenario. Depending on the child's level of development, the child may become concerned about becoming ill in the future. An older child may be better able to understand that not all illnesses lead to death.

Determinants of Grief – How People May Experience Grief:

➢ **Who the deceased was in relation to the mourner**: It may make a difference if the deceased was blood kin (e.g., a parent, sibling) or socially related through marriage or some other situation (e.g., a spouse, a friend).

➢ **What the nature of the attachment to the deceased was:** How strong was the attachment? Was there ambivalence (e.g., a "love-hate" situation) in the relationship?

➢ **Historical and cultural experiences with and expressions of grief:** Grief behavior involves learned behavior as well as personality variables. **Social variables** such as religious/spiritual traditions, and ethnic/racial customs may be impactful. In some societies, for example, individuals may grieve in more demonstrative ways (e.g., loud sobbing, shrieking, dramatic gestures, etc.) while others will grieve more quietly and

➢ **Personality variables:** Individuals with different Myers-Briggs personality traits may experience grief in unique ways, influenced by their distinct preferences and tendencies. For example, an ISTJ, known for their practical and organized nature, might approach grief by focusing on logistical aspects, such as funeral arrangements, to find a sense of order. In contrast, an ESFP, known for being spontaneous and social, may seek comfort in the immediate support of friends and family, engaging in shared memories. INTJs, known for their analytical and independent thinking, might prefer introspection and private mourning. Each personality type brings its own set of coping mechanisms and ways of processing grief, reflecting the diverse and individualized nature of the grieving experience.

Myers-Briggs Personality Trait Types:

- ➢ **ISTJ** (Introverted, Sensing, Thinking, Judging): Practical and organized, focused on details, and reliable.
- ➢ **ESTJ** (Extraverted, Sensing, Thinking, Judging): Efficient, sociable, and natural leaders with a strong sense of duty.
- ➢ **ISTP** (Introverted, Sensing, Thinking, Perceiving): Analytical, hands-on, and adaptable, enjoying practical problem-solving.
- ➢ **ESTP** (Extraverted, Sensing, Thinking, Perceiving): Energetic, action-oriented, and adaptable risk-takers.
- ➢ **ESFP** (Extraverted, Sensing, Feeling, Perceiving): Enthusiastic, social, and spontaneous, enjoying the present moment.
- ➢ **ENTJ** (Extraverted, Intuitive, Thinking, Judging): Visionary leaders, strategic thinkers, and decisive organizers.
- ➢ **INTJ** (Introverted, Intuitive, Thinking, Judging): Strategic, analytical, and independent thinkers with a long-term focus.
- ➢ **ESFJ**: Sociable and nurturing, they thrive on helping others and value harmony in relationships.
- ➢ **ISFP**: Artistic and compassionate, they seek authenticity and enjoy expressing themselves through creative endeavors.
- ➢ **INFJ**: Insightful and empathetic, they are driven by a vision for the future and a commitment to making a positive impact.
- ➢ **INFP**: Idealistic and creative, they are guided by strong values and a desire to contribute to a better world.
- ➢ **INTP**: Analytical and innovative, they are drawn to problem-solving and exploring new ideas with curiosity.
- ➢ **ENTP**: Energetic and inventive, they enjoy challenging the status quo and are natural idea generators.
- ➢ **ENFP**: Enthusiastic and imaginative, they are passionate about exploring possibilities and connecting with others.
- ➢ **INTJ** (Introverted, Intuitive, Thinking, Judging): Strategic and independent, they are known for their visionary thinking, analytical approach, and ability to execute plans with precision.

Using Myers-Briggs As an Example:

a. An **ISTJ** type experiencing grief might tend to blame themselves and repeatedly think about how they could have done things differently or better.

b. An **ESTJ** type experiencing grief would attempt to seem hide their feelings and seem active and competent, taking charge of things and keeping busy to avoid dealing with their emotions.

c. An **ESFJ** type shows some similarity to the ESTJ type, trying to appear active and competent no matter how great their pain. They may feel frustrated because their loved ones "should know how they feel" despite the effort the ESFJ expends to not show distress and without the ESFJ having to actually express themselves, which then can cause more stress and resentment.

d. An **ISTP** type can either seem very reserved and stoic or they can be uncharacteristically emotional and even angry. They may tend to blame themselves and resist seeking support from others.

e. An **ISFP** type may feel emotions and anger intensely and show it, while others may try to hide their emotions from others. They tend to consider fault within themselves first before blaming others. ISFPs may feel exhausted, trapped, have a loss in energy and feel burned out.

f. An **ESTP** type may seem to be calm and in control. They may not ask for help and avoid thinking of the loss, but then are confused if they experience sudden bursts of emotion or anger. An ESTP may become pessimistic if despair becomes chronic.

g. An **ESFP** type would tend to look outside of themselves first in times of grief and search for external sources of blame. Then they will look within and can be more willing to seek support. They are often good at offering support to others who are grieving too. ESFPs are apt to get angry and show it during stressful times. Like an ESTP, an ESFP may also become disillusioned and pessimistic if stress and despair become chronic.

h. An **INTJ** type tends to look inwards first. They prefer to be alone at first to try and process things on their own.

i. An **INFJ** type will also initially look inwards and privately. However, they may try to offer support to others, and even to the extent that they get embroiled in dealing with other people's pain and lose sight of handling their own.

j. An **ENTJ** type will often try to apply logic to a stressful situation, including grief, but they feel upset if it does not work. They may also become withdrawn and in more extreme cases may believe that everyone is against them or that nobody supports them.

k. An **ENFJ** type can find it difficult to express their real feelings and can feel pressure to maintain a sense of calmness.

l. An **INTP** type typically avoids showing grief for a very long period of time. They may find it hard to ask for help and instead withdraw and analyze themselves on what went wrong.

m. An **INFP** type who experiences grief will also desire time alone and privacy to deal with their emotions. However, they may be more willing to work with a counselor.

n. An **ENTP** type may try to use logic to deal with a loss, but then feel resentful if and when it does not work to alleviate their grief. ENTPs may try to rush the grieving process, but this can cause repressed emotions to rise to the surface suddenly and unexpectedly in the future. Interestingly, ENTPs may experience a period of hyper-focusing on details and develop hypochondria symptoms.

o. An **ENFP** type can have one of two reactions to grief. Some ENFPs will want to isolate themselves from others while others will seek out others for support. ENFPs may consider concepts such as the afterlife, the meaning of life, and how short life can be. ENFPs may also experience a hyper-focus on details as a way to deal with their grief and worry about having a life-threatening illness themselves if they feel ill.

➢ **Demographic variables (e.g., age, gender):** For example, the age of the griever as well as the age of the deceased may impact how grief is experienced. One gender may have been taught to express and experience strong emotions, including grief, in particular ways in contrast to how other genders are expected to mourn the loss of a loved one.

- ➢ **Concurrent stresses that the individual may also be experiencing at this time:** For example, a member of the "sandwich generation" (someone who is in between two generations and caring for both, such as caring for parents and children) now has to deal with a loss, possibly in one of those generations. Someone who loses a job and loses a loved one at the same time is grieving two situations of loss simultaneously.

- ➢ **Coping with the public, including possibly the media:** For example, a public figure such as a politician or a celebrity, may not be "allowed" to grieve privately because the eyes of the media are always present to report on anything and everything that happens with such an individual. The media may also be interested in covering a more sensationalistic type of death, disregarding the privacy and wishes of the family.

Mode of Death: How the deceased died can impact the way survivors grieve:

- ➢ **Natural causes:** If there was time to prepare for the death of the deceased, survivors may have had the time to prepare for the death and experience closure. But surprise and shock can occur if the death was unexpected, sudden, or considered premature.
- ➢ **Accidental causes:** May tend to want to blame someone or something else for the death. May also try to determine how the death could have been prevented.
- ➢ **Suicide**: *a deliberate and voluntary act of taking one's life*. Can lead to **complicated grief** – *grief that interferes with normal life functions without progressing towards a resolution.* In some situations, survivors blame themselves or others for the death.
- ➢ **Homicide**: *The killing of one human being by another*. Survivors may desire to place blame elsewhere for this occurrence.
- ➢ **Euthanasia** (the right to die): *An act or practice of allowing or causing the death of a person suffering from a life-limiting condition.* In most states this practice is considered homicide.
- ➢ **Disasters (e.g., from natural disasters or war):** Generally considered when the number of injured and fatalities challenge or exceed an area's ability to handle existing resources. An example of this mode of death was experienced in most major metropolitan areas during the Covid-19 Pandemic.

What is "Normal" Grief? Also see "determinants of grief." Manifestations of "normal" grief can include the following:

- ➢ **Emotional reactions:** Examples: A griever would normally be expected to feel anger, sadness, guilt, self-reproach, anxiety, and so on, though how so is unique to each person. While these emotions are normal, not everyone cries because of a loss. It does not mean that the person is not experiencing painful emotions. A person experiencing a loss may lash out at others, although the real reason behind the anger, frustration, etc. is because of the loss of a loved one. The recipient of the griever's emotions just happens to be in the wrong place at the wrong time ("displaced grief").

> **Physical reactions:** For example, someone grieving a loss may experience dryness of the mouth, headaches and body aches, chest tightness/pain, tightening of the throat, digestive and bowel symptoms, etc. These symptoms are expected to be temporary and an individual experiencing persistent physical symptoms should consult with their medical professionals.

> **Cognitive (thinking) reactions:** For example, a person experiencing a loss may be pre-occupied, distracted, or absent-minded (e.g., "brain fog"). Other cognitive reactions can include disbelief, confusion, a sense of the deceased's presence, hallucinations, etc.

> **Behavioral reactions:** For example, some persons may withdraw from others, cry, experience sleep disturbances, search for the deceased, etc. The person may act as though the deceased will return (e.g., "He always came back from his journeys, and he will come back again. So I will stand by the window and watch for him, as I always do, and he always expects me to be there").

What is "Complicated" Grief? While individuals grieve in unique ways, eventually the expectation is that grief softens and the mourner can progress to a future without the deceased. Mental health professionals typically consider that someone may be experiencing "complicated grief" when grieving continues to be intense, persistent, and debilitating beyond 12 months. Time does not improve symptoms of grief, and professional help may be needed.

Worden listed factors that may contribute to complicated grief that include the following:

> **Relationship with the deceased** such as ambivalence, narcissism, dependency, abuse, etc.
> **Circumstantial factors** such as multiple losses or multiple losses in a short period of time
> **Historical factors** such as previous experiences of complicated grief or impact of early child developmental factors
> **Personality factors** includes the ability to tolerate extreme emotional stress, dependency issues, self-concept, self-efficacy, etc.
> **Social factors** such as a situation where the loss is considered socially unspeakable (e.g., the loss of a previously unknown affair partner), or there is a lack of a social network to commiserate and communicate with, or the death is considered socially unacceptable or negative (e.g., death from suicide or AIDS).

Types of Complicated Grief Reactions:

> **Chronic Grief:** Prolonged and excessive in duration and that might never come to a satisfactory resolution. The American Psychiatric Association (APA) notes that for a diagnosis of chronic (or "persistent") grief, the loss of a loved one must have occurred at least a year ago for adults and at least 6 months ago for children and adolescents.

- ➢ **Delayed Grief**: Inhibited, suppressed, or postponed response to a loss instead of expressing grief immediately after a loss, which could occur, for example, if the bereaved is suppressing grief to support and protect others or to be able to arrange for the funeral and other needs.

- ➢ **Exaggerated Grief**: Excessive and disabling reactions seemingly out of proportion to the circumstances of the death. The exhibition of such grief may be a cultural expectation or a demonstration of an individual's personality.

- ➢ **Masked Grief**: Similar to delayed grief. A mourner attempts to suppress feelings of grief and not address them or allow them to run their natural course. In the immediate aftermath of a loss, this reaction may be helpful, but it is not healthy if experienced over a protracted period of time.

- ➢ **Disenfranchised Grief:** Grief that is not usually openly acknowledged, socially accepted or publicly mourned. For example, the loss of a pet, perinatal losses, loss of a loved one who is not blood kin, the loss of a body part, and even elective abortions may be such losses leading to disenfranchised grief. Examples of a statement that may reveal disenfranchised grief that is hurtful: "It was just a dog." "You had your leg amputated, but at least you're alive." "It wasn't a real baby anyway."

Basic Definitions of Counseling:

- ➢ **ABFSE definition of Counseling**: Professional guidance of the individual by using psychological methods.
- ➢ **Webster Dictionary:** Something that provides direction or advice for a decision or course of action.
- ➢ **American Counseling Association:** A professional relationship that empowers diverse individuals, families, and groups to accomplish mental health, wellness education, and career goals.
- ➢ **Edgar Jackson:** Any time someone helps someone else with a problem.
- ➢ **Carl Rogers:** Founder of client-centered (or person-centered) therapy. Emphasis on reflective listening, empathy, and acceptance instead of interpretation of behaviors or unconscious drives.
- ➢ **Merle Ohlsen:** A therapeutic experience for reasonably healthy people before they develop serious psychological disorders (vs. psychotherapy).

Types and Styles of Counseling (per Raether and Slater): The "counselor" is an individual who provides assistance and guidance:

- ➢ **Informational**: The counselor shares a body of information with the client.

- ➢ **Situational Counseling**: Counseling related to specific situations in life that may create crises and produce human pain and suffering. Additionally, informational counseling is a type of counseling that also addresses significant feelings not produced by life crises.

➢ **Psychotherapy:** Any psychological technique used to facilitate positive changes in a person's personality, behavior, and adjustments. Advanced therapy is provided by professional psychiatrists and psychologists. Not expected of funeral directors, though they may suggest pursuing professional grief therapy for prolonged or complicated grief.

➢ **Grief Counseling:** A short-term process of helping people facilitate grief to a healthy resolution. A funeral director is a type of grief counselor. Funeral directors take the death event and help people begin and engage in their own grieving experience. The funeral director is empathic and provides a safe place for mourners to share their feelings of loss, sadness, and grief. **Empathy** is a capacity for taking another's point of view; the ability to feel what another is feeling.

➢ **Grief Therapy:** Includes specialized techniques used to help people with complicated grief and may be of longer duration than counseling.

Styles of Counseling:

➢ **Directive Counseling**: Counselor-centered counseling in which the professional practitioner takes a more active role in giving advice and problem-solving. This type of counseling can be effective in time-sensitive situations. A directive approach can help to ensure that a decision is made quickly and efficiently. A directive approach may also create more structure in the relationship with the bereaved who may be disorganized and emotional, especially in the immediate aftermath of a loss. A directive approach helps lead the bereaved on a more objective, logical path to a resolution. For example, a widow was very social with her husband before he died, and now she sits in her home feeling alone, abandoned, and isolated but has difficulty in identifying and choosing options. A counselor using the directive approach may suggest participating in activities at the Senior Center or inviting friends over for dinner.

➢ **Non-Directive Counseling**: Person-Centered (or "Client-Centered") counseling approach per Carl Rogers. In this approach, a counselor does not try to solve someone's problems for them. This type of therapy also does not imply that there is no structure whatsoever in the professional relationship. Rather, the counselor works to create an environment in which the client, rather than the counselor, can take the lead for the most part to develop resolutions more independently and without fear of judgment. To accomplish such an objective, a non-directive counselor reflects back to the client their feelings and reactions, asks questions for clarification, and encourages client self-awareness and decision-making. Currently, this type of therapy is the most popular though it is not suitable in crisis situations where speed is of the essence. An example of non-directive counseling would be having the bereaved identify and prioritize goals they want to pursue, such as to decrease feelings of loss and increase the ability to move forward in a world without the deceased.

What is a Crisis? Crisis Intervention Counseling: A **crisis** *is an emotional significant event or radical change of status in a person's life.* It usually occurs suddenly and unexpectedly. A crisis is a highly emotional temporary state in which an individual's feelings of anxiety, grief, confusion or pain impair their ability to act. Specific characteristics of a crisis include the following:

➤ A period of heightened psychological stress that typically lasts approximately four to six weeks. An individual is vulnerable and may be more accepting of outside interventions and change at this time.

➤ Usually initiated by an outside force or emotionally hazardous condition.

➤ Considered a normal reaction to hazardous conditions, not a sign of mental illness.

➤ How an individual perceives the hazardous situation greatly determines the occurrence and seriousness of the crisis. The individual's past history also greatly influences how they perceive the situation.

➤ The more hazardous a situation is perceived to be, the greater the likelihood that more primitive or regressive reactions or coping behaviors such as "fight or flight" will occur.

➤ Persons in crisis may pull away or attempt to separate from significant others and become isolated. Encouragement to seek out support is helpful.

➤ Guilt and shame may occur for certain crises that are not perceived well by society (e.g., suicide, homicide, SIDS; Sudden Infant Death Syndrome, AIDS, etc.).

The ABC Model of Crisis Counseling (Stone, but Previously Caplan and Lindemann):

➤ **A: Achieving rapport:** Initiating and establishing a counseling relationship with the person in crisis by creating a welcoming and safe environment, physically and emotionally. For example, a counselor takes care not to display potentially controversial and upsetting artwork or publications in their office. The counselor faces the client with an open stance (e.g., keeping arms and legs uncrossed) and uses "empathy statements" to express understanding and acceptance of what the client is saying (e.g., "It sounds like you are really angry that your husband died").

➤ **B: Boiling down the problem to its basics:** Identifying and paring down a situation to its core components. The counselor will use open-ended and closed-ended questions to understand accurately what is happening with the client, which is especially critical in a crisis situation in which the counselor may be concerned that the bereaved is so distraught they may be considering harming themselves.

➢ **C: Coping:** Involves working with the client to create a plan of action, including the setting of goals, evaluating accessibility to resources, formulating alternatives, reviewing and refinement of the plan, execution of the plan, and then following up. **A person never gets over losing a loved one… They just learn to cope.**

Defining Grief Counseling Specifically: Grief counseling is a responsibility that funeral directors can be trained to provide, for it involves helping people work through uncomplicated (normal) grief over a reasonably short timeframe. Funeral directors should understand the limits of their skills and knowledge and refer to professional counselors/therapists for prolonged and complicated grief. Funeral directors should NOT attempt to provide therapeutic services; they are untrained and do not have the skill set to diagnose and guide a person through the complexities of complicated grief. The prudent funeral director will have a list of qualified grief counseling professionals who can assist people with this type of grief.

Goals of Grief Counseling (per Worden): In general, the funeral director's grief counseling primary purpose is to help survivors complete unfinished "business" with the deceased and to encourage them to express a final "goodbye." Worden proposes specific goals that correspond with his four tasks of grieving:

➢ **To encourage the acceptance of the reality of the loss:** "Acceptance" does not necessarily mean agreement or approval of what has happened. Instead, acceptance is the point at which the bereaved becomes ready to start coping and healing.

➢ **To help the bereaved deal with their expressed and latent affect (feelings and their expression):** Grief may result in many emotions, including sadness, loneliness, anger, guilt, shame, and others, with many different expressions in different amounts, duration, and order. Worden emphasizes the importance of expressing emotions rather than avoiding them. By allowing the expression of all emotions, they can be properly processed.

➢ **To help the survivor to overcome various impediments to readjustment after a loss:** The bereave's world is forever changed after the loss of a loved one. Adjusting to this "new normal" can take time and include several different adjustments (e.g., internal, external, spiritual). Some impediments may be physical and not just emotional (e.g., handling finances and childcare arrangements that the deceased used to deal with). There are external changes, such as getting used to living alone or doing things alone. Internal changes may include accepting a new identity (e.g., "I used to be Mike's wife and now I am his widow").

➢ **To encourage the survivor to make a healthy emotional withdrawal from the deceased by saying "goodbye" and feeling comfortable in moving forward, including the re-investment of emotion in future relationships.** In other words, life did not stop when the loved one died, which can take time to accept. It is important to encourage the bereaved to maintain the emotional connection to the past while looking forward and experiencing happiness again.

Grief Counseling Principles and Procedures: Funeral directors who engage in grief counseling need to understand the principles and procedures for helping families engage in the process of positive grief work, which might explain why some funeral customs are done. Providing the bereaved with several options will facilitate normal **grief work**, which is *a set of basic tasks that must be completed for successful mourning to take place.* The funeral director's main responsibility is to take the death event and provide a safe environment so people can work through their own grieving experiences. Providing options allows the families to choose the type of funeral activities and rituals that best serves their bereavement needs.

Scenario: Mrs. Thompson comes in for the arrangement conference. In the beginning of the conference, she states that she wishes to cremate her husband. The funeral director says, "Will cremation be before or after the funeral services?" She then states that her husband believed in God, but they were not churchgoers: "Mr. Thompson is spiritual but not religious." The funeral director then adds, we have a "celebrant on staff who could lead a service for your husband." After clarifying what a celebrant function is, Mrs. Thompson decides to give permission for embalming and have a visitation with a funeral service immediately following the calling hours. She then decides to bury her husband's cremated remains on top of his mother's grave, at a later date, with the celebrant leading the committal prayers. Burying her husband's cremated remains on his mother's grave has a special meaning, considering he took care of his mother for eight years prior to her death and during that time, they became extremely close. Now they are close together once again, which brings closure for Mrs. Thompson and her husband's life journey.

Analysis: Many funeral directors complain about how cremation "cuts into their bottom line" for profitability. Such funeral directors immediately assume when they hear the word cremation that the consumer wants direct cremation, which should only be 5 to 7 percent of a funeral home's business. Most cremations should have some type of services that help the bereaved jumpstart their grief work. The problem is not cremation, but rather the funeral directors who do not have options associated with cremation to offer the consumer.

Mrs. Thompson was also provided the option of accompanying her husband to the crematory after the funeral services. She and her two children (and husband's caregiver) rode in precession to the crematory the next day. The celebrant rode in the hearse and gave a final blessing over the closed casket before Mr. Thompson was cremated. Finally, brief committal prayers were said at the grave, and Mr. Thomson's name was inscribed beneath his mother's name.

Closure is an important part of grief work. The bereaved never fully gets over losing a loved one; they just learn to cope with the complexity of the death experience. The funeral director/grief counselor guides the bereaved through the rituals and customs that facilitate normal and healthy grief, which is a new role for funeral directors that has become more and more prevalent in the past 20 years because of the decline in church attendance. Every religion answers one fundamental question: "What happens to us after death?" Each religion has their own set of beliefs and rituals on how to connect the death event with their understanding of the afterlife. As people become disassociated with religions, they also become disconnected from the rituals surrounding final disposition for the dead. The funeral director needs to assume this role that was customarily handled by the clergy prior to the decline in church attendance. Presenting options provides a level of service that the consumer needs and wants from the professional funeral director.

Concepts that Facilitate Positive Grief Work:

Part of the funeral director/grief counselor's job is to console the bereaved and guide the family through the process of caring for the dead, coping with the complexities of the death event, and honoring the life accomplishments of the deceased. On some occasions, some family members will have unresolved conflicts with the deceased that they need to resolve, and the funeral director listens and provides guidance to deal with the reality surrounding the death event. The funeral director does not, however, attempt to resolve or get in the middle of family disputes or disagreements, which is a losing proposition that will offend someone, no matter what the funeral director does to intervene. The funeral director is responsible for maintaining order and setting the ground rules so everyone can grieve the loss while maintaining decorum, as well as respect and dignity for the dead. The funeral service is not the place (while it could be) to mend broken fences that have a history of family separation.

Scenario: Jessie was 94 years old and had health issues. Her daughter Lynne was her caregiver for several years prior to her mother's death. Lynne contracted Covid-19 and subsequently passed the virus to her mother. Due to Lynne and other members of the family's illnesses, caring for her mother was extremely difficult, resulting in her mother having to be taken to a Hospice care center. Shortly afterwards, Jessie died, and Lynne was extremely bereaved and tormented with guilt that she caused her mother's death. In addition, because of Lynne's illness, she could not be present and comfort her mother while she was dying, which complicated her grief experience.

Lynne had little direction on what to do, being sick and having to make funeral arrangements to have her mother sent back to New York from Wisconsin. The funeral director made all the arrangements with Lynne over the phone and three weeks after her mother's death, Lynne and her family held private services in New York.

Among the many conversations Lynne had with the funeral director, her guilt continued to be the main topic. The funeral director allowed her to voice her grief that she was the cause of her mother's death. The funeral director brought reality into the conversation by stating the obvious, that her mother was 94 years old and in failing health before she contracted Covid. The funeral director also consulted with the clergy about Lynne's concern and guilt. The clergy reinforced the funeral director's comments, and over time, Lynne began to grieve her mother's loss in a more balanced manner.

Analysis: The funeral director/grief counselor's role is more about saying the appropriate things at the appropriate time and reassuring the bereaved that what they are experiencing is normal and a part of the grieving process. The funeral director is not a therapist, and when the comments and behaviors appear to be out of the scope of normal grief, they should provide the family with resource information for professional grief therapy. A grief counselor's role is to be a sounding board for the family to vocalize their concerns and feelings while having a sense of being safe to share these thoughts. The funeral director offers their thoughts on why the bereaved is feeling what they are experiencing, based on their knowledge of bereavement counseling, experience in the profession, and their empathetic compassion to listen and be present for the bereaved to grieve. In doing so, these thoughts and bits of advice are grounded and rooted in a comprehensive understanding of concepts, procedures, and principles of bereavement counseling, the topic of this section.

Scenario: Judy died in her apartment, and a few days later was discovered by a neighbor. Judy had a mental illness and because of this condition, her brother and his family were estranged from her for several years. In fact, being present to make his sister's arrangements was the first time he would see his sister in several years. During the time, Peter stated, "I don't want to do this… I was not close to my sister…but I know I have to do it because it's the right thing to do."

The funeral director took this opportunity to be a sounding board for Peter and his wife. He asked Peter open-ended questions that led to Peter's explaining the nature of his relationship to his sister. Finally, after 40 minutes of his sharing thoughts and feelings about his sister, the funeral director said, "You are doing the right thing making these arrangements for your sister. No matter what she has done in the past, this is a time for you and your family to forgive her for what she has done and say goodbye to her in a respectful manner." Then the funeral director shared his story on how he was separated from his sister, and he used her death as an opportunity to forgive and heal from the pains that brought separation in his relationship. The funeral director then suggested that Peter and his wife sit down before the burial and write a letter about their feelings to bring to the committal service.

The funeral director led the committal service and Peter, his wife, and daughter assisted him in carrying the casketed remains to the grave. It was raining that day and as opposed to wiping off the casket before the services commenced, the funeral director left the raindrops on the metal casket. After the committal prayers, Peter's wife read a beautiful letter stating why their relationship was separated and a healing sentence at the end of the letter said, "We love you and rest in peace." At that point, the funeral director handed the letter to Peter and directed him to place the letter on top of the rain-dropped casket and within minutes, the paper absorbed the water, and the ink began to become blurry and illegible. To conclude the services, the funeral director said, "Now is time to say goodbye to your sister. The pain and tears that were shared in life, now go with her in this sign of love and forgiveness." Then with the assistance of the funeral director, Peter and his wife and daughter symbolically lowered the casket into the grave with two straps placed at each end. The lowering device did all the work, and the straps and the family participation helped to facilitate the physical and emotional letting go of their grief and pain.

Analysis: *Funeral directors - Direct! The Bereaved – Grieve. Don't Ever Cross That Line.* This is a deeply rooted tradition in funeral directing and for the most part, one that should be followed. The bereaved come to the funeral director for advice and guidance, and if funeral directors are unable to separate their emotions and conduct themselves professionally, then they could be perceived as ineffective. However, part of **empathy** is being able to sit with and experience some of the pain that the bereaved is experiencing. The compassionate funeral director needs to be able to listen attentively and possesses a genuine concern regarding the feelings of the bereaved. The word **compassion** means to *suffer with,* and while maintaining professionalism, the funeral director needs to demonstrate a willingness to meet the families where they are at in the grieving process and guide them to closure of the death event.

In this scenario, the funeral director listens to the bereaved tell their story and express their feelings. Part of directing is to ask open-ended questions that provides the funeral director with information about the nature of the relationship, which serves to develop an understanding of how to best advise the family towards an appropriate path to closure and healing. The funeral director then shared his story, which was short and relatable. Sharing personal grief experiences, especially when healing is involved, may help the family on their journey towards closure. The important factor for the funeral director/grief counselor to consider is to only present options, and let the family choose what they feel comfortable with for their grief work. What may work for one, may not work for all. That is dependent on the bereave's own comfort level, which always needs to be respected.

The Following are the Principles and Procedures for Grief Work:

- ➢ Help the survivor actualize the loss.
- ➢ Help the survivor to identify and express feelings in a safe environment.
- ➢ Be genuine with the survivor.
- ➢ Discuss what living without the deceased may be like moving forward.
- ➢ Facilitate emotional withdrawal and mitigate stress in doing so.
- ➢ Provide time to grieve, recognizing that each individual is different and no two people grieve in the same manner.
- ➢ Recognize what is considered "normal" behavior and how the survivor may have difficulty in responding to comfort, expressing interest in day-to-day activities, or making future plans.
- ➢ Identify survivor's defensive and coping behaviors.
- ➢ Provide ongoing support.
- ➢ Identify debilitating pathological behaviors and refer to professional services (i.e., a grief therapist).

Funeral Director Responsibilities:

- ➢ **Fulfilling grief counseling responsibilities** requires the funeral director to provide these services throughout the entire process and services. From the moment the family contacts the funeral home, to the aftercare, these responsibilities are an important part of "closing the loop" with the bereaved family.
- ➢ **Following up with "post-funeral" counseling,** which can be critical, demonstrating a caring concern that some families appreciate and welcome.
- ➢ **Providing contacts for support services and groups** to the survivors may be needed, especially in trauma cases or for families experiencing complicated grief.
- ➢ **Organizing and offering community-based education programs on grief** and healthy grieving, which includes sponsoring bereavement support groups and participating in school events, such as Mothers Against Drunk Driving (M.A.D.D); Prom Night Reality Accident Scene demonstrations.
- ➢ **Aftercare** is considered all follow-up care provided by the funeral director after the service. A non-denominational Holiday Hope for the Bereaved service could provide grieving families with an opportunity to mourn the first-year anniversary of the absence of a loved one on a major holiday.

➤ **Some examples of aftercare include the following:**
   a. Phone contact (although personal contact is preferred)
   b. Personal contact is considered the best type of contact.
   c. Postal contact in which letters or cards may be sent after the service such as after 30 days, 90 days, 6 months, and on the one year anniversary of the death.
   d. Providing educational materials (e.g., pamphlets, books, newsletters, audiovisual items)
   e. Free community education programs
   f. Referrals to licensed caregivers and professional aftercare providers
   g. Referrals to support groups and professional therapists.

Personal Characteristics of the Helping Funeral Director (per Wolfelt):

➤ **Empathy:** According to Carl Rogers, empathy is the ability to be figuratively in a survivor's shoes, to deeply understand the survivor's perspective. Funeral directors should consider that if they were actually physically in someone else's shoes, they would be literally looking outward from that person's perspective instead of their own.

➤ **Respect:** The belief that everyone possesses agency and the right to choose alternatives and make decisions. The client is not totally "deficient" because they have a problem. Instead, the successes that the client has had should be identified and acknowledges and skills of success can be used to enable the client to succeed in resolving the current problem.

➤ **Warmth and Caring:** The ability to be sincerely considerate and friendly towards survivors.

➤ **Genuineness:** The capacity to reveal one's authentic self is exhibited through both verbal and nonverbal behaviors that align consistently. Observers perceive the authenticity and truthfulness in what they witness from that individual.

Professional Grief Counseling Skills for the Funeral Director:

➤ **Attending and listening:** Communicating their presence and attentiveness, concentrating on the survivor's needs without distraction, and allowing the survivor to communicate fully and completely before responding. The funeral director should face the survivor and make eye contact. Observing and understanding both verbal and nonverbal clues, demonstrates that the funeral director is truly listening deeply and sincerely to what the survivor needs. Examples of verbal indications of attending and listening can be words (e.g., "I understand," "Please tell me more") or simply sounds indicating such (e.g., "Mm-hmm"). Nonverbal indicators can include said eye contact and facing the survivor, head-nodding, slightly leaning towards the survivor, keeping arms and legs uncrossed, and so on.

➤ **Paraphrasing:** Rewording of survivors' statements, typically in a shorter way, to communicate understanding. There may be times when a funeral director wishes to repeat verbatim what a survivor has said to allow them to hear their own words and realize the potential meaning behind them. But funeral directors are not parrots and should not simply be attempting to repeat everything a survivor has said exactly! All that demonstrates is that they can record rather than trying to understand.

➤ **Clarifying:** To interpret survivors' communications and to request additional details and explanation for clarity. If funeral directors are confused or feel they are lacking the detail to understand something fully, they can ask the survivor for help. Example: "When you said X, did you mean Y?"

➤ **Perception-checking:** Checking with the survivors to ensure the funeral director's perceptions of their communications are accurate. Example: "When you said you were 'fine,' you had tears in your eyes and your teeth were gritted, so are you really 'fine'?" (FINE is an acronym for **F**eelings **I**n **N**eed of **E**motions).

➤ **Leading:** On occasion, anticipating or directing the direction that a survivor "should" go. Such a technique should be used with care, for the survivor should be encouraged to tell his/her/their story without possible manipulation. However, if a survivor is meandering, it may be helpful to provide some structure to a conversation so that all major points are identified and put into a logical order. An emotional survivor or a survivor who feels nervous, guilty, or ashamed may not be able to relate their story in the most logical manner, so the counselor may ask questions and make statements to impart order. For sensitive subjects, leading also helps the survivor to progress forward towards the sensitive subject and then to confront and work through some of the issues.

➤ **Questioning:** Asking open-ended and closed-ended questions to solicit information. A closed-ended question has a definite answer and are often used at the beginning of a counseling relationship to "warm a client up" and prepare them to answer more difficult questions later. Examples of a closed-ended question: "What's your address?" "What's your phone number?" A client can successfully answer such questions and there is a definite answer. An open-ended question allows the client, or in this case, the survivor, to offer any kind of answer. A counselor must be comfortable with the unpredictability of open-ended questions. By asking such questions, the counselor shows respect for the client's choice of what to speak about and how. Example of an open-ended question would be as follows: "What did you feel like when you were told your husband's illness was terminal?" A funeral director may assume that a person will answer this an expected way, but an open-ended question leaves open the possibility of unique and informative answers.

➢ **Reflection:** Attempts to express verbally what the funeral director believes the survivor is feeling or thinking. Example: "When I see you look down at the floor, it gives me the impression that you are uncomfortable with what we are talking about. Am I on the right track?"

➢ **Summarizing:** Tying together several ideas and feelings, including at the conclusion of the funeral director's interactions with a survivor. All of their meetings with a survivor should include time at the end to concisely describe what was covered during the meeting, which is also the time to indicate to the survivor what the funeral director will be discussing in the next meeting (if any). If an interaction is the last meeting with the survivor, the funeral director would summarize, but also express appreciation for the relationship they have had with them and leave the door open for future interactions.

Stages of the Helping Process (per Wolfelt):

There are various stages of helping facilitate the grieving process as a caregiver, which begins with **the initial contact**, and the person answering the phone needs to sound professional and caring, including making a positive impression representing compassion. Trust is gained at early points of contact and the more personal the funeral personnel is to the caller, the more likely that the caller will be assured of high-quality service. Some funeral directors rarely rely on answering services to answer funeral home calls because the person receiving the call may appear to be "scripted." In the age of cell phones, some funeral directors answer their own calls, which demonstrates that they are always available to serve the bereaved's needs, which **starts the helping relationship,** by communicating to the bereaved the funeral director's willingness to help the bereaved through the grieving process. This communication needs to be reassured at several points during the interpersonal experiences with the bereaved. Statements can be, "I am always here for you" or "If you have any concerns, please don't hesitate to call me." Some funeral directors even provide the bereaved with their personal cell phone number so that they can have direct contact with them if a concern arises. While the act is optional, most families respect the gesture and very rarely abuse this direct communication channel.

Funeral directing is built on trust the family bestows upon the funeral director. Breach of that trust in any way, with any negative comments or actions, will result in a family not only not using the funeral home services in the future, but also creating "bad will" within the community as people discuss their poor experiences. Therefore, **building a helpful relationship** continues throughout the grieving process and is the cornerstone for caring for the living and the dead.

When the bereaved states what type of services they want, the professional funeral director helps them **explore the options** that will best care for their dead, while tending to their bereavement needs. When the bereaved states their wish for cremation services, the notion that *direct cremation* is the only services they wish to receive is a false assumption that could complicate their grief process. Furthermore, cremation is only a means of final disposition, and the funeral director needs to provide the consumer with several options that will best fit the family's bereavement needs, which includes a discussion about what to do with the cremated remains after the cremation process has concluded. A growing problem in funeral homes today is abandoned cremated remains in a funeral home attic or dusty, damp basement that demonstrates no respect for the dead and fails to provide closure for the living. Some families wish to wait until the other spouse dies, which may be several years away, and burial needs may change over time. Families need to be guided to deal with the cremated remains so they can fully grieve the loss without conditions or restrictions. Failure to finalize the death without some type of ceremonial ritual could complicate the grief experience. This task is best handled by **consulting and planning** with the survivors to view the cremation process as one part of the final disposition decisions that need to be made during the arrangements.

Sometimes the funeral director needs to "think outside the box" to provide services and merchandise that best accommodates the family's needs and wishes. **Implementing and executing** such events may need to be coordinated with various agencies and groups for their services. **The final goal** in creating funeral services is to help the family take the death event and begin the grieving process, which may require them to tie up "loose ends" and bring closure to the complexity of the death event. However, the funeral director's job is not completed after the funeral/memorial service ended or when the funeral bill is paid. **Post-funeral services** are as important as all the final details attended to before, during, and after the services. The funeral director should follow up with the bereaved with information regarding bereavement services 30-days and one year after the death event. A simple little acknowledgement card stating that the staff at the funeral home is thinking about them on this one-year anniversary is usually a well-received gesture.

Barriers to Effective Helping and Communication (per Wolfelt):

> **Inappropriate domination by the funeral director:** A funeral director may be perceived as being in a position of authority, and so the funeral director must take care to respect the contributions and input of the survivors. Expressing impatience toward the survivors, lecturing or preaching, or attempting to manipulate or coerce the survivors are all unacceptable.

> **Excessive use of questioning vs. prioritizing listening:** If the funeral director fails to provide sufficient time for the survivors to articulate their thoughts, such conduct may be construed as an intrusive interrogation and a lack of concern for the perspectives of the bereaved.

> **Inappropriate level of self-disclosure:** To build rapport, it is appropriate for the funeral director to reveal some personal details about themselves. It is considered fair that if a client is revealing things about themselves that the counselor also prove that they are "human" too. However, choosing what to self-disclose and knowing when to stop are critical. Turning the interaction into a session for the funeral director and their needs is inappropriate. One hint that this breach is happening is if the counselor begins to feel happy that their needs are being met. The survivor's role, however, is not to provide the counselor with assistance that they should more appropriately seek elsewhere.

➢ **Offering insincere platitudes or false reassurances:** It can be offensive to offer clichéd statements of comfort that funeral directors do not believe themselves simply because it is expected for them to say something, they are uncomfortable, or they do not know what to say. If they cannot imagine something or do not have the words to express themselves, it is more honest to say, "I can't imagine what you are going through" or "I have no words," which are honest and genuine. As noted elsewhere, platitudes and false reassurances can be especially confusing for children, who may interpret such statements inaccurately. Example: A child's reaction to "Your dad is in a better place now" might be "Why was being with me not a good enough place?"

➢ **Discouraging the expression of grief and uncomfortable emotions:** Including expressing discomfort or helplessness with survivors' crying or other "negative" emotions (e.g., anxiety, rage, etc.). Some examples of inappropriate statements are the following: "When are you going to get over this already?" "It was just a dog – you can just go out and buy another one."

➢ **Seeming aloof and distant/uncaring:** Example: A woman comes home exhausted from attending her beloved mother's funeral and the woman's boyfriend does not look up from his phone and asks, "What's for dinner?"

➢ **Avoiding discussing painful issues** can prohibit survivors' progress towards confronting their situation and expressing emotion. Example: A survivor is uncharacteristically quiet and seems to be trying to control their facial expressions. Instead of asking "can I help" or "is something wrong?" The funeral director ignores the signs and brings up another less uncomfortable subject. They feel better to the detriment of the survivor's feelings.

Concerns and Cautions for the Funeral Director:

The funeral director's own grief: The funeral director is human too! Funeral directors also experience grief and have grief work to complete. Denial can occur. Funeral directors can also experience anticipatory grief, anxiety, and fear of their own death in the future. Part of the profession requires the funeral director to be grounded in their own belief system; however, pushing that set of beliefs on others could experience resistance and pushback. Again, as a professional, the funeral director needs to focus on the bereaved family's concerns, not their own. The funeral director's grieving and bereavement needs to be addressed outside the arrangement conference. Unresolved grief or bereavement needs will manifest themselves and could interfere with providing the best possible services to the families they serve.

Understanding Stress and Burnout/Characteristics: All forms of compassionate care carry the risk of burnout. Funeral directors can burn out as can other caretakers. Besides regular overall self-evaluations ("…taking one's own temperature"), funeral directors are encouraged to acknowledge and explore specifically their own personal history with loss. They should also evaluate any "unfinished business" in their lives that can be obstacles to performance and the kinds of resources they find useful, including seeking professional counseling services for themselves.

Signs of potential burnout include the following:

➢ Physical and mental exhaustion
➢ Irritability and impatience
➢ Cynicism and detachment
➢ Physical complaints and illnesses
➢ Depression
➢ Disorientation and confusion
➢ Inability to focus and concentrate
➢ Feeling omnipotent and believing in being indispensable
➢ Minimization and denial of negative feelings.

Caring for the Caregiver/Strategies for Self-Care:

One must acknowledge that individuals in the field of funeral service face a heightened risk of experiencing burnout. Currently, the typical period is after 5 years. Developing strategies for self-care is essential, not only for the sake of the funeral director but also so they can provide the optimum level of bereavement support to others. Hence, it becomes crucial for funeral directors to establish regular intervals for rest and rejuvenation. By incorporating vacations and scheduling free time, they contribute to the revitalization of individuals dealing with stress and providing support to others during such challenging times.

Funeral directors should avoid expecting perfection from themselves. Instead, they are encouraged to extend compassion to themselves as they would to others. It is advisable to practice setting personal limits and boundaries, being vigilant about potential boundary violations. Addressing and confronting stressors within one's capacity is essential. Additionally, acquiring and applying effective time management skills, collaborating with technology and others, can contribute to creating time away from work for personal well-being.

The funeral director should develop a personal support system, advocating for others to do the same. Valuable resources include friends, family, and colleagues. Being a member of professional organizations provides opportunities to network and share experiences with those who truly comprehend the challenges in the field.

It is essential for the funeral director to be authentic both personally and professionally. Honesty is crucial, and a thorough examination of motivations for being in the funeral service field is necessary, with a focus on the key motivator as "service."

The funeral director can develop and maintain healthy eating, sleeping and exercise habits. They can be vigilant in recognizing physical and mental signs of stress. Again, seeking professional help when needed is essential.

Bereavement Counseling Glossary

Aftercare (post-funeral counseling) - A means of providing support after the funeral has occurred.

Alternatives (options) - Choices of services and merchandise available to families of the deceased; formulation of different actions in adjusting to a crisis.

Anger - A strong feeling of displeasure and usually of antagonism.

Anomic grief - Grief where mourning customs are unclear due to an inappropriate death and the absence of prior bereavement experience.

Anticipatory grief - Grief in anticipation of death or loss.

Anxiety - Apprehension, dread, or uneasiness similar to fear but based on an unclear threat.

At-need counseling - Consulting with the family from the time the death occurs until the final disposition.

Attachment theory - Theory describing a tendency to make strong affectional bonds with others; derived from the need for security and safety.

Attending (active listening) - Giving undivided attention, demonstrated with verbal and non-verbal behavior.

Attitude: A learned tendency to consider people, objects, or institutions in a positive or negative way.

Bereavement - The experience of grief resulting from the act or event of separation or loss.

Burnout - A work-related condition of mental, physical, and emotional exhaustion.

Chronic grief - Grief that is excessive in duration and has not come to a satisfactory conclusion.

Client-centered (person-centered) counseling - A non-directive method of counseling which stresses the inherent worth of the client and the natural capacity for growth and health.

Cognitive psychology - From the Latin, "to know." The study of the origins and consequences of thoughts, memories, beliefs, perceptions, explanations, and other mental processes.

Communication - A general term for the exchange of information, feelings, thoughts, and acts between two or more people, including both verbal and non-verbal aspects of this process.

Complicated grief - Grief that interferes with normal life functions and does not progress towards resolution.

Coping - Ways of responding and acclimating to stress.

Counseling - Using psychological methods to provide professional guidance to someone.

Crisis - An emotionally significant event or radical change of status in a person's life.

Crisis counseling - A type of intervention that helps those cope with a crisis.

Death anxiety - A learned emotional response to death-related phenomenon characterized by extreme apprehension.

Defense mechanism -A mental process such as repression used (typically unconsciously) to decrease internal stress and avoid anxiety.

Delayed grief - Inhibited, suppressed, or postponed response to a loss.

Denial - Defense mechanism by which a person is unable or refuses to see things as they are because such facts are threatening to the self.

Depression - A state of despondency marked by feelings of powerlessness and hopelessness.

Directive counseling - A type of counseling in which the counselor assumes the initiative and carries a major role in the identification and resolution of problems.

Discrimination - Treating members of groups differently in circumstances where their rights or treatment should be identical.

Disenfranchised grief - Grief experienced due to a loss that society deems unworthy of mourning.

Displacement - Redirecting feelings toward a person or object other than the one who originally caused the feelings.

Emotion(s) - Conscious mental reactions (such as anger or fear) subjectively experienced as strong feelings usually directed toward a specific object and typically accompanied by physical changes in the body.

Emotional intelligence - The ability to perceive, use, understand, and manage emotions.

Empathy - A capacity for deeply understanding another's point of view; the ability to feel what another is feeling.

Euthanasia - An act or practice of allowing or causing the death of a person suffering from a life-limiting condition.

Exaggerated grief - Grief reactions that are excessive, to the point that they may be disabling.

Facilitate - To make easier; help bring about.

Fear - Strong emotion marked by such reactions as alarm, dread, or disquiet.

Funeral service psychology - The study of human behavior and mental processes as related to funeral services.

Grief - An emotion or set of emotions due to loss.

Grief counseling - The process of helping people who have been bereaved to cope with their grief.

Grief syndrome - A set of symptoms associated with loss.

Grief therapy - Specialized techniques used to help people with complicated grief.

Grief work - A set of basic tasks that must be completed for successful mourning to take place.

Guilt - Blame directed toward oneself, which may be derived from oneself.

Homicide - The killing of one human being by another.

Hospice - A program of palliative care for the terminally ill.

Inappropriate death - An unexpected or unnaturally occurring death.

Informational counseling - Counseling in which a body of special knowledge is communicated.

Masked grief - When grievers do not admit their grief or attempt to suppress it; but they may experience physical symptoms or behaviors that can impair normal functioning.

Memorialization - The process of preserving memories of people or events.

Mourning - outward expression of grief.

Non-directive counseling - To listen, support, and advise without directing a course of action.

Non-verbal communication - Expressed by posture, facial expression, actions, or physical behavior rather than via the voice.

Options (alternatives) - see "Alternatives."

Panic - A strong emotion characterized by sudden and extreme fear.

476

Paraphrasing - Expressing a thought or idea in an alternate and shortened form without changing the meaning.

Person-centered (client-centered) counseling - See "client-centered counseling."

Post-funeral counseling (aftercare) - See "aftercare."

Prejudice - Negative attitude towards others based on their gender, religion, race, or membership in a particular group.

Pre-need counseling - Counseling that occurs before a death.

Projection - Attribution of one's unacceptable thoughts, feelings, or behaviors to someone else.

Psychology - The scientific study of human behavior and mental processes.

Psychotherapy - Psychological techniques used to facilitate positive changes in a person's personality, behavior, and attitude.

Rapport - Development of harmonious relations among people.

Rationalization - Attempting to explain or justify an attitude or behavior with a logical reason, even if not appropriate.

Regression - Returning to more familiar and often more primitive modes of coping.

Repression - Involuntary blocking of threatening material from consciousness. Also see "suppression."

Respect - The act of giving particular attention, high regard, and deep admiration for someone or something, elicited by their abilities, qualities, or achievements.

Shame - Feeling of guilt resulting from others' blame.

Situational counseling - Counseling related to specific life situations that may create crises and produce human pain and suffering.

Social comparison -Making judgments about ourselves upon comparison with others.

Social facilitation - Occurs when an individual's performance improves because of the presence of others.

Stress - The mental and physical condition that occurs when a person must adjust or adapt to a stressor.

Stressor - An event capable of producing physical or emotional stress.

Sublimation - Redirection of emotion to culturally or socially appropriate purposes.

Sudden infant death syndrome (SIDS or crib death) - The sudden and unexpected death of an apparently healthy infant, which remains unexplained after a complete autopsy and a review of the circumstances around the death.

Suicide - The deliberate and voluntary act of ending one's own life.

Suppression - The conscious postponement of addressing anxieties and concerns. Also see "repression."

Sympathy - Sincere feelings for a person who is trying to adjust to a serious loss; expression of such feelings.

Thanatology - The study of death, dying, bereavement, and mourning.

Thanatophobia - An irrational, exaggerated fear of death.

Unconscious - The contents of the mind such as impulses and desires beyond awareness.

Verbal communication - Spoken, oral communication.

References

Accounting Section

American Board of Funeral Service Education. (n.d.). *Curriculum.* ABFSE.

https://www.abfse.org/html/curriculum.html

Fritch, J. B. & Altieri, J.C. (2017). *Fundamentals of funeral directing: Building a*

professional cornerstone. Funeral Service Education Resource Center.

Label, W.A. & Henderson, C.K. (2019). *Study guide and workbook for accounting for*

non-accountants: (4th ed.). Solana Dreams Publishing Company.

Taggart, T. R. (2016). *National board examination review book for students of funeral*

service education/mortuary science: Arts. Mesa, Arizona.

Business Law

American Board of Funeral Service Education. (n.d.). *Curriculum.* ABFSE.

https://www.abfse.org/html/curriculum.html

Cleveland, L. J. (2021). *Funeral service law in the United States: A guide for funeral*

service students. Hudson Valley Professional Services.

Communications

American Board of Funeral Service Education. (n.d.). *Curriculum.* ABFSE.

https://www.abfse.org/html/curriculum.html

Pearson, J. C., Nelson P. E., Titsworth S., & Hosek, A. M. (2021). *Human*

communication. (7th ed.). McGraw-Hill.

Wolfelt, A. D. (1990). *Interpersonal skills training.* Routledge/Taylor & Francis

Group.

Ethics

American Board of Funeral Service Education. (n.d.). *Curriculum.* ABFSE.

https://www.abfse.org/html/curriculum.html

Beauchamp, T. & Veatch, R. (1995). *Ethical issues in death and dying (2nd ed.).*

Prentice-Hall, Inc.

Klicker, R. (1995). *Ethics in funeral service.* Thanos Institute.

Federal Trade Commission

Cleveland, L. J. (2021). *Funeral service law in the United States: A guide for funeral*

service students. Hudson Valley Professional Services.

Mevec, E. R., & Cleveland, L. J. (2022). *Funeral Service Business Law: A guide for*

funeral service students. Hudson Valley Professional Services.

Ritchie, J. N. & A., & Staff in the Office of Technology and the Bureau of Competition.

(2023a, February 3). *Complying with the funeral rule.* Federal Trade Commission.

https://www.ftc.gov/business-guidance/resources/complying-funeral-rule

Taggart, T. R. (2016). *National board examination review book for students of funeral*

service education/mortuary science: Arts. Mesa, Arizona.

Funeral Directing and Preparation for Final Disposition

American Board of Funeral Service Education. (n.d.). *Curriculum.* ABFSE.

https://www.abfse.org/html/curriculum.html

Barthuly, C. (2022, May 15). *Masonic funerals: Rituals, service & what to expect.*

Cake Blog. https://www.joincake.com/blog/masonic-

funeral/#h_444271171315732352240056

Cleveland, L. J. (2022a). *Funeral directing in the United States: A guide for funeral service students* (2nd ed.). Hudson Valley Professional Service.

Cleveland, L. J. (2022c). *Funeral service rites and customs: A guide for funeral service student* (2nd ed.). Hudson Valley Professional Services.

Fritch, J. B. & Altieri, J.C. (2017). *Fundamentals of funeral directing: Building a professional cornerstone*. Funeral Service Education Resource Center.

Klicker, R. L. (2020). *21st century funeral directing and Funeral Service Management*. Thanos Institute.

Taggart, T. R. (2016). *National board examination review book for students of funeral service education/mortuary science: Arts*. Mesa, Arizona.

Wood, C., & Hain, R. (2020b, August 22). *How do baha'is deal with death?* BahaiTeachings.org. https://bahaiteachings.org/bahais-deal-death/

Funeral Law

American Board of Funeral Service Education. (n.d.). *Curriculum.* ABFSE. https://www.abfse.org/html/curriculum.html

Cleveland, L. J. (2022). *Funeral service law in New York: A guide for funeral service students* (2nd ed.). Hudson Valley Professional Service.

Cleveland, L. J. (2021). *Funeral service law in the United States: A guide for funeral service students*. Hudson Valley Professional Services.

Mevec, E. R., & Cleveland, L. J. (2022). *Funeral service business law: A guide for funeral service students*. Hudson Valley Professional Services.

Staff in the Office of Technology. (2024, April 24). *FTC announces rule Banning noncompetes*. Federal Trade Commission. https://www.ftc.gov/news-events/news/press-releases/2024/04/ftc-announces-rule-banning-noncompetes

Funeral Service Management & Types of Managements

American Board of Funeral Service Education. (n.d.). *Curriculum.* ABFSE. https://www.abfse.org/html/curriculum.html

Fritch, J. B. & Altieri, J.C. (2017). *Fundamentals of funeral directing: Building a professional cornerstone.* Funeral Service Education Resource Center.

Greenleaf, R. K. (1998). *The power of servant leadership: A series of addresses and a personal testimony.* Berrett-Koehler Publishers

Klicker, R. L. (2020). *21st century funeral directing and funeral service management.* Thanos Institute.

Merchandising and Marketing

American Board of Funeral Service Education. (n.d.). *Curriculum.* ABFSE. https://www.abfse.org/html/curriculum.html

Cleveland, L. J. (2018). *Funeral service marketing and merchandise: A guide for practitioners and mortuary science students.* Hudson Valley Professional Services.

Occupational Health and Safety

Cleveland, L. J. (2021). *Funeral service law in the United States: A guide for funeral service students.* Hudson Valley Professional Services.

Mevec, E. R., & Cleveland, L. J. (2022). *Funeral service business law: A guide for funeral service students.* Hudson Valley Professional Services.

USDOL OSHA public web site search results. (n.d.).

https://search.osha.gov/search?affiliate=usdoloshapublicwebsite&query

Taggart, T. R. (2016). *National board examination review book for students of funeral service education/mortuary science: Arts.* Mesa, Arizona.

Small Business Management

American Board of Funeral Service Education. (n.d.). *Curriculum.* ABFSE.

https://www.abfse.org/html/curriculum.html

Fritch, J. B. & Altieri, J.C. (2017). *Fundamentals of funeral directing: Building a professional cornerstone.* Funeral Service Education Resource Center.

Klicker, R. L. (2020). *21st century funeral directing and Funeral Service Management.* Thanos Institute.

Taggart, T. R. (2016). *National board examination review book for students of funeral service education/mortuary science: Arts.* Mesa, Arizona.

Psychology/Bereavement Counseling

American Board of Funeral Service Education. (n.d.). *Curriculum.* ABFSE.

https://www.abfse.org/html/curriculum.html

Canine, J. (2019). *The psychosocial aspects of death and dying (2nd ed.).* Appleton & Lange.

Wolfelt, A.D. (1990). *Interpersonal skills training; A handbook for funeral home staffs.* Accelerated Development, Inc.

Worden, J. W. (2018). *Grief counseling and grief therapy (5th ed.).* Springer Publishing Company.

Sociology in Funeral Services

American Board of Funeral Service Education. (n.d.). *Curriculum.* ABFSE.

https://www.abfse.org/html/curriculum.html

Fritch, J., & Steward, G. (2016). *One world: Sociology and funeral service.* Funeral

Service Education Resource Center.

Leming, M., & Dickinson, G. (2007). *Understanding dying, death, and bereavement.*

Thompson Higher Education.

Technology

American Board of Funeral Service Education. (n.d.). *Curriculum.* ABFSE.

https://www.abfse.org/html/curriculum.html

Klicker, R. L. (2020). *21st century funeral directing and Funeral Service Management.*

Thanos Institute.

Taggart, T. R. (2016). *National board examination review book for students of funeral*

service education/mortuary science: Arts. Mesa, Arizona.

Tips on How to Pass the National Board Exam

The International Conference of Funeral Service Examining Boards. (2022). *National*

Board Exam arts study guide (Vol. 13). The International Conference of Funeral

Service Examining Boards.

NOTE: Some sections of this book were revised and edited using ChatGPT.

INDEX

\\\